Frontiers of Business Cycle Research

Frontiers of Business Cycle Research

Thomas F. Cooley, Editor

Princeton University Press   Princeton, New Jersey

Library of Congress Cataloging-in-Publication Data

Frontiers of business cycle research / Thomas F. Cooley, editor.
p.   cm.
Includes bibliographical references and index.
ISBN 0-691-04323-X (cl.)
1. Business cycles—Research—History.   I. Cooley, Thomas F.
HB3714.F74   1994
338.5′42—dc20   94-22131

This book has been composed in TEX using Adobe Type 1 versions of Linotype AG's
Times-Roman, The TEXplorators Corporation's MathTimes, and Adobe Type 1 versions
of ITC's Avant Garde Gothic.

Princeton University Press books are printed on acid-free paper and meet the guidelines
for permanence and durability of the Committee on Production Guidelines for Book
Longevity of the Council on Library Resources

Printed in the United States of America

10 9 8 7 6 5 4 3 2 1

To Thomas J. Cooley,
a great humanitarian and a loving father

CONTENTS

ILLUSTRATIONS

TABLES

PREFACE

Business cycles, the recurrent fluctuations in economic activity, have been a well-documented feature of economic life for two centuries or more. The systematic study of business cycles is a more recent enterprise, but one that has undergone important changes in the past few decades. Beginning in the early 1970s, the methods used to study business cycles changed in an important way. In what is often referred to as the new classical revolution, economists, led by the path-breaking work of Robert E. Lucas, Jr., began to study business cycles using the tools of competitive equilibrium theory. This was an important transformation in reasoning about business cycles because it established the view that progress in understanding them could be made using the standard tools of economic analysis, not ad hoc models that are inconsistent with rational behavior and general equilibrium. Beginning in the 1980s, another important development occurred, which has changed the way many economists study business cycles. This was the emergence of the real business cycle approach, as represented by the work of Kydland and Prescott (1972) and Long and Plosser (1983). The most important aspect of the real business cycle development is that it established a prototype and a set of tools for carrying the equilibrium approach forward. It combines general equilibrium theory with a set of tools for computing the equilibria of artificial economies and studying their empirical properties.

The real business cycle approach has been impossible to ignore. It has attracted much attention precisely because it offers a strong challenge to more traditional theories of the business cycle. Most important, the real business cycle approach changed the rules of the game by which we conduct quantitative research in macroeconomics. Most economists now accept as incontrovertible the notion that theories of the business cycle should be consistent with the long-term observations about economic growth and with the principles of competitive equilibrium theory. These ideas have become part of the core curriculum for virtually all students of macroeconomics. Unfortunately, the teaching of this material has been hindered by the lack of a well-organized and careful exposition of the ideas and methods of dynamic general equilibrium modeling. This book attempts to fill that gap. The chapters of this book present a thorough treatment of modern business cycle research. They cover the philosophy underlying this approach, describe the methods that are used to compute the equilibria of business cycle models and study their behavior, and describe applications to virtually all of the important substantive issues in macroeconomics. This approach to studying business cycles and growth has been one of the most active and fast growing in all of economics. By the time this book is in print, many new and important applications of these ideas will exist. Nevertheless, the ideas and methods described here have become standard tools for economists, and they will be useful for a very long time to come.

Many people have been quick to dismiss real business cycle theory because of its emphasis on exogenous shocks to technology as the source of the fluctuations that we associated with the business cycle. The chapters in this book belie that oversimplified view of what modern business cycle research is all about. Written by the leading contributors to research in this area, they provide all of the tools necessary to put the methods of dynamic general equilibrium analysis to work. Moreover, the chapters show how to structure and address important questions in macroeconomics by using these tools. Progress in macroeconomics has been fairly swift over the past two decades in part because of improvements in the mathematical tools we have at our disposal for the study of dynamic stochastic economies. Those tools are well presented in the book *Recursive Methods in Economic Dynamics*, by Stokey and Lucas with Prescott (1989). In designing this book, I took the view that we did not need to present those theoretical tools again, but instead should show how to put them to work empirically to study the business cycle. Accordingly, there is a strong emphasis in this book on computational methods and applications of those computational methods to important problems. The book opens with an overview of the basic ideas. This overview is followed by three chapters describing in detail the methods that are used to compute equilibria. The remaining chapters describe applications of these techniques to various issues in business cycle theory.

Gathering together contributions from the most important researchers in a field is not an easy task, and many people have helped this venture come to fruition. During the course of this project we had two meetings of many of the people involved. Both of these were held at the Federal Reserve Bank of Minneapolis, and they were sponsored by the Institute for Empirical Macroeconomics and the Bradley Policy Research Center at the William E. Simon School of Business at the University of Rochester. I am particularly grateful to Lawrence Christiano, Arthur Rolnick, and Ronald Hansen for their support in securing the funding we needed for these meetings. I am also grateful to Vicki Reupke of the Research Department of the Federal Reserve Bank of Minneapolis, for her support in organizing our meetings. I am indebted to many friends and colleagues for help in editing the volume and my own contributions to it. In particular, I would like to thank Jorge Soares for help with the overall editing and Larry Christiano, John Donaldson, Ed Green, Jeremy Greenwood, Gary Hansen, and Glenn MacDonald for comments and criticisms on the project as a whole and on my own chapters. I thank Lyn Grossman for superb copyediting. I also wish to thank Vicki Mullen and Sue Sullivan for their expert secretarial help. Finally, and most important, I thank Patricia, Aaron, Rikki, Joshua, and Noah for their love and patience.

CONTRIBUTORS

David K. Backus, *New York University*

V. V. Chari, *Northwestern University*

Lawrence Christiano, *Northwestern University*

Thomas F. Cooley, *University of Rochester*

Jean-Pierre Danthine, *University of Lausanne*

John Donaldson, *Columbia University*

Jeremy Greenwood, *University of Rochester*

Gary D. Hansen, *University of California, Los Angeles*

Patrick J. Kehoe, *University of Pennsylvania*

Finn E. Kydland, *University of Texas*

Edward C. Prescott, *University of Minnesota*

José-Víctor Ríos-Rull, *University of Pennsylvania*

Richard Rogerson, *University of Minnesota*

Julio J. Rotemberg, *MIT*

K. Geert Rouwenhorst, *Yale University*

Michael Woodford, *University of Chicago*

Randall Wright, *University of Pennsylvania*

Frontiers of Business Cycle Research

Chapter 1
Economic Growth and Business Cycles

Thomas F. Cooley and Edward C. Prescott

1. Introduction

The intent of this book is to describe the methods and problems of modern business cycle research, using the neoclassical growth framework to study the economic fluctuations associated with the business cycle. Advances in dynamic economic theory and progress in computational methods over the past two decades have provided economists with a new set of tools for the study of important economic issues. These tools have enhanced our ability to construct and study artificial economies that serve as laboratories for economic research. The construction and analysis of equilibrium paths for simple artificial economies based on the neoclassical growth model has proven a very fruitful approach to studying and better understanding the business cycle. In this volume, we present the primary methods and the most important applications of this research.

Research on economic fluctuations has progressed rapidly since Robert Lucas revived the profession's interest in business cycle theory. Prior to the publication of Keynes's *General Theory of Employment, Interest, and Money*, business cycle theory was a well established part of twentieth-century economics. Business cycle theory evolved in the early twentieth century because the empirical study of fluctuations across periods of prosperity and decline had highlighted a remarkable degree of regularity in the characteristics of these cycles. Such economists as Wesley Mitchell, Simon Kuznets, and Frederick Mills carefully documented the characteristics of business cycle fluctuations on the basis of the available data for the United States and other countries. Mitchell was primarily concerned with documenting the simultaneity of movement (comovement) of variables over the cycle, with the view that this could be helpful in learning to predict economic upturns and downturns. Frederick Mills was concerned with documenting the behavior of prices, and in particular the comovement of prices and quantities, over economic expansions and contractions, because he believed that this would yield important clues to the origins of cycles. His view was that if prices appeared to be procyclical, it would be evidence of what he called demand-driven fluctuations, while if they turned out to be countercyclical, it would be indicative of supply-driven fluctuations. Simon Kuznets studied the patterns of both growth and fluctuations. The empirical investigations of these researchers suggested that the defining features of economic fluctuations were surprisingly similar over time and across countries, suggesting that business cycles may be candidates for explanation by "economic laws."

The 1930s was a very active period for business cycle research. The National Bureau of Economic Research (NBER) continued its program (begun by Mills, Mitchell and Kuznets) of empirically documenting the features of cycles. What emerged from the data was the finding that business cycle fluctuations are a recurrent event with many similarities over time and across countries. This finding prompted many attempts to explain the cycle as a natural property or outcome of an economic system. Different views emerged about why cycles occur with regularity in economic systems. One idea, associated mainly with Ragnar Frisch (1933), regarded the cycle as the set of damped oscillations that result from the propagation of random shocks to the economy. The business cycle model of Frisch showed how cycles could arise in the solution of the second-order–difference equations that characterize an economic system. Frisch was heavily influenced by Wicksell in the development of his views. Eugen Slutsky (1937), in an important paper, put forth an alternative theory. He showed how fluctuations resembling business cycles could result from the sum of random shocks to the economy if the economy were characterized by a stable stochastic difference equation with large positive real roots. Additional theories of the cycle were put forth by Kalecki, Schumpeter (who argued that technological innovations can lead to both long-term growth and cycles, and Metzler (who focused on the inventory cycle, among others. This was a period of proliferation of business cycle models without much real progress at resolving important questions.

The first attempts to construct economywide econometric models were motivated by the desire to test competing business cycle theories. Although business cycles are inherently dynamic phenomena, economists did not really have the theoretical tools to deal with rigorous models of the cycle. The search for empirical versions of economic laws appeared to be a more fruitful path to follow. Interest in business cycles per se also waned in the aftermath of the publication of Keynes's *General Theory*. The so called Keynesian revolution that followed the publication of the *General Theory* turned attention away from thinking about cycles. Instead, the intellectual problem for macroeconomists became to explain the forces that determine the level of economic output at a point in time, conditional on the prior history of the economy. This was the research agenda suggested by the *General Theory* and given empirical content by the important contributions of Tinbergen and Klein. The overriding concern with the question of output determination is easy to understand: at the time of these developments, the United States and Britain were emerging from World War II. Many economists were concerned that the prolonged downturn of the Great Depression might recur after the war. An understanding of the determinants of the level of output at a point in time suggested the possibility of designing policies ("stabilization policies") that would influence the level of output, attenuate the business cycle, and possibly prevent the recurrence of large-scale economic crises, such as the Great Depression. One result of this change in focus was that later empirical research was directed almost entirely at the question of output determination at a point in time rather than the study of the whole shape and characteristics of the business cycle. This research agenda, combined with the increased availability of aggregate economic data led to the creation of fully specified artificial economies that were designed to capture the process of output determination. Interest in understanding the business cycle as a recurrent event waned. This remained the state of affairs until Lucas (1972, 1975) and Kydland and Prescott (1982) rekindled interest in the theoretical and empirical investigation of business cycles.[1]

Concurrent with the emergence of Keynesian macroeconomics was a renewed interest in the problem of understanding the long-term laws of motion of modern economies. This was the research agenda of modern growth theory that was initiated by Harrod and Domar and given its preeminent expression in the work of Robert Solow. The modern theory of economic growth evolved from the observation of empirical regularities, as had business cycle theory. As economic data became more available in the Twentieth century, it grew apparent that economic growth displayed striking empirical regularities both over time and across countries. These observations, labeled by Nicholas Kaldor (1957) the "stylized facts" of economic growth, became the benchmarks of the theory of economic growth. These observed regularities suggested economic laws at work that could be captured in formal models. Kaldor's "stylized facts" of growth (as characterized by Solow [1970]) are as follows:

1) Real output grows at a more or less constant rate.

2) The stock of real capital grows at a more or less constant rate greater than the rate of growth of the labor input.

3) The growth rates of real output and the stock of capital tend to be about the same.

4) The rate of profit on capital has a horizontal trend.

5) The rate of growth of output per-capita varies greatly from one country to another.

6) Economies with a high share of profits in income tend to have a high ratio of investment to output.

The third and fourth of these stylized facts imply that capital's share in total income will be constant, while the second and third imply that the investment-output ratio is constant.[2] The first four together describe an economy experiencing "balanced" growth. The scale of an economy experiencing balanced growth will change over time, but the composition of output will not. When Nicholas Kaldor summarized the main observations about economic growth, as they were known in the 1950s, the task of developing a coherent theoretical model of growth became a primary focus of interest for economists in the United States and England. The growth theory that evolved from these observations was concerned primarily with exploring the properties of model economies that exhibit balanced growth or have well-defined steady-state paths and with analyzing whether artificial economies not initially in a steady state would tend to converge to one. The elements of that theory and its evolution are documented in many places. The fifth and sixth stylized facts have posed more difficulty for neoclassical growth theory, and much of the modern endogenous growth literature has been concerned with these features.

The neoclassical model of capital accumulation reproduces many of the stylized facts about economic growth and is consistent with many features of actual growing economies. We also observe that in most industrialized economies, output per capita grows over time, capital per worker grows over time, and productivity grows over time. Robert Solow used the neoclassical growth model as the basis for decomposing the growth in output per capita into portions accounted for by increased inputs and the portion attributable to increases in productivity. Solow's findings prompted much additional research in productivity measurement and considerable development of mathematical growth models with different ways of incorporating technical change.

What is surprising about the development of growth theory is that for a very long time, the theory evolved in an empirical vacuum. It did not much influence, nor was it greatly influenced by, the corresponding developments in empirical macroeconomics. Study of short-term economic behavior or fluctuations and study of long-term growth were divorced. The generally accepted view was that we needed one theory to explain long-term growth and a completely different one to explain short-term fluctuations in output. Several important developments in growth theory established the foundation that made it possible to think about growth theory and business cycles within the same theoretical framework. One of the most important of these developments from the standpoint of the issues addressed in this book was Brock and Mirman's (1972) characterization of optimal growth in an economy with stochastic productivity shocks. A second was the introduction of the labor-leisure choice into the basic neoclassical model. The most thorough and up-to-date treatment of the important theoretical issues in the theory of economic growth is contained in Stokey and Lucas, with Prescott (1989). That theory is the fundamental building block of the modern approach to studying the business cycle. This volume describes both the methods and the findings of this modern approach.

Modern business cycle theory starts with the view that *growth* and *fluctuations* are not distinct phenomena to be studied with separate data and different analytical tools.[3] This theory adheres to the notion, familiar from modern growth theory, that simple artificial economies are useful vehicles for assessing those features of actual economies that are important for business cycles. A distinguishing feature of these model economies is that economic outcomes do not occur arbitrarily, but instead arise as the equilibrium outcomes of fully rational economic agents. The artificial economies described are also in the spirit of the postwar macroeconometric tradition of Tinbergen and Klein in that they are fully specified *empirical* model economies; that is, they are constructed to mimic important aspects of the behavior through time of actual economies. We will show that these artificial economies are useful laboratories for studying the business cycle and for studying economic policy. The goal of this research is to better understand the behavior of actual economies by studying the equilibria of these synthetic economies. The realization of this goal requires a careful marriage of economic theory and empirical observation.

In this chapter, we describe some of the common features of the approach to studying business cycles that unify the chapters in this volume. The most common element is the neoclassical model of economic growth. In the next section, we describe a deterministic economic environment that is designed to capture Kaldor's stylized facts described above. We also describe in some detail a particular competitive equilibrium concept that many of the later chapters and many of the papers in the literature use. Section 3 introduces the stochastic growth environment, and we present the recursive competitive equilibrium concept for this environment. Section 4 describes how the basic neoclassical growth framework can be calibrated to the U.S. economy to yield quantitative statements about the evolution of the model economy. We devote Section 5 to an overview of the solution techniques that are used for computing the equilibria of business cycle models. The known facts about business cycles are described in Section 6; we discuss some of the issues and choices one makes in representing cyclical and growth components in the data. In Section 7, we describe the results of simulating the stochastic growth model.

2. Deterministic Growth

Our purpose in this section is to describe a neoclassical model economy that was designed to capture the features of economies experiencing balanced growth. This environment is the most basic underpinning of all that follows in this book. We are going to be concerned here and throughout the book with *general equilibrium* descriptions of economic growth, so we begin with a deterministic dynamic general equilibrium model.

The Environment

The economy we examine is populated with a large number of identical households, each of which will live forever and each with identical preferences defined over consumption at every date. We assume that preferences are additively separable, with the form

$$u(c_0, c_1, c_2, \ldots) = \sum_{t=0}^{\infty} \beta^t U(c_t), \quad 0 < \beta < 1. \tag{1}$$

The period utility function $U : R_+ \to R$ has the properties that U is continuously differentiable in its arguments, is increasing, is strictly concave, and $\lim_{c \to 0} U'(c) = \infty$. The parameter β is the discount factor that households apply to future consumption.

The households in this economy do not value leisure. We assume that the population size is constant, and we normalize the total time endowment of labor available for production to unity. There is an initial endowment of capital, K_0. Each period, households supply labor, H_t, and capital, K_t, to firms. The latter have access to a technology for producing the single good, Y_t. The aggregate production function is

$$Y_t = F(K_t, H_t), \tag{2}$$

where $F : R_+^2 \to R_+$ has the properties that F is increasing in K and H, is concave in K and H separately, is continuously differentiable in K and H, and is homogeneous of degree one. Moreover,

$$F(0, 0) = F(0, H) = F(K, 0) = 0;$$

$$F_K(K, H) > 0, F_H(K, H) > 0, \forall K, H, > 0;$$

$$\lim_{K \to 0} F_K(K, 1) = \infty, \quad \text{and} \quad \lim_{K \to \infty} F_K(K, 1) = 0.$$

We assume further that capital depreciates at a constant rate $0 < \delta \leq 1$. The aggregate resource constraint implies that consumption, C_t, and gross investment, $K_{t+1} - (1 - \delta)K_t$, have to satisfy the condition

$$C_t + K_{t+1} - (1 - \delta)K_t \leq F(K_t, H_t), \forall t. \tag{3}$$

The Planner's Problem

If we imagine that this economy is governed by a benevolent social planner, the problem faced by the planner is to choose sequences for consumption, labor supply, and the capital stock, $\{C_t, H_t, K_{t+1}\}_{t=0}^{\infty}$, that maximize (1), given K_0, subject to the aggregate resource constraint. The solution to this problem requires that no output be wasted, which in turn implies that equation (3) holds with equality, and that $H_t = 1$ for all t. Accordingly, K_t and Y_t represent capital and output per worker as well as aggregate capital and output.

We can rewrite the aggregate resource constraint as

$$C_t + K_{t+1} = F(K_t, 1) + (1 - \delta)K_t = f(K_t), \forall t. \tag{4}$$

Equation (4) allows us to rewrite the planner's problem as

$$\max_{\{K_{t+1}\}_{t=0}^{\infty}} \sum_{t=0}^{\infty} \beta^t U[f(K_t) - K_{t+1}]$$

$$\text{s.t.} \quad 0 \leq K_{t+1} \leq f(K_t), t = 0, \ldots,$$

$$\text{given } K_0 > 0. \tag{5}$$

One technique for solving dynamic optimization problems of the form (5) is to rewrite them in a recursive form that can be solved by dynamic programming. Let $V(K_0)$ denote the maximum value of the function (5) that could be obtained for any $K_0 > 0$. The planner's problem can then be represented as

$$V(K_0) = \max_{0 \leq K_1 \leq f(K_0)} \{U[f(K_0) - K_1] + \beta V(K_1)\}. \tag{6}$$

The theory of dynamic programming necessary to solve problems like this is discussed in great detail in Stokey and Lucas, with Prescott (1989). The reader should have at least some familiarity with those techniques.

Supporting the Solution to the Planner's Problem as an Arrow-Debreu Competitive Equilibrium

Our interest in the planner's problem is motivated by the fact that for this model economy (and under fairly general assumptions), the solution to the planner's problem is the competitive equilibrium allocation. This result can be established by using the two fundamental theorems of welfare economics. The First Welfare Theorem can be used to conclude that any competitive equilibrium allocation for this economy is a Pareto-optimal allocation. As there is only one Pareto-optimal allocation, if a competitive equilibrium exists it is the solution to the social planner's problem.

One way to establish the existence of a competitive equilibrium is to use the Second Welfare Theorem to support the solution to the social planner's problem as a competitive equilibrium. If there is discounting, the optimum can be supported as a decentralized competitive equilibrium with a price system that has an inner product representation. Stated differently, the value of a commodity bundle is the price of each commodity in the commodity vector times the quantity of that commodity summed over the infinity of the Arrow-Debreu date and event contingent commodities (see Stokey and Lucas, with Prescott 1989, 466, Theorem 15.6; or Harris 1987). This is the valuation equilibrium concept used by Prescott and Lucas (1972) among others.

For our simple economy, the price system just referred to can be found as follows: We assumed that the households own the capital and labor and rent them to firms (if there are constant returns to scale, there need be only one firm). Since the firm needs only to hire capital and labor each period, we can describe the firm as solving a series of static, one-period profit maximization problems:

$$\max_{K_t, H_t} p_t \cdot [F(K_t, H_t) - r_t K_t - w_t H_t], \ \forall t. \tag{7}$$

From the necessary and sufficient marginal conditions for maximization, the real wage rate, w_t, and the real rental price of capital, r_t, in terms of output must be

$$w_t = F_2(K_t, H_t) \tag{8}$$

and

$$r_t = F_1(K_t, H_t), \tag{9}$$

for all t. If we assume constant returns to scale, in equilibrium there are no profits or dividends to distribute to households, and we can ignore issues involving the ownership of firms. Households solve the problem:

$$\max \sum_{t=0}^{\infty} \beta^t U(c_t)$$

$$\text{s.t.} \ \sum_{t=0}^{\infty} p_t[c_t + K_{t+1}] \le \sum_{t=0}^{\infty} p_t[w_t + (r_t + 1 - \delta)K_t],$$

$$c_t \le 0, \ K_{t+1} \ge 0. \tag{10}$$

The first-order conditions for the household's problem imply that prices must make households indifferent between consumption at different dates:

$$p_t/p_{t+1} = U'(c_t)/[\beta \cdot U'(c_{t+1})]. \tag{11}$$

From this we determine the interest rate as $i_t = p_t/p_{t+1} - 1$.

This approach to finding the equilibrium process for the economy is limited. The principal class of economies to which these methods apply is economies with a single type of household and no distortions. This rules out economies with externalities, cash-in-advance constraints, limited contracting technology, monopolistic elements or non–lump sum taxes, among other things. These are all factors that result in nonoptimality of the equilibrium allocation.[4]

Supporting the Solution to the Planner's Problem as a Recursive Competitive Equilibrium

One approach that has proven very useful in the study of business cycle models is to support the allocation given by the planner's problem by using the decentralized stationary recursive competitive equilibrium (RCE) concept suggested by Prescott and Mehra (1980). This equilibrium concept is the one most widely used in this book.[5] Given a set of securities that is sufficient to realize all gains from allocating risks, recursive competitive equilibrium allocations support a state-contingent equilibrium.[6] The recursive competitive equilibrium is particularly convenient for the problem considered here and for the majority of those considered in this book because it fits naturally into the dynamic programming approach to solving optimization problems. It is also very easily applied in a wide variety of settings, including those with distortions, as Chapter 2 and many of the other chapters in this volume will make clear. Another great advantage of the RCE approach is that for an increasingly rich class of model economies, the equilibrium process can be computed and can be simulated to generate equilibrium paths for the economy. These paths can be studied to see whether model economies mimic the behavior of actual economies and can be used to provide quantitative answers to questions of economic welfare.

For the problem at hand, we illustrate the competitive solution, using the recursive competitive equilibrium concept just described. In this approach, we view households and firms as decisionmaking units, and we view individual households as solving dynamic programming problems. We distinguish between the economywide per capita capital stock, K, and the household's own capital stock, k, over which it has control. We further distinguish variables over which the household has control from their aggregate counterparts by using lower-case and upper-case letters, respectively. In equilibrium it will be true that $K = k$, but the problem the household solves makes a distinction between these. The state variables for the household are (k, K). Let $v(k, K)$ be the household's optimum value function and let primes denote next-period values. The household's decision problem is to choose a path for investment, x, and consumption, c, that solves the problem:

$$v(k, K) = \max_{c,x,\geq 0} \{u(c) + \beta v[k', K']\}$$

$$\text{s.t.} \quad c + x \leq r(K)k + w(K),$$

$$k' = (1 - \delta)k + x,$$

$$K' = (1 - \delta)K + X(K). \tag{12}$$

Let $d(k, K)$ be the policy function that gives the optimal decisions for this problem. Because all households are identical it must be the case that in equilibrium $d(k, K) = D(K)$. This leads us to the following definition:

A *recursive competitive equilibrium* is a value function, $v(k, K): \mathbf{R}_+^2 \to \mathbf{R}$; a policy function, $d(k, K): \mathbf{R}_+^2 \to \mathbf{R}_+$, which gives decisions on $c(k, K)$, $x(k, K)$ for the representative household; an aggregate per capita policy function, $D(K): \mathbf{R}_+ \to \mathbf{R}_+$, which gives aggregate decisions $C(K)$ and $X(K)$; and factor price functions, $r(K): \mathbf{R}_+ \to \mathbf{R}_+ w(K): \mathbf{R}_+ \to \mathbf{R}_+$, such that these functions satisfy

1) the household's problem (12);

2) the necessary and sufficient conditions for profit maximization, (8) and (9);

3) the consistency of individual and aggregate decisions, i.e., the condition $d(K, K) = D(K)$, $\forall K$; and

4) the aggregate resource constraint, $C(K) + X(K) = Y(K)$.

If (v, d, D, r, w) is a recursive competitive equilibrium, then the statement that competitive equilibrium allocations are Pareto optimal implies that $v(K, K)$ coincides with the value function $V(K)$ for the social planner's problem discussed earlier and $D(K)$ coincides with the optimal policy function for that problem. This equivalence will be exploited in many of the problems discussed in the ensuing chapters. In the next chapter we show how to solve for a competitive equilibrium by solving the social planner's problem. Equivalence between the competitive equilibrium allocation and the solution to the social planner's problem will not always hold. In some applications, an economy is subject to distortions (because of taxes, money, or other variations in the arrangements), so the competitive equilibrium allocation will not be Pareto optimal. In such cases, we cannot obtain the competitive equilibrium allocation by solving the social planner's problem. In the next chapter we show how to solve a related problem that yields the recursive competitive equilibrium allocation in these situations.

Using the Growth Model

The previous section describes a "model economy" that is explicitly designed to depict how an economy might grow over time in a way that is consistent with the growth facts described at the beginning of this section. It is a competitive general equilibrium economy because we can represent the paths of consumption, investment, output, and hours worked as the market-clearing outcome of individual households and firms responding to prices. An important feature of this economy, from our point of view, is that we can compute the equilibrium and use it to generate data.

To generate time series of the variables of the equilibrium for this economy, we would first assume functional forms for the preferences and technology, assign values to the parameters of those functional forms and assign a value to the initial condition K_0. Given those, we would first use equation (6) to compute K_1. Then equation (4) can be used to compute C_0. Because households do not value leisure and the marginal product of labor is strictly positive, $H_0 = 1$. Equations (7) and (8) are then used to determine the rental prices of the factors r_0 and w_0, and equation (9) is used to determine the interest rate i_t. This process can be repeated to determine the Date 1 values of the variables, along with the Date 2 capital stock. Similarly, the value of each variable can be determined for every subsequent date. This is the sense in which we can operate this artificial economy to study its equilibrium path.

The behavior of economies with these features is well understood. We know that for suitably parametrized preferences and technology, this economy will converge to a balanced growth path that is consistent with the stylized facts described earlier. Producing a balanced growth path is not the main objective of the research and methods described in this book. We view the growth model as a basic building block—a platform that can be extended and elaborated to address richer and more interesting questions.

Robert Solow (1957) addressed one such question when he applied the neo-classical growth model to the U.S. economy to calculate the sources of long-term growth. Using data for the period from 1909 to 1949, Solow estimated that changes in productivity accounted for 87.5 percent of the growth in real output per worker over this period while only about 12.5 percent was accounted for by increased capital per worker.[7] If we were to revisit Solow's calculation of the sources of secular growth but use more recent data we would obtain a breakdown something like that shown in the accompanying table. If we impute the value of the flow of services from consumer durables and add it to measured output, then capital's share in output will be about one-third (we will make these shares more precise in Section 4). Thus approximately one-third of the growth in output per worker is attributable to changes in capital per worker. We also know that there is no trend in the average hours of work per worker in the post–World War II period, so variations in the labor input do not contribute to secular growth. That suggests that the remaining two-thirds of secular growth in output is attributable to improvements in productivity. These are features we would like a model economy to reproduce.

Changes in Output per Worker	Secular Growth	Business Cycle
Due to changes in capital	1/3	0
Due to changes in labor	0	2/3
Due to changes in productivity	2/3	1/3

The primary focus of this book is on business cycles. This leads us to ask how we should modify the basic growth model to see if it can generate cycles. Business cycle accounting is more difficult and the breakdown is more approximate. The decomposition of output fluctuations for the business cycle (again based on the neoclassical growth model) reveals that the sources of business cycle fluctuations are quite different. We know that the capital input fluctuates very little over the cycle and that variations in capital are largely uncorrelated with the cycle. About two-thirds of the fluctuations in aggregate output are attributable to fluctuations in the labor input. Since capital does not vary much, the remaining one-third of fluctuations is attributable to fluctuations in productivity.

This accounting exercise tells us that a model that *integrates* both growth and fluctuations is going to require some features not present in the deterministic growth model. First, we must introduce some mechanism that causes productivity to change at the business cycle frequency. Second, we must introduce labor supply in a way that is consistent with large movements in the labor input over the cycle. Simply stating the problem this way does not make it immediately obvious that there is only one way or a correct way to modify the growth model to produce business cycle–type fluctuations. Kydland and Prescott (1982) and Long and Plosser (1983) explored a number of alternatives, and not all of them were successful. Many alternatives will be explored in the following chapters. In the next section, we describe a modification of the basic growth model that can in principle reproduce these fluctuations. The economy we describe is a stochastic version of the model we have been analyzing here. It also incorporates variations in employment, so it has the potential to explain the features of business cycle fluctuations as well as secular growth. After we have described the model, we will discuss how to use it empirically, describing how we calibrate its parameters from observed features of the U.S. economy, compute an equilibrium, and generate data from that equilibrium.

3. A Stochastic Growth Economy with Labor-Leisure Choice

The Environment

In this section we describe an economic environment that is richer than the one portrayed above. In the basic neoclassical growth model, neither employment nor savings varies over time once the economy has entered its long-run steady state. Here, we modify that economy so that households may vary their consumption and labor supply over time. Their reason for so doing is that in this economy, the agents face uncertainty about their future productivity. The economy is populated by infinitely many identical households that will exist forever. Each of these households has an endowment of time for each period, which it must divide between leisure, ℓ_t, and work, h_t. We normalize the households' time endowment to unity, that is, we set $h_t + \ell_t = 1$. In addition, the households own an initial stock of capital, k_0, which they rent to firms and may augment through investment.

Households' utility for each period is defined over stochastic sequences of consumption and leisure:

$$U[c(\cdot), h(\cdot)] = E\{\sum_{t=0}^{\infty} \beta^t u(c_t, 1 - h_t)\} \quad 0 < \beta < 1, \tag{13}$$

where $c(\cdot)$, $h(\cdot)$ represent the sequences of Arrow-Debreu event-contingent consumptions and labor supplies. We assume that u is continuously differentiable in both arguments, that u is increasing in both arguments, and that u is strictly concave. The households in this economy supply capital and labor to firms, which have access to a technology described by the aggregate production function $F(K_t, H_t) : \mathbf{R}_+ \to \mathbf{R}$. We assume that F is continuously differentiable in K and

H, that F is monotonic in K and H, that F is concave in K and H separately, and that $F(0, 0) = 0$.

Aggregate output is determined by the production function:

$$Y_t = e^{z_t} F(K_t, H_t), \tag{14}$$

where z_t is a random productivity parameter. This productivity shock is the source of uncertainty in the economy. We will make the very specific assumption that z_t evolves according to the law of motion:

$$z_{t+1} = \rho z_t + \epsilon_{t+1}, \quad 0 < \rho < 1. \tag{15}$$

where ϵ is distributed normally, with mean zero and standard deviation σ_ϵ. Brock and Mirman (1972) showed that if the $\{z_t\}$ are identically distributed random variables then there exists a solution to the social planner's problem for this economy.[8]

We assume that the capital stock depreciates exponentially at the rate δ and that consumers add to the stock of capital by investing some amount of the real output each period. Investment in period t produces productive capital in period $t + 1$ so that the law of motion for the aggregate capital stock is

$$K_{t+1} = (1 - \delta)K_t + X_t. \tag{16}$$

As in the previous example, the firms rent capital and hire labor in each period. We can treat this as a single firm that solves a period-by-period profit maximization problem. All relative prices are in terms of output, and we can write the firm's period t problem as

$$\max_{K_t, H_t} p_t \cdot [e^{z_t} F(K_t, H_t) - r_t K_t - w_t H_t], \quad \forall t. \tag{17}$$

This optimization problem yields factor prices (stated in terms of the price of output):

$$r_t = e^{z_t} F_k(K_t, H_t), \tag{18}$$

and

$$w_t = e^{z_t} F_H(K_t, H_t). \tag{19}$$

As in the previous example, given constant returns to scale, in equilibrium profits will be equal to zero.

The households in this economy face a very difficult problem because they must form expectations over future prices. Households will choose consumption, investment, and hours of work at each date to maximize the expected discounted value of utility, given their expectations over future prices subject to sequences of budget constraints and the law of motion for the household's capital stock:

$$\max_{c,x,h} E\{\sum_{t=0}^{\infty} \beta^t u(c_t, 1 - h_t)\} 0 < \beta < 1,$$

$$\text{s.t.} \quad c_t + x_t \leq w_t h_t + r_t k_t,$$

$$k_{t+1} = (1 - \delta)k_t + x_t. \tag{20}$$

Note that for this problem, the prices, w and r, depend on the economywide state variables (z, K). Moreover, the decisions on quantities depend on the individual-level state variables (z, k, K). The equilibrium definition set forth in the next section makes this dependence more precise.

The Recursive Competitive Equilibrium

Again, we will use the recursive competitive equilibrium concept. The state variables for the households in this economy are $s_t = (z_t, k_t, K_t)$, and the aggregate state variables are $S_t = (z_t, K_t)$. The optimality equation for the household's problem can then be written as

$$v(z, k, K) = \max_{c,x,h}\{u(c, 1 - h) + \beta E[v(z', k', K')|z]\}$$

$$\text{s.t.} \quad c + x \leq r(z, K)k + w(z, K)h,$$

$$k' = (1 - \delta)k + x,$$

$$K' = (1 - \delta)K + X(z, K),$$

$$z' = \rho z + \epsilon,$$

$$c \geq 0, 0 \leq h \leq 1. \tag{21}$$

A *recursive competitive equilibrium* for this economy consists of a value function, $v(z, k, K)$; a set of decision rules, $c(z, k, K), h(z, k, K)$, and $x(z, k, K)$, for the household; a corresponding set of aggregate per capita decision rules, $C(z, K)$, $H(z, K)$, and $X(z, K)$; and factor price functions, $w(z, K)$ and $r(z, K)$, such that these functions satisfy:

1) the household's problem (21);

2) The condition that firms maximize and satisfy (18) and (19), that is, $r = r(z, K)$ and $w = w(z, K)$;

3) the consistency of individual and aggregate decisions, that is, the conditions $c(z, K, K) = C(z, K), h(z, K, K) = H(z, K)$, and $x(z, K, K) = X(z, K), \forall(z, K)$; and

4) the aggregate resource constraint, $C(z, K) + X(z, K) = Y(z, K)$, $\forall(z, K)$.

This completes the description of the environment and the equilibrium concept that we will use. This basic framework is consistent with many different model economies, depending on the further restrictions or different arrangements that are added. In order to use this framework to make quantitative statements about business cycles, we need a more explicit structure. In the next section we describe how parameter values are assigned to provide that structure.

4. Calibration

The description of the economic environment and the equilibrium concept together provide a framework that we can use to study business cycles. The environment described in the previous section has features that are motivated by the questions we want to address. In this chapter, the question we address is quite simple: does a model designed to be consistent with long-term economic growth produce the sort of fluctuations that we associate with the business cycle? In subsequent chapters many more complicated questions are addressed, and the basic structures studied in those sections are correspondingly altered. These alterations can take the form of changes in the environment and/or changes in the equilibrium concept.

The framework described in the previous section is consistent with many different equilibrium processes for the variables of interest—output, employment, investment, and so on. To go from that general framework to quantitative statements about the issues of interest is a three-step process. The first step is to restrict these processes to a parametric class. We stress the idea of using a model that is consistent with growth observations to study fluctuations. This requires the use of more economic theory and some observations. The second step in this process is to construct a set of measurements that are consistent with the parametric class of models. With enough theory and observations to define a parametric class of models, we can establish the correspondence between this class and the observed data for the U.S. (or some other) economy. As we will demonstrate, establishing this correspondence may well require that we reorganize the data for the U.S. economy in ways that make them consistent with our class of model economies. The third step is to assign values to the parameters of our models. This involves setting parameter values so that the behavior of the model economy matches features of the measured data in as many dimensions as there are unknown parameters. We observe over time that certain ratios in actual economies are more or less constant. We choose parameters for our model economy so that it mimics the actual economy on the dimensions associated with long term growth. Once this is accomplished we will be in a position to study the quantitative behavior of fluctuations in the particular model economy.

The process just described is called calibration. This approach has a long tradition in economics. This strategy for finding numerical values for parameters uses economic theory extensively as the basis for restricting the general framework and mapping that framework onto the data. As we will see in the chapters that follow, the kinds of restrictions that are used depend very much on the kinds of questions being asked of these artificial economies. If one is interested in studying the behavior of an economy with more than one sector, with distortions due to taxes or money, and/or with different arrangements due to contracting or non-Walrasian elements, the mapping between the theory and the data will be different. The common thread in all of these studies is that they all preserve the neoclassical growth framework.

Restricting the Growth Economy

The distinguishing features of the stochastic growth environment described in Section 3 are the household's labor-leisure choice and the presence of the shocks to technology. These features were added, as we noted earlier, to see if the model designed to explain long-term growth might also be capable of explaining fluctuations. In order to address this question, we are going to restrict our attention to artificial economies that display balanced growth. In balanced-growth consumption, investment and capital all grow at a constant rate while hours stay constant. This behavior is consistent with the growth observations described earlier.

The basic observations about economic growth suggest that capital and labor shares of output have been approximately constant over time even while the relative prices of these inputs have changed. This suggests a Cobb-Douglas production function, which has the form

$$Y_t = e^{z_t} K_t^\theta H_t^{1-\theta}. \tag{22}$$

The parameter θ is referred to as capital's share because if capital is paid its marginal product, it will earn that fraction of output. The Cobb-Douglas assumption defines a parametric class of technologies for this economy.

As with the technology, certain features of the specification of preferences are tied to basic growth observations for the U.S. economy. There is evidence that per capita leisure increased steadily until the 1930s. Since that time, and certainly for the postwar period, it has been approximately constant. We also know that real wages (defined as real average hourly total compensation, including benefits and contributions for social insurance) have increased steadily in the postwar period. Taken together, these two observations imply that the elasticity of substitution between consumption and leisure should be near unity. We consider the general parametric class of preferences of the form

$$u(c_t, \ell_t) = \frac{(c_t^{1-\alpha} \ell_t^\alpha)^{1-\sigma} - 1}{1 - \sigma,} \tag{23}$$

where $1/\sigma$ is the intertemporal elasticity of substitution and α is the share parameter for leisure in the composite commodity. The parameter σ is among the most difficult to pin down because variations in the intertemporal elasticity of substitution affect transitions to balanced growth paths but not the paths themselves. In the sections below, we will further restrict this to the limiting case where $\sigma = 1$, which is $u(c_t, 1 - h_t) = (1 - \alpha) \log c_t + \alpha \log(1 - h_t).$[9]

Defining Consistent Measurements

Calibrating the parametric class of economies chosen requires that we consider the correspondence between the model economy and the measurements that are taken for the U.S. economy. The neoclassical growth framework emphasizes the central role of capital in determining long-term growth in output. Consequently, the first thing we have to consider is the match between the capital as it is conceived in our class of model economies and capital as it is measured and as it is conceptualized in the U.S. National Income and Product Accounts (NIPA).[10]

Our model economy is very abstract: it contains no government sector, no household production sector, no foreign sector and no explicit treatment of inventories. Accordingly, the model economy's capital stock, K, includes capital used in all of these sectors plus the stock of inventories. Similarly, output, Y, includes the output produced by all of this capital. The NIPA are somewhat inconsistent in their treatment of these issues in that the output of some important parts of the capital stock are not included in measured output.[11] For example, the NIPA does not provide a consistent treatment of the household sector. The accounts do include the imputed flow of services from owner-occupied housing as part of GNP. But they do not attempt to impute the flow of services from the stock of consumer durables. The NIPA lump additions to the stock of consumer durables with consumption rather than treating them as investment. Because our model economy does not treat the household sector separately, when we deal with the measured data, we will add the household's capital stock—the stock of residential structures and the stock of consumer durables—to producers' equipment and structures. To be consistent, we will also have to impute the flow of services from durables and add that to measured output. In Chapter 6, where the household production sector is explicitly modeled, the distinction between household capital and the business sector capital will be explicitly preserved, as will the distinction between household output and business sector output.

In a similar vein, although there are estimates of the stock of government capital and estimates of the portion of government consumption that represents additions to that stock of capital, the NIPA make no attempt to impute the flow of services from the government's capital stock and include it as part of output. Nor do the NIPA include government investment as part of measured investment. Because our model economy does not have a government sector, we will add the government capital stock to the private capital stock and the capital stock in the household sector. We will also impute the flow of services from this capital stock and add it to measured output.

Finally, our technology makes no distinction among the roles of reproducible capital, land, and inventories. Some of the later chapters will assign a different role to inventories, but here they are treated as identical to the other forms of capital. When we consider the mapping between the model economy and measured data, it will be important to include the value of land and the value of the stock of inventories as part of the capital stock. The Flow of Funds Accounts, Balance Sheets for the U.S. Economy are the source for estimates of the value of land, and the stock of inventories is reported in the NIPA.[12]

The measurement issues discussed above are central to the task of calibrating any model economy because a consistent set of measurements is necessary to align the model economy with the data. For example, in order to estimate the crucial share parameter in the production function, θ, for our model economy, it is important to measure all forms of capital and to augment measured GNP to include measures of all forms of output. Similarly, when we treat aggregate investment it will be necessary to include in investment additions to all forms of capital stock. For this model economy, the concept of investment that corresponds to the aggregate capital stock includes government investment, "consumption" of consumer durables, changes in inventories, gross fixed investment, and net exports.[13] Making sure that the conceptual framework of the model economy and the conceptual framework of the measured data are consistent, is a crucial step in the process of calibration.

To impute the flow of services from government capital and consumer durables, we will use more economic theory. We know that the income from capital is related to the stock of capital, as follows:

$$Y_{KP} = (i + \delta_{KP})K_P, \tag{24}$$

where Y_{KP} is the income on fixed private capital, K_P is the fixed private capital stock, and δ_{KP} is the depreciation rate of that capital stock. Given measured values of the capital stock, measured values for capital income, and a measured value for depreciation, we can obtain an estimate of i, the return on capital. Measured K_P includes the net stock of Fixed Reproducible Private Capital (*not* including the stock of consumer durables), from Musgrave (1992); the stock of inventories, from the NIPA; and the stock of land, from the Flow of Funds Accounts.

The measured value of income from fixed private capital is taken from the NIPA. There is some judgment involved in defining this because of ambiguity about how much of Proprietors' income and some other smaller categories (specifically, the difference between Net National Product and National Income) should be treated as capital income. We define the measured income in the following way. Let unambiguous capital income be defined as follows:

Unambiguous Capital Income = Rental Income + Corporate Profits

+ Net Interest,

with Rental Income, Corporate Profits, and Net Interest from the NIPA (see table 1.14).

Our strategy is to allocate the ambiguous components of income according to the share of capital income in measured GNP. Let θ_P denote the share of capital in measured GNP. Further, note that the measured value of $\delta_P K_P$ is "Consumption of Fixed Capital" (GNP − NNP) in the NIPA (Table 1.9). We denote this variable as DEP. Define Y_{KP} as follows:

$$Y_{KP} = \text{Unambiguous Capital Income} + \theta_P(\text{Proprietors Income}$$

$$+ \text{ Net National Product} - \text{National Income}) + \text{DEP}$$

$$= \theta_P \cdot \text{GNP}.$$

This equation can be solved for θ_P:

$$\theta_P = \frac{(\text{Unambiguous Capital Income} + \text{DEP})}{(\text{GNP} - \text{Ambiguous Capital Income})}.$$

Multiplying θ_P by GNP, gives us the measured value of Y_{KP}. Given measured Y_{KP}, we use the equation above to determine the interest rate, i:

$$i = (Y_{KP} - \text{DEP})/K_P. \tag{25}$$

Over the sample period, 1954–1992, this yields an average interest rate of 6.9 percent.

To estimate the flow of services from the stock of consumer durables and the stock of government capital we need estimates of the depreciation rates for those portions of the capital stock. These are obtained from the laws of motion for these capital stocks:

$$K_{t+1} = (1 - \delta)K_t + X_t, \tag{26}$$

where X represents investment. Normalizing by output, Y_t, and multiplying by Y_{t+1}/Y_{t+1} yields

$$\frac{Y_{t+1}}{Y_t} \cdot \frac{K_{t+1}}{Y_{t+1}} = (1 - \delta)\frac{K_t}{Y_t} + \frac{X_t}{Y_t}. \tag{27}$$

On a balanced-growth path, $K_{t+1}/Y_{t+1} = K_t/Y_t$, and equation (27) provides the basis for measuring the depreciation rates for consumer durables and government capital. For consumer durables, investment is simply consumption of consumer durables as reported in the NIPA. For government investment the figures also come from the NIPA (table 3.7b). The stock of durables and the government capital stock are taken from Musgrave (1992). If we use the data for 1954–1992, the depreciation rate implied by equation (27) is 0.21 per annum for durables and 0.05 for government capital.[14] The service flows are then estimated as

$$Y_D = (i + \delta_D)K_D,$$

and

$$Y_G = (i + \delta_G)K_G,$$

where the interest rate and the depreciation rates are those estimated above.

The process just described used economic theory to help define a consistent set of measurements. We rearranged and augmented the measured data to correspond to the structure of the model economy. The parameters we used to do this, however, depend only on information in the NIPA and are not specific to the model economy being studied.

Calibrating a Specific Model Economy

The model economy described in Section 3, displays no population growth or long-term productivity growth. The economy we want to match it to is characterized by both. If we let η denote the rate of population growth and let λ denote the long-term real growth rate, then we can rewrite our model economy to take account of these features. If we further restrict the parametric class of preferences so that $\sigma = 1$, we can rewrite the problem in (20) as

$$\max E\left[\sum_{t=0}^{\infty} \beta^t (1 + \eta)^t [(1 - \alpha) \log c_t + \alpha \log(1 - h_t)]\right]$$

s.t. $c_t + x_t = e^{z_t}(1 - \gamma)^{t(1-\theta)} k_t^\theta h_t^{1-\theta},$

$(1 + \gamma)(1 + \eta)k_{t+1} = (1 - \delta)k_t + x_t,$

$z_{t+1} = \rho z_t + \epsilon_t.$ \hfill (28)

All variables are in per capita terms. The parameters η and γ can be measured from the data as the rate of population growth and the rate of growth of real per capita output, respectively. Similarly, given estimates of the missing components of output as described above, capital's share in output, θ, is calibrated as follows:

$$\theta = (Y_{KP} + Y_D + Y_G)/(\text{GNP} + Y_D + Y_G) = 0.40. \hfill (29)$$

Labor's share is $1 - \theta = 0.60$. These estimates are somewhat different than those that appear elsewhere in the literature because they include the imputed income from government capital.[15]

We calibrate the remaining parameters by choosing them so that the balanced-growth path of our model economy matches certain long-term features of the measured economy. Substituting the constraints into the objectives and deriving the first-order condition for k yields

$$\frac{(1 + \gamma)(1 + \eta)}{c_t} = \frac{\beta(1 + \eta)[\theta k_{t+1}^{\theta-1} h_{t+1}^{1-\theta} + 1 - \delta]}{c_{t+1}}. \hfill (30)$$

In balanced growth, this implies that:

$$\frac{(1 + \gamma)}{\beta} + \delta - 1 = \theta \cdot \frac{y}{k}. \tag{31}$$

The first-order condition for hours, h, on a balanced-growth path implies that:

$$(1 - \theta) \cdot \frac{y}{c} = \frac{\alpha}{1 - \alpha} \cdot \frac{h}{1 - h}. \tag{32}$$

Finally, the law of motion for the capital stock in steady state implies that

$$(1 + \gamma)(1 + \eta) \frac{k}{y} = (1 - \delta) \frac{k}{y} + \frac{x}{y}$$

$$\delta = \frac{x}{k} + 1 - (1 + \gamma)(1 + \eta). \tag{33}$$

Equation (33) is the basis for calibrating the aggregate depreciation rate, δ, for this economy, which is seen to depend on the aggregate investment/capital ratio. The steady-state investment/capital ratio for this economy is 0.076. Given the values of γ and η, the parameter δ is calibrated to match this ratio. This yields an annual depreciation rate of 0.048, or a quarterly rate of 0.012. This number depends on the real growth rate, γ, and the population growth rate for the economy. In an economy that does not explicitly include growth this number must be larger to match investment.

Once δ is calibrated, equation (31) provides the basis for determining β. Given values for γ, δ, and θ, β is chosen to match the steady-state output/capital ratio. Under the broad definitions of output and capital consistent with our model economy, the capital/output ratio is 3.32. This yields an annual value for β of 0.947, which implies a quarterly value of about 0.987.

Given an estimate of h, the fraction of time devoted to market activities, equation (32) provides the basis for calibrating the preference parameter, α, based on the steady-state output consumption ratio. The value of h is determined by microeconomic evidence from time allocation studies. Ghez and Becker (1975) and Juster and Stafford (1991) have found that households allocate about one-third of their discretionary time—i.e., time not spent sleeping or in personal maintenance—to market activities. The specific value we use for h is 0.31. Given the broad definition of consumption and output appropriate for this model economy, the steady-state ratio of output to consumption is 1.33. This implies a value of $\alpha/(1 - \alpha) = 1.78$.

Finally, completion of our calibration of this model economy requires parameters of the process that generates the shocks to technology. One approach to calibrating this process would be to do as Robert Solow did and calculate technological change as the difference between changes in output and the changes in measured inputs (labor and capital) times their shares. Using equation (22), we obtain:

$$z_t - z_{t-1} = (\ln Y_t - \ln Y_{t-1}) - [\theta \cdot (\ln K_t - \ln K_{t-1})$$
$$+ (1 - \theta) \cdot (\ln H_t - \ln H_{t-1})] \tag{34}$$

These are the Solow residuals for this economy. Using our estimate of $\theta = 0.4$ and observations on measured output, given a measure of the labor input, we can generate a series for the z_t and their difference. We use a quarterly hours series based on the Establishment Survey for the labor input. An alternative would be to use the hours series based on the Household Survey. The other decision we face is whether to use the broad definition of capital stock consistent with our model economy, and whether to use the broad definition of output, including the imputed service flows from consumer durables and government capital. We elect to use simply measured output (real GNP) and measured labor input, assuming quarterly variations in the capital stock to be approximately zero. We choose this alternative because the capital stock series is only reported annually. Consequently, the imputed service flows that we described above are also annual. One can interpolate quarterly versions of these, but any procedure for doing so is essentially arbitrary and may add to the variability of both output and the residuals. The residuals computed using measured real GNP are highly persistent, and the autocorrelations are quite consistent with a technology process that is a random walk. We assume a value of $\rho = 0.95$, in the law of motion for the technology and use this to define a set of innovations to technology. These innovations have a standard deviation of about 0.007, which is similar to the value calibrated in Prescott (1986).[16]

We summarize our calibrated parameters in the accompanying table.

Technology					Preferences			
θ	δ	ρ	σ_ϵ	γ	β	σ	α	η
0.40	0.012	0.95	0.007	0.0156	0.987	1	0.64	0.012

One of the standard meanings of the word calibration is "to standardize as a measuring instrument." This definition applies to our calibration of the stochastic growth model. Since the underlying structure is the neoclassical growth framework, the choice of parameters and functional forms ensures that this model economy will display balanced growth. This is the standard that we insist on preserving in our study of business cycles. It remains to be seen whether this model economy reproduces anything that looks like business cycles. Before we can address that, we need to describe how the model can be solved for an equilibrium path.

5. Computing the Recursive Competitive Equilibrium

We have motivated our interest in the recursive competitive equilibrium construct in part by arguing that it fits naturally into the dynamic programming language in a convenient way. This connection is also exploited in solving the model. Many methods for solving for the competitive equilibria of these types of economies have been proposed and used in recent business cycle literature. Indeed, this area of research—the study of techniques for solving for the equilibria of dynamic rational expectations economies—has been one of the most active in macroeconomics. This book does not attempt to provide an exhaustive discussion of solution methods. To do so would occupy a whole volume in itself. In the next three chapters we describe a variety of methods for solving such models. Chapter 2, by Gary Hansen and Edward Prescott, describes a set of methods that are among the most important for solving straightforward representative agent economies and overlapping-generations economies. It also describes how those methods may be applied to economies that are subject to distortions where the competitive equilibrium is not a Pareto optimum (i.e., where the Second Welfare Theorem does not apply.) In Chapter 3, Jean-Pierre Danthine and John Donaldson describe a different set of methods, which have been used fruitfully in economies that are subject to distortions and which have computational advantages in a variety of other situations. Chapter 4, by José-Víctor Ríos-Rull describes a set of techniques that are used to solve economies with heterogeneous agents and also shows how to structure economies with overlapping generations so that they can be solved using the methods described in Chapter 2. We do not intend to discuss solution techniques in this chapter, but we do want to present a brief overview of what different solution techniques try to do and provide a taxonomy for understanding where the techniques discussed in the next few chapters fit into the literature.[17]

It is easy to see from the development in the preceding sections that most applications based on the neoclassical growth model result in a stationary dynamic programming problem. The general form of the problem that must be solved in order to obtain an equilibrium path when there is only one type of agent in the economy is:[18]

$$v(z, s) = \max\{r(z, s, d) + \beta E[v(z', s')|z]\}$$

$$\text{s.t.} \quad z' = A(z) + \epsilon'$$

$$s' = B(z, s, d), \tag{35}$$

where $v(z, s)$ is the optimal value function, z is a vector of exogenous state variables (for example, technology shocks), s is a vector of endogenous state variables (for example, the capital stock), d is a vector of decision variables, and $r(z, s, d)$ is the return function for the problem. The two constraints describe the evolution of the state variables.

The object of interest is a function mapping a state space into decisions. Existing solution methods for finding a decision rule fall into two categories. Each seeks to define an operator that will find the fixed point of a particular functional equation. In the first approach the operator maps the space of continuous bounded functions into itself in such a manner that the value function is the unique fixed point of the operator. Since, in addition, this operator can be shown to be a contraction, successive applications of the operator applied to any continuous bounded function will generate a sequence of functions which converges uniformly to the true $v(.)$. Since this process cannot be literally replicated on a computer, computational techniques have been developed that solve for an approximation to the operator's true fixed point. Given this approximation to the true $v(.)$, an approximation to the economy's optimal policy functions or decision rules follows indirectly.

The second approach, the Euler method, goes directly for the decision rules by using the information contained in the necessary and sufficient first-order conditions for an optimum. This approach uses the first-order conditions to define, implicitly, a monotone operator—again, with domain and range the space of continuous bounded functions—for which the unique fixed point is the economy's optimal policy function. These two methods are more precisely contrasted below in the context of problem (35).

Operating Directly with the Value Function

For any $g \in x$, the space of continuous bounded functions defined on an appropriately chosen compact subset of the economy's state space, define the operator, T, as follows:

$$Tg(z, s) = \max_{s' \in B(z,s,d)} [r(z, s, d) + \beta E(g(s', z')|z)]. \tag{36}$$

We summarize the economic environment—i.e., β; the return function, $r(z, s, d)$; and the constraint set, $B(x, s, d)$—by E (not to be confused with the expectation operator). As noted earlier, the search for a $v(.)$ that solves problem (35) is equivalent to searching for a fixed point of the operator, $T : x \to x$. Since the operator acts on an (infinite-dimensional) function space it is impossible to replicate it computationally. Two approaches have been followed in the literature to deal with this issue. Both involve replacing the economy E by an approximate economy $\tilde{E}$ for which a solution is feasible.

The first approach is to simplify the space x by restricting the domain of definition to be only a finite subset, or "grid," of the state space. This amounts to finding an operator T that maps a finite-dimensional subspace. Under suitable regularity conditions, this modified map will also be a contraction with a fixed point approximating the true $v(.)$, provided the approximating grid is chosen finely enough. This approach to computing equilibria has been taken by Danthine and Donaldson (1981), Christiano (1990), and Greenwood, Hercowitz, and Huffman (1988). This technique is not discussed in any great detail in this book.

The second approach to simplifying (35) is discussed in detail in the next chapter, by Hansen and Prescott, and, in a different context, in Chapter 4, by José-Víctor Ríos-Rull. The primary strategy for finding a solution by these methods involves forming a linear quadratic approximation around the steady-state equilibrium path of the original economy and looking for a solution for this approximate linear quadratic economy. This technique was introduced in the literature by Kydland and Prescott (1982) and has been widely explored and applied in subsequent research.

Operating Directly on the Euler Equations

Approaches that operate directly on the Euler equations also involve an operator, T, that maps a function space into itself. The difference here is that the operator is defined by the structure of the necessary and sufficient conditions for an optimum (on which market-clearing conditions have been imposed) that characterize the economy's equilibrium. Nowhere is the value function for the economy, $v(.)$, computed. Indeed, such a $v(.)$ may not exist if the equilibrium being characterized is not optimal because of the presence of taxes or other distortions. One advantage of this approach is that in recursive competitive equilibrium problems where there is a distinction between individual and aggregate state variables, it permits one to operate simply with the aggregate state variables. All implications of the distinction between aggregate and individual variables are lost in the way derivatives are taken to get the Euler equations.

For an economy with one intertemporal decision—say, how much to invest—equilibrium can be described as an aggregate function, $I(z, s)$, that satisfies an integral equation of the form

$$0 = -h[I(z, s), z, s] + \beta \int J[I(z', s'), z', s']dg(z', z). \tag{37}$$

The endogenous state variable, s, for this simple economy is k, and $k' = (1 - \delta)k + I(z, k)$.

Under quite general conditions we can define an operator $T: T(z, k) \rightarrow TI(z, k)$ where $TI(z, k)$ satisfies the conditions:

$$\arg \min | -h[TI(z, k), z, k] + \beta \int J[I(z', k')z', k']dg(z', z)|, \tag{38}$$

and $k' = (1 - \delta)k + I(z, k)$. For the studies in this volume the operator defined above will usually be monotone: successive application of the operator will generate a monotone increasing sequence of functions, which is bounded above and which converges to the fixed point of T.

For any function $I(z, k)$, $TI(z, k)$ is also a function, and the above operator cannot be exactly replicated numerically. As before, two avenues are open. One is to replace the function space by a space of finite-dimensional functions. In this approach, one solves the countable infinity of equations, using functions defined by a finite number of parameters. Clearly, the functional equation cannot be solved exactly. What these methods do is to solve the equation as closely as possible. Solution strategies based on this approach include the method of parametrized expectations of Marcet (1989), the algorithms developed by Danthine and Donaldson (1990) and Coleman (1991), and the minimum weighted residuals technique of Judd (1991). These computational techniques, along with a few others, are discussed in considerable detail in Chapter 3, by Danthine and Donaldson.

Again, as before, we may also substantially simplify the economy's primitive to allow for a simple representation of equation (37). One example of this approach is the strategy adopted by King, Plosser, and Rebelo (1988a) of finding a linear approximation to the first-order conditions characterizing equilibrium. This is related to solution methods proposed much earlier by Blanchard and Kahn (1980). It can also be seen to be related to the "backsolving" method proposed by Sims (1989). The King, Plosser and Rebelo approach is discussed in Chapter 3, by Danthine and Donaldson.

The intent of the next three chapters is to provide a firm grounding in these solution techniques, which can then be used to solve a wide variety of model economies. Throughout the book, special problems arise that require slight modifications to make these methods for computing equilibria work. In Chapter 5, by Finn Kydland, some new wrinkles are needed to solve the models he considers. In Chapter 7, by Cooley and Hansen, special information structures arise that require some modifications to the solution techniques. Where such problems do arise or where the solution procedure is somehow special, we provide further details about how to compute the equilibria.

6. Business Cycle Facts

What features of economic life do we think the stochastic growth economy just described might explain? Lucas, following on the work of Burns and Mitchell, argued that the business cycle should be thought of as apparent deviations from a trend in which variables move together. An examination of the time path of output for any modern industrialized economy quickly reveals that output tends to fluctuate about a long-term growth path. These fluctuations about trend are what we most often think of as the business cycle. The fluctuations are typically irregularly spaced and of varying amplitude and duration. Nevertheless, the one very regular feature of these fluctuations is the way variables move together. It is these comovements of variables that Burns and Mitchell worked so hard to document and that Robert Lucas emphasized as the defining features of the business cycle. These are the features of fluctuations that we would like an artificial economy—a business cycle model—to replicate.

Representing the Business Cycle

Every researcher who has studied growth and/or business cycle fluctuations has faced the problem of how to represent those features of economic data that are associated with long-term growth and those that are associated with the business cycle—the deviations from the growth path. Kuznets, Mitchell, and Burns and Mitchell all employed techniques (moving averages, piecewise trends, etc.) that define the growth component of the data in order to study the fluctuations of variables around the long-term path defined by the growth component. Whatever choice one makes about this is somewhat arbitrary. There is no single correct way to represent these components. They are simply different features of the same observed data.

For a long time, the prevailing view was that we need two different types of theory to explain the different features of the observed data: growth theory to explain the long-term movements; something else to explain the rest. Modern business cycle theory is based on a different premise: the same theory should be capable of explaining both features of the data. It is important to recognize that it was not obvious ahead of time that this premise would be borne out; in choosing a representation, one does not necessarily take a stand on whether a separate theory is needed for both components.

In the chapters that follow and in the modern business cycle literature in general, the authors typically follow one of two procedures to represent the cyclical component in the data. Some assume a stochastic trend and first difference the (logarithms of the) data to remove it. This procedure is well understood by economists. Most of the authors use a technique for representing growth and business cycle components known as the Hodrick-Prescott filter (the H-P filter) a procedure that is less well understood. We describe this filter, explain briefly what it does, and illustrate its effect on the time series of real GNP.

We characterize an observed time series, y_t, as the sum of a cyclical component, y_t^c, and a growth component, y_t^g. Let λ be a parameter that reflects the relative variance of the growth component to the cyclical component. Then, given a value for λ, the H-P filtering problem is to choose the growth component, y_t^g, to minimize the loss function:

$$\sum_{t=1}^{T}(y_t^c)^2 + \lambda \sum_{t=1}^{T}[(y_{t+1}^g - y_t^g) - (y_t^g - y_{t-1}^g)]^2. \tag{39}$$

The nature of this optimization problem is to trade off the extent to which the growth component tracks the actual series (which yields a smaller cyclical component, y_t^c against the smoothness of the trend.[19] For $\lambda = 0$ the growth component is simply the series. As $\lambda \to \infty$, the growth component approaches a linear trend. For quarterly data it is customary to choose $\lambda = 1,600$. The motivation behind this choice is that if the original series were stationary, then the H-P filter with this choice of λ would eliminate fluctuations at frequencies lower than about thirty-two quarters, or eight years. We normally think of the business cycle as fluctuations about the growth path that occur with a frequency of three to five years. This is what Burns and Mitchell (1946) characterized as the usual business cycle frequency. Hence the H-P filter suppresses the really low-frequency fluctuations and emphasizes those in this range. In contrast, the first-difference filter suppresses only the zero frequency and tends to emphasize really high-frequency movements in the data.

Perhaps the easiest way to see what the H-P filter does is to look at the representation of the cyclical component and the growth component that it gives for a typical time series. Figure 1.1 shows a plot of real GNP and its H-P–filtered growth component. The parameter λ was set at 1,600 for this exercise. One can see that the growth component tracks the series reasonably closely but produces a "trend" that highlights cyclical movements, as intended. Figure 1.2 shows the H-P–filtered cyclical component of real GNP, as well as the cyclical component derived from the first-difference filter. It appears from these figures that the first-difference filter leads to more short-term fluctuation than does the H-P filter. This is to be expected since the latter filter emphasizes the high-frequency movements more.

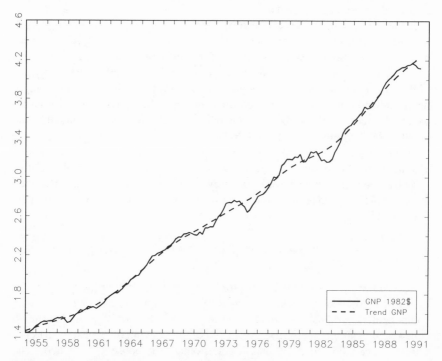

Figure 1.1 Log of Real GNP and Its Growth Component
Trillions of 1982 dollars (log scale).

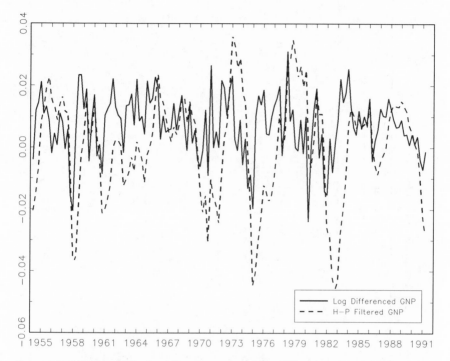

Figure 1.2 H-P–Filtered Cyclical Component and Log-Differenced Real GNP

Correspondingly, it can also be seen that the H-P–filtered data display more serial correlation.

Another alternative for removing fluctuations other than those that occur at the business cycle frequencies is to use a band-pass filter that would eliminate fluctuations at frequencies higher than, say, three years and lower than eight years. Such a filter has been used by some authors, notably Englund, Persson, and Svensson (1992). To implement the filter requires first applying the H-P, or differencing, filter to remove the lowest frequencies, transforming to the frequency domain, and then removing the remaining high-frequency elements. This is fully feasible only with very long data series, and in practice it seems to create no substantive difference in the properties of business cycles.

The Facts

We represent the business cycle facts by calculating several statistics from the H-P filtered time series data for the U.S. economy. We report the amplitude of the fluctuations in aggregate variables in order to assess their relative magnitudes. We also measure the correlation of aggregate variables with real output to capture the extent to which variables are procyclical (positively correlated) or countercyclical

Table 1.1
Cyclical Behavior of the U.S. Economy: Deviations from Trend of Key Variables, 1954:I–1991:II

Variable	SD%	Cross-Correlation of Output with:										
		$x(-5)$	$x(-4)$	$x(-3)$	$x(-2)$	$x(-1)$	x	$x(+1)$	$x(+2)$	$x(+3)$	$x(+4)$	$x(+5)$
Output component												
GNP	1.72	.02	.16	.38	.63	.85	1.0	.85	.63	.38	.16	−.02
Consumption expenditures												
CONS	1.27	.25	.42	.57	.72	.82	.83	.67	.46	.22	−.01	−.20
CNDS	0.86	.22	.40	.55	.68	.78	.77	.64	.47	.27	.06	−.11
CD	4.96	.24	.37	.49	.65	.75	.78	.61	.38	.11	−.13	−.31
Investment												
INV	8.24	.04	.19	.38	.59	.79	.91	.76	.50	.22	−.04	−.24
INVF	5.34	.08	.25	.43	.63	.82	.90	.81	.60	.35	.09	−.12
INVN	5.11	−.26	−.12	.05	.30	.57	.79	.88	.83	.60	.46	.24
INVR	10.7	.42	.55	.65	.72	.74	.63	.39	.11	−.14	−.33	−.43
Ch. INV	17.3	−.03	.07	.22	.38	.53	.67	.51	.27	.04	−.15	−.30
Government purchases												
GOVT	2.04	.03	−.01	−.03	−.01	−.01	.04	.08	.11	.16	.25	.32
Exports and imports												
EXP	5.53	−.48	−.42	−.29	−.10	.15	.37	.50	.54	.54	.52	.44
IMP	4.88	.11	.19	.31	.45	.62	.72	.71	.52	.28	.04	−.18
Labor input based on household survey												
HSHOURS	1.59	−.06	.09	.30	.53	.74	.86	.82	.69	.52	.32	.11
HSAVGHRS	0.63	.04	.16	.34	.48	.63	.62	.52	.37	.23	.09	−.05

HSEMPLMT	1.14	−.10	.04	.23	.46	.69	.85	.86	.76	.59	.40	.18
GNP/HSHOURS	0.90	.06	.14	.20	.30	.33	.41	.19	.00	−.18	−.25	−.24
Labor input based on establishment survey												
ESHOURS	1.69	−.12	.07	.38	.54	.78	.92	.90	.78	.63	.42	.21
ESAVGHRS	0.48	.14	.26	.42	.58	.68	.62	.45	.22	.05	−.15	−.30
ESMPLMT	1.41	−.19	−.01	.22	.47	.72	.89	.92	.86	.73	.55	.34
GNP/ESHOURS	0.73	.35	.44	.44	.45	.34	.34	.10	−.09	−.30	−.38	−.42
Average hourly earnings based on establishment survey												
WAGE	0.757	.20	.35	.47	.58	.66	.68	.59	.46	.29	.12	−.03
Average hourly compensation based on national income accounts												
COMP	0.55	.24	.25	.21	.14	.09	.03	−.07	−.09	−.09	−.09	−.10

Notes: GNP—real GNP, 1982$; CONS—personal consumption expenditure, 1982$; CD—consumption of durables, 1982$; CNDS—consumption of nondurables and services, 1982$; INV—fixed investment, 1982$; INVF—fixed investment, 1982$; INVN—nonresidential fixed investment, 1982$; INVR—residential fixed investment, 1982$; GOVT—government purchases of goods and services, 1982$; EXP—exports of goods and services, 1982$; IMP—imports of goods and services, 1982$; HSHOURS—total hours of work (Household Survey); HSAVGHRS—average weekly hours of work (Household Survey); HSEMPLMT—employment (Household Survey); ESHOURS—total hours of works (Establishment Survey); ESAVGHRS—average weekly hours of work (Establishment Survey); ESMPLMT—employment (Establishment Survey); WAGE—average hourly earning, 1982$ (Establishment Survey); COMP—average total compensation per hour, 1982$ (National Income Accounts). The Establishment Survey sample is for 1964:I–1991:II.

(negatively correlated). Finally, we measure the cross-correlation over time to indicate whether there is any evidence of phaseshift, i.e., evidence that variables lead or lag one another. Table 1.1 shows the standard deviations and correlations with output of the aggregate time series that characterize the *real* U.S. economy. The model economy articulated above contains no monetary elements. These, along with the monetary business cycle facts are discussed in Chapter 7. Here, we focus only on the real economy. The framework of the neoclassical growth model directs our attention to the behavior of output and the inputs that go to produce it. Moreover, it leads us to examine how much factor inputs fluctuate relative to their shadow prices. Several features of the data are worth noting:

1) The magnitude of fluctuations in output and aggregate hours of work are nearly equal. It is well known that the business cycle is most clearly manifested in the labor market and this observation confirms that.

2) Employment fluctuates almost as much as output and total hours of work, while average weekly hours fluctuate considerably less. This suggests that most fluctuations in total hours represent movements into and out of the work force rather than adjustments in average hours of work.

3) Consumption of nondurables and services (CNDS) is smooth, fluctuating much less than output.

4) Investment in both producers' and consumers' durables fluctuates much more than output.

5) The capital stock fluctuates much less than output and is largely uncorrelated with output.

6) Productivity is slightly procyclical but varies considerably less than output.

7) Wages vary less than productivity.

8) The correlation between average hourly compensation and output is essentially zero.[20]

9) Government expenditures are essentially uncorrelated with output.

10) Imports are more strongly procyclical than exports.

These are the some, but clearly not all, of the salient features of the business cycle based on U.S. time series.

To assess whether the stochastic growth economy is useful as a model of the business cycle, we can compute the same statistics for the data generated by our artificial economy and see how they compare. Of course, there are many features we cannot possibly capture because our model economy does not include those elements. It does not allow for a separate choice of hours and employment, it does not include a government sector, and it has no foreign trade sector. These are all elements that will be added and studied in later chapters.

7. The Findings from the Stochastic Growth Economy

Table 1.2 presents the results of simulating the stochastic growth economy using the parameter values discussed above. The model has been simulated 100 times, with each simulation being 150 periods long, to match the number of observations underlying the statistics reported in Table 1.1. The simulated data were filtered by using the H-P filter just as the original data were to give us the same representation of the business cycle. Table 1.2 presents the standard deviations of the key variables from the model economy (with the standard deviations of these statistics across simulations in parentheses below). In addition we present the cross-correlation of each of the variables with output.

What do we learn from this exercise? One question that is answered is: How much of the variation in output can be accounted for by technology shocks? In this artificial economy, output fluctuates less than in the U.S. economy, suggesting that much, but not all, of the variation in output is accounted for by technology shocks. The labor input in this model economy fluctuates only about half as much as in the U.S. economy suggesting that some important feature of the labor market is not captured here. Hours and productivity in the model economy go up and down together, whereas in the data they do not. This also suggests an important missing element in this artificial economy as a business cycle model.

Investment in the model economy fluctuates much more than does output, just as it does in the U.S. economy; in relative magnitudes, it fluctuates about as much as does Fixed Investment but less than does Gross Private Domestic investment. Consumption in the model economy fluctuates much less than does output and less than consumption of nondurables and services do in the U.S. economy. Consumption, investment, and hours in the model economy are all strongly procyclical, as they are in the U.S. economy. Indeed, one of the striking features of the model economy is that all the variables are highly correlated with output. This is an inevitable consequence of the fact that there is only one shock in this economy— only one source of uncertainty. Many of the explorations in the following chapters will explore the consequences of adding other sources of uncertainty.

Judged on the dimension of the composition of output and its comovements, the match between the model economy and the observed data for the U.S. economy is pretty good but clearly not perfect. It does display a business cycle. Our assessment is that this exercise is a success. The broad features of the model economy suggest that it makes sense to think of fluctuations as caused by shocks to productivity. The failures of the model economy tell us there are important margins along which

Table 1.2
Cyclical Behavior of the Artificial Economy: Deviations from Trend of Key Variables, 150 Observations

						Cross-Correlation of Output with:						
Variable	*SD%*	$x(-5)$	$x(-4)$	$x(-3)$	$x(-2)$	$x(-1)$	x	$x(+1)$	$x(+2)$	$x(+3)$	$x(+4)$	$x(+5)$
Output	1.351	-.049	.071	.232	.441	.698	1.0	.6983	.441	.232	.071	-.049
	(0.148)											
Consumption	0.329	.232	.340	.460	.592	.725	.843	.502	.229	.022	-.128	-.234
	(0.041)											
Investment	5.954	-.112	-.007	.171	.389	.664	.992	.713	.470	.270	.115	-.003
	(0.646)											
Hours	0.769	-.130	-.012	.152	.373	.652	.986	.715	.478	.281	.127	.010
	(0.083)											
Productivity	0.606	.055	.175	.325	.512	.732	.978	.649	.376	.160	-.002	-.122
	(0.068)											

Note: Values in parentheses are standard deviations across simulations.

decisions are made that have not been captured in this simple world. They also tell us that in comparing these simple artificial economies to the U.S. economy, we must think about how closely the constructs we measure in this model economy compare to those that are measured in the U.S. economy.

This may seem a very informal approach to assessing the performance of our model economy. Some authors have sought ways to summarize more concretely how well a business cycle model captures the features of the U.S. economy. This involves imposing a metric to measure the distance between summary statistics for the model economy and corresponding statistics for the actual economy. One such procedure is described in Christiano and Eichenbaum (1992). They describe a generalized method of moments interpretation of the calibration exercise that provides them with a metric for assessing the difference between their model and the data. An alternative procedure that aims to come up with something like an R_2 measure for a model economy is described in Watson (1993). Some other techniques are described in Kim and Pagan (1993). Developing formal measures of model fit for general equilibrium model economies is a difficult problem with many dimensions to it. Creators of traditional econometric models struggled for many years to develop formal summary measures of fit for simultaneous equations systems, without a lot of success. In the chapters that follow you will find a variety of ways in which the performance of a model economy is assessed.

8. Conclusion and Summary

This model economy gives us only a glimpse of what it is possible to learn and accomplish by taking the basic neoclassical growth model seriously as a description of how actual economies behave. In the following chapters, we show how this basic framework can be implemented and employed to address many of the substantive questions confronting macroeconomics and business cycle theory today. This book is not intended as a comprehensive survey of the field. The coverage of topics and the treatment of individual contributions is necessarily incomplete because the research program is so active.

The next three chapters are concerned primarily with methodology. In Chapter 2, Gary Hansen and Edward Prescott explain recursive methods for computing the equilibria of business cycle models. They illustrate these methods with a number of examples, which cover many of the applications described later in the book. In Chapter 3, Jean-Pierre Danthine and John Donaldson describe a variety of methods that take a different approach to computing the equilibria of dynamic economies. The methods they describe are widely used for problems where the equilibria are suboptimal and where the dimensionality of the state space would be very large if one used the methods described in Chapter 2. In Chapter 4, José-Víctor Ríos-Rull explains how to structure economies with heterogeneous agents and how to compute their equilibria. He also describes how to compute the equilibria of overlapping-generations economies.

For the most part the remaining chapters deal with applications to substantive issues. Chapter 5, by Finn Kydland, discusses the labor market. As we showed in this chapter, much of the fluctuations at business cycle frequencies are characterized by changes in the labor input. That being the case, it is apparent that an understanding of how that market functions is central to understanding the cycle. In Chapter 6, Jeremy Greenwood, Richard Rogerson, and Randall Wright describe how decisions made by the household sector about the allocation of labor and capital between the household sector and the market sector affects what we observe about fluctuations in the labor market.

Beginning with the important work of Robert Lucas, much of the modern general equilibrium analysis of the business cycle has treated the business cycle as a monetary phenomenon. Real business cycle models like the one described above have been a significant departure from that tradition because they assign a very small role to money. Chapter 7, by Thomas Cooley and Gary Hansen, examines the role of money in business cycle fluctuations. First, using the basic real business cycle model as a vehicle, they examine the quantitative importance of the kinds of information problems (implicitly caused by monetary fluctuations) that Lucas postulated as the source of business cycle fluctuations. Then they look at the potential for rigid wages, resulting from contracting behavior, to act as a propagation mechanism for monetary shocks.

Chapter 8, by Jean-Pierre Danthine and John Donaldson, is an analysis of various types of non-Walrasian economies based on the neoclassical growth model. Danthine and Donaldson construct models designed to assess the quantitative importance of such phenomena as efficiency wages and labor hoarding. More important, they show how the basic framework can be modified to incorporate different arrangements in the economy and provide a quantitative assessment of their importance. Chapter 9, by Julio Rotemberg and Michael Woodford, considers the relation between business cycle fluctuations and noncompetitive elements in the economy. Their findings show that imperfect competition can be important because it significantly affects the way the economy responds to different shocks.

Chapter 10, by K. Geert Rouwenhorst, is devoted to asset-pricing issues. Rouwenhorst shows how the basic real business cycle model can be used to study various contemporary issues in finance. In Chapter 11, David Backus, Patrick Kehoe, and Finn Kydland describe some of the puzzles that arise when we consider the international features of business cycles. They describe a two-country version of the basic real business cycle model that can used to study international business cycles and discuss its ability to explain the international puzzles. Chapter 12, by V. V. Chari, Lawrence Christiano, and Patrick Kehoe shows how the kinds of model developed in this book can be modified to analyze economic policy issues in a rigorous way.

Notes

We thank Larry Christiano, John Donaldson, Ed Green, Jeremy Greenwood, Gary Hansen, Finn Kydland, Glenn MacDonald, and Kevin Salyer for advice and comments and the National Science Foundation for research support.

1. An important exception to this general lack of concern with the business cycle was the famous paper by Adelman and Adelman (1959), who showed that a small econometric model developed by Lawrence Klein displayed business cycle fluctuations when subjected to random shocks. This was consistent with the Slutsky view of how business cycles might get started.

2. To see this, let Y, K, and R_k denote output, capital, and the income from capital, respectively, all of which are functions of time. The third stylized fact implies that $K'/K = Y'/Y$. We could write this equivalently as $[\ln(K)]' = [\ln(Y)]'$, so the fundamental theorem of calculus implies that $\ln(K) = \alpha \ln(Y)$, where α is a time-invariant constant. Equivalently, $K = \exp(\alpha)Y$ so that the ratio K/Y remains constant over time. The fourth stylized fact asserts that R_k/K is constant over time, which in conjunction with the constancy of K/Y implies that capitals' share of income is constant over time.

3. The view that growth and cycles might be integrated phenomena is not unique to this literature. There were earlier theoretical models by Hicks (1949), Goodwin (1955), and Smithies (1957), among others, that treated these together. There were also efforts in the econometric literature of the 1960s to develop economywide econometric models that were consistent with the growth facts.

4. Sometimes there is a "fake" social planner's problem, which is concave and whose first-order conditions coincide with the first-order conditions of the competitive equilibrium. Assuming such a function can be identified, these methods still apply even though there are distortions. An example of such a model is described in Chapter 3.

5. Other decentralized equilibrium concepts have appeared in the literature. Brock (1982) proposed a decentralized equilibrium concept that is very similar to the RCE except that the firm's technology need not be constant returns to scale and the capital stock sequence can be unbounded.

6. One set that is always sufficient are the Arrow securities.

7. Solow also argued that productivity improvements, *not* increasing returns, were the likely explanation for this finding.

8. Stokey and Lucas with Prescott (1989) develop the stochastic growth model under much more general mathematical assumptions about the nature of the shocks. We make these very specific assumptions to facilitate the exposition here.

9. The general specifications of preferences that are consistent with balanced growth are described in King, Plosser, and Rebelo (1988b) and by Caballe and Santos (1993).

10. The most recent measurement of the U.S. fixed reproducible capital stock is reported by Musgrave (1992) in *The Survey of Current Business*. Musgrave distinguishes three major components of the reproducible capital stock: Fixed Private Capital, which includes producers' durables, producers' structures, and residential structures; Government Capital, which includes both equipment and structures at both the federal level and the state & local government level; and Consumer Durables. Another component of the capital stock that we will incorporate is land. A measure of the value of land is reported in the Flow of Funds Accounts, in the Balance Sheets for the U.S. Economy.

11. The complete National Income and Product Accounts for the United States are published in selected issues of *Survey of Current Business*, published monthly by the U.S. Department of Commerce. The complete historical accounts from 1929 through 1988 are contained in the two volumes of *National Income and Product Accounts of the United States*, published by the U.S. Department of Commerce.

12. The value of land reported in the Flow of Funds accounts is an estimate based on current market prices. The measured value of land as a fraction of GNP is quite volatile over time, which suggests that this part of aggregate capital may be poorly measured.

13. Since there is no foreign sector in this economy, net exports are viewed as representing additions to or claims on the domestic capital stock, depending on whether they are positive or negative.

14. These estimates account for the growth in real output and population through the term Y_{t+1}/Y_t.

15. Kydland and Prescott (1982), Prescott (1986), and Hansen (1985) all use a smaller value of θ, .36, because they do not impute the output of government capital.

16. Prescott (1986) argues that the standard deviations of these innovations may be affected by measurement error in the measured labor input. Fortunately, there are two independent estimates of this input, one based on the establishment survey and one based on the household survey. Under the assumption that the measurement errors in these two series are orthogonal, the covariance between the two series is an estimate of the variance of the change in hours. Taking account of this measurement error would actually increase very slightly the standard deviation of the innovations to technology. We chose to ignore it here.

17. The taxonomy in section 5 was suggested by Larry Christiano.

18. Chapters 2 and 4 show how to generalize this to more than one type of agent.

19. One can show that the H-P filter is an optimal signal extractor for y_t^* in the model

$$y_t = y_t^* + v_t (1 - L)^2 y_t^* = \eta_t,$$

where $\lambda = \text{var}(\eta)/\text{var}(\eta)$. This is optimal for a process that is integrated of order 2. Since most macroeconomic time series are not $I(2)$, this has led some researchers to question the use of the H-P filter and advocate a filter that assumes the series are $I(1)$. See King and Rebelo (1993) and Kim and Pagan (1993).

19. The absence of correlation between average hourly compensation and output is related to the lack of correlation between capital stock and output above and to the observation that the correlation between productivity and hours is very small, being slightly positive in the establishment survey data and slightly negative in the household survey data. The latter correlation is not reported in Table 1.1, but it has been stressed by Christiano and Eichenbaum (1992) as an important puzzle. The observation is at odds with the Keynesian view that observed labor market fluctuations take place along a labor demand curve, and it is also at odds with the classical view that they take place along a labor supply curve. For a thorough discussion of this, see Gomme and Greenwood (1993).

Chapter 2
Recursive Methods for Computing Equilibria of Business Cycle Models

Gary D. Hansen and Edward C. Prescott

1. Introduction

In this chapter, we describe some computational methods for computing equilibria of business cycle models. The class of economies for which these methods can be applied is surprisingly large, as we illustrate with a number of examples. Generally, this class consists of economies that fluctuate around a steady-state or balanced-growth path and display local dynamics that are well approximated by a linear law of motion. The methods we describe are designed to economize on the time spent learning to use the techniques and to modify them for a particular application. They are not designed to minimize computing costs, which, in any case, are only a minute or two of personal computer time for most business cycle applications.

The fact that it is not generally possible to compute equilibria of business cycle models analytically led Kydland and Prescott (1982), and subsequently others, to consider a structure for which this is possible. Such a structure is one with a quadratic objective, linear constraints, and exogenous disturbances generated by a first-order, linear, vector-autoregressive process. The particular quadratic objective chosen is the second-order Taylor series expansion of the return function for the deterministic version of the model evaluated at its steady state.

An additional advantage of a linear-quadratic structure is that equilibria can be easily computed even when the dimension of the state variable is large. It does, however, have the added consequence that the resulting equilibrium law of motion is linear. This does not appear to be a serious limitation given that there is little evidence of major nonlinearities in aggregate data. In situations in which the behavior being modeled displays important nonlinearities, methods other than those reviewed here are needed. Some of these will be described in subsequent chapters.

We divide the class of applications where these methods have been used into two subclasses. In the first, competitive equilibria are Pareto optimal and hence solve a social planning problem. In Section 2, we examine the stochastic growth model augmented to have a labor-leisure allocation decision and show how it can be mapped into a basic recursive social planning problem.[1] We also consider a number of extensions of this basic environment to illustrate the flexibility of this mapping. These extensions include time to build, indivisible labor, and geometric growth. In Section 3, we describe computational algorithms for specifying the linear-quadratic social planning problem and for computing the solution to the problem.

The second subclass consists of economies for which distortions due to taxes or externalities typically make it necessary to solve for an equilibrium directly. In Section 4, we deal with homogeneous-agent recursive economies in which the competitive equilibrium need not be Pareto optimal. The first application introduces taxes into our basic business cycle model. The second introduces a cash-in-advance constraint for the purchase of a subset of the consumption goods. In Section 5, we describe algorithms similar to those described in Section 3 for choosing a linear-quadratic recursive economy and for computing the equilibrium stochastic process for that economy. Finally, in Section 6, we demonstrate how these recursive computational methods can be extended to the study of heterogeneous-agent recursive economies. Examples applying these methods will be discussed in Chapter 4.

2. Social Planning Problems

In this section we describe some examples of economies for which competitive equilibrium allocations are identical to the allocations chosen by a social planner that acts to maximize the welfare of a representative agent. For these economies, the Second Welfare Theorem applies. In such situations the equilibrium allocations can be determined by solving a well-behaved concave optimization problem.[2] In addition, the marginal rates of substitution and transformation, evaluated at the optimal allocation, can be used to find equilibrium relative prices.

For each of our examples, the social-planning problem involves solving a dynamic programming problem of the following form (primes denote next-period values):

$$v(z, s) = \max\{r(z, s, d) + \beta E[v(z', s')|z, s]\} \tag{1}$$

$$\text{s.t.} \quad z' = A(z) + \epsilon' \tag{2}$$

$$s' = B(z, s, d). \tag{3}$$

The elements of this program are as follows: z is a vector of exogenous state variables; ϵ is a vector of random variables distributed independently over time with mean zero and finite variance (some components of ϵ may have zero variance); s is a vector of endogenous state variables; and d is a vector of decision variables.[3] Equation (2) is the law of motion for z, where A is a linear function.[4] The realization of z is observed at the beginning of the period. Equation (3) is the law of motion for the endogenous state variables, where B is also linear. Finally, $r(z, s, d)$ is the return function and $v(z, s)$ is the optimal value function for the problem.

An important feature of this problem is that A and B are linear functions, which means that any nonlinear constraints have been substituted into the return function. In Section 3, we describe a method for solving a linear-quadratic approximation of a problem of this form.

The equilibrium business cycle literature is full of applications where dynamic programming problems of this sort are formulated and solved.[5] The examples considered in this section, which are drawn from this literature, include a basic version of the stochastic growth model (the divisible labor model of Hansen [1985]) and a few variants of that model. In particular, we consider adding geometric growth, time to build, and indivisible labor to the basic model.

The Basic Model

This model is an extension of the Brock and Mirman (1972) optimal stochastic growth model upon which much of the equilibrium business cycle literature is based. A representative agent maximizes the utility function

$$E \sum_{t=0}^{\infty} \beta^t U(c_t, \ell_t), \quad 0 < \beta < 1, \tag{4}$$

where U is concave, strictly increasing, and twice continuously differentiable in both arguments. The variables c_t and ℓ_t are consumption and leisure in period t, respectively. The household is endowed with one unit of time, which is divided between work, h_t, and leisure, so that $h_t + \ell_t = 1$.

The representative agent has access to a technology that produces output, y_t, from capital, k_t, and labor:

$$y_t = z_t F(k_t, h_t). \tag{5}$$

The production function, F, is concave, twice continuously differentiable, increasing in both arguments, and displays constant returns to scale. The variable z_t is a technology shock, which is observed at the beginning of the period and follows a first-order linear Markov process:

$$z_{t+1} = A(z_t) + \epsilon_{t+1}, \tag{6}$$

where the ϵ's are i.i.d. random variables with mean zero and finite variance and A is a linear function.

Total output can be freely allocated to either investment, i_t, or consumption:

$$y_t = c_t + i_t, \tag{7}$$

where investment this period becomes productive capital next period. In particular, the capital stock evolves according to the law of motion:

$$k_{t+1} = (1 - \delta)k_t + i_t, \quad 0 < \delta < 1. \tag{8}$$

The problem solved by the social planner is to maximize (4) subject to (5) through (8) with z_0 and k_0 given. We, however, need to express this problem as a dynamic programming problem that is a special case of (1) in order to apply the solution method described in the next section. This is accomplished by combining constraints (5) and (7) to eliminate y_t, solving the resulting equation for c_t, and substituting it into the utility function. This yields a version of problem (1) where $s = k, d = (h, i)$, the return function is

$$r(z, k, h, i) = U[zF(k, h) - i, 1 - h],$$

and the law of motion for s is, $B(z, k, h, i) = (1 - \delta)k + i$.

We now consider three additional examples that are simply elaborations of this basic model.

Geometric Growth

As a second example, we add labor-augmenting technological growth to the basic model.[6] We do this by replacing (5) with

$$y_t = z_t F(k_t, \lambda^t h_t), \quad \text{where } \lambda > 1. \tag{9}$$

In addition, we require that the elasticity of substitution between consumption and leisure equal one so that hours worked is constant on the balanced growth path. An example of such a utility function is the following:

$$U(c_t, \ell_t) = (c_t^\alpha \ell_t^{1-\alpha})^\rho / \rho, \quad 0 < \alpha < 1, \rho < 1 \quad \text{and} \quad \rho \neq 0 \tag{10}$$

All other aspects of the model are the same as for the basic model. The equilibrium allocation is obtained by maximizing (4) subject to (9) and (6)–(8). A property of the solution to this problem is that consumption, investment, output, and capital all grow at the same rate: $\lambda - 1$. In order to solve this problem using our method, we transform the problem so that the solution is stationary over time. The following change of variables achieves this purpose:

$$\hat{y} = y_t/\lambda^t, \quad \hat{c}_t = c_t/\lambda^t, \quad \hat{i} = i_t/\lambda^t \quad \text{and} \quad \hat{k} = k_t/\lambda^t. \tag{11}$$

After this transformation, the social planner's problem is a special case of (1) if $s = \hat{k}, d = (h, \hat{i})$,

$$r(z, \hat{k}, h, \hat{i}) = ([zF(\hat{k}, h) - \hat{i}]^\alpha (1 - h)^{1-\alpha})^\rho / \rho,$$

and

$$B(z, \hat{k}, h, \hat{i}) = [(1 - \delta)/\lambda]\hat{k} + (1/\lambda)\hat{i}.$$

In addition, the discount factor after the transformation, call it $\hat{\beta}$, equals $\lambda^{\alpha\rho}\beta$. We assume that the parameters are such that $\hat{\beta}$ is less than one.

Time to Build

Kydland and Prescott (1982) studied a version of the basic model in which multiple periods are required to build productive capital. This requires that the state vector include stocks of capital goods j periods from completion, u_j, in addition to finished capital. Thus, if it takes J periods to build productive capital, the state and decision variables are $s = (k, u_1, \ldots, u_{J-1})$ and $d = (h, u_J)$.

The laws of motion for these state variables are the following:

$$k' = (1 - \delta)k + u_1,$$

and

$$u'_j = u_{j+1}, \quad \text{for } j = 1, \ldots, J - 1.$$

Letting ϕ_j, for $j = 1, \ldots, J$, be the fraction of resources allocated to the investment project in the jth stage from the last, total investment in the current period is $i = \sum_{j=1}^{J} \phi_j u_j$. With investment defined in this way, the return function for the version of problem (1) corresponding to this economy is given by

$$r(z, k, u_1, \ldots, u_{J-1}) = U[zF(k, h) - i, 1 - h].$$

Indivisible Labor

We now consider an example drawn from Hansen (1985), where indivisible labor, along with Rogerson's (1988) employment lotteries, are introduced into the basic model. For this example, instead of a single representative agent, there is a continuum of ex ante identical agents. All quantities must be interpreted as per capita values in this case. The technology is the same as in the basic model, but the utility function is of the form $u(c) + g(\ell)$, where u and g are increasing, concave, and twice continuously differentiable. Indivisible labor implies that ℓ can take on only two values, $(1 - \hat{h})$ and 1, corresponding to working full time or not at all. An additional difference between this and the basic model is that the competitive equilibrium involves agents' trading employment lotteries that specify a probability of working, rather than hours of work directly.

Letting n equal the probability of working $\hat{h}$ hours, the expected utility of a representative household is

$$n[u(c) + g(1 - \hat{h})] + (1 - n)[u(c) + g(1)]$$

$$= u(c) + ng(1 - \hat{h}) + (1 - n)g(1).[7]$$

Since there is a continuum of households, the equilibrium value of n is also equal to the fraction of households that work. This implies that total hours worked, h, is given by $n\hat{h}$. The utility of the stand-in agent, which enters the objective function of the social planner, is the following (ignoring a constant term):[8]

$$U(c, h) = u(c) + \phi h,$$

where

$$\phi = [g(1 - \hat{h}) - g(1)]/\hat{h}.$$

Therefore, the version of problem (1) for this example is the same as for the basic model except that the return function is linear in hours worked: $r(z, k, h, i) = u(zF(k, h) - i) + \phi h$. Although individual households do not choose hours worked under the competitive equilibrium interpretation of this economy, the decision variables for the social planner are the same as for the basic model.

It is also possible to solve this problem if the utility function is not additively separable in consumption and leisure and takes the form of equation (10). In this case, the commodity traded is an employment lottery that specifies consumption compensation contingent on the employment status. Letting c_1 be consumption when working and c_2 be consumption when not working, the appropriate utility function is

$$nU(c_1, 1 - \hat{h}) + (1 - n)U(c_2, 1).$$

The resource constraint, using the fact that $h = n\hat{h}$, is

$$nc_1 + (1 - n)c_2 + i = zF(k, n\hat{h}).$$

In this case, the planning problem is mapped into the notation employed in problem (1) by setting $s = k$ and $d = (n, c_2, i)$. The return function is

$$r(z, k, n, c_2, i) = nU[\frac{zF(k, n\hat{h}) - (1 - n)c_2 - i}{n}, 1 - \hat{h}] + (1 - n)U(c_2, 1)$$

3. Solving a Social Planning Problem

In this section, we describe a method for solving problems of the form (1) when the return function is quadratic. However, the applications we have considered typically do not deliver quadratic return functions. Therefore, we describe a procedure for approximating a general return function by one that is quadratic. The advantage of solving a linear-quadratic planning problem is that it is possible to solve for an explicit linear policy function, $d_t = d(z_t, s_t)$, which when substituted into (3) yields a linear law of motion for the state variables, $s_{t+1} = g(z_t, s_t)$.

In this discussion, we employ the following convention to refer to the dimension of a particular vector: let $\eta(x)$ equal the dimension of a column vector x, and $\eta(x, y)$ equal the dimension of the stacked vector (x, y). This implies that the vector z of exogenous state variables is of dimension $\eta(z) \times 1$. The dimensions of s (the endogenous state variables) and d (the decision variables) are defined analogously. In addition, $\eta(\epsilon)$ is equal to $\eta(z)$.

Another important convention we employ is to define the first component of z to be constant over time (equal to one, without loss of generality). This assumption will help to simplify accounting later.

Forming the Quadratic Approximation

The quadratic approximation of r corresponds to the first three terms of a Taylor series expansion of this function at the steady state values for (z, s, d), corresponding to the certainty version of problem (1), denoted $(\bar{z}, \bar{s}, \bar{d})$. The vector $\bar{z}$ is the solution to the equation $\bar{z} = A(\bar{z})$. Given $\bar{z}$, the following $\eta(s, d)$ equations are solved for the $\eta(s, d)$ unknowns, $\bar{s}$ and $\bar{d}$:

$$r_d(\bar{z}, \bar{s}, \bar{d}) + \beta r_s(\bar{z}, \bar{s}, \bar{d})[I - \beta B_s(\bar{z}, \bar{s}, \bar{d})]^{-1} B_d(\bar{z}, \bar{s}, \bar{d}) = 0;$$

$$\bar{s} = B(\bar{z}, \bar{s}, \bar{d}). \tag{12}$$

In (12), r_d is the vector of partial derivatives with respect to the elements of d and is of dimension $1 \times \eta(d)$. Similarly, r_s is of dimension $1 \times \eta(s)$. Since $B(z, s, d)$ is actually $\eta(s)$ linear equations, B_s and B_d are of dimension $\eta(s) \times \eta(s)$ and $\eta(s) \times \eta(d)$, respectively. In practice, the first equation in (12) can be made much simpler if one begins by substituting the laws of motion (3) into the return function, eliminating some elements of d. The idea is to rewrite the problem so that next-period state variables, s', are current period decision variables. In this case, all of the elements of B_s are zero.

Let y be the stacked vector (z, s, d) and a superscript T denote the transpose of a vector. The Taylor series expansion of $r(y)$ at the steady-state $\bar{y}$ is

$$\tilde{r}(y) = r(\bar{y}) + Dr(\bar{y})^T(y - \bar{y}) + (1/2)(y - \bar{y})^T D^2 r(\bar{y})(y - \bar{y}), \tag{13}$$

where $Dr(\bar{y})$ is the $\eta(y) \times 1$ vector of first partial derivatives of r and $D^2 r(\bar{y})$ is the $\eta(y) \times \eta(y)$ matrix of second partial derivatives of r, where $\eta(y) = \eta(z, s, d)$. Both are evaluated at the steady state. The first element of $Dr(\bar{y})$ and the elements in the first row and column of $D^2 r(\bar{y})$ are zero, since the first component of y is a constant term and not a variable.

Rather than computing $Dr(\bar{y})$ and $D^2 r(\bar{y})$ algebraically, we approximate the components of these matrices numerically. Let h^i be an $\eta(y) \times 1$ vector, all of the components of which are zero except for the ith component, h_i^i, which is set equal to a small positive number, $\tilde{h}$. The value of $\tilde{h}$ should be chosen to be as small as possible, subject to avoiding computer accuracy problems.[9] The following formulas are used to obtain numerical approximations of the components of $Dr(\bar{y})$ and $D^2 r(\bar{y})$ (recall that the first component of y is constant over time):

$$D_i r(\bar{y}) = [r(\bar{y} + h^i) - r(\bar{y} - h^i)]/(2\tilde{h})$$

$$D_{ii}^2 r(\bar{y}) = [r(\bar{y} + h^i) + r(\bar{y} - h^i) - 2r(\bar{y})]/(\tilde{h}^2)$$

and

$$D_{ij}^2 r(\bar{y}) = [r(\bar{y} + h^i + h^j) - r(\bar{y} + h^i - h^j)$$
$$- r(\bar{y} - h^i + h^j) + r(\bar{y} - h^i - h^j)]/(4\tilde{h}^2)$$

for $i \neq j$ $(i, j = 2, \ldots, \eta(y))$.

Exploiting the fact that the first component of y is equal to one, we can rearrange equation (13) so that $\tilde{r}(y) = y^T Q y$, where Q is a symmetric matrix of dimension $\eta(y) \times \eta(y)$. The elements of Q are given by the following expressions:

$$Q_{1i} = Q_{i1} = [D_i r(\bar{y}) - \sum_{j=2}^{\eta(y)} (D_{ij}^2 r(\bar{y}) \cdot \bar{y}_j)]/2, \quad \text{for } i = 2, \ldots, \eta(y)$$

$$Q_{ij} = Q_{ji} = (1/2) D_{ij}^2 r(\bar{y}), \quad \text{for } i, j = 2, \ldots, \eta(y)$$

and

$$Q_{11} = r(\bar{y}) - \sum_{i=2}^{\eta(y)} D_i r(\bar{y}) \cdot \bar{y}_i + (1/2) \sum_{i=2}^{\eta(y)} \sum_{j=2}^{\eta(y)} D_{ij}^2 r(\bar{y}) \cdot \bar{y}_i \cdot \bar{y}_j$$

For reasons that will be made clear below, it is important for our method that the ordering of y, and hence the ordering of the elements of Q, be exactly as described here. The following is the linear-quadratic dynamic programming problem obtained from this approximation:

$$v(z, s) = \max\{y^T Q y + \beta E[v(z', s')|z]\} \tag{14}$$

subject to (2) and (3).[10]

Solving the Dynamic Program by Successive Approximations

Problem (14) is a standard linear-quadratic dynamic programming problem. Under suitable conditions, the optimal value function, v, exists, solves this functional equation, and is quadratic. Given this, the associated policy functions are linear. In this section, we do not attempt to survey the extensive literature (see, e.g., Hansen and Sargent [forthcoming]) describing efficient techniques for solving such a problem. Instead, we describe a simple algorithm that is easy to implement and understand. A computer program designed to carry out these computations is easy to write and debug. One advantage of this is that it saves time for the researcher. A second advantage is that it will be easy to modify the method to solve for equilibria that are not solutions to social planner's problems, as in economies with taxes or other distortions, or for studying an important class of heterogeneous-agent economies, including those with n-period–lived overlapping generations. These will be described in later sections.

The optimal value function for problem (14) is identical, save for a constant, for any covariance matrix of ϵ. As a result, the optimal policy function is independent of this covariance matrix. Given this, we solve the programming problem for the certainty case, where the covariance matrix has been set equal to zero. In other words, we solve the version of (14) in which the expectations operator has been dropped and ϵ' in (2) has been replaced with its mean, zero.

The method of successive approximations is used to compute the optimal value function, v. Following this method, we generate a sequence of approximations to v that for well-behaved problems will converge to the optimal value function.[11] To solve this problem, an initial quadratic approximation for the value function, v^0, is selected and the standard Bellman mapping is used to obtain the sequence of approximations. In particular, given the nth element of this sequence, the $n + 1$st element is obtained as follows:

$$v^{n+1}(z, s) = \max\{y^T Q y + \beta v^n(z', s')\}$$

$$\text{s.t.} \quad [z', s']_i = \sum_{j \leq \eta(y)} B_{ij} y_j \quad \text{for } i = 1, \ldots, \eta(z, s). \tag{15}$$

The B_{ij}'s in the above constraints are taken directly from equations (2) and (3). To obtain v^{n+1}, we first substitute the constraint into the right side of (15) in order to eliminate z' and s' from the problem. This yields a quadratic expression in (z, s, d). Next, the first order-conditions are used to solve for the vector d as a linear function of z and s. Substituting these into (15), we obtain the next approximation, which is a quadratic function of (z, s). If the problem is well behaved, this procedure is repeated until $\|v^{n+1} - v^n\| < \xi$, where ξ is some small positive real number.

We now describe these iterations in greater detail:

Step 1. Choose some arbitrary negative semidefinite matrix, v^0, of size $\eta(z, s) \times \eta(z, s)$. A possible candidate is a matrix with small negative numbers on the diagonal and zeros for the off-diagonal elements. Once again, the ordering of the columns of this matrix is very important: the first $\eta(z)$ columns contain coefficients corresponding to terms involving elements of z (thus the first column contains the linear terms), and the last $\eta(s)$ columns contain coefficients corresponding to terms involving elements of s.

Steps 2 through 5 describe how to generate successive approximations of the optimal value function. In particular, we describe how to compute v^{n+1} given an approximation v^n. These four steps are repeated until the sequence of approximations has converged.

Step 2. Let x be the stacked vector (y, z', s'), which is equal to (z, s, d, z', s'). Construct a matrix $R^{[\eta(x)]}$, which is of dimension $\eta(x) \times \eta(x)$, that contains the matrix Q (with its elements in the order described above) in the top left corner and the matrix βv^n in the lower right corner. The remaining elements of $R^{[\eta(x)]}$ are set equal to zero. This enables us to write the expression $y^T Q y + \beta v(z', s')$ from (15) as a single quadratic form, $x^T R^{(\eta(x))} x$.

The next two steps describe how to compute $v^{n+1}(z, s)$ by eliminating the variables s', z', and d from $x^T R^{[\eta(x)]} x$, using the constraints in (15) and the first-order conditions. We begin by eliminating the last element of x, and then proceed to eliminate the second-to-last element, and so on, until only the elements of z and s remain. To eliminate a particular element of x, say, x_j, we must be able to express x_j as a linear function of the variables x_i, where i is less than j. This requirement will be satisfied given the particular way in which we have ordered the elements of x.

Each time a linear expression is used to eliminate a component of x, the form of the quadratic objective is altered. For example, when the first variable, which is the last component of x, is eliminated, the quadratic objective becomes $x^T R^{[\eta(x)-1]} x$, where $R^{[\eta(x)-1]}$ is the same array as $R^{[\eta(x)]}$, with the entries changed to reflect the substitution. In particular, the last row and column are now filled with zeros.[12]

To make this more precise, suppose that after some substitutions, we are left with the quadratic form, $x^T R^{(j)} x$, where $j > \eta(z, s)$. The jth component of x must be eliminated next. Using (2), (3), or a first order condition makes it possible to express x_j in terms of x_i, $i < j$, as follows:

$$x_j = \sum_{i<j} \gamma_i x_i. \tag{16}$$

Substituting (16) into the quadratic objective yields a new quadratic objective, $x^T R^{(j-1)} x$, where the components in the first $j - 1$ rows and columns of $R^{(j-1)}$ are given by

$$R_{ih}^{(j-1)} = R_{ih}^{(j)} + R_{jh}^{(j)} \gamma_i + R_{ji}^{(j)} \gamma_h + R_{jj}^{(j)} \gamma_i \gamma_h, \quad \text{for } i, h = 1, \ldots, j-1 \tag{17}$$

The remaining elements of this $\eta(x) \times \eta(x)$ array are equal to zero.

There is a matrix algebraic alternative to (17) that may be easier to implement on the computer, especially if one is using a matrix programming language:

$$R^{(j-1)} = \Gamma^T R^{(j)} \Gamma, \quad \text{where } \Gamma = \begin{bmatrix} I_{j-1} \\ \gamma_1 \ldots, \gamma_{j-1} \end{bmatrix} \tag{18}$$

and I_{j-1} is a $j - 1$ dimensional identity matrix. Note that this formula is written under the assumption that $R^{(j)}$ is of dimension $j \times j$, meaning that the last $\eta(y) - j$ rows and columns of $R^{(j)}$ (which are all zeros) have been eliminated. In all other parts of this chapter, the R matrices are assumed to be padded with zeros so that they are of dimension $\eta(x) \times \eta(x)$.

After repeated application of this procedure, we obtain the quadratic form $x^T R^{[\eta(z,s)]} x$. The matrix v^{n+1}, defined by the mapping (15), is simply the first

$\eta(z, s)$ rows and columns of $R^{[\eta(z,s)]}$. We now describe more precisely the particular substitutions that are made in order to obtain v^{n+1}.

Step 3. In this step, we substitute expressions for s' and z', given by the constraints in equation (15), into the objective. These constraints, which determine the last $\eta(z, s)$ elements of x, are the following:

$$x_i = \sum_{j \leq J} B_{ij} x_j,$$

where

$$i = \eta(z, s, d) + 1, \ldots, \eta(x)$$

and

$$J = \eta(z, s, d).$$

As explained above, we first eliminate $x_{\eta(x)}$, the last element of s'. Using equation 17 with the coefficients $B_{\eta(x),j}$ in place of the γ's, we obtain the matrix $R^{[\eta(x)-1]}$. After all components of s' and z' have been eliminated, we are left with the quadratic form $x^T R^{[\eta(z,s,d)]} x$.

Step 4. The next $\eta(d)$ variables, which are the components of d, are eliminated by using the first-order conditions for the maximization problem on the right side of (15), beginning with $x_{\eta(z,s,d)} = d_{\eta(d)}$. The following is the first-order condition with respect to the jth component of x, assuming that all components of x with index greater than j have already been eliminated:

$$x_j = -\sum_{i=1}^{j-1} (R_{ji}^{(j)} / R_{jj}^{(j)}) x_i, \quad j = \eta(z, s) + 1, \ldots, \eta(z, s, d). \tag{19}$$

At this stage, it is important to examine whether the second-order conditions are satisfied by checking whether $R_{jj}^{(j)}$ is less than zero. In cases where the return function, r, is strictly concave, these conditions will be satisfied if no errors have been made in implementing the algorithm. However, in other cases, say, where the return function is not bounded from above, a violation of the second-order conditions at some stage indicates that a maximum does not exist, and hence indicates a failure of this method to find the optimal value function.

As before, (17) is used to compute $R^{(j-1)}$ where the γ's are given by the coefficients in (19). After all of the decision variables have been eliminated, we are left with the matrix $R^{[\eta(z,s)]}$.

Step 5. Set v^{n+1} equal to the matrix formed by the first $\eta(z, s)$ rows and columns of $R^{[\eta(z,s)]}$. If all the elements of v^{n+1} are sufficiently close to the corresponding elements of v^n (for example, if the biggest difference is less than .00001), stop the iterations.[13] If not, repeat these steps again beginning with Step 2, using v^{n+1} in place of v^n.

Step 6. Once this sequence of successive approximations has converged, the first-order conditions from the last iteration, given by (19), can be used to derive the equilibrium policy functions. Equation (19) can be rewritten as follows:

$$d_j = \sum_{i<K} C_{ij} x_i, \quad j = 1, \ldots, \eta(d),$$

where

$$C_{ij} = \frac{-R_{Ki}^{(K)}}{R_{KK}^{(K)}},$$

and $K = \eta(z, s) + j$.

In this form, the expression for d_j is a function not only of the state variables, z and s, but also of the decision variables with indices from 1 to $j - 1$. These policy functions can be expressed in terms of the state variables alone as follows:

$$d_j = \sum_{i=1}^{\eta(z,s)} D_{ij} x_i, \tag{20}$$

where for each i,

$$D_{i1} = C_{i1},$$

$$D_{i2} = C_{i2} + C_{\eta(z,s)+1,2} D_{i1},$$

and

$$D_{ij} = C_{ij} + \sum_{h<j} [C_{\eta(z,s)+h,j} D_{ih}], \quad j = 3, \ldots, \eta(d).$$

Step 7. Finally, it is wise to check whether the steady state implied by (20) is the same as the steady state for the original nonlinear planner's problem, $(\bar{z}, \bar{s}, \bar{d})$, defined by (12). The simplest way to do this is to substitute $\bar{z}$ and $\bar{s}$ into the right side of (20), and then check whether the resulting vector of decisions equals $\bar{d}$ to, say, six decimal places.

4. Recursive Competitive Equilibrium for Homogeneous-Agent Economies

For many applications, including many in public finance and monetary economics, it is not possible to find equilibrium allocations by solving a planning problem. Instead, it is necessary to solve for equilibrium allocations directly by solving a fixed-point problem.

In this section, we describe two applications where the methods discussed in the previous two sections cannot be applied directly. Our first example is an economy with distorting taxes, and the second is an economy with money introduced by imposing a cash-in-advance constraint. Methods for solving linear-quadratic versions of these two examples are described in Section 5.

The problem faced by households in our tax example, as well as in many other applications involving nonmonetary distortions, is a dynamic programming problem of the following form:

$$v(z, S, s) = \max\{r(z, S, s, D, d) + \beta E[v(z', S', s')|z]\}, \tag{21}$$

$$\text{s.t.} \quad z' = A(z) + \epsilon' \tag{22}$$

$$s' = B(z, S, s, D, d) \tag{23}$$

$$S' = B(z, S, S, D, D) \tag{24}$$

$$D = \mathbf{D}(z, S). \tag{25}$$

As in section 2, z is a vector of exogenous state variables, possibly stochastic, that evolves according to the first-order Markov process (22), where A is a linear function. The variable ϵ is a mean zero random vector with finite variance. In addition, s is a vector of endogenous household-specific state variables, and S is a vector containing their economywide (per capita) values.[14] Similarly, d is a vector of household decision variables, and D is the vector of per capita values of these same variables. Equations (23) and (24) describe the evolution of s and S, where B is a linear function. Note that (24) is obtained from (23) by aggregating over all households.

The function $\mathbf{D}$ in equation (25) expresses the relationship between the per capita values of the decision variables, D, and the state variables, z and S. This function does not describe a feature of the environment but is instead determined as part of the equilibrium. The primary goal of the next section is to describe a computational method for finding a function $\mathbf{D}$ that satisfies our definition of equilibrium.

More specifically, we wish to find a *recursive competitive equilibrium* (RCE), which consists of decision rules for the households, $d = d(z, S, s)$; a rule determining the per capita values of these variables, $D = \mathbf{D}(z, S)$; and a value function, $v(z, S, s)$, such that[15]

1) given the aggregate decision rules, D, the value function, v, satisfies equation (21) and d are the associated decision rules; and

2) the function $\mathbf{D}$ satisfies the relationship $\mathbf{D}(z, S) = d(z, S, S)$.

The Basic Model with Taxes

Our first example is a version of the basic model from Section 2 with taxes on labor and capital income. The particular decentralized economy that we consider consists of a large number, N, of identical households endowed with k_0 units of capital in period 0 and one unit of time in each period, which is spent either working or enjoying leisure. The households receive income in each period from capital and labor, which is used to finance consumption and investments in new capital. Consumption, leisure, and investment are chosen to maximize (4), subject to the following sequence of budget constraints (one for each t from zero to infinity):

$$c_t + i_t = (1 - \tau_h)w_t h_t + (1 - \tau_k)r_t k_t + \tau_k \delta k_t + TR_t. \tag{26}$$

In this equation, the variables w_t and r_t denote the wage rate and rental rate, respectively. The parameters τ_h and τ_k are the tax rate on labor income and the tax rate on capital income net of depreciation, $(r_t - \delta)k_t$. The capital stock owned by a given household evolves according to (8). The last term, TR_t, is a per capita lump sum transfer from the government to the households.

A firm in this economy purchases labor and capital services from the households and uses these to produce output, y_t^f, according to the technology given by (5) and (6). (The superscript f indicates quantities chosen by the firm.) Given that the technology displays constant returns to scale, no loss in generality is incurred by assuming that there is only one firm. The first-order conditions for the firm's profit maximization problem are

$$w_t = z_t F_2(k_t^f, h_t^f)$$

and

$$r_t = z_t F_1(k_t^f, h_t^f),$$

where k_t^f is the amount of capital that the firm rents from the households. Market clearing requires that $k_t^f = K_t N$ and $h_t^f = H_t N$, where N is the number of households, K_t is the per capita stock of capital, and H_t is per capita hours worked. Substituting this into the above first-order conditions, and using the fact that constant returns imply that the marginal products are homogeneous of degree zero, we obtain the following equilibrium expressions:

$$w_t = w(z_t, K_t, H_t) = z_t F_2(K_t, H_t), \tag{27}$$

and

$$r_t = r(z_t, K_t, H_t) = z_t F_1(K_t, H_t). \tag{28}$$

Constant returns also imply that in equilibrium, payments to factors of production fully exhaust revenues and, as a result, dividends are zero.

The role of the government in this economy is simply to collect tax revenue and return it to the households as a lump sum transfer. This implies that the government budget constraint is

$$TR_t = \tau_h w_t H_t + \tau_k (r_t - \delta) K_t. \tag{29}$$

The problem faced by a particular household can be expressed in the form of (21) by making a series of substitutions. First, (29) is substituted into (26) by eliminating TR_t. Next, (27) and (28) are substituted into (26), eliminating w_t and r_t, respectively. Finally, (26) is solved for c_t, and the result is substituted into the utility function (4). After these substitutions, the household's optimization problem can be written as the following dynamic programming problem:

$$v(z, K, k) = \max\{r(z, K, k, I, H, i, h) + \beta E[v(z', K', k')|z]\}$$

$$\text{s.t.} \quad z' = A(z) + \epsilon'$$

$$K' = (1 - \delta)K + I$$

$$k' = (1 - \delta)k + i$$

$$I = \mathbf{I}(z, K) \text{ and } H = \mathbf{H}(z, K). \tag{30}$$

The function $r(z, K, k, I, H, i, h)$ is equal to $U(c, 1 - h)$, where c is given by $w(z, K, H)[h + \tau_h(H - h)] + r(z, K, H)[k + \tau_k(K - k)] + \tau_k^\delta(k - K) - i$.

The functions $\mathbf{I}$ and $\mathbf{H}$ describe the relationship perceived by households between the aggregate decision variables and the state of the economy. We are interested in finding functional forms for $\mathbf{I}$ and $\mathbf{H}$ that satisfy the definition of a recursive competitive equilibrium applied to this example.

This problem can easily be mapped into the framework described at the beginning of the section. The only exogenous state variable is the technology shock, z, and the only endogenous state variable is the capital stock, K.[16] The decision variables are $d = (h, i)$, and the function $B(z, K, k, I, H, i, h)$ for this example is $(1 - \delta)k + i$. Finally, the analog to the function $\mathbf{D}$ in (25) is the pair of functions $\mathbf{I}$ and $\mathbf{H}$.

The Basic Model with Money

Leaving the preferences and technology of our basic model unchanged, fiat money will not be valued in equilibrium.[17] This follows from the fact that money would be dominated in rate of return by privately issued assets. The two most common ways of overcoming this obstacle are to include money as an argument in the utility function or to assume that previously accumulated cash balances are required for the purchase of some consumption goods (cash-in-advance).[18] In this section we will describe an example that illustrates the second approach.

Households choose consumption and leisure to maximize

$$E \sum_{t=0}^{\infty} \beta^t U(c_{1t}, c_{2t}, \ell_t), \quad 0 < \beta < 1, \tag{31}$$

where c_1 is consumption of the "cash good," c_2 is consumption of the "credit good," and ℓ is leisure. The period utility function, U, is bounded, continuously differentiable, strictly increasing, and strictly concave. In addition, Inada conditions are required to ensure that agents consume positive quantities of both consumption goods.

The period budget constraint is

$$c_{1t} + c_{2t} + i_t + \frac{m_{t+1}}{p_t} \leq w_t h_t + r_t k_t + \frac{m_t}{p_t} + \frac{T R_t}{p_t}. \tag{32}$$

This constraint reflects the assumption that c_1 and c_2, in addition to investment, are perfect substitutes in production, and hence sell at the same relative price. Households enter the period with nominal balances equal to m_t, which is augmented with a lump sum transfer of newly printed money, $T R_t$. Using our notational convention, M_t denotes beginning-of-period (pretransfer) per capita money balances, and m_t denotes the money holdings of a particular household. Thus, $T R_t = M_{t+1} - M_t$. The price level is denoted by p_t.

Purchases of the cash good, c_{1t}, must be financed with nominal cash holdings at the beginning of the period (post-transfer). This requirement is formalized by the cash-in-advance constraint,

$$p_t c_{1t} \leq m_t + T R_t. \tag{33}$$

The resource constraint is $c_{1t} + c_{2t} + i_t \leq y_t$, where y_t is produced according to the production function (4). This implies that the equilibrium wage rate and rental rate are given in equations (27) and (28), respectively.

The money supply, M_t, evolves according to the following rule:

$$M_{t+1} = g M_t. \tag{34}$$

The monetary growth factor, g, is constant over time, but, as in the case of the tax rates in the previous example, a natural extension is to model g as an exogenous state variable or as depending on the economy-wide state.

In this example, as well as in most applications involving cash-in-advance models, we impose conditions on the money growth rate such that (33) holds with equality (that is, the Lagrange multiplier associated with this constraint is positive in equilibrium). The precise form that this restriction takes depends on the form of the utility function. In general, this restriction is equivalent to requiring that an appropriately defined nominal interest rate be positive.

Our solution method requires that all variables fluctuate around a constant mean. However, if g is greater than one, both M and p in this example will grow without limit. This motivates introducing the following change of variables:

$$\hat{m}_t = m_t / M_t \quad \text{and} \quad \hat{p}_t = p_t / M_{t+1}. \tag{35}$$

With this change in variables, assuming that the cash-in-advance constraint is binding, the dynamic programming problem solved by households is

$$v(z, K, k, \hat{m}) = \max\{U(c_1, c_2, 1 - h) + \beta E v(z', K', k', \hat{m}')$$

$$\text{s.t.} \quad z' = A(z) + \epsilon'$$

$$K' = (1 - \delta)K + I$$

$$k' = (1 - \delta)k + i$$

$$c_1 + c_2 + i + \frac{\hat{m}'}{\hat{p}} = w(z, K, H)h$$

$$+ r(z, K, H)k + \frac{(\hat{m} + g - 1)}{(g \cdot \hat{p})}$$

$$c_1 = \frac{(\hat{m} + g - 1)}{(g \cdot \hat{p})}$$

$$I = \mathbf{I}(z, K), \quad H = \mathbf{H}(z, K), \quad \hat{p} = \mathbf{P}(z, K). \tag{36}$$

An important feature of this problem, which is absent in (30), is the function
P, which expresses the relationship between the price level and the state of the
economy. Because of this feature, this problem cannot be mapped into the notation
of problem (21). In that problem, there is no analog to relative money holdings,
$\hat{m}$, or the price level, $\hat{p}$. However, the following modified version of problem (21)
incorporates these features. This more general formulation would also apply to
other applications involving money in the utility function or cash-in-advance in
addition to the particular example described above.

$$v(z, S, s, m) = \max\{r(z, S, s, m, D, p, d, m') + \beta E v(z', S', s', m')\} \tag{37}$$

$$\text{s.t.} \quad z' = A(z) + \epsilon' \tag{38}$$

$$s' = B(z, S, s, m, D, d, p, m') \tag{39}$$

$$S' = B(z, S, S, 1, D, D, p, 1) \tag{40}$$

$$D = \mathbf{D}(z, S), p = \mathbf{P}(z, S).$$

In this problem, m and p are the household's nominal money holdings and the
price level, both expressed relative to the per capita money supply. Thus, they
correspond to $\hat{m}$ and $\hat{p}$ in the above example.

A *recursive competitive equilibrium* consists of a set of decision rules for the
household, $d = d(z, S, s, m)$; a decision rule determining the amount of money
the household carries into the next period, $m' = m(z, S, s, m)$; a set of aggregate
decision rules, $D = \mathbf{D}(z, S)$; a function determining the aggregate price level,
$p = \mathbf{P}(z, S)$; and a value function, $v(z, S, s, m)$, such that

1) given the functions $\mathbf{D}$ and $\mathbf{P}$, the value function, v, satisfies equation (37),
and d and m' are the associated decision rules; and

2) given the pricing function, $\mathbf{P}$, individual decisions are consistent with
aggregate outcomes:

$$\mathbf{D}(z, S) = d(z, S, S, 1) \quad \text{and} \quad 1 = m(z, S, S, 1)$$

Note that in equilibrium, m' must equal one since m' is defined to be money holdings relative to the per capita money supply.

It is straightforward to express our cash-in-advance economy in terms of this notation. As in the first example, $d = (i, h)$, and the function B is simply $(1 - \delta)k + i$. The return function, r, is given by

$$r(z, K, k, \hat{m}, I, H, \hat{p}, i, h, \hat{m}') = U(c_1, c_2, 1 - h)$$

where

$$c_1 = \frac{(\hat{m} + g - 1)}{(g \cdot \hat{p})},$$

and

$$c_2 = w(z, K, H)h + r(z, K, H)k - i - \frac{\hat{m}'}{\hat{p}}.$$

5. Solving for a Recursive Competitive Equilibrium

In this section, we describe a method for finding a function $\mathbf{D}$ (for an economy without money) or a pair of functions $\mathbf{D}$ and $\mathbf{P}$ (for a monetary economy) that satisfies the definition of a RCE. As in Section 3, we consider economies for which the return function is quadratic. Since our examples do not generally deliver quadratic objectives, we again make use of the quadratic approximation procedure described in Section 3. We first explain how to compute a RCE for a nonmonetary economy by using methods similar to the successive approximations described in Section 3. Next, we show how essentially the same methods can be applied to economies with money.

We begin by considering an economy where the problem solved by households is (21). As in section 3, z in equation (22) is an $\eta(z) \times 1$ vector of exogenous state variables, the first component of which is assumed to be constant over time (equal to one, without loss of generality). We continue to use the function $\eta(x)$ to denote the length of a column vector, x.

The steady state for the certainty version of this economy, $(\bar{z}, \bar{S}, \bar{s}, \bar{D}, \bar{d})$, which is required in computing the quadratic approximation of the return function, r, is the solution to the following set of equations:

$$\bar{z} = A(\bar{z});$$

$$r_d(\bar{z}, \bar{S}, \bar{s}, \bar{D}, \bar{d})$$

$$+ \beta r_s(\bar{z}, \bar{S}, \bar{s}, \bar{D}, \bar{d})[I - \beta B_s(\bar{z}, \bar{S}, \bar{s}, \bar{D}, \bar{d})]^{-1} B_d(\bar{z}, \bar{S}, \bar{s}, \bar{D}, \bar{d}) = 0$$

$$\bar{S} = B(\bar{z}, \bar{S}, \bar{S}, \bar{D}, \bar{D});$$

$$\bar{d} = \bar{D}, \bar{s} = \bar{S}. \tag{41}$$

Note that in (41) r_d, r_s, etc., have the same definition as (12).

Define y as the stacked vector, $(z, S, s, D_1, d_1, \ldots, D_{\eta(d)}, d_{\eta(d)})$, where the subscript denotes a particular component of D or d. Given the steady state of y, the quadratic approximation can be formed in precisely the manner described in Section 3. From this, we obtain the following linear-quadratic formulation of the household's problem, where the functions $\mathbf{D}_i$ are the unknown aggregate decision rules:

$$v(z, S, s) = \max\{y^T Qy + \beta E[v(z', S', s')|z]\}$$

s.t.   (22)–(24)

$$D_i = \mathbf{D}_i(z, S, D_1, \ldots, D_{i-1}), \tag{42}$$

where the $\mathbf{D}_i$, $i = 1, \ldots, \eta(d)$, are linear functions.

Finding a Recursive Competitive Equilibrium by Successive Approximations

Our computational procedure for finding the functions $\mathbf{D}_i$ that satisfy the requirements of a RCE for a linear-quadratic economy makes heavy use of the methods described in Section 3. As in the earlier section, we focus only on the certainty version of the household's problem (42), since the decision rules will be independent of the variance of ϵ. Successive approximations of the optimal value function, v, are obtained by iterating on the following mapping:

$$v^{n+1}(z, S, s) = \max\{y^T Qy + \beta v^n(z', S', s')\}$$

s.t.   (22)–(24)

$$D_i = \mathbf{D}_i^n(z, S, D_1, \ldots, D_{i-1}), \quad \text{for } i = 1, \ldots, \eta(d). \tag{43}$$

The functions $\mathbf{D}_i^n$ are the linear aggregate decision rules associated with the nth approximation of v. The precise way in which these functions are computed is described in Step 4 below.

Step 1. Choose a negative semidefinite matrix, v^0, of size $\eta(z, S, s) \times \eta(z, S, s)$.

Steps 2 through 7 describe how to obtain successive approximations of the value function, v. Given a matrix v^n, these steps explain how to compute v^{n+1}.

Step 2. Define x to be the stacked vector $(y, z', S', s') = (z, S, s, D_1, d_1, \ldots, D_{\eta(d)}, d_{\eta(d)}, z', S', s')$. Construct a matrix $R^{[\eta(x)]}$, which is of dimension $\eta(x) \times \eta(x)$, and which contains the matrix Q in the top left corner and the matrix βv^n in the lower right corner. All other elements are set equal to zero. The quadratic expression on the right side of (43) can now be written $x^T R^{[\eta(x)]} x$.

Step 3. Eliminate s', S', and z' by using the linear laws of motion, (22)–(24). This is done by using equation (17) from Section 3. After these substitutions, the quadratic expression becomes $x^T R^{[\eta(y)]} x$.

The next three steps are used to eliminate the aggregate and individual decision variables, D_j and d_j. Beginning with $j = \eta(d)$, these steps must be repeated $\eta(d)$ times to eliminate each of the D_j and d_j in turn. The description here assumes that the jth decision variable (D_j and d_j), which corresponds to the $J - 1$st and Jth elements of x, where $J \equiv \eta(z, S, s) + 2j$, is being eliminated. Decision variables with index greater than j are assumed to have already been eliminated.

Step 4. To obtain the function $\mathbf{D}_j^n$, consider the first order condition with respect to d_j:

$$\sum_{i \le J} R_{Ji}^{(J)} x_i = 0, \tag{44}$$

where $J = \eta(z, S, s) + 2j$. At this point it is important to examine if the second-order conditions are satisfied by checking whether $R_{JJ}^{(J)}$ is less than zero.

Substitute the aggregate consistency conditions into (44) by setting $s = S$ and $d_i = D_i$ for $i = 1, \ldots, j$, thereby eliminating s and the remaining components of d. Solving for D_j, we obtain the aggregate decision rule $\mathbf{D}_j^n$:

$$x_{J-1} = D_j = \sum_{i=1}^{J-2} \delta_i x_i, \tag{45}$$

where

$$\delta_i = \begin{cases} R_{Ji}^{(J)}/\bar{R} & \text{for } i = 1, \ldots, \eta(z) \\ (R_{Ji}^{(J)} + R_{J,i+\eta(S)}^{(J)})/\bar{R} & \text{for } i = \eta(z) + 1, \ldots, \eta(z, S) \\ 0 & \text{for } i = \eta(z, S) + 1, \ldots, \eta(z, S, s) \\ (R_{Ji}^{(J)} + R_{J,i+1}^{(J)})/\bar{R} & \text{for } i = \eta(z, S, s) + 1, \ldots, J - 3 \\ & \quad \text{(increments of 2)} \\ 0 & \text{for } i = \eta(z, S, s) + 2, \ldots, J - 2 \\ & \quad \text{(increments of 2)} \end{cases}$$

and

$$\bar{R} = -(R_{J,J-1}^{(J)} + R_{JJ}^{(J)}).$$

The first set of δ's are the coefficients on the components of z in (45). The remaining four sets of δ's are coefficients on the components of S, s, D, and d, respectively. Since (45) is an aggregate decision rule, the coefficients on s and d are equal to zero.

Step 5. Solve equation (44) for x_J and use the resulting linear expression to eliminate $x_J = d_j$ from the right side of (43), using the substitution procedure described in Section 3.

Step 6. Use equation (45) to eliminate $x_{J-1} = D_j$.

Steps 4 through 6 are repeated until all decision variables have been eliminated. After these substitutions, the right side of (43) becomes $x^T R^{\eta(z,S,s)} x$.

Step 7. Define v^{n+1} to be the matrix formed by the first $\eta(z, S, s)$ rows and columns of $R^{\eta(z,S,s)}$. Compare the elements of v^{n+1} with the elements of v^n, ignoring the (1,1) element. If they are sufficiently close, stop the iterations. If not, repeat the procedure beginning with Step 2, using v^{n+1} in place of v^n.

Once the iterations have converged, the equilibrium aggregate decision rules can be computed from the set of $\eta(d)$ equations (45) obtained in the last iteration. The procedure for obtaining these is analogous to the procedure described in Step 6 at the end of Section 3. Finally, one should check whether the steady states obtained from solving (41) are the same as the steady states implied by the linear equilibrium decision rules.

Solving for a Recursive Competitive Equilibrium in a Monetary Economy

We now explain how this method can be modified to solve for a RCE in a monetary model, where money is introduced either through a cash-in-advance constraint, as in the model described in Section 4, or by introducing money directly into the utility function.

The problem solved by households in these models is stated in equation (37). As usual, the first component of z is equal to one. The additional variables, m and p, are defined as in the basic model with money in Section 4. Both of these are one-dimensional variables.

The quadratic approximation of the return function, r, is formed in the same way as above, where the vector y is defined to be the stacked vector $(z, S, s, m, D_1, d_1, \ldots, D_{\eta(d)}, d_{\eta(d)}, p, m')$. The steady state is computed by solving a set of equations analogous to (12) in Section 3 or (41), noting that steady-state money holdings, $\bar{m}$, are equal to one.

The steps involved in generating successive approximations are very similar to those described above for solving a social planning problem. Successive approximations are computed by iterating on the following mapping, which is similar to

(43):

$$v^{n+1}(z, S, s, m) = \max\{y^T Q y + \beta v^n(z', S', s', m')\}$$

s.t.   (38)–(40)

$$D_i = \mathbf{D}_i^n(z, S, D_1, \ldots, D_{i-1}), i = 1, \ldots, \eta(d),$$

$$p = \mathbf{P}^n(z, S, D_1, \ldots, D_{\eta(d)}). \tag{46}$$

The functions $\mathbf{D}_i^n$ and $\mathbf{P}^n$ are the aggregate decision rules and pricing function associated with the nth approximation of v.

Steps 1–3 can be followed almost exactly as described, except that v^0 must be of dimension $[\eta(z, S, s) + 1] \times [\eta(z, S, s) + 1]$ and x is defined to be the stacked vector, $(z, S, s, m, D_1, d_1, \ldots, D_{\eta(d)}, d_{\eta(d)}, p, m', z', S', s', m')$. Notice that m' appears in this vector twice since it enters the value function for the next period as well as the current return function. The second m' is eliminated in Step 3 by using the equation $x_{\eta(x)} = x_{\eta(y)}$, that is, by setting the second m' equal to the first m'.

Step 4 for this problem differs from the nonmonetary case since the pricing function, $\mathbf{P}^n(z, S, D_1, \ldots, D_{\eta(d)})$, must be obtained in addition to the aggregate decision rules, denoted by $\mathbf{D}_i^n, \ldots, \mathbf{D}_{\eta(d)}^n$. The function $\mathbf{P}^n$ is computed from the first-order condition associated with m' by imposing the aggregate consistency conditions—$s = S, m = m' = 1$, and $d_i = D_i, i = 1, \ldots, \eta(d)$—and then solving for p. The expression $p = \mathbf{P}^n[z, S, D_1, \ldots, D_{\eta(d)}]$ is used to eliminate $x_{\eta(y)-1}$ as described in Step 6.

The rest of the procedure is unchanged from the nonmonetary one except that the accounting is slightly different because of the additional components of x. The decision variables, d and D, are eliminated as explained in Steps 4–6, and v^{n+1} is computed. Successive approximations of v are computed until they converge. Finally, the equilibrium decision rules and pricing function are computed from the functions $\mathbf{P}^n$ and $\mathbf{D}_i^n, i = 1, \ldots, \eta(d)$, associated with the last approximation of v.

6. Extensions to Heterogeneous-Agent Economies

An advantage of the methods we have described in this chapter is that they can be extended in a straightforward manner to an important class of economies in which agents are not ex ante identical. In this final section, we describe how to compute an equilibrium for an extension of the basic model in which agents differ according to preferences and initial capital holdings. More complicated heterogeneous-agent environments, including economies with n-period–lived overlapping generations, can be studied with methods similar to the one used for this example.[19]

Suppose that the economy consists of N types of households, with λ_i being the fraction of type $i = 1, \ldots, N$. It follows that the total measure of households is one. A household of type i solves the following problem:

$$\max E \sum_{t=0}^{\infty} \beta^t U_i(c_{it}, \ell_{it}), \quad 0 < \beta < 1 \tag{47}$$

s.t. $\quad h_{it} + \ell_{it} = 1$

$$z_{t+1} = A(z_t) + \epsilon_{t+1} \tag{48}$$

$$c_{it} + x_{it} = w_t h_{it} + r_t k_{it} \tag{49}$$

$$k_{i,t+1} = (1 - \delta)k_{it} + x_{it} \tag{50}$$

$$w_t = z_t F_H(K_t, H_t) \tag{51}$$

$$r_t = z_t F_K(K_t, H_t). \tag{52}$$

The initial k_{i0} is given as well as the stochastic process generating sequences $\{K_t, H_t\}_{t=0}^{\infty}$.

The variables c_{it}, x_{it}, h_{it}, ℓ_{it}, and k_{it} denote consumption, investment, hours worked, leisure, and capital stock of household i in time t.[20] Equations (51) and (52) are the equilibrium wage and rental rates as derived for the basic model with taxes in Section 4 under the assumption that there is a single constant-returns-to-scale technology. As usual, $K_t = \sum \lambda_i K_{it}$ and $H_t = \sum \lambda_i H_{it}$ are the per capita capital stock and hours worked, respectively, where K_{it} and H_{it} are the per capita capital stock and hours for households of type i. Equation (48) is the law of motion for the technology shock, where A is a linear function and ϵ is an i.i.d. random variable with finite variance.

As can be seen from the budget constraint (49), agents are permitted to use income from capital and labor to purchase units of current-period output (consumption and investment goods) only. They are not permitted to purchase (or sell) state-contingent claims to next-period units of output. This is not necessarily an innocuous assumption, as it is in economies where agents are identical. In addition, allowing these trades does complicate the solution procedure somewhat. Ríos-Rull (1992a) describes how to compute a recursive competitive equilibrium of an overlapping-generations economy in which these sorts of trades are permitted.

In our recursive formulation of this economy, we utilize the following notational conventions: k_i is the capital stock of a particular household of type i; K_j, for $j = 1, \ldots, N$, are the per capita capital stocks of households of types j; and $\mathbf{K} = (K_1, \ldots, K_N)^T$ is a vector describing the entire distribution of capital stocks. These same conventions apply to the decision variables, hours, h, and investment, x.

If we substitute (51) and (52) into (49), solve (49) for c_{it} and substitute the resulting function into the utility function, household i's optimization problem can be expressed as the following dynamic program:

$$v_i(z, \mathbf{K}, k_i) = \max\{r_i(z, \mathbf{K}, k_i, \mathbf{X}, \mathbf{H}, x_i, h_i) + \beta E[v_i(z', \mathbf{K}', k_i')|z]\} \tag{53}$$

s.t. $z' = A(z) + \epsilon';$

$$k_i' = (1 - \delta)k_i + x_i; \tag{54}$$

$$K_j' = (1 - \delta)K_j + X_j, \text{ for } j = 1, \ldots, N; \tag{55}$$

$$H_j = H_j(z, \mathbf{K}), X_j = X_j(z, \mathbf{K}) \text{ for } j = 1, \ldots, N. \tag{56}$$

Notice that although factor prices depend only on the per capita capital stock, the state of the economy includes the vector of per capita stocks held by each type. Equation (55) is the law of motion for the K_j. Equation (56) states that the per capita hours and per capita investment (for each j) are given functions of the state of the economy.

A *recursive competitive equilibrium* for this economy consists of a set of decision rules for households of type i, $h_i(z, \mathbf{K}, k_i)$ and $x_i(z, \mathbf{K}, k_i)$ for $i = 1, \ldots, N$; a set of per capita decision rules, $H_i(z, \mathbf{K})$ and $X_i(z, \mathbf{K})$, for each i; and a set of value functions, $v_i(z, \mathbf{K}, k_i)$ for each i, such that

1) given the per capita decision rules, the value function for type i, v_i, satisfies equation (53), and h_i and x_i are the associated decision rules; and

2) $H_i(z, \mathbf{K}) = h_i(z, \mathbf{K}, K_i)$ and $X_i(z, \mathbf{K}) = x_i(z, \mathbf{K}, K_i)$ for each i.

To compute an equilibrium, we approximate the return function of each type by a quadratic function, using the quadratic approximation procedure described in Section 3. To obtain successive approximations of the value function for type i we iterate on the following mapping, where y_i, is the stacked vector $(z, \mathbf{K}, k_i, \mathbf{X}, \mathbf{H}, x_i, h_i)$:

$$v_i^{n+1}(z, \mathbf{K}, k_i) = \max\{y_i^T Q_i y_i + \beta v_i^n(z', \mathbf{K}', k_i')\}$$

s.t. $z' = A(z)$, (54), (55),

$$X_j = X_j^n(z, \mathbf{K}) \text{ and } H_j = H_j^n(z, \mathbf{K}) \text{ for } j = 1, \ldots, N. \tag{57}$$

To compute v_i^{n+1}, X_i^n, and H_i^n for a household of type i given a quadratic function v_i^n, we first employ the substitution procedure described in Section 3 to eliminate z', $\mathbf{K}'$, and k_i', using the linear equations $z' = A(z)$, (55) and (54), respectively. This must be done for each i.

Next, for each type i, we take the first-order conditions with respect to x_i and h_i. Substituting the aggregate consistency conditions—$x_i = X_i$, $h_i = H_i$, and $k_i = K_i$ for each i—into these first order conditions, we obtain $2N$ equations that are used to solve for the $2N$ unknowns $\mathbf{X}$ and $\mathbf{H}$ as functions of z and $\mathbf{K}$. These are the functions X_j^n and H_j^n, for $j = 1, \ldots, N$, that appear in the mapping (57).

The third step is to use the first-order conditions to solve for x_i and h_i as a function of $(z, \mathbf{K}, k_i, \mathbf{X}, \mathbf{H})$ for each i. The resulting functions are used to eliminate x_i and h_i from the right side of the mapping (57). The final step is to eliminate $\mathbf{X}$ and

H by using the linear functions, X_j^n and H_j^n, for each j. From this, we obtain a quadratic function of z, **K**, and k_i, which is used as the next approximation of v_i, v_i^{n+1}. The procedure is repeated until the iterations have converged.

Notes

We are grateful to Mariano Cortes and Rajeev Dhawan for research assistance. This research was supported in part by NSF Grants SES-8921346 and SES-6205417.

1. This repeats some of the material covered in Chapter 1, but this seemed to us to be useful for carrying out the purposes of the current chapter.

2. See Stokey and Lucas with Prescott (1989) for details on the dynamic general equilibrium theory underlying the approach employed in this section. It is worth noting that in some special cases a similar approach can be used when equilibrium allocations are not Pareto optimal. In these cases, equilibrium allocations are the solution to *some* dynamic optimization problem that is different from the problem that gives the optimal allocation. See Becker (1985) for an example where this approach is employed.

3. Distinguishing between z and s is not important in cases where a social-planning problem is to be solved. However, it is important in cases where the Second Welfare Theorem does not hold. We make this distinction here so that the notation will be consistent throughout the chapter.

4. Although it is clear that (2) allows for the possibility that components of z evolve as a continuous-state Markov process, it is not difficult to modify the solution method described in this section to allow for components of z to follow a finite-state Markov chain. In this case, instead of solving for a single value function, $v(z, s)$, there is a separate value function, $v_z(s)$, for each z in the state space.

5. Examples from this literature include Cho and Rogerson (1988), Christiano (1988), Greenwood, Hercowitz, and Huffman (1988), Kydland (1984a), Kydland and Prescott (1982, 1988), Hansen (1985), Hansen and Sargent (1988), and King, Plosser, and Rebelo (1988a). In each of these papers, numerical methods are used to solve a planning problem, such as (2.1). Long and Plosser (1983) consider an example where the planning problem can be solved analytically so that numerical methods are not required.

6. In this example we show how to add deterministic growth to the model. It is also possible to introduce stochastic growth by assuming that the technology shock evolves as a random walk with drift. The details are given in Hansen (1989).

7. We have imposed the result that with utility separable in consumption and leisure, optimal consumption is the same for those who work and for those who do not work.

8. Notice that although n, and not h, is a decision variable for an individual household, the social planner does choose h.

9. In practice, we recommend choosing $\tilde{h}$ so that the steady state computed from the linear decision rules are the same (up to, say, six decimal places) as the steady state for the nonlinear economy. In addition, if the steady states for the components of y differ significantly in absolute value, it may be desirable to set h_i^i proportional to the steady state, $h_i^i = \tilde{h}\bar{y}_i$, as long as $\bar{y}_i$ is different from zero.

10. In the rest of this section, unless we say otherwise, references to v are to the optimal value function for this linear-quadratic problem, as opposed to the optimal value function for problem (1).

11. The return function, r, given that the utility function is strictly concave, is bounded from above. See Stokey, Lucas, and Prescott (1989) for a discussion of discounted dynamic programming with returns bounded from above.

12. In practice, one could just as well eliminate this last row and column. However, we have chosen to fill this last row and column with zeros to simplify notation.

13. In practice, one should ignore the constant term of v^{n+1} and v^n (the (1,1) element) when doing this comparison. The reason is that this term takes relatively longer to converge and has no effect on the policy functions.

14. Here, and in the rest of the paper, we use lower-case letters (e.g., h and k) to denote quantities associated with a particular household. Capital letters (H and K) denote economy-wide (per capita) quantities that are determined in equilibrium but are not influenced by the actions of any individual household.

15. The notion of a recursive competitive equilibrium is developed in Prescott and Mehra (1980).

16. A natural extension of this example would be to model the tax rates as exogenous stochastic processes, or as depending on the endogenous state variables. See Braun (1990), Chang (1990), Greenwood and Huffman (1991), and McGrattan (1989) for applications of this sort to equilibrium business cycle theory.

17. See Sargent (1987) for a detailed discussion of this issue.

18. Both of these types of models are discussed in Sargent's (1987) textbook, and standard references are provided. Papers that contain applications of these monetary models to equilibrium business cycle theory include Cooley and Hansen (1989), Huh (1993), and Kydland (1989).

19. Ríos-Rull (1992a) extends and applies these methods to the study of models with n–period lived overlapping generations.

20. Notice that we have switched notation from previous sections. Previously, investment was denoted by i_t, but the letter i is now used to index type of household. Therefore, we now use x_t to denote investment.

Chapter 3
Computing Equilibria of Nonoptimal Economies

Jean-Pierre Danthine
and John B. Donaldson

1. Introduction

By the Second Welfare Theorem, every Pareto-optimal allocation can be expressed as a competitive equilibrium under appropriate assumptions. Recent work by Prescott and Lucas (1972), Prescott and Mehra (1980), and Brock (1979) has extended this equivalence to the general setting of the infinite-horizon stochastic growth paradigm. Unlike the traditional valuation equilibrium concept of Debreu (1954), where all trading occurs at a single date, these "decentralization" concepts provide for the more natural sequential, period-by-period exchange of commodities and securities appropriate to macroeconomic analyses. The enormous significance of this work cannot be overemphasized. Under quite general circumstances, it allows researchers to exploit straightforward contraction mapping techniques to solve central-planning infinite-horizon optimum formulations knowing all the while that the intertemporal allocations thereby obtained can be interpreted as decentralized competitive equilibria. Without such a concept, the use of variants of the stochastic growth paradigm for macroeconomic studies would be inappropriate: no modern economy of interest is overseen by an all-powerful central planner.

But what if we choose to incorporate features that force the model's equilibrium to be Pareto suboptimal? This will occur, e.g., with such additions as income taxes and production externalities, borrowing or lending constraints, noncompetitive pricing behavior, or monetary phenomena. For a number of reasons, the dominant trend in the literature appears to be in this direction. First, it is of interest to examine the impact of various tax regimes on the dynamic time path of the economy (e.g., Bizer and Judd [1989a]; Coleman [1991]; and Dotsey [1990]). Second, it has been argued that the incorporation of many of these features may be critical to the ability of this model class to replicate adequately the set of business cycle stylized facts (e.g., Danthine and Donaldson [1991b]; Rotemberg and Woodford [1991]). Third, the suboptimality of equilibrium affords a necessary rationale for countercyclical policy intervention studies (e.g., Greenwood and Huffman [1991]). Fourth, the impact of monetary phenomena can be studied only in the setting of non optimal economies. Fifth, the abovementioned features are obviously present in real-world economies, and the accuracy of our models and the resultant persuasiveness of their implications must thus depend significantly on their inclusion.

Since the equilibria of economies with these features can rarely be characterized as solutions to optimization problems, the methods of Chapter 2 do not generally apply. Rather, equilibrium for this general class of models can typically be characterized as the solution to a system of first-order conditions on which certain market-clearing conditions have been imposed. For the model specifically considered in this essay, equilibrium, if it exists, can generally be summarized as the solution function $X(s, z)$ to an integral equation of the form

$$0 = g[X(s, z), s, z] + \int h[X(s', z'), s', z']Q(dz'; z)$$

$$X(s, z) \in B(s, z)$$

$$s' = F(X(s, z), s, z), \tag{1}$$

where s denotes an endogenous "state" of the economy with $s \in S$, the endogenous state space; $g()$ and $h()$ are continuous functions from $R^N \mapsto R^1_+$; and $Q(dz'; z)$ is a continuous transition density function on the economy's exogenous state variables $z \in Z$, the exogenous state space. The set $B(s, z)$ will typically be a compact subset of the overall state space and represents the set of possible actions feasible for the economy's agents to undertake given the current state. Lastly, $F[X(s, z), s, z]$ represents the level of the endogenous state variables next period (indicated by a prime, $'$) conditional on the state and action taken today.

It is the objective of this chapter to describe the methods that have been developed to solve such equations in a computationally manageable way. In the notation of the preceding paragraph, the typical strategy will be to define an operator, T, acting on a well-defined space of continuous functions, such that the solution function $X(s, z)$ is a fixed point of that operator. The form of equation (1) above suggests the following natural definition of the operator: for every $s \in S$ and every $z \in Z$ and any $\hat{X}(s, z) \in B(s, z)$, define $T\hat{X}(s, z)$, if it exists, as the function that satisfies

$$0 = g[T\hat{X}(s, z), s, z] + \int h[\hat{X}(s', z'), s', z']Q(dz'; z)$$

$$\hat{X}(s, z), T\hat{X}(s, z) \in B(s, z)$$

$$s' = F[T\hat{X}(s, z), s, z].$$

In order for this operator to be implementable by a computer-based routine, it must be somehow modified to act only on objects that can be identified with points in finite-dimensional space. This can be accomplished in a number of different ways. For example, all relevant functions can be restricted to being defined only on a discrete partition of the overall state space; in this case, the operator is effectively defined over n-dimensional vectors, where n identifies the cardinality of the partition. These methods become of additional interest when we recognize that they are equally well suited to the solution of more standard optimal formulations, thereby providing a (sometimes computationally advantageous) alternative to the traditional value-iterative approach.

In what follows, all the principal methodologies are illustrated in the context of an economy with a simple tax distortion. This economy is first detailed in Section 2. It is important to understand how these equilibrium characterizations arise, and the tax setting is the simplest illustration available. In Sections 3 through 8, we introduce alternative solution methodologies, while Section 9 concludes the chapter.

2. An Illustration of a Nonoptimal Economy

We consider an economy with an explicit income tax. Since the tax drives a wedge (forces inequality) between the payments made by the firm to the factors of production and the payments actually received by those factors, equilibrium cannot be optimal, and thus is not expressible as the solution to a straightforward infinite-horizon maximization problem. We must, rather, begin with an entirely decentralized formulation and construct the equilibrium characterization. The model we review is a simplification of one considered by Coleman (1991), and we parallel his development; variants are to be found in work by Danthine and Donaldson (1985), Bizer and Judd (1989a), and Dotsey (1990).

For convenience of notation, we consider an economy populated by a large number of consumer-investor households, indexed by $\gamma \in [0, 1]$ and a single firm which behaves competitively (takes prices as given). The timing of events is discrete. At the start of each period, the households rent their capital and labor services (supplied inelastically) to the firm, which employs them in a constant-returns-to-scale (CRS) production process to produce (identical) consumption and capital goods. At the end of the period, after production has occurred, the firm returns to the households the remaining undepreciated portion of their capital stock, while also providing (competitively determined) rental payments for the use of both factors. All income payments to the households are taxed by the government at a flat rate, which may depend on the state of the economy. These tax payments are then rebated in a lump sum fashion to the households. Since each household is of measure zero relative to the overall economy, it is assumed that the households do not recognize the implicit (equilibrium) identity between what they pay in taxes and the per capita rebate they receive. Finally households use their net after-tax incomes to purchase consumption and investment goods from the firm. The undepreciated capital plus the new investment goods are then carried over by the households into the following period to be rented to the firms once again, and the cycle repeats itself.

More formally, let K_t denote aggregate economywide capital held in total by all households at the start of period t (by definition, $\int_0^1 k_t d\gamma = K_t$, where k_t

is the period t individual capital holdings of a representative household), and let z_t denote the economywide period t shock to technology. Under the scenario described above, the firm solves a series of one-period problems; in particular, the firm's profit-maximizing production decisions solve

$$\max_{\{c_t^f, z_t^f, k_t^f, h_t^f\}} P_c(K_t, z_t)c_t^f + P_x(K_t, z_t)x_t^f - r(K_t, z_t)k_t^f - w(K_t, z_t)h_t^f$$

$$\text{s.t.} \quad c_t^f + x_t^f \leq f(k_t^f, h_t^f)z_t,$$

where $P_c(K_t, z_t)$, $P_x(K_t, z_t)$, $r(K_t, z_t)$, and $w(K_t, z_t)$ denote, respectively, the economywide price of the consumption good and the investment good, the rental rate for capital, and the wage rate. As is customary c_t^f stands for the consumption good, x_t^f stands for the investment good, and h_t^f stands for labor services (hours); the superscript "f" identifies these quantities as either outputs produced by or inputs purchased by the firm. The CRS production function $f(\cdot, \cdot)$ is subject to a random technology shock, z_t, whose probabilistic process is known to all the economy's agents. In general an upper-case variable will represent economywide levels of that variable, while a lower-case variable denotes the firm- or individual-specific value of that variable. Assuming an interior solution, the first-order conditions are given by:

$$P_c(K_t, z_t) = P_x(K_t, z_t) \equiv_{def} 1, \tag{2}$$

$$f_1(k_t^f, h_t^f)z_t = r(K_t, z_t), \tag{3}$$

and

$$f_2(k_t^f, h_t^f)z_t = w(K_t, z_t), \tag{4}$$

where $f_i()$ indicates the partial derivative with respect to the ith variable. Note that under CRS, the firm's profits will be zero. Throughout this chapter the following assumptions will be understood to hold.

Assumption 1. $z_t \in [z_1, z_2] \in R_+^1$, where $z_1 > 0$, $z_2 < \infty$; z_t follows a Markov process with continuous transition density $Q(dz'; z)$. For notational economy, let $[z_1, z_2]$ be represented by $\mathfrak{Z}$.

Assumption 2. The CRS production function $f(\cdot, \cdot)R_+^2 \mapsto R_+^1$ is twice continuously differentiable, strictly increasing, and strictly concave with $f(0, h) = f(k, 0) = 0$ and $\lim_{k \mapsto 0} f_1(k, h) = \infty$ for $h > 0$. Furthermore, there exists some capital stock level $\bar{K} > 0$ such that $f(\bar{K}, 1)z + (1 - \delta)\bar{K} \leq \bar{K}$ for all z. Again for notational economy let $\mathfrak{C} = [0, \bar{K}]$.

In Assumption 2, δ denotes the period capital depreciation rate and the inequality restriction ensures that if initial aggregate capital is below $\bar{K}$, then it will never exceed $\bar{K}$.

Turning next to the problem faced by a representative consumer-worker household, these participants are assumed to solve

$$\max_{\{c_t\},\{x_t\}} E\left[\sum_{t=0}^{\infty} \beta^t u(c_t)\right]$$

s.t. $P_c(K_t, z_t)c_t + P_x(K_t, z_t)x_t \leq [r(K_t, z_t)k_t$

$\qquad + w(K_t, z_t)h_t](1 - \tau(K_t, z_t)) + \pi(K_t, z_t)$

$\qquad h_t \leq 1,$

$\qquad k_{t+1} = (1 - \delta)k_t + x_t,$ and given the equation of motion

$\qquad$ on aggregate capital

$$K_{t+1} = (1 - \delta)K_t + X(K_t, z_t), \qquad (5)$$

where $X(K_t, z_t)$, aggregate investment, is assumed to be known to the consumer investor households. The choice of notation is again customary: E denotes the expectations operator, β denotes the agent's subjective discount factor, δ the period depreciation rate, $\tau(K_t, z_t)$ denotes the (state-contingent) rate of income tax, and $\pi(K_t, z_t)$ denotes the period transfer payment to the household from the government. Two more assumptions are now required:

Assumption 3. $\tau : R^+ \times [z_1, z_2] \mapsto [0, 1]$ is continuously differentiable; so also for $\pi()$. In addition $[1 - \tau(K, z)]f_1(K, 1)z$ is decreasing as a function of K.

Assumption 4. The period utility function $u() : R_+ \mapsto R$ is bounded, continuously differentiable, strictly concave, and strictly increasing with $\lim_{c \mapsto 0} u_1(c) = +\infty$.

As is well known, the solution to problem (5) is equivalent to finding a $v(k_t, K_t, z_t)$ that solves

$$v(k_t, K_t, z_t) = \sup_{x_t, h_t}\{u([r(K_t, z_t)k_t + w(K_t, z_t)h_t](1 - \tau(K_t, z_t))$$

$$+ \pi(K_t, z_t) - x_t)$$

$$+ \beta \int v((1 - \delta)k_t + x_t, K_t(1 - \delta)$$

$$+ X(K_t, z_t), z_{t+1}) Q(dz_{t+1}; z_t)\}$$

s.t. $0 \leq h_t \leq 1$

$$0 \leq x_t \leq [r(K_t, z_t)k_t + w(K_t, z_t)h_t](1 - \tau(K_t, z_t))$$

$$+ \pi(K_t, z_t), \tag{6}$$

where we have imposed the normalization $P_c(K_t, z_t) = P_x(K_t, z_t) = 1$. It is well known that such a $v()$ exists under quite general circumstances:

> **Theorem 1.** Given assumptions 1–4, and provided that $X(K, z) : \mathfrak{C} \times 3 \mapsto R^+$ is continuous, then there exists a bounded continuous function $v(k, K, z)$, which is strictly increasing and strictly concave in its first argument. Furthermore, for every $(k, K, z) \in \mathfrak{C} \times \mathfrak{C} \times 3$, the sup is attained by a unique $x = x(k, K, z)$, which is continuous in its first argument.

> **Proof.** Standard in the literature; see Stokey, Lucas, and Prescott (1989, Ch. 9).

These assumptions are also sufficient to guarantee (i) an interior solution for problem (6), which follows, in particular, from $\lim_{c \to 0} u_1(c) = \infty$, and $f(0, 1)z = 0$, for all z, and (ii) that the requirements of Benveniste and Scheinkman (1979, theorem 1) hold. Thus $v(k, K, z)$ is differentiable with respect to its first argument, and the necessary and sufficient first-order condition for problem (6) is

$$u_1([r(K_t, z_t)k_t + w(K_t, z_t)1](1 - \tau(K_t, z_t)) + \pi(K_t, z_t) - x_t)$$

$$= \beta \int v_1((1 - \delta)k_t + x_t, (1 - \delta)K_t + X(K_t, z_t), z_{t+1}) Q(dz_{t+1}; z_t) \tag{7}$$

Equilibrium for this economy may now be defined.

> **Definition.** An equilibrium for the economy described above is a pair of continuous pricing functions, $r(K, z)$ and $w(K, z)$; a continuous aggregate transfer function, $\Pi(K, z)$; and a continuous aggregate investment function, $X(K, z)$ such that

1) market clearing occurs, i.e.,

$$k_t^f = K_t = \int_0^1 k_t d\gamma (= k_t)$$

$$c_t^f = C_t = \int_0^1 c_t d\gamma (= c_t)$$

$$h_t^f = H_t = 1 = \int_0^1 h_t d\gamma (= h_t = 1)$$

$$x_t^f = X_t = \int_0^1 x_t d\gamma (= x_t)$$

2) all agents are optimizing given these prices and the equation of motion on aggregate capital stock, i.e., equations (3), (4), and (7) are satisfied;

3) $\int_0^1 \pi(K_t, z_t) d\gamma = \Pi(K_t, z_t) = \tau(K_t, z_t) f(K_t, 1) z_t$, i.e., all tax revenues are lump sum rebated to the households; and

4) the individual agent's decision rule is consistent with the law of motion on aggregate capital stock, that is, $x_t = x(k_t, K_t, z_t) = X(K_t, z_t)$. In other words, the aggregate investment function assumed by the households coincides with what they actually plan to invest in the aggregate.

Our assumptions allow a convenient characterization of this equilibrium. By the envelope theorem,

$$
\begin{aligned}
v_1(k_t, K_t, z_t) &= u_1([r(K_t, z_t)k_t + w(K_t, z_t)h_t]((1 - \tau(K_t, z_t)) \\
&\quad + \pi(K_t, z_t) - x_t) \cdot ((1 - \tau(K_t, z_t))r(K_t, z_t) \\
&\quad + \beta(1 - \delta) \int v_1((1 - \delta)k_t + x_t, (1 - \delta)K_t \\
&\quad + X(K_t, z_t), z_{t+1})Q(dz_{t+1}; z_t) \\
&= u_1([r(K_t, z_t)k_t + w(K_t, z_t)h_t](1 - \tau(K_t, z_t)) \\
&\quad + \pi(K_t, z_t) - x_t) \\
&\quad \cdot [(1 - \tau(K_t, z_t))r(K_t, z_t) + (1 - \delta)], \quad (8)
\end{aligned}
$$

where, in the second equality, we have eliminated $\int v_1[(1 - \delta)k_t + x_t, (1 - \delta)K_t + X(K_t, z_t), z_{t+1}]Q(dz_{t+1}; z_t)$ by substituting from the optimality equation (7). Replacing $v_1()$ in equation (7) with (8) in turn yields

$$
\begin{aligned}
&u_1([r(K_t, z_t)k_t + w(K_t, z_t)h_t](1 - \tau(K_t, z_t)) + \pi(K_t, z_t) - x_t) \\
&= \beta \int u_1([r(K_{t+1}, z_{t+1})k_{t+1} + w(K_{t+1}, z_{t+1})h_{t+1}](1 - \tau(K_{t+1}, z_{t+1})) \\
&\quad + \pi(K_{t+1}, z_{t+1}) - x_{t+1}) \\
&\quad \cdot [r(K_{t+1}, z_{t+1})(1 - \tau(K_{t+1}, z_{t+1})) + (1 - \delta)]Q(dz_{t+1}; z_t) \quad (9)
\end{aligned}
$$

Since, in equilibrium, aggregate and individual values of the various variables coincide, and since with CRS, the factor payments exhaust output, equation (9) reduces to

$$u_1(f(K_t, 1)z_t - X(K_t, z_t)) = \beta \int u_1(f(K_{t+1}, 1)z_{t+1} - X(K_{t+1}, z_{t+1}))$$

$$\cdot [r(K_{t+1}, z_{t+1})(1 - \tau(K_{t+1}, z_{t+1}))$$

$$+ (1 - \delta)]Q(dz_{t+1}; z_t) \qquad (10)$$

where $K_{t+1} = (1 - \delta)K_t + X_t$. Substituting the equilibrium expression for $r(K_{t+1}, z_{t+1})$ yields a final simplification:

$$u_1(f(K_t)z_t - X(K_t, z_t)) = \beta \int u_1(f(K_{t+1})z_{t+1} - X(K_{t+1}, z_{t+1}))$$

$$\cdot [f_1(K_{t+1})z_{t+1}(1 - \tau(K_{t+1}, z_{t+1})) + (1 - \delta)]Q(dz_{t+1}; z_t), \qquad (11)$$

where $f(K_t)z_t = f(K_t, 1)z_t$. Equivalently,

$$u_1(C(K_t, z_t)) = \beta \int u_1(C(K_{t+1}, z_{t+1}))(f_1(K_{t+1})z_{t+1}(1 - \tau(K_{t+1}, z_{t+1}))$$

$$+ (1 - \delta))Q(dz_{t+1}; z_t). \qquad (12)$$

Proving the existence of equilibrium for the economy just described is thus equivalent to demonstrating the existence of a continuous $X(K, z)$ that solves equation (11). We also require that the equilibrium existence proof be constructive, in a manner that can be conveniently replicated by a computer-based numerical routine. A number of authors have studied variations on equation (11), and a review of their work, as applied to the above model, provides an overview of the solution methods currently available.

3. Method 1: The Equivalent Optimum Formulation

In certain special cases, the equation defining the equilibrium investment function, equation (11), is also the necessary and sufficient first-order condition of a modi-fied, though closely related, optimum formulation. First to exploit this approach were Becker (1985) (certainty) and Danthine and Donaldson (1985) (uncertainty), who studied a special case of (11) where (i) $\delta = 1$, and (ii) a fixed tax rate, $\tau(K, z) = \hat{\tau}$ for all $(K, z) \in \mathfrak{C} \times \mathfrak{Z}$, is applied (iii) only to capital income. With labor supplied inelastically every period, the last modification (iii) has no impact on the basic first-order condition, which in this case reduces to

$$u_1(f(K_t)z_t - X(K_t, z_t))$$

$$= \beta \int u_1[f(K_{t+1})z_{t+1}$$

$$- X(K_{t+1}, z_{t+1})](1 - \hat{\tau})f_1(K_{t+1})z_{t+1}Q(dz_{t+1}; z_t), \qquad (13)$$

or

$$u_1[C(K_t, z_t)] = \beta(1-\hat{\tau}) \int u_1[C(K_{t+1}, z_{t+1})]f_1(K_{t+1})z_{t+1}Q(dz_{t+1}; z_t). \quad (14)$$

Under our maintained assumptions, Becker (1985) and Danthine and Donaldson (1985) recognized that equation (14) is the necessary and sufficient first-order condition for the following problem:

$$\max_{(C_t)} E\{\sum_{t=0}^{\infty}[\beta(1 - \hat{\tau})]^t u(C_t)\}$$

$$\text{s.t.} \quad C_t + X_t \leq f(K_t)z_t$$

$$K_{t+1} = X_t. \qquad (15)$$

Under these special-case assumptions, we are thus informed that a competitive economy with a fixed capital income tax rate will experience a time path identical to that of a centrally planned economy for which the discount factor of the representative agent is reduced to $\beta(1 - \hat{\tau})$. As a result, investment will be lower and the mean levels of aggregate consumption, capital stock, and output will be less than in an analogous untaxed economy despite the full lump sum tax rebate (see Danthine and Donaldson [1985]). Applying the decentralization equivalence of Prescott and Mehra (1980), we can further conclude that the time path of a competitive economy subject to a fixed proportional tax rate with lump sum redistribution is identical (for the same shocks) to that of an untaxed economy with a lower subjective discount factor. Of more immediate significance from our perspective, the optimal $X(K, z)$ that solves equation (13) can be found by applying the standard value iterative procedures to problem (15).

The simple correspondence noted above is obviously dependent on the fact that $\delta = 1$. Yet, the aggregate dynamics of our income-taxed economy will coincide with those of a related optimum problem even in the case of $\delta \neq 1$. Consider the following optimum formulation:

$$\max E\left(\sum_{t=0}^{\infty} \beta^t u(C_t)\right)$$

$$\text{s.t.} \quad C_t + X_t \leq \hat{f}(K_t)z_t + e_t$$

$$K_{t+1} = (1 - \delta)K_t + X_t, K_0 \text{ given}, \qquad (16)$$

where $\hat{f}(K_t)z_t = (1 - \hat{\tau})f(K_t, 1)z_t$ and (e_t) is an exogenous endowment sequence. Under our original assumptions the above problem will have a solution for any sequence (e_t) where $e_t \geq 0$ and $e_t \leq M$, for some $M > 0$. Let us denote the optimal investment function for the above problem by $X_t = X(K_t, z_t, e_t)$, where we make its dependence on the endowment sequence explicit. Given quite reasonable restrictions, it can be shown that there exists an endowment sequence $(e_t^*), 0 \leq e_t^* \leq M$ such that $e_t^* = \tau f(K_t^*)z_t$, for all t, where $K_t^* = (1 - \delta)K_{t-1}^* + X(K_{t-1}^*, z_{t-1}^*, e_{t-1}^*)$ is the optimal capital sequence given K_0, $\{z_t^*\}$, and $\{e_t^*\}$. See Jones and Manuelli (1990) for a full discussion. With $(e_t) = (e_t^*)$, the aggregate investment function for problem (16) coincides with the aggregate investment function of our suboptimal economy with income taxation. While this method can be easily adapted to prove the existence of equilibrium for a wide class of suboptimal economies, it is of limited computational usefulness as a method for constructing the critical endowment sequence (e_t^*) is not specified. In some cases, however, the (e_t^*) sequence can be constructed. See Kehoe, Levine, and Romer (1989) for a discussion of other examples for which this technique is useful.

A second illustration of this perspective considers a dynamic model in which there is present a production externality of the type introduced by Romer (1986). Under this scenario, the production technology available to firms is hypothesized to be of the form $f(k_t, \bar{K}_t)z_t = k_t^\alpha(\bar{K}_t)^{1-\alpha}z_t$, where $\bar{K}_t$ denotes the level of knowledge or production skill available in the economy. Firms take $(\bar{K}_t)$ as given; following Romer (1986), it is assumed that $\bar{K}_t$ is proportional to the level of capital stock available in the aggregate to all firms in the economy, that is, $\bar{K}_t = Nk_t$, where k_t is the capital stock level in any one of the N identical firms. A representative consumer-investor in this economy solves

$$\max E\left(\sum_{t=0}^{\infty} \beta^t u(c_t)\right)$$

$$\text{s.t.} \quad c_t + x_t \leq f(k_t, \bar{K}_t)z_t$$

$$k_{t+1} = x_t$$

$$k_0, (\bar{K}_t) \text{ given}, \tag{17}$$

where we assume the number of consumer-investors equals the number of firms without loss of generality. Under the customary concavity, boundedness, and differentiability assumptions, the necessary and sufficient first-order condition for this problem is given by

$$u_1(c_t) = \beta \int u_1(c_{t+1})f_1(k_t, \bar{K}_t)z_t Q(dz_{t+1}; z_t) \tag{18}$$

If we further assume that $u(c_t) = \ell n(c_t)$ and that (z_t) is i.i.d. with $Ez_t = 1$, equation (18) reduces to

$$\frac{1}{c_t} = \beta \int \left(\frac{1}{c_{t+1}}\right)\alpha k_{t+1}^{\alpha-1}(Nk_{t+1})^{1-\alpha}Q(dz_{t+1}), \tag{19}$$

where we have imposed the equilibrium condition, $\bar{K}_t = Nk_t$. With these functional forms, it is to be expected that investment, x_t, will be a fixed fraction of output, $x_t = \gamma k_t^\alpha (Nk_t)^{1-\alpha} z_t$ for some $\gamma > 0$. Substituting this expression for $x_t = k_{t+1}$ together with the concomitant relationship $c_t = (1 - \gamma)[Nk_t^\alpha (nk_t)^{1-\alpha}]z_t$ into equation (19) and simplifying yields the familiar $\gamma = \alpha\beta$. A quick check of the first-order conditions confirms that the identical savings function applies to the following optimum problem in which agents are presumed to know the dependency of $(\bar{K}_t)$ on their own capital stock decisions:

$$\max E \left(\sum_{t=0}^{\infty} (\alpha\beta)^t u(c_t) \right)$$

$$\text{s.t.} \quad c_t + x_t \leq f(k_t, Nk_t)z_t$$

$$K_{t+1} = x_t$$

$$k_0 \text{ given.} \tag{20}$$

As in our tax formulation, the required modification is to reduce the discount factor. The depressing effect on the level of savings this modification has just offsets the savings enhancement that would otherwise result from "internalizing" this externality. Other distortions can be accommodated for this choice of functional forms, although the precise equivalence detailed here is once again crucially dependent on the presence of complete depreciation ($\delta = 1$) and the Cobb-Douglas form of the production technology. The function that relates individual capital stocks to the aggregate level of knowledge, $\bar{K}_t$, may, however, assume more general forms.

If the approach of finding an equivalent optimum formulation fails—and, in practice, this is more often the case than not—a number of other solution techniques are available. Referring again to our analysis of the tax problem, these different strategies may be first differentiated by the focus of their application: either the original problem statement (5), or the equivalent Bellman formulation (6), or the equilibrium Euler formulation (11). Furthermore, some researchers work with an approximated economy (for example, quadratically approximating the utility function), while others discretize the state space and leave the economy's primitives (for example, preferences) unaltered. In our earlier operator language, these latter techniques involve a modification of the operator itself while the former leave the operator unchanged but modify the economy that defines its domain of application. We summarize these methods and our understanding of the literature in Table 3.1, where we also note the section of this chapter in which the indicated method is discussed.

Not all possible formulations are considered in detail as suggested by the empty cells in Table 3.10. This decision was made for the following reasons: First, the Kydland (1989b) method discussed in Section 7 is clearly also amenable to discrete state space methods. An elaborate discussion of the discrete space analog

Table 3.1
Taxonomy of Solution Methods

	Euler Equation–Based	*Bellman Equation–Based*	*Original Problem Formulation*
Approximated Operator discrete state space methods)	(1) Baxter, Crucini, and Rouwenhorst 1990 (2) Coleman 1991 (3) Danthine and Donaldson 1990, 1991b (4) Lucas 1978		
Approximated Economy	(1) Judd 1991 (2) Marcet 1989 and den Haan and Marcet 1990	(1) Cooley and Hansen 1989 (2) Kydland 1988	(1) King, Plosser, and Rebelo 1988a, 1988b

is therefore unnecessary. Second, the principal merit of the approach advocated by King, Plosser, and Rebelo (1988a, 1988b) lies in the simplicity of interpreting their linearization of the first-order conditions around the economy's certainty steady state. This simplicity would be lost and it is not clear what would be gained by marrying their approach to a discrete state space formulation.

4. Method 2: The Monotone Operator Euler Equation Approach

We begin by describing in detail the most widely used approach for computing nonoptimal economies, which, in this sense, can be viewed as the principal workhorse of this model class. The focus is on computing a solution to the Euler equation characterizing the equilibrium of the artificial economy. The state space will be discretized and the computation undertaken on the basis of the economy's original functional forms. We continue our discussion in the context of the tax equilibrium of Section 2.

The idea here is to generate the equilibrium $X(K, z)$ as the uniformly convergent limit of a sequence of approximating functions $\{X_n(K, z)\}$. These approximating functions are generated recursively from the second equilibrium condition in the following way: let $X^n(K, z)$ be defined for all $(K, z) \in \mathfrak{C} \times \mathfrak{Z}$; for any $(\hat{K}, \hat{z}) \in \mathfrak{C} \times \mathfrak{Z}$, define $X^{n+1}(\hat{K}, \hat{z})$ as the solution $\hat{X}$, if it exists, to the equation

$$u_1[f(\hat{K})\hat{z} - \hat{X}] = \beta \int u_1[f(K')z' - X^n(K', z')]$$

$$\cdot \{f_1(K')z'[1 - \tau(K', z')] + (1 - \delta)\} Q(dz'; \hat{z}). \quad (21)$$

$K' = (1 - \delta)K + X$. In our operator language, the solution $X = X(K, z)$ defines the image of an operator T acting on $X^n(K, z)$.

Such a procedure will be most useful if the following three assertions are true. First, the sequence $\{X^n(K, z)\}$, so constructed, must in fact be a monotone sequence of functions. Since the sequence $\{X^n(K, z)\}$ is uniformly bounded above (by the maximum output the production function can achieve) and below (by zero, as investment can never be negative), this sequence must converge and the limit is a candidate solution for (11). Second, the limit function, call it $X^*(K, z)$, should not be degenerate if it is to be of interest; that is, $X^*(K, z) \neq 0$, and $X^*(K, z) \neq f(K)z$ for all $(K, z) \in \mathfrak{C} \times \mathfrak{Z}$. Third, we would like $X^*(K, z)$ to be the unique solution to (11); this property is especially important if we are to be able to make simple, straightforward statements about the economy's dynamic properties.

We respond to these concerns in Theorem 2. Following its statement, we outline that portion of the proof in which the candidate solution is constructed. We do this because the numerical algorithm that will be proposed to solve equation (11) is based directly on this construction.

For simplicity of presentation, we choose $\delta = 1$. See Greenwood and Huffman (1993) and especially Coleman (1991) for more general treatments and associated full proofs and details. Our outline follows Greenwood and Huffman (1993).

Theorem 2. Under Assumptions 1–4, there is a unique nontrivial solution $X^*(K, z)$ to (11). Furthermore, $X^*(K, z)$ is continuous in its first argument.

Proof outline. Constructing a candidate solution.

Define $X^0(K, z) \equiv 0$ on $\mathfrak{C} \times \mathfrak{Z}$. By construction, $X^0(K, z)$ is continuously differentiable with respect to its first argument and satisfies $X_1^0(K, z) \leq f_1(K)z$. For the induction step, suppose $X^J(K, z)$ exists, is continuously differentiable for $K > 0$, and satisfies $X_1^J(K, z) \leq f_1(K)z$ and $X^J(K, z) = 0$ if $K = 0$. For each $(K, z) \in \mathfrak{C} \times \mathfrak{Z}$, $K > 0$, define $X^{J+1}(K, z)$, if it exists, as the $X = X(K, z)$ that satisfies

$$u_1[f(K)z - X] = \beta \int u_1[f(X)z' - X^J(X, z')]$$

$$\cdot \{[f_1(X)z'[1 - \tau(X, z')]\}Q(dz'; z). \tag{22}$$

If $K = 0$, define $X^{J+1}(K, z) = 0$ for any $z \in \mathfrak{Z}$. For an arbitrary $(\hat{K}, \hat{z}) \in \mathfrak{C} \times \mathfrak{Z}$, $\hat{K} > 0$, the left-hand side of (22) is monotone increasing in X and growing without bound as X approaches $f(K)z$, since $\lim_{c \to 0} u_1(c) = \infty$. Furthermore, for each $z' \in \mathfrak{Z}$, the right-hand side of (22) is monotone decreasing in X. This latter fact follows from the observations that $\tau(K, z)$ is nondecreasing in K, that $f_1(K)$ is decreasing in K, and that $f(X)z - X^J(X, z)$ is nondecreasing in X by the induction assumption. Since the right-hand side grows without bound as X approaches zero, there is an $\hat{X} = X(\hat{K}, \hat{z}) > 0$ that solves (22) as per Figure 3.1.

Furthermore, since all the functions defining (22) are continuously differentiable with respect to K, $K > 0$, $X^{J+1}(K, z)$ is continuously differentiable on $[\xi, \bar{K}]$ for any $\xi \in (0, \bar{K}]$ by an application of the implicit function theorem. Suppose the induction hypothesis fails; that is, $X_1^{J+1}(\tilde{K}, \tilde{z}) > f_1(\tilde{K})\tilde{z}$ for some $\tilde{K} > 0$ and some $\tilde{z} \in \mathfrak{Z}$. Then this latter inequality must be true in a neighborhood of $\tilde{K}$; but then equality (22) cannot be satisfied for some $K > \tilde{K}$. Hence $X_1^{J+1}(K, z) \leq f_1(K)z$ for $K > 0$.

Finally, by the structure of (22), if $X^J(K, z)$ is replaced by a function everywhere greater than or equal to itself, then the corresponding solution to (22) must be larger. Since $X^1(K, z) \geq X^0(K, z)$, this means $X^2(K, z) \geq X^1(K, z)$ and, in general, $X^{J+1}(K, z) \geq X^J(K, z)$ so that $\{X^J(K, z)\}$ is a monotone increasing sequence. Since it is bounded above by $\bar{K}$, it has a pointwise limit, which we will call $X^*(K, z)$. Since for all J, $X^J(K, z) = 0$ if $K = 0$, the same is true for $X^*(K, z)$.

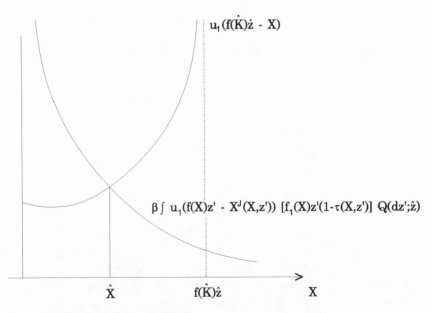

Figure 3.1 Monotone Operator Solution

To prove continuity of $X^*(K, z)$ with respect to its first argument, the convergence must be shown to be uniform. To see this, we note that since $X_1^J(K, z) \leq f_1(K)z \forall J$, for any $K_1, K_2 \in [\xi, \bar{K}], \xi > 0$, the following inequality must hold for any J:

$$|X^J(K_1, z) - X^J(K_2, z)| \leq M|K_1 - K_2|,$$

where $M = \max_{K \in [\xi, \bar{K}], z \in \mathfrak{Z}} f_1(K)z$. This latter inequality informs us that the family of functions $\{X^J(K, z)\}$ is equicontinuous on $[\xi, \bar{K}]$ as a function of K, for any $\xi > 0$. Since $\{X^J(K, z)\}$ is equicontinuous and converges pointwise on $[\xi, \bar{K}]$, it converges uniformly. Hence, $X^*(K, z)$ is continuous on any closed interval $[\xi, \bar{K}]$, $\xi > 0$. By construction $X^*(K, z)$ satisfies (21) and is a strong candidate for the equilibrium aggregate investment function. Clearly, if $k = K$, the agent's $x(k, K, z)$ coincides with $X^*(K, z)$, provided $0 < X^*(K, z) < f(K)z$, for all $(K, z) \in \mathfrak{C} \times \mathfrak{Z}$; $X^*(K, z)$ is also an interior solution which the agent's problem demands. This latter property is proved by Greenwood and Huffman (1993); a slightly stronger result is proved by Coleman (1991). Thus $X^*(K, z)$ defines the equilibrium investment function. Coleman (1991) demonstrates uniqueness of $X^*(K, z)$ as well. We do not detail these arguments, as they are involved and do not directly affect the form of the solution algorithm.

Constructing the aggregate equilibrium investment function in this way has considerable intuitive appeal for a number of reasons. Recall that for the first element of the recursively defined sequence, we chose $X^0(K, z) \equiv 0$. This choice may be interpreted as representing the equilibrium aggregate investment for a finite horizon economy analogous to the one described above but with zero periods remaining. Clearly, nothing would be saved in the final period of existence. Following on this interpretation, $X^1(K, z)$, constructed as per (21), would define the equilibrium level of investment in an economy with one period remaining. Thus $X^n(K, z)$ would represent the equilibrium level of aggregate investment for a finite economy with n periods remaining, etc. Viewed this way, our recursive approach is the exact counterpart of the more customary value-function iteration.

Other economic principles come to the fore as well. The fact that the sequence $\{X^n(K, z)\}$ can be shown to be monotone increasing is simply a reflection of the fact that the longer an agent's time horizon, the more the agent will save. The crucial property that $0 \leq X_1^J(K, z) \leq f_1(K)z$, $\forall J$, simply formalizes the notion that both savings and consumption are normal goods. Provided the above properties hold for the agent undertaking the investment decision, recursive Euler techniques will be applicable irrespective of how complex the nature of equilibrium may be.

Such a solution concept is easy to implement numerically and we shall detail how this may be done in the context of our paradigm.

Step 1. Selecting the State Space. All approximating functions will be defined on a neighborhood of the certainty steady-state capital stock and shock values. Without loss of generality we can assume $Ez = 1$. For the model under consideration, the certainty steady-state capital stock value is defined by the equation

$$1 = \beta\{f_1(K_{ss})[1 - \tau(K_{ss}, 1)] + (1 - \delta)\}, \tag{23}$$

which has a unique solution under our assumptions. Construct a partition, $\mathcal{P}_K \subseteq \mathcal{C}$, as per

$$\mathcal{P}_K = \{K_{ss}\} \cup \{K_{ss} - i\Delta K : i = 1, 2, \ldots, N_1\}$$
$$\cup \{K_{ss} + i\Delta K : i = 1, 2, \ldots, N_2\},$$

where ΔK, the "norm" of the partition, is a choice variable, as is the breadth of the partition, as captured by the choices of N_1 and N_2. Of course N_1 and N_2 should be such that $K_{ss} - N_1 \Delta K \geq 0$, and $K_{ss} + N_2 \Delta K \leq K^*$, where K^* denotes an upper bound to the stationary capital stock distribution.

With regard to the shock process, it is customary in this literature to represent it either by a finite-state Markov chain with unconditional mean of one or by a simple first-order autoregressive process, also with an unconditional mean of 1. In the former case, a two-state chain with symmetric transition matrix of the form

$$
\begin{array}{cc}
 & \begin{array}{cc} z_1 & z_2 \end{array} \\
\begin{array}{c} z_1 \\ z_2 \end{array} & \left(\begin{array}{cc} \rho & 1 - \rho \\ 1 - \rho & \rho \end{array} \right)
\end{array}
$$

is usually adequate. With $z_1 = 1 + \xi$ and $z_2 = 1 - \xi$, ρ and ξ can be chosen to give any desired unconditional variance and serial autocorrelation combination. In the latter case, the shock process is usually specified to be of the form

$$z_{t+1} = \rho z_t + \tilde{\epsilon}_t \tag{24}$$

with $\tilde{\epsilon}_t \sim N(1 - \rho, \sigma_\epsilon^2)$. The variance σ_ϵ^2 is chosen so as either (1) to match the variance of the Solow residual for the U.S. economy (e.g., Hansen 1985) or (2) to allow the standard deviation of the economy's output series to match its corresponding value for the U.S. economy. Such a process must also be approximated by a discrete Markov chain in order for the monotone operator approach to be operational; a systematic procedure for obtaining this approximation is detailed in Tauchen (1986).

Let P_z denote the (discrete) set of possible shock values. In what follows, all the approximating functions $\tilde{X}^n(K, z)$—as distinguished from their theoretical counterparts $X^n(K, z)$—will be understood to be defined on $\mathcal{P}_K \times P_z$.

Step 2. *Calibration.* This model would in general be calibrated in a manner identical to what has been proposed in earlier chapters. The only added feature is the tax function, which should be constructed so that the average share of income going to taxes in the model matches the data for the U.S. economy or some other reference economy under study.

Step 3. *Constructing the Approximating Sequence.* Construct an approximating sequence, $\{\tilde{X}^n(K, z)\}$, as follows. As noted in the theoretical discussion, let $\tilde{X}^0(K, z) \equiv 0$ for all $(K, z) \in \mathcal{P}_K \times \mathcal{P}_z$, and suppose $\tilde{X}^{n-1}(K, z)$ has been constructed. Define $\tilde{\psi}^n(K, z) : \mathcal{P}_K \times \mathcal{P}_z \mapsto \mathcal{P}_K$ as the solution to the following minimization problem: For each $(\hat{K}, \hat{z}) \in \mathcal{P}_K \times \mathcal{P}_z$,

$$\tilde{\psi}^n(\hat{K}, \hat{z}) = \underset{\substack{\psi \in \mathcal{P}_K \\ (1-\delta)\hat{K} \leq \psi \leq f(\hat{K})\hat{z}+(1-\delta)\hat{K} \\ \psi^{n-1}(\hat{K},\hat{z}) \leq \psi}}{\arg\min} u_1[f(\hat{K})\hat{z} + (1 - \delta)\hat{K} - \psi]$$

$$- \beta \sum_{z' \in P_z} u_1[f(\psi)z' - \tilde{X}^{n-1}(\psi, z')]$$

$$\cdot \{f_1(\psi)z'[1 - \tau(\psi, z')] + (1 - \delta)\} \text{Prob}(z'; \hat{z})|$$

where we solve for next period's capital stock, $\tilde{\psi}^n(K, z)$, rather than this period's investment, a practice that eliminates the need for interpolation. The associated investment function, $\tilde{X}^n(K, z)$, is then defined by

$$\tilde{X}^n(K, z) = \tilde{\psi}^n(K, z) - (1 - \delta)K.$$

Notice that the minimization calculation is substantially abbreviated because of the presence of the $\tilde{\psi}^{n-1}(\hat{K}, \hat{z}) \leq \psi$ constraint. This constraint reflects the monotonicity property the sequence $\{\tilde{X}^n(K, z)\}$ must have. Clearly, the accuracy with which $\tilde{X}^n(K, z)$ approximates $X^n(K, z)$ will depend on the fineness of the capital stock partition and any methods of interpolation we may employ. Given $\tilde{X}^n(K, z)$, we repeat the process to construct $\tilde{X}^{n+1}(K, z)$ in a like fashion.

Step 4. *Convergence.* Choose $\epsilon > 0$, $\epsilon < \Delta K$. The iterative process detailed in Step 2 would cease whenever

$$\max_{(K,z)\in\mathcal{P}_K \times P_z} |\tilde{X}^N(K, z) - \tilde{X}^{N-1}(K, z)| < \epsilon$$

for some N. We approximate $X^*(K, z)$ by $\tilde{X}^N(K, z)$.

Step 5. *Time Series Computation.* Construct a shock sequence, $\{\tilde{z}_t\}$, for $t = 0$ through some T that respects the assumed probability transition matrix. (We choose $T = 4,999$.) This is accomplished as follows. Use the computer's random number generator to create a random series of real numbers, θ_t, in the range $(0, 1)$ of desired length T. Let P_{ij} represent $\text{Prob}(z_{t+1} = z_j | z_t = z_i)$,

z_i, z_j, $\in \{z_1, z_2\}$ (we maintain, for simplicity, the two shock assumption). Since $P_{i1} = \text{Prob}[\theta_t \in (0, P_{i1})]$ and $P_{i2} = \text{Prob}(\theta_t \in [P_{i1}, 1])$, if $\tilde{z}_t = z_i$, then $\tilde{z}_{t+1} = z_1$, provided $\theta_t \in (0, P_{i1})$; and $\tilde{z}_{t+1} = z_2$, provided $\theta_t \in [P_{i1}, 1]$. Use this sequence of shock values to generate the associated capital stock sequence, $\{\tilde{K}_t\}$, according to

$$\tilde{K}_0 = K_{ss}, \quad \tilde{K}_{t+1} = \psi^*(\tilde{K}_t, \tilde{z}_t), \quad 0 \leq t \leq T$$

where $\psi^*(\cdot, \cdot) = \tilde{\psi}^N(K, z)$. Given the capital stock sequence, the output sequence $\{\tilde{Y}_t\}$, aggregate consumption sequence $\{\tilde{C}_t\}$, aggregate investment sequence $\{\tilde{X}_t\}$, aggregate tax sequence $\{\tilde{\tau}_t\}$, and wage sequence $\{\tilde{w}_t\}$ may be constructed according to

$$\tilde{Y}_t = f(\tilde{K}_t)\tilde{z}_t,$$
$$\tilde{C}_t = \tilde{Y}_t - \psi^*(\tilde{K}_t, \tilde{z}_t) + (1 - \delta)\tilde{K}_t,$$
$$\tilde{X}_t = \psi^*(\tilde{K}_t, \tilde{z}_t) - (1 - \delta)\tilde{K}_t,$$
$$\tilde{\tau}_t = \tau(\tilde{K}_t, \tilde{z}_t)\tilde{Y}_t, \text{ and}$$
$$\tilde{w}_t = \tilde{Y}_t - \tilde{K}_t f_1(\tilde{K}_t)\tilde{z}_t$$

In order to be assured that the statistics so computed are calculated for series values that lie in the range of their respective stationary probability distributions, we usually drop the first one thousand elements of each series. As noted in earlier chapters, it is standard practice to detrend the remaining time series by using the Hodrick-Prescott (1980) filter (H-P filter) and to compute the customary statistical summaries with respect to these detrended series.

Step 6. *Bounds Check and Partition Norm Reduction.* Our work is not yet complete. Consider the set $K_s = \{K : K \in \mathcal{P}_K, \text{and } \exists \text{ some } t, 1000 \leq t \leq 4999$ such that $\tilde{K}_t = K\}$; K_s represents the set of (undetrended) stationary capital stock values. If either $K_{ss} - N_1 \Delta K \in K_s$ or $K_{ss} + N_2 \Delta K \in K_s$, there is a possibility that the upper and/or lower bounds of the capital stock partition are constraining the economy's investment choices, thereby resulting in a biased stationary capital stock distribution. If this is the case, N_1 and/or N_2 must be increased as necessary and the exercise repeated until neither of the partition bounds is present in the stationary set. Finally, it has been our practice at this juncture to recompute the entire model for a smaller choice of ΔK. We continue to reduce the size of ΔK until there was no effect in the first two decimal points of the detrended series statistical summaries.

Remark. State space methods are highly numerically intensive, especially for a state space of large cardinality. This fact prompts us to consider whether quadratic approximation procedures are suitable for the class of models in question. Since there is no standard nonoptimal paradigm, however, it is a question that cannot be answered with any generality. For a tax model close in structure to the one considered here, Dotsey and Mao (1992) compare the accuracy of various quadratic approximation procedures with the standard state space methodology. Their results are somewhat discouraging. While the approximation methods were "fairly accurate in terms of capital, output and labor hours,. . . [they failed]. . . to some extent with regard to other variables"(53). Furthermore, for more complex model formulations, the functional relationships influencing the construction of the $\{\tilde{X}^n(K, z)\}$ sequence may not have explicit closed form expressions. This is the case in Danthine and Donaldson (1990, 1991b). Quadratic approximation methods are thus not immediately applicable.

5. Method 3: Contraction Operator Approaches to Solving the Euler Equation

As noted in the introduction and expanded upon in Section 4, the equilibrium aggregate investment function—which is the heart of model dynamics for nonoptimal and optimal economies alike—can typically be defined as the fixed point of an appropriately defined operator acting on a modified first-order condition. In the case of a production economy with distortionary income taxation, the relevant operator generates a monotone increasing uniformly convergent sequence of functions. The monotonicity property rests on the observation that for finite economies, the longer the time horizon the more will be saved (ceteris paribus). Without it, the solution method would be useless.

For a narrower set of circumstances, it is sometimes possible to define the first-order condition operator for which the fixed point is the economy's aggregate equilibrium investment function in such a way that it is a contraction on a space of continuous, bounded functions. Experience suggests that this is most likely to be possible when the models under study are nonproduction models, of the type often used to study asset pricing or monetary issues. A contraction operator is stronger than a monotone operator in the sense that precise bounds on the distance to the fixed point from any stage in the iteration can be easily computed.

We illustrate the possibility of characterizing equilibrium as the fixed point of a contraction operator in two cases: Lucas's (1978) familiar asset-pricing model, and Giovannini and Labadie's (1991) approach to solving cash-in-advance constrained monetary models.

The Lucas (1978) Asset Pricing Model

Lucas (1978) hypothesizes a model in which claims to exogenous real-income streams are priced. The behavior of a representative agent in his economy can be described as the solution to the following maximization problem (all notation is as in earlier sections except as noted):

$$\max_{\{c_t\},\{x_t\}} E\left[\sum_{t=0}^{\infty} \beta^t u(c_t)\right]$$

$$\text{s.t.}\quad c_t + p(Y_t)x_{t+1} \le [Y_t + p(Y_t)]x_t$$

$$0 \le x_t \le 1,$$

$$0 \le c_t \le Y_t, \tag{25}$$

where $p(Y_t)$ is the period t competitive price of the perfectly divisible share claim to all the economy's output, Y_t, and x_t is the fraction of the share owned by the agent. Output is assumed to follow an exogenous Markov process with transition probability function $\hat{Q}(dY'; Y)$.

Under quite weak conditions, Lucas (1978) proves that the necessary and sufficient first-order condition for the agent's problem has the form

$$u_1(c)p(Y) = \beta \int u_1(c')[p(Y') + Y']\hat{Q}(dY'; Y). \tag{26}$$

In equilibrium $x = 1$, and $c = y = Y$ for all t (the entire share is owned and all output consumed); it follows that (26) specializes to

$$u_1(Y)p(Y) = \beta \int u_1(Y')Y'\hat{Q}(dY'; Y) + \beta \int u_1(Y')p(Y')\hat{Q}(dY'; Y). \tag{27}$$

The equilibrium asset-pricing function, if it exists, must satisfy (27). Defining $h(Y) = u_1(Y)p(Y)$, (27) can be expressed as

$$h(Y) = \beta \int u_1(Y')Y'Q(dY'; Y) + \beta \int h(Y')\hat{Q}(dY'; Y), \tag{28}$$

which suggests an operator T_c defined by

$$T_c h(Y) = \beta \int u_1(Y')p(Y')\hat{Q}(dY'; Y) + \beta \int h(Y')\hat{Q}(dY'; Y) \tag{29}$$

Under assumption 4 and the assumption that $\int g(Y')\hat{Q}(Y'; Y)$ is continuous as a function of Y for any continuous $g(Y)$, $T_c : \mathbf{C} \mapsto \mathbf{C}$, where $\mathbf{C}$ is the space of continuous bounded functions.

Furthermore, if $h_1(Y), h_2(Y) \in \mathbf{C}$ and $h_1(Y) \ge h_2(Y)$, then $T_c h_1(Y) \ge T_c h_2(Y)$; also, for any constant ξ, $T_c(h(Y) + \xi) \le T_c h(Y) + \beta\xi$, $\beta < 1$. By Blackwell's Theorem, T_c is a contraction and thus has a fixed point $h^*(Y) \in \mathbf{C}$, from which the equilibrium price function can be recovered as per

$$p(Y) = \frac{h^*(Y)}{u_1(Y)}. \tag{30}$$

By the well-known properties of a contraction operator, for any initial $h^0(Y) \in C, T^n h^0(Y) \mapsto h^*(Y)$ where the convergence is uniform; $h^*(Y)$ is also guaranteed to be unique.

Contractions are the easiest operators to implement numerically. Modeling the process on output as a discrete Markov chain with states $\{Y_1, Y_2, \ldots, Y_n\} = P_Y$, the iterative process would be defined as per

$$h_n^0(Y_i) \equiv 0, \ Y_i \in P_Y,$$

and

$$T_c h^n(Y_i) = \beta \sum_{Y_j \in P_Y} u_1(Y_j) Y_j p_{ij} + \beta \sum_{Y_j \in P_Y} h^n(Y_j) p_{ij} = h^{n+1}(Y_i),$$

where

$$p_{ij} = \text{Prob}(Y' = Y_j | Y = Y_i). \tag{31}$$

Giovannini and Labadie's Technique for Solving for Monetary Equilibria

Monetary economies of the type considered in this volume are normally classified as nonoptimal for a specific reason. In general, a monetary equilibrium will be nonoptimal whenever the specified money supply rule is nonoptimal. As a result, there will be a distortionary inflation tax. In particular, if the growth rate in the money supply is not chosen so as to equate the rate of return on money and the rate of return on investment, money will be costly to hold, and agents will seek to economize on its use relative to the optimum.

Giovannini and Labadie (1991) propose a contraction-based solution methodology to compute equilibria for the monetary exchange models of Lucas (1982) and Svensson (1985). Both of these models are characterized by an infinitely-lived representative agent maximizing the present value of discounted utility of consumption subject to a liquidity constraint (which motivates the holding of money) and a wealth constraint. In each of the models, the real endowment and money supply levels are governed by exogenous stochastic processes. It is in the timing of the transactions in the goods and asset markets that these models differ.

Since the solution technique in both models is the same, we choose, somewhat arbitrarily, to focus again on Lucas's formulation. The representative agent in his model solves

$$\max_{\{c_t\},\{x_t\},\{M_t^d\}} E \left[\sum_{t=0}^{\infty} \beta^t \frac{1}{1-\sigma} c_t^{1-\sigma} \right]$$

$$\text{s.t.} \quad 0 \le c_t \le M_t^d \pi_t$$

$$M_t^d \pi_t + x_t q_t \leq \left(\frac{\pi_t}{\pi_{t-1}} Y_{t-1} + q_t \right) x_{t-1} + (\mu_t - 1) M_{t-1} \pi_t$$

$$+ \left(M_{t-1}^d \pi_t - c_{t-1} \frac{\pi_t}{\pi_{t-1}} \right). \tag{32}$$

The endowment sequence, $\{Y_t\}$, and the money supply sequence, $\{M_t\}$, evolve according to

$$Y_t = \eta_t Y_{t-1},$$

and

$$M_t = \mu_t M_{t-1}, \tag{33}$$

where the gross growth rates, η_t and μ_t, follow stationary stochastic processes. The term π_t denotes the inverse of the price level, that is, $1/p_t$, while q_t denotes the real share price, and x_t, as before, denotes the fraction of the perfectly divisible share held by the agent. Ownership of this share gives the agent title to the entire endowment sequence. Additions to the money supply are distributed in a lump sum fashion.

The terms in the right-hand side of the second budget constraint merit some interpretation, and this can be done in the context of a discussion of the timing of events. The middle term, $(\mu_t - 1) M_{t-1} \pi_t$, represents the period t, real value of the money transfer the agent receives at the start of period t while the final term, $(M_{t-1}^d \pi_t - c_{t-1} \frac{\pi_t}{\pi_{t-1}}) = (M_{t-1}^d - c_{t-1} p_{t-1}) \frac{1}{p_t}$, denotes the period t real value of the agent's unspent money holdings carried over from the prior period. The first term, $(\frac{\pi_t}{\pi_{t-1}} Y_{t-1} + q_t) x_{t-1} = (\frac{p_{t-1} Y_{t-1}}{p_t} + q_t) x_{t-1}$, represents the real dividend payments according to the fractional share purchased in the prior period plus the value of that fractional share itself relative to period t prices. These resources are also available at the start of period t for the purchase of shares and the acquisition of new money balances. Following these asset market transactions, the agent enters the goods market and purchases consumption goods with the agent's just-acquired period t money balances, M_t^d (see first constraint). Note that the total period t nominal dividend payments, $p_{t-1} Y_{t-1}$, represent the value of (equilibrium) consumption purchases in the prior period. These money balances are thus held by the "firm" until the next period (period t), when they are paid out to the shareholder-agent. As they may suffer an inflationary devaluation while in the firm's possession, the inflation tax is viewed as being levied on the firm itself.

In equilibrium, the market-clearing conditions hold and are of the form $c_t = Y_t$, $M_t^d = M_t$, and $x_t = 1$. Following our earlier examples, this equilibrium is characterized by the set of first-order conditions to the agent's problem on which the market-clearing conditions have been imposed. Let $\lambda_1(s_t)$ and $\lambda_2(s_t)$ denote the multipliers associated with, respectively, the first and second constraints; for economy of notation, we follow Giovannini and Labadie (1991), and let s_t represent the economy's state (η_t, μ_t). These equilibrium conditions, after some routine manipulations, are as follows:

$$Y_t^{-\sigma} = \lambda_2(s_t) \tag{34}$$

$$\lambda_2(s_t)\pi(s_t) = \beta \int \lambda_2(s_{t+1})\pi(s_{t+1})\hat{Q}(ds_{t+1}; s_t) + \lambda_1(s_t)\pi(s_t), \tag{35}$$

and

$$\lambda_2(s_t)q(s_t) = \beta \int \lambda_2(s_{t+1})(q(s_{t+1}) + Y_t \frac{\pi(s_{t+1})}{\pi(s_t)})\hat{Q}(ds_{t+1}; s_t). \tag{36}$$

Not only are these equations essentially linear, but they also bear a more than passing resemblance to the equation defining equilibrium in Lucas's asset pricing model. We thus have hope that their solution can also be expressed as the fixed point of a contraction operator. In particular, if the function $\pi(s_t)$ can be obtained from equations (34) and (35), then equation (36) is exactly of the form of equation (28), and $q(s_t)$ can thus be found in a manner analogous to the determination of the $p(Y)$ function in the Lucas asset pricing model.

Giovannini and Labadie (1991) begin by defining a function $\hat{K}(s_t)$ by

$$\pi(s_t) = \frac{Y_t \hat{K}(s_t)}{M_t}. \tag{37}$$

It is clear that $\pi(s_t)$ is "recoverable" from a knowledge of $\hat{K}(s_t)$, since both Y_t and M_t follow known processes. In equilibrium, $c_t = Y_t$, and the cash-in-advance constraint becomes $Y_t \leq M_t\pi(s_t)$; hence $\hat{K}(t) \geq 1$ in all states, with strict inequality holding when the cash-in-advance constraint is nonbinding. Substituting the above expression for $\pi(s_t)$ and the known form of $\lambda_2(s_t)$ into equation (35) yields

$$\hat{K}(s_t)\lambda_1(s_t) = Y_t^{-\sigma}\left[\hat{K}(s_t) - \beta \int \frac{\eta_{t+1}^{1-\sigma}\hat{K}(s_{t+1})}{\mu_{t+1}}\hat{Q}(ds_{t+1}; s_t)\right]. \tag{38}$$

If the cash-in-advance constraint is not binding for a particular state s_t, then $\lambda_1(t) = 0$, and equation (38) reduces to

$$\hat{K}(s_t) = \beta \int \frac{\eta_{t+1}^{1-\sigma}\hat{K}(s_{t+1})}{\mu_{t+1}}\hat{Q}(ds_{t+1}; s_t). \tag{39}$$

If $\lambda_1(t) > 0$ for state s_t, however, then $\hat{K}(s_t) = 1$. Uniting these two observations allows us to define $\hat{K}(s_t)$ recursively by the equation

$$\hat{K}(s_t) = \max\left[1, \beta \int \frac{\eta_{t+1}^{1-\sigma}\hat{K}(s_{t+1})}{\mu_{t+1}}\hat{Q}(ds_{t+1}; s_t)\right]. \tag{40}$$

The form of equation (40) suggests that the solution function $K^*(s_t)$ is expressible as the fixed point of the operator $\hat{T}_c$, defined by

$$\hat{T}_c K(s_t) = \max \left[1, \beta \int \frac{\eta_{t+1}^{1-\sigma} \hat{K}(s_{t+1})}{\mu_{t+1}} \hat{Q}(ds_{t+1}; s_t) \right].$$

It is easy to check that $\hat{T}_c : \mathbf{C} \mapsto \mathbf{C}$ and that it possess the monotonicity property, that is, if $f_1(), f_2() \in \mathbf{C}$, and $f_1() \geq f_2()$, then $\hat{T}_c f_1() \geq \hat{T}_c f_2()$. The discounting property is less easily satisfied, however. In a clever, indirect approach to this question, Giovannini and Labadie (1991) first demonstrate that there exists an integer N such that $\hat{T}_c^N$ is a contraction on the space of bounded continuous functions provided for every $(\eta_t, \mu_t) = (s_t)$, $\int \frac{\eta_{t+1}^{1-\sigma}}{\mu_{t-1}} Q(ds_{t+1}; s_t) < \frac{1}{\beta}$. It is well known that if $\hat{T}_c^N$ is a contraction for some N, than $\hat{T}_c$ is itself a contraction. Hence $\hat{T}_c$ has a fixed point, $\hat{K}^*(s_t)$, from which we extract the corresponding $\pi^*(s_t)$ function via equation (37).

It remains to determine the equilibrium equity price function $q(s_t)$ and this can be found as the fixed point of a contraction as well. Substituting $\hat{K}^*(s_t)$ into equation (36), as well the representation for $\lambda_2(s_t)$ via equation (34), yields

$$q(s_t)/Y_t = \beta \int (q(s_{t+1})/Y_{t+1}) \hat{Q}(ds_{t+1}; s_t)$$

$$+ \beta \int \left(\frac{\eta_{t+1}^{1-\sigma}}{\mu_{t+1}} \right) \frac{\hat{K}^*(s_{t+1})}{\hat{K}^*(s_t)} \hat{Q}(ds_{t+1}; s_t). \tag{41}$$

If we let $\xi(s_t) = \frac{q(s_t)}{Y_t}$, the above equation allows us to define an operator $T_c^* : \mathbf{C} \mapsto \mathbf{C}$ by

$$T_c^* \xi(s_t) = \beta \int \xi(s_{t+1}) \hat{Q}(ds_{t+1}; s_t) + \beta \int \left(\frac{\eta_{t+1}^{1-\sigma}}{\mu_{t+1}} \right) \frac{\hat{K}^*(s_{t+1})}{\hat{K}^*(s_t)} Q(ds_{t+1}, s_t). \tag{42}$$

In a manner similar to the operator $\hat{T}_c$, T_c^* can also be demonstrated to be a contraction with modulus β. If $\xi^*(s_t)$ is the fixed point of T_c^*, then the equilibrium asset-pricing function follows as per $q^*(s_t) = \xi^*(s_t)Y_t$. Given a hypothesized Markov chain defined on a finite-state space of pairs (η, μ) both operators, $\hat{T}_c$ and T_c^*, can be numerically implemented in a manner exactly analogous to the procedures of Lucas's asset pricing model. We thus determine the asset price and price level functions via jointly operating contraction mappings. As noted earlier, such techniques are usually applicable in exchange settings, of which this is a second illustration.

6. Nonfinite State Space Methods

Marcet (1989) and Judd (1991) also work with the economy's equilibrium conditions, though in a manner very different from the monotone operator approach. Their methods involve approximating either the equilibrium investment function (Judd 1991) or the entire right-hand side of equation (12) (Marcet 1989; den Haan and Marcet 1990) by a function of the form

$$\sum_{i=1}^{n} a_i \phi_i(K, z), \tag{43}$$

or by a monotone transformation thereof. In the above expression the $\{\phi_i(K, z)\}_{i=1}^{n}$ functions serve as "basis vectors" in the space of approximating functions, while the constants $\{a_i\}_{i=1}^{n}$ identify the particular approximation chosen. Note that given a selection of basis functions (which remains unchanged in the course of any algorithmic procedure), the choice of the optimal approximation reduces to choosing the optimal set $\{a_1^*, a_2^*, \ldots, a_n^*\}$. Thus, an infinite-dimensional problem—that of finding an $X(K, z)$ functional solution to (11)–(12)—again reduces to selecting a point in finite-dimensional space, a search that the computer is ideally suited to perform.

The methods of den Haan and Marcet (1990) and Judd (1991) differ not only in the choice of basis vectors but also in the objects of approximation. As the den Haan–Marcet method has, to date, been employed more frequently in the literature, it is detailed first. One minor caution is appropriate, however: the current literature contains only a few preliminary applications of their method to tax distorted equilibria similar to those considered in this chapter. While these results appear very promising, no complete assessment can thus yet be made as to the method's accuracy and rapidity of convergence vis-à-vis equilibria of this type.

Den Haan and Marcet's 1990 Method of Parameterized Expectations

For convenience of reference, let us first restate equation (12):

$$u_1[C(K_t, z_t)] = \beta \int u_1[C(K_{t+1}, z_{t+1})]\{f_1(K_{t+1})z_{t+1}[1 - \tau(K_{t+1}, z_{t+1})]$$

$$+ (1 - \delta)\}Q(dz_{t+1}, z_t), \tag{44}$$

where $K_{t+1} = (1 - \delta)K_t + X(K_t, z_t)$. Den Haan and Marcet's (1990) strategy is to approximate the right-hand side of (44) by a function $\Psi()$ of the form

$$\Psi(K_t, z_t; \vec{a}) = a_1 K_t^{a_2} z_t^{a_3} = \exp(\ell n a_1 + a_2 \ell n K_t + a_3 \ell n z_t), \tag{45}$$

where the functions $\ell n a_1$, $\ell n K_t$, and $\ell n z_t$ correspond, respectively, to $\phi_1(K_t, z_t)$, $\phi_2(K_t, z_t)$ and $\phi_3(K_t, z_t)$ of the introductory discussion. The idea is to choose the vector of parameters $\vec{a} = (a_1, a_2, a_3)$ so that the approximation is very good. But how is this to be judged?

By employing expression (45), and for some choice of $\vec{a}$, the set of equations

$$u_1(C_t) = \beta \Psi(K_t, z_t; \vec{a}) \tag{46}$$

and

$$C_t + K_{t+1} = f(K_t)z_t + (1 - \delta)K_t, \ K_0 \text{ given}, \tag{47}$$

can be jointly solved (two equations in two unknowns) to construct a time series $\{C_t(\vec{a}), K_t(\vec{a})\}_{t=0}^{T}$ for a given sequence of random shocks $\{z_t\}_{t=0}^{T}$ (den Haan and Marcet choose $T = 2,500$) that respects the conditional density $Q(dz_{t+1}; z_t)$. Den Haan and Marcet (1990) view $\Psi()$ as a good approximation to the right-hand side of (44), provided the time series thus generated as per equations (46) and (47) also solve (44), to as close an approximation as possible. For this to be so, the parameters $\vec{a} = (a_1, a_2, a_3)$ should be chosen as the fixed point of the operator $A = A(\vec{a}) : R^3 \mapsto R^3$, defined by

$$A(\vec{a}) = \arg\min_{\vec{a}^*}(1/T) \sum_{t=1}^{T} \left[u_1[C_t(\vec{a})]\left(f_1[K_t(\vec{a})]z_{t+1}\left\{ 1 - \tau[K_{t+1}(\vec{a}), z_{t+1}] \right\} \right. \right.$$
$$\left. \left. + (1 - \delta) \right) - \exp(\ell n a_1^* + a_2^* \ell n K_t + a_3^* \ell n z_t) \right]^2 \tag{48}$$

For a given $\vec{a}$, the operator $A()$ in effect generates a new $\vec{a}^*$, which best allows $\Psi(K_t, z_t, \vec{a}^*)$ to approximate, in a time series sense, the sequence

$$\{u_1[C_t(\vec{a})][f_1[K_t(\vec{a})]z_{t+1}\{1 - \tau[K_{t+1}(\vec{a}), z_{t+1}]\} + (1 - \delta)]\}_{t=1}^{T},$$

generated as per (46) and (47). The image of $\vec{a}$ under $A()$, $A(\vec{a})$, is obtained via a nonlinear regression of

$$\{u_1[C_t(\vec{a})][f_1[K_t(\vec{a})]z_{t+1}\{1 - \tau[K_{t+1}(\vec{a}), z_{t+1}]\} + (1 - \delta)]\},$$

on a first-order power series representation of $\exp(\ell n a_1^* + a_2^* \ell n K_t + a_3^* \ell n z_t)$.

In actual practice, the fixed point itself, $\vec{a}_f = A(\vec{a}_f)$, is approximated by the final element in a sequence $\{\vec{a}^n\}$, generated recursively according to $\vec{a}_0$ given, and

$$\vec{a}^n = (1 - \lambda)\vec{a}^{n-1} + \lambda A(\vec{a}^{n-1}), \tag{49}$$

where the parameter λ governs the speed of convergence. The iterative process concludes when $\vec{a}^{n+1} \approx \vec{a}^n$ (equivalently, $A(\vec{a}^n) \approx (\vec{a}^n)$) according to the user's choice of convergence criterion. Drawbacks to the procedure include the need to choose wisely both the initial guess, $\vec{a}$, and the parameter λ, lest the algorithm fail to converge. Nevertheless, for the standard optimal growth model without taxes, the method performs very well vis-à-vis the alternatives.

Judd's Minimum Weighted Residuals Method

Judd's (1991) method is similar in spirit to den Haan and Marcet's (1990) strategy but procedurally very different. In particular, Judd emphasizes the importance of choosing basis vectors that are orthogonal vis-à-vis the inner product defined on the chosen function space. This has the objective of maximizing the global accuracy of the approximating function by increasing the power of the basis vectors to effectively complete the space. His procedure for choosing the optimal parameter vector $\vec{a}$ is also very different from that of den Haan and Marcet.

To illustrate his method in the context of our tax paradigm, first rewrite equation (12) as

$$0 = C(K, z) - u_1^{-1}[\beta \int u_1(C[f(K)z - C(K, z), z'])\{f_1[f(K)z - c(K, z)]z'$$

$$\cdot (1 - \tau[f(K)z - C(K, z), z']) + (1 - \delta)\}Q(dz'; z)]. \tag{50}$$

Judd approximates the optimal $C(k, z)$ by an approximation $\hat{C}(K, z)$ of the form

$$\hat{C}(K, z) = \sum_{i=1}^{M_k} \sum_{j=1}^{M_z} a_{ij} \psi_{ij}(K, z), \tag{51}$$

where

$$\psi_{ij}(K, z) = T_{i-1}\left[2\left(\frac{K - K_m}{K_M - K_m}\right) - 1\right] T_{j-1}\left[2\left(\frac{z - z_M}{z_M - z_m}\right) - 1\right], \tag{52}$$

and

$$T_{i-1}\left[2\left(\frac{K - K_m}{K_M - K_m}\right) - 1\right] = \cos\left\{(i - 1) \arccos\left[2\left(\frac{K - K_m}{K_M - K_m}\right) - 1\right]\right\} \tag{53}$$

Basis vectors of the form $\psi_{ij}(K, z)$ above can be shown to satisfy a desirable orthogonality property. The parameters $\{K_m, K_M, z_m, z_M\}$ are chosen so that the stationary distribution on K will be confined to $[K_m, K_M]$ (in particular, $[K_m, K_M]$ must contain the certainty steady-state capital stock value) and $z_m = z_2, z_M = z_1$. The objective is to choose constants $\{a_{ij}\}_{i=1,\ldots,n_K; j=1,\ldots,n_z}$ (a finite-dimensional vector) that satisfy

$$0 = \hat{C}(K, z) - u^{-1}\{\beta \sum_{z'} u_1(\hat{C}[f(K)z - \hat{C}(K, z), z'])$$

$$\cdot \{f_1[f(K)z - \hat{C}(K, z)]z'$$

$$\cdot (1 - \tau[f(K)z - \hat{C}(K, z), z']) + (1 - \delta)\} \text{Prob}(z'; z)\} \qquad (54)$$

as closely as possible.

As Judd (1991) notes, there are two principal approaches to obtaining a "best" set $\{a_{ij}\}$. The most obvious is the "collocation method": pick a partition of n_K capital stock values of the interval $[K_m, K_M]$ ($n_z = 2$ under our standard two-state shock process), and evaluate equation (54)'s right-hand side for each of these $n_K x n_z$ pairs. This yields an $n_K \times n_z$ system of non linear equations in the unknowns $\{a_{ij}\}$, which can be solved using standard off-the-shelf routines. Note, however, that although the approximation is naturally exact at these $n_K \times n_z$ points, there is no guarantee that it will be accurate elsewhere.

Alternatively, Judd (1991) champions the Galerkin approach. Under this option, we solve for those $\{a_{ij}\}_{i=1,2,...,m_K; j=1,2}$ that satisfy the orthogonality conditions,

$$\sum_{i=1}^{m_K} \sum_{j=1}^{2} R(K_i, z_j; \{a_{ij}\}) X_{ij}(K_i, z_j) = 0 \qquad (55)$$

for specially chosen $\{K_i\}_{i=1}^{m_K}$ (see Judd 1991) and $z_j \in \{z_1, z_2\}$. In the above equation, $R(K_i, z_j; \{a_{ij}\})$ represents the right-hand side of equation (54), evaluated at the indicated values. For Judd's method, once the policy function has been approximated, the time series can be constructed in the obvious manner. See Judd (1991) for details and a fuller justification, along with a comparison of his method with others considered in this chapter.

7. Kydland's Bellman Equation-Based Approach

This approach was first proposed by Kydland (1989b) and subsequently employed by Cooley and Hansen (1989) for computing equilibria of monetary economies. Very much in the spirit of optimum model formulations, these authors work principally at the level of the Bellman equation (6). The key difference is, of course, that a suboptimal economy cannot be fully described at this level alone. As noted earlier, the solution to the Bellman problem provides only the optimal decision rules of the representative agent. To obtain the equilibrium, it is necessary to confront these decision rules with the market-clearing conditions. Kydland's (1989b) method is to approximate, quadratically, the representative agent's utility function inclusive of all nonlinear constraints, and to iterate on the Bellman equation, all the while requiring the market-clearing conditions and the other linear constraints to be satisfied at each step of the iteration. Since this method is fully described in Chapter 2 of this book, it need not be detailed here any further. Note, however, that in principle the same approach could be employed by replacing the need to approximate the objective function in the Bellman equation by a discretization of the state space in a manner similar to that proposed in the earlier sections. We know, however, of no existing application of this latter alternative. For a discrete state space solution to Bellman's equation, see Danthine, Donaldson, and Mehra (1989) or Christiano (1990).

8. King, Plosser, and Rebelo's Linearized First-Order Equation Approach

The final approach that we wish to highlight is the one first proposed by King, Plosser, and Rebelo (1988a) and described in detail in King, Plosser, and Rebelo (1987, 1988a, 1988b). As applied to our tax equilibrium problem, the method starts with reformulating the representative agent's original problem statement, (5), as follows:

$$\max_{\{c_t\}\{k_t\}} E \left[\sum_{t=0}^{\infty} \beta^t u(c_t) \right]$$

$$\text{s.t.} \quad c_t + k_{t+1} \leq f(k_t)z_t[1 - \tau(K_t, z_t)] + \Pi(K_t, z_t) + (1 - \delta)k_t$$

$$(1 - \delta)k_t \leq k_{t+1}$$

$$k_0 \text{ given.} \tag{56}$$

The necessary and sufficient first-order conditions for this problem are given by

$$\beta^t u_1(c_t) - \Lambda_t = 0, \tag{57}$$

$$-\Lambda_t + E_t\{\Lambda_{t+1}[f_1(K_{t+1})z_{t+1}(1 - \tau(K_t, z_t)) + (1 - \delta)]\} = 0, \tag{58}$$

$$c_t + k_{t+1} = f(k_t)z_t(1 - \tau(K_t, z_t)) + \Pi(K_t, z_t) + (1 - \delta)k_t, \tag{59}$$

and

$$\lim_{t \mapsto \infty} E_0\{\Lambda_t k_{t+1}\} = 0, \quad \text{for all } t = 0, 1, 2, \ldots. \tag{60}$$

At equilibrium, $c_t = C_t$, $k_t = K_t$, $x_t = X_t$, and $\pi_t = \Pi_t = \tau(K_t, z_t)f(K_t)z_t$. The above first-order conditions can thus be transformed into the economy's equilibrium characterization under the imposition of the obvious substitutions:

$$\beta^t u_1(C_t) = \Lambda_t, \tag{61}$$

$$E_t(\Lambda_{t+1}\{f_1(K_{t+1})z_{t+1}[1 - \tau(K_{t+1}, z_{t+1})] + (1 - \delta)\}) = \Lambda_t, \tag{62}$$

$$C_t + K_{t+1} = f(K_t)z_t[1 - \tau(K_t, z_t)] + (1 - \delta)K_t + \Pi(K_t, z_t),$$

$$= f(K_t)z_t + (1 - \delta)K_t, \tag{63}$$

and

$$\lim_{t \mapsto \infty} E_0 \Lambda_t K_{t+1} = 0, \forall t = 1, 2, 3, \ldots. \tag{64}$$

The essence of the King, Plosser, and Rebelo (1988a, 1988b) method is to transform equations (61)–(63) into an approximating first-order autoregressive linear system. For our model, this is accomplished as follows. First rewrite equation (61) as

$$u_1(C_t) = \frac{\Lambda_t}{\beta^t} \overset{\text{def}}{\equiv} \psi_t. \tag{65}$$

If we denote the steady-state levels of consumption and the transformed multiplier by, respectively, C^* and ψ^*, equation (65) can be approximated by

$$u_1(C^*) + u_{11}(C^*)C^* \left(\frac{C_t - C^*}{C^*} \right) = \psi^* + \psi^* \left(\frac{\psi_t - \psi^*}{\psi^*} \right) \tag{66}$$

where, for example, $\left(\frac{C_t - C^*}{C^*} \right) \approx \ell n C_t - \ell n C^*$. If we let $\hat{C}_t = \left(\frac{C_t - C^*}{C^*} \right)$, and $\hat{\psi}_t = \left(\frac{\psi_t - \psi^*}{\psi^*} \right)$, equation (66) can be rewritten as

$$\hat{C}_t = \frac{\psi^*}{u_{11}(C^*)C^*} \hat{\psi}_t \equiv \xi_1^* \hat{\psi}_t, \tag{67}$$

where we have used the fact that $u_1(C^*) = \psi^*$.

Next, rewrite the certainty version of equation (62) as

$$\beta\{f_1(K_{t+1})z_{t+1}[1 - \tau(K_{t+1}, z_{t+1})] + (1 - \delta)\} = \frac{\psi_t}{\psi_{t+1}}. \tag{68}$$

Letting $G(K_{t+1}, z_{t+1})$ represent the left-hand side of (68), King, Plosser, and Rebelo approximate $G(K_{t+1}, z_{t+1})$ by the expression

$$[G(K^*, z^*) + G_1(K^*, z^*)K^*\hat{K}_{t+1} + G_2(K^*, z^*)z^*\hat{z}_{t+1}],$$

where $\hat{K}_{t+1} = (K_{t+1} - K^*)/K^*$, and $\hat{z}_{t+1} = (z_{t+1} - z^*)/z^*$, K^*, z^*, steady-state values of K and z respectively. Representing the right-hand side by $H(\psi_t, \psi_{t+1})$ and expanding $H()$ analogously yields an approximation to equation (68):

$$\beta\{f_{11}(K^*)z^*[1 - \tau(K^*, z^*)] - f_1(K^*)z^*\tau_1(K^*, z^*)\}K^*\hat{K}_{t+1}$$
$$+ \beta\{f_1(K^*)[1 - \tau(K^*, z^*)] - f_1(K^*)z^*\tau_2(K^*, z^*)\}z^*\hat{z}_{t+1}$$
$$= \hat{\psi}_t - \hat{\psi}_{t+1}. \tag{69}$$

The same procedure can be applied to equation (63). This yields

$$C^*\hat{C}_t + K^*\hat{K}_{t+1} = [f_1(K^*)z^* + (1 - \delta)]K^*\hat{K}_t + f(K^*)z^*\hat{z}_t. \tag{70}$$

Substituting for $\hat{C}_t$ via equation (67) gives

$$C^*\xi_1^*\hat{\psi}_t + K^*\hat{K}_{t+1} = [f_1(K^*)z^* + (1 - \delta)]K^*\hat{K}_t + f(K^*)z^*\hat{z}_t. \tag{71}$$

Under the substitutions

$$\xi_2^* = \beta\{f_{11}(K^*)z^*[1 - \tau(K^*, z^*)] - f_1(K^*)z^*\tau_1(K^*, z^*\}$$

and

$$\xi_3^* = \beta\{f_1(K^*)[1 - \tau(K^*, z^*)] - f_1(K^*)z^*\tau_2(K^*, z^*)\},$$

the essential equations, (69) and (71), become

$$\hat{K}_{t+1} = \frac{-C^*}{K^*}\xi_1^*\hat{\psi}_t + [f_1(K^*)z^* + (1 - \delta)]\hat{K}_t + \frac{f(K^*)}{K^*}z^*\hat{z}_t, \qquad (72)$$

and

$$\hat{\psi}_{t+1} = \hat{\psi}_t - \xi_2^*K^*\hat{K}_{t+1} - \xi_3^*z^*\hat{z}_{t+1} \qquad (73)$$

respectively. Substituting (72) into (73) gives

$$\hat{\psi}_{t+1} = \hat{\psi}_t - \xi_2^*C^*\xi_1^*\hat{\psi}_t - \xi_2^*K^*[f_1(K^*)z^* + (1 - \delta)]\hat{K}_t$$
$$- \xi_2^*f(K^*)z^*\hat{z}_t - \xi_3^*z^*\hat{z}_{t+1}. \qquad (74)$$

Equations (72) and (74) may also be compactly written in matrix form:

$$\begin{bmatrix} \hat{K}_t \\ \hat{\psi}_t \end{bmatrix} = \begin{bmatrix} a_{11} & a_{12} \\ a_{21} & a_{22} \end{bmatrix} \begin{bmatrix} \hat{K}_{t-1} \\ \hat{\psi}_{t-1} \end{bmatrix} + \begin{bmatrix} b_{11} & b_{12} \\ b_{21} & b_{22} \end{bmatrix} \begin{bmatrix} \hat{z}_t \\ \hat{z}_{t-1} \end{bmatrix}, \qquad (75)$$

via the following identifications: $a_{11} = [f_1(K^*)z^* + (1 - \delta)]$, $a_{12} = \frac{-C^*}{K^*}\xi_1^*$, $b_{11} = 0$, $b_{12} = \frac{f(K^*)}{K^*}z^*$, $a_{21} = 1$, $a_{22} = -\xi_2^*K^*[f_1(K^*)z^* + (1 - \delta)]$, $b_{21} = -\xi_2^*f(K^*)z^*$, and $b_{22} = -\xi_3^*z^*$. Also appended to this system are the two boundary conditions: the initial condition, $\hat{K}_0$, and the transversality condition, $\lim_{t \mapsto \infty} \beta^t(\hat{\psi}_t + \hat{K}_t) = 0$.

Focusing first on the equation of motion for capital stock, it is well known (see, e.g., Sargent 1979) that system (75) can be re-written as

$$(1 - \phi_1 L - \phi_2 L^2)\hat{K}_t = \theta_1\hat{z}_{t-1} + \theta_2\hat{z}_{t-2}, \qquad (76)$$

for constants $\phi_1, \phi_2, \theta_1, \theta_2$, where L denotes the lag operator.

Equivalently,

$$(1 - \mu_1 L)(1 - \mu_2 L)\hat{K}_t = \theta_1\hat{z}_{t-1} + \theta_2\hat{z}_{t-2} \qquad (77)$$

for constants μ_1, μ_2. Suppose without loss of generality that $\mu_1 < 1, \mu_2 > 1$; then,

$$-\mu_2^{-1}L^{-1}(1 - \mu_1 L)(1 - \mu_2 L)\hat{K}_t = -\mu_2^{-1}L^{-1}(\theta_1\hat{z}_{t-1} + \theta_2\hat{z}_{t-2}), \qquad (78)$$

or

$$(1 - \mu_2^{-1}L^{-1})(1 - \mu_1 L)\hat{K}_t = -\mu_2^{-1}(\theta_1\hat{z}_t + \theta_2\hat{z}_{t-1}). \qquad (79)$$

Since $\mu_2^{-1} < 1$, it is possible to invert the first operator on the left-hand side of (79) to obtain

$$(1 - \mu_1 L)\hat{K}_t = \hat{K}_t - \mu_1 \hat{K}_{t-1} = -\mu_2^{-1} \left[\sum_{j=0}^{\infty} \left(\frac{1}{\mu_2} \right)^j (\theta_1 \hat{z}_{t+j} - \theta_2 \hat{z}_{t+j-1}) \right],$$

(80)

or

$$\hat{K}_t = \mu_1 \hat{K}_{t-1} - \mu_2^{-1} \left(\sum_{j=0}^{\infty} \left(\frac{1}{\mu_2} \right)^j [\theta_1 \hat{z}_{t+j} + \theta_2 \hat{z}_{t+j-1}] \right) \qquad (81)$$

King, Plosser, and Rebelo then replace $\{\hat{z}_{t+j}\}$ and $\{\hat{z}_{t+j-1}\}$ in the above series by their expectations conditional on information available in period $t - 1$, that is, the realization z_{t-1}. If the shock process $\{z_t\}$ follows a simple first-order autoregressive process, then these expectations can be explicitly computed, and the second term on the right-hand side of (81) reduces to $\theta_K \hat{z}_t$, for some constant θ_K. In like fashion, the equation of motion on $\hat{\psi}_t$ can be expressed as

$$\hat{\psi}_t = \Delta_1 \hat{\psi}_{t-1} + \theta_z \hat{z}_t, \qquad (82)$$

for constants Δ_1 and θ_z.

Given an exogenously generated sequence $\{\hat{z}_t\}$, equations (81) and (82) can be used to construct time series $\{K_t\}$ and $\{\psi_t\}$. From $\{K_t\}$, $\{z_t\}$ we can obtain the output sequence, $\{Y_t\}$, and the consumption sequence, $\{C_t\}$. The usual summary time series statistics can then be easily computed. Note that this procedure is not applicable when the shock process is a discrete Markov process, since the aforementioned conditional expectations may not be easy to compute. Tauchen (1986), however, describes how a discrete Markov process can be approximated by an autoregressive process.

9. Concluding Comments

In this essay we have sought to introduce the reader to several techniques that have proved useful for computing the equilibria of nonoptimal economies. These techniques have wide applicability. It should be clear from the context of our discussion that they also serve as potential solution techniques for optimal economies. More significantly, the tendency toward analyzing ever more complex economies with non-Walrasian frictions, imperfect competition, or monetary features guarantees that they will be relied upon increasingly frequently in quantitative theory.

Which of the described approaches is the most appropriate to use? While this is a natural question to raise, it is unlikely to have a single, straightforward answer. Indeed, performance criteria may conflict—speed of convergence versus precision of estimation, for example. Furthermore, the performance of a given technique is likely to depend upon the choice of the particular model under study. The task of fully comparing the properties of the various techniques we have outlined above is, to a large extent, still before us.

Note

We thank Jordi Gali, Edward Prescott, and the editor, Thomas Cooley, for helpful conversations and comments.

Chapter 4
Models with Heterogeneous Agents

José-Víctor Ríos-Rull

1. Introduction

Some questions addressed in the business cycle literature require environments with multiple agents. One obvious question we need to ask is, How robust are the findings of this literature to modifications of the model that incorporate observed heterogeneity of agents in characteristics such as age and skill level, as well as imperfect insurance markets? Other, more specific questions involve the cyclical behavior of the distribution of income and wealth, or the role played by liquidity constraints, and of asymmetric information. Moreover, multiagent models are being used to address certain features of the data that are difficult to explain within the representative-agent framework. These include the cyclical behavior of the factor shares of national income, and the risk premium puzzle, which is a related issue in financial economics.

Computable models that are capable of dealing with multiagent environments have been developed to address many of these questions. Computation of equilibria in these models is usually substantially more difficult than in standard representative-agent models, as equilibrium laws of motion become functions not only of aggregate variables, but also of the distribution of these variables across different types of agents. Solving for the laws of motion of such distributions is a nontrivial task.

We review these models by grouping them according to the criteria that give rise to the heterogeneity. Section 2 deals with economies where agents face some idiosyncratic shocks to productivity, and where there are no markets to insure such risks. In Section 3, overlapping generations economies are reviewed. In these two sections, there are a large number of agent types. Section 4 is about a variety of two-agent models, each addressing a specific question, while Section 5 gives some indications regarding the course of future research.

2. Models with Uninsurable Individual Risks

Potential Uses

The existence of a full set of Arrow-Debreu markets makes the distribution of income irrelevant, as agents only face one budget constraint in the initial period. A property of this class of complete-markets economies is that all individual risks get perfectly insured at no cost. The existence of an insurance industry in the United States that accounts for a nontrivial portion of output reminds one that whatever insurance is available is not free. If instead of complete markets, trading arrangements only include asset holdings with returns that cannot be made contingent upon the realization of individual shocks, then agents trade every period, and they will insure themselves against adverse realizations by holding assets that will be depleted during bad times. These arrangements represent an alternative, and perhaps more accurate, description of the trading opportunities in actual economies. In contrast with complete-markets arrangements they give an important role to the distribution and intertemporal movements of income and wealth.

One interesting use of such models has been to evaluate the cost of business cycles when the model accounts for some of the observed heterogeneity of people in the data. Another use has been to assess the welfare properties of various monetary policies when money is modeled as a store of value. Finally, they have been used to assess the properties of a variety of government policies, such as unemployment insurance, and social security, that operate as a substitute for perfect insurance.

General Description

In these economies, agents differ on how they are affected by some idiosyncratic risk, as well as in the assets they are able to hold. The key feature that makes these economies different from representative-agent models is that the set of possible trades available for agents is restricted.[1] Typically, agents cannot write contracts contingent on their individual shocks, and in some cases, they cannot hold negative quantities of any asset. This prevents various aggregation results from holding[2] (see, e.g., Deaton 1992), and thus computing the equilibrium requires keeping track of the distribution of agents. At any point in time, the state of the economy is characterized by how agents are positioned across levels of asset holdings, individual shocks, and, perhaps, an aggregate exogenous shock to the economy. In general, equilibrium prices and quantities depend on both the distribution of agents and the aggregate shock. The individual agents, when solving their maximization problem, have to be able to predict future prices, and thus they have to use the distribution of agents and its law of motion as an input to their decisionmaking process. Note that the aggregate level of asset holdings would not be enough to characterize the individual state, since in order to predict next period's level, we would also have to know today's distribution, as different agents accumulate different amounts, depending on their individual states.

These considerations imply that computing the competitive equilibrium amounts to finding a fixed point in the space of functions from a set of measures into itself, an unmanageable computational problem. The key computational difficulties arise when solving the problem of the agent because a measure becomes a state variable. A measure is not a standard state variable, such as, say, aggregate physical capital; it is a far more complex mathematical object. Its characterization, even if it is approximated, demands that a lot of information be stored. This means that the individual state space is a large set, and that decision rules have to be solved for a large variety of circumstances. Furthermore, inherent features of the problem (for example, the restrictions imposed in the set of feasible trades) prevent the use of the cheapest computational method, linear-quadratic approximations, because the optimal solution sometimes hits a corner. The other standard methods available, discretization of the state space, parameterized expectations, backward solving, and so on, have severe shortcomings in environments with a large set of state variables.

Note also that solving the problem of the agent for a given law of motion of the distribution is not enough. The correct law of motion of the distribution has to be found. This requires iterating at this level too, which introduces another layer of computational complexity into the process.

For all these reasons, it is necessary to reduce the dimensionality of the problem of the agent. Typically, the procedure followed is to prevent the distribution of agents from affecting relative prices, in particular, the relative wage and the rate of return of capital. This drastically simplifies the problem of the agent and completely avoids iterations on the law of motion of the distribution, which can then be computed residually. In this fashion, İmrohoroğlu (1989) utilizes a storage technology that pins down exogenously the rate of return of savings. In Díaz-Giménez and Prescott (1989) and Díaz-Giménez (1990), the government commits itself to a certain inflation rate policy that does not depend on the asset distribution.

The approach that these models use to compute the equilibrium is to create a grid in the set of possible asset holdings, and to have a finite number of possible realizations of both individual and aggregate exogenous variables. In this case, the maximization problem of the agent, if written in the form of a value function, becomes a finite problem, as the value function and the distribution of agents become vectors.

Next, we develop a general structure that encompasses as special cases most of the papers in the area.

A General Heterogeneous-Agent Model with Liquidity Constraints

The economy consists of a continuum of agents that is taken to be of measure one. They have standard preferences over streams of consumption and leisure, which can be represented by $E_0\{\sum_{t=0}^{\infty} u(c_t, n_t)\}$, where for each period t, the pair (c_t, n_t) is restricted to belong to C, the per-period consumption possibility set of the agent, which might specify nonnegative consumptions and restrict the choice of possible hours worked by the agent. There is a limited set of markets to which agents have access. Every period, they engage in production activities, and accumulate assets, which are restricted to be in a set $A \subset \mathbf{R}^{n_a}$. We can think of $a \in A$ as including real assets, which we generically label as a_1, and which affect production possibilities, and a variety of financial assets, such as money, a_2, and bonds, a_3, which differ in their denomination sizes and rates of return. For convenience, we measure these assets in real terms at their acquisition values for the previous period; for instance, real capital is measured in goods of the period it was acquired. All these assets are not identical, and therefore they might command different rates of return. We thus think of r_1 as the real rate of return on capital, while $\frac{1}{r_2} - 1$ is the inflation rate.

The after-tax production capability of the agents depends partly on an exogenous idiosyncratic shock, $s \in S$, and on an economywide shock, $z \in Z$. We assume that both s and z can only take a finite number of values N_S and N_Z. These shocks are assumed to be Markov processes, with transition matrix $\pi(s', z' \mid s, z)$. The problem of the agents is to maximize expected utility subject to a sequence of budget constraints, such as $c_t + e^T \cdot a_{t+1} = a_t^T \cdot r_t + n_t w_t + tr_t$, where $a_t \in A$ is the vector of asset holdings; r_t is the vector of gross after-tax rates of return on those assets (or one plus the rate of return); e is just a vector of ones used to aggregate (and the superindex T indicates that the vector is transposed, that is, that it is a row vector); w_t is the after-tax real wage; and tr_t are government transfers, which might depend on the agents' actions (unemployment insurance is the obvious example). Given processes for w_t, r_t, and tr_t, the agents are characterized by (z_t, s_t, a_t), but in order to be able to solve their maximization problem, those processes have to be specified. For the reasons noted above, the processes r_t, w_t, and tr_t have to be independent of the distribution of agents, but they can depend on the particular state of each agent, and, even on the agents' labor decisions.

There is a government in this world that commits itself to policies $w(z, s, a, n)$, $r(z, s, a, n)$, and $tr(z, s, a, n)$. The government can do this through a variety of fiscal, monetary, and debt policies. With this arrangement, the government is restricted by technology considerations, and by its budget constraint. It operates in asset markets, and it imposes taxes on capital and labor income that guarantee that labor and capital prices, w and r, and transfer payments, tr, are independent of the distribution of agents across individual states. In this fashion, the policies that are implemented by the government have to be functions of the aggregate state of the economy. They do not enter, however, into the problem of the agent, as the after-tax pricing functions that agents use to make their decisions are not functions of the aggregate state. In fact, this is what the government does: it implements policies that prevent the distribution of agents from affecting agents' decisions.

At any point in time, the economy is characterized by the aggregate shock, $z \in Z$, and a distribution of agents according to their asset holdings and individual states. Mathematically, this can be represented by a pair, (z, μ), where μ is a measure defined over $\mathcal{B}$, an appropriate family of subsets of $(S \times A)$, the set of possible states for individual agents. The problem of the agents' is to maximize utility, subject to their budget constraint and to the trading restrictions, and taking as given the after-tax pricing functions, $w(z, s, a, n)$ and $r(z, s, a, n)$, and the transfer function, $tr(z, s, a, n)$.

Production possibilities depend on the total amount of capital and labor input, and the aggregate shock, z. The labor input is constructed by aggregating hours worked over agents that have idiosyncratic shock, s. Let (K, N) be the total amount of factor inputs; then total output is given by a constant-returns-to-scale production function, $f(K, N, z)$.

Equilibrium Defined

We have completed the characterization of the environment, so we are ready to define equilibrium. It consists of a set of government policies; after-tax real wages, $w(z, s, a, n)$, after-tax rates of return for real capital, $r_1(z, s, a, n)$, for money, $r_2(z, s, a, n)$, and for bonds, $r_3(z, s, a, n)$; and for transfers $tr(z, s, a, n)$; tax rates on capital income, $\tau(z, \mu, s, a, n) \in \mathbf{R}^{n_a}$; tax rates on labor income, $\tau_0(z, \mu, s, a, n)$; government expenditures, $G(z, \mu) \geq 0$, bonds issued by the government, $b_g(z, \mu)$, and monetary policy, $m_g(z, \mu)$; decision rules of the agents for consumption, hours worked, and asset holdings, $\{c(z, s, a), n(z, s, a), a'(z, s, a)\}$; the value function of the agents' problem, $v(z, s, a)$; functions for aggregate inputs, $K(z, \mu)$ and $N(z, \mu)$; and a law of motion for the distribution of agents in the economy, $\mu' = g(z, \mu, z')$, such that

1) given $r(z, s, a, n)$, $w(z, s, a, n)$, and $tr(z, s, a, n)$, agents' decision rules, $\{c(z, s, a), n(z, s, a), a'(z, s, a)\}$, solve their problem:

$$v(z, s, a) = \max_{\{a',c,n\}} u(c, n) + \beta E\{v(z', s', a' \mid s, z\}$$

s.t. $a' \in A$

$(c, n) \in C$

$a^T \cdot r(z, s, a, n) + n\, w(z, s, a, n) + tr(z, s, a, n)$

$$\geq e^T \cdot a' + c \tag{1}$$

for all $(z, s, a) \in Z \times S \times A$;

2) The goods market clears, and government expenses are positive:

$$\int_{A,S} \left[a_1'(z, s, a) + c(z, s, a) \right] d\mu + G(z, \mu) = f[K(z, \mu), N(z, \mu), z],$$

$$\tag{2}$$

for all (z, μ).

3) The money market clears:

$$\int_{A,S} a_2'(z, s, a)d\mu - m_g(z, \mu) = 0, \qquad (3)$$

for all (z, μ);

4) The bonds markets clear:

$$\int_{A,S} a_3'(z, s, a)d\mu - b_g(z, \mu) = 0, \qquad (4)$$

for all (z, μ);

5) Aggregate factor inputs are generated by decision rules of the agents:

$$K(z, \mu) = \int_{A,S} a_1 \, d\mu,$$

and

$$N(z, \mu) = \int_{A,S} s \, n(z, s, a)d\mu, \qquad (5)$$

for all (z, μ);

6) Pretax factor prices are marginal productivities:

$$w(z, s, a, n) = [1 - \tau_0(z, \mu, s, a, n)] \, s \, f_2[K(z, \mu), N(z, \mu), z],$$

and

$$r(z, s, a, n) = [1 - \tau_1(z, \mu, s, a, n)] f_1[K(z, \mu), N(z, \mu), z]; \qquad (6)$$

and

7) Individual and aggregate behavior are consistent:

$$\mu'(S_0, A_0) = g(S_0, A_0)(z, \mu, z')$$

$$= \int_{S_0, A_0} \left\{ \int_{S,A} 1_{a'=a'(z,s,a)} \pi(s' \mid s, z, z')d\mu \right\} da'ds', \qquad (7)$$

for all $(S_0, A_0) \in \mathcal{B}$, and all (z, μ, z'), with $1_{a'=a'(z,s,a)}$ being an indicator function that takes the value one if the statement is true and zero otherwise.

An important feature that we have avoided is the budget constraint of the government—nowhere in this definition have we talked about it. This is because Walras's law takes care of it. Typically, equilibrium is defined by requiring that all agents satisfy their budget constraints, and by requiring that all markets except one clear, with aggregation (Walras's law) taking care of the last market. Here, we have required that all markets clear, and that all agents except the government satisfy their budget constraint. Aggregation implies that the government's budget constraint is also satisfied.

An Example without Aggregate Endogenous Variables

"Cost of Business Cycles with Indivisibilities and Liquidity Constraints" (İmrohoroğlu 1989) is perhaps the first published paper where the equilibrium of an artificial economy with heterogeneous agents, calibrated to match some key U.S. observations, is computed. Its purpose is to find whether measurements of the social cost of business cycles that treat every person as perfectly insured against idiosyncratic risks—in particular, the evaluation made by Lucas (1987)—severely understates such cost relative to an economy where liquidity constraints are pervasive. İmrohoroğlu considers three different environments. The first is one with liquidity constraints, where the assets of the agents cannot be negative and where there is no possibility of writing contingent contracts. Another institutional market arrangement allows for the existence of credit markets but not contingent markets for idiosyncratic or aggregate risks. In this economy, holding assets remains the only mechanism of insurance. Finally, she considered an economy where perfect insurance prevails. For all three economies, the allocation with and without aggregate fluctuations is computed. Comparisons between the allocations of the economy with aggregate fluctuations and the economy without them permit the computation of the additional consumption required to make agents indifferent between the two. If this difference is similar across institutional market arrangements, we could conclude that the existence of liquidity constraints in an economy is not an important feature for welfare considerations. It is very easy to specialize our general model described above to her environment. In particular, there is no need to introduce a government since relative prices do not depend on the total amount of assets held in the economy.

Technology and preferences are identical across economies. Labor is inelastic, so $C = \mathbf{R}_+ \times 1$, and preferences are $E_0\{\sum_{t=0}^{\infty} \beta^t u(c_t)\}$. Agents face two possible individual states, $s \in S = \{e, u\}$; in state e there is an employment opportunity, and in state u there is none. An agent with an individual state s produces $w(s)$ units of output, where $w(e) > w(u)$. One can think of $s = e$ as being employed and $s = u$ as being unemployed, but being able to work at home. The transition of this state depends on the state of the economy as a whole, $z \in Z = \{g, b\}$, which can be in either good or bad times. The matrix $\pi(s', z' \mid s, z)$ is the transition matrix of the aggregate state of the economy and the individual state. The difference between economies that have business cycles and those that do not is determined by the specification of π. In economies with business cycles, the transition matrix depends on z, while in economies without business cycles it does not. In these economies, as in the data, recessions are characterized by agents' having both a higher probability of losing a job and a higher probability of not finding a job than in booms. Of course, this difference shows up not only in individual transition probabilities, but also in the aggregate level, with unemployment typically building up during recessions, and falling during booms. There is a publicly available storage technology that transforms a units of the time t good into $a\,r$ units in $t + 1$. These considerations imply that we can write the production function as $\int_{A,S}[ra_1 + w(s)]d\mu$, since the only asset available is the storage good.

Liquidity Constraints

The first market arrangement considered has liquidity constraints and no contracts contingent on either individual states or the aggregate state. In this economy, the only means that agents have to smooth consumption over time is to store the good as a precaution against future bad times. Since there is no money ($a_2 = 0$), or bonds ($a_3 = 0$), the set of possible asset holdings becomes $A = \mathbf{R}_+ \times \{0\} \times \{0\}$. The return of the unique asset is that of the storage technology, r. The problem of the agent can be written in the form of a value function as

$$v(z, s, a_1) = \max_{\{a_1', c\} \geq 0} u(c) + \beta E\{v(z', s', a_1') \mid s, z\}$$

$$\text{s.t.} \quad a_1 r + w(s) = a_1' + c. \tag{8}$$

An equilibrium for this economy consists of decision rules $c(z, s, a_1)$ for consumption and $a_1'(z, s, a_1)$ for inventory holdings, together with the value function, v, and a law of motion of the population, $g(z, \mu)$, such that

1) $c(z, s, a_1)$ and $a_1'(z, s, a_1)$ solve problem (8) given $w(s)$; and

2) The goods market clears:

$$\int_{A,S} \left[a_1'(z, s, a_1) + c(z, s, a)\right] d\mu = \int_{A,S} \left[a_1(z, s, a_1) + w(s)\right] d\mu, \tag{9}$$

Notice that the first condition guarantees that the second condition is satisfied. Condition 1 requires that the budget constraint be satisfied for every agent, which is just another way of requiring it to be satisfied for every pair (s_1, a_1). Then it will also be satisfied for the integral with respect to the measure that that describes the state of the economy. This is another way of saying that storage and the budget constraint guarantee that the goods market will clear.

Conditions 3–6 in the definition of equilibrium for the general problem are irrelevant, as there are no bonds, no labor, and no marginal productivities.

A version of condition 7 in the definition of equilibrium for the general problem has to be satisfied. All that is required is that the law of motion, g, of the distribution of agents across asset holdings, a_1, and individual shocks, s, evolve according to agents' choices and the stochastic properties of s and z. We write this condition as

$$\mu'(S_0, A_0) = g(S_0, A_0)(z, \mu, z')$$

$$= \int_{S_0, A_0} \left\{ \int_{S, A} 1_{a'_1 = a'_1(z, s, a_1)} \pi(s' \mid s, z, z') d\mu \right\} da'_1 ds', \quad (10)$$

Pure Credit

The second market arrangement allows for noncontingent loan contracts. In the model, the rates at which the agent can borrow and lend are different, since intermediation uses real resources. The problem of the agent becomes slightly different than in the first market arrangement, since the agent's choice set is enlarged by allowing for negative assets. We model this arrangement by letting borrowing simply be negative bond holdings ($a_3 \leq 0$), with gross rate of return bigger than one. Here, $A = \mathbf{R}_+ \times \{0\} \times \mathbf{R}_-$, where the first component is the amount stored or lent, with gross return r, and the third component is the amount borrowed with interest rate i. Note that both rate r and rate i can be considered parameters since both are technologically determined, r by storage and i by the sum of both storage and intermediation costs, since lending and storing have to be perfect substitutes in equilibrium. The problem of the agent is

$$v(z, s, a_1, a_3) = \max_{\{a'_1, -a'_3, c\} \geq 0} u(c) + \beta E\{v(z'_1, s'_1) \mid z, s)$$

$$\text{s.t.} \quad a_1 r + a_3(1 + i) + w(s) = a'_1 + a'_3 + c. \quad (11)$$

The definition of equilibrium is similar to the definition of the first market arrangement, except that in order to guarantee feasibility, total asset holdings cannot be negative, $\int_{A,S}(a_1 + a_3) \, d\mu \geq 0$. This implies that if the interest rate is too low, and the rate differential too small, equilibrium might not exist because aggregate savings cannot be negative. Savings can be positive because of the storage.

Complete Markets

The last market arrangement considered allows for perfect insurance, or complete markets. The allocation of this economy can be found as the solution to a planner's problem, as the welfare theorems hold for this economy. The planner's problem chosen is the one that treats everyone equally. The allocation found this way corresponds to the equilibrium when the initial condition is equal initial wealth distribution. It is found by solving the following maximization problem:

$$v(z, N, a_1) = \max_{a'_1 \geq 0} u[ra + Nw(e) + (1 - N)w(u) - a'_1]$$

$$+ \beta E\{v(z', N', a'_1) \mid z\}$$

$$\text{s.t.} \quad N'(N, z') = N\pi(e, z' \mid e, z) + (1 - N)\pi(e, z' \mid u, z), \quad (12)$$

where N is aggregate employment, and its law of motion is given in the constraint.

Calibration of this economy is standard except for the transition, π, and the ratio between unemployment and employment income, $w(u)/w(e)$. The values of π are chosen so that the aggregate state is symmetric and the average length of a cycle 4 years, and so that the average length of a spell of unemployment matches what we see in the United States in both good and bad times. With these considerations, π is completely pinned down. To choose a value for the relative income between the individual states, observations on the size of unemployment insurance and on how widespread it is are used.

The equilibria for these artificial economies are computed, and their statistical properties are empirically determined. It is found that among the properties of these models are that the cost of the business cycle in economies with liquidity constraints is at least three times bigger than in economies with perfect insurance.[5]

Computing the Equilibrium

The most popular approach to solving this type of model is to discretize the state space. A grid on $\{Z \times S \times A\}$ is constructed. Agents' choices are restricted to belong to a finite set. This property determines that the value function of agents can be represented as a vector of size, $(N_Z \times N_S \times N_A)$, where N_A is the total number of grid points in A, an element of a finite-dimensional Euclidean space. Decision rules specify for each of the elements in $\{Z \times S \times A\}$ elements in A, and C, and this can be represented not only by means of a real-valued vector, but by an integer-valued vector, as there are only a finite number of possible choices. All this implies that the Bellman equation is one with finite states, whose solution can be found using numerical methods.

The computations required to obtain the value function and the decision rules are as follows:

Step 1. Initialize value functions $v_0 \in \mathbf{R}^{N_z \times N_s \times N_a}$ to arbitrary initial values. Note that decision rules are also vectors, as there are only a finite number of states. Moreover, they can be represented as integers, as there are only N_a possible saving levels and typically only a decision of whether to work or not to work on the part of the agent.

Step 2. For all $(z, s, a) \in Z \times S \times A$, solve the following problem:

$$\max_{\{1 \le i \le N_a, 0 \le j \le 1\}} u[a^T \cdot r(z, s, a, n) + n_j \, w(z, s, a, n) + tr(z, s, a, n)$$

$$- e^T \cdot a'_i, n_j] + \beta E\{v_0(z', s', a'_i) \mid z, s\} \quad (13)$$

Step 3. For all $(z, s, a) \in Z \times S \times A$, update the value function:

$$v_1(z, s, a) = u[a^T \cdot r(z, s, a, n) + n_{j*} \, w(z, s, a, n) + tr(z, s, a, n)$$
$$- e^T \cdot a'_{i*}, n_{j*}] + \beta E\{v_0(z', s', a'_{i*} \mid z, s) \qquad (14)$$

where the stars refer to the solutions obtained in Step 2. Obviously, these solutions are functions of the state (z, s, a).

Step 4. Check for convergence. If $\max_{\{z,s,a\}} |v_1(z, s, a) - v_0(z, s, a)| > \epsilon$, then $v_0 = v_1$, and go back to Step 2. Otherwise we will assume convergence, and therefore that the solution of the agent's problem has been found.

Once the problem of the agent has been solved, we still have to compute the tax policies, $\tau(z, \mu, S, a, n)$, that equate pretax relative prices to marginal productivity of factor inputs. The required government expenditures needed to implement government policies are computed and checked to be nonnegative.

The remaining object of the equilibrium to be computed is the law of motion of the distribution, $\mu' = g(z, \mu)$. There is no need to compute the function g as such. Given a distribution, μ, and aggregate shock, z, in order to compute next period's distribution, all that is needed is the transition matrix, π, and the decision rule, $a'(z, s, a)$. First note that with a finite state space, a distribution is a nonnegative vector of $(N_S \times N_A)$, elements that sum up to one. In order to compute $\mu'(s', a')(z, \mu)$, the measure of agents that have assets a' and individual shock s' tomorrow given that today the distribution is μ and the aggregate shock z, we look over all pairs $(\bar{s}, \bar{a})$ such that $a' = a'(\bar{s}, \bar{a})$, and we add $\pi(s' \mid \bar{s})\mu(\bar{s}, \bar{a})$.

It is hard to say what is in general a sufficient number of points. One possible rule is to keep increasing them until the findings are no longer sensitive to finer grids. In İmrohoroğlu (1989), for example, the grid considered for the set A has 301 points (for economies 1 and 3), and the one for economy 2 has 602, although they are all equally spaced. Computing the value function is solving a finite-state Bellman equation, which always has a solution. Given the two individual states, the two aggregate states, and the size of the grid in İmrohoroğlu (1989), the value function becomes a vector with 1,204 entries.

An Example with Aggregate Endogenous Variables

In the previous example, relative prices (rates of return of assets) were pinned down by technological factors. This is typically not the case, as the interactions among agents typically play a crucial role in determining prices. For example, in "The Risk Free Rate in Heterogeneous-Agents, Incomplete Markets Economies," Huggett (1993) asks the question, What is the interest rate of an economy where there are no insurance possibilities, and no capital? Equivalent versions of his economy with perfect insurance have an interest rate of $i = 1/\beta - 1$. He argues that a puzzle in the U.S. data is that the risk free interest rate is too low in the post–World War II period (in fact, this rate is about half a percentage point, real, per year). Huggett tries to assess the importance of the role played by the lack of insurance. His paper does not have aggregate uncertainty, but to solve for the equilibrium of his economy a nontrivial market-clearing condition has to be satisfied. Another reason to look at this model is the fact that Huggett developed a different computational method, which proves very useful when market-clearing conditions are important. In his environment, agents can lend and borrow up to certain limits at a rate that is endogenously determined by market-clearing conditions. Agents are subject to idiosyncratic labor market shocks of the same type that İmrohoroğlu's agents' experience. In this case, all assets can be thought of as bonds, a_3, which can be either positive or negative, and the problem of the agent can be written as

$$v(s, a_3; i) = \max_{\{a_3', c\} \geq 0} u(c) + \beta E\{v(s', a_3'; i) \mid s\}$$

$$\text{s.t.} \quad a_3(1 + i) + w(s) = a_3' + c \tag{15}$$

Note the explicit dependence of the value function on the interest rate i. A key element will be, of course, determination of the interest rate that clears the bond market.

In this economy, we can define stationary equilibria, as there is no aggregate uncertainty. This definition would be a pair of decision rules for bonds holdings, $a_3'(s, a_3; i^*)$, and consumption, $c(s, a_3; i^*)$, together with a value function, $v(s, a_3; i^*)$, that solve the problem of the agent, an interest rate, i^*, and a stationary distribution, μ^*, that clears the bonds market:

$$\int_{S,A} a_3'(s, a_3; i^*) \, d\mu^* = 0, \tag{16}$$

Let us consider what a nonstationary equilibrium would look like. The first thing to note is that we would need a law of motion for the distribution of agents: $\mu' = g(\mu)$. Also, the agents would need to know the relevant interest rate, i, every period, and this has to be a function of μ, $i(\mu)$. However, in this case, the distribution of agents would enter the problem of the agent, making it a computational nightmare. The nice property about a stationary equilibrium is that it is a fixed point of the function $g(.)$, and we can find it without computing the whole function.

To compute a stationary equilibrium for this type of economy, we define an aggregate excess demand for bonds function, $\varphi(i)$, in the following steps:

Step 1. Fix i.

Step 2. Solve the problem of the agent and obtain $a_3'(s, a_3; i)$.

Step 3. Fix μ_0.

Step 4. Iterate on the following mapping from distributions to distributions of agents across bonds holdings, a_3 and idiosyncratic shock, s: $\mu_{n+1}(S_0, A_0) = \int_{S,A} 1_{a_3'(s,a_3;i)\in\{S_0,A_0\}} \, d\mu_n$. Huggett proves that this procedure converges to the unique stationary distribution, $\mu^*(i)$.

Step 5. Obtain $\varphi(i) = \int_{A,S} a_3'(s, a_3; i) \, d\mu^*(i)$.

An equilibrium is a zero of φ. It can be found with a one-equation solver routine.

Huggett does not obtain decision rules by restricting the agents' choices to belong to a finite partition. He uses piecewise linear functions to approximate the decision rules of the agent. For this he makes a grid in the asset space, and he performs the following operations:

Step 1. Initialize $vv_2(s, a_3; i)$, (the derivative of the value function with respect to the second argument) at every point in the grid of asset holdings.

Step 2. Then use this value of the derivative of the value function to solve for the optimal level of asset holdings by solving for a_3':

$$-u'(a_3(1 + i) + w(s) - a_3') + E\beta\{vv_2(s', a_3'; i) \mid s\} = 0. \tag{17}$$

This gives functions $a_3'(s, a_3; i)$ (linear interpolation is used in between points), which are in turn used to update the derivatives of the value function vv_1: $vv_2(s, a_3; i) = (1+i) \, u'[a_3(1+i)+w(s)-a_3'(s, a_3; i)]$. This iterative procedure converges to a solution of the agent's problem.

Other Examples

In the next few subsections we will review some of the issues studied, using the methodology described above. For each economy, we redefine the sets C, the per-period consumption possibility set, A, the set of admissible asset holdings, (S, Z), the set of exogenous states, π, their transition function, and the government policies.

Liquidity Constraints in Economies with Aggregate Fluctuations

Javier Díaz-Giménez and Edward Prescott (1989) elaborate a model designed to study heterogeneous-agents economies where money and bonds are used to smooth consumption in the tradition of overlapping-generation models and of the permanent income hypothesis. They use it to address some issues regarding the dominance of the rate of return of government bonds. The structure of the model is similar to İmrohoroğlu's, as the economy does not have capital. There are, however, important differences: agents care about leisure, intertemporal prices are not fixed by arbitrarily chosen technologies, but by explicit monetary policies followed by the government, and there are two assets, bonds and money, that command different rates of return since bonds are indivisible and they are issued in larger denominations than money.

Agents have standard preferences over expected discounted streams of consumption and leisure. They choose whether to work or not, but the length of the working day is fixed, becoming a discrete choice. Therefore, $C = \mathbf{R}_+ \times \{0, 1\}$. Their one-period production possibility set depends on a personal state, $s \in S = \{s_1, s_2, \ldots, s_{N_s}\}$. In this model, they choose not to have aggregate movements in productivity. There is also a time-invariant tax rate on labor income, $\tau_0 = .2$; therefore $w(z, s) = w(s)$. Not all agents are born identical: there are two different human capital types, one being eight times more productive than the other, and each type faces a personal shock to productivity that makes it vary with a ratio of 3 to 1. The aggregate state just characterizes the bond return policy of the government, so $r_2(z) = r$, and all $z \in Z$, while $r_3(z_1) = 1.00$ in the low-return state, z_1, and $r_3(z_2) = 1.03$ in the high return-state. With these properties, π can be decomposed into $\pi_z(z' \mid z)$, and $\pi_s(s' \mid s)$; this last matrix is a block diagonal matrix, as agents do not change their human capital type. The set of possible asset holdings becomes $A = \{0\} \times \{0, \bar{m}, 2\bar{m}, \ldots, (n_m - 1)\bar{m}\} \times \{0, \bar{b}, 2\bar{b}, \ldots, (n_b - 1)\bar{b}\}$, where $\bar{m}$, and $\bar{b}$ are the indivisible units in which the assets can be traded, with $\bar{b} = \psi\bar{m}, \bar{m}$ corresponding to approximately 100\$ and $\psi = 100$.

Díaz-Giménez and Prescott (1989) find that inflation/nominal interest rate policies with implied similar rates of return to those observed in the United States are feasible in heterogeneous-agent consumption-smoothing models. They also find that unfrequent policy changes of the type described have large real effects and that these effects are distributed over a long period of time.

Uninsured Idiosyncratic Risks and Aggregate Fluctuations

Javier Díaz-Giménez (1990) explored the business cycle implications of alternative insurance technologies. He found that limited monetary arrangements entail larger fluctuations in aggregate hours than do perfect insurance arrangements in otherwise identical economies. He calculated the welfare costs of the monetary arrangement, which amounted to 1.25 percent of output in zero-inflation economies. To obtain these conclusions, Díaz-Giménez compared two environments: perfect insurance and a monetary arrangement with pervasive liquidity constraints. The model can be implemented as follows. Let $C = \mathbf{R}_+ \times \{0, 1\}$, with standard preferences. Let $A = \{0\} \times \{0, \bar{m}, 2\bar{m}, \ldots, n_m\bar{m}\} \times \{0\}$, where $\bar{m}$ is calibrated to imply the equivalent of \$36 of 1989. Agents are born identical and are subject to an idiosyncratic shock that depends on the aggregate state as in İmrohoroğlu. The difference here is that individual productivity, $w(s, z)/(1 - \tau_0)$, depends on the economywide state, z. This causes procyclical productivity, which is calibrated to the U.S. business cycle. The government follows a monetary policy that sets the inflation rate equal to $r_2(z)^{-1}$ (recall that in our notation r_2 is the real rate of return of a_2, money). This inflation policy either takes the form of a "Phillips curve" (procyclical investment with a 4 percent average and a 2 percent premium in good times) or is at a constant 4 percent rate, it also imposes a labor income tax of $\tau_0 = .25$. The equilibrium of this economy can now be computed, as well as the process for government expenditures. In order to make meaningful comparisons with a perfect insurance environment, the two economies must share the government policies regarding expenditures and labor income taxes. For this, the optimal arrangement that agents can achieve is the maximum utility of the average agent, taking as given the tax sequences and the necessary transfers that the government has to make to balance its budget. This becomes a static problem and it is easily solved once the first-order maximization conditions are specified. Then the results of the simulations of the two environments that share economic policy are processed to obtain meaningful statistics that can be compared.

The Size of Precautionary Savings

The issue of precautionary savings, in particular, those motivated by self-insurance against idiosyncratic risk, has a long tradition in economics. There have been very few attempts to measure the size of this factor. One such attempt is Aiyagari (1993), which sets forth a model similar to that of Huggett (1993). Obviously, this question can be addressed only in an environment where aggregate savings can exist (note that Huggett's is an endowment economy, meaning that there are no possibilities for the economy as a whole to save). There is also a sense in which the level of aggregate savings should affect society's abilities to provide for goods. Aiyagari incorporates these two features by using the technological framework of the standard neoclassical growth model. In this economy, the market-clearing condition is similar to (16)). We write it as

$$\int_{S,A} a_1'(s, a; R(K)) \, d\mu^* = K, \tag{18}$$

where $R(K)$ is the real rate of return associated with a level of aggregate capital K. This condition can be stated by saying that in equilibrium, such a level of aggregate capital generates a real rate of return that induces agents' decisions that in turn generate such a level of aggregate capital.

Aiyagari found that the effect of precautionary savings is small: uninsured idiosyncratic risk accounts for only a 3 percent increase in the aggregate savings rate, at least for moderate and empirically plausible parameter values.

Related Non–Business Cycle Research

The type of models described in this paper can also be used to investigate other issues that involve abstraction from aggregate fluctuations. For example, they have been used to study the real cost of inflation when money plays a well-defined precautionary role and to study the welfare properties of such insurance schemes as unemployment compensation in the presence of moral hazard considerations that arise from the fact that the shock, s, is not observed; only the employment choice, n, is observed.

In the type of economies that we have been reviewing, there is a natural role for public policies that provide some kind of insurance that is infeasible for private agents. For example, an unemployment insurance scheme is Pareto improving in such an environment. However, one of the main criticisms of public insurance mechanisms is that if moral hazard is widespread, private agents will not have the incentives to follow the unrestricted social optimum. Hansen and İmrohoroğlu (1992) attempt to make a quantitative assessment of how important these moral hazard considerations are for the welfare implications of unemployment insurance. In their model, in every period agents get a realization of an idiosyncratic variable that is interpreted as receiving or not receiving a job offer. Moral hazard is modeled as a situation in which the government audits only a fraction of those that claim the insurance. They find that the optimal level of insurance (the fraction of the wage to be paid when unemployed) is very low in the presence of even very small amounts of moral hazard. In İmrohoroğlu the welfare cost of inflation is investigated when money is held for precautionary purposes.

3. Overlapping-Generations Models

Overlapping-generations models provide a natural partition of the population according to features that can be readily observed. Standard data-collecting procedures provide a variety of descriptions of individual behavior by age group. For instance, the cyclical behavior of hours worked varies by age group. It is natural to ask whether these are features that arise naturally in equilibrium models of the business cycle type.

In the absence of measures of how the population is distributed with respect to its attitude toward risk, overlapping-generations models also provide an environment in which to assess the properties of risk sharing in an economy. In these economies it is usually assumed that agents live a large number of periods in order to relate the length of the periods for which the data are collected to the length of the life of people.

A Simple Overlapping-Generations Model

The demographics of this model will be kept at the most simple level. There is a maximum number of periods that an agent can live, I. Compared to the frequencies that interest business cycle researchers, the age structure of the population moves very slowly; therefore populations are taken to have a fixed age distribution. We normalize the size of the first cohort, μ_1, to one. The size of age i cohort, μ_i, becomes $(1 + \lambda_\mu)^{-i}$, where λ_μ is the rate of growth of the population.[11] Agents are endowed with one unit of time per period, which can be enjoyed as leisure or can be used as an input to produce, jointly with capital, a consumption good. One unit of time of an age i agent can be transformed into ϵ_i units of labor input, where $\epsilon = \{\epsilon_1, \ldots, \epsilon_I\}$ is a vector of exogenously given parameters. Preferences are standard, and are represented by the expected discounted sum of a strictly concave current utility function of leisure and a consumption good. For a newborn agent this can be written as

$$E\left\{ \sum_{i=1}^{I} \beta^{i-1} u(c_i, l_i) \right\}, \tag{19}$$

while an agent of age i has remaining utility of $E\left\{ \sum_{j=i}^{I} \beta^{j-1} u(c_j, l_j) \right\}.$[12]

There is a neoclassical production function, $f(K, N)$, that is affected by a multiplicative shock, $z \in Z = \{z_1, z_2, \ldots, z_{N_z}\}$. This shock follows a Markov process with transition matrix π and is observed at the beginning of the period. Output can be used either for consumption in the same period that production takes place or for increasing the capital stock next period. Capital depreciates at rate δ, and for notational simplicity, we will assume that undepreciated capital can also be used for consumption purposes. If we denote next period's variables by primes, all this can be written as

$$\sum_{i=1}^{I} c_i \, \mu_i + K' = z \, f(K, N) + (1 - \delta)K. \tag{20}$$

These models are used, among other things, to explore the quantitative relevance of different market arrangements. This is done by comparing the equilibrium allocations of these alternative market institutions. In particular, these models are very useful in exploring the issue of whether the existence of possibilities of insurance against aggregate fluctuations is quantitatively important or not. A useful way of formulating the market structure is to allow trade in securities that deliver one unit of the capital good next period. At the beginning of the period, the shock is observed, then the contracts for the securities are honored, and finally, production takes place. This choice of timing of delivery is somehow nonstandard, as the securities do not deliver units of consumption, but units of the capital good before production takes place. As we will see, this timing implies simple restrictions on security prices. A general way of setting up different degrees of market completeness is to allow for trade on securities contingent on the elements of $\mathcal{F} = \{\varphi_1, \varphi_2, \ldots, \varphi_{n_\varphi}\}$, a partition[13] of Z, with $n_\varphi \leq N_z$, as for all $n \in \{1, \ldots, N_z\}$, there exists $m \in \{1, \ldots, n_\varphi\}$, such that $z_n \in \varphi_m$. When $\mathcal{F} = \{Z\}$, savings can only be made uncontingent, as there are no possibilities of signing contracts that depend in any ways on the value of next's period's shock.

When $\mathcal{F} = \{z_1, z_2, \ldots, z_{N_z}\}$, the full set of securities can be traded. This implies that agents face the following budget constraints:

$$a_1 = 0, \tag{21}$$

$$a_i R + W(1 - l_i)\epsilon_i = \sum_{\varphi \in \mathcal{F}} b_i^\varphi q^\varphi + c_i, \tag{22}$$

$$a'_{i+1}(z') = b_i^{\varphi(z')}, \quad \text{for } \varphi \in \mathcal{F}, \ i = 1, \ldots, I, \tag{23}$$

and

$$b_I^\varphi \geq 0, \tag{24}$$

where a_i is the net wealth accumulated so far by an age i agent, b_i^φ constitutes the amount of state-contingent capital goods bought by agents of age i, q^φ is the price of the state-contingent assets, R is the return on asset holdings, and W is the price of one unit of labor input in terms of the consumption good. Condition (23) specifies that net wealth tomorrow depends on the realization of the shock tomorrow.

Note that aggregate gross savings (including undepreciated capital) are $zf(K, N) + (1 - \delta)K - \sum_i \mu_i c_i$, and they become next period's aggregate capital, K'. The decisions that lead to the determination of K' are all made this period; therefore K' cannot depend in tomorrow's value of the shock, z'. On the other hand, aggregate savings can also be obtained by adding up contingent savings of all individuals: $(\sum_i \mu_i b_i^\varphi)$. Note that this is true for every φ. This implies that aggregate contingent savings has to be the same for all $\varphi \in \mathcal{F}$, as their size is determined today by the total amount of nonconsumed real resources. In other words, next period's aggregate capital stock cannot be made contingent on tomorrow's shock, although its distribution can. This is just another way of stating the market-clearing condition for the securities. Hence, the aggregate feasibility constraint becomes:

$$\sum_i \mu_i(b_i^\varphi + c_i) = zf(K, N) + (1 - \delta)K, \quad \text{for all } \varphi \in \mathcal{F}, \text{ all } z \in Z. \tag{25}$$

In the feasibility constraint, aggregate inputs are, respectively,

$$N = \sum_i \mu_i (1 - l_i)\epsilon_i \quad \text{and} \quad K = \sum_i \mu_i a_i. \tag{26}$$

Note that the price of a unit of capital for sure for next period can be acquired by the purchase of one unit of b^φ for all $\varphi \in \mathcal{F}$, at a price of $\sum_\varphi q^\varphi$. Note also that this capital good can be obtained by staying outside the market and saving one unit of the good. Obviously, this restricts the set of possible prices of the securities. If $\sum_\varphi q^\varphi > 1$, an agent could sell arbitrarily large amounts of these securities by buying the good, and delivering it next period while making arbitrarily large profits. If $\sum_\varphi q^\varphi < 1$, an agent could do the opposite operation and also obtain arbitrarily big consumption possibilities. These two properties together imply that in equilibrium it must be the case that $\sum_\varphi q^\varphi = 1$, since unbounded consumption possibilities cannot be feasible.

Equilibrium Defined

Equilibrium is defined recursively. The state of the economy is characterized by the economywide shock, $z \in Z$, and by the distribution of asset holdings by agents in each age group, $k \in \mathcal{A} \subset \mathbf{R}^I$. The state variables for any given agent are the agent's own asset holdings, $a \in \mathcal{A}_i \subset \mathbf{R}$, and the economywide state, (z, k). Note that since all agents of the same age share the same strictly concave utility function and convex choice set, they do the same thing in equilibrium, that is, $a_i = k_i$. Therefore, the aggregate laws of motion for the economy depend only on the decision rules of the agents and the process for the shock, and, since the latter follows a Markov process, its current value is all the information needed to know tomorrow's distribution. With the type of securities chosen, next period's state, k', depends on next period's shock, z'. Then $k'(z') = b^\varphi$, where $\varphi(z')$ is the element of $\mathcal{F}$ that contains z'. The value functions involved in the definition are indexed by the age of the agent, and their value is expected remaining utility. A recursive competitive equilibrium is a set of decision rules, $b_i^\varphi(z, k, a), c_i(z, k, a)$, $l_i(z, k, a)$, for all $i = 1, \ldots, I, \varphi \in \mathcal{F}, z \in Z, k \in \mathcal{A}, a \in \mathcal{A}_i$; a set of pricing functions $W(z, k), R(z, k), q^\varphi(z, k)$, for all $\varphi \in \mathcal{F}, z \in Z, k \in \mathcal{A}$; a set of value functions, $v_i(z, k, a), i = 1, \ldots, I, z \in Z, k \in \mathcal{A}, a \in \mathcal{A}_i$; a law of motion for the capital stocks, $k'_{i+1}(z') = g_i^{\varphi(z')}(z, k), i = 1, \ldots, I - 1, z \in Z, k \in \mathcal{A}$, $z' \in Z$; and a pair of functions for aggregate variables. $K(z, k), N(z, k), z \in Z$, $k \in \mathcal{A}$, such that the following conditions are satisfied:

1) The allocation is feasible, that is, for all z, k, and all φ,

$$\sum_i \left[b_i^\varphi(z, k, k_i) + c_i(z, k, k_i) \right] \mu_i = zf[K(z, k), N(z, k)]$$

$$+ (1 - \delta) \sum_i k_i \mu_i. \quad (27)$$

2) Factor prices are competitive, that is, they are the marginal productivities:

$$W(z, k) = zf_2[K(z, k), N(z, k)], \quad (28)$$

and

$$R(z, k) = 1 - \delta + zf_1[K(z, k), N(z, k)]. \quad (29)$$

3) Given the law of motion for capital stocks, the price functions, and the transition for z, decision rules for age i agents solve their maximization

problem:

$$\left\{b_i^\varphi(z, k, a), c_i(z, k, a), l_i(z, k, a)\right\} \in$$

$$\arg\max_{b^\varphi, c, l} u(c, l) + \beta E\left\{v_{i+1}\left(z', g^{\varphi(z')}(z, k), b^{\varphi(z')}\right) \mid z\right\}$$

$$\text{s.t.} \quad aR(z, k) + (1 - l)\epsilon_i W(z, k) = c + \sum_{\varphi \in \mathcal{F}} b^\varphi q^\varphi(z, k). \quad (30)$$

4) The value functions are generated by the policy functions and $v_{I+1} = 0$, and the budget constraint is satisfied:

$$v_i(z, k, a) = U\left[c_i(z, k, a), l_i(z, k, a)\right]$$

$$+ \beta E\left\{v_{i+1}\left[z', g^\varphi(z, k), b_i^\varphi(z, k, a)\right] \mid z\right\}, \quad (31)$$

and

$$aR(z, k) + [1 - l_i(z, k, a)]W(z, k)\epsilon_i$$

$$= c_i(z, k, a) + \sum_{\varphi \in \mathcal{F}} b_i^\varphi(z, k, a)q^\varphi(z, k). \quad (32)$$

5) The law of motion of the capital stocks is generated by the decision rules of the agents:

$$b_i^\varphi(z, k, k_i) = g_{i+1}^\varphi(z, k), \quad \text{for all } z' \in Z, \text{ all } i = 1, \ldots, I - 1. \quad (33)$$

6) Aggregate functions K and N are generated by aggregation and the decision rules of the agents:

$$K(z, k) = \sum_i \mu_i k_i, \quad (34)$$

and

$$N(z, k) = \sum_i \mu_i [1 - l_i(z, k, k_i)] \epsilon_i. \quad (35)$$

If the agent problem (30) of condition 3 has been explicit about the fact that agents can arbitrage by storing the capital good themselves, then a requirement on prices that prevents arbitrage opportunities does not have to be imposed as it is implicit in the fact that there is a well-defined solution to (30), which can only happen if $\sum_{\varphi \in \mathcal{F}} q^\varphi(z, k) = 1$. If we are not explicit about that fact we can impose such a requirement as an equilibrium condition. It is also a good idea to impose such a condition for computational reasons. We write this as equilibrium condition 7:

7) There are no arbitrage opportunities:

$$\sum_{\varphi \in \mathcal{F}} q^{\varphi}(z, k) = 1, \text{ or } q(z, k) \in \Delta^{n_{\varphi}}, \quad \text{for all } z \in Z, \ k \in \mathcal{A}. \quad (36)$$

It is also important to explain the role played by market-clearing conditions. The above definition includes only those for the factors of production, but we also have markets for securities, so where are their market clearing conditions? The answer is, of course, that it is implicit in condition 1, the feasibility requirement. Note that as it is written, it has to hold for all φ. Thus every period, we have not only one feasibility requirement but n_{φ} of them. Therefore, if we have a set of functions, $b^{\varphi}(z, k, a)$ that satisfy condition 1, then they will also satisfy

$$\sum_{i} \mu_i b_i^{\varphi}(z, k, k_i) = \sum_{i} \mu_i b_i^{\varphi'}(z, k, k_i), \quad \text{for all } \varphi, \varphi' \in \mathcal{F}. \quad (37)$$

Computation of the Equilibrium

The typical procedure used to compute the equilibrium law of motion for these economies consists in calculating a linear-quadratic approximation of a set of reduced-form utility functions around the steady state. This requires us first to find the steady state. As Auerbach and Kotlikoff (1987) show, this involves finding the solution of a nonlinear equation of one variable. The easiest way to do it is to define an equation that given a capital-labor ratio, returns the capital-labor ratio that is generated by the economy.[14]

Once this is done, we know the levels of asset holdings, consumption, and leisure at every age. We then substitute factor prices for the expressions of marginal productivities in terms of the shock, z, the asset distribution, k, and aggregate employment, N. We set contingent prices, q^{φ}, equal to the conditional probabilities of the events the associated securities are contingent on (which will depend on the current shock, z), and contingent security holdings, b_i^{φ}, equal to the steady state levels of asset holdings at each age. All this allows us to use the budget constraint to substitute for current consumption, and we obtain a current utility function $R_i(z, k, a, N, q^{\varphi}, b^{\varphi}, l)$. We approximate these functions by quadratic functions. Next, iterations are performed on the set of value functions. In each iteration, expressions for $(N, q^{\varphi}, k'^{\varphi})$ as functions of the aggregate state (z, k) have to be found. This requires the inversion of a large matrix. Chapter 2 gives a generic description of how to perform these procedures. However, for a detailed explanation of how to compute the equilibria in overlapping-generation economies with a variety of market structures, see Ríos-Rull (1993a). For details on how to incorporate sophisticated demographic structures, see Ríos-Rull (1992b).

Altig and Carlstrom (1991) used a different procedure, which can be described not as computing the exact (up to computer accuracy) equilibria of an approximated economy, but as an approximation to the equilibria of the original economy. Their method is based on the algorithm developed by Auerbach and Kotlikoff

(1987) to compute transition paths between steady states. The process can be described in the following way. Starting from the steady state, an innovation in the exogenous shock occurs. Assume that from that period on the economy will behave deterministically, with the value of future shocks set at their conditional expectation. Then compute the transitional path to the steady state. From this transition, obtain the value of prices and quantities for the first period. Next, a new value for the exogenous shock is obtained, and the process is repeated. This method presents two problems. The first is that it applies the notion of certainty equivalence in a context where it does not apply. The other problem is that it is very computer intensive, with the computations proportional to the length of the sample that is produced.

Special Calibration Issues

In these economies some special calibration issues arise. The production side of the economy is the same as that of representative-agent economies, so the same calibration considerations apply. The important difference is that the demographic structure has to be specified. For this, the procedure is to construct a stable population that shares the U.S. birth rates and age-specific mortality. (To explicitly include mortality requires certain adjustments in the model, as we should face the issue of the possible role played by markets for annuities; see Ríos-Rull [1992a] for details). The demographic structure has strong implications for the preference parameters. The discount rate, β, no longer should be calibrated to match historical average rates of return. Its value must be chosen, based on estimation from individual data. In this respect, Hurd (1989) estimates individual preference parameters, taking into account demographic features that make his estimates very attractive for our purposes. The values for the per-period utility function also must be chosen from microeconomic studies, but these are not typically detailed enough to be able to make the parameters age dependent.

A very important set of parameters is that given by ϵ, the vector of efficiency units of labor by age group. Its value can be obtained from different sources: Ríos-Rull (1992a) uses Hansen's (1993) Consumer Population Survey (CPS) data to construct it, while Auerbach and Kotlikoff (1987) and Altig and Carlstrom (1991) use Welch's (1979) regression coefficients. It is also important to note that under this assumption of how individual hours aggregate into the labor input, the standard measure of the Solow residual is no longer valid, and its process has to be reevaluated. Details of these and related issues are discussed in Ríos-Rull (1992a).

Review of the Literature

Life Cycle Economies and Aggregate Fluctuations

It is a well-known fact that the volatility of hours worked is not constant across age groups, but is highest for the youngest and the oldest. Ríos-Rull (1992a) studies the general business cycle properties of these economies and, in particular, the relative volatility of hours across age groups. His findings were that the business cycle properties of these economies are very similar to those of the representative-agent models, which are discussed elsewhere in the book. With respect to the behavior of hours worked, he found that aggregate hours have small volatility, a finding that is similar to other business cycle models with no nonconvexities in the labor choice. The relative volatility of hours worked across age groups shows some differences between the data and the model. While volatility of the hours worked by young agents in the model is greater than that of prime-age agents, as they are in the data, agents between 45 and 64 years of age show a much higher volatility of hours than that of the 25–44 age group, contradicting the behavior observed in the data.

Inflation, Personal Taxes, and Real Output: A Dynamic Analysis

The objective of Altig and Carlstrom (1991) is to answer the question, What consequences do interactions between inflation and the nominal taxation of capital income have for the cyclical behavior of the economy? In their model, there is no role for money. Inflation simply introduces a distortion in the measurement of individual capital income. In particular, an inflation rate of π overstates capital income in an amount equal to $\pi/(1 + \pi)$ per unit. They impose a progressive tax structure that mimics the 1965 U.S. tax code. Given the role that inflation has in this model, it is sufficient to calibrate its process with a univariate representation. They estimate an autoregressive process of order two, with an associated average inflation of 4 percent. They find that with progressive taxes, the volatility of inflation, on top of the exogenous variation in the Solow residual, drastically increases the volatility of hours worked, compared to a constant inflation process (about 80 percent more), and moderately increases the volatility of consumption, while leaving the volatility of investment, output, and capital roughly unchanged.

The inclusion of the inflation effects transforms equation (21) into

$$[a_i R + W(1 - l_i)\epsilon_i]\{1 - \tau[a_i R \frac{1 + 2\pi}{1 + \pi} + W(1 - l_i)\epsilon_i]\}$$

$$- \tau[a_i R \frac{1 + 2\pi}{1 + \pi} + W(1 - l_i)\epsilon_i]a_i R \frac{\pi}{1 + \pi} + tr = \sum_{\varphi \in \mathcal{F}} b_i^\varphi q^\varphi + c_i, \quad (38)$$

where the first term is the after-tax income, taking into account the progressive nature of the tax, the next term reflects the distortion that inflation induces on the tax base through the capital income and the last term of the right-hand side is the transfer required to balance the government budget given that there are no public expenditures.

The state space has to be enlarged to include current and lagged inflation since inflation is supposed to follow a second-order autoregressive process.

The market structure considered does not include contingent markets; therefore, $\mathcal{F} = \{Z\}$. The definition of the equilibrium also requires a transfers function, $tr(z, k, \pi, \pi_{-1})$, that the agents use to solve their problem, and that has to balance the government budget.

On the Quantitative Importance of Market Completeness

In Ríos-Rull (1993a), the question explored is, How different are the equilibrium allocations across economies that differ only in whether there are Arrow securities for economywide productivity shocks in the absence of idiosyncratic shocks of any kind? The economies studied vary only on the specification of $\mathcal{F}$, ranging from $\mathcal{F} = \{Z\}$, where savings can only be made noncontingent, to $\mathcal{F} = \{z_1, z_2, \ldots, z_{N_z}\}$, where markets are dynamically complete. The answer found is that the aggregate series obtained for the various market specifications are very similar to one another, to the point that it would be almost impossible to identify the type of economy from this type of data alone. If data on individual allocations are observed, slight differences across economies arise as agents actively engage in risk sharing trades. These differ, of course, depending on the trade possibilities allowed in each economy. In any case, differences are very small. There are differences across individual asset holding data, that can be readily observable. This seems to indicate that different market structures offer different mechanisms that allow an economy to reach almost the same objective: an allocation as close as possible to a Pareto optimum.

Related Non–Business Cycle Research

The ability to compute nonstationary equilibria in overlapping-generations economies where agents live a large number of periods makes it possible to address some other interesting questions. For example, we can study the role that demographic changes play in the economy. Of special interest is their influence on capital accumulation and social insurances. The methods developed can address these because they take into account the effect that the induced changes in prices have on the behavior of agents. Ríos-Rull (1992b) assesses the magnitude of the changes in savings rates that can be expected the result from the current aging of the Spanish population. Similar topics have been studied by Auerbach et al. (1989) and by Danthine and Surchat (1991), where certain shortcuts have been assumed to simplify calculations. Ríos-Rull (1993b) uses a simple computable overlapping-generations model with two-period–lived agents to study some joint facts about the relation between wages and hours worked from four different points of view: cross-section, long-term, cyclical, and age-specific. This model gives some insights into how heterogeneity arises in environments where all agents start equal, but it is very different from the models in this book, as there is no physical capital and periods are very long compared with the quarterly or yearly frequency typical of business cycle models.

4. Other Types of Heterogeneity

The Cyclical Behavior of Factor Shares

Economies with agents differing in preferences have been used to address some additional business cycles issues. Gomme and Greenwood (1993) use such an economy to study the cyclical behavior of factor shares. The long-term behavior of the factor shares is basically constant, as is the capital output ratio, and the rate of return on capital. This restricts the elasticity of substitution between capital and labor to be one, and leaves Cobb-Douglas as the primary candidate for the production function. But this production function implies that factor shares are constant at every frequency, while the data show that labor share moves countercyclically, while profits are procyclical. To address this issue, Gomme and Greenwood introduce labor contracts as risk-sharing arrangements between two types of agents: workers and entrepreneurs.

In their model, agents are born being of one of the two types. Entrepreneurs operate a constant-returns-to-scale stochastic technology, which requires their own labor input as well as workers' labor input and real capital. Preferences are of the type described by Epstein (1983) as stationary cardinal utility, which allows deterministic economies to have a unique invariant distribution of wealth across agents. The key property of these preferences is that future discount factors become a decreasing function of current utility. Preferences of the two types are calibrated so that the entrepreneurs constitute the rich agents, owning 25 percent of the wealth, and constitute 1 percent of the population. A competitive equilibrium with a full set of Arrow securities is calculated. We can think of this equilibrium as having spot markets for labor and capital and Arrow securities, or as the Arrow securities' being embodied in the labor contract, which now is contracted one period in advance, or as the entrepreneurs issuing bonds, which are held by the workers, to acquire capital. Any of these market structures implements the complete-markets allocations, although they imply very different behavior for wages, and consequently for the labor share. The first implementation gives a constant labor share, while the second and the third result in a countercyclical behavior.

Heterogeneous Agents and the Risk Premium

One of the great puzzles in aggregate economics is the size of the premium that risky assets (namely, stocks) have over relatively riskless assets, such as government bonds (see Mehra and Prescott 1985). Standard models (that is, representative-agent endowment economies with time-separable preferences and a process for consumption that shares the stochastic properties of aggregate consumption in the post World War II United States) systematically generate premiums that are far too small. In trying to account for this anomaly, the standard representative-agent model has been modified along several dimensions. The one direction that is relevant to us tries to explore the issue of whether the size of the premium can be accounted for by lack of markets in multiagent worlds where their endowments are not perfectly correlated. In independent research. Lucas (1990), Ketterer and Marcet (1989), Marcet and Singleton (1990), and Telmer (1992) have constructed models with two agents where individual endowment processes are not perfectly correlated. They explore the nature of the equilibrium allocations and prices under various market structures that include trading on some assets and find that they are very similar to the ones obtained in complete market settings. This result can be explained by noting that in economies that are calibrated to quarterly periods, the average value of their income stream (which is of the order of magnitude of the returns of the assets that agents can use to smooth consumption) is around twenty times the value of average quarterly consumption. This is a very big cushion for smoothing consumption in the presence of reasonable perturbations on the endowments stream. A related paper of Danthine, Donaldson, and Mehra (1992), studies the implications of the fact that stockholders bear a disproportionate share of output uncertainty in a model with non-walrasian features.

Asymmetric Information and Limited Commitment

Marcet and Marimon (1992) have studied the set of implementable allocations in environments where the actions of an infinitely-lived borrower are unobservable and there is no commitment technology to repay the loans. They do this in the context of a small country where the allocation of national output between consumption and investment and the technological shock are both unobservable. They are able to characterize and compute the optimal contract between risk–neutral agents and the small country. They find that when the rationale for borrowing is to increase the capital stock, there is no improvement over autarky. However, when loans are used to smooth consumption, the optimal contract scheme improves significantly over autarky.

5. Current Research Agenda

So far, all models with idiosyncratic shocks and an absence of complete insurance possibilities are either silent on the distribution of wealth (in the sense that it is imposed ex ante) or have no capital. As distributional issues become more interesting (among other features, they have tremendous relevance for public finance and the nature of the tax system), the key innovation will be to develop methods to compute equilibria in economies with capital where the distribution of wealth and income is endogenous. With such a tool, the cyclical behavior of the distributions of income and wealth can be addressed. Also, the redistributional effect of a variety of policies can be quantitatively evaluated, as such methods allow one to compute not only the optimal reaction of agents to the policies but also the ultimate outcome that results from their interaction. To this end, there is some very preliminary work that tries to approximate the distribution of wealth in different ways that might be able to keep both computational costs and the accuracy at reasonable levels.

The radical technological change that affects the computer industry provides economists with increasingly cheaper and more powerful machines. At the same time, computational literacy of economists provides strong externalities in terms of an accumulated body of procedures that become available for all researchers. This is one of the main reasons for the rapid development of this class of models over the last two or three years. As there are no indications of these processes stopping or slowing down, the outlook for future success seems very bright.

Notes

Part of this material has been used to teach a Ph.D. course in Carnegie Mellon University. I am grateful to its students. Thanks also to the comments of Paul Gomme, Jeremy Greenwood, Mark Huggett, Pat Kehoe, Finn Kydland, Lee Ohanian, and the editor of this book, Tom Cooley.

1. This literature takes the fact that some markets are missing as given and studies the properties of such economies; it does not attempt to explain why they are missing.

2. Constantinides and Duffie (1991) and Zin (1992) have examples of heterogeneous-agent models with incomplete markets that can be represented as homogeneous-agent ones. They require the shocks to be such that even in the presence of markets, agents do not gain anything by trading. In other words, in these markets, there is no consumption smoothing, as marginal utilities are restricted to remain constant.

3. As of early 1994, there is preliminary work suggesting that using a small set of moments to approximate the distribution is a promising avenue. In particular, Krusell and Smith (1994) suggest that an affine law of motion for aggregate wealth works very well. Castañeda, Díaz-Giménez, and Ríos-Rull (1994) are using these ideas to study the cyclical behavior of the income distribution. See also den Haan (1993).

4. The reason why μ' is also a function of z' is because π, the joint law of motion of (s, z), might have the property that the distribution of s' can be jointly conditional on $\{s, z, z'\}$ so that the measure of agents with each shock might vary with z'. Of course, the marginal distribution over asset holdings $\mu'(A_0, S)$ for $A_0 \subset A$ will not depend on z'.

5. İmrohoroğlu (1989) actually does not compute the equilibrium of the economy with perfect insurance, but of an economy that does not have storage technology, so her calculations actually provide a lower bound for the difference of the cost of business cycles, as storage can only reduce the costs in perfect-insurance economies.

6. It is possible to pose this type of problem as a linear maximization problem, whose solution is found with the simplex algorithm.

7. Note that by Walras's Law, clearing of the bonds market implies clearing of the goods market.

8. Chapter 3 in this book discusses related computational methods based on approximations to the Euler equation.

9. Actually, this condition is not exactly true. If for all a_3 above the lower bound, equation (17), is negative, then the a_3' that is chosen is precisely the lower bound, and equation (17) is not set to 0.

10. Note that since with perfect insurance, there is no inflation tax and total output is typically different than in the liquidity-constrained environment, there is a need for these transfers to balance the budget.

11. For simplicity, we abstract from early death of the agents. See Ríos-Rull (1992b) for a discussion of the demographics in this type of economy.

12. We could think of more general preference structures by indexing the current return utility function, u, by age, obtaining $u_i, i \in \{1, \cdots, I\}$, by noting that combinations of consumption and leisure are not regarded equally across different ages. Also, we could substitute a common discount factor, such as β, for a system of weights that treat each age's utility in a different manner.

13. Given a set Z, a partition $\mathcal{F}$ of Z is a family of subsets, $\varphi_j, j \in J$, of Z, such that their union is the set Z, $(\cup_j \varphi_j = Z)$, and they have pairwise empty intersection $(\varphi_j \cap \varphi_{j'} = \emptyset$, for all $j, j' \in J)$.

14. Given K/N, we obtain relative prices W and R. If we assume them constant forever, it is straightforward to find the amounts of asset holdings and labor input that agents want at each age. Aggregating factors of production, and obtaining their ratio yields a new capital-labor ratio.

Chapter 5
Business Cycles and Aggregate Labor Market Fluctuations

Finn E. Kydland

1. Introduction

Central to business cycle theory as well as to growth theory is the aggregate production function, which relates the nation's output of goods and services to the inputs of capital and labor. Of prime importance to business cycle theory is the behavior of the labor input. For growth, most of the output change is accounted for by changes in technology and in capital. In contrast, perhaps on the order of two-thirds of the business cycle is accounted for by movements in the labor input and one-third by changes in technology. Thus, most business cycle theorists agree that an understanding of aggregate labor market fluctuations is a prerequisite for understanding how business cycles propagate over time.

Table 5.1 lists statistics describing the cyclical behavior of key U.S. aggregates that are related to the labor input. The table includes measures of cyclical volatility, as well as correlations with cyclical real GNP, contemporaneously and at leads and lags of up to five quarters. The logarithms of the original series were detrended using the Hodrick-Prescott filter before the statistics were computed. (See Kydland and Prescott [1990] for details.) Some of the cyclical series are plotted against cyclical real GNP in figures 5.1–5.6.

Notable regularities related to the labor market are as follows:

1) Total hours, whether measured by the household or the establishment (payroll) survey, is almost as volatile as real GNP.

2) The household survey indicates that approximately two-thirds of the total-hours fluctuation is in the form of variation in employment and one-third is in hours per worker.

3) Total hours is highly procyclical, as indicated by the contemporaneous correlation coefficients with real GNP of nearly 0.9.

4) Total hours displays a slight phase shift in the direction of lagging the cycle, especially in the employment component. Hours per worker displays almost no phase shift.

Table 5.1
Cyclical Behavior of U.S. Labor Market Aggregates, 1954:I–1991:II

Variable	Volatility (% SD)	Cross-Correlation of Real GNP with:										
		$x(-5)$	$x(-4)$	$x(-3)$	$x(-2)$	$x(-1)$	x	$x(+1)$	$x(+2)$	$x(+3)$	$x(+4)$	$x(+5)$
Real Gross National Product	1.72	−.02	.16	.38	.63	.85	.86	.85	.63	.38	.16	−.02
Hours (Household Survey)	1.49	−.10	.05	.25	.46	.70	.83	.85	.74	.58	.38	.17
Employment	1.09	−.17	−.03	.16	.38	.63	.83	.88	.80	.65	.46	.25
Hours per Worker	0.54	.07	.20	.36	.49	.64	.70	.58	.42	.28	.12	−.02
Hours (Establishment Survey)	1.66	−.23	−.07	.14	.39	.67	.88	.91	.80	.63	.42	.22
GNP/Hours (Household Survey)	0.87	.12	.23	.33	.47	.50	.51	.22	−.01	−.24	−.32	−.34
GNP/Hours (Establishment Survey)	0.82	.41	.47	.51	.53	.44	.32	−.06	−.30	−.47	−.50	−.49
Average Hourly Real Compensation (Business Sector)	0.93	.35	.39	.41	.43	.41	.35	.25	.16	.05	−.07	−.18
Real Employee Compensation (NIPA)/ Hours (Household Survey)	0.65	−.11	−.11	−.13	.06	.02	.10	.13	.14	.10	.08	.04
Real Employee Compensation (NIPA)	1.54	−.14	.00	.18	.41	.67	.88	.88	.76	.59	.38	.18
Employee Compensation (NIPA)/GNP		−.21	−.32	−.44	−.53	−.51	−.46	−.13	.13	.32	.39	.38

Source of basic data: Citicorp's Citibase data bank.

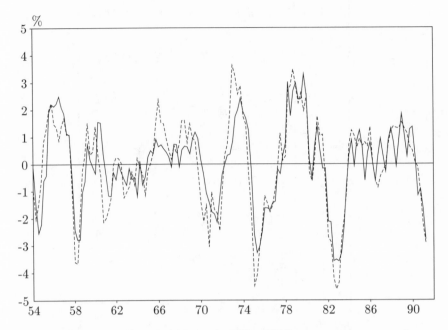

Figure 5.1 Total Hours (Household Survey) and Real GNP

Solid line shows hours and broken line shows real GNP. In Figures 5.1 through 5.6, data are quarterly from 1954:I to 1991:II and H-P filtered.

5) Average labor productivity is somewhat procyclical and leads the cycle. The degree of procyclicality is greater when output is divided by hours measured according to the household survey. The hours from the establishment survey indicate the longest lead: two to three quarters.

6) The statistics for average real hourly compensation in the business sector (which produces about 85 percent of GNP) are quite similar to those for productivity. If, on the other hand, we divide total employees' compensation from the national income accounts by total hours from either survey, series result whose correlations with real GNP are much lower.

7) Some writers have focused instead on the correlation of compensation (or productivity) with hours rather than with GNP (e.g., Christiano and Eichenbaum 1992). As a reflection mainly of the longer phase shift, the compensation series are less correlated contemporaneously with hours than with real GNP.

8) Real labor income is procyclical, but labor income as a fraction of GNP is countercyclical.

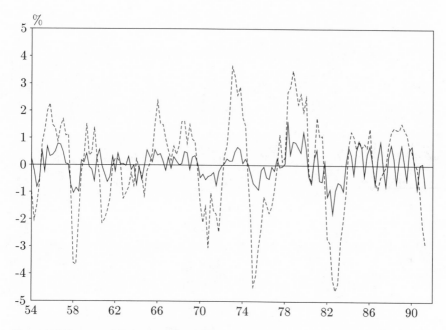

Figure 5.2 Hours per Worker and Real GNP
Solid line shows hours; broken line shows real GNP.

9) Over time, real hourly compensation has risen dramatically while hours worked per household has remained about constant. Cross-sectionally, however, there is a clear positive correlation between hours worked and the real wage. Moreover, the volatility of annual hours of work is much higher for wage earners in the two lowest quintiles than in the two highest (see Kydland 1984a; Ríos-Rull 1993b).

10) Benhabib, Rogerson, and Wright (1991) and Murphy, Shleifer, and Vishny (1989) argue that hours allocated to the production of consumption goods are procyclical. While direct observations based on a clear classification of the goods produced are not readily available, empirical evidence reported by Murphy, Shleifer, and Vishny points in that direction.

At various stages of the recent development of business cycle theory, some of these cyclical patterns have been regarded as deviations from existing theory. An application of real business cycle theory has been to address the question, How much of postwar business cycles would have remained if technology shocks were the only source of fluctuations? Major deviations along dimensions central to this question obviously could reduce one's confidence in the quantitative answer obtained. Through the interaction of theory and measurement, the deviations

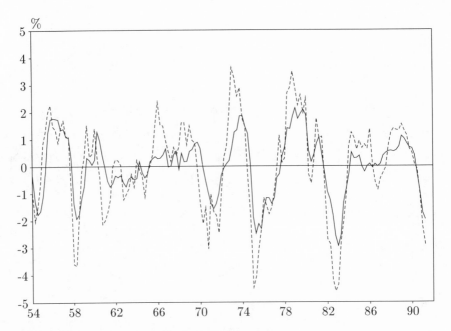

Figure 5.3 Total Employment and Real GNP
Solid line shows employment; broken line shows real GNP.

or anomalies relative to theory have led to stronger theory as well as to better measurements.

This chapter has two main objectives. The first is to give examples of the perceived deviations relative to theory, especially those related to labor market fluctuations, and of how researchers have attempted to resolve them. In the process, it will become clear that some of the proposed modifications still leave open important theoretical and measurement issues. The second objective is to present in detail an example of a model environment that is reasonably rich in its description of the labor market. It will incorporate movements of labor inputs in the forms of hours per worker as well as employment—both the intensive and the extensive margins.

In the next section, we present as a benchmark the standard neoclassical stochastic growth model, extended to include an explicit role for time allocation. It can be regarded as the starting point for the purpose of addressing business cycle questions. Then we review some of the developments in theory and measurement that have been motivated by perceived deviations from established theory. One such development is consideration of the use of nonmarket time in the household, possibly jointly with other inputs, to produce nonmarket goods. This is the subject of Section 3. Section 4 considers the fact that the work force consists of workers with a wide range of skills, whose behavior over the cycle differs substantially.

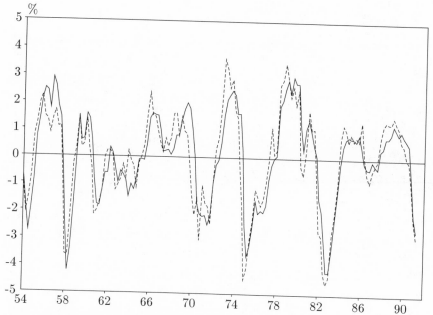

Figure 5.4 Total Hours (Establishment Survey) and Real GNP
Solid line shows hours; broken line shows real GNP.

This issue is discussed both from a modeling standpoint and from the perspective of measuring the labor input in aggregate production. The model formulations described in Sections 3 and 4 represent, with today's methods, tractable extensions of basic neoclassical theory.

Section 5 deals with the implications for the business cycle of the fact that labor input changes take the forms of both hours-per-worker and employment changes. The significance of introducing the employment margin became clear from the important paper by Hansen (1985) based on the theoretical insight of Rogerson (1984, 1988). The methodological foundation permitting the introduction of both margins has been developed only recently. A fundamentally new issue in this context is what shape the production function should take. In the business sector, the change of output associated with a given change of total hours in a given period surely is different when the change is in the number of hours a plant is being used rather than in the number of workers operating the plant.

In this chapter, several ways are presented in which the roles of market and nonmarket time for business cycles have been modeled. Section 6 provides a comparison of four of these in terms of the main business cycle characteristics. Section 7 contains an example of how one can extend one of these model economies (the one presented in section 5) to incorporate a new feature, in this case, learning by doing.

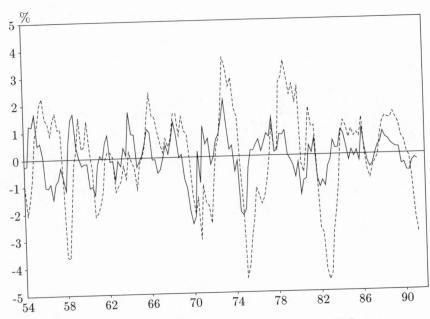

Figure 5.5 Average Productivity (Establishment Survey) and Real GNP
Solid line shows productivity; broken line shows real GNP.

Finally, in the last section we attempt an assessment of where we stand, particularly regarding the labor market's contribution to the propagation of shocks.

2. Basic Business Cycle Framework

Neoclassical growth theory has become the dominant theoretical framework in quantitative business cycle theory, as well as in most other areas of aggregate economics. It represents an environment that includes household and business sectors, and, for some questions, a government sector as well. The simplest growth model ignores time allocation decisions (see Stokey and Lucas with Prescott [1989, ch. 2] or Section 2 of Chapter 1 of this volume). A version that still is simple, but contains enough ingredients potentially to address business cycle questions, is as follows. The economy is inhabited by a large number of identical households, whose preferences are represented by a utility function:

$$E \sum_{t=0}^{\infty} \beta^t u(c_t, \ell_t),$$

where c_t is consumption, ℓ_t is time spent in nonmarket activity, or leisure for short, and β is the subjective discount factor. The production technology uses as

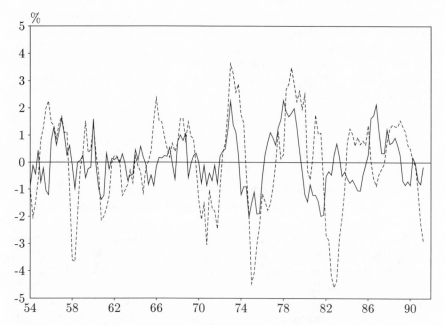

Figure 5.6 Average Hourly Real Compensation and Real GNP
Solid line shows hours; broken line shows real GNP.

inputs capital, k_t, and labor, h_t. There is perfect substitution in production between investment, x_t, and consumption. The constraints on the uses of output and time are

$$c_t + x_t \leq z_t f(h_t, k_t),$$

and

$$h_t + \ell_t \leq 1,$$

where, for simplicity, total discretionary time (net of sleep and personal care) is normalized to one. Laws of motion for the capital stock and technology are

$$k_{t+1} = (1 - \delta)k_t + x_t,$$

$$z_{t+1} = \rho z_t + \epsilon_{t+1}, \tag{1}$$

where ϵ_{t+1} is a random disturbance with positive mean.

This framework departs from the simplest neoclassical growth framework in two ways. Leisure is included in the utility function, a feature from which models designed to address growth questions usually abstract. The emphasis on the time allocation decision distinguishes business cycle theory from growth theory. Another extension is the inclusion of stochastic technology shocks, which have been considered in the theoretical growth literature by Brock and Mirman (1972) and by Danthine and Donaldson (1981). With these features included, one could use the model to address, for example, questions about the role of technology shocks. Following Solow (1957), the z's can be measured as the residual in output variation after the capital and labor inputs have been accounted for. With the Cobb-Douglas production function,

$$f(h_t, k_t) = h_t^\theta k_t^{1-\theta} \tag{2}$$

one can write

$$\log z_t = \log \text{GNP}_t - \theta \log h_t - (1 - \theta) \log k_t.$$

The value of θ corresponds to the average labor share in GNP. By studying the resulting series of z's, one can characterize statistically their persistence, as reflected in the parameter ρ in (1), as well as the volatility of the innovations, ϵ.

With explicit forms for the u and f functions and numerical values for the parameters of these functions and of the laws of motion, one can compute the solution in the form of decision rules for the variables c_t, n_t, and x_t. These decision rules, along with the laws of motion for the state variables, k_t and z_t, and the stochastic specification of the random shocks, can be used to perform computational experiments with the aim of yielding quantitative answers to business cycle questions.

A standard utility function is

$$u(c_t, \ell_t) = (c_t^\alpha \ell_t^{1-\alpha})^{1-\sigma} / (1 - \sigma). \tag{3}$$

Here, the elasticity of substitution between consumption and leisure is one. In the general class of constant-elasticity-of-substitution (CES) functions, this is the only value consistent with the observation that in spite of a large increase in the average real wage over the past few decades, there has been little change in long-run hours per household in market activity. In a model of this type, this fraction of long-run time spent in market work typically turns out to be close to the value of the parameter α. Thus, with measurement of this fraction from data on individuals or households, its average value implies a value for α. Such time allocation measurements were reported by Ghez and Becker (1975), who, when defining the total discretionary time available for market and nonmarket activity, were careful to measure and to exclude time devoted to sleep and personal care.

Determining values of θ and α as well as those of the elasticities of substitution in the utility and production functions are examples of calibrating the model economy. The curvature parameter, σ, is harder to quantify with confidence. Studies of attitudes towards risk may suggest a reasonable range for this parameter.

Business cycle theory organizes quarterly national income and product accounts (NIPA) data. With this period length, however, it makes a difference that building new factories takes much longer than one quarter. Accordingly, Kydland and Prescott (1982) assume that the construction of productive capital in the business sector takes J quarters, where J on the average may be 3 or 4, but with resources used throughout the construction period. The law of motion for the productive capital stock then is

$$k_{t+1} = (1 - \delta)k_t = s_{1t}, \tag{4}$$

where the notation is to let s_{jt}, $j = 1, \ldots, J$ be capital (in units of finished capital) that is j periods from completion. Thus,

$$s_{j,t+1} = s_{j+1,t}, \qquad j = 1, 2, \ldots, J - 1. \tag{5}$$

The amount of resources used at each stage when building one unit of new productive capital is φ_j. Total investment, the sum of fixed investment and inventory investment, then is

$$x_t = \sum_{j=1}^{J} \varphi_J s_{jt} + y_{t+1} - y_t, \tag{6}$$

where y_t is the inventory stock at the beginning of period t. Including inventories is another way of extending the standard growth model. In a period with high productivity, for instance, people may wish to smooth consumption and carry into the subsequent quarter some finished goods in the form of inventories. Moreover, as motivated in Kydland and Prescott (1982), the inventory stock may be treated as an input in aggregate production. A specification of the resource constraint then is

$$c_t + x_t \le [(1 - \gamma)(z_t h_t^\theta k_t^{1-\theta})^{-\nu} + \gamma y_t^{-\nu}]^{-1/\nu}.$$

With these features added, the model environment accounts quite well for the key properties of postwar U.S. business cycles, including relative volatility of investment and consumption, the procyclicality of most aggregates, and the contemporaneously uncorrelated capital stock. The model yields the preliminary estimate that technology shocks account for more than half of postwar U.S. business cycles. This estimate follows from computational experiments that use as an input the volatility of Solow residuals obtained for the U.S. economy; it is based on the fraction of U.S. output volatility implied by the model economy. This finding is supported by the model behavior of other aggregates, such as relative consumption and investment fluctuations. The key deviation relative to theory is that in this simple model with everyone working the same number of hours, the percentage standard deviation of the hours is substantially smaller than that of the model's real GNP.

3. Household Production

The realization that the empirical procyclical volatility of hours may be a problem for a general equilibrium theory of the cycle dates back at least to Lucas and Rapping (1969). Confronting this issue, they were led to the question, Are there reasons to substitute intertemporally, not captured by the standard specification of the household problem, that give rise to greater procyclical hours volatility? Lucas and Rapping suggest the theoretical possibility that future utility may depend, in part, directly on this period's choice of hours of work.

Kydland and Prescott (1982) make this idea operational and represent preferences in such a way that current utility is a function of a weighted average of current and past choices of nonmarket time:

$$u[c_t, \mu(L)\ell_t] = \frac{1}{1-\sigma} [c_t^\alpha (\sum_{i=0}^{\infty} \mu_i \ell_{t-i})^{1-\alpha}]^{1-\sigma}.$$

With weights summing to one, as can be assumed without loss of generality, their choice of parameter values was to let as much as one-half of the weight fall on current leisure ($\mu_0 = 0.5$), with the remainder spread over the past with geometrically declining weights. Thus, continuing with this numerical example, if the weights decline by 10 percent per quarter, then $\mu_1 = 0.05$, $\mu_2 = 0.045$, and so on. With that specification, the dependence of utility on current and past leisure choices is characterized by two parameters, μ_0 and v, where v is the rate of decline of the weights, that is, $\mu_{i+1} = (1-v)\mu_i$ for all $i \geq 1$.

Kydland (1984a) interprets this utility function as a stand-in for household production, in which part of nonmarket time is used to accumulate household capital, which yields utility in the future. Examples of such capital may be quality of children, health, and perhaps the quality of the residence and other durable household property. The relatively large weight, α_0, on current nonmarket time then reflects the notion that a substantial portion of nonmarket time yields immediate pleasure. The remainder represents an investment in a form of household capital, which depreciates at a rate of v. This analog of the specification above to the household production idea is exact when the two uses of nonmarket time are in fixed proportions and leisure and the durable home good are perfect substitutes in preferences. These are conservative assumptions. Relaxing them presumably would make market hours more responsive to changes in market opportunities.

With this feature included, not only does the volatility of hours increase relative to those of productivity and output, but technology shocks are also more potent in generating overall business cycle volatility. Referring to those findings, Kydland (1984b) concludes: "Using a standard time-separable utility function, about two-thirds of the fluctuations in the data were accounted for. If households are assumed to value leisure more if they have consumed less leisure in the past, the growth model explained nearly all."

This preliminary statement was not based on direct measurements of the volatility of the technology shocks. A more precise estimate uses Prescott's (1986) measurements. They are based on Solow's (1957) method for measuring technological change as the residual after the inputs have been accounted for. Subsequently, the resulting estimate of the volatility of the Solow residual has been used in computational experiments with a variety of model economies. The statistical properties of these residuals indicate that they are highly persistent—have high serial correlation. On the basis of these estimates, the "two-thirds" in the above quotation instead would have been 55 percent.

The fact remains that the quantitative importance of household capital formed by past nonmarket time can make a substantial difference to the estimate of the role of technology shocks. An attempt at assessing independently the magnitude of this form of household capital is made in Hotz, Kydland, and Sedlacek (1988). Using annual panel data for 482 men who in the first year of the twelve-year sample period were between the ages of 23 and 52, they estimate the parameters characterizing the role of household capital for life cycle behavior, taking into account differences in age, number of children, and other demographic factors. The estimates are consistent with the parameter values for μ and ν used by Kydland and Prescott (1982). It is probably fair to say, however, that this feature of household production has not been verified sufficiently by measurements to be regarded as necessary for a reliable estimate of the role of technology shocks for the cycle.

This formulation of time as an input into producing a form of household capital is simple and abstracts from the possibility that market-produced goods may be required as a joint input. The general idea, however, that attention to household production is important for understanding labor market fluctuations is an appealing one. It has been pursued in greater detail in two recent papers, by Benhabib, Rogerson, and Wright (1991) and by Greenwood and Hercowitz (1991). Both these papers consider the use in the household of physical capital (residential housing and/or consumer durables) that, along with nonmarket time, can be used to produce consumption goods. Greenwood and Hercowitz focus on the joint pattern of capital accumulation in the business and household sectors. Although this question has indirect implications for the labor input in market production, we shall leave a discussion of that topic for another chapter. Benhabib, Rogerson, and Wright, on the other hand, address issues that have a more direct bearing on the labor market. For example, they are motivated partly by the impression that fact (10) on the list in Section 1 represents a deviation from standard business cycle theory.

A key feature in the Benhabib, Rogerson, and Wright (BRW) model is the inclusion of a commodity made in the home using time and capital as inputs in a way analogous to the production of the market good. This home-produced consumption good is an imperfect substitute for market goods. Home production is a function of technology shocks in a manner analogous to that for the business sector.

The utility function is similar to (3), except that the variable c_t is replaced by a CES aggregator function representing a composite consumption good, which depends on c_{mt} and c_{nt}, where the subscripts m and n stand for market and nonmarket, respectively. Leisure in the utility function is net of time allocated to market and nonmarket production: $\ell_t = 1 - h_{mt} - h_{nt}$. Investment goods are produced in the market sector only. Capital can be moved between the two sectors. In practice, this reallocation takes place in the form of new investment. The home and business technologies both are Cobb-Douglas, with share parameters calibrated separately. The laws of motion for the technology shocks in the two sectors are identical, including a serial correlation coefficient of 0.95.

In addition to the motivation already mentioned, Benhabib, Rogerson, and Wright (1991) refer to measurements indicating that the fraction of nonmarket time devoted to production in the household is large. An interesting question, then, is whether household production may interact with market production in such a way that, combined, technology shocks to market and household production account for a considerably larger fraction of the business cycle than do those of the market sector alone. The answer hinges on three parameters—an elasticity of substitution in preferences, the standard deviation of the home technology shock, and its correlation with the business one. Indeed, a main contribution of the article is to demonstrate this fact. Since measurements of these parameters are either lacking or rudimentary at best, it underlines the importance of such measurements for a reliable answer.

Among those three parameters, the key one is the elasticity of substitution in preferences between market- and home-produced consumption, which BRW set equal to 5. This figure is based, in part, on estimates in Eichenbaum and Hansen (1990), according to which there is little statistical evidence against the hypothesis of perfect substitution elasticity between nondurables and durables. This empirical result can be interpreted as having a bearing on the model at hand. The estimate, however, is hard to reconcile with the observation that over time the price of durables relative to nondurables and services has fallen while the expenditure share has remained roughly constant. This fact would suggest an elasticity much closer to one than to infinity. Thus, one may doubt whether the elasticity in the BRW model will hold up under empirical scrutiny. Clearly, it plays a significant role for the model properties.

Other new parameters in the home-production specification are the standard deviation of the innovation to home technology and its contemporaneous correlation coefficient with the innovations in business sector technology. Again, good measurements upon which to base the values are not available. It seems much less likely, however, that the findings hinge upon future measurements of these parameters. For one thing, the authors make a good case for their reasonableness. Also, the theoretical findings appear to be not nearly as sensitive to variations within a moderate range of these parameters.

Benhabib, Rogerson, and Wright find that for their economy in comparison with the standard growth model, the volatility of output rises from 1.29 to 1.71 percent, which is very close to that observed for the postwar U.S. economy. The volatility of hours in relation to that of GNP, $std(h_m)/std(GNP)$, rises from 0.50 to 0.75, where std is short for percentage standard deviation.

The correlation in the model between real GNP and hours spent producing consumption goods in the market sector is 0.10. This magnitude may strike the reader as quite disappointing. One contribution of the article, however, is to show that this correlation can be turned from a large negative value to this slightly positive value simply through the introduction of household production. The simplicity of the model environment in other respects accounts for the negative correlation in the benchmark model. There are several reasons. Most important perhaps is the omission of inventories. Changes in business inventories have been procyclical and highly volatile, and a large part of those changes in every quarter has been in consumption goods. For instance, if inventory changes were divided between consumption and investment goods in the same proportion as are their average fractions of GNP (about three-fourths and one-fourth, respectively), then a standard business cycle model without explicit household production, such as that described at the end of Section 2, would imply a positive correlation between real GNP and the hours spent producing consumption goods. With the introduction of the BRW household production function in that environment, the correlation would presumably be substantially higher than the BRW model's 0.10. A numerical comparison is discussed in Section 6.

Another issue is whether the statistics that serve as a basis for fact (10) in Section 1 include consumer durables. Empirically, this aggregate shares many of the properties of business investment: it is highly volatile and strongly procyclical. Most model economies abstract from consumer durables and, one may argue, cannot hope to produce very procyclical hours in the consumption sector. In the BRW economy, consumer durables are, to a larger extent, the empirical counterpart to household capital, yet the hours spent producing them are not allocated to the consumption sector. For the BRW benchmark parameter values, household investment is strongly countercyclical. This fact leaves some doubt as to how much has been resolved with regard to accounting for the procyclical hours in the consumption sector.

We have discussed two approaches to modeling household production, each of which may have an important bearing on labor market fluctuations. The first emphasizes the use of nonmarket time to accumulate a durable, which is not necessarily tangible, in the home sector. The other approach is to think of nonmarket time as being combined with tangible market-produced durables to produce another consumption good. In either case, if these features can be shown to be of quantitative importance, they will help to account for a considerable part of output and, in particular, hours variability. Both cases share the characteristic, however, that the underpinnings in the form of measurements are still shaky.

Another model motivated by home production, or by the interaction between home and market production, is presented in Cho and Cooley (1994). Their idea is that a fixed cost is associated with each day when people work. This cost can be motivated, in part, by the notion that some home production, such as child care, needs to be replaced. Moreover, Cho and Cooley assume an externality in the sense that this cost depends on the aggregate number of workers. They then show that introducing this feature potentially can lead to a substantial increase in the volatility of hours relative to that of productivity. Strict calibration of the model to micro observations gives less encouraging results, however, and the authors conclude that the evident deviation shows that some important feature still is missing from their model environment.

4. High- and Low-Wage Earners

Theory

The model environments discussed so far assume that all workers are homogeneous. If there are substantial differences in cyclical behavior across demographic groups, then this assumption could bias considerably the estimate of the role of technology shocks. As fact (9) in Section 1 indicates, an example of such a difference is the greater hours volatility of the low-wage earners as compared with high-wage workers.

A simple way to introduce heterogeneity in this class of economies is to divide the model population into groups according to skills. Kydland (1984a) considers two equal-sized groups, where the first is better skilled for market production than the second. The resource constraint then can be written as

$$c_{1t} + c_{2t} + x_t \leq z_t f(h_t^e, k_t),$$

where c_{1t} and c_{2t} are consumption by the high- and low-skilled workers, respectively, and $h_t^e = \omega h_{1t} + h_{2t}$ is total labor input measured in quality-weighted units. If we divided the work force in two according to skills and used average per-person labor compensation to compute this weight, the numbers in Kydland (1984a) or in Ríos-Rull (1993b) suggest a value for ω of 2 or higher. The equilibria studied are those corresponding to the Pareto problem of maximizing the weighted utilities of the two groups (see Negishi 1960). The weights are calibrated to yield average hours spent in market activity comparable to those in the U.S. data when workers are divided into two similar-sized groups according to human capital.

The associated equilibrium is such that average consumption less labor income is greater for the low-wage earners than for those with high wages. Steady-state aggregate consumption has to satisfy the constraint

$$c_1 + c_2 = w_1 h_1 + w_2 h_2 + b_1 + b_2$$

where b_i stands for net nonlabor income for workers of type i. It consists of net capital income as well as any net transfers, τ_i, from the other skill group, that is, $\tau_1 = -\tau_2$. Thus, total steady-state nonlabor income, $b_1 + b_2$, is simply the real interest rate, r, multiplied by the capital stocks. For each skill group, b_i is defined so that $c_i = w_i h_i + b_i$. For the equilibriums reported in Kydland (1984a), the steady-state magnitude of b_2 exceeds that of b_1 by nearly 4 percent of GNP. Given what we know about relative capital income for the two groups, this means that some of b_2 has to be a transfer from the high-wage to the low-wage earners. In view of the amounts of such transfers that take place through the government as well as within the household, this magnitude does not appear unreasonable.

The paper compares the case in which ω, the wage of the skilled workers relative to that of the unskilled, is constant with the case in which this relative wage is allowed to move countercyclically by a small amount, say, with a standard deviation of .25 percent. A finding is that in the latter case, the standard deviation of aggregate unweighted hours rises by more than 20 percent relative to that of productivity. On the other hand, the fraction of output volatility accounted for by Solow residuals declines by about 10 percent. The model's cyclical relation between the relative wages of the skill groups is consistent with that reported by Reder (1962), although it would be interesting to have this empirical regularity investigated again using more recent, perhaps higher-frequency, data. Intuitively, it seems reasonable that the high-skilled workers are more adaptable in recessions, but that the skills of some, such as certain engineers, become obsolete in periods of rapid technological advance. There are, of course, numerous microstudies of the interaction in production of such categories as white- and blue-collar workers or workers with different levels of training.

This model economy introduces heterogeneity in a way that makes it tractable within a framework with infinitely lived agents. It illustrates a channel through which skill differences may have a bearing on the role of technology shocks for the cycle in general and for the implied volatility of hours of work in particular. A sharper assessment of this importance will depend on measurements such as those suggested in the preceding paragraph. Moreover, since the equilibria studied require transfers from the skilled to the unskilled of particular magnitudes, the reliability of the findings may depend on the presence of similar magnitudes in the actual economy. Although sizable transfers clearly do take place, their exact quantities are not easy to determine for the appropriate classification of people.

We have described an environment with the population divided into two different infinitely lived groups. It abstracts from life cycle behavior, for instance. Such behavior for mortal consumers can be built into an overlapping-generations framework. Until recently, however, it was difficult to see how one could calibrate such models while at the same time maintaining computational tractablity.

Economists' perspective on the feasibility of using aggregate equilibrium models with life cycle behavior now has changed, in part as a consequence of research that develops further the quantitative-theoretic approach pioneered for such models by Auerbach and Kotlikoff (1987).

In the past few years, Ríos-Rull has led the way in developing and using overlapping generations models in order to obtain quantitative answers to a variety of questions. Of particular interest in our context is his paper (1993b) on the interaction between household production and the choice of whether or not to become better skilled for market production. His paper is motivated to a large extent by fact (9) in Section 1. The driving forces are the presence of a home-produced good with poor market substitutes, and the possibility of choosing whether or not to acquire skills through schooling. In this model economy, meaningful heterogeneity arises even though everyone is born alike. The model accounts well for some of the key movements both cross-sectionally and secularly. Cyclically, however, a remaining discrepancy is that in contrast to the U.S. data, in the model, the hours volatility of the unskilled workers does not exceed that of the skilled.

Measurement

An alternative to modeling explicitly the heterogeneity of workers in terms of skills for market production is to take account of these differences in the measurements to which models are compared. Given the central role played by the production function for aggregate theory in general and for business cycle theory in particular, an important question is, How reliable are the available measurements of the labor input? For output and its components, the principles behind the measurements are those pioneered by Kuznets (1946a) and Stone (1947) for national income and products accounts. According to these principles, steady-state or base-year prices are used to weight the different goods being summed up to form the aggregate real quantities. A similar approach is used for the capital stock. The difficulties for capital are perhaps even more severe, as the capital controversy between the two Cambridges illustrated. It is clear, however, that while Cambridge, England, was right in theory, Cambridge, U.S., prevailed in practice. The capital stock measurements have contributed to the important developments and insights in growth theory in the past thirty or forty years (see Solow 1970). In contrast, the same NIPA principles typically have not been applied to the measurement of the labor input. Standard practice is to give equal weight to the hours of all workers, including people with dramatically different stocks of human capital. If the cyclical behavior of these workers differs widely, then the standard procedure of simply adding up the hours may produce a poor measure of the labor input.

From the viewpoint of a theory in which the production function is a central feature, it is natural to think of the labor input in efficiency units. One would then like to weight the hours of different individuals by their relative base-year prices in the same way that other NIPA quantity data are constructed. The urgency of this task is demonstrated in Kydland (1984a). Using data from the Panel Study of Income Dynamics (PSID) on about 1000 men over the age of 30, which presumably is the least volatile major category of the labor force, and dividing the subjects into five nearly equal groups according to years of schooling, he estimates that over the eleven-year period of the sample, those with the least formal education changed their annual hours on the average by about 100 hours more for each percentage point change in the unemployment rate than did those with the most formal education.

A more detailed study of this measurement issue is reported in Kydland and Prescott (1993). Using a sample from the PSID of nearly 5,000 people consisting of all major demographic groups, they compared the cyclical behavior of two alternative measures of the labor input as follows. Let N_t be the number of people in the population in year t, and let h_{it} be person i's hours of work in that year. The standard measure is simply to add up, in each period, the hours across all workers: $H_t = \sum_i h_{it}$. Another measure is to multiply the hours of each individual by relative human capital weights that do not change cyclically: $L_t = \sum_i \phi_i h_{it}$. For the sample period, there was little secular change in average real compensation per hour. Therefore, a fixed relative weight for person i was constructed by dividing his or her total real labor earnings over all the years by total hours worked in those same years; that is, $\phi_i = \sum_t e_{it} / \sum_t h_{it}$, where e_{it} is real labor earnings of individual i in year t, and the summations are over all the years of the sample period for which observations for that person were available. This measure of the worker's "normal" efficiency is used in every period as the stand-in for his or her relative efficiency in market production.

The finding is that if the sample were representative for the entire population, the standard measure of labor input would overstate the labor input volatility by about 40 percent. This is a large number from the standpoint of business cycle theory. Another finding is that the real hourly compensation of the quality-adjusted labor input is more procyclical than the corresponding average compensation per unweighted hour.

5. Hours versus Employment Behavior

Indivisible Labor

An important development in the understanding of hours volatility was the article by Hansen (1985). In the models discussed so far, all the variability in hours takes place in the form of changes in hours per worker. Hansen went to the opposite extreme. In his environment, all the labor-input volatility takes the form of employment changes. There is a fixed cost of working, with the implication that everyone works either zero hours or some positive number h_1.

As an illustration, assume that the utility function is logarithmic (corresponding to $\sigma = 1$ above):

$$u(c_t, \ell_t) = \log c_t + \alpha \log \ell_t$$

To get around the nonconvexity implied by the binary choice of hours of work, assume instead that individuals choose the probability π_t of working. In other words, a contract to work h_1 hours with probability π_t and 0 hours with probability $1 - \pi_t$ is traded between workers and firms. This means that workers get paid whether they work or not. (Hansen discusses in an appendix the interpretation in terms of insurance).

Individuals are identical ex ante, but the ex post outcome in every period depends on the lottery. Expected utility is

$$U(c_t, \ell_t) = \pi_t[\log c_t + \alpha \log(1 - h_1)] + (1 - \pi_t)(\log c_t + \alpha \log 1)$$

$$= \log c_t + \alpha \pi_t \log(1 - h_1).$$

Per capita hours worked are simply $h_t = \pi_t h_1 = 1 - \ell_t$, implying that $\pi_t = (1 - \ell_t)/h_1$. Substituting this expression for π_t into the utility function, we obtain the representative individual's utility function:

$$U(c_t, \ell_t) = \log c_t - \frac{\alpha \log(1 - h_1)}{h_1} \ell_t + \text{constant}.$$

In other words, the planner's utility function is linear in ℓ_t. Thus, the startling finding is that the intertemporal elasticity of substitution in the aggregate can be very large even though, as a property of each individual's utility function, this elasticity has the much smaller value associated with the logarithmic utility function. On the basis of this model economy, Hansen found that Solow residuals could produce business cycles even more volatile than those observed in the postwar U.S. economy.

With the extreme assumption that the employment margin is where all the hours variability takes place, the implied estimate naturally overstates the role of technology shocks for the cycle. An economy that permits variation along both margins—employment and hours per worker—presumably would yield an estimate somewhere in between those of Hansen's model and those of a model with only hours-per-worker variation. Such an estimate is provided in Kydland and Prescott (1991).

Two Margins

The goal here is to construct a business cycle model in which there is variation in labor input along both the hours-per-worker margin and the employment margin. In order to provide a credible estimate of the role of technology shocks, this model ought to mimic to a reasonable degree facts (2) and (4) in the list in Section 1.

In this economy, the obvious analogue of the standard production function is $z_t f(h_t n_t, k_t)$, where n_t is the number of workers and h_t is hours per worker. This production function implies that the marginal product of labor input is the same no matter which of the two forms the change takes. A better assumption is that a fixed number of workers are assigned to each machine or, more generally, to each unit of capital input. Adding workers to a fixed stock of capital then reduces the marginal product in the usual way, while letting the existing workers operate the machines longer hours would, to a reasonable approximation, increase output in the same proportion; the production function is $z_t h_t f(n_t, k_t)$.

Another issue is how to deal with the labor indivisibility analogous to that in Hansen's economy. The economy still is inhabited by a large number of ex ante identical individuals, although some will not work ex post in every period. Some preliminary insight can be gained from a related one-period example from Hornstein and Prescott (1993).

Each agent is endowed with $\bar{k} > 0$ units of capital. Preferences with respect to consumption-work pairs, (c, h), are represented by their expected utility, $E[u(c, h)]$, where h is the fraction of time allocated to market activity. For simplicity, we assume that $s = (c, h, k)$ is a member of $S = C \times H \times K$, where C, H, and K are finite sets. In practice, these sets could be constructed as a grid of values in the relevant range for each of the variables. For each individual, the commodity bundle is interpreted as a contract that obliges him or her to provide k units of capital and h units of time, for which he or she receives c units of the consumption good. The probability of an event $s = (c, h, k)$ is x_s.

In the business sector, add the finite set N, and let $A = H \times K \times N$ with elements of the type $a = (h, k, n)$. The choice is how many plants z_a to operate for h hours using k units of capital and n workers. An allocation satisfies the resource constraints if

$$\sum_s cx_s - \sum_a hf(n, k)z_a \leq 0,$$

$$-\sum_s kx_s + \sum_a kz_a \leq 0,$$

and

$$-\sum_{c,k} x_s + \sum_{k,n} nz_a \leq 0 \quad \text{for all } h \in H.$$

The first constraint says that the amount consumed is less than or equal to the quantity produced. According to the second constraint, the quantity of capital used in production cannot exceed the quantity available. The last constraints (one for each value of h) say that the number of people working in plants that are operated h hours does not exceed the number of people working h hours.

For this economy, as shown by Hornstein and Prescott (1993), the competitive equilibrium can be obtained by solving a stand-in Pareto problem. This problem is a linear programming (LP) problem with the x_s as variables:

$$\max_{x \geq 0} \sum_s u(c, h) x_s$$

$$\text{s.t.} \quad \sum_s x_s = 1$$

$$\sum_s [c - f(1, k)h] x_s \leq 0$$

$$\sum_s k x_s \leq \bar{k}.$$

A general property of the solution to an LP problem with three constraints is that at most three variables are positive. That is, there are no more than three combinations of $s = (c, h, k)$ such that $x_s > 0$.

Now consider the utility and production functions given by (3) and (2), respectively, with standard parameter values. It turns out that when the grids of the points in S are made successively finer, the solutions to the corresponding planner's problems tend to cluster in such a way that at least two of the points that receive positive x_s get closer and closer. As Hornstein and Prescott (1993) show, this pattern reflects the property that when the sets C, H, and K contain infinitely many points (S is a subset of $\mathbb{R}_+^3$), then the solution to the LP problem implies mass on either two points or only one point depending on the parameter values for the utility and production functions.

When the equilibrium consumption vector places mass on only one point ($x_s = 1$ for some $s = s_1$), it is of the form $s_1 = (c_1, h_1, k_1)$. Since $h_1 > 0$, everyone works the same number of hours. When there is mass on two points, s_0 and s_1, then the value of h_0 in s_0 is zero. Thus, some fraction of people work h_1 hours and receive consumption c_1, while for everyone else h_0 is zero and consumption is c_0.

Business Cycle Model

We shall now embed an analogous structure within a fully dynamic business cycle model. This model will be calibrated to correspond to that with mass on two points. The variable n_t will be the fraction of people who work in period t. A person working h hours and using k units of capital produces $zhk^{1-\theta}$ units of some intermediate good. This good, along with inventory services, y, is an input to a CES production function.

For this economy, the aggregate resource constraint in period t is

$$c_t + x_t + m_t \leq [(1 - \gamma)(z_t h_t n_t^{\theta} k_t^{1-\theta})^{-\nu} + \gamma y_t^{-\nu}]^{-1/\nu} \tag{7}$$

where m_t is the aggregate cost of moving people between the market and non-market sectors. This cost will be approximated by a quadratic function, $m_t =$

$\mu(n_t - n_{t-1})^2$. As suggested by Kydland and Prescott (1991), this specification is a stand-in for an environment in which there is a distribution of moving costs across the population, and those with the smallest cost are moved first. The moving-cost distribution is independent over time. This formulation gives rise to labor hoarding in this economy.

The cost of getting to work every day may also play a role. Most of that cost probably is in the form of time that neither is enjoyed as leisure nor contributes as an input in the production of goods. Such a cost is allowed for in the original model. Although it affects the calibration somewhat, it makes little difference to the cyclical properties, and we ignore it here.

As in Section 2, the inventory stock is included as an input. This assumption is made partly for analytic reasons. One can then ignoore the nonnegativity constraint for inventories and use a linear-quadratic economy. The assumption that larger inventories economize on the other two inputs can be justified in several ways. For example, by making longer production runs and thus holding larger inventories on the average, firms reduce equipment downtime associated with shifting from producing one good to producing another. For this economy, the observed procyclical behavior of the aggregate inventory stock is mimicked reasonably well.

The remainder of the model specification is analogous to that in Section 2. The laws of motion for finished and unfinished capital stocks are given by (4) and (5), and total investment is given by (6). Finally, we use the law of motion given by (1) for the technology level.

An implication analogous to that in Hornstein and Prescott (1993) is that the equilibrium can be computed by solving a social planner's problem:

$$\max E \sum_{t=0}^{\infty} \beta^t [n_t u(c_{1t}, 1 - h_t) + (1 - n_t)u(c_{0t}, 1)]$$

$$\text{s.t.} \quad c_t = n_t c_{1t} + (1 - n_t)c_{0t}$$

and to the constraints just mentioned. The utility function, u, is the standard one given by (3), where the elasticity of substitution already has been calibrated to equal one for reasons discussed in Section 2.

Steady State and Calibration

The steady state for this economy is its deterministic rest point, that is, the point resulting when the variance of the shock is zero. The steady state is important for two reasons. First, since this highly nonlinear model will be represented by a quadratic approximation, the steady state represents the point about which this approximation is made. More important, however, the properties of the steady state for the model economy correspond to analogous long-run relations in the actual economy that in many cases can be measured with high signal-to-noise ratios and are used in the calibration.

Some relations do not require much analysis of the model. Examples are NIPA relations for the model environment. Without loss of generality, we choose units such that steady-state output is one. Steady-state consumption and investment shares of GNP are set to 0.75 and 0.25, respectively. For the United States in the postwar period, the inventory stock has been about a quarter of annual GNP. Thus, we set $y = 1$. Steady-state n corresponds to the long-run fraction of the working-age population who actually work and is taken to be 0.75, while h, the steady-state fraction of time spent working, conditional on being in the market sector, is 0.40. As an average of the entire population of the model economy, then, the time spent in market activity is 0.30, or just over thirty hours per week. This is a standard magnitude for this relation and in line with the measurements by Ghez and Becker (1975).

The elasticities of substitution between consumption and leisure in utility and between capital and labor in production have been discussed already. Both equal one. There is less clear-cut evidence on which to base the value of the elasticity $1/(1 + \nu)$ between inventories and the composite input. It is probably quite small, and ν is therefore probably substantially larger than zero. We choose $\nu = 3$. If the question dictates it, one should of course investigate the robustness of the answer to this choice.

A value for J of 3 (quarters) is a reasonable compromise. Some capital, of course, takes more time, and some less, to build. There is little evidence that the average time to build varies over the cycle. We assume that the resources needed are used up evenly throughout the construction period, that is, $\phi_j = 1/J$ for all j. The evidence is that the yearly depreciation rate is in the range of 8–10 percent. Since we assume no growth, we shall use the upper end of this range and assume that $\delta = 0.025$. This value, along with an investment share of output of 0.25, corresponds to a yearly capital/output ratio of 2.5 ($k = 10$). Also, with no growth, the steady-state real interest rate, r, equals $(1 - \beta)/\beta$. A value for r of 0.01 per quarter implies that β is approximately 0.99.

Before we consider the remaining parameter values, we need to derive the steady-state implications of equilibrium behavior for the model environment. For this purpose it is convenient to work with the decentralized problems of the household and of the firm separately. (For a discussion of decentralization of the standard growth model, see Chapter 1 of this volume.) We think of firms as being owned by the households, and the input factors as being rented or hired from these same households. For either problem, we initially take hours per period, h, as given. The remaining decision variables for the firm, then, are n, k, and y, and those for the household are c_0, c_1, and n. In the end, we determine h from the equilibrium condition that the marginal product of working h hours equals the negative of the ratio of marginal utilities with respect to hours and consumption.

The Firm's Problem

The firm is endowed with a technology whereby it uses labor, capital, and inventories as inputs to produce output of goods and services. Defining q_k and q_y to be the rental prices of capital and inventories, respectively, and $w_h = wh$ to be a worker's real earnings per period conditional on working h hours, the firm maximizes in every period

$$F(zhn^\theta k^{1-\theta}, y) - q_k k - q_y y - w_h n.$$

In the steady state, the equilibrium q_y equals r and, with no additional time to build (that is, with $J = 1$), the rental price of capital would be $r + \delta$. For multiple-period construction ($J > 1$), however, the real price, p_k, of newly produced capital exceeds one because resources are tied up during the construction period. Defining the prices of s_j, the capital being built, to be p_j, for $j = 1, \ldots, J - 1$, we must have $p_{J-1} = \phi_J$. The other prices are determined recursively as

$$p_{j-1} = (1 + r)p_j + \phi_j, \qquad j = 2, \ldots, J - 1.$$

The equilibrium steady-state price of a unit of productive capital, then, is

$$p_k = \sum_{j=1}^{J} \phi_j (1 + r)^{j-1},$$

implying a steady-state rental price of $q_k = (r + \delta)p_k$.

Units in which to measure output, such that its steady-state quantity is one, are chosen by selecting the average z appropriately. To turn to the inventory decision, the condition $F_y = q_y$ yields

$$y = q_y y^{\nu+1}$$

Similarly, from the condition $F_k = q_k$ one obtains

$$1 - \theta = q_k k/(1 - \gamma y^{-\nu}) = q_k k/(1 - ry).$$

That is, the parameter $1 - \theta$ equals the capital share of income net of the income share of the inventory input. Thus, both γ and θ are quantified from relations between variables or parameters whose values we already have determined. In particular, γ equals 0.01 (implying that 1 percent of the model's national income can be attributed to inventories), and θ is approximately equal to 0.64. Finally, the wage rate w, which is a parameter of the household's problem, is implied by $w_h = wh = F_n$.

The Household's Problem

The household's problem treats the capital income parametrically. Steady-state net capital income is

$$b = q_y y + (q_k - \delta)k,$$

which also can be written as

$$b = ry + rp_k k + rp_1 \delta k + rp_2 \delta k,$$

that is, the interest rate times each of the values of the four capital stocks. Given this steady-state net capital income, the household maximizes discounted utility subject to an infinite-period budget constraint. The resulting values of the variables c_{0t}, c_{1t}, n_t and h_t clearly are date independent. Consequently, we can drop the time subscripts. The steady-state problem of the household then can be written as

$$\max (1 - n)u(c_0, 1) + n \cdot u(c_1, 1 - h)$$

$$\text{s.t.} \quad (1 - n)c_0 + nc_1 \leq whn + b.$$

Maximization yields first-order conditions with respect to the variables c_0, c_1, and n. Moreover, hours per worker, h, has to satisfy the condition $-u_h/u_{c_1} = F_h$. These four conditions and the budget constraint determine the Lagrange multiplier along with four additional unknowns. These four will be α and σ from the utility function, and c_0 and c_1. The resulting values are $\alpha = 0.29$, $\sigma = 2.41$, $c_0 = 0.57$, and $c_1 = 0.81$. We note that in the steady state, those who work consume about 40 percent more than do those who are not in the market sector.

The value of σ warrants a comment. This value is larger than the value of 2.0 used in Kydland and Prescott (1991) and results mainly from a lower calibrated value of h, namely, 0.40 rather than 0.44. With a total time allocation of about 100 hours per week, the value of 0.44 probably was a little too high. It may be easier to think about σ in relation to the empirical finance literature if we multiply $1 - \sigma$ by α, thus obtaining the overall exponent on c in the utility function. This exponent (whose value here is -0.4) should be comparable conceptually to what is used in finance studies that abstract from the time allocation decision, so that the implied degree of relative risk aversion is in the ballpark of what those studies find.

6. Cyclical Properties of Model Economies

The purpose of this section is to compare cyclical properties of four of the economies that we have discussed:

1) a homogeneous-worker economy similar to that in Kydland and Prescott (1982), but with standard utility function;

2) as in economy 1, but with part of nonmarket time used to produce a durable household good;

3) as in economy 1, but including a household technology for using capital and labor as inputs to producing consumption goods (similar to the BRW model); and

4) as in economy 1, but with two margins for changing the labor input, as described in Section 5.

All four environments include inventories in the same ratio to GNP. It takes three quarters to build new productive capital. Other sources of calibration that are common to these economies also are assigned the same values. These magnitudes are presented and motivated in the preceding section.

The differences in calibration across economies are as follows. In economies 1, 2, and 3, the fraction of time devoted to market activity is 0.3, as in section 5, but all in the form of h, since by assumption n is one. In economy 2, the magnitude of μ_0 is set equal to 0.60, which gives slightly more weight to current leisure in the utility function than in Kydland and Prescott (1982). The depreciation rate η for household capital equals 0.10. In economy 3, the parameters of the aggregator function for consumption in the utility function and those of the household technology are assigned the same values as in the BRW model. In other respects, the economy is analogous to economy 1. For example, it includes the same curvature parameter σ, which is greater than that used by Benhabib, Rogerson, and Wright (1991), who employ a logarithmic utility function.

The statistics on which we focus, in addition to output and its two main components, are those corresponding to the aggregates listed in Table 5.1. They are summarized in Table 5.2, borrowing the format in BRW. The notation h_c represents the hours spent producing consumption goods in the market economy, while c_m denotes consumption goods produced in the market economy. This distinction is relevant only for economy 3.

In the simplest version of the growth model, as modified in Section 2, the standard deviation of cyclical output is 1.25 percent. Introducing household capital produced solely by leisure raises the figure to 1.39 percent. The increase in hours volatility is substantially greater, however, while productivity volatility is lower, so that for economy 2, hours volatility actually is larger than that for productivity.

The household technology shock evidently has the potential to account for a substantial fraction of the business cycle. The comparison of economy 3 with economy 1, where the introduction of the household technology is the only difference, indicates a rise in output volatility from 1.25 to 1.60 percent. Moreover, productivity becomes substantially less correlated with the cycle.

The introduction of a distinction between employment and hours-per-worker variation, along with the modified production function in (7), raises the standard deviation of output from 1.25 to 1.55 percent. The latter figure was produced with

Table 5.2
Statistical Properties of Model Economies

	c_m	i	h_m	n	$GNP/h_m n$	h_c
			$x =:$			
			Model Economy 1: std(GNP) = 1.25			
std(x)/std(GNP)	.40	2.49	.41		.60	
Corr.(x,GNP)	.97	0.95	.99		.99	
			Model Economy 2: std(GNP) = 1.39			
std(x)/std(GNP)	.37	2.57	.53		.49	
Corr.(x,GNP)	.95	0.95	.98		.98	
			Model Economy 3: std(GNP) = 1.60			
std(x)/std(GNP)	.66	2.59	.69		.46	.82
Corr.(x,GNP)	.73	0.90	.91		.79	.48
			Model Economy 4: std(GNP) = 1.55			
std(x)/std(GNP)	.43	2.61	.20	.46	.47	.28
Corr.(x,GNP)	.98	0.95	.75	.86	.97	.17

the same value of the standard deviation of innovations to technology as in the other experiments. Allowing for variable capacity utilization, however, means that the standard expression for determining the Solow residuals no longer is theoretically correct. A way of checking the size of the bias is to use the standard method in the model economy to see if the variance estimate is different from the variance of ϵ (0.0076^2) used as input to the experiments. The resulting bias suggests that the estimate of the standard deviation for economy 4 should be reduced from 1.55 to 1.49.

For economies 3 and 4, we have computed the statistics for h_c, hours devoted to the production of consumption goods. This variable, which in part motivated the BRW model, no longer has a straightforward definition because of the presence of inventory changes. A considerable fraction of these changes presumably are in the form of consumption goods. The assumption made in Table 5.2 is that in every period the fraction of inventory change that is in the form of consumption goods is the same as that in final sales. This is probably a conservative assumption.

Then even economy 4 implies procyclical h_c, indeed with a greater correlation coefficient with cyclical GNP than in the BRW model. But for the modified BRW economy, our economy 3, this correlation coefficient is as high as 0.48. Had the model economy included market-produced consumer durables in a way implying that they were procyclical as in the data, then an even larger correlation coefficient presumably would result. Thus, it seems safe to say that fact 10 in the list in Section 1 no longer can be regarded as a fact from which the theory deviates.

7. On-the-Job Learning

In constructing a model environment with heterogeneous workers, Kydland (1984a) assumes that the division of human capital between the two groups is given. That assumption precludes consideration of issues that relate to the timing of the accumulation of human capital over the cycle. As Mincer (1962, S73) concludes, "Investment in on-the-job training is a very large component of total investment in education in the United States economy." Human capital of this form thus is large enough that abstracting from its accumulation when evaluating the role of technology shocks, one risks omitting a potentially important propagation mechanism. One may guess a priori that introducing on-the-job training will change the cyclical properties of several aggregates, perhaps of labor input and productivity variables in particular. The main question, however, is to what extent the estimate of the cyclical role of technology shocks is affected.

An example of a tractable specification is to assume that workers enter the labor force at the lowest efficiency level and accumulate skills through the process of learning for I periods. Let e_{it}, $i = 0, \ldots, I$, be the number of workers at efficiency level i at time t, where e_{0t} represents the bottom of the skill distribution. Consider the following laws of motion:

$$e_{i+1,t+1} = (1 - \eta)e_{it}, \qquad i = 0, \ldots, I - 2,$$

and

$$e_{I,t+1} = (1 - \eta)(e_{I-1,t} + e_{It}).$$

In other words, a fraction η of the workers at each level lose their previously accumulated skills or "die." In the steady state, a corresponding number reenter at the inexperienced level. The total number of workers in period t is $n_t = \sum_{i=0}^{I} e_{it}$. If the relative efficiencies are $\pi_0 < \pi_1 < \cdots < \pi_I$, where we normalize π_0 to one, then the corresponding quality-adjusted number is $e_t = \sum_{i=0}^{I} \pi_i e_{it}$. This variable replaces n_t in the production function.

The rest of the model is as in Section 5. Indeed, that economy is a special case (for $\Delta \pi = 0$) of the one considered here. With on-the-job learning, I state variables are added. With the computational method used, computer time increases a little, but there is no practical difficulty in setting up the computational experiments.

Assume that the absolute increments to π_i are equal at all stages, that is, $\Delta\pi_i = \pi_i - \pi_{i-1}$ are the same for all i. This means, of course, that the percentage increases get smaller at each higher stage. We choose $I = 8$ and $\Delta\pi = 0.05$, so that the most highly skilled workers are 40 percent more productive than those just entering the market sector. This is a compromise. Measurements probably would indicate steeper growth of efficiency at the initial stages and flatter growth at the later ones, with growth of some magnitude continuing after two years. The attrition rate, η, is set equal to 0.08 per quarter. Consequently, in the steady state, about half of the model's working population is in the highest-earning group.

The comovements of the various aggregates with GNP and most of the relative volatilities are quite similar to those for the case of $\Delta\pi = 0$. The main difference is that the standard deviation of output drops by 0.10; in other words, Solow residuals account for a slightly smaller fraction of the business cycle.

It has been suggested that with human capital, different measurements are needed for the Solow residuals. This is not necessarily so. The situation is analogous to that in Kydland and Prescott (1991), where the authors permit variation in the number of hours a plant is operated, while the measurements of Solow residuals do not assume this. The magnitudes of the technology shocks going into the model are known. One can then measure the shocks in the model in the same way that they are measured in the data and estimate the magnitude of the bias. In the Kydland and Prescott (1991) study, this procedure led to a slight reduction in the estimate of the fraction of the output variance accounted for.

8. Conclusion

This chapter has presented variants of what can be regarded as the dominant framework of shared knowledge in aggregate economics. It is a framework within which one can organize and interpret NIPA data. The particular choice of model environment within this framework, of course, depends on the question to be addressed. The question of the role of shocks to aggregate production technology for the business cycle has received considerable attention in the past ten years. In this chapter we have focused on the extent to which the estimate of this role depends on the model specification as it relates to the labor market in particular. To some extent, the different environments represent a progression over time in our understanding of the role of the labor input.

As we have seen, in spite of using an identical stochastic process for the impulse—the technology shock in the market sector—in each of the economies, the resulting volatility of GNP across models can be quite different. In other words, the roles of the propagation mechanisms are of central importance. In choosing models to consider, we have focused on the extent to which they represent different specifications of features that affect aggregate behavior as reflected more or less directly in the labor market.

In the initial development and use of this framework, some features of the workings of the labor market in the U.S. data, especially the volatility of aggregate hours of work and the correlation between hours and productivity, were regarded as important deviations relative to theory. As theory and measurements have progressed, however, the status of these features as deviations has diminished. Better abstractions have been developed, for instance, to indicate that a great deal of aggregate intertemporal substitution of hours is what the theory predicts. From a measurement standpoint, evidence suggests that the volatility of the labor input, which one would like to measure by weighting the hours of different workers according to their normal efficiency, is considerably less than the unweighted hours variability. The high correlation between hours and productivity, of course, is to be expected in environments with only technology shocks as a source of impulse. As illustrated in the model with shocks to household production added, the presence of other impulses will reduce that correlation. This has also been demonstrated with government shocks as the additional impulse (Christiano and Eichenbaum 1992).

Among other things, we have discussed ways in which the propagation of shocks via the labor market is affected through interaction of the business and household production. It is probably fair to say that we know mainly about the *potential* for household production to play a sizable role. A clearer answer about its actual role, however, will have to await measurements that have not yet been carried out. This is an important area of future research. Another area is consideration of whether the findings using environments with adjustment along both the intensive and extensive margins are affected by the degree of insurance assumed in those models.

Many recent contributions to the understanding of the labor market and the cycle have been omitted from this overview. For example, while Hansen (1985) shows that intertemporal substitution in the aggregate may be much larger than that reflected in individuals' preferences, Smith (1989) finds a tendency in the same direction due to asymmetric information between workers and firms about the workers' skills. We did not focus on the countercyclical labor share of national income observed in the data. Ways of accounting for this fact are studied in Danthine and Donaldson (1990), who use a contracting set-up, and in Gomme and Greenwood (1993).

It may be surprising to some that we make few references to micro labor studies, given that such studies are potential sources of calibration. The main reason is that much of that literature has been occupied by the goal of measuring such things as supply and demand elasticities for labor. With modern general equilibrium language, measurements of such elasticities do not map naturally into model parameters. Moreover, to the extent that one can interpret low elasticities as evidence of limited willingness, according to individual preferences, to substitute intertemporally, the insight from Hansen's (1985) economy suggests that this has little or no relevance to aggregate questions.

We have already listed some interesting measurement issues that remain for future research. On the theory side, many features of the labor market have received little attention and also represent interesting research areas for the future. Examples are the role of the differences of skills across workers for market production, the role of variation in capacity utilization and its implications for the aggregate production function, and the role of less than perfect insurance for workers against shocks.

Note

The National Science Foundation and the Federal Reserve Bank of Cleveland has provided research support. Christian Zimmermann assisted with the computational experiments.

Chapter 6
Household Production in
Real Business Cycle Theory

Jeremy Greenwood, Richard
Rogerson, and Randall Wright

1. Introduction

A central objective of the real business cycle research program is to construct
models consistent with observed fluctuations in aggregate economic variables.
These models typically assume that all economic activity takes place in the market.
The thesis of this chapter is that for some purposes, it is useful to also explicitly
consider nonmarket activity—or *household production*.

As a factual matter, the household sector is sizable, both in terms of the labor
and capital inputs used in home production and in terms of home-produced output.
Consider the following evidence for the U.S. economy:

> **1)** Studies such as the Michigan Time Use Survey indicate that a typical
> married couple allocates about 25 percent of its discretionary time to work
> in household production activities, including cooking, cleaning, child care
> and so on; by comparison, the typical couple spends about 33 percent of its
> discretionary time working for paid compensation (see Hill [1984] or Juster
> and Stafford [1991] for descriptions of the time use data).
>
> **2)** The postwar national income and product accounts indicate that invest-
> ment in household capital, defined as purchases of consumer durables and
> residential structures, actually exceeds investment in market capital, defined
> as purchases of producer durables and nonresidential structures, by about
> 15 percent (see Section 3 for details concerning the data and more precise
> calculations).
>
> **3)** Attempts to measure the value of the output of home production come up
> with numbers between 20 and 50 percent of the value of measured market
> GNP (see the survey by Eisner [1988]).

Despite these facts, household production has only recently been incorporated
into macro models. It has, however, been part of the standard paradigm in labor
economics for some time (fundamental references include Becker [1965], Pollak and Wachter [1975], and Gronau [1977, 1986]. In his presidential address

to the American Economic Association, Becker (1988) advocated the introduction of home production into macroeconomics, and several subsequent papers have pursued this. Ríos-Rull (1993b) includes home production in a dynamic general equilibrium model and analyzes life cycle, business cycle, and cross-sectional wage behavior. Nosal, Rogerson, and Wright (1992) show that adding home production to two models of the labor market can affect the interpretation of unemployment and underemployment. Benhabib, Rogerson, and Wright (1991) and Greenwood and Hercowitz (1991) explicitly incorporate household sectors into real business cycle theory. McGrattan, Rogerson and Wright (1992) and Fisher (1992) generalize these models and estimate their structural parameters econometrically. Fung (1992) introduces money into a home production model.

This research demonstrates that there can be interesting interactions between household and market activity. In this chapter, we try to communicate and extend some of the findings in these papers. Our starting point is the basic neoclassical growth model, modified to include a home production function that transforms household labor and capital into home-produced output, just as the usual production function transforms market labor and capital into market output. Although it entails a relatively minor increase in complexity, the addition of a household sector implies a much richer model. For example, with home production, agents must allocate their time among leisure, market work, and home work, rather than simply between leisure and labor, as in the standard model. Similarly, they must allocate output between consumption, investment in market capital, and investment in household capital, rather than simply between consumption and investment. This increase in generality can be significant for the analysis of both long-run and business cycle issues.

We calibrate the model to match certain key first moments in the data, including the amount of time and capital allocated to both market and household activity. One finding that emerges from this exercise is that models with household production can more easily reconcile the evidence on the capital stock, labor's share of income, and taxation. We then simulate several alternative specifications of the model. The standard real business cycle model can be nested within our framework, in the sense that one can choose parameter values so that Hansen's (1985) model is a special case. For the parameter values that emerge from our calibration, however, the home production model does a better job than the standard model of accounting for the following aspects of the data:

1) the volatility of output;

2) the relative volatilities of output, consumption, investment, and hours;

3) the correlation between hours and productivity; and

4) the correlation between the investments in home and market capital.

The rest of the paper is organized as follows. In Section 2, we lay out a household's decision problem in a dynamic model with home production, and discuss how explicitly incorporating the household sector can make a difference in a qualitative sense. In Section 3, we embed this decision problem into a general equilibrium setting, and introduce functional forms and parameter values. In Section 4, we report the results of simulating alternative specifications of the model and compare them with the data. In Section 5, we present an extension of the analysis designed to better capture certain long-run growth facts. Some concluding remarks are contained in Section 6. The basic message is that household production models perform reasonably well (that is, better than models without home production) along many dimensions, although there remain some deviations between facts and theory that seem worthy of further investigation.

2. The Household Problem

Consider a decisionmaker with preferences described by

$$U = \sum_{t=0}^{\infty} \beta^t u(c_{Mt}, c_{Ht}, h_{Mt}, h_{Ht}), \qquad (1)$$

where $\beta \in (0, 1)$ is the discount factor. The instantaneous utility function, u, is defined over four arguments at each date: c_{Mt} is consumption of a market-produced commodity, c_{Ht} is consumption of a home produced commodity, h_{Mt} is labor time spent in market work, and h_{Ht} is labor time spent in home work. We normalize the total amount of discretionary time available in a period to unity, and define leisure to be the time remaining after market and home work: $\ell_t = 1 - h_{Mt} - h_{Ht}$. All variables are constrained to be nonnegative, although we suppress these constraints in what follows. We assume that u is continuously differentiable and concave, and that $u_1 > 0$, $u_2 > 0$, $u_3 < 0$, and $u_4 < 0$.[1]

At each date, the individual is subject to a market budget constraint that allocates total income between three uses: the purchase of the market consumption good, the purchase of household capital, and the purchase of market capital. Capital goods purchased in one period are brought forward and become usable in the next period. Household capital, k_{Ht}, is used in home production, whereas business capital, k_{Mt}, is rented to firms and used in market production. If δ_M and δ_H are the depreciation rates on the two types of capital, w_t is the wage rate, and r_t is the rental rate on market capital, then (ignoring taxation, for now) the budget constraint can be written as

$$c_{Mt} + k_{Mt+1} + k_{Ht+1} = w_t h_{Mt} + r_t k_{Mt} + (1 - \delta_M)k_{Mt} + (1 - \delta_H)k_{Ht}. \qquad (2)$$

The relative prices of the consumption and two capital goods equal unity, as we assume they can be transformed back and forth freely at a point in time.

The individual is also subject to the home production constraint at each date:

$$c_{Ht} = g(h_{Ht}, k_{Ht}, z_{Ht}). \tag{3}$$

The home production function, g, yields consumption of the home good as a function of the time spent in home work and the household capital brought into the period, plus a stochastic term, z_{Ht}, representing technological change. We assume that g is increasing and concave in labor and capital. Note that (3) implies that there are no uses for home-produced output other than consumption—it cannot be sold or transformed into capital, for example, the way that market-produced output can. This is a key asymmetry between the market and home sectors: only the former can produce capital.[2]

We now define a reduced-form utility function, by substituting the home production constraint into the momentary utility function and maximizing with respect to time spent in home work, taking the values of the other variables as given:

$$V(c_M, h_M, k_H, z_H) \equiv \max_{h_H} u[c_M, g(h_H, k_H, z_H), h_M, h_H]. \tag{4}$$

It is straightforward to show that the reduced-form utility function is continuous, increasing in c_M and k_H, decreasing in h_M, and concave in its first three arguments. Hence, V defines a well-behaved preference ordering over (c_M, h_M, k_H), conditional on z_H.

Now consider the following two individual decision problems:

$$\max \sum_{t=0}^{\infty} \beta^t u(c_{Mt}, c_{Ht}, h_{Mt}, h_{Ht})$$

$$\text{s.t.} \quad (2) \text{ and } (3); \tag{5}$$

and

$$\max \sum_{t=0}^{\infty} \beta^t V(c_{Mt}, h_{Mt}, k_{Ht}, z_{Ht})$$

$$\text{s.t.} \quad (2). \tag{6}$$

Given the definition of V, problems (5) and (6) yield identical solutions for the variables c_{Mt}, h_{Mt}, k_{Ht}, and k_{Mt}. This implies the following observational equivalence result: for any model with momentary utility function u and home production function g, there is an alternative model with utility function V that makes no explicit reference to home production, except that k_{Ht} enters V directly, and delivers identical predictions for all variables that are traded in the market.[3]

One can conclude from this that there is nothing we can do with a home production model, in terms of explaining market quantities, that cannot be done, in principle, with a model that does not explicitly include home production. In practice, however, the home production approach provides us with direction and discipline in the specification of functional forms and parameter values, something that is obviously critical in the quantitative-theoretic real business cycle framework. Moreover, the interpretation of the results can hinge on whether we explicitly include home production, as can be seen from the following discussion.

Suppose that the momentary utility function is $u = \log(C) + A \cdot \log(\ell)$, where $C = C(c_M, c_H)$ is a composite of the two consumption goods and $\ell = 1 - h_M - h_H$ is leisure. In the following cases, the reduced-form utility function can be obtained analytically.

Case 1: $C = c_M + c_H$ and $g = a_0 k_H + a_1 h_H$ implies

$$V = \log[c_M + a_0 k_H + a_1(1 - h_M)].$$

Case 2: $C = c_M^a c_H^{1-a}$ and $g = a_0 k_H + a_1 h_H$ implies

$$V = a \log(c_M) + (1 - a + A) \log[a_0 k_H + a_1(1 - h_M)].$$

Case 3: $C = c_M^a c_H^{1-a}$ and $g = k_H^\eta h_H^{1-\eta}$ implies

$$V = a \log(c_M) + (1 - a)\eta \log(k_H)$$

$$+ [(1 - a)(1 - \eta) + A] \log(1 - h_M).$$

Notice how V can be very different, starting from the same preferences over C and ℓ, depending on the degree of substitutability between the two types of consumption in the utility function and between the two inputs in the home production function. Case 3 delivers a reduced form that is equivalent to a model that has the same utility function, $u = \log(C) + A \cdot \log(\ell)$, and ignores the home production process—that is, a model that sets $C = c_M$ and $\ell = 1 - h_M$—but then simply adds the $\log(k_H)$ term.[4] Case 1, on the other hand, yields a reduced form in which c_M, k_H and $1 - h_M$ are perfect substitutes—very different from the underlying utility function. Case 2 is intermediate, in the sense that $1 - h_M$ and k_H are perfect substitutes, while c_M enters separately.

An interesting feature of Case 1 is that although leisure, as measured by $\ell = 1 - h_M - h_H$, is a normal good according to u, the wealth effect on the quantity $1 - h_M$ is identically zero according to V. That is, an increase in wealth leads to a reduction in $h_M + h_H$ but no change in h_M. A version of this functional form is used by Greenwood, Hercowitz, and Huffman (1988) in their business cycle model, and it has desirable properties resulting from the fact that it implies a large labor supply elasticity because the wealth effect on h_M is zero.[5] Without considering the underlying home production model, however, one could question a choice of functional form that implies a zero wealth effect on h_M. In particular, how can it be reconciled with the fact that h_M has displayed no trend growth over long periods despite large increases in market productivity and real wages?

To understand this, note that this long-run fact implies that the substitution and wealth effects on market hours offset each other (see King, Plosser, and Rebelo 1987), and therefore the wealth effect must be negative. Starting with a zero wealth effect specification appears to be inconsistent with this observation. However, in a home production model with the above specification, market hours will be constant as long as productivity in the home and productivity in the market increase at the same rate on average. That is, a home production model can generate a balanced growth path with no trend in h_{Mt} and h_{Ht} even though the reduced-form utility function implies a zero wealth effect on h_{Mt}. The growth in home productivity shows up in the reduced form as trend growth in the marginal utility of leisure. Of course, one can assume directly that preferences are changing over time in a particular way but incorporating home production suggests an arguably more palatable interpretation.[6]

Another implication is that whenever the home technology is stochastic, we end up with what look like preference shocks in the reduced-form utility function, V. This can improve the performance of business cycle models along some dimensions.[7] Positive shocks to the marginal utility of leisure or the home technology reduce labor supplied to the market, which tends to induce a negative relation between market hours and productivity. This counteracts the positive relation between hours and productivity induced by shocks to the market technology. Models with shocks to both technologies can generate patterns of hours versus productivity closer to the data than those with only market shocks. Of course, to make these arguments precise in a quantitative sense, we need a fully specified general equilibrium model; this is what we provide in the next section.

3. The General Equilibrium Model

This section specifies and calibrates the general equilibrium model with household production. There is a large number of identical infinitely-lived agents, with instantaneous utility function specified by

$$u = b \log(C_t) + (1 - b) \log(\ell_t),\tag{7}$$

where

$$C_t = [ac_{Mt}^e + (1 - a)c_{Ht}^e]^{1/e}\tag{8}$$

and $\ell_t = 1 - h_{Mt} - h_{Ht}$. The elasticity of substitution between c_{Mt} and c_{Ht} is given by $1/(1 - e)$. For simplicity, the two types of work are always assumed to be perfect substitutes in what follows.

There is a representative firm with a constant-returns-to-scale technology described by the market production function,

$$f(h_{Mt}, k_{Mt}, z_{Mt}) = k_{Mt}^{\theta}(z_{Mt}h_{Mt})^{1-\theta}.\tag{9}$$

All households have access to the home production function,

$$g(h_{Ht}, k_{Ht}, z_{Ht}) = k_{Ht}^{\eta}(z_{Ht}h_{Ht})^{1-\eta}.\tag{10}$$

Here, θ and η are the capital share parameters and z_{Mt} and z_{Ht} represent labor augmenting technological change. Technical change occurs as follows: $z_{Mt} = \lambda^t \tilde{z}_{Mt}$, and $z_{Ht} = \lambda^t \tilde{z}_{Ht}$, where λ^t is a deterministic component, and $\tilde{z}_{Mt}$ and $\tilde{z}_{Ht}$ are stochastic processes with

$$\log(\tilde{z}_{Mt+1}) = \rho_M \log(\tilde{z}_{Mt}) + \epsilon_{Mt+1}, \tag{11}$$

and

$$\log(\tilde{z}_{Ht+1}) = \rho_H \log(\tilde{z}_{Ht}) + \epsilon_{Ht+1}. \tag{12}$$

We assume that $|\rho_M|$ and $|\rho_H|$ are less than unity. The innovations ϵ_{Mt} and ϵ_{Ht} are independent and identically distributed over time, with standard deviations σ_M and σ_H and contemporaneous correlation γ.

For reasons that will become apparent in the calibration exercise, it is important to include taxation. We therefore assume that each period the government levies proportional taxes on labor and capital income (net of depreciation) at the constant rates τ_h and τ_k, transfers the lump sum T_t back to individuals, and consumes the surplus. Hence, government consumption is given by

$$G_t = w_t h_{Mt} \tau_h + r_t k_{Mt} \tau_k - \tau_k \delta_M k_{Mt} - T_t, \tag{13}$$

where $\tau_k \delta_M k_{Mt}$ is a depreciation allowance. For simplicity, we assume from now on that all revenue is rebated as a lump sum back to consumers, so that $G_t = 0$ in what follows.[8]

Feasibility implies that market output, $y_t = f(h_{Mt}, k_{Mt}, z_{Mt})$, is allocated across market consumption, c_{Mt}, investment x_t, and government spending G_t:

$$y_t = c_{Mt} + x_t + G_t. \tag{14}$$

Investment augments the capital stock according to the law of motion

$$k_{t+1} = (1 - \delta_M) k_{Mt} + (1 - \delta_H) k_{Ht} + x_t. \tag{15}$$

The aggregate stock can be divided between business and household capital at a point in time according to $k_t = k_{Mt} + k_{Ht}$. Although capital can be freely transformed between its two uses, it may depreciate at different rates in its two uses. Investment in each of the two capital goods is defined residually by[9]

$$x_{Mt} = k_{Mt+1} - (1 - \delta_M) k_{Mt} \tag{16}$$

and

$$x_{Ht} = k_{Ht+1} - (1 - \delta_H) k_{Ht}. \tag{17}$$

A competitive equilibrium for this economy is defined in the usual manner.[10] The representative firm solves a sequence of static problems at each date: maximize instantaneous profit Π_t, where

$$\Pi_t = f(h_{Mt}, k_{Mt}, z_{Mt}) - w_t h_{Mt} - r_t k_{Mt}, \tag{18}$$

taking as given w_t, r_t, and z_{Mt}. The representative consumer maximizes EU where U is given by (1), subject to a budget constraint modified to include taxes,

$$c_{Mt} + x_{Mt} + x_{Ht} = w_t(1 - \tau_h)h_{Mt} + r_t(1 - \tau_k)k_{Mt} + \delta_M \tau_k k_{Mt} + T_t, \quad (19)$$

and the home production constraint (3), taking as given stochastic processes for $\{w_t, r_t, T_t, z_{Mt}, z_{Ht}\}$. Given stochastic processes for the exogenous variables (technology shocks) and initial capital, an equilibrium is a set of stochastic processes for prices and transfer payments $\{w_t, r_t, T_t\}$ and quantities $\{c_{Mt}, c_{Ht}, h_{Mt}, h_{Ht}, k_{Mt}, k_{Ht}\}$ that solves both the producer and the consumer problems.

In order to calibrate the model, we need to derive some properties of the balanced-growth path (that is, the equilibrium path to which the economy converges when $z_{Mt} = z_{Ht} = \lambda^t$ for all t). When $z_{Mt} = z_{Ht} = \lambda^t$, given the initial conditions, the equilibrium converges to a path where $h_{Mt} = h_M$ and $h_{Ht} = h_H$ are constant, while all other endogenous variables grow at rate λ, so that $y_t = y\lambda^t$ for some constant y, $c_{Mt} = c_M \lambda^t$ for some constant c_M, and so on. To describe this in more detail, substitute the budget and home production constraints into the consumer's objective function, and then differentiate to obtain the first-order conditions:

$$h_{Mt} : u_1(t)w_t(1 - \tau_h) = -u_3(t), \quad (20)$$

$$h_{Ht} : u_2(t)g_1(t) = -u_4(t), \quad (21)$$

$$k_{Mt} : u_1(t)[r_t(1 - \tau_k) + 1 - \delta_M + \delta_M \tau_k] = u_1(t - 1)/\beta, \quad (22)$$

and

$$k_{Ht} : u_1(t)(1 - \delta_H) + u_2(t)g_2(t) = u_1(t - 1)/\beta, \quad (23)$$

where the notation $\xi(t)$ means that the function ξ is evaluated at its arguments as of date t.

If we use the first-order conditions for the firm's problem, $w_t = f_1(t)$ and $r_t = f_2(t)$, then given our functional forms, the above expressions can be simplified to yield

$$abc_M^{e-1}C^{-e}y(1 - \theta)(1 - \tau_h) = (1 - b)h_M/\ell, \quad (24)$$

$$(1 - a)bc_H^e C^{-e}(1 - \eta) = (1 - b)h_H/\ell, \quad (25)$$

$$\theta(1 - \tau_k)y/k_M = \lambda/\beta - 1 + \delta_M(1 - \tau_k), \quad (26)$$

and

$$\eta(1 - a)c_H^e c_M^{1-e}/ak_H = \lambda/\beta - 1 + \delta_H. \quad (27)$$

Additionally, equations (16) and (17) imply

$$x_M/k_M = \lambda - 1 + \delta_M, \quad (28)$$

and

$$x_H/k_H = \lambda - 1 + \delta_H. \tag{29}$$

We now proceed to choose parameter values, setting some numbers on the basis of a priori information and setting the others according to the balanced-growth conditions. Since we interpret the period as one quarter, we set $\lambda = 1.005$ in order to match the quarterly growth rate of output in the U.S. data.[11] The discount factor is set so that the annual real rate of return on assets in the model is about 6 percent, which yields $\beta = 0.9898$. We set the labor income tax rate to $\tau_h = 0.25$, the average value in the series in McGrattan, Rogerson, and Wright (1992), which is based on the definitions in Joines (1981). The effective tax rate on capital income is more controversial, and there is a wide range of estimates in the literature. For example, the series in McGrattan, Rogerson, and Wright (1992) implies that τ_k is about 0.50 on average, while Feldstein, Dicks-Mireaux and Poterba (1983) estimate that τ_k is between 0.55 and 0.85 in the period 1953–1979.

We use the mean of the Feldstein, Dicks-Mireaux, and Poterba estimates, and set $\tau_k = 0.70$. This is higher than in some other studies in the real business cycle literature, but two reasons suggest that it is the right number for our purposes. First, given that we are trying to model both market and nonmarket investment, we want τ_k to capture all forms of government regulation, interference, or any other institutional disincentive to invest in business capital, not only direct taxation. Second, the capital's share coefficient in the market production function, θ, which is calibrated below, turns out to be sensitive to the choice of the capital income tax rate. Setting $\tau_k = 0.70$ implies a value for θ that is consistent with independent evidence from the national income accounts (we will return to this issue in what follows).

We now use (24)–(29) to match the following six observations: the two capital/output ratios, the two investment/output ratios, and labor hours in the two sectors. The postwar national income and product accounts yield $k_M/y = 4$, $k_H/y = 5$, $x_M/y = 0.118$, and $x_H/y = 0.135$, on average, where home capital is measured by consumer durables plus residential structures and business capital is measured by producer durables plus nonresidential structures. Averaging data from the 1971 and 1981 time use surveys, we find $h_H = 0.25$ and $h_M = 0.33$ for a typical household, where these numbers are defined as fractions of discretionary time (twenty-four hours per day minus personal care, which is mainly sleep). These six observations determine δ_M, δ_H, θ, η, and two of the three preference parameters, a, b, and e.

The system (24)–(29) has a simple recursive structure. Equations (28) and (29) yield $\delta_M = 0.0247$ and $\delta_H = 0.0218$, which we approximate by setting the two depreciation rates to a common value of $\delta = 0.0235$. Equation (26) yields $\theta = 0.29$, and then (27) yields $\eta = 0.32$.[12] The value $\theta = 0.29$ is also exactly what we compute from the national income and product accounts.[13] Three preference parameters remain to be specified, a, b, and e, but we only have two equations left. In what follows, we consider several alternative values of e, which is the parameter that determines the elasticity of substitution between c_M and c_H, and for each we solve for the values of a and b from (24) and (25). As e varies, a and b will change, but the values of δ_M, δ_H, θ, and η will not.

Finally, we need to specify the parameters describing the stochastic elements of the model. As in much of the literature, we set $\rho_M = 0.95$, and set σ_M so that the innovation in $z_{Mt}^{1-\theta}$ has a standard deviation of 0.007. We then set $\rho_M = \rho_H$ and $\sigma_M = \sigma_H$, so that the home shock mimics the market shock. This leaves γ, which is the correlation between the innovations ϵ_{Mt} and ϵ_{Ht}. Unfortunately there is little independent evidence to guide us in choosing this parameter. In what follows, as with the preference parameter e, we report the results of experiments with different values of γ.

To summarize, all of the parameters except e and γ have been set. The parameter e measures agents' willingness, and the parameter γ measures agents' incentive, to move economic activity between the home and market. Higher values of e mean that agents are more willing to substitute consumption of one sector's output for consumption of the other sector's output. Lower values of γ mean that the technology shocks more frequently take on different values across sectors, which implies a greater incentive to move resources across sectors. As will be shown in the next section, changing either the willingness or incentive to substitute between the home and the market can affect the implications of the model for business cycles.

To close this section, we return to the interaction between taxes and household production. Consider a model without taxation under the standard assumption that the entire capital stock enters into the market production function, so that k_M/y is about 9. Then, calibrating the model as we did above, we find $\theta = 0.34$, which is close to the value implied by the national income accounts and typically used in the real business cycle literature.[14] However, zero taxes are clearly counterfactual. If we set $\tau_k = 0.70$, then in order to get $k_M/y = 9$ we need to set $\theta = 0.66$, which seems far too high. Even a more conservative tax rate of $\tau_k = 0.50$ implies $\theta = 0.48$, which still seems too high. Intuitively, we must assume that when capital income is taxed the marginal product of capital is big, in order to get agents to accumulate a stock as large as $k_M/y = 9$, and θ is the key parameter governing this marginal product. In a home production model we do not interpret all capital as market capital; therefore, k_M/y is 4 rather than 9. This in combination with taxation implies $\theta = 0.29$, which is just what we observe in our data.

4. Simulation Results

Table 6.1 lists some summary statistics for the U.S. economy, and for several versions of the model to be described below.[15] We focus on the following statistics: the standard deviation (in percent) of y; the standard deviations relative to y of x,

Table 6.1
Summary Statistics

	σ_y	σ_x/σ_y	σ_{c_M}/σ_y	σ_{h_M}/σ_y	σ_w/σ_y	σ_{h_M}/σ_w	$c(h_M, w)$	$c(x_M, x_H)$
Data	1.96	2.61	.54	.78	.73	1.06	−.12	.30
Model 1	1.36	2.82	.41	.41	.60	0.68	.96	−.09
Model 2	1.60	2.34	.61	.52	.52	1.00	.86	−.82
Model 3	1.59	2.44	.53	.48	.53	0.91	.95	−.75
Model 4	1.21	2.95	.38	.39	.62	0.63	.95	.50

Notes: y = Gross National Product minus Gross Housing Product; x_M = fixed nonresidential private investment; x_H = private residential investment plus personal consumption expenditure on durable goods; $x = x_M + x_H$; c_M = personal consumption of nondurables plus services minus Gross Housing Product; h_M = manhours of employed labor force (Household Survey); $w = y/h_M$. All series are quarterly and are from the period 1947:1–1987:4. Nominal variables are deflated into 1982 dollars. The series were divided by population, logged, and detrended by using the Hodrick-Prescott filter. The statistic σ_j is the standard deviation of series j (expressed as a percentage), and $c(j, j')$ is the correlation between series j and j'. Model statistics are sample means over 50 simulations, each the same length as our data.

All models use $\lambda = 1.004674$, $\beta = 0.9898$, $\tau_h = 0.35$, $\tau_k = 0.70$, $\delta_M = \delta_H = 0.0235$, $\theta = 0.2944$, $\eta = 0.3245$, a and b determined so that $h_M = 0.33$ and $h_H = 0.25$, $\rho_M = \rho_H = 0.95$, and $\sigma_M = \sigma_H$ determined so that the innovation in $\tilde{z}_M^{1-\theta}$ has standard deviation 0.007. Model 1 sets $e = 0$, $\gamma = 2/3$. Model 2 sets $e = 2/3$, $\gamma = 2/3$. Model 3 sets $e = 0.40$, $\gamma = 0$. Model 4 sets $e = 2/3$, $\gamma = 0.99$, and uses a CES home production function with $\psi = -0.5017$.

c_M, h_M, and w; the correlation between h_M and w; and the correlation between x_M and x_H. The variable w can be interpreted either as the real wage or, equivalently, as the average product of hours worked in the market, since the wage equals the marginal product in equilibrium and the marginal product is proportional to average product with a Cobb-Douglas technology. Investments in the two capital stocks are defined by letting business capital be producer structures plus equipment and letting home capital be residential structures plus consumer durables. Total investment is the sum. Consumption is defined to include nondurables plus services minus the service flow imputed to the housing stock. Market output is defined to be consumption plus investment and government spending. Market hours are from the household survey.

In Model 1, we set $e = 0$, implying that the elasticity of substitution between c_M and c_H is unity. We also set the correlation between the shocks ϵ_M and ϵ_H to $\gamma = 2/3$, as in Benhabib, Rogerson, and Wright (1991) (although when $e = 0$ the value of γ does not matter for the results). Except for minor details, Model 1 is the benchmark model in Greenwood and Hercowitz (1991), and is designed to minimize the role of household production. This can be seen from Case 3 in the examples analyzed in Section 2, which is the current specification with $e = 0$.

Recall that in this case the reduced-form utility function is

$$V = a \log(c_M) + (1 - a)\eta \log(k_H) + [(1 - a)(1 - \eta) + A] \log(1 - h_M).$$

If $\eta = 0$, this reduces to the standard utility function, which ignores home production. Hence, the home production model replicates the results of the standard model exactly when $e = \eta = 0$. Even if $\eta > 0$, when $e = 0$, the home production model generates results that are close to the standard model.

As is well known, the statistics generated by the standard model, and therefore the results generated by Model 1, differ from the data along several dimensions. First, output is less volatile in the model than in the data. Second, in the model, investment is too volatile and consumption is not volatile enough relative to output. Third, in the model, hours worked are not volatile enough relative to either output or productivity. Fourth, hours worked and productivity are highly positively correlated in the model but not in the data. Fifth, the two investment series are positively correlated in the data but not in the model. See Chapter 5, Hansen and Wright (1992), and Benhabib, Rogerson, and Wright (1991) for discussions. Although the results generated by Model 1 are perhaps somewhat better than the prototypical real business cycle model, such as Hansen's (1985) divisible labor model, the model still differs from the data along the five dimensions listed above.

In Model 2, we set $e = \gamma = 2/3$. This corresponds to a situation where consumers are much more willing to substitute between c_M and c_H than in Model 1. Notice, first, that in comparison to Model 1, the volatility of output in Model 2 has increased. Second, the relative volatility of investment has decreased, and that of consumption has increased. Third, hours have become more variable relative to output and to productivity. Fourth, the correlation between hours and productivity has decreased slightly, although not very much. Fifth, the correlation between the two investment series is lower. As found by Benhabib, Rogerson, and Wright (1991), increasing the value of e moves the model in the right direction vis à vis the data, except for the correlation between x_M and x_H.

Benhabib, Rogerson, and Wright (1991) set e and γ more or less arbitrarily. Another approach is to estimate the model by using maximum likelihood techniques, as in McGrattan, Rogerson, and Wright (1992). This procedure yields $e = 0.4$ and $\gamma = 0$ (after rounding), which we use in Model 3. These parameter values correspond to a situation where, as compared to Model 2, consumers are less willing to substitute between the two sectors but there is more of an incentive to do so. Notice that Models 2 and 3 yield similar results. This illustrates the interaction between assuming that individuals are more willing to substitute (a higher value of e) and assuming that they have greater incentives to do so (a lower value of γ): raising e for a given γ is very similar to lowering γ for a given e.[16]

Although neither Model 2 nor Model 3 does well in terms of the correlation between h_M and w, this is a statistic that can in principle be matched by introducing home production. Intuitively, the standard model with shocks only to the market technology is driven by a shifting labor demand curve, so simulations trace out in

(h_M, w) space a stable, upward-sloping labor supply curve and yield a correlation between the two variables close to unity. What is needed is a second shock to shift labor supply, such as a preference or home technology shock.[17] Home technology shocks change the amount people are willing to work in the market at a given wage, shifting the labor supply curve and reducing the hours-productivity correlation. In Models 2 and 3 this effect is present but small. Increasing the standard deviation of the home technology can reduce the correlation between hours and productivity much more, however; see Hansen and Wright (1992) for further discussion.

We now turn to the correlation between x_M and x_H, which the above models do not capture well at all. The problem is that in times of high relative market productivity, agents want to move inputs out of the home and into the market (since that is where they can build capital in order to spread the effects of a temporary productivity rise into the future). The movement of resources between the two sectors is part of what makes a home production model work: the reallocation of hours from nonmarket to market labor, rather than exclusively from leisure to labor, as in the standard model, increases the volatility of h_M for a given technology shock. But it also leads to a problem: how can we make agents want to invest in both business and home capital at the same time, especially when the market and home labor inputs are moving in opposite directions over the cycle?

Greenwood and Hercowitz (1991) approach the problem by assuming a more general home production function:

$$g(h_H, k_H, z_H) = [\eta k_H^{\psi} + (1 - \eta)(z_H h_H)^{\psi}]^{1/\psi}; \qquad (30)$$

note that $\psi = 0$ reduces to the Cobb-Douglas case we have considered so far. They also assume that the shocks z_H and z_M are highly correlated, so that when a positive technology shock hits the market it also hits the home. When a positive shock arrives, since z_H is labor augmenting, it is possible to move hours out of the home and into the market and still end up with more *effective* hours in the home. That is, $z_H h_H$ can increase while h_H decreases. Thus, effective hours in home production can increase during upswings in market activity and, depending on ψ, this can imply a desire to increase capital in the home.

Model 4 uses the technology in (30), with $\psi = -1/2$, $\gamma = 0.99$, and $e = 2/3$, and otherwise keeps the parameters as described above. As can be seen, this does generate a positive correlation between x_M and x_H. However, it requires a high correlation between the shocks, and if the two shocks are very highly correlated, the model does not entail frequent incentives to substitute between household and market activity. Therefore, generating a positive correlation between x_M and x_H involves sacrificing at least part of the other improvements that can be achieved by introducing home production. It is not obvious how to resolve this tension. Additionally, the U.S. data display a clear phase shift, with investment in household capital leading investment in business capital. Building a model that better accounts for these phenomena remains to be done.

Let us summarize the findings from these experiments. With $e = 0$, the model generates second moments that are similar to but somewhat better than those of a standard model without home production. By increasing e for a given γ we can affect the volatility of output, investment, consumption, and hours in the right direction. A similar effect can be obtained by decreasing γ for a given e. These results do not require a large home shock, and we point out that the model performs about as well if the home technology is nonstochastic.[18] However, the larger the home shock the better the resulting correlation between hours and productivity. The correlation between investments in the two sectors can also be improved by considering a more general home technology, although this tends to reduce the impact of home production along other dimensions.[19]

5. An Extension

In this section, we briefly discuss an extension of the framework that is capable of replicating the following fact: over time, the relative prices of consumer durables and producer durables have declined, while expenditures on these items have remained roughly constant. Therefore, we do not actually observe balanced growth in the data, since the stocks of both producer and consumer durables are faster-growing than the other series. Following Greenwood, Hercowitz and Krusell (1994), we address this by assuming that technological change is embodied in the form of new capital goods—in our context, in the home sector as well as the market sector. We also allow capital utilization to be a variable factor of production. Utilizing capital more intensively implies that it depreciates more quickly. We will not completely solve the model sketched here and we have not attempted calibration or simulation; the discussion is only meant to suggest future research topics.

Let the market and home technologies be described by the following functional forms:

$$f(h_M, \mu_M k_M) = (\mu_M k_M)^\theta h_M^{1-\theta}, \tag{31}$$

and

$$g(h_H, \mu_H k_H) = (\mu_H k_H)^\eta h_H^{1-\eta}, \tag{32}$$

where μ_M and μ_H are capital utilization rates. Higher utilization results in increased depreciation: $\delta_M = \delta_M(\mu_M)$ and $\delta_H = \delta_H(\mu_H)$, where $\delta'_M, \delta''_M > 0$ and $\delta'_H, \delta''_H > 0$. Notice that these technologies are deterministic. The shocks enter via the relative prices of capital goods, so that

$$k_{Mt+1} = [1 - \delta(\mu_M)]k_{Mt} + x_{Mt} z_{Mt}, \tag{33}$$

and

$$k_{Ht+1} = [1 - \delta(\mu_H)]k_{Ht} + x_{Ht}z_{Ht}. \tag{34}$$

For example, a high value of z_{Mt} indicates a favorable rate at which market output can be transformed into market capital next period. The shocks follow the usual processes: $z_{Mt} = \lambda^t \tilde{z}_{Mt}$ and $z_{Ht} = \lambda^t \tilde{z}_{Ht}$, where $\tilde{z}_{Mt}$ and $\tilde{z}_{Ht}$ are given by (11) and (12).

For simplicity, ignore taxation. Then the equilibrium can be found as the solution to the planner's problem of maximizing EU, where U is given by (1), subject to the home production constraint (3) and

$$c_{Mt} + x_M + x_H = f(h_M, \mu_M k_M). \tag{35}$$

To describe the deterministic growth path, consider the case where $z_{Mt} = z_{Ht} = \lambda^t$ for all t. Then the first-order conditions imply

$$h_{Mt} : u_1(t)f_1(t) = -u_3(t), \tag{36}$$

$$h_{Ht} : u_2(t)g_1(t) = -u_4(t), \tag{37}$$

$$k_{Mt} : u_1(t)f_2(t)\mu_{Mt} + u_1(t)[1 - \delta_M(\mu_{Mt})]/z_{Mt} = u_1(t-1)/\beta z_{Mt-1}, \tag{38}$$

$$k_{Ht} : u_2(t)g_2(t)\mu_{Ht} + u_1(t)[1 - \delta_H(\mu_{Ht})]/z_{Ht} = u_1(t-1)/\beta z_{Ht-1}, \tag{39}$$

$$\mu_M : f_2(t) = \delta'_M(\mu_{Mt})/z_{Mt}, \tag{40}$$

and

$$\mu_H : g_2(t)u_2(t)/u_1(t) = \delta'_H(\mu_{Ht})/z_{Ht}. \tag{41}$$

Assume that the instantaneous utility function is defined by (7) and (8), with $e = 0$—that is, with a unitary elasticity of substitution between c_M and c_H. Then it is straightforward, if somewhat tedious, to verify that the model has an "almost balanced" growth path with the following properties. First, h_{Mt}, h_{Ht}, μ_{Mt} and μ_{Ht} are all constant. Second, y_t, c_{Mt}, x_{Mt} and x_{Ht} all grow at the same rate, which is $\lambda^{\theta/(1-\theta)}$. Third, k_{Mt} and k_{Ht} both grow at the rate $\lambda^{1/(1-\theta)}$, which is greater than the growth rate of market output because $\theta < 1$. Fourth, c_{Ht} grows at the rate $\lambda^{\eta/(1-\theta)}$, which can be greater than or less than the growth rate of market output, depending on whether η is greater than or less than θ. We conclude that this model is capable of rationalizing the observation that the growth rates of the capital stocks exceed the growth rates of other market variables. It also has a home sector that can either grow or shrink relative to the market, depending on parameter values.

Although we have not done so, it may be worth pursuing the business cycle implications of this structure. Suppose, for example, that the shocks z_{Mt} and z_{Ht} are highly correlated. Then positive shocks reduce the cost of acquiring both consumer and producer durables and therefore tend to increase both investments; see (38) and (39). To the extent that home consumption goes up by more than market consumption, because market output is being invested rather than consumed, x_H

will go up by less than x_M; see (39). There will also be an increase in capacity utilization and hours worked in the market sector to take advantage of the lower cost of putting capital in place. Furthermore, positive shocks encourage greater capital utilization in order to accelerate the depreciation of the existing stock, since replacing it is now cheaper; see (40) and (41). Of course, this discussion is only meant to be suggestive, and the net quantitative effects generated by such a model remain to be seen. We leave exploration of this to future research.

6. Conclusion

We have argued that home production is empirically sizable, and further suggested that there may be interesting interactions between the household and market sectors. We have shown how to incorporate home production into an otherwise standard real business cycle model and how to calibrate it. With reasonable parameter values, it is possible to replicate first-moment properties of the U.S. data, including the observed allocation of capital and time to both market and home production. In terms of the dynamic properties of the model, it does a good job of accounting for the standard features of observed business cycles. There do remain deviations between the theory and data, such as some aspects of the behavior of the two investment series. As should be expected, the exact results depend on the willingness and incentive to substitute between the home and market sectors and on the functional form of the home technology. There is, unfortunately, not a lot of independent evidence on the parameters dictating these features of the model, and it would seem worthwhile to try to uncover more such information from microstudies. In summary, we have tried in this chapter to illustrate both the strengths and the weaknesses of incorporating home production into macroeconomic models, and to make suggestions for future research projects.

Notes

We thank Thomas Cooley, who edited this volume, as well as Gary Hansen, Ellen McGrattan, Edward Prescott, and Warren Weber for suggestions or comments. Ellen McGrattan allowed us to use her computer programs. Lorrenzo Giorgianni and Shawn Hewitt provided research assistance. Much of this work is based on previous research with Jess Benhabib and Zvi Hercowitz, and we thank them for their input. The National Science Foundation provided research support. The views expressed are those of the authors and not those of the Federal Reserve Bank of Minneapolis or the Federal Reserve System.

   1. Following Becker (1965), Greenwood and Hercowitz (1991) assume that there is no direct disutility to labor; following Gronau (1975), Benhabib, Rogerson, and Wright (1991) assume that there is direct disutility to labor, as we do for the most part in this chapter. Excluding labor from u has the advantage of theoretical and computational parsimony, but including it can generate some additional insights. Note that there are direct measures of

all three variables—market work, home work, and leisure—in the time use survey data, and measures of both market work and home work in some panel data (such as the PSID).

2. The appropriate decisionmaking unit in reality is a household or family, which may, of course, consist of more than one individual. This implies that it may be possible to consume a home-cooked meal, for example, without actually cooking it. At the level of abstraction adopted here, the family is taken to be a single decisionmaking unit with no internal bargaining or disagreement. This may not be particularly realistic, but it does make things simpler. Pollak and Lundberg (1991) discuss bargaining within the family and provide references to the related literature.

3. A converse result also holds: for any model without home production but with home capital entering the utility function directly, there is a model with a utility function of the form (1) and a well-behaved home production function that delivers the same predictions for all market variables.

4. This is what has often been done in the literature on consumer durables; see Macklem (1989), for example.

5. Devereaux, Gregory, and Smith (1992) also show how these preferences can be used to reconcile the puzzle that observed cross-country consumption correlations in the data are lower than those predicted by conventional open-economy real business cycle models.

6. This analysis bears on another issue in real business cycle theory. The indivisible labor model of Rogerson (1984, 1988), as used by Hansen (1985) and several others, has the following property: unemployed workers enjoy greater utility than do their employed counterparts, not only for the particular functional forms used in those studies, but for any utility function that implies that leisure is a normal good. If we incorporate home production, however, the model need not have this implication; see Nosal, Rogerson, and Wright (1992) for details.

7. For example, Bencivenga (1991) introduces preference shocks.

8. More generally, G could enter the utility function, and we could assume that G in the model mimics government spending in the data (either its stochastic properties, or at least its long-run average behavior). Note, however, that if we assume that government consumption is a perfect substitute for market consumption in the utility function, then a model with $G \neq 0$, generates exactly the same statistics as does a model with $G = 0$, except for the fact that c_M will change one-for-one to offset changes in G.

9. Although capital is freely mobile between home and market at a given point in time in the experiments that we conducted it is rare for any capital to physically move between sectors, since typically gross (if not net) investment in each is positive. Hence, free mobility seems to play little role. What is important, however, is that capital does not have to be committed to either sector until the shocks have been observed. Greenwood and Hercowitz (1991) assume that capital does have to be allocated in advance, which has some advantages in terms of the results. We adopt the specification in the text for simplicity.

10. Because of the presence of distorting taxes, equilibrium allocations are not generally Pareto optimal, so we have to work with the equilibrium directly rather than with the social planner's problem. The discussion here is not intended to be particularly rigorous. Greenwood and Hercowitz (1991) define a recursive competitive equilibrium for the model more carefully, along the general lines of Hansen and Prescott's analysis in chapter 2. The solution procedure that we use is described in detail in McGrattan (1991).

11. Table 6.1 below reports exact parameter values; in the text, we round off most parameters to a few digits.

12. It looks as though one needs to know the parameter a in order to determine η from (27); however, a can be eliminated from (27) by using other conditions.

13. To compute θ from the national income accounts, we subtract proprietors' income from total income, as is standard, and also subtract the service flow attributed to the housing stock from output since this is household and not market output. The result is $\theta = 0.29$ in our sample.

14. Depending on details, such as how one treats proprietors' income, the national income accounts indicate that θ could be anywhere between 0.25 and 0.43; see Christiano (1988), for example. Prescott (1986) argues for $\theta = 0.36$, while, as indicated earlier, we find $\theta = 0.29$.

15. The U.S. data are quarterly and are from the period 1947:1–1987:4. Often in the literature, only data after 1955 are considered, presumably to eliminate the effect of the Korean War; summary statistics are similar in the two periods (see Hansen and Wright 1992). We take logarithms and detrend using the Hodrick-Prescott filter (see Chapter 1) before computing statistics, both for the U.S. data and for data generated by the models. The notes to the table provide more details.

16. One might think that the parameter values from McGrattan, Rogerson, and Wright (1992) would do even better than indicated by the results in Table 6.1 since, after all, they were estimated by fitting the model to the aggregate time series. Several points are relevant in this regard. First, the model in that paper differs from the one here in certain respects, such as the fact that it includes stochastic taxation and government consumption. Second, although we use the same e and γ, some of the other parameter values are different. Finally, the likelihood function takes into account aspects of the time series other than the small number of second moments computed from filtered data considered in Table 6.1; for example, estimation trades off the fit at business cycle frequencies against the fit at other frequencies.

17. Christiano and Eichenbaum (1992) argue for including government spending. The idea is that as long as government spending is less than a perfect substitute in utility for private consumption, an increase in G entails a negative wealth effect, which shifts labor supply. Stochastic tax shocks, as in McGrattan (1989) or Braun (1990), can have similar effects in terms of shifting labor supply.

18. This is because, even if the home technology is nonstochastic, shocks to the market production function obviously still induce relative productivity differentials between the sectors.

19. Combining indivisible labor with home production may be interesting, since this should increase the volatility of hours, and help with the correlation between hours and productivity, given the second shock. Combining home production with stochastic tax or government spending shocks may have similar effects.

Chapter 7
Money and the Business Cycle

Thomas F. Cooley and Gary D. Hansen

1. Introduction

A prominent feature of the business cycle in the United States and many other countries is the striking coherence between movements in monetary aggregates and aggregate output. The strength of this association has been sufficiently persuasive that many economists have focused on monetary instability as a cause of the Great Depression of the 1930s and have searched for purely monetary explanations of the business cycle. The problem has always been to show how monetary forces can be an important cause of business cycle fluctuations in a world where agents are assumed to behave rationally. There are two predominant modern theories about how money becomes important for business cycle fluctuations. The first, formulated by Robert Lucas, treats monetary shocks as a source of confusion that makes it difficult for agents to separate relative price changes from aggregate price changes. The second explanation holds that monetary shocks have important real effects because of rigidities in prices or wages.

Our intention in this chapter is to illustrate how the basic neoclassical business cycle model can be modified to capture these two predominant explanations of how monetary factors could influence real output. We then use these models to assess the quantitative importance of monetary shocks, operating through these different channels, for fluctuations in output and employment. Our principal finding in this analysis is that monetary shocks do not appear to play a quantitatively important role in driving the business cycle in a model based on the first theory. However, monetary shocks do play an important role when they are propagated by some form of rigidity in wages or prices.

Macroeconomic theories have been divided over the years on whether the impulses that cause economic fluctuations should be viewed as demand shocks or supply shocks. Much of the business cycle research of the past fifty years has been based on the view that the shocks that get propagated as business cycles are mainly shocks to demand. In particular, shocks originating in monetary policy have been viewed by much of the profession as prime candidates. This idea has been highly influenced by the comprehensive historical research of Friedman and Schwartz (1963). They documented a very strong association between the periods of severe economic decline they observed over ninety-three years of U.S. history and sharp declines in the stock of money. Although it would be difficult to firmly establish the direction of causality in this association, and monetary shocks appear to operate with "long and variable lags," this association is interpreted by the authors, as well as others, as evidence that monetary forces are important for aggregate fluctuations in real variables.[1]

Modern views of the business cycle have also been heavily influenced by the evidence for some form of Phillips curve relationship in post–World War II data. Providing an equilibrium theory based on rational behavior that accounts for this relationship is the motivation behind the work of Robert Lucas (1972). Lucas faced two important challenges, as would anyone who views macroeconomic outcomes in terms of general equilibrium theory and is motivated by the apparent strong relationship between money and real activity. The first challenge is to provide a theory in which money is valued in equilibrium. The second and more difficult challenge is to show how changes in the supply of money could have a significant effect on the real economy in a world where economic agents are behaving rationally without simply asserting some *ad hoc* form of money illusion.

Many models have been developed that show how money can be valued in equilibrium. All have the feature that money either facilitates existing trades or permits new ones. The overlapping-generations model of Samuelson, which was employed by Lucas (1972), is a model where money accomplishes both. Models where money is treated symmetrically with other goods by placing real money balances in the utility function also result in money's being valued in equilibrium. The approach employed in this chapter is to simply assume that currency must be used for certain transactions by imposing a cash-in-advance restriction. This approach has proven particularly useful for the kind of quantitative analysis carried out here because, as we illustrate below, the theory implies a set of strong restrictions that help to calibrate the model.

Robert Lucas (1972,1975) solved the second challenge by showing that monetary shocks could have real consequences by creating information problems for rational economic agents. His basic insight was that monetary shocks could be important for real fluctuations if they caused economic agents to be confused about whether changes in observed prices were the result of changes in relative prices or changes in the aggregate price level. Lucas showed in elegant detail how monetary shocks could have real effects in an economy where agents face the problem of extracting signals from prices and where monetary shocks are a source of confusion. This theoretical breakthrough led to a flood of papers that explored this paradigm both theoretically and empirically.

A second approach, which deviates somewhat from the extreme rationality assumption adhered to by Lucas, explored the possibility that monetary shocks get propagated not by informational problems but by price rigidities. This view has strong intellectual precedents in Keynes *General Theory*. Gray (1976), Fischer (1977), and Taylor (1979) described economies in which wage rigidities arise because workers and firms enter into contracts that fix nominal wages in advance. They developed the implications of such arrangements for the propagation of monetary shocks. In recent variations, Mankiw (1985), Parkin (1986) and others have suggested that the more important phenomenon is that prices for goods are rigid because of the costs associated with changing prices. Common to all of this literature is the view that nominal rigidities are the mechanism by which monetary shocks get propagated.

Our goal in this chapter is to describe and explore the properties of models that attempt to capture these two alternative views about how monetary shocks may come to have an important influence on real activity. The economies we describe will conform to the basic principles that unify this book; that is, they will be dynamic general equilibrium models that are based on the neoclassical growth framework described in Chapter 1. In evaluating these models we offer a quantitative assessment of two issues: (1) How important are monetary shocks for the business cycle when propagated by the mechanism in question? and (2) How do the fluctuations and comovements that we observe in the data compare with those displayed by the artificial economies?

In the next section of this chapter we review the post–World War II evidence about the relation between money and business cycles. We begin by presenting the relation between money and real output in postwar quarterly U.S. data. We then present summary statistics that describe the nominal features of the business cycle. In subsequent sections we consider three different economies. In the first, agents face signal extraction problems of the sort envisioned by Lucas. In this economy, confusion arises because of the presence of noise (interpreted to be due to monetary policy) that causes agents to be uncertain about their productivity. In the second model, agents simply hold money because cash is required to purchase some consumption goods. In this model, monetary shocks have real effects because inflation acts as a distorting tax on the holding of money; we explore the business cycle implications of this feature. Lastly, we consider an economy with nominal rigidities. The model is the same as the previous one with the additional feature that agents enter into contracts that specify the nominal wage one period in advance. We use this model to illustrate the quantitative importance of the nominal contracting mechanism for the propagation of monetary shocks.

2. Stylized Facts

In Chapter 1, we characterized the volatility and comovements among real variables that are associated with the business cycle. Other chapters have presented additional statistics, which highlight other features of observed aggregate fluctuations. In this section, we describe those features of the cycle that are uniquely monetary. The strength of the association between monetary and real variables over the cycle is such that many economists view the cycle as a purely monetary

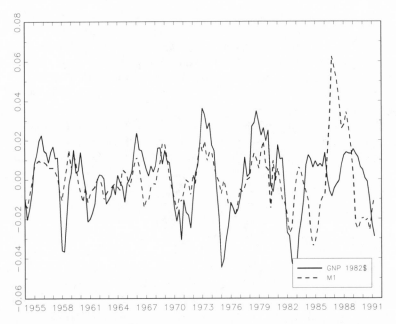

Figure 7.1 Detrended GNP and M1
Trillions of 1982 dollars (log scale).

phenomenon. What are the associations between real and nominal variables that lead one to this notion?

Figure 7.1 shows the behavior of detrended real GNP and M1 for the postwar period plotted against time (both variables are expressed in logarithms).[2] The relation between money and GNP is pretty striking, and it seems fair to say that this coherence has prompted a large part of the post–World War II research on the business cycle. Figure 7.2 shows the same relationship between GNP and M2, a broader concept. Again the apparent strength of the relation is quite striking. No inference about the direction of causality can be made simply because these variables are highly correlated. The causality could run in either direction. Nevertheless, models that seriously explore the role of monetary shocks are going to look for channels of causality from money to output.

A more complete representation of the relations among real and nominal variables is presented in Table 7.1.

Table 7.1 shows the standard deviations, cross-correlations with real GNP, and correlations with the growth in M1 of several macroeconomic aggregates. The table includes the most important real variables as well as nominal variables.[3] Several features are important in characterizing the business cycle. Here, we discuss briefly those that have been regarded as the most significant monetary features.

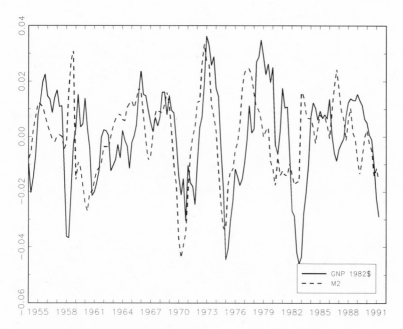

Figure 7.2 Detrended GNP and M2
Trillions of 1982 dollars (log scale).

Monetary aggregates and velocity are procyclical.

The correlations in Table 7.1 show that virtually all of the monetary aggregates and M1 velocity are procyclical. The simple correlation between money and output has, as we noted above, been one of the most compelling features of aggregate data. One of the early attempts to understand this relationship in the context of a simple equilibrium business cycle model is the paper by King and Plosser (1984). One of the findings to emerge from the simple model they consider is that inside money, which they measure as real deposits, should be correlated with output growth, but that outside money should not be. The results of Friedman and Schwartz (1963) also suggested this possibility, although they were less conclusive. The statistics in Table 7.1 bear this out to some extent in that broader definitions of money exhibit stronger correlations with GNP, as well as more volatility. This distinction may be an important one to explore, but it is not addressed in the monetary models described in this chapter.

There is a pronounced phase shift in the correlation between output and monetary aggregates.

The cross correlations of output with the monetary aggregates show that output is more highly correlated with lagged values of the aggregates, implying that the monetary aggregates peak before output. The ability to capture this dynamic

Table 7.1
Cyclical Behavior of the U.S. Economy: Deviations from Trend of Key Variables, 1954:I–1991:II

Variable	SD%	Cross-Correlation of Output with:											Correlation with M1 Growth
		$x(-5)$	$x(-4)$	$x(-3)$	$x(-2)$	$x(-1)$	x	$x(+1)$	$x(+2)$	$x(+3)$	$x(+4)$	$x(+5)$	
Output component													
GNP	1.72	−.02	.16	.38	.63	.85	1.0	.85	.63	.38	.16	−.02	−.12
Consumption Expenditures													
CNDS	0.86	.22	.40	.55	.68	.78	.77	.64	.47	.27	.06	−.11	.02
CD	4.96	.24	.37	.49	.65	.75	.78	.61	.38	.11	−.13	−.31	.07
Investment													
INV	8.24	.04	.19	.38	.59	.79	.91	.76	.50	.22	−.04	−.24	−.18
Ch.INVENT	17.3	−.03	.07	.22	.38	.53	.67	.51	.27	.04	−.15	−.30	−.34
Labor input based on Household Survey													
HSHOURS	1.59	−.06	.09	.30	.53	.74	.86	.82	.69	.52	.32	.11	−.15
Prices													
GNPDEF	0.88	−.52	−.63	−.69	−.70	−.65	−.57	−.44	−.31	−.17	−.04	.08	−.16
CPI	1.43	−.57	−.66	−.71	−.72	−.65	−.52	−.35	−.17	.02	.19	.34	−.22
INFLATION	0.57	−.32	−.23	−.10	.01	.19	.34	.43	.44	.47	.43	.34	−.29
Monetary Aggregates													
MB	0.84	.22	.33	.39	.42	.37	.30	.21	.15	.07	.03	.02	.18
M1	1.52	.16	.24	.33	.41	.39	.33	.21	.12	.05	.03	.02	.25
M2	1.46	.51	.58	.62	.62	.50	.33	.10	−.08	−.21	−.29	−.37	.37
Velocity of money													
M1V	1.94	−.38	−.33	−.24	−.08	.15	.37	.39	.33	.22	.09	0.0	.01

Interest rates

GB10YR	0.66	-.51	-.46	-.39	-.26	-.09	.10	.08.	.11	.10	.08	.07	-.37
TB1MO	1.29	-.55	-.41	-.27	-.03	.20	.40	.42	.44	.36	.32	.25	-.27

Note: GNP—real GNP, 1982$; CNDS—consumption of nondurables and services, 1982$; CD—consumption of durables, 1982$; INV—gross private domestic investment, 1982$; Ch.INVENT—change in inventories, 1982$; HSHOURS—total hours of work (Household Survey); GNPDEF—implicit GNP deflator; CPI—Consumer Price Index, all items; INFLATION—ΔLN(CPI); MB—monetary base; M1—Money Supply 1; M2—Money Supply 2; M1V—velocity for M1; GB10YR—10-year government bond yield; TB1MO—1-month Treasury bill rate.

response pattern of output to monetary innovations is an important challenge for macroeconomists.[4]

There is a negative correlation between output and prices.

Table 1 shows that prices are counter-cyclical. This fact has been discussed in Kydland (1989), Cooley and Ohanian (1991), and Kydland and Prescott (1991) in some detail. It is worthy of note because it is one of those business cycle facts that has been the subject of much confusion. A survey of most textbooks in macroeconomics would probably lead one to suspect that the consensus view is that prices are procyclical. In part this is genuine confusion, caused by carelessness on the part of the profession. In part it has to do with what is being measured.

There is a positive correlation between output and inflation.

While prices are countercyclical, the data in Table 7.1 clearly indicate that the detrended inflation rate is procyclical over this postwar period. There is also a pronounced phase shift in this relationship, with future inflation rates more highly correlated with current output than contemporaneous inflation rates.

There is a positive correlation between output and nominal interest rates.

Table 1 show that short-term nominal interest rates are strongly positively correlated with output, and long-term rates somewhat less so. In addition, short rates are considerably more volatile than long rates.[5]

There is a negative correlation between M1 growth and both output and hours.

There is also a modest contemporaneous correlation between M1 growth and the price level and the inflation rate.

There is a contemporaneous negative correlation between money growth and nominal interest rates.

This feature is often attributed to the liquidity effect of a monetary shock. Some recent research on monetary business cycle models has been directed at constructing economic environments specifically designed to capture this liquidity effect.[6] We will not be exploring these models in this chapter.

These are the primary facts that characterize what one might call the nominal business cycle. In the next three sections, we focus on the extent to which the basic neoclassical growth model, with money introduced, can explain the observed features of business cycles, as represented by these few observations as well as the other statistics provided in Table 7.1.

3. Money as a Source of Confusion

The first model we consider in this chapter is one designed to capture the monetary non-neutrality present in the "Lucas island model." This model originally appeared in Lucas (1972) as way of interpreting the positive correlation between the inflation rate and the level of output, a relationship referred to in textbooks as the Phillips curve. This paper was influential because it was the first to provide an example of a model economy in which agents have rational expectations, all markets clear, and this correlation is displayed. In subsequent work, Lucas (1975, 1977) modified the model so that it could also explain, at least qualitatively, additional comovements of aggregate variables observed over the business cycle. Thus, the Lucas model is an example of an equilibrium business cycle model in which monetary shocks, rather than technology shocks, are the impulses leading to aggregate fluctuations. Our purpose in this section is to explore the quantitative implications of monetary shocks in this type of economy.

In this model, changes in the growth rate of money have real effects because agents in the economy have incomplete information. In particular, agents are spatially separated and are unable to perfectly distinguish movements in relative prices from movements in the aggregate price level. Agents are assumed to observe the price of output on their own island, but do not directly observe the economywide price level. Therefore, an unanticipated change in the growth rate of money, which leads to an unanticipated change in the inflation rate, causes these imperfectly informed agents to confuse these purely nominal movements with changes in relative prices. Thus, purely nominal shocks, as long as they are unanticipated, will have real effects.

It is important to recognize that there is nothing inherently monetary about the Lucas story. There is really no need to posit an explicit motive for holding money to capture the essentials of this story. The essential features can be reproduced in a real economy with a technology shock that is observed with noise, where the noise is only informally interpreted as resulting from monetary policy. The important aspect is that agents face the same kind of informational (signal extraction) problem as in the Lucas model.

In this section we illustrate how to set up and solve such an economy. We then describe the quantitative implications of assuming that technology shocks are observed with noise. We find that these noise shocks have relatively small effects on the fluctuations exhibited by the model. In fact, introducing noise shocks can actually *reduce* the size of the fluctuations.[7] We interpret this as implying that an explanation of business cycles based on this sort of monetary nonneutrality is not likely to succeed. This may partially explain why the profession has largely abandoned this model of the business cycle in favor of models based on real technology shocks.

An Economy with Imperfectly Observed Shocks to Technology

The model we study in this section is similar to one studied in Kydland and Prescott (1982, 1988).[8] This is a model designed to capture the monetary surprise shocks described by Lucas. Kydland and Prescott accomplish this by assuming that the technology shock in the standard real business cycle model is observed with noise. In addition, to be true to the Lucas model, technology shocks are assumed to be the sum of a persistent and transitory component. That is,

$$z_t = z_{1t} + z_{2t},$$

$$z_{1t+1} = \rho z_{1t} + \epsilon_{1t+1},$$

and

$$z_{2t+1} = \epsilon_{2t+1}, \tag{1}$$

where ρ is less than, but close to, one. The random variables ϵ_1 and ϵ_2 are i.i.d. normal with mean zero and standard deviations σ_1 and σ_2, respectively.

For later convenience, we rewrite this system using matrix notation. Let $\tilde{z}_t = [z_{1t}, z_{2t}]^T$ and $\tilde{\epsilon}_t = [\epsilon_{1t}, \epsilon_{2t}]^T$. Then, with primes denoting next-period values,

$$\tilde{z}' = A\tilde{z} + \tilde{\epsilon}', \quad \tilde{\epsilon} \sim N(0, \Sigma), \quad \text{where } A = \begin{bmatrix} \rho & 0 \\ 0 & 0 \end{bmatrix} \text{ and } \Sigma = \begin{bmatrix} \sigma_1^2 & 0 \\ 0 & \sigma_2^2 \end{bmatrix}.$$

At the beginning of period t, agents observe a noisy signal, π_t, where

$$\pi_t = z_t + \epsilon_{3t} = B\tilde{z}_t + \epsilon_{3t}, \tag{2}$$

where B is the row vector $[1, 1]$. The random variable ϵ_3 is also i.i.d. normal with mean zero and standard deviation σ_3.

After observing π_t, agents make employment and capital investment decisions. After the output has been produced, agents are able to observe $z_t = B\hat{z}_t$ directly, but they are still unable to observe z_{1t} and z_{2t} individually.

If we were to assume, as in Chapter 1, that all output is either invested in new capital or consumed, consumption in this model would be quite variable; in particular, it would be more variable than it would be if agents could observe z_t at the beginning of the period. This is because consumption must absorb any undesired changes in output due to ϵ_3. Thus, the incomplete information aspect of this economy induces a buffer role for inventories.[9] To incorporate this, we assume that

$$c_t + x_t + s_{t+1} - s_t \leq y_t, \tag{3}$$

where y_t is output in period t, c_t is consumption, x_t is investment in physical capital, and s_t is the stock of inventories in period t. All these variables are subject to nonnegativity constraints.

If this buffer role were the only role played by inventories, the restriction $s_t \geq 0$ would likely bind in many periods. However, the solution methods used here and in Kydland and Prescott (1982, 1988) do not allow for constraints that bind in some periods but not others.[10] Therefore, we follow Kydland and Prescott by assuming that inventories also serve as a factor of production. This permits inventory stocks to be large enough on average that the nonnegativity constraint never binds.[11] This leads us to assume the following form for the production function, which is the same as that assumed in Kydland and Prescott (1988):

$$y_t = [(e^{zt}k_t^{\theta}h_t^{1-\theta})^{-\nu} + \sigma s_t^{-\nu}]^{-1/\nu}, \tag{4}$$

where $0 < \theta < 1, \sigma > 0$ and $\nu > -1$. We also assume that it takes one period to produce productive capital, so

$$k_{t+1} = (1 - \delta)k_t + x_t, \quad 0 < \delta < 1. \tag{5}$$

The representative household maximizes expected discounted utility, given by

$$U = E \sum_{t=0}^{\infty} \beta^t u(c_t, 1 - h_t), \quad 0 < \beta < 1. \tag{6}$$

We assume that $u(c_t, 1 - h_t) = \log c_t - \gamma h_t$, where γ is a positive constant. The fact that this utility function is linear in hours worked is due to an implicit assumption that labor is indivisible in this model and that a market for employment lotteries is used to allocate labor. This is explained more fully in Hansen (1985), Rogerson (1988), and Chapter 5 in this book.

Since there are no distorting taxes or externalities in this economy, the competitive equilibrium allocation can be obtained by solving a social planning problem consisting of maximizing (6) subject to (1)–(5). Of course, the social planner is subject to the same information limitations as the agents in the economy. Our goal in the remainder of this section is to formulate this problem as a standard stochastic dynamic programming problem so that the solution methods described in Chapter 2 can be applied.

To do this, we need to define a state vector for this problem. Since $\tilde{z}$ is not observable, it cannot be included as part of the state. Instead, we require variables that characterize the conditional distribution of current and future $\tilde{z}$'s given the information available. Since $\tilde{\epsilon}$ is normally distributed, this conditional distribution is completely characterized by its mean and covariance matrix. At the beginning of a period, the information set of an agent relevant for predicting current and future $\tilde{z}$'s, call it I_0, consists only of past values of $z = B\tilde{z}$. That is, $I_0 = \{z_j, j < t\}$. Define $m_0 \equiv E[\tilde{z}|I_0]$ and $V_0 \equiv \text{Cov}[\tilde{z}|I_0]$. This mean and covariance matrix summarizes completely the information contained in I_0.

Prior to the choice of hours and capital investment, the noisy signal π is observed. Thus, the information set is now $I_1 = \{\pi, I_0\}$, and the conditional mean and covariance are denoted m_1 and V_1. Similarly, before the choice of inventories and consumption, z_t is observed; the information set now includes the current as well as past values of z, so $I_2 = \{z_j, j \le t\}$. The conditional mean and covariance are denoted m_2 and V_2.

Applying conditional probability formulas for the multivariate normal distribution, the covariance matrices V_1, V_2, and V_3 can be obtained recursively from the following equations:[12]

$$V_1 = V_0 - (BV_0)^T(BV_0B^T + \sigma_3^2)^{-1}BV_0;$$

$$V_2 = V_1 - (BV_1)^T(BV_1B^T)^{-1}BV_1;$$

$$V_0 = AV_2A^T + \Sigma. \tag{7}$$

These conditional covariances do not depend on the realizations of the observables π or z; they are constant over time. Hence, they need not be included as part of the state vector for the social planning problem. The conditional means, however, do depend on the realized values of the observables according to the following formulas:

$$m_1 = m_0 + (BV_0)^T (BV_0 B^T + \sigma_3^2)^{-1} (\pi - Bm_0);$$

$$m_2 = m_1 + (BV_1)^T (BV_1 B^T)^{-1} (z - Bm_1);$$

$$m_0' = Am_2. \tag{8}$$

The state of the economy at the beginning of a period is (m_0, k, s); before the first set of decisions is made, the state becomes (m_1, k, s); before the second set of decisions, it becomes (m_2, k, s, h, x). Bellman's equation for the social planning problem is the following, where $v(m_0, k, s)$ is the value function evaluated at the beginning of a period:

$$v(m_0, k, s) = \max_{s', c} \left\{ E \left[\max_{h, x} \{ E[(\log c - \gamma h) + \beta v(m_0', k', s') | m_1] \} m_2 \right] \right\},$$
$$\tag{9}$$

where the maximization is subject to (3)–(5) and (8).

A solution to this functional equation yields a set of stationary optimal policy functions of the following form:

$$h = \mathbf{h}(m_1, k, s);$$

$$x = \mathbf{x}(m_1, k, s);$$

$$s' = \mathbf{s}'(m_2, k, s, h, x);$$

$$c = \mathbf{c}(m_2, k, s, h, x). \tag{10}$$

Solution and Simulation Method

We will use the methods described in Chapter 2 to solve for linear approximations of the decision rules for h, x, and s'.[13] Since we will be working with a linear-quadratic approximation of the dynamic programming problem (9), we can appeal to certainty equivalence. That is, the coefficients of the decision rules for a certainty version of this problem, one in which the variance of $\epsilon_{it} (i = 1$ to 3) is set equal to zero, are the same as the coefficients obtained if the variances are positive. These coefficients are the same whether the decision is a function of m_1, m_2, or $\tilde{z}$. The decision rules and the computational procedure used to obtain them are unaffected by the signal extraction problem resulting from the imperfectly observed technology shocks. However, the method used for *simulating* artificial time series when the σ_i's are positive must explicitly take into account the estimates of $\tilde{z}$ formed by agents given the information available.

A linear-quadratic approximation of (9) can be formed by first substituting (3) and (4) into the utility function, eliminating c. Chapter 2 describes how to compute a quadratic approximation of the resulting return function at the nonstochastic steady state. Denote this function by $Q(z_1, z_2, k, s, h, i, s')$. Since we are now solving a linear-quadratic approximation of (9), the optimal decision rules are not affected by the variance of the shocks. Therefore, using the procedures described in Chapter 2, the decision rules can be obtained by solving the following functional equation where the variance of the ϵ's have been set equal to zero:

$$v(z_1, z_2, k, s) = \max\{Q(z_1, z_2, k, s, h, x, s') + \beta v(z'_1, z'_2, k', s')\}$$

$$\text{s.t. } z'_1 = \rho z_t$$

$$z'_2 = 0$$

$$k' = (1 - \delta)k + x. \tag{11}$$

In this case, $m_1 = m_2 = (z_1, z_2)$, and the decision rules will be linear functions of z_1, z_2, k and s.

Since we are interested in simulating this economy with the σ_i's strictly positive, decision rules of this form are not sufficient. Given the sequential nature of decisionmaking in this model, we require decision rules for h and x that are functions of (z_1, z_2, k, s), which we have, and a decision rule for s' that is a function of (z_1, z_2, k, s, h, x), which we do not have. However, when we use the procedure described in Chapter 2, obtaining this decision rule is very easy: after eliminating the next-period state variables (Step 3 of the successive-approximations procedure in Section 3 in Chapter 2), the first-order condition for s' can be arranged to express s' as a function of (z_1, z_2, k, s, h, x). In this way we obtain linear decision rules of the following form that can be used to simulate the model:

$$h = d_{10} + d_{11}m_{11} + d_{12}m_{12} + d_{13}k + d_{14}s;$$

$$x = d_{20} + d_{21}m_{11} + d_{22}m_{12} + d_{23}k + d_{24}s;$$

$$s' = d_{30} + d_{31}m_{21} + d_{32}m_{22} + d_{33}k + d_{34}s + d_{35}h + d_{36}x. \tag{12}$$

Finally, before the simulation, equation (7) needs to be solved to obtain values for V_0, V_1, and V_2. We do this by choosing a candidate for V_0 and then iterating, using equation (7) to obtain successive candidates. The iterations are continued until convergence is obtained.

Suppose now that we wish to simulate the economy for T periods. First, realizations for z_{1t}, z_{2t}, and π_t ($t = 1$ to T) are derived from equations (1) and (2) by setting z_{1t} for $t = 0$ equal to zero (its unconditional mean) and drawing values for ϵ_{1t}, ϵ_{2t}, ϵ_{3t} ($t = 1$ to T) from a random number generator. Next, these realizations, along with equation (8), are used to form realizations for m_{1t} and m_{2t} ($t = 1$ to T). Third, given values for k_0 and s_0 (generally we set these equal to their nonstochastic steady-state values), we can use equations (5) and (12) to simulate k_t, s_t, h_t, and x_t for $t = 1$ to T. Finally, equations (3) and (4) are used to obtain values for c_t and y_t, as well.

Calibration

The strategy used to calibrate the model is the same as that described in detail in Chapter 1. Of course, since this model differs from the one studied in that chapter, this strategy will lead to different values for many of the parameters.[14] However, as in Chapter 1, the parameters θ, δ, β, and γ are calibrated so that the nonstochastic steady state of the model matches a set of long-run averages computed from post–Korean War U.S. time series and microstudies. These include the average value of capital's share of income, the investment-output ratio, the capital-output ratio, and the fraction of time households spend working in the market. The same U.S. time series used in Chapter 1 are used for the variables of this model except that inventories are modeled differently here. Hence, they are not included as part of the empirical measure of the capital stock, k_t, and inventory investment is not part of x_t. Consequently, the average investment-output and capital-output ratios used here are smaller than those used in Chapter 1. In addition, since inventories are a separate factor of production here, capital's share of income is also lower than in Chapter 1. In particular, the value for capital's share used here is .39, the investment-output ratio is .243, the quarterly capital-output ratio is 12.4, and the fraction of time spent working is .31 (the latter is the same value used in Chapter 1).

In addition to these parameters, the share parameter, σ, was calibrated so that the steady-state inventories-output ratio is .88, which is equal to the average quarterly inventories-output ratio in the U.S. economy. The parameter, ν, which determines the elasticity of substitution between inventories and the composite capital-labor input, is set equal to 3, as in Kydland and Prescott (1988), on the grounds that these substitution opportunities are quite limited.

Finally, we need to assign values for the parameters of the technology shock process. The parameters ρ and σ_1, which relate to the persistent component z_1, are dictated by the properties of the aggregate Solow residuals described in Chapter 1. This led us to choose the same values, .95 and .007, for these parameters as were employed in Chapter 1. The choices of σ_2 and σ_3 are more difficult to justify. We would like the latter parameter to somehow reflect the uncertainty created by monetary shocks but, it is difficult to make that connection without an explicit model of money holding. The strategy we adopt here is to proceed with somewhat arbitrary values and see whether this particular factor—the signal extraction problem—appears to be an important source of fluctuations. If it turns out to be important, then more work must be done to calibrate these parameters. Hence, in our experiments we assigned the same values to σ_2 and σ_3 as were used in Kydland and Prescott (1988).

We summarize our parameter choices and the resulting linear decision rules in the accompanying table.

Parameter Values						
θ	v	σ	δ	β	γ	ρ
.394	3.00	.007	.020	.988	2.55	.95

Decision Rules
$h = 0.44582 + 0.42744m_{11} + 0.63500m_{12} - 0.00695k + 0.00053s$
$x = 0.45169 + 1.48754m_{11} + 3.24776m_{12} - 0.06995k + 0.93797s$
$s' = -0.39938 + 1.14598m_{21} + 1.46033m_{22} - 0.00171k + 0.94196s$
$\quad\quad + 2.85415h - 0.96257x$

Case	σ_1	σ_2	σ_3
A. Persistent Shock Only	0.007	0	0
B. Persistent and Transitory Shocks	0.007	0.00154	0
C. Persistent, Transitory, and Noise Shocks	0.007	0.00154	0.007
D. Islands Economy (only aggregate shock is noise)	0.007	0.00154	0.007

Findings

Table 7.2 presents the results of simulating the economy just described. The statistics shown in the table are averages of statistics computed from 100 simulations. Each simulation consists of 150 periods, which is equal to the number of quarters in the U.S. sample used in constructing Table 7.1. Statistics are computed from artificial time series that have been first logged and then detrended by using the Hodrick-Prescott filter (see Chapter 1). Standard deviations have been multiplied by 100 to denote percent deviations from trend.

Part A of Table 7.2 shows the business cycle features of the economy when it is subject only to persistent shocks. The behavior of this economy is the same, subject to differences in calibration, as the behavior of the basic real business cycle model with the indivisible labor assumption, as described in Chapter 5 or in Hansen (1985). This is not surprising given that the signal extraction feature plays no role when there is only one type of shock. In addition, Figure 7.3 shows the response of output, consumption, investment and hours worked to a one standard deviation innovation to the persistent shock.

Part B of Table 7.2 shows the effects of adding transitory shocks. The transitory shocks increase the volatility of output and all of the aggregate variables except capital, while changing the cross-correlation structure slightly. Figure 7.4 shows that the response of the economy to these temporary shocks, although quite short-lived, is just as described by Lucas (1977): the temporary shock causes people to

Table 7.2
Simulated Signal Extraction Economies

							Cross-Correlation of Output with:					
Variable	SD%	x(−5)	x(−4)	x(−3)	x(−2)	x(−1)	x	x(+1)	x(+2)	x(+3)	x(+4)	x(+5)
A. Economy with Only Persistent Shocks												
Output	1.623	−.049	.074	.236	.439	.693	1.000	.693	.439	.236	.074	−.049
Consumption	0.406	−.295	−.186	−.027	.191	.479	.845	.739	.623	.505	.389	.281
Investment	5.019	−.029	.090	.244	.438	.676	.964	.832	.511	.258	.062	−.084
Capital stock	0.357	−.496	−.494	−.460	−.380	−.247	−.048	.224	.453	.586	.643	.645
Hours	1.254	.029	.148	.301	.488	.717	.988	.644	.361	.142	−.025	−.146
Productivity	0.431	−.269	−.155	.010	.233	.525	.894	.737	.604	.474	.351	.240
Inventories	0.647	−.297	−.218	−.100	.068	.291	.579	.937	.750	.580	.426	.291
B. Economy with Persistent and Transitory Shocks												
Output	1.646	−.048	.070	.226	.423	.669	1.000	.669	.423	.226	.070	−.048
Consumption	0.407	−.294	−.190	−.035	.176	.455	.838	.734	.618	.501	.386	.279
Investment	5.049	−.027	.087	.238	.428	.661	.968	.806	.494	.248	.057	−.084
Capital stock	0.357	−.488	−.487	−.452	−.375	−.243	−.047	.227	.450	.578	.634	.635
Hours	1.276	.028	.143	.290	.471	.692	.988	.615	.343	.132	−.029	−.144
Productivity	0.433	−.267	−.158	.002	.218	.502	.890	.731	.598	.470	.348	.238
Inventories	0.648	−.293	−.219	−.106	.057	.273	.553	.932	.748	.579	.426	.291

C. Economy with Persistent Transitory, and Noise Shocks

Output	1.557	−.048	.081	.253	.469	.736	1.000	.736	.469	.253	.081	−.048
Consumption	0.393	−.291	−.171	.002	.236	.546	.843	.736	.622	.505	.388	.281
Investment	5.268	−.032	.079	.228	.414	.638	.926	.834	.500	.255	.065	−.078
Capital stock	0.355	−.504	−.505	−.471	−.393	−.259	−.061	.216	.459	.596	.658	.660
Hours	1.225	.007	.199	.267	.450	.667	.949	.738	.435	.197	.015	−.121
Productivity	0.549	−.151	−.032	.123	.328	.598	.715	.440	.361	.280	.199	.134
Inventories	0.660	−.272	−.183	−.052	.127	.362	.668	.898	.672	.516	.375	.249

D. Islands Economy

Output	0.295	−.050	−.057	−.063	−.078	−.089	1.000	−.089	−.078	−.063	−.057	−.050
Consumption	0.017	−.156	−.193	−.232	−.279	−.338	.259	.405	.315	.243	.183	.134
Investment	1.498	−.033	−.039	−.043	−.054	−.059	.977	−.297	−.067	−.054	−.049	−.041
Capital stock	0.032	−.121	−.151	−.181	−.216	−.263	−.316	.590	.302	.235	.181	.135
Hours	0.499	−.044	−.050	−.055	−.068	−.077	.999	−.110	−.090	−.073	−.064	−.055
Productivity	0.205	.035	.039	.042	.053	.059	−.995	.140	.107	.087	.075	.063
Inventories	0.075	.017	.008	.004	.003	.006	.002	−.964	.207	.165	.132	.108

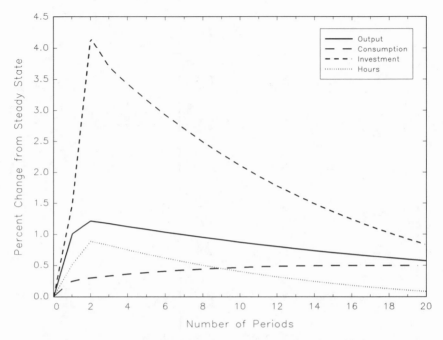

Figure 7.3 Confusion Model: Response to a Persistent Shock

work harder when they are temporarily more productive, and then increase their consumption of leisure in the future. This same sort of intertemporal substitution is also displayed by investment. These effects are also seen in the increased volatility of hours and investment shown in part B of Table 7.2. In addition, the serial correlation in the economy is decreased by the response to temporary shocks, as measured by the cross-correlations with output. The total magnitude of these temporary effects is, however, quite small.

Part C of Table 7.4 presents summary statistics for an economy with all three shocks operating. Contrary to what one might expect, the addition of noise to this economy actually dampens the fluctuations in output. Consumption and aggregate hours also fluctuate less, while investment, productivity, and inventories fluctuate more. Agents fail to react as strongly to noisy signals than when shocks are observed directly. This fact increases the serial correlation in the economy as well.

So far, we have simply added noise to a standard representative-agent real business cycle model. The Lucas story, however, envisioned an economy with many islands, in which agents are subject to island-specific real shocks that are uncorrelated across islands. Hence, if the real shocks on each island could be observed without noise, there would be no aggregate fluctuations. However, aggregate fluctuations will result if aggregate noise is added. We are able to simulate the aggregate behavior of this island's economy with our representative-agent economy

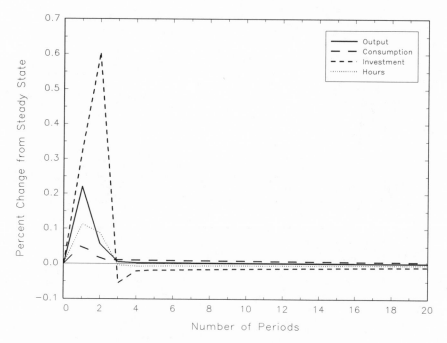

Figure 7.4 Confusion Model: Response to a Transitory Shock

by setting ϵ_1 and ϵ_2 equal to zero for every t in our simulation and drawing nonzero values for ϵ_3. Of course, the parameters σ_1 and σ_2 are set equal to their nonzero calibrated values when we compute the agents' conditional expectations of z_1 and z_2, which we have denoted m_{11}, m_{12}, m_{21}, and m_{22}. Part D of Table 7.2 presents summary statistics for this environment. In this world, output does not fluctuate very much, nor do investment and consumption. In addition, hours fluctuate more than output does, which is a property not shared by the actual economy. The serial correlation properties are also inconsistent with what we observe in the data. The reason for this can be seen in Figure 7.5, which shows that the response of the economy to a noise shock of one standard deviation dies out after only one period. Shocks in this economy are simply not propagated across time.

Taken together, these findings suggest that introducing monetary shocks in this manner yields real fluctuations that are quantitatively too small to be a major source of business cycle fluctuations. In fact, introducing these shocks into a real business cycle model actually reduces the size of the aggregate fluctuations. In addition, the comovements among real variables are relatively unaffected by the addition of the noise shocks. Thus, the results presented in part C of Table 7.2 indicate that introducing imperfectly observed technology shocks into a real business cycle model does not significantly change the business cycle properties of the model. The results presented in part D indicate that if noise were the only aggregate shock,

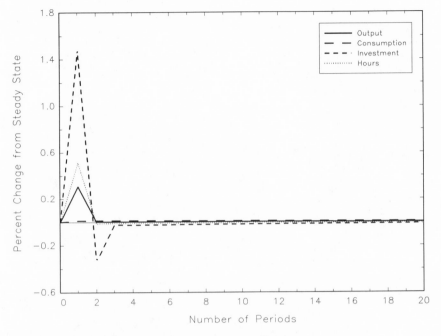

Figure 7.5 Confusion Model: Response to a Noise Shock

we would observe aggregate fluctuations that look nothing like those we observe in actual economies.

These findings confirm those of a similar study by Kydland (1989a). He found (for a slightly different economic environment) that only when one assumes a very small persistent technology shock, does the addition of noise shocks actually increase the volatility of the economy. Again, the quantitative magnitude of the effect he found is small.

4. An Explicit Monetary Economy

The economy explored in the previous section is designed to be a stand-in for a monetary economy where money would be neutral except for the informational problems that it creates for agents. In this section we want to study the features of an economy where money is valued in equilibrium. To introduce money explicitly, one has to take a stand on why money is held, and this in turn will have a bearing on how money affects output. It also has important implications for how one calibrates an abstract monetary model to features of an actual economy. There are three general approaches to introducing money into the neoclassical growth framework: (1) real money balances can be entered directly as an argument in the utility function; (2) money can be assumed to save on the transactions costs associated with purchasing goods; or (3) money can be required to purchase consumption goods or some subset of consumption goods.[15] In this section we describe an economy in which money is held for the latter reason, a cash-in-advance economy. The theoretical foundations of the basic cash-in-advance model of money are carefully laid out in Lucas and Stokey (1983, 1987) and Svensson (1985). The model has been empirically implemented in Cooley and Hansen (1989, 1991, 1992).

We introduce the cash-in-advance motive for holding money into the basic "indivisible labor" real business cycle model. As in the previous section, we are interested in exploring the quantitative effects of monetary shocks for real aggregate fluctuations. However, in contrast with the previous section, there will be no money illusion in this economy. Nonneutralities will arise only because anticipated inflation acts as a distorting tax on activities involving the use of cash. The economy is neutral with respect to unanticipated changes in the money supply. In addition, because we are studying an explicit monetary economy, we are also able to explore whether the economy displays the same comovements among real and nominal variables as documented in Section 2.

Although the economy is similar to the one studied in Chapter 1 and in the previous section, the competitive equilibrium is no longer Pareto optimal because of the distortion introduced by forcing agents to hold money. Therefore, we cannot simply solve a social planning problem to obtain the equilibrium allocations, as we have done previously. Instead, we use the recursive competitive equilibrium concept described in detail in Chapter 1 and apply the methods described in Chapter 2 to obtain equilibrium decision rules.

The outline of this section is as follows. We first describe the basic features of the economy and define an equilibrium. Next, we discuss the calibration issues. The final subsection describes the business cycle properties of the economy.

A Cash-in-Advance Model

Aggregate output, Y_t, is produced according to the following constant returns-to-scale technology, where K_t and H_t are the aggregate capital stock and labor input, respectively:[16]

$$Y_t = e^{z_t} K_t^{\theta} H_t^{1-\theta}, \quad 0 < \theta < 1. \tag{13}$$

Given the assumption of constant returns, we can assume, without loss of generality, that there is only one competitive firm. In addition, the firm will make zero profits in equilibrium. The technology shock, z_t, consists of a single persistent component that evolves according to the law of motion:

$$z_{t+1} = \rho z_t + \epsilon_{t+1}, \quad 0 < \rho < 1. \tag{14}$$

The random variable ϵ is normally distributed with mean zero and standard deviation σ_ϵ.

The portion of output that is not consumed is invested in physical capital.[17] As before, investment in period t produces productive capital in period $t + 1$, so

$$K_{t+1} = (1 - \delta)K_t + X_t, \quad 0 < \delta < 1. \tag{15}$$

The firm seeks to maximize profit, which is equal to $Y_t - w_t H_t - r_t K_t$. The first-order conditions for the firm's problem yield the following functions for the wage rate and rental rate of capital:

$$w(z_t, K_t, H_t) = (1 - \theta)e^{z_t} \left(\frac{K_t}{H_t} \right)^{\theta}, \tag{16}$$

and

$$r(z_t, K_t, H_t) = \theta e^{z_t} \left(\frac{H_t}{K_t} \right)^{1-\theta}. \tag{17}$$

The economy is populated by a large number of identical households, which obtain utility from consumption and leisure. Their preferences are summarized by the following utility function:

$$E_0 \sum_{t=0}^{\infty} \beta^t [\alpha \log c_{1t} + (1 - \alpha) \log c_{2t} - \gamma h_t], \quad 0 < \beta < 1 \text{ and } 0 < \alpha < 1. \tag{18}$$

There are two types of consumption goods; c_1 is a "cash good" and c_2 is a "credit good." The difference is that previously accumulated cash balances are required in order to purchase units of c_1. As in the previous section, hours worked enters linearly in the utility function. This is a reduced-form utility function, which results from the "indivisible labor" assumption. We will be employing this assumption throughout the chapter.

In the beginning of any period t, a representative household has currency holdings equal to $m_t + (1 + R_{t-1})b_t + T_t$, where m_t is currency carried over from the previous period and the second term is principal plus interest from government bond holdings, b_t.[18] The third term is a nominal lump sum transfer (or tax) paid at the beginning of period t. Households then acquire bonds, which they carry into the next period, b_{t+1}. This leaves the household with $m_t + (1 + R_{t-1})b_t + T_t - b_{t+1}$ units of currency for purchasing goods; the household has no access to additional currency after this point. Thus, purchases of cash goods must satisfy the cash-in-advance constraint,

$$P_t c_{1t} \leq m_t + (1 + R_{t-1})b_t + T_t - b_{t+1}, \tag{19}$$

where P_t is the price level in period t.[19] It turns out that this constraint will hold with equality as long as the nominal interest rate is always positive. This requirement will be satisfied throughout our analysis.

Household allocations must also satisfy the following sequence of budget constraints:[20]

$$c_{1t} + c_{2t} + x_t + \frac{m_{t+1}}{P_t} + \frac{b_{t+1}}{P_t} \leq w_t h_t + r_t k_t + \frac{m_t}{P_t} + \frac{(1 + R_{t-1})b_t}{P_t} + T_t. \quad (20)$$

The household expenditures include purchases of the two consumption goods, investment (x_t), money to be carried into the next period (m_{t+1}), and government-issued bonds. The funds available for these purchases include income from capital and labor, currency carried over from the previous period, the principal and interest from bond holdings, and nominal transfers.

Real government consumption, G_t, and the per capita stock of money, M_t, are assumed to be realizations of exogenous stochastic processes. In addition, a government policy also includes sequences of nominal transfers net of taxes, T_t, and nominal government debt, B_t, that satisfies the following government budget constraint for each period t:

$$P_t G_t + T_t = M_{t+1} - M_t + B_{t+1} - (1 + R_{t-1})B_t, \quad (21)$$

where the initial stock of government debt, B_0, is given. In addition, the government policy must satisfy the condition that $(1 + R_{-1})B_0$ plus the expected present value of government purchases and net transfer payments equals the expected present value of seignorage revenues.

Since we are interested in studying the impact of monetary shocks and not the impact of changes in government spending, we set G_t equal to a constant for all $t \geq 0$. In particular, we set $G_t = 0$. In this case, a money injection can be used to directly finance lump sum transfers or to retire existing government debt. The first of these is analogous to the "helicopter drop" described in Friedman (1969), and the second is a standard open market operation. An implication of Ricardian equivalence in this economy is that given B_0 and a particular realization of the money supply process, as long as the present-value government budget constraint is satisfied, the time path of $B_t (t \geq 1)$ and $T_t (t \geq 0)$ does not matter for the equilibrium allocations. Thus, these two methods for injecting new money are equivalent in this economy.[21] Hence, with no loss in generality, we assume that $B_t = 0$ for all $t \geq 1$. In addition, we assume that B_0 is equal to zero. Together these assumptions imply that no bonds are held in this economy and that $T_t = M_{t+1} - M_t$ for each t.

The per capita money supply is assumed to grow at the rate $e^{\mu_t} - 1$ in period t. That is,

$$M_{t+1} = e^{\mu_t} M_t, \quad (22)$$

where μ_t is revealed at the beginning of period t. Therefore, $T_t = (e^{\mu_t} - 1)M_t$. The random variable μ_t is assumed to evolve according to the autoregressive process,[22]

$$\mu_{t+1} = \eta\mu_t + \xi_{t+1}, \quad 0 < \eta < 1. \tag{23}$$

The random variable ξ is log-normally distributed with mean $(1-\eta)\bar{\mu}$ and standard deviation σ_ξ. The average growth rate of money is equal to $\bar{\mu}$. With this specification, μ_t is guaranteed to be positive in every period; thus, the cash-in-advance constraint (19) is always binding.[23]

The problem solved by the representative household is to maximize (18) subject to (14)–(17), (19)–(23), where (19) and (20) are assumed to hold with equality, and the law of motion for the household's own capital stock, $k_{t+1} = (1-\delta)k_t + x_t$. In order to put this problem into a form for which the solution procedure described in Chapter 2 can be applied, we transform variables so that all variables in the deterministic version of the household's problem converge to a steady state. To accomplish this, we define $\hat{m}_t \equiv m_t/M_t$, $\hat{P}_t \equiv P_t/M_{t+1}$ and use this to eliminate m_t and P_t from the problem. Given the particulars of the government policy employed, the Bellman's equation for the household's problem can now be written as follows:

$$v(z, \mu, K, k, \hat{m}) = \max\{\alpha \log c_1 + (1-\alpha) \log c_2$$
$$- \gamma h + \beta E v(z', \mu', K', k', \hat{m}')\}$$

s.t.   (14), (16), (17), (23)

$$c_1 = \frac{\hat{m} + e^\mu - 1}{e^\mu \hat{P}}$$

$$c_2 + k' + \frac{\hat{m}'}{\hat{P}} = w(z, K, H)h + (r(z, K, H) + 1 - \delta)k$$

$$K' = K'(z, \mu, K), \ H = H(z, \mu, K), \text{ and } \hat{P} = P(z, \mu, K). \tag{24}$$

The last line of (24) gives the perceived functional relationship between the aggregate state, (z, μ, K), and per capita investment, per capita hours, and the price level. In equilibrium, these functions must satisfy the requirements of the following definition:

A *recursive competitive equilibrium* consists of a set of decision rules for the household, $c_1(s)$, $c_2(s)$, $k'(s)$, $\hat{m}'(s)$ and $h(s)$, where $s = (z, \mu, K, k, \hat{m})$; a set of per capita decision rules, $K'(z, \mu, K)$ and $H(z, \mu, K)$; pricing functions $P(z, \mu, K)$, $w(z, K, H)$, and $r(z, K, H)$; and a value function, $v(s)$, such that;

1) Households optimize: Given the pricing functions and the per capita decision rules, $v(s)$ solves the functional equation in (24), and c_1, c_2, k', $\hat{m}'$, and h are the associated decision rules;

2) The firm optimizes: The functions w and r are given by equations (16) and (17); and

3) Individual decisions are consistent with aggregate outcomes:

$$k'(z, \mu, K, K, 1) = K'(z, \mu, K), h(z, \mu, K, K, 1) = H(z, \mu, K),$$

and

$$\hat{m}'(z, \mu, K, K, 1) = 1 \text{ for all } (z, \mu, K).$$

We solved for the linear per capita decision rules for a linear-quadratic approximation of this economy. The methods employed are described in detail in Sections 4 and 5 of Chapter 2, so there is no point in repeating the details here.

Calibration

Again, we follow the procedure of calibrating the model by mapping the model economy into observed features of the data, as described in Chapter 1. Just as in that chapter and in the previous section, the values of θ, δ, β and γ are chosen so that certain features of the nonstochastic steady state of the model match average values from post-Korean War U.S. time series. In particular, parameter values are chosen to match average values for capital's share of income, the investment-output ratio, the capital-output ratio, and the fraction of time households spend working in the market. In contrast with the previous section, inventories are not treated as a separate factor of production in this economy. Hence, each of these ratios takes on the same values as in Chapter 1: capital's share is .4, the ratio of investment to output is .25, the quarterly ratio of capital to output is 13.28, and the fraction of time spent working is .31. Again, the resulting parameter values are different from those found in Chapter 1 since this model does not explicitly incorporate productivity and population growth, and indivisible labor is assumed rather than divisible labor.

The properties of the Solow residuals implied by this calibration have virtually the same statistical properties as do the Solow residuals implied by the model of Chapter 1. Hence, the same values for ρ and σ_ϵ are employed here. We now proceed to calibrate the additional parameters introduced by incorporating money into the model. These include the preference parameter, α, and the parameters describing the money supply process.

The parameter α, which determines the relative importance of the cash and credit good in the utility function, is calibrated by considering two kinds of evidence. First, we take an approach similar to that of Lucas (1988). He considers a cash-in-advance model and shows how the parameters of conventional money demand functions are related to the parameters of preferences. To illustrate this, the first-order conditions for the household's problem can be used to obtain the following expression:

$$\frac{C_t}{C_{1t}} = \frac{1}{\alpha} + \frac{(1 - \alpha)}{\alpha} R_t, \tag{25}$$

where $C_t = C_{1t} + C_{2t}$. Per capita real money balances held during period t are equal to C_{1t}, given that the cash-in-advance constraint (19) holds with equality. This implies that the velocity of money with respect to consumption (VEL) is

$$\text{VEL}_t = \frac{1}{\alpha} + \frac{1 - \alpha}{\alpha} R_t. \tag{26}$$

To give empirical content to (26), one must identify the appropriate measure of consumption and the appropriate measure of money from which to construct the velocity. For consumption we use consumption of nondurables and services, taken from the National Income and Product Accounts. Choosing a measure of money presents problems. Conventional monetary aggregates that one might use to capture quantities subject to the inflation tax—the monetary base, or the non–interest-bearing portion of M1—have the drawback that they are too large. They imply velocities of less than unity, which is inconsistent with the model. Instead, we use the portion of M1 that is held by households.[24] To obtain a value for α, we compute the regression implied by (26) using these data.[25] For the sample period, 1970–1986, the estimated equation is:

$$\text{VEL} = \begin{array}{cc} 1.1392 & + & 0.1165 \; * \text{RTB} \\ (0.0265) & & (0.0133) \end{array}$$
$$D - W = 0.297 \qquad R^2 = 0.549,$$

where RTB is the rate on three-month Treasury bills stated on a quarterly basis.

The intercept of this regression implies an estimate of $\alpha = 0.88$. But, it must be noted that the conclusions of this regression analysis are sensitive to the choice of sample period.

An alternative way to approach this calibration problem is to estimate α from survey studies of how people actually make their transactions. In 1984, and again in 1986, the Federal Reserve commissioned surveys of consumer transactions (Avery 1986, 1987). The purpose of these surveys was to determine how people use cash and other means of payment in making their transactions. The proportions for 1984 and 1986 are virtually identical. We take as our estimate of the "cash goods" transactions those purchases made with cash, main checking, other checking, and money orders. This constitutes 84 percent of all transactions. If we denote this percentage by v, then the relation between the preference parameter α and this percentage v is given by the following expression:

$$\alpha = \frac{e^\mu v}{\beta(1 - v) + e^\mu v}. \tag{27}$$

This expression is obtained from the steady-state version of the first-order conditions of the model. Use of $\beta = 0.99$, $\mu = 0$, and $v = 0.84$ implies an estimate of $\alpha = 0.84$. Since 0.84 is close to the number obtained from the regression above, this is the number that is used.

Clearly, neither of the approaches to calibrating the model described above is entirely satisfactory. The first is sensitive to the sample period used and requires using data with velocity implications different from those of the model. The second does not really identify transactions with the precision that the model does. The advantage of the cash-in-advance model is that there is a direct connection between the parameters of that model and empirical relationships (such as the demand for money) that have been widely explored. Trying to calibrate the model in the way we have described highlights shortcomings of the available data on monetary aggregates and the features of the model that appear unrealistic from the point of view of the observed data. This empirical discipline is useful in thinking about extensions of the model and ways to improve our measurement. In any event, the business cycle features of this model that are reported on below are simply not very sensitive to this parameter.

The monetary growth rate is calibrated by estimating an autoregression for M1 growth over the sample period, 1954:I to 1991:II. That estimation produces the following equation:

$$\Delta \log M_t = \underset{(0.0012)}{0.0066} + \underset{(0.072)}{0.491} \, \Delta \log M_{t-1}, \quad \hat{\sigma}_\xi = 0.0089.$$

The implied average growth rate of money is 1.3 percent per quarter.

We summarize our parameter choices and the resulting equilibrium per capita decision rules in the accompanying table.

Parameter Values							
θ	δ	β	γ	α	$\bar{\mu}$	ρ	σ_ϵ
.40	.019	.989	2.53	.84	.015	.95	.007

Decision Rules	
A. Constant Money Growth	$\ln \hat{P} = 1.74085 - 0.39517z + 0\mu - 0.58217 \ln K$
$\nu = 0$	$\ln K' = 0.13235 + 0.12130z + 0\mu + 0.95784 \ln K$
$\sigma_\xi = 0$	$\ln H = 0.25843 + 1.51199z + 0\mu - 0.45540 \ln K$
B. Stochastic Money Growth	$\ln \hat{P} = 1.73386 - 0.39517z + 0.46620\mu - 0.58217 \ln K$
$\eta = .49$	$\ln K' = 0.13206 + 0.12130z + 0.01911\mu + 0.95784 \ln K$
$\sigma_\xi = .0089$	$\ln H = 0.25932 + 1.51199z - 0.05950\mu - 0.45540 \ln K$

Findings

Tables 7.3 and 7.4 show the results of simulating this economy. We compute these statistics in the same way that we compute those in Table 7.2. We compute 100 simulations of 150 periods in length, take logarithms, and filter each simulated time series using the H-P filter.[26] The statistics reported are averages of the statistics computed for each of the 100 simulations. In Table 7.3, we display summary statistics for an economy with only technology shocks operating; in Table 7.4, we present the results for the economy with both monetary and technology shocks. In addition, Figure 7.6 shows the response of output, consumption, investment, and hours worked to a one–standard deviation shock to the money growth process (23).

The behavior of the real variables shown in Table 7.3 is very similar to the behavior of the same variables shown in Table 7.4. Introducing money with a constant growth rate causes very little change in the behavior of the real business cycle economy with indivisible labor. This economy is slightly more volatile than the economy of Table 2, but it is otherwise very similar. The addition of money does enable one to study the behavior of nominal variables, and on this dimension the performance of the model economy is decidedly mixed. The price level in this model economy is countercyclical and velocity is procyclical, as in the U.S. economy, and both display a pattern of cross correlations similar to that shown in Table 7.1. But the price level in the model economy is considerably less variable than the price levels presented in Table 7.1. In addition, the inflation rate in the model economy is negatively correlated with output, in contrast to what is observed in U.S. time series. Finally, the nominal interest rate in the model economy shows almost no correlation with output and is considerably less volatile than in the U.S. economy.

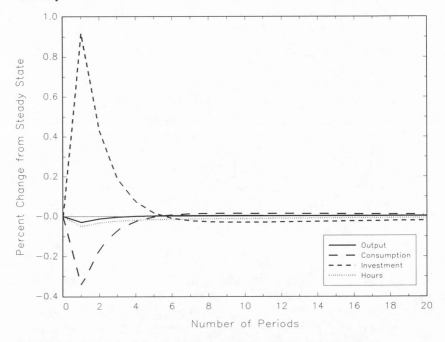

Figure 7.6 Cash-in-Advance Model: Response to a Money Growth Shock

Table 7.3
Simulated Monetary Economy with Only Technology Shocks and Constant Money Growth

								Cross-Correlation of Output with:					
Variable	*SD%*	$x(-5)$	$x(-4)$	$x(-3)$	$x(-2)$	$x(-1)$	x	$x(+1)$	$x(+2)$	$x(+3)$	$x(+4)$	$x(+5)$
Output	1.69	−.033	.083	.240	.444	.693	1.000	.693	.444	.240	.083	−.033
Consumption	0.42	.286	.390	.504	.625	.741	.852	.486	.202	−.016	−.175	−.281
Investment	5.83	−.102	.012	.171	.385	.652	.989	.707	.477	.285	.136	.023
Capital stock	0.38	.635	.647	.610	.507	.320	.028	−.191	−.342	−.436	−.486	−.502
Hours	1.35	−.131	−.017	.145	.363	.638	.988	.716	.493	.306	.158	.046
Productivity	0.42	.289	.392	.508	.630	.749	.863	.493	.205	−.016	−.176	−.283
Price level	0.42	−.289	−.392	−.508	−.630	−.749	−.863	−.493	−.205	.016	.176	.283
Inflation	0.26	.167	.182	.191	.186	.181	−.579	−.451	−.349	−.253	−.173	−.115
Nominal interest rate	0.39	.006	.010	.012	.007	−.007	−.017	−.007	.001	.004	.001	−.003
Velocity	1.35	−.131	−.017	.145	.363	.638	.988	.716	.493	.306	.158	.046

Table 7.4
Simulated Monetary Economy with Money and Technology Shocks—Autoregressive Money Process

Variable	SD%	Cross-Correlation of Output with:											Correlation with Money Growth
		$x(-5)$	$x(-4)$	$x(-3)$	$x(-2)$	$x(-1)$	x	$x(+1)$	$x(+2)$	$x(+3)$	$x(+4)$	$x(+5)$	
Output	1.69	-.033	.083	.240	.444	.692	1.000	.692	.444	.240	.083	-.033	-.01
Consumption	0.53	.220	.307	.397	.488	.582	.676	.378	.153	-.013	-.131	-.217	-.60
Investment	5.90	-.098	.012	.169	.381	.643	.975	.699	.473	.282	.133	.022	.16
Capital stock	0.38	.630	.641	.604	.501	.316	.026	-.191	-.342	-.436	-.485	-.500	.00
Hours	1.35	-.131	-.016	.145	.362	.637	.987	.715	.492	.305	.158	.046	-.03
Productivity	0.42	.288	.391	.505	.628	.745	.859	.491	.204	-.017	-.177	-.284	.06
Price level	1.88	-.078	-.109	-.135	-.161	-.190	-.218	-.126	-.064	-.021	.010	.040	.43
Inflation	1.23	.047	.040	.040	.045	.042	-.138	-.093	-.065	-.049	-.046	-.029	.92
Nominal interest rate	0.58	.011	.008	.010	.011	-.002	-.014	.003	.011	.007	-.004	-.004	.72
Money growth rate	0.87	.011	.001	.001	.005	-.000	-.008	.008	.011	.002	-.011	-.008	1.00
Velocity	1.40	-.122	-.015	.141	.351	.613	.948	.691	.477	.295	.150	.042	.27

Table 7.4 summarizes the behavior of this monetary economy under the assumption that the money supply follows an autoregressive stochastic process. Comparing Tables 7.3 and 7.4, we find that the results for the real variables are almost unchanged. Monetary shocks do increase somewhat the standard deviation of consumption and lower its correlation with output. Some intuition for this result is provided by Figure 7.6, which shows that the monetary shock has almost no effect on output or hours, but has a more sizable, although still quite small, effect on consumption and investment.

Adding monetary shocks does, however, change the statistical properties of some of the nominal variables. Although the behavior of velocity and the nominal interest rate are about the same in Tables 7.3 and 7.4, the price level and inflation rate are more variable in the second economy. In fact, the model displays significantly more variability in the price level and inflation than is observed in the U.S. data. In addition, although inflation in the Table 7.4 economy is not procyclical, as in the data, it is less negatively correlated with current output than in the Table 7.3 economy.

The model economy displays very little correlation between money growth and real variables except consumption. We also observe little correlation with real variables in the data, but this includes consumption. In addition, money growth is negatively correlated with inflation, the price level and nominal interest rates in Table 7.1, but positively correlated with these variables in the model. In general, even after allowing for stochastic money growth, the cyclical behavior of nominal variables in the model economy are quite different from the behavior of nominal variables in the U.S. economy.

The results for the real variables confirm what is shown in Cooley and Hansen (1989). Monetary growth shocks do not contribute much to the fluctuations in real variables displayed by a basic neoclassical growth model when money is introduced by requiring cash-in-advance. Monetary growth does distort allocations in this economy because of the tax associated with inflation. The welfare costs of this distortion have been explored extensively in Cooley and Hansen (1989, 1991, 1992). Nevertheless, we have shown here that these monetary shocks are quantitatively unimportant for the real business cycle. What is missing is some mechanism by which monetary shocks have significant real consequences at business cycle frequencies. In the next section we describe a model in which such a mechanism exists.

5. An Economy with Nominal Rigidities

The possibility that nominal contracts may play an important role in the propagation of monetary shocks has been perhaps the most popular alternative to the signal extraction models that we considered in Section 3. Price rigidity resulting from nominal wage contracts has been regarded as an important propagation mechanism because of the prevalence of wage agreements observed in labor markets: a relatively large portion of the labor force consists of salaried workers, and a significant portion of the manufacturing labor force participate in long-term contracts. The importance of wage contracts is also often inferred from the observation that aggregate hours fluctuate more than wages do.[27]

There are several papers in the equilibrium business cycle literature that have studied the implications of nominal wage contracts as well as nominal price contracts for the transmission of monetary shocks. Cho (1990) examines the quantitative implications of one-period nominal wage and price contracts. Cho and Cooley (1992) study the properties of economies with multiperiod wage and price contracts. Robert King (1991) also studies multiperiod wage and price contracts but in an economy that does not incorporate any specific motive for money holding. In this section of the paper, we consider a particularly simple version of a contracting economy, one with one-period nominal wage contracts. We show how to specify and solve such an economy and illustrate the impact this has on the propagation of monetary shocks.

The economy we study is identical to the one described in the previous section, but we consider a variation on the standard recursive competitive equilibrium concept that is motivated by the work of Gray (1976) and Fischer (1977). In this arrangement, households and firms agree to specify the nominal wage in advance, and households cede to firms the right to determine aggregate hours, leaving firms free to maximize profits. We beg the important question of why firms and workers enter into such a contract. Our objective here is to illustrate the quantitative impact of such arrangements. Having agreed to the arrangements just described, households and firms behave as typical rational neoclassical agents: they solve for the equilibrium and form their expectations using the equilibrium decision rules of the economy.

An Economy with Wage Contracting

The economic environment studied in this section is the same as the cash-in-advance model studied in Section 4, with one additional feature: the nominal wage rate for period t is agreed to one period in advance.[28] At the end of period $t - 1$, the nominal wage rate for period t is competitively determined on the basis of expectations about the technology and monetary shocks (z_t and μ_t). Then, in period t, after z_t and μ_t are revealed, households choose consumption and investment. In addition, firms unilaterally choose employment to equate the marginal product of labor to the realized real wage. Under these assumptions, the nominal wage rate, W_t^c, will be a function of z_{t-1}, μ_{t-1} and K_t, in contrast with the model of the previous section, where the nominal wage is a function of z_t, μ_t, and K_t. Individual households' consumption and investment choices are functions of the state $s_t = (z_{t-1}, \epsilon_t, \mu_{t-1}, \xi_t, K_t, k_t, m_t)$, while per capita consumption, investment, and employment are functions of the aggregate state $S_t = (z_{t-1}, \epsilon_t, \mu_{t-1}, \xi_t, K_t)$. In what follows we will drop time subscripts and denote z_{t-1} and μ_{t-1} by z_{-1} and μ_{-1}. In addition, we denote the information set available to agents when W^c is determined at the end of period $t - 1$ by ω, where ω is a subset of the state s, consisting of z_{-1}, μ_{-1}, K, k, and m. The equilibrium contract wage is a function of the aggregate information set Ω, consisting of z_{-1}, μ_{-1}, and K.

The commodity for which W^c is the market-clearing wage is the expected labor input given Ω, which we denote by $\tilde{H}$. Taking W^c as given, households choose their desired labor supply, $\tilde{h}$, as a function of ω. In addition, the firm, also taking W^c as given, chooses its demand for the expected labor input by maximizing expected profits given the information set Ω. With this market structure, the equilibrium contract wage will equal the conditional expected value given Ω of the marginal product of labor multiplied by the price level. Employing the same functional forms as in Section 4 (see equation [16]), this implies that

$$\log W^c = \log(1 - \theta) + \theta(\log K - \log \tilde{H}) + E[z + \log P|\Omega].^{29} \quad (28)$$

Once S is revealed, actual hours worked, H, is chosen by the firm so that the marginal product of labor is equal to the realized real wage. In conjunction with equation (16), this implies that

$$H(S) = \left[\frac{(1 - \theta)e^z P}{W^c(\Omega)} \right]^{\frac{1}{\theta}} K. \quad (29)$$

Taking logs and using (28) to eliminate $\log W^c$, we obtain the following expression for H:

$$\log H = \log \tilde{H} + \frac{1}{\theta} (\log P - E[\log P|\Omega]) + \frac{1}{\theta} \epsilon. \quad (30)$$

Equation (30) implies that $\log H - \log \tilde{H}$ is an i.i.d. random variable with zero mean. Households are assumed to understand that whatever choice they make for $\tilde{h}(\omega)$, their actual hours worked, $h(s)$, will differ from this by the realization of this random variable. Thus,

$$\log h = \log \tilde{h} + \frac{1}{\theta} (\log P - E[\log P|\Omega]) + \frac{1}{\theta} \epsilon. \quad (31)$$

As in the previous section, we introduce a transformation of variables so that all variables are stationary in the limit ($\hat{m}_t \equiv m_t/M_t$ and $\hat{P}_t \equiv P_t/M_{t+1}$). With this transformation, the dynamic programming problem solved by a representative household, (24), as modified to incorporate nominal contracts, is the following:

$$v(s) = \max_{\hat{m}'k'} \left\{ E\left[\max_{\tilde{h}}\{E[(\alpha \log c_1 + (1-\alpha)\log c_2 - \gamma h + \beta v(s'))|\omega]\}|s \right] \right\}$$

s.t.   (14), (17), (23)

$$c_1 = \frac{\hat{m} + e^{\mu} - 1}{e^{\mu}\hat{P}}$$

$$c_2 + k' + \frac{\hat{m}'}{\hat{P}} = (1-\theta)\left[\frac{K}{H}\right]^{\theta} h + [r(S) + 1 - \delta]k$$

$$\log h = \log \tilde{h} + \frac{1}{\theta}[\log \hat{P} - E(\log \hat{P}|\Omega)] + \frac{1}{\theta}\epsilon + \frac{1}{\theta}[\xi - (1-\eta)\bar{\mu}]$$

$$\log H = \log \tilde{H} + \frac{1}{\theta}[\log \hat{P} - E(\log \hat{P}|\Omega)] + \frac{1}{\theta}\epsilon + \frac{1}{\theta}[\xi - (1-\eta)\bar{\mu}]$$

$$K' = K'(S), \ \tilde{H} = \tilde{H}(\Omega), \ \text{and} \ \hat{P} = P(S). \tag{32}$$

The budget constraint on line 4 of (32) incorporates the fact that the realized real wage equals the equilibrium marginal product of labor by virtue of the way actual hours, H, is determined (see equation [29]).

A *recursive competitive equilibrium* for the wage-contracting model consists of a set of decision rules for the household, $c_1(s)$, $c_2(s)$, $k'(s)$, $\hat{m}'(s)$, and $\tilde{h}(\omega)$; a set of per capita decision rules, $K'(S)$ and $\tilde{H}(\Omega)$; pricing functions, $P(S)$ and $r(S)$; and a value function $v(s)$, such that

1) Households optimize: Given the pricing functions and the per capita decision rules, $v(s)$ solves the functional equation in (32), and $c_1, c_2, k', \hat{m}'$, and $\tilde{h}$ are the associated decision rules;

2) The firm optimizes: The rental rate, r, is given by equation (17), and hours worked, H, is determined by equation (30); and

3) Individual decisions are consistent with aggregate outcomes:

$$k'(z_{-1}, \epsilon, \mu_{-1}, \xi, K, K, 1) = K'(z_{-1}, \epsilon, \mu_{-1}, \xi, K),$$

$$\hat{m}'(z_{-1}, \epsilon, \mu_{-1}, \xi, K, K, 1) = 1,$$

and

$$\tilde{h}(z_{-1}, \mu_{-1}, K, K, 1) = \tilde{H}(z_{-1}, \mu_{-1}, K), \ \text{for all } S.$$

Calibration and Solution Method

The nonstochastic steady state for this model is identical to the steady state of the economy studied in Section 4. For this reason, we employ the same parameter values as in the previous section. We also employ the same processes for the technology shock, z, and the money growth rate, μ. Thus, since there are no additional calibration issues, we can proceed to describe the modifications we make to our solution procedure described in Chapter 2 that enable us to solve for a recursive competitive equilibrium for this economy.

The nonlinear return function, which we approximate by a quadratic function, is formed by using the cash-in-advance constraint and budget constraint in (32) to eliminate c_1 and c_2 from the utility function. Since the rule determining H, given by the sixth line in (32), is a log-linear function rather than a linear function, it is convenient to form the quadratic approximation of the return function as a function of the logs rather than the levels of the variables.

At this point, problem (32) has been reduced to one of maximizing a quadratic objective subject to linear constraints. Since the individual and per capita decision rules obtained from a linear-quadratic problem are independent of the variance of the shocks, we can set these to zero without loss of generality. The equilibrium pricing function $P(S)$—actually log $P(S)$—and equilibrium decision rules for log K' and log $\tilde{H}$ can then be obtained by straightforward application of the methods described in Chapter 2.[30] However, the resulting decision rule for $\tilde{H}$ will be a function of S rather than Ω. The correct decision rule for log $\tilde{H}$ is simply the conditional expectation of this rule given Ω. This can be obtained by setting ϵ and ξ equal to their means, thereby making log $\tilde{H}$ a function of the elements of Ω only. Finally, the decision rule for actual hours employed, log $H(S)$, is formed from the functions log $P(S)$ and log $\tilde{H}(\Omega)$ by using the formula on the sixth line of equation (32).

Applying this procedure, we obtained the linear decision rules shown in the accompanying table, which were used to simulate the economy.

Decision Rules for Economy with Nominal Contracts
$(\eta = .49, \sigma_\xi = .0089)$
$\ln \hat{P} = 1.73457 - 0.37541 z_{-1} - 0.39517\epsilon + 0.22844\mu_{-1} + 0.37346\xi - 0.58217 \ln K$
$\ln K' = 0.13089 + 0.11523 z_{-1} + 0.12130\epsilon + 0.00937\mu_{-1} + 0.17170\xi + 0.95784 \ln K$
$\ln H = 0.23260 + 1.43640 z_{-1} + 1.51208\epsilon - 0.02916\mu_{-1} + 3.43365\xi - 0.45540 \ln K$

Findings

The results of simulating this economy are shown in Table 7.5 and Figure 7.7. It is immediately obvious that nominal contracts enable monetary shocks to have significant real effects; real output, investment, hours, and productivity are all vastly more volatile than in the same economy without contracts (see Table 7.4). Indeed, hours are more variable than output, a finding that is at odds with the U.S. data but might be anticipated given the response of these variables to a money growth shock shown in Figure 7.7. The correlations of real variables with output are lower in

Table 7.5
Simulated Monetary Economy with Nominal Contracts

							Cross-Correlation of Output with:						Correlation with
Variable	SD%	x(−5)	x(−4)	x(−3)	x(−2)	x(−1)	x	x(+1)	x(+2)	x(+3)	x(+4)	x(+5)	Money Growth
Output	2.37	−.037	.019	.098	.202	.320	1.000	.320	.202	.098	.019	−.037	.61
Consumption	0.49	.233	.300	.363	.392	.346	.261	.304	.131	−.004	−.097	−.157	−.42
Investment	9.00	−.077	−.028	.047	.154	.289	.986	.298	.198	.108	.039	−.011	.67
Capital stock	0.43	.464	.488	.481	.431	.327	−.087	−.210	−.293	−.342	−.363	−.365	.00
Hours	3.10	−.072	−.040	.001	.066	.142	.937	.189	.128	.070	.025	−.010	.77
Productivity	1.21	.113	.146	.197	.236	.279	−.422	.159	.079	.018	−.023	−.047	−.78
Price level	1.79	.048	.053	.053	.055	.041	−.011	−.361	−.266	−.191	−.132	−.083	.42
Inflation	1.15	−.007	.000	−.003	.022	.078	.561	−.145	−.117	−.093	−.076	−.067	.92
Nominal interest rate	1.04	−.029	−.020	−.019	.012	.079	.475	−.069	−.053	−.039	−.035	−.039	.71
Money growth rate	0.87	−.045	−.038	−.015	.064	.236	.608	−.091	−.076	−.069	−.067	−.067	1.00
Velocity	2.39	−.087	−.043	.022	.122	.254	.975	.254	.172	.097	.038	−.007	.74

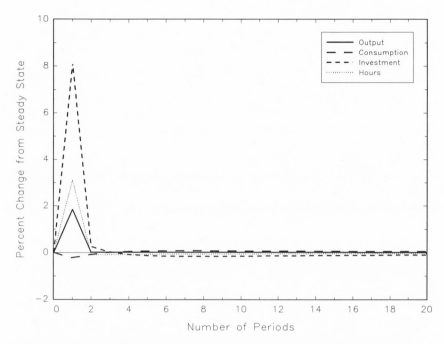

Figure 7.7 Model with Nominal Contracts: Response to a Money Growth Shock

this economy than in the previous one, except the correlation between investment and output, which is larger. The most striking change is that the correlation of productivity and output fell from .86 in the cash-in-advance economy to −.42 in the economy with nominal contracts.

Comparing Figures 7.6 and 7.7, which were both constructed by using the same-sized innovation to money growth, we see that the response of investment, for example, is on the order of ten times larger in the economy with nominal contracts than in the cash-in-advance economy. In addition, the response of output and hours to an increase in the growth rate of money is positive in this economy. The response was negative in the economy of the previous section. In fact, the response to a money growth shock shown in Figure 7.7 looks quite similar to the response to a noise shock in the signal extraction economy shown in Figure 7.5. The main difference is that the response shown in Figure 7.7 is much larger.

The correlations with money growth shown in Table 7.5 differ significantly from those shown in Table 7.4. The most striking difference is that the correlations between money growth and the real variables are much larger. Still, these look nothing like the correlations shown in Table 7.1. The correlations between money growth and the nominal variables are quite similar in the two model economies, with the exception of velocity, which is more highly correlated with money growth in the nominal contracting economy. Again, this is a property not shared with the U.S. economy.

There are, however, dimensions along which the economy with nominal contracts displays properties that are closer to those of U.S. business cycles. In particular, inflation and nominal interest rates are both positively correlated with output in the economy with nominal contracts (these correlations were negative in the basic cash-in-advance economy), and the magnitude of these correlations are similar to those shown in Table 7.1. In addition, nominal interest rates are more volatile in this economy than in the economy without contracts; they are almost as volatile as the interest rate on one-month Treasury bills. On the other hand, the nominal contracting model does not account very well for the countercyclical behavior of prices reported in Table 7.1, a feature that the basic cash-in-advance model does capture.

The nominal contract also alters the serial correlation structure of this economy. However, because the contract in this economy is only one period long, most of the impact of the monetary shock occurs in the first few periods. With longer-term contracts this response will be spread out over several periods. This is important because one of the features of U.S. data that was noted in Section 2 of this chapter is that there is a phase shift in the correlation between output and monetary variables. That is not apparent in Table 7.5. The results of Cho and Cooley (1992) suggest that there may be some pattern of multiperiod contracts that leads to a correlation structure with this feature.

The results just displayed are intended to be suggestive of the possible impact of wage contracts on the economy. A more extensive exploration of economies with nominal contracting is contained in papers by Cho (1990), Cho and Cooley (1992), Cho and Phaneuf (1993), and Cho, Cooley, and Phaneuf (1994). Cho and Cooley (1992) explore the properties of multiperiod wage and price contracts, as well as those of staggered contracts. Briefly, their findings are as follows: (1) the volatility of the economy increases with contract length; (2) price contracting can cause far more volatility than wage contracting can, although the amount depends on the exact nature of the arrangements employed; and (3) monetary shocks propagated by nominal contracts of either sort are unlikely to be the sole or even the most important source of fluctuations because monetary shocks by themselves produce correlations in the generated data that are inconsistent with observed U.S. data.

6. Summary and Conclusions

The goal of this chapter was to illustrate how the basic real business cycle model can be adapted to study the role of monetary shocks in business cycles. We constructed economic environments that were designed to capture what we take to be the two predominant modern theories about how monetary shocks cause fluctuations in real activity. We then assessed the quantitative importance of monetary shocks in these environments. In addition, the explicit monetary environments of the last two sections enabled us to study nominal features of the business cycle. These include the comovements of output and other real variables with the price level, inflation, nominal interest rates, the money growth rate, and so on.

Our findings can be summarized as follows. First, of the three models considered in the chapter, only the nominal contracting model has the feature that monetary shocks have a significant effect on the properties of the real business cycle. However, in the version of that model considered here, as well as in more complicated versions studied in Cho and Cooley (1992), the comovements induced by monetary shocks are inconsistent with what we observe in U.S. data. Thus, none of these models considered here can be interpreted as providing a strong theoretical argument for money growth shocks' being the key impulses driving aggregate fluctuations. Monetarists must look elsewhere for a general equilibrium theory consistent with their interpretation of U.S. time series.

Our second basic finding is that neither of the two monetary economies considered are particularly successful in accounting for the features of the business cycle that are purely monetary. One feature that particularly stands out is that in both of our models, the correlation between money growth and nominal interest rates is quite high, around .7, while in the U.S. data, this correlation is negative. Hence, there is a need for additional research aimed at discovering and incorporating the specific features needed for a quantitative general equilibrium model to account for the properties of nominal variables over the business cycle. Without such a model, we must conclude that questions concerning the importance of monetary shocks for the business cycle are still very much unresolved.

In fact, the study of monetary economies by means of the dynamic general equilibrium methods described in this book is at an early stage. There is a great deal of ongoing research in this area.[31] For example, some recent work has focused on the use of models with liquidity effects to account for the negative correlation between money growth and nominal interest rates. In particular, Christiano and Eichenbaum (1993) have explored in some detail the quantitative implications of a model with liquidity effects based on the theoretical work of Lucas (1990c) and Fuerst (1992). Other research has explored the business cycle effects of additional monetary nonneutralities ignored by the models studied in this chapter. Altig and Carlstrom (1991), for example, study the effects of the interaction of inflation with the nominal taxation of capital income.

Finally, others have used quantitative theory to explore monetary environments that differ significantly from the ones we have focused on here and address questions that differ from the business cycle issues that motivate this chapter. However, these papers emphasize roles for money and mechanisms through which money affects real variables that may prove important for the sorts of questions raised in this paper. For example, İmrohoroğlu (1992) describes an economy where individual households hold nominal assets as insurance against idiosyncratic shocks because they are liquidity constrained. İmrohoroğlu and Prescott (1991),

Díaz-Giménez (1990), Díaz-Giménez and Prescott (1989), and Díaz-Giménez et al. (1992) have studied a variety of monetary issues, including the role of financial intermediation, using heterogenous-agent monetary economies that are extensions of the environment considered by İmrohoroğlu.[32]

Notes

We are grateful to Larry Christiano and Edward Prescott for helpful discussions and comments. We acknowledge research support from the National Science Foundation and from the John M. Olin Foundation.

1. Friedman and Schwartz (1965) are careful to distinguish between the behavior of "outside" money and that of "inside," or high-powered, money. King and Plosser (1984) also stress the importance of this distinction. The evidence reported by Friedman and Schwartz is consistent with the view that both kinds of money play an important role, with perhaps somewhat stronger evidence in favor of the importance of inside money. However, in this chapter we will be describing models with outside money only.

2. Throughout this chapter we represent the business cycle features by using the H-P filter described in Chapter 1.

3. All variables except the inflation rate, interest rates, and M1 growth rate are logged before filtering with the H-P filter.

4. King (1991) has emphasized that the ability to capture this dynamic response is an important test of monetary models. In a similar vein, Sims (1991) has suggested that the sluggish response of prices to monetary innovations is of crucial interest.

5. A feature of nominal interest rates that is not captured in these statistics is the tendency of the slope of the yield curve to vary over the cycle. The behavior of real interest rates and the real yield curve over the business cycle have been extensively documented in a number of papers. Donaldson, Johnsen and Mehra (1990) describe the behavior of the real yield curve over the business cycle. Chapman (1992) describes the movements of both real and nominal interest rates and real and nominal yield curves over the business cycle and the extent to which this behavior can be captured in simple dynamic general equilibrium models of the type considered in this paper. For that reason and because the behavior of asset prices in such models is also explored extensively by Rouwenhorst in Chapter 10, we do not emphasize these features here.

6. See Fuerst (1992); Christiano (1991); and Christiano and Eichenbaum (1993).

7. An exercise similar to this one was originally carried out by Kydland (1989), who obtained very similar results.

8. The model studied here differs from Kydland and Prescott's (1988) model in three important respects. First, Kydland and Prescott assume it takes multiple periods to build productive capital, while it takes just one period in our economy. Second, their specification permits the rate of capital utilization to vary; ours does not. Third, they assume that labor is divisible and that past leisure affects the current period utility, while we assume that labor is indivisible.

9. Christiano (1988) also analyzes an economy with a buffer role for inventories and an information structure similar to that considered by Kydland and Prescott (1982).

10. There are several ways to solve models with occasionally binding constraints. Fisher and Christiano (1994) compare several algorithms for solving models with this feature. They conclude that a version of the method of parameterized expectations described in Chapter 3 performs best.

11. Kydland and Prescott (1982) provide the following additional motivation for including inventories as a factor of production: "With larger inventories, stores can economize on labor resources allocated to restocking. Firms, by making larger production runs, reduce equipment down-time associated with shifting from producing one type of good to another" (p. 1350).

12. For a derivation of these formulas, as well as those in equation (8), see Mood, Graybill, and Boes (1973).

13. This section is written under the assumption that the reader is familiar with the material in Chapter 2.

14. In addition to the fact that this model includes unobserved technology shocks and inventories, this economy differs from the one described in Chapter 1 in that productivity and population growth are not explicitly incorporated, and labor is assumed to be indivisible rather than divisible.

15. There is a formal equivalence between the different motives, discussed by Feenstra (1986).

16. Recall that the notational convention used in this book is to use capital letters, such as K and H, to denote aggregate (or per capita) quantities. Lower-case letters, such as k and h, denote quantities demanded or supplied by an individual household.

17. In contrast with the economy described in the previous section, there is no role for inventories in this model given that all information is revealed at the beginning of the period and inventories are not a factor of production.

18. In this section we assume that all bonds are issued by the government. It would not be difficult to allow for privately issued bonds as well, but since all households are identical, no privately issued bonds would be held in equilibrium.

19. We do not consider the possibility of a cash-in-advance constraint on investment as in Stockman (1981).

20. This budget constraint incorporates the fact that both consumption goods and the investment good sell at the same price even though one is a cash good and the others are credit goods. This is because all goods are produced by using the same technology and, from the point of view of the seller, sales of both credit goods and cash goods result in cash that will be available for spending at the same time in the following period. Although sales of cash goods in a given period result in cash receipts in the same period, this cash cannot be spent until the next period.

21. These are not the only ways that new money could be injected. For example, following Lucas (1982), an asset could be introduced that entitles the bearer to a share of all seignorage revenues generated by the central bank. It can be shown that in equilibrium this scheme would lead to the same allocations as in the economy where new money is introduced using lump sum transfers.

22. This is a very simple policy rule, which does not react to changes in other state variables, such as the technology shock. The view that monetary policy reacts to real shocks, or that it ought to react in specific ways, is widely held. Unfortunately, there is little empirical evidence that changes in the money growth rate are correlated with technology shocks, so it is difficult to calibrate a model with these features.

23. With this monetary policy, the equilibrium nominal interest rate is given by

$$R_t = \left[\beta E_t \left(\frac{1}{e^{\mu_{t+1}}} \right) \right]^{-1} - 1.$$

The fact that μ is always greater than zero guarantees that R_t is always greater than zero and that the cash-in-advance constraint always binds.

24. These data are obtained from the Flow of Funds Accounts. Unfortunately these data are also flawed because of the way they treat currency. Currency held by households is treated as the residual of total currency outstanding and currency held by businesses and governments. The resulting figure is undoubtedly too high.

25. The data reveal a strong trend in velocity. For this regression to be valid, it would have to be matched by a trend in interest rates. We test the null hypothesis that velocity and nominal interest rates are cointegrated. We cannot reject the null hypothesis that velocity and interest rates are cointegrated at the .05 level of confidence. Unfortunately, there is also evidence of a remaining spurious trend in the residuals of this regression.

26. As in constructing Table 7.1, variables that are already expressed as rates are not logged. These include the inflation rate, the nominal interest rate, and the money growth rate. All other variables are logged before filtering.

27. More recently, attention has shifted to the importance of rigid goods prices. Mankiw (1985), Parkin (1986), Akerlof and Yellen (1985), and others have stressed the importance of price rigidities that arise as a consequence of the costs of changing prices. Here as well, the importance of the phenomenon is frequently inferred from the observation that in the aggregate, quantities seem to fluctuate more than prices. Cho and Cooley (1992) explore the role of price rigidities in a setting similar to that considered here.

28. The extension to multiperiod contracts is not a trivial extension of the environment considered here. See Cho and Cooley (1992).

29. In this expression we approximate the log of the expected value of the marginal product with the expected value of the log.

30. In fact, given that the same parameter values are being used, the linear rules obtained for $\log P$, $\log \tilde{H}$, and $\log K'$ will be identical to those obtained in Section 4 except that the state vector will include z_{-1}, μ_{-1}, ϵ, and ξ, rather than simply z and μ.

31. In this chapter, we have made no attempt to provide a complete survey of the literature in this area and will not attempt to remedy this situation now.

32. Ríos-Rull discusses some of this research, as well as the work of Altig and Carlstrom (1991), in Chapter 4.

Chapter 8
Non-Walrasian Economies

Jean-Pierre Danthine
and John B. Donaldson

1. Introduction

In the first decade since its inception, the Real Business Cycle (RBC) research program has been viewed as having a clear "new classical" bias. Some have sought to interpret its initial attempts to rationalize business cycle fluctuations in the context of model economies where equilibrium allocations are Pareto optimal as an unwarranted challenge to the notion that government intervention can be beneficial. The perspective of seeking to explain observed fluctuations in employment as resulting exclusively from movements along the labor supply curve has provoked even stronger reactions. These reactions are perhaps epitomized by the oft-cited quip that the RBC theory requires us to interpret "the Great Depression as a prolonged bout of laziness."

As is clear from previous chapters, however, the RBC methodology has much broader applicability than our introductory paragraph would suggest: being scientific in nature, it should lead us to prefer the model or set of models that best helps us to understand the business cycle observations irrespective of any ideology associated with its (their) constituent building blocks. Given this perspective, the natural strategy for the RBC program was to begin first with an analysis of the most thoroughly understood dynamic macromodel: the neoclassical stochastic growth model. The fact that certain implications of the model are inconsistent with observed business cycle regularities has led to a number of proposals for its substantial modification (e.g., Kydland and Prescott 1982, Hansen 1985). In addition, one cannot rule out, at the current state of development, the possibility that two models of substantially different structure may equally well explain the accepted set of stylized facts. The choice between such models must therefore be based on their relative performance vis-à-vis new facts as they become known.

For the better part of this century, economists have disagreed about which macroeconomic facts are most significant and how some of them should be interpreted. Perhaps subject to more differing interpretations than any other economic phenomenon are the characteristics of unemployment in modern economies: (1) a fraction of the labor force is unemployed at any given time, (2) this fraction varies over time, and (3) it assumes different average values in different economies. In particular, a significant portion of the economics profession insists that these observations cannot be rationalized in a market-clearing framework. While attempts to vindicate this assertion are unsatisfying if they result from exogenous fixed-price (or wage) assumptions, several justifications have been provided for the failure of prices and wages to adjust in certain circumstances. These include (without attempting to be complete) precontracting in nominal or real terms, efficiency wage considerations, credit rationing resulting from asymmetric information, and pure distributional issues.

The main assertion of this chapter is that the RBC modeling perspective provides, in principle, a coherent and unbiased procedure for "testing" these alternative views of the labor market: the idea is to construct dynamic equilibrium models that incorporate the features of special interest and to evaluate whether they empower the model better to replicate qualitatively and quantitatively the major business cycle facts.[1] The qualification "in principle" refers only to current limitations in formulating complex dynamic economies and computing their equilibria.

In this chapter, we illustrate this perspective by specifying two economic models into which distinctly different non-Walrasian features of the labor market have been inserted. Our goal is not to be "non-Walrasian" per se. Rather, it is to amend the canonical model in the hope of remedying one of its well-known deficiencies: the inability to account for the relative variability of employment and productivity. While modifications other than those discussed here have also been proposed, we believe that our decision to incorporate labor market frictions or efficiency wage considerations is a direction for resolving this puzzle that many economists would consider natural. It is thus also reasonable to use the machinery of the RBC construct to evaluate these alternative constructs. A second objective of this chapter is therefore to show how this can be accomplished and to show how the canonical model can be adapted to accommodate a variety of non-Walrasian features. We conclude this introduction with a few reflections on the definition and usefulness of the "non-Walrasian" label.

In a strict sense, a Walrasian general equilibrium model is one in which the allocation of resources is fully effected at prices which clear frictionless competitive markets and in which preferences, consumption, and production sets satisfy normal regularity conditions. A non-Walrasian economy, then, would be any economy in which one of these conditions is not met. It is clear that in our context this definition is too broad to be useful: most of current business cycle research and proposed future work in the RBC program would have to be reviewed in the present chapter.[2]

We elect, therefore, to delineate the notion of a non-Walrasian economy much more narrowly. In conformity with the usage in at least part of the macroeconomics literature, we define a non-Walrasian economy as one in which, for reasons that may vary, some market transactions are effected at nonclearing prices. Our choice of a rather narrow focus is dictated by the general thrust of this book and its primary concentration on methodological issues. The discussion has close counterparts in the imperfect competition model discussed in Chapter 10, and in other models not represented in this book, such as models of incomplete markets or transactions costs (Telmer 1992; Aiyagari and Gertler 1991).

Armed with this definition, we next model two economies with non-Walrasian features in the labor markets. Following our original perspective, we then evaluate their relative performance along the customary business cycle dimensions.

1. An Economy with Labor Contracting and a Wage Floor

This section presents a detailed illustration of the way non-Walrasian considerations may be incorporated in a real business cycle model within the general formal structure provided by the neoclassical growth paradigm. Here, as in the following section, the main challenge is to propose a business cycle model where (sufficient) employment variability is generated exclusively by movements in and out of employment—with a fixed labor supply—rather than along the labor supply curve, as in Walrasian models.

The Firms

Consider an economy with a large number of identical firms. Firms are owned by infinitely lived dynasties of shareholders and undertake all investment and hiring decisions.[3] All firms produce the unique commodity with the same constant-returns-to-scale (CRS) technology, as described by a production function of the form $f(k, n_p, n_s)z$, where k represents an individual firm's capital stock, z is the economywide shock to technology common to all firms, and n_p and n_s, respectively, denote firm levels of primary and secondary labor employed. (More on this distinction presently.) Firm owners (stockholders) receive the residual income from production, that is, the value of output net of the wage bill and taxes. We write $\pi(k, K, z)$ to represent the (thus defined) income function of a firm owner with individual capital, k, when the state of the economy is summarized by the aggregate level of capital stock, K, and the technology shock, z. In general, a capital letter will indicate the economywide level of the variable, while lower-case variables denote firm-specific levels. With this notation, the representative shareholder's consumption and savings decisions are assumed to solve the following problem:

$$\max_{\{(c_t,(x_t))\}} E\left(\sum_{t=0}^{\infty} \beta^t u(c_t)\right)$$

$$\text{s.t.} \quad c_t + x_t \leq \pi(k_t, K_t, z_t)$$

$$k_{t+1} = (1 - \delta)k_t + x_t$$

$$k_0 \text{ given.} \tag{1}$$

Note that problem (1), which will be the heart of the dynamics for our economy, is formally very similar to the standard neoclassical growth problem.

Workers in the Primary Sector

Let us make the admittedly extreme assumption that workers do not have access to financial markets: they do not own shares in firms, and they can neither borrow nor lend. A useful technical implication of this assumption is that the workers' decision problem is static. We are thus able to introduce agent heterogeneity in a convenient way, without the challenge of having to keep track of wealth distributions: only one agent effectively accumulates wealth. However, this heterogeneity is nontrivial, and we shall see that the choice of preference parameters for the workers has a significant impact on the properties of equilibrium.

As to the economic motivation for the above assumption, let us make the following two observations. First, workers' main wealth is in the form of their human capital. Yet human capital cannot collateralize loans in modern economies. Second, a large fraction of the population does not own stocks. Mankiw and Zeldes (1991), in fact, report that for the U.S. economy, only one-quarter of all families own stocks. These comments together suggest that our modeling device of excluding workers from the capital markets could be a useful abstraction of reality.

The hypothesis of restricted access effectively prevents an optimal allocation of risks via financial markets: workers in our model economy consume their period income and are likely to experience substantial income risk. Modern economies, however, have developed substitute mechanisms for smoothing consumption. In this chapter, we shall focus on the labor market and related institutions as instruments for doing so. One of our primary objectives will be to demonstrate that this enlarged role of labor institutions and arrangements is not without consequences for the dynamics of the economy.

We want to introduce two types of equilibrium wage functions, and for that purpose, two types of relationships between firms and workers are postulated. Labor services are provided by a stationary population of workers; we assume for simplicity that each worker supplies one unit of labor inelastically in each period of the worker's life (there is no disutility to work). Workers in the primary sector benefit from a lifelong association with the firm. They are permanent members of the organization, or "insiders." Suppose, for instance, that these permanent workers (managers) are considered by firm owners as being "part of the family," in such a way that their utility is included directly in the firm owner's objective function. The period utility function of a firm owner with labor force n_p could then be written as $u(c) + \nu n_p \bar{u}(w_p)$, where w_p is the compensation offered the typical permanent worker, and ν is the altruistic parameter. Clearly $w_p(k, K, z)$ will be such that

$$\nu n_p \bar{u}_1[w_p(k, K, z)] = u_1[c(k, K, z)]. \qquad (2)$$

Each of the large number of identical firms employs its share of the primary sector work force. Here $c(k, K, z)$ solves problem (1), and $\bar{u}()$ denotes the period utility of (both types of) workers. Under this first interpretation, the magnitude of the parameter ν will reflect the relative position of permanent workers vis-à-vis shareholders in the organization, as manifested by their respective income shares.

The sharing rule summarized by equation (2) can be rationalized on other grounds. Suppose, indeed, that the commitment technology in our economy is such that firm-owners and permanent workers can precommit to the terms of a contract negotiated at the beginning of their association to be in effect for the indefinite future. The objective of the contract would again be to provide income insurance to permanent workers. An optimal lifetime contract of this nature must be such that in exchange for each worker's supplying one unit of labor in each period of working life, workers receive a state-contingent compensation such that the ratio of their ex post marginal utility of consumption to the marginal utility of consumption of the firm owners is a constant, ν, across all states of nature and across time. This is exactly what (2) implies.[4]

The parameter ν again determines the relative income shares. With (adversarial) contracting, incentive compatibility demands that ν be chosen so that the expected utility of firm owners under this risk-sharing arrangement exceeds the expected utility they would obtain at Walrasian equilibrium wages. This allows us to assert that both firms and workers would voluntarily enter into such arrangements.

The effect of (2) is to reduce primary workers' consumption volatility both within the period and intertemporally. The latter smoothing results from the fact that shareholders are able to smooth their consumption intertemporally and the fact that the relationship defined by equation (2) de facto imparts some of this smoothing to the primary workers.[5] In effect, the contract serves as a substitute for a complete securities market in which primary workers and shareholders trade risks.[6]

Secondary Sector Workers

At the other extreme, let us assume that workers in the secondary or "casual" sector do not have tenure with a firm, but, rather, only a short-term relationship, which may or may not be renewed depending on the realization of the firm's productivity shock.

In this chapter, we assume that workers of both types are of equal measure, which we normalize to be one. Firms take the wage level of secondary workers as given. Their hiring is determined by the standard condition that marginal productivity should cover the real wage. Anticipating the fact that with CRS production functions, an equilibrium can be characterized as though there were only one firm (employing the economywide stock of capital and all employed workers), the level of employment of secondary sector workers, $N_s(K, z)$, will be given by

$$w_s(k, z) = f_3[K, 1, N_s(K, z)]z, \tag{3}$$

where $w_s(K, z)$ is the wage level of secondary workers.

It is here that we want to introduce a non-Walrasian flavor to our model. We have set up the model in such a way that there are several possible options for doing this. We could specify that the secondary labor market clears in each state at the Walrasian equilibrium wage given by

$$w^*(K, z) = f_3(K, 1, 1)z.$$

But there are of other ways to close the model. One such way would be to observe that this "Walrasian" solution would entail considerable income variation for secondary workers. All modern economies have adopted a variety of redistributive schemes, such as minimum wage laws, welfare payments, unemployment compensation, and so on, which can be interpreted as having the objective of preventing these extremes of income variation. Could it be that these pervasive institutions matter in terms of the dynamic behavior of an economy? The RBC approach offers us an ideal procedure for answering this question. Let us assume the existence of a legal minimum wage or some rule or customs acting as an effective wage floor and postulate that

$$w_s = \max[w^*, w_m], \tag{4}$$

with w_m, the minimum wage, a constant (for example, chosen as a fixed proportion of the average wage paid to the primary workers). With this modification, the dynamic equilibrium time path could be computed and its properties studied.

It is clear that this abstraction allows us to mirror not only what prevails in that segment of the labor market directly affected by minimum wage restrictions but also what prevails in all those professions where union activity significantly affects the compensation level of workers (thereby preventing, in certain circumstances, a full equilibration of the corresponding market). An arrangement such as (4) would represent the simplest modeling of a wage floor.

More ambitiously, we may follow Drèze (1989), as in Danthine and Donaldson (1991b), in trying to rationalize the existence of the institutions mentioned above by assuming that the wage floor, $w_f(K, z)$, and the transfer payments, $t(K, z)$, to the unemployed (if any) are determined, on a state-contingent basis, as the solution to the maximization of a weighted sum of agents' period utilities. For every (K, z), $w_f(K, z)$ and $t(K, z)$ solve

$$\max_{\{w_f, t\}} \psi u(c(K, K, z)) + \bar{u}(w_p(K, z)) + N_s(K, z)\bar{u}(w_f) + (1 - N_s(K, z))\bar{u}(t)$$

$$\text{s.t.} \quad w_f \geq t; 1 \geq N_s(K, z). \tag{5}$$

In problem (5) above, $N_s(K, z)$ is determined by equation (3), while $w_p(K, z)$ satisfies equation (2). The unemployment compensation transfer $t()$ will be financed by a lump sum tax on shareholder income, as will be made clear shortly, when the income function of the shareholders is made explicit. Note that the structure of problem (5) ensures that $w_f(K, z) = t(K, z)$ for all those states of nature for which $w_f(K, z) \neq w^*(K, z)$, the Walrasian wage. As in Hansen (1985), the employed and unemployed secondary workers thus enjoy the same consumption. By altering the first constraint to take the form $\phi w_f(K, z) \geq t(K, z)$, with $\phi > 1$, however, a utility differential could be introduced. We have not imposed this constraint, as it would not alter the basic message of this chapter.

The parameter ψ is the firm owner's weight factor in the government objective function. It will be calibrated to ensure that capital income's share of total income in the model economy approximates its observed real-world counterpart. The wage paid to the secondary workers is thus given by

$$w_s(K, z) = \max\{w_f(K, z), w^*(K, z)\}, \tag{6}$$

where $w^*(K, z)$ is the Walrasian wage. Problem (3) is appealing because on a period-by-period basis, it produces an allocation of resources (with unemployment) that is socially preferred to the Walrasian solution of the secondary labor market. Of course, (5) presupposes (not unrealistically, some would argue) that the government acts myopically by failing to take account of the depressing effect of its wage floor policy on the investment function of the firm owners. Note that some form of myopia has to be assumed on the part of government or society if a nonoptimal level of employment is to be rationalized in the context of this model.

Equilibrium

Our setup can now be summarized as follows. Firm owners determine their investment policy, $X()$, by solving problem (1), taking as a given the state-contingent wage of the secondary workers, $w_s(K, z)$, and the state-contingent (lump sum) tax function, $T(k, K, z) = (k/K) \cdot t(K, z) \cdot (1 - n_s(k, z))$. They are also committed through an indefinite contract to employing their share (k/K) of permanent workers, with a compensation scheme given by $w_p(k, K, z)$.

These constraints are subsumed in the definition of a representative firm owner's income:

$$\pi(k, K, z) = \max_{n_s}\{f(k, n_p, n_s)z - w_p(k, K, z)n_p - n_s w_s(K, z) - t(k, K, z)\}. \tag{7}$$

Note that optimal risk sharing between workers and shareholders may force the residual shareholder income to differ from the return on capital even in the presence of constant returns. Thus we view shareholders as entrepreneurs who contribute whatever capital they have to the production process every period and who receive in return the residual income after wages and taxes have been paid.

Taking the investment policy as a given—thus ignoring the impact of its policies on the shareholder's investment function—the government imposes a wage floor, $w_f(\cdot)$, and a tax (and transfer) policy, $T(K, z)$. In effect, we assume that society precommits itself to a social contract—summarized by problem (5)—which is invariant across all future time periods and which benefits secondary workers. As in the case of primary workers, the (social) contract is not renegotiated on a period-by-period basis and in that sense may be viewed as an element of the constitution of the society. This assumes a precommitment technology which differentiates our formulation from that of, for example, Kydland and Prescott (1977) and Chari, Kehoe, and Prescott (1989).

In equilibrium, individual quantities and aggregate quantities coincide: $K = k$, $T(K, K, z) = t(K, z) \cdot [1 - n_s(K, z)]$, $N_s = n_s$, and $N_p = n_p = 1$. With the identifications $x(K, K, z) \equiv X(K, z)$, $C(K, K, z) \equiv c(K, z)$, and $w_p(K, K, z) \equiv w_p(K, z)$, we are now in a position to state our definition of equilibrium.

Definition. An equilibrium in this model is a continuous investment policy, $X(\cdot)$, and a continuous government policy, $[w_f(\cdot), T(\cdot)]$, such that, given $X(\cdot)$, $[w_f(\cdot), T(\cdot)]$ solves (5) for all (K, z), while given $[w_f(\cdot), t(\cdot)]$, $X(\cdot)$ is the solution to (1) with profit defined in (7).

The existence of equilibrium can, in general, be guaranteed provided the technology and preferences satisfy certain substantially restrictive assumptions, which are detailed in Danthine and Donaldson (1991b). A brief overview of the technique (and its computational analogue) is as follows.

The necessary first-order condition for problem (1) is given by

$$u_1[C(K, z)] = u_1[\pi(K, z) - X(K, z)] = \beta \int u_1[\pi(K', z')$$
$$- X(K', z')]\{f_1[K', 1, N_s(K', z')]z' + (1 - \delta)\}Q(z, dz'), \qquad (8)$$

where $Q(\cdot, \cdot)$ denotes the conditional probability transition function for the Markov process on the shocks to technology. Let $\mathbf{C}$ denote the set of bounded continuous functions defined on $R^+ \times R^+$, and for $X(K, z) \in \mathbf{C}$, define the operator $\mathbf{W}()$: $\mathbf{C} \to \mathbf{C} \times \mathbf{C} \times \mathbf{C}$ by

$$\mathbf{W}[X(K, z)] = [w_p(K, z), w_s(K, z), T(K, z)], \qquad (9)$$

where the right-side set of functions solves (5) together with (3) and (6), given $X(K, z)$. We next define a second operator, $\chi : \mathbf{C} \times \mathbf{C} \times \mathbf{C} \to \mathbf{C}$, by

$$\chi[w_p(K, z), w_s(K, z), T(K, z)] = X(K, z), \qquad (10)$$

where $X(K, z)$ solves equation (8) given $[w_p(K, z), w_s(K, z), T(K, z)]$. Equilibrium for this economy can then be expressed as a function $\hat{X}(K, z) \in \mathbf{C}$, for which

$$\hat{X}(K, z) = \theta[\hat{X}(K, z)] \equiv \chi[\{\mathbf{W}(\hat{X}(K, z)]\}, \qquad (11)$$

that is, for which $\hat{X}(K, z)$ is a fixed point of the composition operator, $\theta()$.

A simple iterative scheme that generated a sequence, $\{X_n(K, z)\}$, $X_n(K, z) = \theta[X_{n-1}(K, z)]$, allowed us to compute the equilibrium, $\hat{X}(K, z)$, as the limit of a monotone-increasing sequence of functions.

Model Calibration, Numerical Procedures, and Results

Heterogeneous-agent models, such as the one just described, are especially difficult to calibrate because most empirical measures (for example, measures of risk aversion) are obtained from aggregate data, which do not account for individual differences. In particular, there is, to our knowledge, no convincing study that attempts to measure the coefficient of relative risk aversion of shareholder-entrepreneurs vis-à-vis nonshareholder workers. In conformity with earlier custom in the literature, let us choose $u(c) = \ln(c)$. We further adopt the intuitive assumption that those who choose not to be entrepreneurs are more risk averse than those who do. The results reported below correspond to a period utility function for both primary and secondary workers of $\bar{u}(c) = \frac{c^{\sigma}}{\sigma}$, with $\sigma = -6$. This latter parameter choice is centered in the admissible range, $[-10, -2]$, as identified in earlier microstudies, most notably that of Drèze (1981), and allows for the correct relative variability of stockholder and worker consumption.

As for the production technology, $f(K, N_p, N_s)z$ was assumed to be of the form $[MK^{\theta}(N_p^{1-\gamma}N_s^{\gamma})^{1-\theta}z]$, which is a straightforward generalization typical of this literature. The parameter θ was fixed at 0.36. While other mechanisms in our model determine the share of income going to labor, this choice is not at variance with U.S. data in that regard and is customary in the literature. In the absence of hard empirical evidence on γ, the fraction of total labor income going to secondary workers as opposed to permanent workers under contract, we fixed $\gamma = 0.5$. The technology shock process was required to follow a two-state Markov process, with the transition probability matrix given by

$$
\begin{array}{cc}
 & \begin{array}{cc} z_1 & \quad\; z_2 \end{array} \\
\begin{array}{c} z_1 \\ z_2 \end{array} &
\left(\begin{array}{cc} \rho & 1-\rho \\ 1-\rho & \rho \end{array} \right),
\end{array}
$$

with z_1, z_2, and ρ fixed at 1.025, 0.975, and 0.975, respectively. Under this assignment, the persistence and mean of the process coincide with those of the autoregressive process, $z_{t+1} = \phi z_t + \tilde{\epsilon}_{t+1}$, $\phi = 0.95$, $\tilde{\epsilon}_t \sim$ Normal $(0.05, 0.00712)$, while the standard deviation is approximately half as great. This specific reference process has been used extensively in the literature to drive Walrasian model formulations, in particular, Hansen's (1985) elegant indivisible labor formulation. The fact that the shock variance required to match the standard deviation of model output to that of U.S. output data is half as great for non-Walrasian formulations reflects an important property of the model class—less flexible prices give rise to proportionately greater quantity variations. In effect, the "transmission mechanism" in an economy with the type of trading restrictions in this model is more powerful than its analogue for purely Walrasian models. In light of the fact that with proper accounting (in the Solow tradition), existing Walrasian paradigms are unable to account fully for the observed variability of output, we view the preceding observation as supportive of this modeling perspective.

Only a few parameters remain to be determined. Following Kydland and Prescott (1982), we choose $\beta = 0.99$ and $\delta = 0.025$; these choices imply that our model period corresponds to one quarter. The technology parameter, M, is purely a scale parameter, which was chosen to fix the level of secondary labor unemployment; in particular, to obtain an unemployment rate of 10 percent for secondary workers (our choice), $M = 0.49$ was necessary. As noted earlier, the parameter ν was determined entirely endogenously within the model to ensure that the expected utility of entrepreneurs in the presence of risk-sharing contracts for primary workers did not fall short of their expected utility in the absence of such contracts with primary workers receiving the Walrasian wage. Both comparisons were undertaken in the presence of the income stabilization for secondary workers. For the results reported below, $\nu = 16$. Lastly, the parameter ψ, which determines the relative income shares of firm owners and workers, was also endogenously determined, in this case to maintain the share of income going to capital at approximately 0.36; in particular, $\psi = 7$.

The recursive iterative procedure we employed to compute model equilibrium acts on the form of the equilibrium investment function. This is in the spirit of the existence argument outlined earlier in equations (9), (10) and (11). All the approximating functions were defined on a discrete partition of the state space in a neighborhood of the certainty steady state. An overview of the algorithm is as follows. First choose $X_0(K, z) \equiv 0$. Using this $X_0(K, \Gamma)$, solve problem (5) to determine the corresponding wage and employment functions, $w_s^0(K, z)$, $w_p^0(K, z)$, and $N_s^0(K, z)$. This is a matter of solving a system of two nonlinear equations for which standard subroutines are available.

Using these latter functions, next solve equation (8)—which characterizes the contingent (on the wage and employment functions) equilibrium investment function—to obtain an $X_1(K, z)$. This $X_1(K, z)$ is obtained in a somewhat novel way. Since the solution process for problem (5) requires an explicit functional form for the $X_1(K, z)$ function and since the standard procedure for solving equation (8) provides an equilibrium, $\tilde{X}_1(K, z)$, defined only on a discrete set (the partition of the state space), we chose to approximate the true $X_1(K, z)$ in the following manner. Using the $\tilde{X}_1(K, z)$, we generated economic time series of investment, capital stock, and shocks to technology for 3,000 time periods. In order to consider only stationary capital stock values, we dropped the first 1,000 entries for each of the series. Using the remaining 2,000 data points, we regressed investment as a function of the capital stock and the shock to technology to obtain an expression of the form $X_1(K, z) = \hat{A} + \hat{B}K + \hat{D}z$. Work by Christiano (1990) is persuasive that the $X_1(K, z)$ so obtained is a good approximation to $\tilde{X}_1(K, z)$. Our procedures for obtaining $\tilde{X}_1(k, z)$ as the discrete solution to equation (8) follow the line of techniques proposed by Coleman (1991) and are discussed in Chapter 3 of this volume.

Using the $X_1(K, z)$, we next solve problem (5) again to secure a new set of wage and employment functions, $w_s^1(K, z)$, $w_p^1(K, z)$, and $N_s^1(K, z)$. From these latter functions, a new $X_2(K, z)$ is obtained as a solution to equation (8), and the process repeats itself. We thereby construct a sequence of monotone-increasing functions that is bounded above and thus converges. The corresponding sequences of wage functions $\{w_p^n(K, z)\}$ and $\{w_s^n(K, z)\}$, are both monotone-decreasing and converge; $\{N_s^n(K, z)\}$ is also monotone-increasing and convergent.

Table 8.1 summarizes the performance of the model with regard to the behavior of the basic macroeconomic aggregates. As in U.S. data, investment is more variable than output, which is in turn more variable than total consumption. The presence of non-Walrasian labor market features is clearly not inconsistent with the most basic characteristics of the business cycle. Nevertheless, there is evidence of excessive consumption smoothing, as is typical of RBC models. With regard to the relative variability of hours vis-à-vis average productivity, the model performs quite well. Unlike most pure Walrasian formulations, this formulation can be viewed as solving the employment-productivity variability paradox of U.S. data.

Shareholder consumption is seen to vary proportionately much more than worker consumption does. This is to be expected in light of the fact that workers are substantially more risk averse than shareholders and that as a consequence, substantial income risk is transferred from workers of both types to shareholders in regions of unemployment. Mankiw and Zeldes (1991) provide empirical support for the

Table 8.1
The Non-Walrasian Model

	U.S. Economy		Non-Walrasian Model	
	SD(%)	Correlation with Output	SD(%)	Correlation with Output
Output	1.73		1.76	
Total consumption	1.22	.85	0.34	.69
Shareholder consumption	—	—	5.36	.98
Worker consumption	—	—	0.22	.10
Total investment	5.21	.90	6.08	.99
Capital stock	0.63	.04	0.54	.03
Employment	1.38	.83	1.26	.98
Average productivity	0.97	.60	0.61	.91
Unemployment rate	—	—	—	—

Source: U.S. statistcs were computed from IFS data except for the capital stock series, which is taken from Hansen (1985). Model statistics were computed from model data, which were detrended by means of the H-P filter.

assertion that shareholder consumption varies more than nonshareholder consumption by examining the ratio of the standard deviation of consumption growth for shareholders to that of nonshareholders and finding it to be about 1.5 for the data they examine. In our model, this same ratio assumes a value of 1.6 (unfiltered data). To our knowledge, this statistic has no counterpart in other model formulations.

The model just described is one in which all quantities and prices are measured in real terms. Other authors, notably Cho and Cooley (1992), have devised RBC models with nominal wage and price contracts (rigidities) in the presence of an exogenous stochastic money supply process. Consistent with the results of our own real model, Cho and Cooley (1992), in particular, find that nominal wage contracts, posited in an environment of both monetary and technology shocks, allow their model to replicate the stylized facts of the U.S. business cycle quite well. Nominal price contracts, however, produce results somewhat at variance with U.S. data.

Another employment perspective that has been addressed within a dynamic context is that of search equilibrium. Included in this general area are works by Andolfatto (1992), Mortensen and Pissarides (1992), and Mortensen (1990). Andolfatto's (1992) model most closely resembles the RBC paradigm, although his formulation does not include physical capital. Methods similar to the ones employed here (the monotone operator approach) are the focus of his solution algorithm as well.

Summary

The key to the successful incorporation of non-Walrasian labor market features into the RBC paradigm is to incorporate them in such a way that only one model agent solves an intertemporal problem. As in the formulation above, this can usually be done in such a way that the other model participants nevertheless possess substantial influence over the precise nature of the equilibrium. If we respect this caveat, most contracting formulations of the labor market can be successfully analyzed in a RBC setting.

No less amenable to RBC analysis is the other major strand of non-Walrasian labor market behavior—the efficiency wage perspective. It is to this literature that we now turn. In the next section we demonstrate how one prominent efficiency wage perspective can be successfully matched to an RBC paradigm in a way that is formally very similar to the model just discussed.

1. An Efficiency Wage Model

Introductory Remarks

The efficiency wage literature constitutes another major non-Walrasian labor market perspective. At least four modeling approaches have been considered. Each relies on the notion that an increase in a firm's wage or a decrease in the "reference wage" (the competing alternative available to the worker if the worker chooses to separate from the firm) increases the margin of excess utility of the employed over the unemployed and thus the cost of job loss. In particular, an increase in the wage offer of the firm (above the level of competitive equilibrium) may (1) reduce shirking by workers and thus increase productivity in the event that work effort is not completely monitorable (this is the perspective of Shapiro and Stiglitz [1984]); (2) reduce the probability of workers' voluntarily quitting the firm and thus reduce the turnover costs (retaining expenses) associated with a given size of the labor force (see Salop [1979] for a discussion); (3) improve the average quality of job applicants and thus of the firm's labor force by increasing the excellence of the applicant pool (see Stiglitz [1976]); or (4) induce greater worker efforts via morale improvements (Akerlof's [1982] gift exchange perspective).

Given our objectives, the essential common implication of each of these four perspectives is that it may not always be in the best interest of the firm to lower its wage offer in the face of low demand or unfavorable productivity shocks—at least not to the extent necessary to clear the labor market. This means, in effect, that there may be quantity rationing of labor.

In Danthine and Donaldson (1990), we explored the gift exchange concept of Akerlof. Under this hypothesis, it is assumed that by extending to workers the "gift" of a wage rate in excess of some reference norm (typically the worker's reservation wage, which may be equivalent to either the level of wages generally prevailing in the economy or to the level of unemployment compensation), the firm may expect in return a degree of effort in excess of some acceptable level. While demonstrating the feasibility of taking such considerations into account in the standard RBC setting, our analysis revealed that the unemployment and quantity rationing in the labor market created under this motivation are not synonymous with wage sluggishness. In particular, most of the adjustment to productivity shocks continues to take place through prices (wages), and too little through quantities (employment), relative to what is observed in U.S. data. We thus concluded that efficiency wage considerations based on the gift exchange paradigm are not sufficient to resolve the business cycle puzzle.

Here we propose to outline how the shirking perspective of Shapiro and Stiglitz (1984) could be incorporated and tested via the same standard RBC methodology. In harmony with the contracting model detailed earlier, the heart of the model will remain the dynamic optimization problem of the firm shareholder-owners.

The idea underlying the shirking perspective is that workers will naturally shirk and that perfect monitoring of worker performance is prohibitively costly. With imperfect monitoring, there is nevertheless a positive probability (exogenous) that any worker who is shirking will get caught and be fired. If there is full employment, however, there is no mechanism to discourage shirking: if fired, the worker simply takes another job immediately. In the presence of unemployment, however, there is a cost to being fired, and thus a disincentive to shirk. Furthermore, the higher the wage paid by the firm, everything else being fixed, the greater the disincentive to shirk as the greater is the relative penalty for shirking.

Model Formulation

We retain as much of the structure and notation of our contract equilibrium formulation as possible while specializing our model to the setting of Shapiro and Stiglitz (1984). Workers now are assumed to live two periods, supply one unit of labor inelastically every period, and experience disutility from providing effort.[7] If they are caught and fired in some period, they do not assume alternative employment in that period, but engage in home activities (or receive unemployment compensation). Since workers are assumed not to reapply for work in the period in which they are fired, they do not care about that period's unemployment rate. The "stigma" of being fired, rather, shows up via the fact that a worker fired when young is viewed as an inexperienced old worker, and thus receives a lower wage. Once again, workers are prohibited from participating in the capital markets, with the consequence that all savings investment decisions are, as before, the exclusive province of the profit-earner dynasties, which are assumed to exist forever. In order to present the model as economically as possible, we will assume aggregation has already occurred. Our notation is thus consistent with one firm, one shareholder-owner, and a continuum of old and young workers who have already been aggregated. All agents act competitively.

Old Workers

We first consider the problem confronting the old workers. These workers consume their wages; since everything will be expressed in real terms, we can continue to equate wages and consumption. There are a number of circumstances in which old workers may find themselves:

> **1)** *If the old worker is unemployed,* the worker's utility is $\bar{u}(b)$, where b, a constant, can be viewed as the return on home effort. Alternatively, we could view b as an unemployment insurance payment financed by a tax on employers. Purely for expositional simplicity, we adopt the home effort interpretation.

> **2)** *If the old worker is employed,* there are four possible subcases:

>> **a)** *The worker is experienced and does not shirk.* In this event, the worker's utility is $\bar{u}[w_e^0(K_t, \Gamma_t)] - D_1$, where D_1, a constant, captures the disutility of working for the experienced old worker and $w_e^0(K_t, z_t)$ represents the state-contingent wage of the experienced old generation.

>> **b)** *The worker is experienced and shirks.* The (expected) period utility of an old worker in this set of circumstances is given by

$p\bar{u}(b) + (1 - p)\bar{u}[w_e^0(K_t, z_t)]$, where p denotes the exogenous probability of being caught while shirking.

c) *The worker is inexperienced and does not shirk.* In this case the worker's period utility is assumed to be $\bar{u}[w_i^0(K_t, z_t)] - D_2$, where D_2, another constant, measures the disutility of work for the inexperienced worker, and $w_i^0(K_t, z_t)$ measure the worker's state-contingent equilibrium wage. One could reasonably argue $D_1 > D_2$, since this will ensure that in equilibrium $w_e^0(K_t, z_t) > w_i^0(K_t, z_t)$.

d) *The worker is inexperienced and shirks.* This is the final possibility. In the spirit of (b) above, expected utility in this case is given by $p\bar{u}(b) + (1 - p)\bar{u}[w_i^0(K_t, z_t)]$.

In equilibrium, the wages $w_e^0(K_t, z_t)$ and $w_i^0(K_t, z_t)$ are set according to the requirement that no one shirks (indeed this is the only reasonable possibility for a model in which all workers are the same). Thus $w_e^0(K_t, z_t)$ and $w_i^0(K_t, z_t)$ will be set to satisfy, respectively,

$$\bar{u}[w_e^0(K_t, z_t)] - D_1 = p\bar{u}(b) + (1 - p)\bar{u}[w_e^0(K_t, z_t)], \qquad (12)$$

or

$$w_e^0(K_t, z_t) \equiv w_e^0 = \bar{u}^{-1}\left[\frac{p\bar{u}(b) + D_1}{p} \right], \qquad (13)$$

and

$$u[w_i^0(K_t, z_t)] - D_2 = p\bar{u}(b) + (1 - p)\bar{u}[w_i^0(K_t, z_t)], \qquad (14)$$

or

$$w_i^0(K_t, z_t) \equiv w_i^0 = \bar{u}^{-1}\left[\frac{p\bar{u}(b) + D_2}{p} \right]. \qquad (15)$$

Note that the unemployment rate does not enter into the determination of w_i^0 and w_e^0 functions since these wages apply only to those who are working. Thus we see that the wages paid to the old will be constant across all states of nature. When calibrating the model, the parameter b should be set at a level that is not too low; otherwise, the demand for labor may exceed its supply. Let $N_e^0(K_t, z_t)$ and $N_i^0(K_t, z_t)$ denote, respectively, the employment levels of the experienced and inexperienced old workers; $N_e^0(K_t, z_t)$ and $N_i^0(K_t, z_t)$ must satisfy, respectively,

$$f_2[K_t, N_e^0(K_t, z_t), N_i^0(K_t, z_t), N(K_t, z_t)]z_t = w_e^0, \qquad (16)$$

and

$$f_3[K_t, N_e^0(K_t, z_t), N_i^0(K_t, z_t), N(K_t, z_t)]z_t = w_i^0. \qquad (17)$$

As will be apparent shortly, the precise form of our production function explicitly takes account of the fact that the productivity of shirking workers is less than the productivity of nonshirking workers, although in equilibrium, no one shirks. In the above equations, $N(K_t, z_t)$ represents the employment level of the young workers.

Young Workers

We now turn to a consideration of the more complex problem facing these young workers. Characterizing the behavior of the young workers is a good deal more complicated. Once again, we need to consider a number of cases.

(1) *The young worker is unemployed.* For a young worker in these circumstances, the present value of lifetime expected utility is given by

$$
\bar{v}_u(K_t, z_t) = \bar{u}(b) + \beta \int \{[\bar{u}(b) \left[1 - \frac{N_i^0(K_{t+1}, z_{t+1})}{1 - N(K_t, z_t)} \right]
$$

$$
+ \frac{N_i^0(K_{t+1}, z_{t+1})}{1 - N(K_t, z_t)} \left[\bar{u}(w_i^0) - D_2 \right] \} Q(dz_{t+1}; z_t). \quad (18)
$$

Viewing workers of each generation as being distributed uniformly on [0,1], the expression $\left[1 - \frac{N_i^0(K_{t+1}, z_{t+1})}{1 - N(K_t, z_t)} \right]$ describes the probability that an old worker will be unemployed given that the worker is inexperienced (unemployed while young), the next period's state is (K_{t+1}, z_{t+1}), and the level of employment of the young is $N(K_t, z_t)$ this period. The employment level term is present because the number of inexperienced workers in period $t + 1$ is limited to the number of workers not hired in period t; thus $N_i^0(K_{t+1}, z_{t+1}) \leq 1 - N(K_t, z_t)$, and $N_i^0(K_{t+1}, z_{t+1})$ must be normalized by $1 - N(K_t, z_t)$ in order to express a probability. These relationships produce a second intertemporal constraint beyond the capital accumulation equation and substantially complicate the simulation.

Notice that the use of w_i^0 in the above formulation assumes that the old worker, if hired, will not shirk, as is guaranteed by the equilibrium. As in the contracting model, $K_{t+1} = (1-\delta)K_t + X(K_t, z_t)$, where investment, $X(K_t, z_t)$, is determined by the profit earner's consumption/savings problem, to be considered shortly.

(2) *The young worker is employed and decides to shirk.* In this case the present value of lifetime expected utility is given by a more complex expression:

$$
\bar{v}_{e,s}(K_t, z_t) = p\bar{u}(b) + (1 - p)\bar{u}(w(K_t, z_t))
$$

$$
+ \beta \int \{(1 - p) \left[1 - \frac{N_e^0(K_{t+1}, z_{t+1})}{N(K_t, z_t)} \right] \bar{u}(b)
$$

$$
+ (1 - p) \left[\frac{N_e^0(K_{t+1}, z_{t+1})}{N(K_t, z_t)} \right] [\bar{u}(w_e^0) - D_1]
$$

$$+ p \left[1 - \frac{N_i^0(K_{t+1}, z_{t+1})}{1 - N(K_t, z_t)} \right] \bar{u}(b)$$

$$+ p \left[\frac{N_i^0(K_{t+1}, z_{t+1})}{1 - N(K_t, z_t)} \right] [\bar{u}(w_i^0) - D_2]\} Q(dz_{t+1}; z_t), \quad (19)$$

where $w(K_t, z_t)$ denotes the equilibrium wage of the young workers. By way of interpretation, the two terms outside the integral measure a worker's expected utility while young (either the worker is caught and fired or not), while the first two terms under the integral give the worker's expected utility next period given that the worker is not caught shirking today and thus is viewed by employers as an experienced worker. The final two terms under the integral give the worker's expected utility next period given that the worker is caught shirking today.

(3) *The young worker is employed and decides not to shirk.* If we let D_1 also measure the disutility of the young, our final present value of utility expression has the following form:

$$\bar{v}_{e,ns}(K_t, z_t) = \bar{u}[w(K_t, z_t)] - D_1 + \beta \int \{ \frac{N_e^0(K_{t+1}, z_{t+1})}{N(K_t, z_t)} [\bar{u}(w_e^0) - D_1]$$

$$+ \left[1 - \frac{N_e^0(K_{t+1}, z_{t+1})}{N(K_t, z_t)} \right] \bar{u}(b)\} Q(dz_{t+1}; z_t). \quad (20)$$

The first-period equilibrium wage should be high enough so that none of the employed young workers will want to shirk; that is, $w(K_t, z_t)$ must be such that $v_{e,ns}(K_t, z_t) \geq v_{e,s}(K_t, z_t)$. Equating expressions (19) and (20) and solving for the resultant $w(K_t, z_t)$ gives, after simplification and manipulation, the following equilibrium wage for the young:

$$w(K_t, z_t) = \bar{u}^{-1}\{ \frac{1}{p} [D_1 + p\bar{u}(b) + \beta \int \{ \frac{N_e^0(K_{t+1}, z_{t+1})}{N(K_t, z_t)} [-p(\bar{u}(w_e^0) - D_1)]$$

$$- p \left(1 - \frac{N_e^0(K_{t+1}, z_{t+1})}{N(K_t, z_t)} \right) \bar{u}(b)$$

$$+ p \left(1 - \frac{N_i^0(K_{t+1}, z_{t+1})}{1 - N(K_t, z_t)} \right) \bar{u}(b)$$

$$+ p \left(\frac{N_i^0(K_{t+1}, z_{t+1})}{1 - N(K_t, z_t)} \right) (\bar{u}(w_i^0) - D_2)\} Q(dz_{t+1}, z_t)\} \quad (21)$$

Notice that the unemployment rate of the young enters into this calculation only insofar that it determines the size of the pool of experienced and inexperienced workers next period. This is so because the nonshirking wage, $w(K_t, z_t)$, today applies only to those at work. Furthermore, since fired workers are assumed to be unable to obtain alternative employment for the period in which they are fired, their immediate prospects are unaffected by the current unemployment rate. The "stigma" of being fired shows up not only in lost present utility but also via the fact that a fired worker is viewed by future employers as an inexperienced old worker, with a lower probability of being hired.

Profit Earners

To complete our discussion of the economic participants, we need to consider the intertemporal decision problem confronting the profit earners. Our discussion so far has formally justified replacing traditional labor supply curves by specific wage-employment schedules: $w(K, z)$, w_e^0, w_i^0, $N_e^0(K, z)$ $N_i^0(K, z)$, and $N(K, z)$. Under these new constraints, profit earners allocate output remaining after wages have been paid (and possibly unemployment taxes) between consumption and investment to maximize their present value of discounted utility of consumption. Assuming one perfectly competitive firm, which takes wage rates as given, this is equivalent to solving for a $v(K_t, z_t)$ that satisfies:

$$v(K_t, z_t) = \max_{X_t, N_e^0(K_t, z_t), N_i^0(K_t, z_t), N(K_t, z_t)} \{u[f(k_t, N_e^0(K_t, z_t),$$

$$N_i^0(K_t, z_t), N(K_t, z_t))z_t - N_e^0(K_t, z_t)w_e^0$$

$$- N_i^0(K_t, z_t)w_i^0 - w(K_t, z_t)N(K_t, z_t) - X_t]$$

$$+ \beta \int v[(1 - \delta)K_t + X_t, z_{t+1}]Q(dz_{t+1}; z_t)\}, \qquad (22)$$

where $w(K_t, z_t)$ is viewed as given. The first-order conditions and intertemporal constraints for this problem are, in addition to equations (16) and (17), which define the optimal employment levels for old workers,

$$N(K_t, z_t) : f_4[K_t, N_e^0(K_t, z_t), N_i^0(K_t, z_t), N(K_t, z_t)]z_t = w(K_t, z_t), \qquad (23)$$

and

$$X_t : u_1(C_t) = \beta \int u_1(C_{t+1})\{f_1[K_{t+1}, N_e^0(K_{t+1}, z_{t+1}), N_i^0(K_{t+1}, z_{t+1}),$$

$$N(K_{t+1}, z_{t+1})]z_{t+1} + (1 - \delta)\}Q(dz_{t+1}; z_t), \qquad (24)$$

where

$$C_t = f[K_t, N_e^0(k_t, z_t), N_i^0(K_t, z_t), N(K_t, z_t)]z_t - N_e^0(k_t, z_t)w_e^0$$

$$- N_i^0(K_t, z_t)w_i^0 - w(K_t, z_t)N(K_t, z_t) - X_t. \qquad (25)$$

Lastly,

$$K_{t+1} = (1 - \delta)K_t + X_t, \quad N_e^0(K_t, z_t) \le N(K_{t-1}, z_{t-1}),$$

and

$$N_i^0(K_t, z_t) \leq 1 - N(K_{t-1}, z_{t-1}). \tag{26}$$

Notice that the origin of the nonoptimality of intertemporal equilibrium lies in the nonmonitorability of workers' efforts. The price to be paid for this is unemployment, which is suboptimal if at equilibrium, the productivity of the marginal worker exceeds the disutility to work—which must be the case.

Equilibrium

Equilibrium in this model is a collection of strictly positive, continuous, invariant wage, employment, and investment functions, $w(K_t, z_t)$, $N(K_t, z_t)$, $N_e^0(K_t, z_t)$, $N_i^0(K_t, z_t)$, and $X(K_t, z_t)$, and a pair of constants, w_e^0 and w_i^0, which together satisfy equations (13), (15), (16), (17), (21), (23) and (24) together with the equation of motion on capital stock and the intertemporal employment constraints (26).

The structure of equilibrium for this economy is formally identical to the one detailed in the discussion of equilibrium in Section 2. Given an $X(K, z) \in C$, define the operation $\hat{W} : C \mapsto C \times C \times C \times C$ by

$$\hat{W}[X(K, z)] = [N_e^0(K, z), N_i^0(K, z), N(K, z), w(K, z)], \tag{27}$$

where this quadruple set of functions solves equations (16), (17), (21) and (23) conditional on X(K,z). Next, define a second operator, $\hat{\chi} : C \times C \times C \times C \mapsto C$, by

$$\hat{\chi}[N_e^0(K, z), N_i^0(K, z), N(K, z)w(K, z)] = X(K, z), \tag{28}$$

where $X(K, z)$ solves equation (24) given the vector of functions $[N_e^0(K, z), N_i^0(K, z), N(K, z), w(K, z)]$.

As before, equilibrium for this economy can be summarized as a function $X^*(K, z) \in C$ for which

$$X^*(K, z) = \hat{\theta}[X^*(K, z)] = \hat{\chi}\{\hat{W}[X^*(K, z)]\}. \tag{29}$$

Again the equilibrium investment function is representable as the fixed point of a composition operator, in this case, $\hat{\theta} : C \mapsto C$. The formal existence of such a function can be proved along the lines detailed in the monotone operator subsection of Chapter 3.

Model Calibration, Numerical Procedures, and Results

By now it is obvious that this efficiency wage model is closely related to the contracting model of Section 2. In both formulations, only one group of agents solves an intertemporal consumption-savings problem (no borrowing or lending for workers). In both formulations, worker preferences directly affect wage and employment levels, which in turn affect the intertemporal consumption-savings problem. As a result, the numerical routines will also be similar in structure: iterate on the form of the aggregate investment function, while simultaneously updating the wage and employment functions to keep them formally consistent. As in the contracting model, all functions are defined on a partition $\wp_K \times \wp_z$ of the state space surrounding the certainty ($z_t \equiv 1$) steady-state capital stock. In addition, all functional forms except the production technology coincide with their counterparts in the earlier model; in particular $u(c) = \ln c$ and $\bar{u}(c) = \frac{c^\sigma}{\sigma}$. The shock process is also two-state Markovian; as a result $\wp_z = \{z_1, z_2\}$. For the production technology, we assumed, for reasons that will be made clear shortly, the functional form

$$f(K, N_e^0, N_i^0, N)z = MK^\theta[\gamma_1(N_e^0)^{1-\theta} + \gamma_2(\gamma_3 + N_i^0)^{1-\theta} + \gamma_4 N^{1-\theta}]z. \quad (30)$$

An overview of the routine is as follows. First, construct a partition, $\wp_N$, of the range of possible employment levels for young workers (this will be a uniform partition of [0,1]). Let $X_0(K, z) = A + BK + Cz$, and suppose that for every $K \in \wp_K, z \in \{z_1, z_2\}$, and $N^* \in \wp_N$, the nth investment function, $X_n(K, z; N^*)$, iterate has been computed. Using this investment function, compute, for every $N^* \in \wp_N$, the functions $N_e^0(K, z; N^*)_n$, $N_i^0(K, z; N^*)_n$, $N(K, z; N^*)_n$, and $w(K, z; N^*)_n$ as the solution, for all $(K, z) \in \wp_K \times \wp_z$, to the following system of equations and constraints:

$$f_2[K, N_e^0(K, z; N^*)_n, N_i^0(K, z; N^*)_n, N(K, z; N^*)_n]z$$
$$= w_e^0; N_e^0(K, z; N^*)_n \le N^*, \quad (31)$$

and

$$f_3[K, N_e^0(K, z; N^*)_n, N_i^0(K, z; N^*)_n, N(K, z; N^*)_n]z$$
$$= w_i^0; \quad N_i^0(K, z; N^*)_n \le 1 - N^*. \quad (32)$$

Under our assumptions on the form of $f()$, $N_e^0(K, z; N^*)_n$ and $N_i^0(K, z; N^*)_n$ can be solved independently of $N(K, z; N^*)_n$ and $X_n(K, z)$, and will in fact be invariant to the iteration n. The presence of the parameter N^* in the preceding expressions represents the prior period's level of young-worker employment; in effect, these employment functions must be computed for every employment history. They are also used in the joint computation of $N(K, z; N^*)$ and $w(K, z; N^*)$ as per equations (33) and (34) below:

$$f_4[K, N_e^0(K, z; N^*)_n, N_i^0(K, z; N^*)_n, N(K, z; N^*)_n]z = w(K, z; N^*)_n, \quad (33)$$

and

$$w(K, z; N^*)_n = \bar{u}^{-1}[\frac{1}{P}\{D_1 + p\bar{u}(b)$$

$$+ \beta \sum_{z_{t+1}} \{ \frac{N_e^0[(1-\delta)K + X_n(K, z; N^*), z_{t+1}; N(K, z; N^*)]}{N(K, z; N^*)}$$

$$- p(\bar{u}(w_e^0) - D_1)]$$

$$- p \left(1 - \frac{N_e^0[(1-\delta)K + X_n(K, z; N^*), z_{t+1}; N(K, z; N^*)]}{N(K, z; N^*)} \right) \bar{u}(b)$$

$$+ p \left(1 - \frac{N_i^0[(1-\delta)K + X_n(K, z; N^*), z_{t+1}; 1 - N(K, z; N^*)]}{1 - N(K, z; N^*)} \right) \bar{u}(b)$$

$$+ p \left(\frac{N_i^0[(1-\delta)K + X_n(K, z; N^*), z_{t+1}; 1 - N(K, z; N^*)]}{1 - N(K, z; N^*)} \right)$$

$$(\bar{u}(w_i^0) - D_2)\} \mathrm{Prob}(z_{t+1}; z)]. \tag{34}$$

This system of equations can be solved using a standard numerical subroutine. The final step of the algorithm is to obtain a $X_{n+1}(K, z; N^*)$ by using these auxiliary functions and the prior $X_n(K, z; N^*)$ via equation (37); that is; $X_{n+1}(K, z; N^*)$ is defined for every $K \in \wp_K, z \in \{z_1, z_2\}$, and $N^* \in \wp_N$ as the solution to

$$u_1(f(K, N_e^0(K, z; N^*)_n, N_i^0(K, z; N^*)_n, N(K, z; N^*)_n)z - N_e^0(K, z; N^*)w_e^0$$

$$- N_i^0(K, z; N^*)w_i^0 - w(K, z; N^*)_n N(K, z; N^*)_n - X_{n+1}(K, z; N^*))$$

$$= \beta \sum_{z_{t+1}} u_1(f\{(1-\delta)K + X_{n+1}(K, z; N^*), N_e^0[(1-\delta)K$$

$$+ X_{n+1}(K, z; N^*), z_{t+1}; N(K, z; N^*)]_n,$$

$$N_i^0((1-\delta)K + X_{n+1}(K, z; N^*), z_{t+1}; 1 - N(K, z; N^*)]_n,$$

$$N[(1-\delta)K + X_{n+1}(K, z; N^*))_n, z_{t+1};$$

$$N(K, z; N^*)]_n\}z_{t+1} - N_e^0[(1-\delta)K$$

$$+ X_{n+1}(K, z; N^*), z_{t+1}; N(K, z; N^*)]_n w_e^0$$

$$- N_i^0[(1-\delta)K + X_{n+1}(K, z; N^*), z_{t+1}; N(K, z; N^*)]_n w_i^0$$

$$- w[(1-\delta)K + X_{n+1}(K, z; N^*), z_{t+1}; N(K, z; N^*)]_n$$

$$\cdot N[(1-\delta)K + X_{n+1}(K, z; N^*), z_{t+1}; N(K, z; N^*)]_n$$

$$- X_n[(1-\delta)K + X_{n+1}(K, z; N^*), z_{t+1}; N(K, z; N^*)])$$

$$\cdot [f_1(\text{same arguments as } f)z_{t+1} + (1-\delta)]\mathrm{Prob}(z_{t+1}; z_t). \tag{35}$$

Given the $X_{n+1}(K, z; N^*)$, equations (31)–(34) can be resolved to obtain new $N_e^0(K, z; N^*)_{n+1}, N_i^0(K, z; N^*)_{n+1}$, etc., and the process repeats itself.

Theoretical explorations of this model imply that such a process will give rise to monotonic sequences in all the relevant functions that converge to the true equilibrium functions. See again the monotone operator approach detailed in Chapter 3. Let these limit functions be denoted, respectively, by $X(K, z; N^*)$, $N_e^0(K, z; N^*)$, $N_i^0(K, z; N^*)$, $N(K, z; N^*)$, and $w(K, z; N^*)$. The raw time series are then generated in the following way. First construct a sequence of 3,000 technology shocks, $(z_t)_{t=0}^{t=2999}$, which respect the transition matrix, $Q(dz_{t+1}; z_t)$, and choose a K_0 and N_{-1}^* equal to their certainty steady state values. Given this shock sequence, aggregate capital stock evolves according to $K_{t+1} = (1 - \delta)K_t + X(K_t, z_t; N_t^*)$, where the $\{N_t^*\}$ sequence itself evolves according to $N_{t+1}^* = N(K_t, z_t; N_t^*)$. All other output, wage, employment, etc., series are computable from $\{K_t\}_{t=0}^{t=2999}$, $\{z_t\}_{t=0}^{t=2999}$, and $\{N_t^*\}_{t=0}^{t=2999}$. A statistical summary of this exercise is shown in Table 8.2 for the indicated parameters.

As with the contracting formulation, the performance of the model is strikingly good. First, the relative variability of all the major aggregates in the model matches the U.S. data: investment is more variable than output, which, in turn, is more variable than total consumption. The absolute level of investment and capital stock variability is somewhat too low, however. An exaggerated resolution of the wage-employment variability paradox is also illustrated: all of the employment series are substantially more variable than average productivity. Correlations are generally in the acceptable range as well, and the pattern of hours volatilities of the various worker groups is not unreasonable. Mention should also be made of the fact that the indicated level of required output variation is achieved by means of even smaller shock variation than in the earlier contracting formulation.

The shirking formulation imposes even greater demands on the calibration procedure than did the contracting model, because the shirking model must be calibrated not only on the basis of specific observations on the rates of risk aversion of firm owners and workers but also on the basis of data relevant to the fraction of workers in our various employment categories. In addition, the shirking economy will clearly depend on utility parameters, (D_1, D_2), and on parameters linked with the shirking construct, (p, b); for both, little is known or likely to be known. For that reason, the model must be anchored at a different level and its interpretation adapted accordingly.

One potentially useful anchor is the average level and the dynamic properties of the various unemployment rates. In essence, this amounts to asking the following question: is there a set of parameter values that enable the shirking (or contracting, or efficiency wage) construct to match the main stylized facts of the business cycle while also rationalizing a plausible average level of unemployment and a real-world-like dynamic behavior of the unemployment index? If this is the case, what can be said about the plausibility of this set of parameter values? The choice of production function parameters γ_1, γ_2, γ_3, and γ_4, in part, was governed by exactly these sorts of considerations. It seemed plausible to assume that the unemployment

Table 8.2
The Shirking Model

| | U.S. Economy | | Non-Walrasian Model | | |
	SD(%)	Correlation with Output	SD(%)	Correlation with Output	Rate (%)
Output	1.73		1.74		
Total consumption	1.22	.85	1.23	.99	
Investment	5.21	.90	3.32	.99	
Capital stock	0.63	.04	0.30	.04	
Employment (hours)	1.38	.83			
Old experienced	—	—	2.17	.71	
Old inexperienced	—	—	8.16	.03	
Young	—	—	2.17	.95	
Total	1.66	.94	1.70	.98	
Average productivity	0.97	.60	0.29	.24	
Unemployment					
Old experienced	—	—	—	—	0
Old inexperienced	—	—	—	—	11.9
Young	—	—	—	—	23
Overall	—	—	—	—	13.1

$\theta = .36, \beta = .99, \sigma = -2, z_1 = 1.019, \rho = .97,$
$\gamma_1 = .49, \gamma_2 = .45, \gamma_3 = .50, \gamma_4 = .45, M = .205,$
$\delta = 0.25, p = .40, D_1 = 3.0, D_2 = 2.5, b = .10$

Source: U.S. statistcs were computed from IFS data except for the capital stock series, which is taken from Hansen (1985). Model statistics were computed from model data, which were detrended by means of the H-P filter. For all series, the raw data were limited to $t = 999$ through $t = 2,999$; that is, the first 1,000 points were dropped to ensure stationarity of the data.

rates for experienced old workers (with highest seniority) should be less than those for inexperienced old workers. Also, the unemployment of the young should reasonably be the highest of all worker groups. As shown in Table (8.2), the computed rates appear reasonable and respect this intuition.

Of course, the less ascertainable the parameter values, the more important it is to undertake sensitivity analysis. An excessive sensitivity to specific values of the unobservable or difficult-to-determine parameters would be undesirable. There is no single way to proceed, and tailor-made approaches have to be developed in view of the issues raised by particular models.

4. Concluding Comments

We have illustrated the non-Walrasian approach to business cycle models through representations of the labor markets involving contracts and shirking considerations. Other viewpoints are amenable to this general methodology, which then offers a testing ground for partial equilibrium theories of labor market frictions. The benefit of the methodology lies in a more disciplined confrontation of such theories with the business cycle facts. Furthermore, alternative views of the fundamental mechanisms at the origin of business cycle fluctuations are thus proposed. We have shown elsewhere that the confrontation of existing Walrasian and non-Walrasian models with additional stylized facts, in the financial arena in particular, tended to reinforce the relevance of these alternative views (Danthine, Donaldson, and Mehra (1992)).

These benefits do not come free however. First, new informational requirements are raised within the calibration procedure. In several instances, full calibration would demand collection of hitherto unavailable elements of information. In some others, there is little hope of obtaining precise and reliable observations on some new parameters. It is then necessary to proceed with systematic sensitivity analysis, as well as attempting to anchor the model in other ways. In the case of the labor market models discussed above, matching the time series behavior of the unemployment series seems a good way to proceed.

One alleged trump card of the Walrasian approach is that it is a unique reference paradigm. On the contrary, there are many ways, often complementary, to be non-Walrasian; that is, there are many types of frictions that one may want to take into account, and it is often not plausible to claim that a single one is solely responsible for the phenomenon to be explained. We may think of alternative theories of unemployment as an example of this. It would be overly ambitious at this stage, however, to try to incorporate more than one, or at most two, such frictions into a single model. This raises questions in interpreting model results, which are, however, not unlike those raised by the exclusive reliance of past RBC models on technological shocks (see Kydland and Prescott 1991).

Finally, non-Walrasian models are not limited to labor market frictions. In principle, non–market-clearing theories of product markets could also be incorporated. More promising, and in close connection with other developments in macroeconomics, it would be interesting to model, and to test the business cycle implications of, credit markets with rationing equilibrium. In addition, to extend somewhat our quite restrictive definition of the "non-Walrasian," imperfect competition models must be mentioned as being close cousins of the models we have illustrated. The reader is referred to Chapter 10 for a discussion.

Notes

1. This approach is of course not limited to evaluating alternative theories of the labor market.

2. This work typically includes at least one of the following features: money and financial intermediation, imperfect competition, contracts, nonconvex consumption sets.

3. We intend that the infinitely lived dynasty be a proxy for a family for which each generation internalizes the utility of its heirs. Barro (1974) demonstrates that such an organization will behave collectively like the infinitely lived agent we postulate.

4. Could an arrangement between firm owners and permanent workers with a sharing parameter, v, changing over time, be a Pareto-superior arrangement to the one we have specified? The answer is no, and for the following reason: a constant v effectively implies that the intertemporal marginal role of substitution of permanent workers and firm owners will be the same and this condition is necessary to a Pareto-optimal allocation. With v's changing through time, the marginal rates of substitution will differ, implying further gains to intertemporal exchanges between the two types of agents.

5. In fact equation (2) implies that workers' and firm owners' marginal utilities will be equally variable. Since we shall assume that workers are more risk averse than firm owners, the previous condition will imply that their consumption levels will be smoother.

6. To see why this is so, notice that the problem of the primary workers and shareholders is essentially a variant of the following:

$$\max E \left(\sum_{t=0}^{\infty} \beta^t [v n_p \bar{u}(w_p(K_t, z_t)) + u(C(K_t, z_t))] \right)$$

$$\text{s.t.} \quad C(K_t, z_t) + n_p w_p(K_t, z_t) + X_t \leq f(K_t) z_t$$

$$K_{t+1} = (1 - \delta) K_t + X_t, \quad K_0 \text{ given.}$$

The value function $v(K_t, z_t)$ for this problem which exists, is continuous etc., and, under the normal regularity conditions, satisfies

$$v(K_t, z_t) = \max_{C(K_t, z_t), X(K_t, z_t)} \{ v n_p \bar{u}(f(K_t) z_t - C(K_t, z_t) - X(K_t, z_t)) + u(C(K_t, z_t))$$

$$+ \beta \int V((1 - \delta) K_t + X_t, z_{t+1}) Q(dz_{t+1}; z_t) \}.$$

The necessary first-order conditions for this problem are thus

$$C(K_t, z_t) : v \bar{u}_1(w_p(K_t, z_t)) = u_1(C(K_t, z_t)),$$

and

$$X(K_t, z_t) : v \bar{u}_1(w_p(K_t, z_t)) = v \beta \int u_1(w_p(K_{t+1}, z_{t+1}))[f_1(K_{t+1}) z_{t+1}$$

$$+ (1 - \delta)] Q(dz_{t+1}; z_t),$$

which together also imply

$$u_1(C(K_t, z_t)) = \beta \int u_1(C(K_{t+1}, z_{t+1}))[f_1(K_{t+1})z_{t+1} + (1 - \delta)]Q(dz_{t+1}; z_t).$$

This maximization problem can be interpreted as a complete markets model. Since its first-order-conditions are identical to the conditions imposed under our contracting formulation, we must conclude that our contract substitutes for a securities market where primary workers and shareholders trade risks.

     7. It will be clear from what follows that it would be prohibitively complicated to assume otherwise. This hypothesis, however, creates difficulties for model calibration. See Section 3.3.

Chapter 9
Dynamic General Equilibrium Models with Imperfectly Competitive Product Markets

Julio J. Rotemberg and
Michael Woodford

1. Introduction

In this chapter, we discuss the consequences of introducing imperfectly competitive product markets into otherwise standard neoclassical growth models. We are particularly interested in the effects of imperfect competition on the way the economy responds at business cycle frequencies to various shocks. The literature on equilibrium modeling of aggregate fluctuations has mainly assumed perfectly competitive firms. While that represents an obvious starting point for analysis, we argue that there are important reasons for allowing competition to be imperfect.

One reason is that imperfect competition makes equilibrium possible in the presence of increasing-returns technologies.[1] This increased flexibility in the specification of technology may be of great importance in modeling fluctuations, in particular, for understanding cyclical variations in productivity. Empirical evidence on increasing returns is discussed in Section 4 below. We argue that not only is imperfect competition necessary if one wishes to assume increasing returns, but that, conversely, if market power is important, one is virtually required to postulate increasing returns, in order to account for the absence of significant pure profits in such economies as that of the United States. Increasing returns may also make possible new sources of aggregate fluctuations—in particular, fluctuations due solely to self-fulfilling expectations.

Allowing for market power (and hence prices higher than marginal cost) and increasing returns may have important consequences for the interpretation of business cycles, although we do not argue for a particular theory of the cycle in this chapter. In the real business cycle literature, technology shocks have usually been assigned a dominant role as the source of fluctuations. But the existence of market power and increasing returns implies that the Solow residual, interpreted in the Real Business Cycle (RBC) literature as a measure of exogenous technology shocks, contains an endogenous component. As Hall (1987, 1988b) has emphasized, this endogenous component may be unrelated to true changes in technology. For example, we show below in a complete dynamic model that increases in government purchases in the presence of imperfect competition result in a positive Solow residual, as well as an increase in output and hours. Thus, if one assumes that firms are perfectly competitive when they are not, one can be led to attribute to random technical progress a fraction of the increase in output that is in fact generated by increased government purchases, or other types of shocks that raise equilibrium output other than through an effect upon production possibilities. Various empirical puzzles regarding the behavior of Solow residuals suggest that this endogeneity may be important, as we discuss in Section 5.

Imperfect competition also changes the predicted effects of technology shocks when they occur. As shown by Hornstein (1993), the ability of increases in productivity to stimulate increased employment is greatly reduced in the case of even rather moderate degrees of market power and increasing returns (we discuss this further in section 6). Hence if imperfect competition is important, it seems likely that other types of shocks will have to be assigned a major role in the explanation of business cycle variations in employment.

The hypothesis of imperfect competition does not in itself point one toward any particular alternative source of shocks. However, it does introduce new potential sources of employment fluctuations, as well as providing a channel through which the importance of other shocks is increased. Imperfect competition not only implies that price generally differs from marginal cost, but is also consistent with variations over time in the gap between price and marginal cost. We show that an increase in this gap results in a reduction in the level of labor input that firms demand at a given real wage. The effect upon labor demand is thus similar to an adverse technology shock, while there need not be so large an offsetting wealth effect upon labor supply. Thus changes in the markup of price over marginal cost are potentially an important determinant of employment. We show that fluctuations in these markups, of a size that is not implausibly large given data on the U.S. economy, can generate employment variations of the size observed.[2]

One view of the source of markup fluctuations is that they result from exogenous changes in market structure—for example, in the context of the model of monopolistic competition developed in Sections 2–3, variations in the degree of substitutability between the differentiated goods. Under this view, imperfect competition introduces a new source of shocks. But it is also possible for markups to vary endogenously in response to aggregate shocks, with no direct relation to market structure. In that case, the effects of markup variation become an additional channel through which such shocks can affect aggregate activity. As we will show, this channel may be particularly important in understanding cyclical variations in employment. We discuss several theories of endogenous variation in markups in Section 8, giving particular attention to theories in which it is possible for the markup to fall when there is an increase in aggregate demand. We then illustrate the potential importance of allowing for endogenous markup variation by showing how these theories affect the response of equilibrium employment to changes in government purchases.

Finally, the assumption of imperfect competition can lead to equilibrium aggregate fluctuations in the absence of any shocks at all. In standard real business cycle models, there exists a unique equilibrium (which corresponds to the solution to a planning problem). This equilibrium is necessarily independent of "sunspot" variables. But the introduction of imperfect competition implies that rational expectations equilibria no longer correspond to the solution of a planning problem; indeed, several distinct equilibria can exist. These equilibria may include "sunspot" equilibria, in which fluctuations result from self-fulfilling shifts in expectations. The quantitative plausibility of this possibility has been analyzed by Benhabib and Farmer (1992), Gali (1992), and Farmer and Guo (1993).

A further aim of this chapter is to show how existing empirical studies using data at various levels of aggregation can be used to obtain estimates of the departures from perfect competition and from constant returns. While our survey of this literature is far from complete, we show how existing evidence bears upon the calibration of certain of the key parameters of imperfectly competitive models.

Finally, the chapter shows that incorporating imperfect competition into equilibrium business cycle theory is easy. It is true that because the resulting allocation is not Pareto optimal, it is not possible to compute the equilibrium by considering the solution to a planning problem. However, familiar methods for the computation of dynamic general equilibrium models, which make use of an Euler equation characterization of equilibrium (as discussed in detail in the next chapter) can also be applied when markets are not perfectly competitive.

The chapter proceeds as follows. In Section 2, we first develop a basic imperfectly competitive model, in which firms are monopolistic competitors and there is no intertemporal aspect to their pricing problem. We show that under quite general conditions, firms will choose to charge a price that represents a constant markup over marginal cost. We also discuss the connections between imperfect competition and increasing returns. In Section 3 we embed this model of firm behavior in a complete dynamic general equilibrium model, and discuss the way in which the resulting model generalizes a standard real business cycle model. Section 4 provides a brief overview of the microeconomic evidence on the importance of imperfect competition. We then discuss the numerical solution of the response to shocks. In Section 5, numerical results are presented for shocks to the level of government purchases, while section 6 concentrates on technology shocks. These sections illustrate the importance of taking account of imperfect competition. They also show how a comparison of the U.S. data and the model's responses can be used to obtain estimates of the quantitative importance of the departures from imperfect competition. Section 7 shows that for some parameter values (involving a sufficiently large degree of imperfect competition and increasing returns), the equilibrium response to shocks becomes indeterminate. This opens up a new potential source of aggregate fluctuations, namely, fluctuations due solely to self-fulfilling expectations, which may occur even in the absence of any stochastic disturbances in economic "fundamentals."

Sections 8 and 9 then discuss models with markup variations. In section 8, we consider the consequences of exogenous variations in the degree of market power (here modeled as due to exogenous changes in the substitutability of differentiated products) in a model of the kind treated in sections 5 and 6. We show that shocks of this kind can produce an overall pattern of comovement of aggregate variables that captures several features of observed aggregate fluctuations, and that they are, in particular, able to produce large movements in employment. We estimate the size of the markup fluctuations that would be required to account for observed business cycle variations in employment in the United States, and compare this with independent calculations of the degree of cyclical variation in markups in the U.S. economy. In Section 9, we discuss models in which endogenous variations in markups occur in response to other kinds of shocks. We develop two models in detail, the "customer markets" model of Phelps and Winter (1970) and the model of oligopolistic collusion used in our own previous work. In this section, we also illustrate the predictions of these two models regarding the effects of changes in the level of government purchases. Here, we particularly emphasize the ability of shocks other than technology shocks to produce variations in labor demand. We also briefly discuss the model of Gali (1992), in which the equilibrium markup depends on the composition of aggregate demand. In the context of this model we discuss the possibility of aggregate fluctuations in the absence of any shock at all.

2. The Behavior of Monopolistically Competitive Firms

We suppose that there exists a continuum of potentially producible differentiated goods indexed by the positive real line. At any point in time, only the subset whose index runs from zero to I_t is actually produced. These goods are bought by consumers, the government, and firms. The firms buy the differentiated goods both as materials that are used in current production and in the form of investment goods that increase the capital stock available for future production. To simplify the model, and to make it comparable to the standard perfectly competitive model, we assume that all of these ultimate demanders are interested in a single "composite good." In other words, the utility of consumers, the productivity of materials inputs, and the addition to the capital of firms depends only upon the number of units of the composite good that are purchased. An agent whose purchases of individual differentiated goods are described by a vector, B_t, obtains Q_t units of the composite good, where Q_t is given by

$$Q_t = f_t(B_t). \tag{1}$$

We assume that the aggregator, f_t, is an increasing, concave, symmetric, and homogeneous of degree one function of the measure B_t. By a symmetric function, we mean a function whose value is unchanged if one exchanges the quantities purchased of any of the individual goods, so that the value Q_t depends only upon the *distribution* of quantities purchased of individual goods, and not upon the identities of the goods purchased. The aggregator is the same for all of the purposes mentioned above; we allow, however, for variation over time, as the set of differentiated goods being produced changes. The producer of each of the differentiated goods sets a price for it; the collection of these prices describes a price vector, P_t, conformable with the vector of goods purchases. Consider an agent (be it a consumer, government, or firm) wishing to buy G_t units of the composite good. The agent will distribute its purchases over the various differentiated goods so as to minimize the total cost, $< P_t, B_t >$, of obtaining G_t. Because f_t is homogeneous of degree one, this cost-minimizing demand is equal to G_t times a homogeneous of degree zero vector–valued function of the price vector:

$$B_t = G_t \Delta_t(P_t).$$

Hence, for a given vector of prices, P_t, all agents will choose scalar multiples of the same vector, $\Delta(P_t)$. This allows us to aggregate the demands of all types to obtain

$$B_t = Q_t \Delta_t(P_t),$$

where Q_t denotes total demand for the composite good for all purposes.

Furthermore, because f_t is symmetric, the component $\Delta_t^i(P_t)$ indicating purchases of goods i must depend only upon the price, p_t^i, charged for that good and the overall distribution of prices charged. We will be concerned here only with symmetric equilibria. We will thus consider situations where all firms (with the possible exception of firm i) charge a price of p_t at t while firm i charges p_t^i. In this case $\Delta_t^i(P_t)$ can be written in the form $D_t(p_t^i/p_t)/I_t$, where D_t is a decreasing function, the same for all i, and I_t denotes the number of goods produced at date t. D_t depends only on the ratio of the two prices because Δ is homogeneous of degree zero. (The normalization by I_t is simply for convenience.) The demand for firm i's product is then given by

$$d_t^i = \frac{Q_t}{I_t} D_t \left(\frac{p_t^i}{p_t} \right). \tag{2}$$

By monopolistic competition we mean that each firm i takes as given aggregate demand, Q_t, and the price charged by other firms, p_t, and chooses its own price, p_t^i, taking into account the effect of p_t^i on its sales indicated by (2).[3] We are therefore interested in the properties of the demand curve, D_t.

Let us assume as a normalization of f_t in each period that $f_t(M) = I_t$ for all t, where M is a vector of ones (or, in the continuum case, the uniform measure). Then since f_t is symmetric, one must have $D_t(1) = 1$ for all t. We furthermore assume that D_t is differentiable at one, and that the value $D_t'(1) < -1$ is similarly independent of t. The latter assumption means that the degree of substitutability between different differentiated goods, evaluated in the case of equal purchases of all goods, remains the same as additional differentiated goods are added, and the common elasticity of substitution is greater than one. Finally, we assume that for each t, $D(\rho) + \rho D'(\rho)$ is a monotonically decreasing function of the relative price, ρ, over the entire range of relative prices for which it is positive. This implies the existence of a downward-sloping marginal revenue curve for each producer of a differentiated good. The result of these assumptions is that at a symmetric equilibrium, firms face a time-invariant elasticity of demand. It is worth stressing that we have obtained this result without having to make global assumptions on preferences, as is done, for instance, by Dixit and Stiglitz (1977).[4]

We now turn to a discussion of the technology with which firms produce output. When considering an economy with imperfectly competitive firms, it no longer makes sense to assume the kind of technology specification that is standard in the real business cycle literature. First of all, it is common in that literature to assume a production function using only capital and labor inputs, ignoring produced materials. In the case of perfectly competitive firms, this involves no loss of generality, as the output measure that one is concerned with is total value added (the total product net of the value of materials inputs), and this can indeed be expressed as a function of capital and labor inputs. Suppose that the production function for good i is given by

$$q_t^i = G(K_t^i, z_t H_t^i, M_t^i), \tag{3}$$

where z_t is an index of labor-augmenting technical progress at t, while q_t^i denotes the output, K_t^i denotes the level of capital services, H_t^i denotes the hours employed, and M_t^i denotes the materials inputs of firm i in period t. In a symmetric equilibrium, the price of materials is the same as the price for output, so that value added is given by $q_t^i - M_t^i$. In an equilibrium with perfect competition, this will necessarily equal

$$F(K_t^i, z_t H_t^i) = \max_{M_t^i}[G(K_t^i, z_t H_t^i, M_t^i) - M_t^i]. \tag{4}$$

This follows from profit maximization by price-taking firms. Thus there exists a pseudo-production function for value added with only capital and labor inputs as its arguments. Furthermore, by the envelope theorem, the derivatives of F with respect to its two arguments equal the marginal products of those two factors, which must be equated to their prices (deflated by the price of output) in equilibrium. Thus one obtains correct equilibrium conditions if one simply treats F as the true production function. This is implicitly what is being done in the real business cycle literature (as in other common growth models).

But with imperfect competition, (4) is no longer correct. A monopolistically competitive firm will choose its materials inputs to maximize

$$\frac{p_t^i}{p_t} G(K_t^i, z_t H_t^i, M_t^i) - M_t^i, \tag{5}$$

given the relation (2) between its sales and its price. Because p_t^i is not independent of the quantity sold, materials inputs are not chosen as in (4), even though in a symmetric equilibrium $p_t^i = p_t$. If (1.3) is a smooth neoclassical production function, the first-order condition for choice of materials inputs implies that in a symmetric equilibrium,

$$G_M(K_t^i, z_t H_t^i, M_t^i) = [1 + D'(1)^{-1}]^{-1},$$

so that the use of materials inputs depends upon the degree of market power. Of course, we can still solve this equation for M_t^i as a function of $(K_t^i, z_t H_t^i)$, and thus obtain an expression for value added as a function of those two inputs alone. But apart from the fact that this function would not represent the economy's true production possibilities, it would also change in the case of changes in the degree of market power. In general, in the presence of imperfect competition the economy will be strictly inside its production possibilities frontier (and not simply at an inefficient point on it given preferences over consumption and leisure), and the degree to which it is inside will depend upon the degree of market power.[5]

This complication can be avoided if one assumes a fixed-coefficient technology as far as materials inputs are concerned. Suppose that (3) takes the form

$$q_t^i = \min\left[\frac{V(K_t^i, z_t H_t^i)}{1 - s_M}, \frac{M_t^i}{s_M} \right].$$

Here $0 < s_M < 1$ corresponds to the share of materials costs in the value of gross output (in a symmetric equilibrium). In this case, firm i will always choose materials inputs $M_t^i = s_M q_t^i$ regardless of the degree of market power, and there exists a production function for value added that is independent of the degree of market power, namely, $V(K_t^i, z_t H_t^i)$. We will in fact assume a production function of this form in what follows, insofar as it seems realistic to assume that opportunities to substitute capital or labor inputs for materials are relatively small; but in so doing, we neglect effects that may actually be of importance.

With imperfect competition, materials inputs matter also for another reason, and they continue to matter for this reason even in the case of a fixed-coefficients production function. With imperfect competition, materials inputs affect the size of the wedge between the marginal product of labor and the wage. For a given degree of market power, that is, a given slope $D'(1)$, and hence a given markup of price over marginal cost, this wedge is greater the larger the share of materials. Hence, taking account of materials inputs is important when we wish to calibrate our model on the basis of evidence about typical degrees of market power.

To see this, note that in the case of the fixed-coefficients production function, capital and labor inputs are chosen to maximize

$$\frac{p_t^i}{p_t} q_t^i - w_t H_t^i - r_t K_t^i - s_M q_t^i,$$

where w_t represents the wage deflated by the price of the composite good and r_t represents the rental price of capital deflated in the same way, again given (2). (Because the present paper is concerned solely with imperfectly competitive product markets, we assume that firms are price-takers in factor markets.) In a symmetric equilibrium, the first-order conditions for factor demands take the forms

$$[1 + D'(1)^{-1} - s_M] V_1(K_t^i, z_t H_t^i) = (1 - s_M) r_t \tag{6}$$

and

$$[1 + D'(1)^{-1} - s_M] z_t V_2(K_t^i, z_t H_t^i) = (1 - s_M) w_t \tag{7}$$

We assume that

$$s_M < 1 + D'(1)^{-1},$$

so that a symmetric equilibrium of this kind is possible. (We also defer discussion of second-order conditions for the moment.) The wedge between marginal products and factor prices is observed to be

$$\mu = \frac{1 - s_M}{1 - s_M + D'(1)^{-1}} > 1.$$

This is a monotonic function of $(1 - s_M) D'(1)$, higher when the latter is a smaller negative quantity. Hence $s_M > 0$ has an effect equivalent to making each firm's degree of market power higher.

We now consider the relation between price and marginal cost in a monopolistically competitive equilibrium. In period t, each firm's marginal cost of production (using the composite good as numeraire) is

$$(1 - s_M) \frac{w_t}{z_t V_2(K_t^i, z_t H_t^i)} + s_M.$$

Comparing this with (7), we observe that each firm's markup (ratio of price to marginal cost) will equal

$$\gamma = [1 + D'(1)^{-1}]^{-1} > 1. \tag{8}$$

Note that in this simple model, the markup is a constant, regardless of any changes that may occur in equilibrium output due to technology shocks or for other reasons. This conclusion depends crucially on the homogeneity of the aggregator function, f, as well as upon the assumption of monopolistically competitive behavior on the part of firms. Without homogeneity, each firm's markup can depend on the level of output itself. But abandoning homogeneity also makes the aggregation of different buyers' demands more complicated. For this reason, our entire analysis is conducted with a homogeneous f. We do consider departures from monopolistic competition in Section 9, which result in endogenous variations in markups.

If $s_M > 0$, the inefficiency wedge, μ, is larger than the individual firm's markup γ, although the two are closely related. The former can be thought of as the ratio between the price of value added (the difference between the price of output and the cost of materials) and its marginal cost. This is larger than the ratio of price to marginal cost γ because firms mark up their materials inputs as well. For a given value of s_M, μ is a monotonically increasing function of γ, given by

$$\mu = \frac{(1 - s_M)\gamma}{1 - s_M\gamma}.$$ (9)

This relation is important when we consider below the effects of variations in market power. (Recall that s_M is a parameter of the production technology, rather than an endogenous variable.) It is also important for understanding the relation between different measures of the degree of market power found in the empirical literature, as we discuss further in Section 4.

We now discuss the relationship between the inefficiency wedge introduced by market power and the degree of returns to scale. We mentioned earlier that imperfect competition makes equilibrium possible even in the case of an increasing-returns technology, we have more flexibility in the specification of V. In fact, once we have assumed market power, assuming increasing returns is not only possible but also more reasonable. In the case of a constant returns production function (V homogeneous of degree one), Euler's theorem together with (6) and (7) implies that

$$q_t^i - M_t^i = \mu(r_t K_t^i + w_t H_t^i).$$ (10)

Hence $\mu > 1$ implies pure profits (the value of output exceeds the sum of materials costs, capital costs, and labor costs). Yet studies of U.S. industry generally find evidence of little, if any, pure profits on average (we discuss this further in Section 4). Hence if market power is significant (as evidence discussed below suggests), we must conclude that constant returns do not exist.

Let us use as a measure of returns to scale in the production of value added the quantity

$$\eta_t^i = \frac{V_1(K_t^i, z_t H_t^i)K_t^i + V_2(K_t^i, z_t H_t^i)z_t H_t^i}{V(K_t^i, z_t H_t^i)}.$$ (11)

Here increasing, decreasing, or constant returns correspond to η_t^i greater than, less than, or equal to one. Note that this is a purely local measure that may vary over time as production varies; in the case that V is homogeneous of some degree, then η^i is a constant and corresponds to that degree of homogeneity. Note also that this is a measure of the *short-run* returns to scale associated with changes in the factors employed while the number of differentiated goods being produced remains fixed; it has no implication regarding the *long-run* returns to scale in a growing economy with growth in the number of types of goods being produced as well as in the total quantity of factors employed. Finally, note that this is a measure of increasing returns in the production of *value added* rather than of gross output. A standard (local) measure of increasing returns in the production of gross output would instead be the ratio of average to marginal cost for firm i, that is,

$$
\rho_t^i = \frac{r_t K_t^i + w_t H_t^i + M_t^i}{[(1 - s_M) \frac{w_t}{z_t V_2(K_t^i, z_t H_t^i)} + s_M] q_t^i}
$$

$$
= \frac{\eta_t^i \mu^{-1}(1 - s_M) + s_M}{\mu^{-1}(1 - s_M) + s_M}
$$

Note that if $s_M > 0$, the measure η_t^i will be larger than ρ_t^i, though the two coincide when there are no intermediate inputs.[6]

Abandoning the assumption of short-run constant returns ($\eta = 1$), we find instead of (10) the more general result

$$
\eta_t^i (q_t^i - M_t^i) = \mu (r_t K_t^i + w_t H_t^i).
$$

Hence zero pure profits on average are consistent with $\mu > 1$ if the average returns to scale are $\eta = \mu > 1$. Thus increasing returns (in the sense just explained) are required. Note that $\eta > 1$ also means $\rho > 1$, so there are also increasing returns in the production of gross output, of a magnitude

$$
\rho_t^i = [\mu^{-1}(1 - s_M) + s_M]^{-1} = \gamma.
$$

The intuition is simple. With increasing returns, average cost exceeds marginal cost, so price can be equal to average cost and profits be zero even if price exceeds marginal cost. It is important that these increasing returns be internal to the firm, rather than due to externalities of the kind postulated by Baxter and King (1991). Even if there are also external returns to scale, the firm will make positive profits unless its own average costs exceed its own marginal cost.

The existence of increasing returns of this size is furthermore not merely fortuitous, but follows from economic principles, as Chamberlin (1933) pointed out. If $\eta_t^i \neq \mu$ in any period, then there are non-zero pure profits. This is consistent with profit maximization, assuming that the number of differentiated goods being produced, and the identities of their producers, cannot change. (Negative short-run profits are possible if it is assumed that it is not possible to simply shut down at zero cost, perhaps because fixed costs have been paid in advance.) But it does not make sense that such a situation should persist. Recall that we have assumed that the aggregator f_t depends upon the number of goods sold I_t in such a way that the elasticity of demand for each good, $-D'(1)$, remains the same after I_t changes.

With this assumption, an entrepreneur that produces an additional product earns the same profits on the new product as the profits earned on all existing products. The reason is that the entrepreneur's optimal markup is the same as that of all existing firms and their optimal markup does not change either. Hence sustained positive profits in the production of existing goods give entrepreneurs a reason to introduce new goods. Sustained negative profits should correspondingly eventually lead to exit of some producers. Hence it is reasonable to assume that in the long run, profits return to the zero level, as a result of adjustment in the number of produced goods I_t.

A simple specification for the production function (3) that makes this possible is

$$q_t^i = \min\left[\frac{F(K_t^i, z_t H_t^i) - \Phi}{1 - s_M}, \frac{M_t^i}{s_M} \right], \tag{12}$$

where F is assumed to be homogeneous of degree one, and $\Phi > 0$ indicates the presence of fixed costs.[7] This is a production function in which marginal cost is independent of scale, but average cost is decreasing because of the existence of the fixed costs; it generalizes the specification that is standard in the equilibrium business cycle literature in a way that involves the introduction of only one new parameter. In the case of production function specification (12), the index of increasing returns is given by

$$\eta_t^i = \frac{Y_t^i + \Phi}{Y_t^i},$$

again by Euler's theorem, where Y_t^i denotes value added in industry i in period t. Profits become zero in the long run if Y_t^i in each industry tends toward a particular value, namely, $\Phi/(\mu - 1)$. This in turn can be brought about by having the right number of differentiated goods I_t relative to the aggregate quantity of capital and labor inputs used in production; specifically, we require that in the long run

$$\frac{I_t}{F(K_t, z_t H_t)} = \frac{\mu - 1}{\mu \Phi}, \tag{13}$$

where K_t and H_t denote aggregate quantities of capital and labor inputs respectively. This condition requires that the steady-state number of differentiated goods grow at the same rate as the capital stock, the quantity of effective labor inputs, and aggregate output.[8]

Let us now collect our equations describing aggregates in a symmetric equilibrium. Aggregate value added is determined by aggregate factor inputs through the relation

$$Y_t = F(K_t, z_t H_t) - \Phi I_t. \tag{14}$$

(This is of course the output concept for which we have aggregate data.) Aggregate factor demands are related to factor prices through the relations

$$F_1(K_t, z_t H_t) = \mu r_t \tag{15}$$

and

$$z_t F_2(K_t, z_t H_t) = \mu w_t, \tag{16}$$

where the inefficiency wedge, μ, is determined by (8)-(9). Because our interest is in the short-run effects of shocks, we will treat both of the processes $\{z_t\}$ and $\{I_t\}$ as exogenous, even though we recognize that in the long run macroeconomic conditions may affect both technical progress (for reasons stressed in the literature on endogenous growth) and the number of differentiated products that are produced (for reasons sketched above). Our specification of these exogenous processes, however, will be such as to imply that our equilibria will involve only transitory deviations from a scale of operations at which (13) holds.

These equations jointly describe the production side of our model. Note that in the case that $\mu = 1$ and $\Phi = 0$, these are the equilibrium conditions of a standard real business cycle model. Hence our specification nests a standard competitive model as a limiting case.

3. A Complete Dynamic Equilibrium Model with Monopolistic Competition

The economy also contains a large number of identical infinitely lived households. At time t, the representative household seeks to maximize

$$E_t \left\{ \sum_{\tau=0}^{\infty} \beta^\tau N_{t+\tau} u(c_{t+\tau}, h_{t+\tau}) \right\}, \tag{17}$$

where E_t takes expectations at time t, β denotes a constant positive discount factor, N_t denotes the number of members per household in period t, c_t denotes per capita consumption by the members of the household in period t, and h_t denotes per capita hours worked by members of the household in period t. By normalizing the number of households at one, we can also use N_t to represent the total population, $C_t = N_t c_t$ to denote aggregate consumption, and so on. We assume, as usual, that u is a concave function, increasing in its first argument, and decreasing in its second argument. (The class of utility functions is further specialized below.)

Rather than make assumptions about the parameters of u directly, it turns out to be more convenient to make assumptions about the Frisch demand functions for consumption and leisure. These Frisch demand functions depend on the marginal utility of wealth, λ_t, which is given by

$$\lambda_t \equiv u_1(c_t, h_t). \tag{18}$$

Assuming that households can freely sell their labor services for the real wage w_t, they must satisfy the first order condition

$$\frac{u_2(c_t, h_t)}{u_1(c_t, h_t)} = w_t = \frac{u_2(c_t, h_t)}{\lambda_t}, \tag{19}$$

where the second equality follows from the definition (18). Combining (18) with the second equality of (19), we can solve for c_t and h_t as functions of λ_t and w_t which gives the Frisch demand curves

$$c_t = c(w_t, \lambda_t) \tag{20}$$

and

$$h_t = h(w_t, \lambda_t). \tag{21}$$

One advantage of using the Frisch demand functions is that the effects of all future variables (and their expectations) on current choices are captured by the marginal utility of wealth, λ_t. In terms of these functions, the condition for market clearing in the labor market is

$$H_t = N_t h(w_t, \lambda_t), \tag{22}$$

while that for the product market is

$$Y_t = N_t c(w_t, \lambda_t) + [K_{t+1} - (1 - \delta)K_t] + G_t, \tag{23}$$

where G_t represents government purchases of produced goods, and δ is the constant rate of depreciation of the capital stock, satisfying $0 < \delta \leq 1$. Equation (23), with Y_t representing value added is the standard GNP accounting identity, except that we do not count value added by the government sector as part of either G_t or Y_t. This equation says that one unit of the composite good at t can be used to obtain one unit of capital at $t + 1$. It follows that the purchase price of capital, just like that of materials, is equal to one. We assume that households, like firms, have access to a complete set of frictionless securities markets. As a result, the expected returns to capital must satisfy the asset-pricing equation,

$$1 = \beta E_t \left\{ \left(\frac{\lambda_{t+1}}{\lambda_t} \right) \left[r_{t+1} + (1 - \delta) \right] \right\}.$$

Substituting (15), we obtain

$$1 = \beta E_t \left\{ \left(\frac{\lambda_{t+1}}{\lambda_t} \right) \left[\frac{F_1(K_{t+1}, z_{t+1} H_{t+1})}{\mu} + (1 - \delta) \right] \right\}. \tag{24}$$

A rational expectations equilibrium is a set of stochastic processes for the endogenous variables $\{Y_t, K_t, H_t, w_t, \lambda_t\}$ that satisfies (14), (16), and (2)–(24), given the exogenous processes $\{G_t, z_t, N_t, I_t\}$.[9] We analyze the response of this model to changes in z_t and government purchases, using essentially the method of King, Plosser, and Rebelo (1988a). This involves restricting our attention to the case of small stationary fluctuations of the endogenous variables around a steady-state growth path. Let us first consider the conditions under which stationary solutions to these equations are possible. Given the existence of trend growth in the exogenous variables, the equilibrium requires that variables such as $\{Y_t, w_t, \ldots\}$ exhibit trend growth as well. However, a stationary solution for transformed (detrended) variables can exist if the equilibrium conditions in terms of these transformed variables do not involve any of the trending exogenous variables (that is, the levels of z_t or N_t as opposed to their growth rates).

As in King, Plosser, and Rebelo (1988a), this requires only that there exist a $\sigma > 0$ such that $h(w, \lambda)$ is *homogeneous of degree zero* in $(w, \lambda^{\frac{-1}{\sigma}})$, and $c(w, \lambda)$ is *homogeneous of degree one* in $(w, \lambda^{\frac{-1}{\sigma}})$. Given these conditions, there exists an equilibrium in which the detrended endogenous state variables,

$$\tilde{Y}_t = \frac{Y_t}{z_t N_t}, \quad \tilde{K}_t = \frac{K_t}{z_{t-1} N_t}, \quad \tilde{H}_t = \frac{H_t}{N_t}, \quad \tilde{w}_t = \frac{w_t}{z_t}, \quad \tilde{\lambda}_t = \lambda_t (z_t)^\sigma,$$

are stationary, given stationary processes for the exogenous random variables,

$$\tilde{G}_t = \frac{G_t}{z_t N_t}, \quad \tilde{I}_t = \frac{I_t}{z_t N_t}, \quad \gamma_t^z = \frac{z_t}{z_{t-1}},$$

and a constant population growth rate so that $\frac{N_{t+1}}{N_t} = \gamma^N$ in all periods. The equilibrium conditions in terms of the stationary variables become

$$\tilde{Y}_t = F\left((\gamma_t^z)^{-1} \tilde{K}_t, \tilde{H}_t\right) - \Phi \tilde{I}_t, \tag{25}$$

$$F_2\left(\frac{\tilde{K}_t}{\gamma_t^z}, \tilde{H}_t\right) = \mu \tilde{w}_t, \tag{26}$$

$$\tilde{H}_t = H(\tilde{w}_t, \tilde{\lambda}_t), \tag{27}$$

$$c(\tilde{w}_t, \tilde{\lambda}_t) + [\gamma^N \tilde{K}_{t+1} - (1 - \delta)(\gamma_t^z)^{-1} \tilde{K}_t] + \tilde{G}_t = \tilde{Y}_t, \tag{28}$$

and

$$1 = \beta E_t \left\{ \left(\gamma_{t+1}^z\right)^{-\sigma} \left(\frac{\tilde{\lambda}_{t+1}}{\tilde{\lambda}_t}\right) \left[\frac{F_K((\gamma_{t+1}^z)^{-1} \tilde{K}_{t+1}, \tilde{H}_{t+1})}{\mu} + (1 - \delta) \right] \right\} \tag{29}$$

These equilibrium conditions involve only the detrended state variables, and thus admit a stationary solution in terms of those variables.[10]

Like King, Plosser, and Rebelo (1988a), we furthermore seek to characterize such a stationary equilibrium only in the case of small fluctuations of the detrended state variables around their steady-state values, that is, the constant values that they take in a deterministic equilibrium growth path in the case that γ_t^z, $\tilde{I}_t$, and $\tilde{G}_t$ are constant. This steady state can be found by solving the 5 equations (2.9)-(2.13) for the five unknowns, $\tilde{Y}$, $\tilde{H}$, $\tilde{w}$, $\tilde{\lambda}$, and $\tilde{K}$. Since these solutions vary continuously with $\tilde{I}$, we can then find a value for $\tilde{I}$ for which (13) holds and profits are zero. At this solution, $\tilde{I}\Phi$ equals $(\mu - 1)\tilde{Y}$.

Given a steady state, we approximate a stationary equilibrium involving small fluctuations around it by the solution to a log-linear approximation to the equilibrium conditions. This linearization uses derivatives evaluated at the steady-state values of the state variables.[11] In writing the log-linear equations, we use the notation $\hat{Y}_t$ for $\log(\tilde{Y}_t/\tilde{Y})$, $\hat{w}_t$ for $\log(\tilde{w}_t/\tilde{w})$, and so on, where the $\tilde{Y}$, $\tilde{w}$, and so on, denote steady-state values. The log-linear approximation to the Frisch consumption demand (20) and labor supply (21) functions can be written as

$$\hat{C}_t = \epsilon_{Cw}\hat{w}_t + \epsilon_{C\lambda}\hat{\lambda}_t \tag{30}$$

and

$$\hat{H}_t = \epsilon_{Hw}\hat{w}_t + \epsilon_{H\lambda}\hat{\lambda}_t, \tag{31}$$

where the coefficients represent the elasticities of the Frisch demands. Thus the only way in which the specification of preferences affects our equilibrium conditions is in the values implied for these elasticities, and so we calibrate the model by specifying numerical values for these elasticities directly. Our homogeneity assumptions furthermore imply that

$$\epsilon_{Hw} - \sigma\epsilon_{H\lambda} = 0, \tag{32}$$

$$\epsilon_{Cw} - \sigma\epsilon_{C\lambda} = 1 \tag{33}$$

and

$$\frac{\epsilon_{Cw}}{\epsilon_{Hw}} = \frac{\sigma - 1}{\sigma} \frac{\tilde{w}\tilde{H}}{\tilde{C}}. \tag{34}$$

The three restrictions, (32), (33), and (34), imply that there are only two independent parameters among ϵ_{Cw}, $\epsilon_{C\lambda}$, ϵ_{Hw}, $\epsilon_{H\lambda}$, and σ. To preserve comparability with earlier studies, we calibrate σ and ϵ_{Hw}. The former is the inverse of the intertemporal elasticity of consumption growth with hours worked held constant, while the latter is the intertemporal elasticity of labor supply.

The log-linearized equilibrium conditions can then be written as

$$\hat{Y}_t = \mu s_K \hat{K}_t + \mu s_H \hat{H}_t - \mu s_K \hat{\gamma}_t^z - (\mu - 1)\hat{I}_t, \tag{35}$$

$$\frac{s_K}{\epsilon_{KH}}(\hat{K}_t - \hat{\gamma}_t^z - \hat{H}_t) = \hat{w}_t, \tag{36}$$

$$\hat{H}_t = \epsilon_{Hw}\hat{w}_t + \epsilon_{H\lambda}\hat{\lambda}_t, \tag{37}$$

$$s_C(\epsilon_{Cw}\hat{w}_t + \epsilon_{C\lambda}\hat{\lambda}_t) + s_I[\left(\frac{\gamma_n\gamma_z}{\gamma_n\gamma_z + \delta - 1}\right)\hat{K}_{t+1}$$

$$-\left(\frac{1 - \delta}{\gamma_n\gamma_z + \delta - 1}\right)(\hat{K}_t - \hat{\gamma}_t^z)] + s_G\hat{G}_t = \hat{Y}_t, \tag{38}$$

and

$$-\sigma\hat{\gamma}^z_{t+1} + E_t\left\{\hat{\lambda}_{t+1} - \hat{\lambda}_t + \left(\frac{r+\delta}{1+r}\right)\frac{s_H}{\epsilon_{KH}}(\hat{H}_{t+1} - \hat{K}_{t+1} + \hat{\gamma}^z_{t+1})\right\} = 0. \quad (39)$$

This system may be further simplified as follows. We can solve (35), (36) and (37) for $\hat{H}_t$, $\hat{Y}_t$, and $\hat{w}_t$ as functions of $\hat{K}_t$ and $\hat{\lambda}_t$. Substitution of these solutions into (38) and (39) gives a system of two difference equations of the form

$$A\begin{pmatrix} E_t\hat{\lambda}_{t+1} \\ \hat{K}_{t+1} \end{pmatrix} = B\begin{pmatrix} \hat{\lambda}_t \\ \hat{K}_t \end{pmatrix} + C\begin{pmatrix} \hat{\gamma}^z_t \\ \hat{G}_t \\ \hat{I}_t \end{pmatrix} + D\begin{pmatrix} E_t\hat{\gamma}^z_{t+1} \\ E_t\hat{G}_{t+1} \\ E_t\hat{I}_{t+1} \end{pmatrix}. \quad (40)$$

We assume that the exogenous variables $\{\gamma^z_t, \hat{G}_t, \hat{I}_t\}$ are subject to stationary fluctuations. Thus, as shown, for example, by Blanchard and Kahn (1980), (40) has a unique stationary solution if and only if the matrix A is nonsingular and the matrix $A^{-1}B$ has one eigenvalue with modulus less than one and one with modulus greater than one. Woodford (1986) shows that this is also the case in which the original nonlinear equilibrium conditions have a locally unique stationary solution. Moreover, when perturbed by exogenous shocks whose support is sufficiently small, this solution involves only small fluctuations around the steady state. For the calibrated parameter values discussed in the next section, and for all sufficiently nearby values, we find that there is indeed exactly one stable eigenvalue. We thus focus much of our analysis on this case. In Section 7, we discuss alternative parameter values that lead both eigenvalues to be smaller than one.

In the case where there is only one stable eigenvalue, there is a unique equilibrium response to the shocks with which we are concerned. We can approximate this unique response by calculating the solution to the log-linear system (40), using the formulas of Blanchard and Kahn (1980) or Hansen and Sargent (1980). The resulting solution is a linear function of the exogenous variables. This means that we can decompose fluctuations in the state variables into the contributions from each of the shocks that affect our exogenous variables. It also means that the analysis of the effect of any one shock would not be affected by the inclusion of additional exogenous shocks.

The coefficients in the log-linear equation system (36)–(39) have been written in terms of the parameters shown in Table 9.1. Column 2 of the table gives the formulas that, when evaluated at the steady-state values of the detrended state variables, allow us to compute the values of these parameters. With the exception of population growth and the parameters related to the lack of perfect competition, the values we have assigned follow those presented in King, Plosser, and Rebelo (1988a). Note that in the case where μ is equal to one, the model we have presented reduces to the standard real business cycle model. We survey some of the evidence relating to values for the average inefficiency wedge, μ (for now, taken to be a

Table 9.1
The Calibrated Parameters

Parameter	Defined by:	Values	Description
γ_z		1.004	Steady-state quarterly growth rate of technology
γ_N		1.004	Steady-state quarterly growth rate of population
s_C	$\frac{\tilde{C}}{\tilde{Y}}$	0.587	Share of private consumption expenditure in value added
s_G	$\frac{\tilde{G}}{\tilde{Y}}$	0.117	Share of government purchases of goods in value added
s_I	$(\gamma_z \gamma_N - 1 + \delta)\frac{\tilde{K}}{\tilde{Y}}$	0.296	Share of private investment expenditure in value added
δ		0.025	Rate of depreciation of capital stock (per quarter)
s_H	$\frac{F_H \tilde{H}}{F}$	0.58	Share of labor costs in total costs
s_M		0.5	Share of materials in total costs
r	$\frac{F_K}{\mu} - \delta$ or $\gamma_z^\sigma \beta^{-1} - 1$	0.016	Steady-state real rate of return (per quarter)
$1/\sigma$		1	Intertemporal elasticity of substitution of consumption with hours worked held constant
ϵ_{H_w}		4	Intertemporal elasticity of labor supply
ϵ_{KH}	$\frac{F_K F_H}{F_{KH} F}$	1	Elasticity of substitution between capital and hours
μ		1, 1.4	Steady-state value-added markup (efficiency wedge)
κ		0.02	Rate at which entry adjust to changes in technology
ϵ_μ	$\frac{\tilde{X}\mu'}{\tilde{Y}\mu}$	$-1, 0.39$	Elasticy of the markup (endogenous markup model)
α		0.9	Probability that future sales depend on price history
ρ^G		0.9	Serial correlation of government purchases
ρ^μ		0, 0.9	Serial correlation of μ (Exogenous markup model)

Notes: Except for population growth, the first twelve parameters take the values in King, Plosser, and Rebelo (1988a).

constant) in the next section. The same evidence is equally relevant for calibration of the steady-state markup in the case of the variable markup models discussed later.

4. Evidence on the Size of Markups and Increasing Returns

Evidence on the size of markups and increasing returns comes from several distinct sources. First, there is a literature that attempts to measure the degree of increasing returns from engineering studies of the average costs of different plants. Most of this literature, which is summarized in Panzar (1989), has concerned itself with returns to scale in regulated industries. The returns to scale found in the telecommunications industry tend to be substantial, with most studies finding returns to scale corresponding to a value of η in (11) of the order of 1.4. Those found for electric power generation seem to be somewhat sensitive to the exact specification. Christensen and Greene (1976) found that only half the 1970 plants were operating at a scale where marginal cost was below average cost. By contrast, Chappell and Wilder (1986) found much more substantial returns to scale when taking into account the multiplicity of outputs of many electric utilities.

These findings are of only limited relevance to our analysis. These studies seek to measure the degree of long-run returns to scale, that is, the rate at which average costs decline as one goes from a small plant to a larger one. However, constant returns in this sense are perfectly consistent with large gaps between short-run average costs and short-run marginal costs. This would happen, in particular, if plant size exceeded the size that minimizes costs. Firms would rationally make such capacity choices if, for instance, producing at an additional location or introducing an additional variety raised a firm's sales for any given price, as in the Chamberlinian model of monopolistic competition. This is in essence what occurs in our model. We stipulated a fixed cost per plant so that lowest average cost would be obtained by having a single plant. In equilibrium there are several plants, all of which have the same average cost, and nonetheless, marginal cost is below average cost.

Second, there is a literature that attempts to measure the elasticity of demand facing individual products produced by particular firms. This literature is relevant because, as is clear from the derivation of (8), it is never profit maximizing to set the markup γ lower than one over one plus the inverse of the elasticity of demand for the product. There are many estimates of the elasticity of demand for particular products in the marketing literature. Tellis (1988) surveys this literature, and reports that the median measured price elasticity is just under 2. This suggests that the markup γ of these individual firms would equal 2 if they behaved like monopolistic competitors. If our symmetric model were correct, the demand elasticity estimated in the marketing literature would correspond to the elasticity of demand faced by the typical firm. In practice, elasticities of demand probably differ across products, and the elasticity of demand of those products studied in the marketing literature is probably atypically low. This is because the marketing literature focuses on the demand for branded consumer products, which are more differentiated than unbranded products, so their demand is probably less price sensitive. Thus, the typical product in the economy probably has a price elasticity of demand that exceeds 2.

Finally, there is a literature that tries to obtain econometric estimates of marginal cost and, in some cases, combine them with econometric estimates of the elasticity of demand. The aim of this approach is to obtain simultaneous, independent estimates of the markup and of the degree of increasing returns. Morrison (1990) follows this approach. She estimates a flexible functional form cost function, using data on gross industry output and materials inputs. Her estimates of γ and of η range between 1.2 and 1.4 for sixteen out of her eighteen industries. One notable feature of these estimates is that her industry estimates of the ratio of average to marginal cost closely resemble her estimates of the markup itself. Thus the relation between these two parameters that we imposed through our zero-profit condition appears to be validated.

Hall (1988b, 1990) proposes a variant of this approach in which, essentially, equation (35) is estimated by using instrumental variables. The share coefficients are treated as known (from measured factor payments), rather than estimated, so that only μ need be estimated; instruments are used that are believed a priori to be orthogonal to exogenous technological progress, γ_t^z; and endogenous variation in $\hat{I}_t$ is ignored. Hall obtains large estimates of μ for many U.S. manufacturing sectors; it is over 2 for six out of seven one-digit sectors. We discuss this approach and related estimates at the end of the next section. Here, we wish simply to note that one reason that Hall's estimates of the "markup ratio" are larger than those obtained by such authors as Morrison is that he is estimating μ rather than γ.

Before closing this section, it is worth discussing the basis on which we state that profits in the U.S. economy are zero, so μ must equal η.[12] Total tangible assets minus durables in 1987 were equal to 2.25 times that year's private value added. Since private investment (again excluding durables) equaled about 18 percent of private value added and the yearly growth rate is about 3 percent, it follows that the yearly depreciation of this capital stock must be about 5 percent (to obtain this, one must subtract the growth rate from the ratio of investment to capital, which equals 8 percent). The share of payments going to capital has been 25 percent on average. These payments can be decomposed into the product of the capital output ratio and the sum of the rate of depreciation and an implied rate of return on capital. Thus, this implied rate of return to capital has been about 6 percent per annum. It is the fact that this rate of return is close to the rate of return on stock market securities that leads us to say that there are no profits in the economy. If owners of capital also received some pure profits, the payments to capitalists would exceed the product of the stock market rate of return and the actual capital stock.

Yet another way of making the same point is to note that, on average, Tobin's q is one (Summers 1981). This again says that the present value of payments to the owners of capital discounted at the required rate of return on equity shares equals the cost of replacing the capital stock.

In the next two sections we study the effects of having a constant markup different from one for the effects of shocks to government purchases and of technological shocks.

5. Responses to Government Purchases

The first exercise we consider is a change in government purchases, G_t. To perform this exercise, we must postulate a stochastic process for G_t, because the behavior of the agents in the model depends also on their expectation of future government purchases of goods. We assume that $\hat{G}_t$ is given by

$$\hat{G}_t = \rho^G \hat{G}_{t-1} + v_t^G \qquad\qquad |\rho^G| < 1. \tag{41}$$

In this section we assume constant growth of z_t and N_t; hence (41) specifies an exogenous stochastic process for G_t. For the purposes of analyzing the response of the economy to the shock, v_t^G, we assume that the number of firms, I_t, does not respond to the shock. In the perfectly competitive case where μ equals one and Φ is equal to zero, this involves no loss of generality since the number of firms is indeterminate. For this case we just set I_t equal to one. In the case of imperfect competition, changes in G_t do change the profits of the existing firms. We nonetheless assume that I_t continues to grow exogenously at the same rate as $z_t N_t$ (so that $\tilde{I}_t$ is constant). Abstracting from variations in the rate of entry is reasonable as an approximation because entry decisions involve relatively long lead times.

In a model with constant markups, a change in G increases output only through an increase in the supply of hours at a given real wage. This is apparent from (16). This equation is, for a given constant inefficiency wedge, μ, a relationship between the wage and the marginal product of labor, where the latter depends on employment, the state of technology, and capital. Since technology and capital are fixed, the willingness of firms to hire labor at a given real wage does not change. However, there are two reasons, emphasized by Barro (1981), why labor supply will change. The first is that the increase in government purchases makes households less wealthy. The second is that government purchases tend to increase real interest rates. Both of these effects raise the marginal utility of wealth, λ_t, and thus raise H_t for any given w_t. Thus the real wage falls and employment rises.

We compute simulations of the model's response to changes in v_t^G for the case where ρ^G is equal to .9. We chose this value of ρ^G because changes in government purchases are persistent but also have large mean-reverting components.[13] We assume that the share of materials in total output, s_M, equals one-half. This is a conservative choice, since value added in manufacturing is only about half of the value of gross output in manufacturing. This parameter plays no role in our perfectly competitive model but is crucial in the imperfectly competitive case. We compute results both for μ equal to one and for μ equal to 1.4.; with s_M equal to 0.5, (9) implies that the latter corresponds to a markup γ equal to 1.17. This markup is fairly low relative to those that have been estimated in the literature. The other parameter values are listed in Table 1; they are taken from King, Plosser, and Rebelo (1988a).

Figures 9.1 and 9.2 show the percentage response in hours, output, and the real wage to a 1 percent change in v_t^G. We see in the figures that the qualitative response of hours, output, and the wage is the same when the μ equals one as in our imperfectly competitive case where $\mu = 1.4$. Output and hours rise in both cases, and as was suggested by the earlier discussion, real wages decline. But there is a change in the magnitude of these effects for given values of the model's other parameters. We see that output rises by about 0.04 percent in the case of perfect competition, while it increases by 0.05 percent when $\mu = 1.4$. Because government purchases equal 11.7 percent of GNP, the multiplier for government purchases is less than one-half in both cases, but it is larger with imperfect competition. On the other

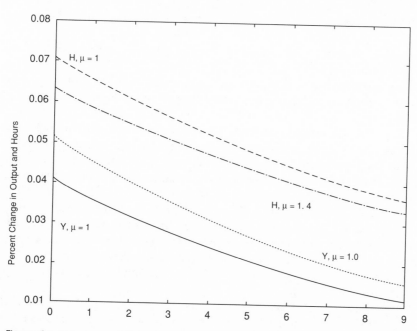

Figure 9.1 Response of Output and Hours to a 1 Percent Shock to Government Purchases

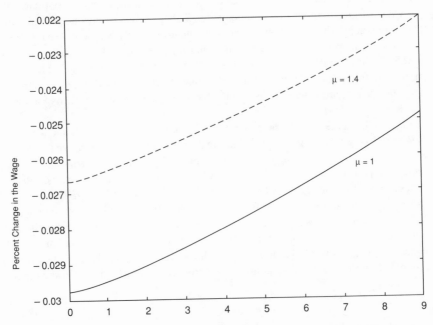

Figure 9.2 Response of Real Wage to a 1 Percent Shock to Government Purchases

hand, the percentage response in hours and real wages is smaller when μ equals 1.4 than when it equals one.

The difference in the responsiveness of hours and output does cast some doubt on the accuracy of the common view that the presence of imperfect competition, in itself, magnifies the short-run effect of government purchases on economic activity.[14] This is argued to reflect the presence of "aggregate demand spillovers" on consumption demand. The idea is that the increase in output induced by the rise in government purchases raises the profits of the imperfectly competitive firms, and the resulting increase in income makes consumers purchase more. It is argued that these effects amplify the response of economic activity through a "multiplier" process of the Kahn/Keynes type. It is true that in our model, a larger μ, magnifies the response of output for given values of the other parameters. But this is solely due to the fact that imperfectly competitive firms set the wage below the marginal product of labor, which causes a 1 percent increase in hours to raise output by μs_H percent rather than by s_H percent.[15] On the other hand, a larger μ reduces the response of hours.

The reason for this is easily seen. Hours become less responsive when μ is increased because the (negative) wealth effect of an increase in government purchases become smaller. For given prices (wages and interest rates), labor supply depends upon the present value of after-tax income net of wages. In either case, the direct effect of an increase in G is to increase the present discounted value of taxes (and hence reduce after-tax income) by exactly the amount of the increase in G. But, potentially, changes in G have an additional effect on the present value of income. If they lead equilibrium hours and output to rise, income net of wages increases by the amount by which the increase in output exceeds the increase in the wage bill. To first order, this amount is zero when the marginal product of hours equals the real wage, but it is positive if the marginal product of hours exceeds the real wage (that is, if firms have market power). Thus in the case of perfect competition, a one-dollar increase in G lowers the present value of income by one dollar, while in the case of imperfect competition it lowers it by less than one dollar.

In a sense, the "demand spillover" literature is correct in arguing that the increased profits in the case of imperfect competition give an additional boost to household income. Where this argument errs is in supposing that the stimulative effects of government purchases result from a *positive*, rather than a *negative* effect of government purchases on household income. It also errs in supposing that the direct determinant of equilibrium employment is the effect of household income on *consumption demand*, rather than the effect of income on *labor supply*.

Another implication worthy of note concerns the effect of government purchases on measured labor productivity. Since output increases more and hours increase less, in the case of μ greater than one (see Figure 9.1), it is obvious that measured productivity rises more (falls less) in the case of imperfect competition. The behavior of the Solow residual, which is used as a measure of exogenous productivity growth in the real business cycle literature, is especially noteworthy. Recall that the Solow residual is given by

$$\Delta Y_t - s_H \Delta H_t - s_K \Delta K_t, \tag{42}$$

where ΔY_t represents the change in the logarithm of Y_t, and analogously for ΔH_t and ΔK_t. By contrast, differentiation of (14) by using (15) and (16) and keeping I constant establishes that

$$\gamma_t^z = \frac{\Delta Y_t - \mu s_H \Delta H_t - \mu s_K \Delta K_t}{\mu s_H}. \tag{43}$$

The numerator of (43) thus must be invariant (to first order) to changes in G_t. But this implies that if μ is greater than one and $\hat{H}_t$ rises for any reason other than a technological shift (so that γ_t^z is unchanged), the expression in (42) will rise. In other words, an increase in hours induced by an increase in government purchases or any other nontechnology shock raises the standard Solow residual. The reason is that with imperfect competition, an increase in the labor input must necessarily raise the value of output by more than it raises labor costs (since firms make profits on the marginal units). This results in an increase in measured productivity.

This shows that ignoring imperfect competition when it is actually present is dangerous. It leads to incorrect measures of total factor productivity. If one wants to measure true changes in z, one must use the formula of (43), which depends on μ in addition to depending on observable magnitudes.

The fact that the Solow residual (42) is not a correct measure of true technical progress may explain some observed anomalies concerning Solow residuals. For example, a number of authors have observed that in postwar U.S. data, Solow residuals are correlated with various measures of government purchases (Hall 1988b; Baxter and King 1991; Burnside, Eichenbaum, and Rebelo 1993). One might argue that this simply indicates that government purchases are not exogenous with respect to technology shocks. This might be true of some components of government purchases, especially spending by local governments that are forced to have balanced budgets. But it is hard to defend the "reverse causation" thesis in the case of national defense–related goods, which have moved mainly in response to changed perception of the threat posed by communist regimes. Yet this component is positively correlated with Solow residuals, as Hall (1988b) and Baxter and King (1991) show. Our model can explain this observation insofar as it predicts that hours should increase in response to an exogenous increase in government purchases and, as a result, the Solow residual should increase as well if $\mu > 1$.[16]

Imperfect competition might similarly explain the observations of Hall (1988b) that changes in world oil prices (which, again, should be exogenous with respect to the state of U.S. productivity) are correlated with Solow residuals,[17] and the findings of Evans (1990) that various measures of monetary policy shocks forecast future Solow residuals.[18]

The ability of imperfect competition to explain these anomalies not only provides an argument that imperfect competition is important but may also be the basis for a quantitative estimate of its importance. Indeed, this is the basis for Hall's (1988b) estimates of μ. The parameter μ can be estimated by using (43) if one observes a variable, v_t, such as military purchases or changes in the world oil price, that is correlated with both output and hours changes and is known to be orthogonal to the change in technology, γ_t^z. Then v_t should be orthogonal to the right-hand side of (43). In particular,

$$\text{Cov}(v_t, \Delta Y_t - \mu s_H \Delta H_t - \mu s_K \Delta K_t) = 0. \tag{44}$$

Hall's proposal is to estimate μ so as to minimize (under an appropriate metric) the extent to which the moment condition (4.4) fails to hold. In the case where v_t is a single variable, the expression in (4.4) is actually zero if μ is replaced by the instrumental variable estimate

$$\mu^e = \frac{\sum_t v_t \Delta Y_t}{\sum_t v_t (s_H \Delta H_t + s_K \Delta K_t)}.$$

Hall's estimates indicate estimates of the wedge, μ, of over 1.8 for all seven one-digit-SIC industries that he considers. Subsequent work by Domowitz, Hubbard, and Petersen (1988), uses gross industry output so that it estimates the markup, γ. Their estimates of γ range between 1.4 and 1.7 for seventeen out of their nineteen industries. These two sets of estimates do not contradict each other because as long as the materials share, s_M, is positive, μ is greater than γ, as can be seen from (9). For example, μ equal to 2.3 (a typical value for Hall's industries) and a materials share of 0.5 (which is also typical for those industries) imply $\gamma = 1.4$, which is in the range of those estimated by both Domowitz, Hubbard, and Petersen (1988) and Morrison (1990).

6. Responses to Technology Shocks

In this section, we show that the level of the average markup matters when it comes to the response of the economy to changes in technology. Before we can compute the economy's response, we must postulate a stochastic process for the level of technology itself and for the number of firms. It is not enough to simply compute the size of the technology shocks by using (43). The reason is that, once again, households' decisions of how much labor to supply and output to consume depend upon their expectations of the future state of productivity. We are also unable, in this case, to ignore the issue of variation in the rate of entry of new firms, as we do not wish to assume that technology shocks have a purely transient effect on productivity. In fact, in this section, we follow King, Plosser, and Rebelo (1988b) and Plosser (1989) in assuming that productivity is a random walk, so that γ_t^z is an independently distributed random variable.[19]

As we showed in (13), the number of firms must grow with z for profits to remain equal to zero in the steady state. On the other hand, we do not believe that the number of firms adjusts very rapidly to a technology shock. We thus wish to concentrate on short-run effects of technology shocks by assuming that entry plays only a small role in these short-term dynamics. To do this, we let I_t follow an error correction process of the form

$$\log I_t = \kappa \log(I z_t N_t) + (1 - \kappa) \log I_{t-1}, \tag{45}$$

where I and κ are positive constants, with $\kappa < 1$. This process implies that with a stationary, $\{\gamma_t^z\}$, $\{\tilde{I}_t\}$ is itself stationary as we assumed in Section 3. By letting κ be small we ensure that there is little immediate entry in response to a technology shock, even when the latter is permanent. We conjecture that our results hinge mainly on the fact that the response of entry with a small κ is slow and not on the precise specification of (45). In particular, a small κ preserves comparability between our results and those obtained by Hornstein (1993) for a model without permanent technology shocks in which the effects of technology shocks on entry are ignored.

Differencing (45), we obtain

$$\Delta I_t = \kappa(\gamma_t^z + \gamma^N) + (1 - \kappa)\Delta I_{t-1},$$

which implies that

$$\Delta \hat{I}_t = \sum_{j=0}^{\infty} \kappa (1 - \kappa)^j \hat{\gamma}^z_{t-j}, \tag{46}$$

where $\Delta \hat{I}_t$ denotes ΔI_t minus the unconditional mean of that stationary variable, while, as before, $\hat{\gamma}^z_t$ denotes γ^z_t minus its mean.[20]

Differentiation of (14) now yields

$$\gamma^z_t = \frac{\Delta Y_t - \mu s_H \Delta H_t - \mu s_K \Delta K_t + (\mu - 1)\Delta I_t}{\mu s_H}. \tag{47}$$

This implies that the change in the number of firms affects the measurement of the corrected Solow residual (analogous to (43)), in the case of imperfect competition. This is because the entry of firms increases fixed costs and thus requires an increase in productivity if a given quantity of output is to be produced with the same inputs. Thus an assumption such as (45) is necessary in order to measure technology shocks. Removing means from (47) and substituting (46), we obtain

$$\hat{\gamma}^z_t = \Omega(L) \left[\Delta \hat{Y}_t - \mu s_H \Delta \hat{H}_t - \mu s_K \Delta \hat{K}_t \right], \tag{48}$$

where $\Omega(L)$ is a polynomial in the lag operator whose coefficients depend on μ and κ. This polynomial has no roots inside the unit circle; in particular, it equals one when μ is one. Using (48), we construct a series for γ^z_t for the U.S. economy, using quarterly data from the first quarter of 1947 through the last quarter of 1989 on private output and private sector hours, while assuming that the change in capital is constant.[21] The construction of our output and hours series is discussed in Rotemberg and Woodford (1992).

The first part of Table 9.2 shows the measured variance of γ^z_t for various values of μ. It shows that the measured variance of technology falls as we increase the markup. The reason is that typical U.S. business cycles involve procyclical movements in output, hours, and the standard Solow residual. If μ is greater than one, one expects the Solow residual to move procyclically, even in the absence of technology shocks, as explained in the previous section. Thus a model with μ greater than one can explain some fraction of the variation in the Solow residual leaving smaller unexplained variations in total factor productivity.

We computed the model's responses to shocks in γ^z using the King, Plosser, and Rebelo (1988a) parameters listed in Table 9.1, a materials share of one-half, and, again, values for μ equal to 1 and 1.4. We assumed that κ is equal to 0.02 to make sure that immediate entry had a relatively trivial effect on the results. The model's prediction for the effect on output and hours of a 1 percent shock to γ^z_t is presented in Figure 9.3. We see that for a given increase in z, the response of output is higher under imperfect competition. The reason is that an increase in z represents, in effect, an increase in the effective units of labor that firms hire. Because firms with market power set the marginal product of labor higher than the

Table 9.2
The Effect of Technology Shocks: Predicted versus Actual Second Moments

μ	Variance of Measured Total Factor Productivity	Output Statistics				Hours Statistics			
		(1)	(2)	(3)	(4)	(1")	(2")	(3")	(4")
1.0000	2.1653	1.3216	1.2263	0.5286	−.2379	.8282	.1833	.9365	−.3520
1.2000	1.5132	1.3216	0.9448	0.6332	−.1940	.8282	.0271	.8658	−.0780
1.4000	1.1510	1.3216	0.7745	0.7632	−.1635	.8282	.0010	.8383	−.0134
1.6000	0.9365	1.3216	0.6685	0.8980	−.1853	.8282	.0076	.8055	.0182
1.8000	0.8038	1.3216	0.6016	1.0288	−.2336	.8282	.0218	.7644	.0507
2.0000	0.7192	1.3216	0.5596	1.1522	−.2952	.8282	.0373	.7187	.0872

Note: (1)—var$[dY(t)]$; (2)—var$[dYth(t)]$; (3)—var$[dY(t) - dYth(t)]$; (4)—rho $= 2*\text{cov}(dYth, dY - dYth)/[\text{var}(dYth) + \text{var}(dY - dYth)]$; (1")—var$[dH(t)]$; (2")—var$[dHth(t)]$; (3")—var$[dH(t) - dHth(t)]$; (4")—rho $= 2*\text{cov}(dHth, dH - dHth)/[\text{var}(dHth) + \text{var}(dH - dHth)]$.

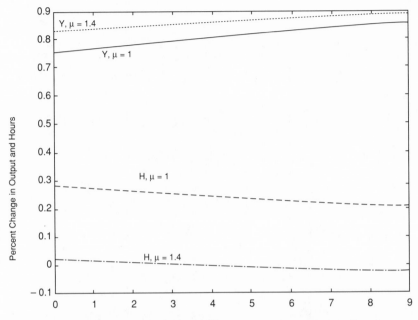

Figure 9.3 Response of Output and Hours to a 1 Percent Technology Shock

wage, an increase in the effective labor input raises output more under imperfect competition. This can be seen directly from equation (35), which shows that the change in output for given hours and capital input is equal to μs_H times γ^z. This is why a higher μ raises the response of output.

By contrast, the response of hours worked is smaller when the markup is higher. Indeed, for our chosen value of μ, hours are nearly insensitive to changes in technological possibilities. That the response of hours to a change in technological opportunities is ambiguous is well known. Because capital is fixed in the short run, an increase in z raises temporarily the marginal product of labor and the wage, and this leads workers to substitute current work for future leisure. On the other hand, an increase in z also makes people wealthier, and this reduces labor supply. The net effect depends on whether the intertemporal substitution or the wealth effect is larger. Imperfect competition increases the size of the wealth effect, as discussed in the previous section, and so reduces the extent to which labor supply increases. If μ is made slightly larger than 1.4, a positive technology shock actually reduces equilibrium hours, though output still increases.

This result, that employment fluctuations are smaller with imperfect competition, is also obtained by Hornstein (1993), who discusses it in terms of the variances of output and hours that can be explained by technology shocks. We next turn to the consequences of imperfect competition for this type of exercise.

There are two different ways of computing the variance of output and hours that can be attributed to changes in z. They both rely on the impulse response functions plotted in Figure 9.3. Let the impulse response functions be written as

$$\Delta \hat{Y}_t = \sum_{i=0}^{\infty} \xi_i^Y \hat{\gamma}_{t-i}^z,$$ (49)

and

$$\Delta \hat{H}_t = \sum_{i=0}^{\infty} \xi_i^H \hat{\gamma}_{t-i}^z.$$ (50)

Then one estimate of the implied variance of the change in output is

$$\sum_{i=0}^{\infty} (\xi_i^Y)^2 \text{Var}(\gamma_t^z),$$ (51)

where $\text{Var}(\gamma_t^z)$ is the variance of the technology shock shown in Table 9.2. The variance of the change in hours can be computed analogously.

An alternative computation of the variances of output and hours relies on the historical time series for the technology shock, which can be computed by using (48). Like Plosser (1989), we can compute the values of output and hours that these time series for technology shocks predict. If $\bar{\gamma}_t^z$ gives the (de-meaned) historical series for technology shocks, the predicted series for (de-meaned) changes in output and hours are, respectively,

$$\Delta \bar{Y}_t = \sum_{i=0}^{\infty} \xi_i^Y \bar{\gamma}_{t-i}^z,$$

and

$$\Delta \bar{H}_t = \sum_{i=0}^{\infty} \xi_i^H \bar{\gamma}_{t-i}^z.$$ (52)

We can then compute the sample variance of the series $\{\Delta \bar{Y}_t\}$ and $\{\Delta \bar{H}_t\}$.

The second and third parts, of Table 9.2 show the empirical variances of output and hours growth, ("1" and "1"," respectively), and give their theoretical variances ("2" and "2""), computed by using the sample variances of (52). We do not report the variances computed by using (51) because they are nearly identical.[22] For the standard case where μ is equal to one, the predicted variance of output is somewhat smaller than the actual variance, while the predicted variance of hours is quite a bit smaller than the actual variance. Increases in μ lower both predicted variances, though they have a more substantial effect on the variance of hours for the reasons that we gave above.

We also present in Table 9.2 a statistic that provides a further test of the empirical plausibility of the model's predictions regarding the effects of technology shocks. This statistic ("3" and "3'") relates to the orthogonality of the predicted movements in output and hours on the one hand, and the prediction errors on the other. We have mentioned above that a correct measure of technical progress should be independent of the other shocks that affect the economy. In the previous section, we showed that if some of the other shocks can be directly measured, this gives rise to an orthogonality condition that can be used to test the validity of the method of measuring technology shocks. But even when the other shocks cannot be directly measured, the independence principle can be used as the basis for a specification test of a model of the effects of technology shocks. Because if the technology shocks are correctly measured and the theoretical impulse response coefficients, ξ^Y and ξ^H, are correct, then the prediction errors, $\Delta Y - \Delta \bar{Y}$ and $\Delta H - \Delta \bar{H}$, should be expressible as distributed lags of the other exogenous shocks.[23] It follows that

$$\text{Cov}\{\Delta \bar{Y}_t, (\Delta Y_t - \Delta \bar{Y}_t)\} = 0, \tag{53}$$

and

$$\text{Cov}\{\Delta \bar{H}_t, (\Delta H_t - \Delta \bar{H}_t)\} = 0. \tag{54}$$

Testing the validity of these moment conditions provides a specification test that does not require knowledge of the other types of shocks. To provide a convenient measure of the extent to which the moment conditions, (53) and (54), are violated, we decompose the variance of actual changes in output as follows:

$$\text{Var}(\Delta Y_t) = \text{Var}(\Delta \bar{Y}_t) + \text{Var}(\Delta Y_t - \Delta \bar{Y}_t) + 2\text{Cov}\{\Delta \bar{Y}_t, (\Delta Y_t - \Delta \bar{Y}_t)\},$$

so that

$$1 = \frac{\text{Var}(\Delta \bar{Y}_t)}{\text{Var}(\Delta Y_t)} + \frac{\text{Var}(\Delta Y_t - \Delta \bar{Y}_t)}{\text{Var}(\Delta Y_t)} + \omega^Y,$$

where

$$\omega^Y = \frac{2\text{Cov}\{\Delta \bar{Y}_t, (\Delta Y_t - \Delta \bar{Y}_t)\}}{\text{Var}(\Delta Y_t)}.$$

Thus ω^Y measures the extent to which the sum of the variance of output that the model attributes to technology shocks and the variance it attributes to other sources fails to equal the total variance of output. The size of the departure of ω^Y from zero thus gives one some idea of how seriously one can take a statistic such as $\text{Var}(\Delta \bar{Y}_t)/\text{Var}(\Delta Y_t)$ as a measure of the degree to which observed variations in output growth can be explained by technology shocks.

The last column of Table 9.2 shows values of ω^Y and of the analogously defined ω^H for different values of μ. For the model to be correct, both ω's ought to be zero. Hence, these provide additional moment restrictions, which can be used to estimate μ. Such an estimate is then based entirely upon the way in which one parameter value as opposed to another improves the model's ability to produce empirically plausible predictions regarding the part of aggregate fluctuations that is attributable to aggregate technology shocks.

As we can see, raising μ from 1 to 1.4 lowers both ω's, which reach a minimum for μ between 1.4 and 1.6. Thus the results of this estimation procedure also yield relatively important departures from perfect competition. What is perhaps even more interesting is that the resulting estimate of μ implies that technology shocks lead to practically no fluctuations in hours worked. Thus, essentially, the entire movement in hours worked must be due to some other type of shock.

7. Fluctuations Due to Self-Fulfilling Expectations

The introduction of imperfect competition and increasing returns also makes possible an entirely new source of equilibrium fluctuations in economic activity. In particular, equilibria may exist in which economic activity fluctuates in response to random events that do not involve any change in underlying fundamentals ("sunspots"). These fluctuations are caused simply by changes in people's expectations of the future path of the economy. This need not be because individual agents' expectations are incorrect—instead, in such a "sunspot equilibrium," it is correct to expect a different future path for the economy, if everyone else's expectations and actions change in response to the event in question. Equilibria of this kind are now known to be possible in many kinds of intertemporal equilibrium models (see, e.g., Guesnerie and Woodford 1992). They are not, however, possible in the case of the standard neoclassical growth model. For there, the equilibrium allocation of resources must maximize the expected utility of the representative household, and there is a unique allocation with this property.

Once we introduce imperfect competition, as above, the First Welfare Theorem no longer holds, and as a result, one cannot show in such a simple way that equilibrium must be unique. Indeed, it need not be, as Benhabib and Farmer (1992) show in the case of a model with monopolistic competition, like that described here in Sections 2 and 3.[24] Recall that in Section 3 we observed that for our calibrated parameter values, the matrix $A^{-1}B$, where A and B are the matrices in (40), has one real eigenvalue with absolute value less than one, and another with absolute value greater than one; this allows us to compute a locally unique stationary solution to (40). This need not be true, however, for all parameter values, and Benhabib and Farmer show that if μ and η are sufficiently large, $A^{-1}B$ instead has two eigenvalues with modulus less than one (which for some parameter values are a complex pair). In this case, there exists a large multiplicity of stationary rational expectations equilibria, including equilibria in which output fluctuates in response to "sunspot" events.

Consider, for simplicity, the case in which there are no stochastic variations in any of the exogenous "fundamentals," $\{\gamma_t^z, \hat{G}_t, \hat{I}_t\}$. Then (40) becomes simply

$$
A \begin{pmatrix} E_t \hat{\lambda}_{t+1} \\ \hat{K}_{t+1} \end{pmatrix} = B \begin{pmatrix} \hat{\lambda}_t \\ \hat{K}_t \end{pmatrix}.
$$

A stationary solution is given by the bivariate stochastic process:

$$
\begin{pmatrix} \hat{\lambda}_{t+1} \\ \hat{K}_{t+1} \end{pmatrix} = A^{-1} B \begin{pmatrix} \hat{\lambda}_t \\ \hat{K}_t \end{pmatrix} + \begin{pmatrix} u_{t+1} \\ 0 \end{pmatrix},
$$

where $\{u_t\}$ is a mean-zero white noise "sunspot" variable, and the realization of u_{t+1} becomes known only at date $t + 1$.[25] In fact, all stationary solutions must be of this form (for some "sunspot" variable $\{u_t\}$). Thus the multiplicity of equilibria does not mean that the theory lacks testable implications about the character of aggregate fluctuations. In the absence of exogenous shocks and to the extent that the log-linear approximation is accurate, all of the stationary equilibria are simply scalar multiples of a single equilibrium. Thus the model does not predict the amplitude of the fluctuations, but one is able to obtain definite numerical predictions about the *relative* variability of output, hours, investment, real wages, and so on, as well as definite predictions about the serial correlation and cross correlation of all these series.[26] Even when other shocks are added, the set of stationary equilibria is a set of finite dimension (linear combinations of a small number of possible types of fluctuations), which places relatively strong restrictions on the data.

Farmer and Guo (1993) show that in the case of a model of this kind that is "calibrated" in a relatively standard fashion, except for the large values assumed for μ and η, the predicted fluctuations in aggregate quantities, in the absence of any exogenous shocks, exhibit relative variabilities and comovements similar to those observed in detrended U.S. data. They argue that in this respect the model's predictions are not clearly less consistent with the facts than those of a standard RBC model, with perfect competition, constant returns, and exogenous technology shocks. The standard model, of course, also seeks to explain the amplitude of aggregate fluctuations, given that measured Solow residuals can be taken to indicate the size of the exogenous technology shocks, while the amplitude of fluctuations remains unexplained in the Farmer and Guo model. The Farmer-Guo model, however, can in principle explain the comovement of measured Solow residuals with other aggregate variables; for the model predicts variation in measured Solow residuals in response to "sunspot" events that cause variations in output, for the reasons discussed in Section 5.[27]

The degree of market power and increasing returns assumed by Farmer and Guo ($\mu = 1.72, \eta = 1.61$) is not completely outside the range of values suggested by the empirical evidence discussed in Sections 4 and 5. However, it should be noted that in their model, assuming somewhat lower values does not simply reduce the *magnitude* of the equilibrium response to the "sunspot" events; it eliminates it altogether.[28] This is because the stationary "sunspot" equilibria exist only if both eigenvalues are inside the unit circle. Since one of them must be outside the unit circle in the case of perfect competition (because of the First Welfare Theorem), and since the eigenvalues vary continuously as one varies the parameters μ and η toward one, there must be a point at which μ and η still exceed one but one eigenvalue has a modulus greater than one. The quantitative reasonableness of Farmer and Guo's assumptions about μ and η is therefore a critical issue, more so than in the case of other consequences of imperfect competition and increasing returns, such as Hall's interpretation of productivity variations. The reason is that, as shown by Hall, any departures from perfect competition will generate *some* procyclical productivity even if the departures are not big enough to explain all the variations in productivity. On the other hand, Farmer and Guo require that the departures be significant. Indeed, in the case of Farmer and Guo's calibration, μ and η cannot be made much smaller than the values that they assume. Further research on the magnitude of these parameters thus seems crucial to establish the empirical validity of their model.

8. Models with Exogenously Varying Markups

Up to this point we have considered a model in which, as in the perfectly competitive model, the markup is constant. One benefit of considering models with imperfect competition is that this class of models also contains models where markups vary over time. This leads to specifications that are considerably richer than those with constant markups. In particular, markup variations may play an important role in generating fluctuations in equilibrium employment. To show this, we first consider the effect of exogenous changes in markups. In the next section, we take up models of endogenous markup variation.

Suppose that there are exogenous variations in each firm's elasticity of demand, $D'(1)$, resulting from variations in the degree of substitutability of the various differentiated goods. Giving this elasticity a subscript t, equation (8) becomes

$$\gamma_t^i = [1 + 1/D_t'(1)]^{-1}. \tag{55}$$

Equation (9) then implies that the value-added markup varies as well. This variation in the markup implies a variation in the ratio of the marginal product of labor to the wage. In particular, (16) becomes

$$z_t F_2(K_t, z_t H_t) = \mu_t w_t. \tag{56}$$

Thus varying markups imply labor demand shifts, that is, changes in the amount of labor that firms will hire at a given real wage. In this respect, changes in markups are similar to changes in the productivity parameter z_t. In terms of the detrended variables (56) becomes

$$F_2 \left(\frac{\tilde{K}_t}{\gamma_t^z}, \tilde{H}_t \right) = \mu_t \tilde{w}_t. \tag{57}$$

The variability of markups also changes equation (29), which becomes

$$1 = \beta \left(\gamma_t^z \right)^{-\sigma} E_t \left\{ \left(\frac{\tilde{\lambda}_{t+1}}{\tilde{\lambda}_t} \right) \left[\frac{F_K(\tilde{K}_{t+1}/\gamma_{t+1}^z, \tilde{H}_{t+1})}{\mu_t} + (1 - \delta) \right] \right\}. \tag{58}$$

These are the only equilibrium conditions affected by the variability of the markup. Their linearization yields

$$\frac{s_K}{\epsilon_{KH}} (\hat{K}_t - \gamma_t^z - \hat{H}_t) = \hat{w}_t + \hat{\mu}_t, \tag{59}$$

and

$$-\sigma \hat{\gamma}_t^z + E_t \left\{ \hat{\lambda}_{t+1} - \hat{\lambda}_t + \left(\frac{r + \delta}{1 + r} \right) \frac{s_H}{\epsilon_{KH}} (\hat{H}_{t+1} - \hat{K}_{t+1} + \hat{\gamma}_{t+1}^z) \right.$$

$$\left. - \left(\frac{r + \delta}{1 + r} \right) \hat{\mu}_t \right\} = 0, \tag{60}$$

where $\hat{\mu}_t$ is the logarithmic deviation of the markup from its steady state value (which we shall denote by μ). To solve the current model, we substitute (35), (59) and (37) into (38) and (60) to obtain two difference equations, which now also involve the stationary random variable $\hat{\mu}_t$.

To compute how the system responds to markup shocks, we postulate a stochastic process for $\hat{\mu}_t$. In particular, we assume that

$$\hat{\mu}_t = \rho^\mu \hat{\mu}_{t-1} + v_t^\mu. \tag{61}$$

We use the same parameter values as in previous simulations.[29] For the markup, we assume, as before, that the mean of μ is 1.4. We experiment with a variety of values of ρ^μ. Figure 9.4 shows the response of output, hours, consumption, and investment to a unit shock to v^μ when ρ^μ equals 0.9, while Figure 9.5 shows the same responses when ρ^μ equals zero. Figure 9.6 shows the response of real wages for both values of ρ^μ. The instantaneous responses of all three variables do not depend to any significant extent on ρ^μ. Not surprisingly, the higher value of ρ^μ makes the responses of output, hours and wages more persistent.

Figure 9.6 shows that real wages decline when markups rise. This is to be expected since increases in markups lower labor demand. What is important about this is that it shows that real wages move procyclically in response to markup shocks.

One notable feature of the results shown in Figures 9.4 and 9.5 is that in the immediate aftermath of the shock, consumption moves less than output does, while

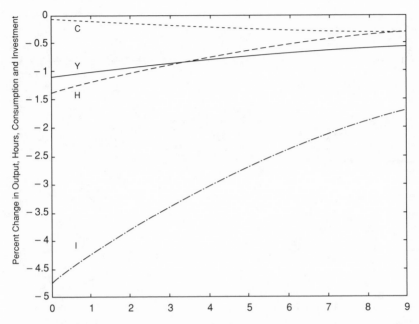

Figure 9.4 Response of Output, Hours, Consumption, and Investment to a 1 Percent Markup Shock, $\rho^\mu = 0.9$

investment moves more. Thus, our model with markup shocks makes consumption less variable than output, whereas investment is more variable. This higher relative variability of investment is a robust feature of business cycles, which the model reproduces. The success of the model along this dimension is due to the relative unwillingness of consumers with concave utility functions to substitute their consumption intertemporally, coupled with the small sensitivity of the marginal product of capital to short-run changes in investment. These also account for the relative variability of consumption and investment in standard real business cycle models.

We also observe that the short-run impact on hours of a markup shock exceeds that on output. When ρ^μ equals zero, a unit increase in ν^μ lowers hours by 1.38, while output falls only by 1.13. This rather large change in hours must be contrasted with the negligible effect of a unit technology shock. The reason that hours fall so dramatically when μ rises, even though they hardly change when z rises, is that in the latter case, wealth and substitution effects work in opposite directions. In particular, an increase in z raises wealth, which discourages work. By contrast, increases in μ have only very small effects on wealth. The reason is that, to first order, the increase in firm's profits is exactly offset by the losses to consumers.

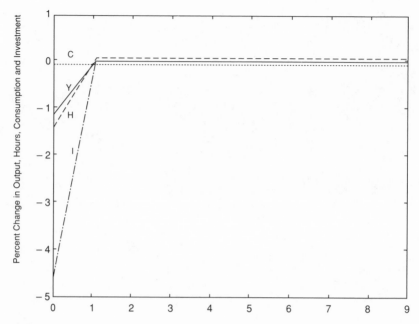

Figure 9.5 Response of Output, Hours, Consumption, and Investment to a Markup Shock, $\rho^{\mu} = 0$

Thus, the main effect of increases in μ is to lead households to substitute leisure for consumption. The small importance of wealth effects probably accounts also for the similarity of the responses to temporary and more persistent changes in μ.

The difference between the response of output and that of hours is due to the value of μs_H. For our choice of parameters, $\mu s_H < 1$. As a result, (35) implies that, when z is held constant, the change in output is smaller than the change in hours. This conclusion would be reversed if μs_H were greater than one.

We have also computed the variance of the log changes in hours and in output for a variety of values of μ and ρ^{μ}. In Table 9.3 we display these variances as ratios of the variance of the log changes in μ. We normalize by the variance of the changes in μ so that the variances will not grow spuriously as we raise ρ^{μ}. We see that for large values of μ, which imply that μs_H is greater than one, the variance of output actually exceeds the variance of hours. However, for smaller values of μ the variance of hours changes exceeds the variance of output changes. If parameter values of this type are entertained, markup shocks cannot possibly be the only shocks impinging on the economy. The reason is that, as we saw earlier, the variance of hours is in fact smaller than the variance of output. However, a

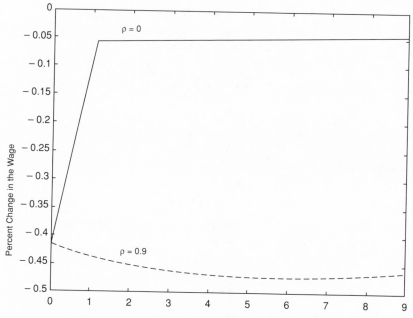

Figure 9.6 Response of Real Wage to Markup Shocks

larger predicted variance of H can be reconciled with the model as long as markup shocks coexist with technology shocks. Since the latter affect mainly the variance of output, a combination of the two types of shocks can potentially explain both why hours fluctuations are significant and why output variability is larger than the variability of hours.

This discussion raises the question of whether average markups actually vary, and thus of how much of the observed variation in hours can be attributed to them. Important markup variations, with markups being much lower in booms than in recessions, were found by Bils (1987) and Rotemberg and Woodford (1991). Using a somewhat different specification of technology, Rotemberg and Woodford (1991) found that the assumption of an average markup of 1.6 implies that the variance of quarterly changes in markups equals 1.33 percent. This number is not directly comparable to the variance in markups in our theoretical model because of differences in specification and because the actual stochastic process for markups is not (61). Nonetheless, it is worth noting that the values shown in Table 9.3 suggest that such a large variability in markups implies that output and hours should vary even more than they actually do.

Table 9.3
Variance of the Log Difference of Output, Hours, and Wage

Variance of Output Changes Divided by Variance of Markup Changes				
μ	$\rho^\mu = 0$	$\rho^\mu = 0.3$	$\rho^\mu = 0.6$	$\rho^\mu = 0.9$
1.2000	0.9269	0.9363	0.9580	1.0577
1.4000	1.2285	0.2295	1.2317	1.2430
1.6000	1.5626	1.5494	1.5210	1.4145
1.8000	1.9262	1.8926	1.8216	1.5726
2.0000	2.3166	2.2559	2.1303	1.7180

Variance of Hours Changes Divided by Variance of Markup Changes				
μ	$\rho^\mu = 0$	$\rho^\mu = 0.3$	$\rho^\mu = 0.6$	$\rho^\mu = 0.9$
1.2000	2.0055	2.0244	2.0672	2.2589
1.4000	1.9681	1.9676	1.9664	1.9597
1.6000	1.9316	1.9128	1.8720	1.7159
1.8000	1.8960	1.8601	1.7840	1.5151
2.0000	1.8613	1.8094	1.7020	1.3480

Variance of Wage Normalized by Variance of Markup				
μ	$\rho^\mu = 0$	$\rho^\mu = 0.3$	$\rho^\mu = 0.6$	$\rho^\mu = 0.9$
1.2000	0.1498	0.1484	0.1455	0.1367
1.4000	0.1521	0.1533	0.1562	0.1704
1.6000	0.1564	0.1584	0.1668	0.2030
1.8000	0.1571	0.1634	0.1775	0.2340
2.0000	0.1596	0.1685	0.1881	0.2634

9. Models of Endogenous Markups

In the last section, we showed that markup variations of a plausible magnitude can explain the fluctuation in hours worked. The problem with the analysis of that section is that exogenous changes in markups do not appear to be particularly plausible. Models of imperfect competition would be more attractive if markup changes could themselves be explained by changes in other variables. Of particular interest in this regard are changes in aggregate demand, that is, changes in desired purchases away from the future and toward the present.[30] Changes in aggregate demand include many of the variables traditionally held responsible for business fluctuations, including changes in current government purchases, changes in the expected future profitability of current investment (as opposed to changes in the productivity of the existing capital stock), and changes in "consumer sentiment."

In this section we briefly describe three models of endogenous markup determination and their ability to fit business cycle facts. These models can be separated into two types. The first has markups depend only on the size of aggregate demand at different points in time but makes the markup independent of the composition of demand. In this category are the models of markup determination discussed by Rotemberg and Woodford (1991). The second type of model makes markups depend on the composition of demand but not on the level of aggregate demand itself. In the latter category are the models of Bils (1989) and Gali (1991).

We first consider two models of the first type. The first is a customer market model based on Phelps and Winter (1970), which is similar to that of Phelps (1992), the second is an implicit collusion model based on Rotemberg and Woodford (1992). Then we consider a model with demand-composition effects, that is, a model of the second type.

The Customer Market Model

The customer market model we consider is based on Phelps and Winter (1970). As before, firms maximize profits with respect to their own markups, taking the markup charged by all other firms as given. This model differs from the earlier one in that demand has a dynamic pattern. A firm that lowers its current price not only sells more to its existing customers, but also expands its customer base. Having a larger customer base raises future sales for any given future price. It would be attractive to obtain such a specification of demand from underlying aggregator functions for consumers, such as (1), which would depend on previous purchases. Unfortunately, we are unable to do so and capture the basic idea by simply writing the quantity demanded from firm i at time t, q_t^i, as

$$q_t^i = \frac{Q_t}{I_t} \psi\left(\frac{\mu_t^i}{\mu_t}\right) m_t^i, \qquad \psi' < 0, \quad \psi(1) = 1. \tag{62}$$

The variable m_t^i is the fraction of average demand, Q_t/I_t, that goes to firm i if it charges the same price as all other firms. The ratio of markups in (62) represents the relative price of firm i's good, since marginal cost is independent of the scale of operation and the same for all firms (as in Section 2). Thus (62) is a straightforward generalization of (2). The market share, m^i, depends on past pricing behavior according to the rule

$$m_{t+1}^i = g\left(\frac{\mu_t^i}{\mu_t}\right) m_t^i \qquad g' < 0, \quad g(1) = 1, \tag{63}$$

so that a temporary reduction in relative price raises firm i's market share permanently. Equations (62) and (63) are intended to capture the idea that customers have switching costs, in a manner analogous to the models of Gottfries (1986), Klemperer (1987), Farrell and Shapiro (1988), and Beggs and Klemperer (1992). A reduction in price attracts new customers, who are then reluctant to change firms for fear of having to pay these switching costs. One obvious implication of (62) and (63) is that the long-run elasticity of demand, that is, the response of eventual demand to a permanent increase in price, is larger than the short-run elasticity of demand. In our case, a firm that charges a higher price than those of its competitors eventually loses all its customers, though this is not essential for our analysis.

Ignoring fixed costs, firm i's profits at t are given by

$$\frac{\gamma_t^i - 1}{\gamma_t} \frac{Q_t}{I_t} \psi\left(\frac{\mu_t^i}{\mu_t}\right) m_t^i.$$

Using (9) and an analogous condition for individual markups, as well as the fact that Y equals $(1 - s_M)Q$, these profits also equal

$$\frac{\mu_t^i - 1}{\mu_t} \frac{Y_t}{I_t} \psi\left(\frac{\mu_t^i}{\mu_t}\right) m_t^i. \tag{64}$$

Thus, the firm's expected present discounted value of profits from period t onward is

$$E_t \sum_{j=0}^{\infty} \alpha^j \beta^j \frac{\lambda_{t+j}}{\lambda_t} \left(\frac{\mu_{t+j}^i - 1}{\mu_{t+j}}\right) \frac{Y_{t+j}}{I_{t+j}} \psi\left(\frac{\mu_{t+j}^i}{\mu_{t+j}}\right) m_t^i \prod_{z=0}^{j-1} g\left(\frac{\mu_{t+z}^i}{\mu_{t+z}}\right), \tag{65}$$

where our earlier analysis implies that $\beta^j \frac{\lambda_{t+j}}{\lambda_t}$ is the pricing kernel for valuing contingent securities that pay off in period $t + j$. The quantity $1 - \alpha$ represents the probability that a firm will, for random reasons, be assigned a market share in the next period that is independent of its past pricing behavior. For example the firm might cease to exist with this probability. Firm i chooses μ_t^i to maximize (65), taking as given the stochastic processes $\{\mu_t\}$, $\{\lambda_t\}$ and $\{Y_t/I_t\}$. Therefore,

$$\psi\left(\frac{\mu_t^i}{\mu_t}\right) \frac{Y_t}{I_t} + \psi'\left(\frac{\mu_t^i}{\mu_t}\right)\left[\frac{\mu_t^i - 1}{\mu_t}\right] \frac{Y_t}{I_t} + g'\left(\frac{\mu_t^i}{\mu_t}\right) \tag{66}$$

$$\times E_t \sum_{j=1}^{\infty} \alpha^j \beta^j \frac{\lambda_{t+j}}{\lambda_t} \left[\frac{\mu_{t+j}^i - 1}{\mu_{t+j}}\right] \psi\left(\frac{\mu_{t+j}^i}{\mu_{t+j}}\right) \frac{Y_{t+j}}{I_{t+j}} \prod_{z=1}^{j-1} g\left(\frac{\mu_{t+z}^i}{\mu_{t+z}}\right) = 0.$$

At a symmetric equilibrium, where all firms charge the same price, each has an equal share, m^i, equal to one, and g equals one in all periods. Thus the expectation term in (66) is equal to X_t/I_t where

$$X_t = I_t E_t \sum_{j=1}^{\infty} \alpha^j \beta^j \frac{\lambda_{t+j}}{\lambda_t} \left(\frac{\mu_{t+j} - 1}{\mu_{t+j}}\right) \frac{Y_{t+j}}{I_{t+j}}. \tag{67}$$

Note that X_t can be interpreted as the aggregate profits expected in the future by all the existing firms. By using (67), equation (66) can be transformed so that

μ_t is expressed as

$$\mu_t = \mu(X_t/Y_t) \equiv \frac{\psi'}{1 + \psi' + g'(1)X_t/Y_t}. \tag{68}$$

Because ψ' and $g'(1)$ are both negative, the derivative of μ with respect to X/Y is negative. An increase in X_t means that profits from future customers are high, so each firm lowers its price in order to increase its market share. An increase in Y_t means that profits stem mostly from current sales, so increasing market share is relatively unimportant. The result is that firms raise their prices.

Equation (68) replaces the exogenous stochastic process (61) that we employed in Section 8. The other equations of Section 8, however, continue to hold.

The Implicit Collusion Model

The model in this section is a simplified presentation of Rotemberg and Woodford (1992), which is itself based on Rotemberg and Saloner (1986). In this model, two levels of aggregation are needed to go from individual products to aggregate output. First, there is an aggregator function, such as (1), that gives total output as a function of the output of a measure of industries. The output of each industry is itself given by a homogeneous of degree one aggregator function, which depends on the output of n constituent firms. The goods produced by each of the n firms that constitute a particular industry are very good substitutes for one another, and to prevent what would seem the inevitable fall in price until price is close to marginal cost, the firms in each industry collude implicitly. Collusion is implicit in the sense that there is no enforceable cartel contract, but only an implicit agreement that firms that deviate from the collusive understanding will be punished.

The firms in each industry, even when acting in concert, take other industries' prices, the level of aggregate demand, and the level of marginal cost as given. We will consider symmetric equilibria and the profitability of deviation from this equilibrium by either a single firm or by an industry as a whole. We thus consider the demand for the product of firm i in industry j at t, when its price corresponds to an inefficiency wedge of μ_t^{ij}, all other firms in its industry charge a price that corresponds to μ_t^{j}, and all firms in other industries charge a price that corresponds to μ_t. Given the homogeneity of demand, we can write the demand faced by firm i in industry j as

$$q_t^{ij} = D^i\left(\frac{\mu_t^{ij}}{\mu_t}, \frac{\mu_t^{j}}{\mu_t}\right)\frac{Q_t}{I_t} \qquad D^i(1, 1) = 1/n. \tag{69}$$

Using the same substitution that led to (64), profits for this firm equal

$$\pi_t^{ij} = \frac{\mu_t^{ij} - 1}{\mu_t} D^i\left(\frac{\mu_t^{ij}}{\mu_t}, \frac{\mu_t^{j}}{\mu_t}\right)\frac{Y_t}{I_t}. \tag{70}$$

If each firm existed for only one period, it would maximize (70) with respect to its own markup, treating the markups of all other firms as given. The resulting Bertrand equilibrium would have relatively low prices and low profits. If the firms in an industry charge more than the Bertrand price, individual firms would benefit from undercutting the industry's price. Higher prices, with their attendant higher profits, can be sustained as a subgame-perfect equilibrium only if deviators are punished after a deviation. If firms interact repeatedly and have an infinite horizon, there are many equilibria of this type and these differ in the price that is charged in equilibrium.

We assume that firms succeed in implementing the symmetric equilibrium that is jointly best for them. That is, their implicit agreement maximizes the present discounted value of expected equilibrium profits for each firm in industry j, taking as given the stochastic processes for $\{\mu_t\}$, $\{\lambda_t\}$, and $\{Y_t/I_t\}$. As shown by Abreu (1986), this requires that the punishment for any deviation be as severe as possible. Because of the possibility of exit, the voluntary participation of the firm that is being punished precludes its earning an expected present value lower than zero after a deviation. This leads us to assume that a deviator earns a present discounted value of zero after its deviation. Sufficient conditions for this punishment to be feasible and subgame perfect are given in Rotemberg and Woodford (1992).

Because the punishment is independent of the size of the deviation, a deviating firm sets its price at t to maximize (70). Let X_t^j denote, by analogy to (66), the expected present discounted value of the profits that each firm in industry j can expect to earn in subsequent periods if there are no deviations. Then, if the expected present value of profits after a deviation equals zero, firms in industry j will not deviate as long as

$$\max_{\mu_t^{ij}} \pi_t^{ij} \leq \pi_t^j + X_t^j, \tag{71}$$

where π_t^j is the value of π_t^{ij} when firm i charges the same price as the other firms in its industry. We consider the case where the incentive compatibility constraint, (71), is always binding. Thus, firms are indifferent between the additional profits from deviating in the present and the future loss of X. Since X is what firms who deviate give up, α can be given a different interpretation. The quantity $(1 - \alpha)$ remains the probability that sales will be independent of the history of prices. This can now mean that $(1 - \alpha)$ is the probability that the collusive arrangement will be renegotiated and a firm that has deviated in the past and has exited to avoid punishment will be able to reenter.[31]

At a symmetric equilibrium, all industries have the same markup, so each firm sells Q_t/nI_t, and X_t^j equals X_t/nI_t. Assuming that (71) holds with equality, (70) implies that

$$\max_{\rho}\left[\rho - \frac{1}{\mu_t}\right] D(\rho, 1) \frac{Y_t}{I_t} = \left[1 - \frac{1}{\mu_t}\right] \frac{Y_t}{nI_t} + \frac{X_t}{nI_t}, \tag{72}$$

where ρ represents the relative price chosen by the deviating firm. Equation (72) can be solved for μ_t, yielding once again

$$\mu_t = \mu(X_t/Y_t). \tag{73}$$

In this case, however, the derivative of μ with respect to X/Y is positive. The reason is that an increase in X/Y raises the size of the punishment (the forgone profits represented by X_t) relative to the size of current sales (as represented by Y_t). It thus allows the firms in each oligopolistic industry to charge higher markups without fearing deviations. The theoretical model also implies an upper bound on the elasticity of the markup with respect to X/Y. We show in Rotemberg and Woodford (1992) that this upper bound is equal to $\mu - 1$.

The two models we have presented both make the markup depend on X_t/Y_t. Because the sign of the effect of X/Y differs, they are empirically distinguishable; this is pursued in Rotemberg and Woodford (1991). Here, we are interested in seeing what this dependence of the markup on X/Y implies about the effect of aggregate demand.

The Response of the Model to Exogenous Changes in Government Purchases

To compute the responses of the model to exogenous changes in aggregate demand we have to linearize (67) and (73) around their steady states. For this purpose, we assume that $\tilde{X}_t$ is given by $\frac{X_t}{z_t N_t}$, while $\tilde{X}$ and $\tilde{\mu}$ give the steady-state level of expected profitability and of the markup, respectively. We then let $\hat{X}_t$ and $\hat{\mu}_t$ represent the logarithmic deviations of $\tilde{X}_t$ and μ_t from their respective steady-state values. In terms of these values, and assuming a constant number of firms, I_t, equations (67) and (73) become approximately

$$\hat{X}_t = E_t\left\{\hat{\lambda}_{t+1} - \hat{\lambda}_t + \left(\frac{1 - \alpha\gamma_z\gamma_n}{1+r}\right)\left(\frac{1}{\mu - 1}\hat{\mu}_{t+1} + \hat{Y}_{t+1}\right) + \left(\frac{\alpha\gamma_z\gamma_n}{1+r}\right)\hat{X}_{t+1}\right\}, \tag{74}$$

and

$$\hat{\mu}_t = \epsilon_\mu(\hat{X}_t - \hat{Y}_t), \tag{75}$$

respectively.

The linearized model now consists of (35), (59), (37), (38), (60), (74), and (75). Since we are interested in the effect of temporary changes in government spending, we shall assume that the number of firms stays constant so that $\hat{I}_t$ is zero in these equations. We can solve (59) and (37) for $\hat{H}_t$ and $\hat{w}_t$ as functions of $\hat{\lambda}_t$, $\hat{K}_t$, and $\hat{\mu}_t$. Substitution into (35) gives $\hat{Y}_t$, and substitution into (75) then allows us to solve for $\hat{X}_t$, both again as functions of the same three state variables. We can then eliminate these four state variables from the remaining three equilibrium conditions, obtaining a system of difference equations of the form (40) except that it has three endogenous variables, $\{\lambda, K, \mu\}$, instead of only $\{\lambda, K\}$.

Assuming once again that the stochastic process for government purchases takes the form given in (41), with ρ^G equal to 0.9, we can compute the economy's response to the shock, v_t^G. These responses are computed by using the parameters shown in Table 9.1, with the average inefficiency wedge, μ, set equal to 1.4. We have set α equal to 0.9 because this is consistent with (71), holding as an equality with about ten firms. Finally, we have looked at two values of ϵ_μ. In the first case, it has the sign suggested by the customer market model and equals -1. In the second, it has the sign implied by the implicit collusion model and equals 0.39. We chose 0.39 because it is just below the upper bound of 0.4, which applies for our average markup.

The response of output and hours is displayed in Figure 9.7, while Figure 9.8 displays the response of real wages. We see in Figure 9.7 that the response of output and hours is most pronounced in the case where ϵ_μ equals $\phi.39$ and least pronounced in the case where it equals -1. The constant markup case of Figure 9.1 yields an intermediate answer. The reason is easy to understand. An increase in military purchases requires that individuals postpone their consumption, so interest rates rise. This lowers X. Since the increase in military purchases also raises

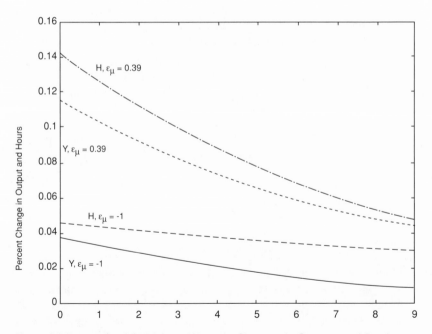

Figure 9.7 Response of Output and Hours to Changes in Government Purchases: The Case of Endogenously Varying Markups

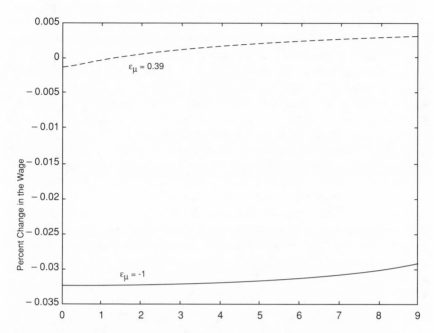

Figure 9.8 Response of Real Wage to Changes in Government Purchases: The Case of Endogenously Varying Markups

Y, X/Y unambiguously falls. Thus in the customer market model, markups rise, which by (56) lowers the demand for labor at any given real wage. The result is that output and the labor input do not rise as much as in the case where the markup is constant. By contrast, in the implicit collusion model, the fall in X/Y lowers markups, which raises the demand for labor. This accentuates the increase in output.

The difference between the models' implications for the demand for labor is even more apparent in Figure 9.8, where we plot the responses of the real wage, w_t, to changes in v_t^G. We see that the customer market model accentuates the reduction in real wages that we displayed in Figure 9.2 for the constant markup case. The reason is that, as we saw, the reduction in X/Y lowers the demand for labor at any given real wage. By contrast, in the implicit collusion model with ϵ_μ equal to 0.39, the real wage actually rises, albeit only slightly. This occurs because the fall in X/Y is so pronounced that the increased demand for labor from the fall in the markup actually exceeds the increase in labor supply. In Rotemberg and Woodford (1992), we obtained much more pronounced rises in real wages by assuming a smaller elasticity of labor supply, ϵ_{Hw}.

The conclusion from this exercise is that the implicit collusion model can generate procyclical movements in real wages in response to changes in government purchases of goods. Because the key ingredient in generating these responses is the increase in interest rates that leads to a fall in X/Y, similar responses would be observed to other shocks that increase aggregate demand, such as increases in firms' desire to invest because of changing perceptions of future profitability.

In Rotemberg and Woodford (1992), we considered the actual response of real wages to changes in military purchases. We showed that, indeed, real wages have tended to rise in the United States following increases in military purchases. That paper also considers alternative explanations for the finding, such as the fact that the government raises the size of its military personnel at the same time that it increases its national defense purchases of produced goods. It shows that even after this is taken into account, reductions in markups of the sort implied by the implicit collusion model are needed to explain the reaction of real wages. In Rotemberg and Woodford (1993), we demonstrated that increases in oil prices tend to raise markups in this type of model. We showed that this is consistent both with the large size of output reductions that follow actual oil price increases and with the failure of the value added deflated real wage to rise on these occasions.

A Model with Demand-Composition Effects

In this subsection, we describe an example of a model (that of Gali [1992]) in which markups are affected by the composition of aggregate demand. In Gali's model, both households and firms purchase the entire range of differentiated goods, but (in contrast to our assumption in Section 2) their aggregator functions, f_t, are different. In particular, the elasticity of substitution between different goods, again evaluated at the case of uniform prices for all goods, is different for the two types of purchasers. In all other respects, the model is one of static monopolistic competition, like that described in Sections 2 and 3.

Profit maximization by price-setting firms now implies a markup that depends on the share, θ_t, of aggregate demand that consists of demand by firms so that

$$\gamma_t = \gamma(\theta_t) \equiv \left\{ 1 + \left[\theta_t D'_f(1) + (1 - \theta_t) D'_h(1) \right]^{-1} \right\}^{-1},$$

where D'_f and D'_h indicate the elasticities of demand of firms and households, respectively. This reduces to (8) in the case where $D_f = D_h = D$. In the case argued by Gali to be of greatest interest, that in which $D'_f(1) < D'h(1) < -1$, one finds that γ is a monotonically decreasing function of θ_t. Because the inefficiency wedge, μ_t, remains the same function of γ_t as before, as given by (9), μ_t is also a monotonically decreasing function of θ. Finally, identifying

$$\theta_t = \frac{I_t + M_t}{Q_t} = s_M + (1 - s_M)s_{It},$$

where s_{It} is the share of investment spending in value added, we obtain

$$\mu_t = \mu(s_{It}) \tag{76}$$

where $\mu(s_I)$ is a monotonically decreasing function. Gali's model is then essentially the model of Section 8 with (76) added in place of the exogenous markup process.

In this model, shocks that affect the composition of aggregate demand affect equilibrium markups. This introduces a channel through which some kinds of increases in aggregate demand may have additional expansionary effects (for example, an increase in investment due to a change in tax incentives). But, it is not a model where increases in aggregate demand *as such* have an expansionary effect through a change in desired markups. It depends entirely on the category of demand increase. For example, if the government uses the same aggregator as households (an issue not discussed in Gali), an increase in government purchases will *increase* markups. This would imply that government purchases are even less expansionary than in the constant markup model.

The predictions of such a model depend critically upon the elasticities of demand of different purchasers. Gali provides no direct evidence on this although he does show that the average markup (measured by means of a method similar to that of Rotemberg and Woodford [1991]) shows a strong negative association with the investment share, even when one controls for the levels of aggregate output and hours. (Thus the association is not simply a reflection of the fact that the average markup is countercyclical).

Another consequence of Gali's model is that for some choices of the parameters, aggregate fluctuations can occur in equilibrium in the absence of exogenous shocks. He shows that low expected future markups increase current investment demand. The reason is that the low expected markups raise the expected demand for labor and thereby increase the expected marginal product of capital for any given capital stock. In addition, the reduction in expected markups lowers the wedge between the marginal product of capital and its user cost. This means that low expected future markups raise current investment, which in turn reduces current markups. For some parameter values, this effect is so strong as to make the expectation of low markups self-fulfilling. Gali demonstrates this possibility, and analyzes the character of the fluctuations that can result from self-fulfilling expectations, using techniques similar to those discussed in Section 7.

10. Conclusions

In this chapter, we have shown that imperfect competition matters; it affects the way in which the economy responds to a great variety of shocks. It is thus not possible to ignore departures from perfect competition if one wants quantitatively accurate assessments of the importance of various disturbances. The reason imperfect competition matters so much is that it affects the relationship among the marginal product of labor and the real wage. It thus affects the relationship between output, the labor input, and the wage. Because so many of the puzzles in macroeconomics, including Okun's law and the Dunlop-Tarshis observation, relate to these three variables, imperfect competition is central to the concerns of business cycle analysis.

We have also shown that incorporation of imperfectly competitive product markets into standard dynamic models of aggregate fluctuations is relatively simple. The models that we have presented can still be analyzed numerically by means of standard techniques. At most, a small increase in the state space is required. We have also shown that imperfect competition need introduce only a small number of additional parameters to be calibrated and that both empirical evidence and theoretical considerations can be used to bound the plausible range of variation in the new parameters. The degree to which this direction of generalization of standard models can improve the ability of such models to explain observed aggregate fluctuations is the subject of continuing research.

Notes

We wish to thank David Backus, Roland Benabou and participants at the Frontiers of Business Cycle Research for comments, Stephanie Schmitt-Grohë and Martin Uribe for research assistance and the NSF for research support.

1. Increasing returns are compatible with competitive firms if the increasing returns are external, rather than internal to the firm, as in the model of Baxter and King (1991). We believe, however, that there is much more reason to believe that internal increasing returns are important.

2. It is also worth pointing out that the assumption that producers have market power in their product markets is an essential element in models of nominal price rigidity. Such price rigidity enhances the role of monetary policy shocks as a source of aggregate fluctuations. For examples of completely specified dynamic models, see Hairault and Portier (1992) and Yun (1993).

3. This equilibrium concept is an obvious one, given that we eventually wish to assume the existence of a continuum of goods in each period, identified with an interval $[0, I_t]$ on the real line. In the continuum limit, the price charged for an individual good obviously has no effect upon any agent's intertemporal allocation of total expenditure, and thus has no effect upon the equilibrium processes, $\{p_t, Q_t\}$. Even in the case of a finite number of goods, we can *define* equilibrium in this way, just as one can define Walrasian equilibrium for an economy with a finite number of traders. However, the equilibrium concept becomes compelling only as a formal representation of the outcome of competition in the limit of an infinite number of traders. For rigorous development of this equilibrium concept for the finite case, see Benassy (1991, sec. 6.4 and references cited therein). It has become common in the literature in macroeconomics and international trade to assume a continuum of differentiated goods, especially when, as here, one wishes to treat the number of goods as an endogenous variable.

4. In the Dixit-Stiglitz model, $f_t(B_t)$ is equal to $I_t^{-\frac{\sigma}{1-\sigma}} \left[\sum_{i=1}^{I_t} (b_t^i)^{1-\sigma} \right]^{\frac{1}{1-\sigma}}$, where $0 < \sigma < 1$. They thus assume a globally constant elasticity of substitution equal to $1/\sigma$.

This means that $D_t(\rho)$ is equal to $\rho^{-\frac{1}{\sigma}}$, so $D_t'(1) = -1/\sigma$ for all t. We also observe that the condition of decreasing marginal revenue is satisfied for all ρ. However, a globally constant elasticity of substitution of this kind is nowhere essential to our conclusions, which depend only on the assumption that the elasticity of demand in the case of uniform prices is independent of scale.

5. For further development of this point, see Basu (1992).

6. One reason that we emphasize the measure η here is that most studies in the real business cycle literature simply assume a production function for value added, and so when these authors calibrate the degree of increasing returns, they are in fact specifying η rather than ρ.

7. Alternative specifications are possible. In particular, one can assume that the fixed costs take the form of some fixed amount of labor, or capital. The current specification assumes that both labor and capital can be used as fixed costs and that the proportions in which they are employed for this purpose depend on factor prices.

8. In this formulation, the output of each firm stays constant in the steady state; the entire growth in output is accounted for by growth in firms. An alternative formulation that preserves a constant steady-state markup and degree of increasing returns is to assume, as we did in Rotemberg and Woodford (1992), that

$$q_t^i = \min\left[\frac{F(K_t^i, z_t H_t^i) - \Phi_t}{1 - s_M}, \frac{M_t^i}{s_M} \right],$$

and that Φ_t has the same steady-state growth rate as z_t and hence the same growth rate as K_t and Q_t. In this case, an equilibrium with a constant steady-state markup has no growth in the number of firms. The entire growth in output is reflected in growth in each firm's output. One could probably also construct intermediate models with constant steady state markups where the number of firms as well as output per firm grow over time.

9. The variables Y_t, H_t, w_t, and λ_t must be measurable with respect to information available at time t, while K_t must be measurable with respect to information available at time $t - 1$. Information available at time t consists of the realizations at time t or earlier of the variables G_t, z_t, N_t, and I_t. In Section 7, we allow the information set to also contain "sunspot" variables.

10. Note that equilibrium conditions in terms of stationary variables can be obtained with this technique even if the model has multiple steady-state equilibria.

11. The method is the same as in King, Plosser, and Rebelo (1988a). This can be made rigorous, and justified as an application of a generalized implicit function theorem, as shown in Woodford (1986). It should be understood that when we refer to small fluctuations around the steady-state values, we have in mind stationary random variables with a sufficiently small bounded support.

12. For a more complete discussion along similar lines, with independent estimation of the degree of increasing returns, see Hall (1990).

13. In our analysis of military purchases we found these to follow a very persistent but stationary AR(2) process. For simplicity and comparability with previous literature we consider a persistent AR(1) here.

14. See, e.g., Dixon (1987); Mankiw (1988); Startz (1989); and Silvestre (1993).

15. One can also understand from (35) the basis of Startz's (1989) argument that this is just a short-run effect. A permanent increase in G would permanently increase profits,

requiring an eventual increase in the number of firms, I. In a comparison of steady-state equilibria (in which I is assumed to adjust so as to keep profits equal to zero), the percentage increase in output equals only s_H times the percentage increase in the labor input.

16. Alternative possible explanations of the anomaly that do not depend on imperfect competition are proposed by Baxter and King (1991) and Burnside, Eichenbaum, and Rebelo (1993).

17. For a complete dynamic equilibrium model of the effects of oil prices that is constructed along the lines of this chapter, see Rotemberg and Woodford (1993).

18. Explicit development of an explanation for this effect of monetary policy would require, of course, a model where monetary policy shocks affect economic activity, a topic we do not take up here. Imperfect competition in product markets does not in itself imply any real effect of monetary policy. On the other hand, as we mentioned in note 2, imperfect competition is often a crucial element of models in which monetary nonneutrality results from price rigidity.

19. We assume technology follows a random walk in part because the results we obtained for the case where z_t is stationary were unsatisfactory. We show below that there are two different methods of computing the variance of output implied by the model as a response to technology shocks. While the methods are different, they ought to give the same answer for the volatilities of output and hours. The two methods do so when we assume that z is a random walk, but we obtain very different theoretical variances for output and hours when we assume that z is stationary. For more on the sensitivity of theoretical variances of output as one varies the stochastic process for the technology shocks, see Eichenbaum (1991).

20. Note that with this notation, if a variable X is stationary, then $\Delta \hat{X}$ is the first difference of $\tilde{X}$.

21. This is not strictly correct, but because investment is such a small fraction of capital, it does not induce a large bias into our calculation.

22. As we said in note 19, this is not true when technology shocks are assumed to induce only transitory changes in technology. When we assumed that z_t followed an autoregressive process, we obtained much smaller theoretical variances for output changes when using the method of Kydland and Prescott (1982) than when we asked about the variability of output generated by the model in response to the entire time series of Solow residuals. This was true even when we made the autoregressive coefficient equal to .99.

23. Here we rely on the validity of the log-linear approximation introduced in Section 3.

24. The indeterminacy of rational expectations equilibrium, and the possibility of endogenous equilibrium fluctuations, were first discussed in the context of a model of this kind by Hammour (1988). For other examples of stationary "sunspot" equilibria in models with imperfectly competitive product markets and increasing returns, see Woodford (1991), Hammour (1991), and Gali (1992).

25. This solution to the log-linearized equilibrium conditions (40) approximates a solution to the exact equilibrium conditions, if the amplitude of "sunspot" fluctuations are sufficiently small. See Woodford (1986) for details.

26. Early illustrations of this were given in Woodford (1988, 1991).

27. The possibility that the observed comovement of measured Solow residuals with output could be consistent with a model in which all fluctuations are due to self-fulfilling expectations was first illustrated in Woodford (1991).

28. The notion that the possible amplitude of the sunspot equilibria is unaffected by the parameter values is to some extent an artifact of the log-linear approximation used here. In the case of the log-linear equilibrium conditions (40), if any "sunspot" solution exists, solutions exist with fluctuations of arbitrary amplitude. In the case of the exact equilibrium conditions instead, it is possible that the set of possible stationary "sunspot" equilibria includes only fluctuations over a certain range of amplitudes, the bounds of which collapse to zero as one approaches the critical parameter values at which local "sunspot" equilibria cease to be possible. However, the general point derived from analysis of the log-linear system, that stationary "sunspot" equilibria cease to be possible while some amount of market power and increasing returns still exist, remains valid.

29. Hence, as earlier, the matrix $A^{-1}B$ has exactly one eigenvalue with a modulus less than one, and so the equilibrium response to the markup variations is determinate, just as in the case of the responses to variations in government purchases and to technology shocks.

30. From a macroeconomic perspective another potentially important determinant of average markups, and hence of aggregate activity, is the level of inflation. Benabou (1992) shows both that many search models imply a connection between inflation and markups, and that markups in the retail sector constructed along the lines of Rotemberg and Woodford (1991) are in fact negatively correlated with the rate of inflation.

31. In Rotemberg and Woodford (1992) we give conditions under which a deterministic steady state exists in which (71) is always binding. We also show that, for small enough stochastic shocks, there continues to exist a perturbed equilibrium in which (71) always binds. This case is clearly most plausible if X_t^j is not too large a multiple of a single period's profits, which is to say, if α is considerably less than one.

Chapter 10
Asset Pricing Implications of Equilibrium Business Cycle Models

K. Geert Rouwenhorst

1. Introduction

Research problems on the boundary of finance and macroeconomics are rapidly emerging as central to the evolution of each field. In finance it is now well established that expected returns on securities do not depend on idiosyncratic risks, but rather on nondiversifiable components, as predicted by the standard Capital Asset Pricing Model (CAPM) of Sharpe (1964) and Lintner (1965). There is much less agreement on which aggregate factors are relevant to the determinants of expected returns or how these factors change over time. Rather, detailed analysis of asset pricing issues requires a general equilibrium model, as stressed by Cox, Ingersoll, and Ross (1985) and Breeden (1986). In macroeconomics, much recent research has been oriented toward development and simulation of small-scale dynamic equilibrium models, as in Kydland and Prescott (1982) and Long and Plosser (1983), but few papers have explored the asset pricing relationships of these general equilibrium macroeconomic models.[1]

A frequently debated issue in finance has been whether discount rates or expected returns are sufficiently constant to permit application of the CAPM of Sharpe (1964) and Lintner (1965) in research and decisionmaking. The early literature on stock price volatility, for instance, suggested that stock prices were too volatile relative to the present value of dividends, discounted at a constant rate (LeRoy and Porter 1981, Shiller 1981). Although most finance scholars will agree that discount rates vary over time, relatively little work has been done toward understanding the extent to which they vary, and the sources of this variation. Recently, a large number of authors have argued that there exists important variation in expected returns and return variances, and that this variation is linked to the stages of the business cycle. For instance, Schwert (1989) finds that equity returns are more volatile during recession periods. Fama and French (1988b, 1989) present evidence that the dividend-to-price ratio captures cyclical variation in returns and risk premiums on stocks.

The relationship between business cycles and asset prices poses a challenge for parsimonious equilibrium asset pricing models to explain. The starting point of this chapter is the standard neoclassical growth model, studied by Brock and Mirman (1972), modified to incorporate the endogenous choice of labor and leisure. This model has been relatively successful in replicating many features of business cycles, such as the comovement of output, consumption, and investment over time, as well as the relative variability of these aggregates (e.g., King, Plosser, and Rebelo 1988a, 1988b; Hansen 1985). By using arguments along the lines of Brock (1982) and Lucas (1978), these models of business cycles can easily be turned into asset pricing models. This illustrates the promise of developing the asset pricing implications of simple dynamic equilibrium models. Notably, the strategy can provide financial economists with a list of candidate state variables, or "factors," whose evolution determines the evolution of expected asset returns. Further, the strategy can provide macroeconomics with additional implications about cyclical variation in asset prices, which can be used to evaluate equilibrium macroeconomic models.

As is natural for an initial investigation, the model economy studied is very simple, with a single source of uncertainty (technology shocks). It abstracts completely from the influence of inflation, government spending and taxation, or incomplete markets, although it would be possible to study the implications of these modifications, by using the recent methodological advances of Baxter (1988) and Coleman (1988).[2] In a long-run strategy of developing knowledge about asset pricing, however, the model studied here is a necessary first step.

The organization of the chapter is as follows. In Section 2, some basic facts about average returns on common stocks and bonds are reviewed by using quarterly data from the post–World War II United States. This section also discusses some empirical regularities in the cyclical behavior of returns and return volatility that have emerged from recent studies of Schwert (1989), Fama and French (1988a, 1988b, 1989), Poterba and Summers (1988), and Campbell and Shiller (1987). In Section 3, the economic model is described and the general nature of asset pricing relations is developed. In Section 4, a variety of simulation experiments are conducted within a parametric version of this model. Explorations with these simulations reveal how asset pricing implications of the model are influenced by variations in the parameters of technology and preferences. Related research, including that of Mehra and Prescott (1985) on the equity premium puzzle, is reviewed in the light of these results. The chapter concludes with a brief summary of the main findings and suggestions for future research directions.

2. Stylized Facts about Returns

Before discussing the formal model, we present a set of "stylized facts" that have received much attention and debate in the finance literature. This set is by no means exhaustive, but can serve as a benchmark to evaluate the asset pricing implications of equilibrium business cycle models. Part A of Table 10.1 gives the sample moments of U.S. postwar time series on real returns on stocks and bonds. The returns are measured at quarterly frequency and expressed in percentage per quarter. Data are taken from Ibbotson and Associates (1993). The average real return on one-month Treasury bills has been 0.23 percent per annum, slightly lower than the real return on long government bonds, which have provided 0.38 per cent per annum. The return on long bonds has been much more volatile than Treasury bills, but investors have not been compensated for this extra variation during the postwar period. Stocks have grossed 2.23 percent in real terms, with a standard deviation of 7.74 per cent. Part B of the table lists the correlations between these variables and provides the correlation between the various returns and risk premiums.

Table 10.1
Sample Moments of U.S. Quarterly Time Series of Realized Real Returns

A. Mean Returns, 1948:I–1992:IV		
	Mean	*Rule*
Treasury bills	0.23	0.79
Long Government bonds	0.38	5.07
Corporate bonds	0.51	4.91
SP500	2.23	7.74
Government bond premium	0.14	4.76
Default premium	0.29	1.54
Equity premium	1.99	7.63

B. Correlations of Real Returns							
	(1)	(2)	(3)	(4)	(5)	(6)	(7)
(1) Treasury bills		.44	.44	.17	.30	−.04	.06
(2) Long Government bonds			.95	.34	.99	−.25	.29
(3) Corporate bonds				.39	.94	.06	.34
(4) SP500					.33	.13	.99
(5) Government bond premium						−.26	.30
(6) Default premium							.14
(7) Equity premium							

Notes: All returns are measured at the quarterly frequency and expressed in percent per quarter. The equity premium is computed as the ration of one plus the return on the SP500 divided by one plus the return on Treasury bills. Other risk premiums are computed in a similar fashion. The government bond premium and default premium compare the return on long government bonds and corporate bonds to the return on Treasury bills. The averages are computed as arithmetic means. For a complete description of the data, see Ibbotson Associates (1993).

Several papers have discussed the inability of consumption-based asset pricing models to explain these *cross-sectional* differences in returns (Hansen and Singleton 1983; Mehra and Prescott 1985). This chapter will primarily focus on evidence about the *time series* variation in relative rates of return and return variability, in particular on those papers that suggest that these movements are related to the stage of the business cycle. Schwert (1989) provides evidence that equity returns are more variable during recession periods. His estimates indicate a major increase in volatility during recessions: 60 percent over the period 1953–1986 and 227 percent over 1927–1986. Schwert documents a similar increase in volatility in short-term interest rates, yields on corporate bonds, and the growth rate of industrial production. He concludes that the cyclical variation in return volatility can be only partially accounted for by movements in leverage, dividend yields, and macroeconomic variables. Flood, Hodrick, and Kaplan (1986), Fama and French (1988a, 1988b), and Poterba and Summers (1988) discuss the presence of negative autocorrelation in equity returns, which is more pronounced the longer the return interval. Fama and French (1988a, 1988b) argue that mean reversion in stock returns signals important time variation in expected returns, and that this time variation is tracked by the dividend and the earnings-to-price ratio. One explanation is that shocks to the economy have little or no effect on expected dividends or expected returns in the distant future, and the cumulative effect of the shocks has offsetting effects on expected returns and the current price. Since these negative autocorrelations are present in all size and industry portfolios, they argue that the explanation for this phenomenon can likely be found in a common factor, notably business cycles. In a subsequent paper, Fama and French (1989) find that excess returns on bonds and stocks can be forecast by the term spread, the default spread, and dividend yields, and that the predictive power increases with the return interval. Because the forecasting variables are related to business cycle conditions (typically high during recessions and low at business cycle peaks), Fama and French interpret this as evidence of capturing cyclical variation in expected returns. An important question is whether this variation of expected returns reflects rational pricing in an efficient market.

A final set of regularities links the information in asset prices to expectations about future real activity. Work by Stock and Watson (1988), and Estrella and Hardouvelis (1991) suggests that the slope of the term structure is an important leading indicator, and helps to predict future real activity.

These findings pose a challenge for parsimonious equilibrium asset pricing models to explain. The next section presents a simple equilibrium model commonly used in the literature on real business cycles, which can be turned into an asset pricing model with arguments along the lines of Lucas (1978) and Brock (1982). The evolution of the investment opportunity set is important for asset payoffs and valuation of these payoffs, but fundamentally these are governed by trade-offs agents make in production and consumption. Rather than posit a stochastic process for consumption, as in Mehra and Prescott (1985) or Kandel and Stambaugh (1991), the model economy endogenizes the decisions to produce, invest, and consume. First, this allows pricing of portfolios of contingent claims apart from those that pay off the aggregate endowment, which leads from a finance perspective to a more natural definition of certain complex securities, such as equity shares. Second, this makes it possible to evaluate whether the stylized facts mentioned above can be accounted for by models that restrict the relations between the behavior of macroeconomic variables and returns in mutually consistent ways, and in which asset prices reflect rational optimizing behavior by economic agents.

3. Model Economies

The model we study is a version of the standard neoclassical growth model which includes variable labor supply. The economy consists of many identical, infinitely lived households that derive utility from the consumption of goods and leisure. All production in the economy takes place in firms that own the stock of physical capital in the economy. Agents receive their income from supplying labor services to firms, and from dividends on the shares they hold in the firms. The market structure of the economy is as follows. At time 0 there exists a complete set of markets in which households and firms can trade contracts for future delivery of units of the single consumption good and labor services contingent on the state of the economy. The state of the economy at time t can be thought of as a "history" of the economy between dates 0 and t. Let s_t denote the state of the economy at time t, and let $\pi(s_t)$ denote the date 0 probability of the history s_t. The date 0 price of a unit of the consumption good in history t is $p(s_t)$, and the date 0 price of one unit of labor services is $p(s_t)w(s_t)$, where $w(s_t)$ denotes the real wage rate.

Firms

Firms combine capital with labor services rented from households to produce a single good, according to a constant-returns-to-scale production function, $y = zF[k, \lambda h]$, where k represents the capital stock, h represents the amount of labor services, and λ is an index of technological progress, which, for now, is assumed to grow at a constant rate. $F(\cdot)$ is assumed to be a concave, increasing, and twice continuously differentiable function of k and h. The output of the economy is uncertain because of a random shock to total factor productivity, z, which is assumed to follow a first-order Markov process. The information structure of the economy is such that the inputs into the production process have to be decided before the realization of this random shock is known. This dating is slightly different from the usual convention in the business cycle literature, which assumes that labor inputs can be chosen after the uncertainty about factor productivity has been resolved. Output in history s_t can therefore be written as

$$y(s_t) = z(s_t)F[k(s_{t-1}), \lambda^{t-1}h(s_{t-1})]. \tag{1}$$

The capital stock is assumed to depreciate at a constant rate, δ. Because firms own the capital in the economy, they decide on the amount of investment, x, that is necessary to maintain the capital stock for production in future periods. The evolution of the capital stock is given by:

$$k(s_t) = (1 - \delta)k(s_{t-1}) + x(s_t). \tag{2}$$

The dividend of the firms, d, is the residual of the value of the output produced after the factor payments to labor have been made and investment has been financed. Dividends in history s_t are given by

$$d(s_t) = y(s_t) - w(s_t)h(s_{t-1}) - x(s_t). \tag{3}$$

It will be assumed that firms maximize their net present value:

$$V = \sum_{t=1}^{\infty} \sum_{s_t} \pi(s_t)p(s_t)[y(s_t) - w(s_t)h(s_{t-1}) - x(s_t)]$$

s.t. (1) and (2). $\tag{4}$

The first-order condition for the efficient allocation of labor is

$$z(s_{t+1})\lambda^t D_2 F[k(s_t), \lambda^t h(s_t)] = w(s_{t+1}), \tag{5}$$

where D_i denotes the derivative of a fuction with respect to its ith argument. Defining $\pi(s_{t+1}; s_t)$ as the conditional probability of history s_{t+1} given s_t, efficient allocation of capital requires that

$$\sum_{s_{t+1}} \pi(s_{t+1}; s_t)p(s_{t+1})\{z(s_{t+1})\lambda^t D_1 F[k(s_t), \lambda^t h(s_t)]$$

$$+ (1 - \delta)\} = p(s_t). \tag{6}$$

These efficiency conditions state that the wage rate in history s_{t+1} equals the marginal product of labor, and that the price of one unit of capital equals the conditional expectation of its net marginal value product next period.

Households

The consumers in the economy are assumed to maximize their expected lifetime utility, defined over the consumption of goods, c, and leisure, l:

$$\max U = \sum_{t=1}^{\infty} \beta^t \sum_{s_t} \pi(s_t)u[c(s_t), l(s_{t-1})]. \tag{7}$$

Instantaneous utility is such that both consumption and leisure are "goods." β is the discount factor applied to future utilities, reflecting the preference on the part of agents, all else equal, to consume earlier rather than later. Household finance their consumption expenditures from the proceeds of renting labor services to firms and the dividends they receive from their ownership of shares. If we use $P(s_t)$

and $Z(s_t)$ to denote the relative price and the number of shares in history s_t, and normalize the endowment of time per period $h + l = 1$, the budget constraint of households can be written as

$$\sum_{t=1}^{\infty} \sum_{s_t} \pi(s_t) p(s_t)[c(s_t) + P(s_t)Z(s_t)]$$

$$\leq \sum_{t=1}^{\infty} \sum_{s_t} \pi(s_t) p(s_t)\{w(s_t)h(s_{t-1}) + Z(s_{t-1})[P(s_t) + d(s_t)]\}. \quad (8)$$

The consumer's first-order conditions are as follows. Efficient consumption plans require

$$\beta^t D_1 u[c(s_t), 1 - h(s_{t-1})] = \Lambda p(s_t); \quad (9)$$

efficient allocation of work effort implies that

$$\beta^{t+1} \sum_{s_{t+1}} \pi(s_{t+1}; s_t) D_2 u[c(s_{t+1}), 1 - h(s_t)]$$

$$= \Lambda \sum_{s_{t+1}} \pi(s_{t+1}; s_t) p(s_{t+1}) w(s_{t+1}); \quad (10)$$

and asset holdings are chosen such that

$$p(s_t)P(s_t) = \sum_{s_{t+1}} \pi(s_{t+1}; s_t) p(s_{t+1})[P(s_{t+1}) + d(s_{t+1})], \quad (11)$$

where Λ denotes the Lagrange multiplier on the household's budget constraint. From Swan (1963) it is known that a constant returns to scale technology with labor-augmenting technological progress allows a feasible steady state (under certainty) in which all variables grow at the rate of technological progress, $\lambda - 1$. King et al. (1988a) demonstrate that additional restrictions are required on preferences in order for this feasible steady state to be compatible with the efficiency conditions of the economy. The reason is that effort cannot grow in the steady state, since time in a period is in fixed supply. We follow King, Plosser, and Rebelo (1988) by assuming that preferences belong to a class that is compatible with steady-state growth:

$$u(c, 1 - h) = \begin{cases} \dfrac{1}{1 - \sigma} c^{1-\sigma} v(1 - h), & \text{if } \sigma \neq 1, \\ \log(c) + \phi \log(1 - h), & \text{if } \sigma = 1, \end{cases}$$

where σ is the inverse of the elasticity of intertemporal substitution, or the coefficient of relative risk aversion.

Equilibrium

The equilibrium in the economy is a set of prices, $p(s_t)$, $P(s_t)$, $w(s_t)$, and quantities, $c(s_t)$, $h(s_t)$, $k(s_t)$, $x(s_t)$, $d(s_t)$, $y(s_t)$, $x(s_t)$, $Z(s_t)$, that satisfies the efficiency conditions of firms, (5) and (6), and households, (9), (10) and (11); as well as the economywide resource constraints, (1), (2) and (3); and

$$y(s_t) = c(s_t) + x(s_t) \tag{12}$$

and

$$Z(s_t) = 1, \tag{13}$$

for all $s_t, t = 1, 2, \ldots, \infty$, and given k_0, h_0, z_0, and $Z_0 = 1$.

Asset Prices

Although the equilibrium prices and quantities in the economy are all determined in a single market-clearing operation at date 0, it is straightforward to derive the implied "shadow" asset prices at intermediate dates. Since the purpose of this chapter is to study the behavior of asset prices over time, we will derive the equilibrium prices that agents would be willing to pay for trading one unit of consumption between states s_t and s_{t+j}. At date 0 this would be the relative price, $\pi(s_{t+j})p(s_{t+j})/\pi(s_t)p(s_t)$. However, not all histories s_{t+j} are feasible for a given history s_t. For the purpose of studying bond prices, we will be interested in the relative price of one unit of consumption in state s_{t+j} given that the history s_t has been realized at date t. This price is $\pi(s_t)\pi(s_{t+j}; s_t)p(s_{t+j})/\pi(s_t)p(s_t) = \pi(s_{t+j}; s_t)p(s_{t+j})/p(s_t)$. We are now ready to define the price of a j-period bond in state s_t as the relative price of a payoff of one unit of consumption at $t + j$, by summing over all histories s_{t+j} that are feasible for a given history, s_t up to time t:

$$
\begin{aligned}
B^j(s_t) &= \frac{\sum_{s_{t+j}} \pi(s_{t+j}; s_t)p(s_{t+j})}{p(s_t)} = \frac{E_{s_t} p(s_{t+j})}{p(s_t)} \\
&= \frac{E_{s_t}\beta^j D_1 u[c(s_{t+j}), 1 - h(s_{t+j-1})]}{D_1 u[c(s_t), 1 - h(s_{t-1})]}. \tag{14}
\end{aligned}
$$

By similar reasoning we can derive the relative price in state s_t of a dividend payment in state s_{t+j}, conditional on the history s_t, as $\pi(s_{t+j}; s_t)p(s_{t+j})d(s_{t+j})/p(s_t)$. The value of a claim in state s_t to all future dividends can be found analogously by summing over all feasible future histories:

$$
\begin{aligned}
P(s_t) &= \frac{\sum_{j=1}^{\infty} \sum_{s_{t+j}} \pi(s_{t+j}; s_t)p(s_{t+j})d(s_{t+j})}{p(s_t)} \\
&= \frac{E_{s_t} p(s_{t+j})d(s_{t+j})}{p(s_t)}
\end{aligned}
$$

$$= \frac{E_{s_t}\beta^j D_1 u[c(s_{t+j}), 1 - h(s_{t+j-1})]d(s_{t+j})}{D_1 u[c(s_t), 1 - h(s_{t-1})]}. \tag{15}$$

Equation (15) is simply a restatement of the first-order condition (11) solved forward. It states that the price of a share is the present value of the expected future dividends. If we assume constant-returns-to-scale in production, it is easy to show that the share price must also be equal to the capital stock. Substituting (2) and (5) into (3) and assuming constant returns to scale gives

$$d(s_{t+1}) = y(s_{t+1}) - w(s_{t+1})h(s_t) - x(s_{t+1})$$

$$= k(s_t)z(s_{t+1})D_1 F[k(s_t), \lambda^t h(s_t)] - k(s_{t+1}) + (1 - \delta)k(s_t). \tag{16}$$

Rearranging terms yields

$$\frac{d(s_{t+1}) + k(s_{t+1})}{k(s_t)} = z(s_{t+1})D_1 F[k(s_t), \lambda^t h(s_t)] + (1 - \delta). \tag{17}$$

By substituting this into (6), we get (11) for $P(s_t) = k(s_t)$.

Time-Varying Expected Returns

To understand why equilibrium business cycle models are natural candidates for the study of issues of time variation in expected returns and risk premiums, consider the net return, r_k, from holding one unit of capital between states s_t and s_{t+j}:[3]

$$r_k(s_{t+1}; s_t) = z(s_{t+1})D_1 F[k(s_t), \lambda^t h(s_t)] - \delta. \tag{18}$$

The realized return can be decomposed into its expected and unexpected components:

$$r_k(s_{t+1}; s_t) = E_{s_t} r_k(s_{t+1}; s_t) + b(s_t)\epsilon(s_{t+1}), \tag{19}$$

where $b(s_t) = D_1 F[k(s_t), \lambda^t h(s_t)]$, and $\epsilon(s_{t+1}) = z(s_{t+1}) - E_{s_t}z(s_{t+1})$. The return on productive investments therefore follows a one-factor representation, with the productivity shock z as the single factor. Equation (19) states that the return deviates from its expectation by the unexpected component of the factor realization, ϵ, multiplied by the sensitivity, b, to this factor. This factor sensitivity, or "asset beta," is itself state dependent because it is a function of the time-varying marginal product of capital. The risk premium on productive capital can be derived by rewriting the Euler equation, (6), as

$$E_{s_t}\{[1 + r_k(s_{t+1}; s_t)]\frac{p(s_{t+1})}{p(s_t)}\} = 1. \tag{20}$$

Using the definition of the covariance and substituting in (19), we get:

$$1 + E_{s_t} r_k(s_{t+1}; s_t) = \frac{p(s_t)}{E_{s_t} p(s_{t+1})} - b(s_t)\frac{E_{s_t}\epsilon(s_{t+1})p(s_{t+1})}{E_{s_t} p(s_{t+1})} \tag{21}$$

$$= \frac{D_1 u[c(s_t), h(s_{t-1})]}{\beta E_{s_t} D_1 u[c(s_{t+1}), h(s_t)]}$$

$$+ b(s_t) \frac{-E_{s_t} \epsilon(s_{t+1}) D_1 u[c(s_{t+1}), h(s_t)]}{\beta E_{s_t} D_1 u[c(s_{t+1}), h(s_t)]}. \tag{22}$$

The conditional expected return on capital is therefore the sum of two components. The first is the inverse of the one-period bond price in state s_t, as defined in equation (14) for $j - 1$. It is therefore equal to one plus the conditional one-period "risk-free" rate. The second term is the product of the factor sensitivity and the risk premium on the factor. The sign of the factor risk premium is determined by $E_{s_t} \epsilon(s_{t+1}) D_1 u[c(s_{t+1}), h(s_t)]$, or the conditional covariance between the technology shock and the marginal utility of consumption. Because an unexpectedly high realization of the technology shock will generally lead to an increase in consumption, this covariance will be negative, and the risk premium on the return on capital will be positive. It is important to note that all the components of the expected return, that is, *i.e.* the risk-free rate, the factor risk premium, and the "beta," are time varying. It is in this sense that the equilibrium business cycle models are natural candidates for the study of the links between variation in expected returns and fluctuations in the economic fundamentals.

Firms and Leverage

It has become common practice in the literature to compare the time series properties of equity shares in model economies to the behavior of stock market indices. Our current definition of equity shares has at least two aspects that do not mirror stock prices in reality. First, the share of capital and labor in the model are equally risky, as both represent constant fractions, θ and $1 - \theta$, of output. As noted by Donaldson and Mehra (1984), in practice the share of capital is riskier than the share of labor, which is largely negotiated prior to the realization of output, which creates *operating* leverage. Because in the model economy, both inputs are chosen before the realization of the productivity shock, a natural way to capture this insurance aspect of labor services is to modify the contract structure and pay labor its expected utility-denominated marginal product instead of its actual marginal product. The fixed wage, $\overline{w}(s_t)$, contracted for one period ahead solves

$$E_{s_t} p(s_{t+1}) z(s_{t+1}) D_2 F[k(s_t), h(s_t)] = \overline{w}(s_t) E_{s_t} p(s_{t+1}). \tag{23}$$

Incorporating operating leverage in this manner has the effect that capital income provides an insurance to labor income. This insurance is partial in the sense that it only pertains to the one-period-ahead realization of the productivity shock. Labor income will still vary with the level of the capital stock, but its share will covary negatively with the realization of z.

A second unrealistic aspect of the equity definition is that it represents an unlevered claim to the stock of capital, whereas many firms rely in part on debt to finance productive investments. Because the economy is one in which the Modigliani and Miller propositions hold, there is, strictly speaking, no role for debt financing. By the same token, however, because capital structure does not alter the equilibrium allocations, we can simply assume a particular financial structure and use the complete markets framework to study two sets of contingent claims, corporate debt, and levered equity, that add up in value to the capital stock. Following this approach, we define a one-period risky bond in the firm that promises to pay a fraction, ψ, of average firm value over all states, $\overline{V}$, or future firm value, whichever is lower. This definition emphasizes the option characteristics of corporate debt. If the value of the firm falls below a fraction of its average value, shareholders sell the firm to bondholders for the face value of the bond. The payoff to holders of the risky bond if the economy goes from state s_t to s_{t+1} is

$$\min\left[\psi\overline{V},\ P(s_{t+1}) + \theta(s_{t+1}; s_t)y(s_{t+1}) - x(s_{t+1})\right], \tag{24}$$

where $\theta(s_{t+1}; s_t)$ is the share of capital after accounting for operating leverage. The price of this bond, $B^c(s_t)$, is therefore given by

$$\frac{E_{s_t}\min\left[\psi\overline{V},\ P(s_{t+1}) + \theta(s_{t+1}; s_t)y(s_{t+1}) - x(s_{t+1})\right]p(s_{t+1})}{p(s_t)}. \tag{25}$$

Note that the face value of the risky bond, $\psi\overline{V}$, is constant across all states. Consequently leverage, defined as the value of the risky bond relative to the value of the unlevered firm, will be high in states where firm value is low (recessions). The end of period cum dividend value of a levered equity share is given by the firm's cash flows net of the payments on the one-period risky bond:

$$\max\left[0,\ P(s_{t+1}) + \theta(s_{t+1}; s_t)y(s_{t+1}) - x(s_{t+1}) - \psi\overline{V}\right]. \tag{26}$$

The contingent ex-dividend value of the levered equity, $P^l(s_t)$, is simply the value of an unlevered share minus the value of the risky bond, $P(s_t) - B^c(s_t)$. The dividend on the levered equity share, $d^l(s_{t+1})$, therefore equals the cum dividend value of the levered equity share minus its ex-dividend value:

$$\max\left[0,\ P(s_{t+1}) + \theta(s_{t+1}; s_t)y(s_{t+1}) - x(s_{t+1}) - \psi\overline{V}\right]$$
$$- \left[P(s_{t+1}) - B^c(s_{t+1})\right]. \tag{27}$$

It is perhaps important to point out that the component we call dividends in the model does not directly correspond to its empirical counterpart. It bears closer resemblance to a measure of net cash flows of the firm, after taking into account the effects of investment and debt financing. Approximating dividends by net cash flows is therefore likely to overstate their variability.

Term Spread, Default Spread, and D/P-Ratio

We conclude this section by defining the model equivalent of three financial variables that have been empirically shown to have predictive power for (excess) returns. The term spread is defined as the difference between the yield to maturity on a five-year (twenty-period) pure discount bond and that on a bond that matures in one quarter, which can be found from the bond pricing equation, (14), for $j = 1, 20$. The default spread compares the yield to maturity on the one-period risky bond to the yield on the pure discount bond of equal maturity. The dividend price ratio is defined as the dividend on the levered equity scaled by the price of levered equity.

4. A Numerical Evaluation

Parameter Values

This section contains a numerical simulation of the model. We choose parameters of technology and preferences such that the steady state under certainty coincides with the average behavior of per capita U.S time series. The certainty steady state can be thought of as the limiting case of an economy with uncertainty, in which the shocks become arbitrarily small, and the stationary distribution degenerates to a single point. It will be assumed that the production function is Cobb-Douglas $F[k, h] = k^\theta h^{1-\theta}$. First, $1 - \theta$ was chosen to be 0.65, on the basis of estimates of labor's share in GNP by Christiano (1988),[4] and λ was set to 1.004, the average common (gross) growth rate of per capita output, consumption, and investment during the postwar period. Substituting the estimated investment-to-capital ratio of 0.0255 into (2), implies a depreciation rate of 2.2 percent per quarter. An estimate of the capital-to-output ratio of 10.57 can be used to compute the utility discount factor in the "transformed" economy $\hat{\beta}$ of 0.993. In Chapter 2, Hansen and Prescott show how to transform a growth economy into a stationary economy. We choose ϕ such that the effort in the steady state equals 0.20, which is the average time devoted to market work in the postwar period. The remaining preference parameter, σ, plays an important role in the determination of asset returns. The model will be simulated for $\sigma = \{1, 5\}$, which is within the range suggested by Hall (1988a), but considerably lower than the value of 28 proposed by Kandel and Stambaugh (1991) for reasons that will become clear later. The degree of leverage, ψ, is set to 0.40, as proposed in Kandel and Stambaugh (1991); this choice is close to estimates by Bodie, Kane, and McDonald (1983), who estimate the proportion of stocks in investors' portfolios to be around 60 percent.

Technology shocks

On the basis of these parameter values, the productivity shock, z_t, can be "inverted" from the data as $\log(z_t) = \log(y_t) - \theta \log(k_{t-1}) - (1 - \theta) \log(h_{t-1})$. The autocorrelation in these Solow residuals was estimated to be 0.96. Because it is not possible to reject the hypothesis of a unit root in technology, the model will be simulated under two assumptions about the persistence of $\log(z_t)$. The deterministic trend (DT) model assumes that growth evolves according to a deterministic trend, λ^t. Deviations from this trend occur from stationary but correlated technology shocks with $\rho = 0.96$. In the difference stationary (DS) model the shock process has a unit root, which is equivalent to assuming that the growth rate of technology, λ, is stochastic and independently distributed over time. In the DT model, the natural logarithm of z (or λ in the DS model) can take on three values, $\{\mu - \epsilon, \mu, \mu + \epsilon\}$, and follows a first-order Markov process with transition probability matrix

$$
\Pi_{\mathbf{z}} = \begin{bmatrix} p^2 & 2p(1 - p) & (1 - p)^2 \\ p(1 - q) & pq + (1 - p)(1 - q) & (1 - p)q \\ (1 - q)^2 & 2q(1 - q) & q^2 \end{bmatrix}. \tag{28}
$$

This process mimics a discrete first-order autoregressive model with autoregressive parameter $p + q - 1$, as discussed in more detail in the appendix to this chapter. I choose ϵ to closely match the model's implied variance of output to its U.S. postwar sample counterpart. This shock process is used for two reasons. First, its simplicity makes the interpretation of the parameters p and q transparent. The term p^2 is the probability that $\log z_{t+1} = \mu - \epsilon$ given that $\log z_t = \mu - \epsilon$, and $(1 - p)^2$ is the conditional probability of a transition from the lowest state to the highest state. Similarly, q^2 is the probability that $\log z_{t+1} = \mu + \epsilon$ given that $\log z_t = \mu + \epsilon$ and $(1 - q)^2$ is the conditional probability of a transition from the highest state to the lowest state. Hence, p governs the conditional probabilities of moving up after a low realization of the technology shock and q governs the conditional probabilities of moving down after a high realization. Second, it provides a simple description of business cycle conditions, because the choice of p and q affects the expected duration of contractions and expansions. In particular, choosing p to be smaller than q implies that bad shocks occur less frequently than good shocks, and that the conditional probabilities of leaving the lowest state are higher than the probabilities of leaving the highest state, which reduces the expected length of contractions relative to expansions. If $p = q = 0.98$, the stationary distribution of (28) is $\{0.25, 0.50, 0.25\}$, and hence the average time spent in the bad state and the good state are equal. The average time of reaching the highest state from the lowest state is about twenty periods, which is longer than the duration of the average postwar expansion. For $p = 0.97$, $q = 0.99$ the stationary distribution becomes $\{0.0625, 0.3750, 0.5625\}$, making recessions shorter than expansions. Also, for a symmetric shock process $\{\mu - \epsilon, \mu, \mu + \epsilon\}$, this would introduce conditional heteroskedasticity in the shocks.[5] In the simulations of the DT model, p and q are both set to 0.98. In the DS model, z_t is assumed to have a unit root. This can be modeled by simulating a Markov process for λ, as in (28), with p and q both equal to 0.50, where these probabilities now apply to transitions of λ.[6]

Finally, the simulations assume that labor is inelastically supplied, with h set to 0.2, the average time devoted to market work during the postwar period.[7] Utility reduces to $u(c) = \frac{1}{1-\sigma} c^{1-\sigma}$. Because this objective function is time separable, past consumption of goods and leisure does not affect current utility. Also, the time required to build new capital goods is one-period. These properties, combined with the fact that uncertainty is Markov, imply that the state of the economy can be described by the pair $s' = \{k, z'\}$.

Solution Methods

The model can be solved using a variety of numerical methods (see Chapter 2 for a discussion). We use a technique called value function iteration as described in Bertsekas (1976). This technique attempts to find a pointwise approximation to the solution for $k' = k'(k, z')$, by restricting the capital stock to a discrete grid, $\{k_1, k_2, \ldots, k_n\}$. In our numerical solutions we set $n = 1,000$. It is sometimes difficult to assess the accuracy of discrete approximation techniques. Taylor and Uhlig (1990) compare the relative performance of a variety of solution techniques, and report important discrepancies across methods. Also the relative accuracy may be different across policy functions. For instance, consumption is an order of magnitude smaller than capital, and is computed as the difference between output and investment. Because investment is approximately the time derivative of the capital stock, small approximation errors in the policy for capital become relatively more important for consumption and investment.

Table 10.2 gives an indication of the importance of approximation error in the model, by comparing on a state-by-state basis the accuracy of the Euler equation that plays a central role in the pricing of assets. Entries in the table give the left side of (20), which should be unity in the continuous economy. Although the average is close to unity substantial deviations occur across states. The averages in Table 10.2 are not probability weighted. Because the largest deviations occur in the tails of the distribution of the capital stock and receive low weight in the stationary distribution, the table probably overstates the importance of the approximation error. Nevertheless, these errors can contaminate some of the results, especially when we focus on small quantities, such as excess returns.[8]

Quantity Dynamics

To understand the response of asset prices to shifts in the investment opportunity set, it is useful to briefly describe the dynamics of output, consumption, and investment. The model dynamics in this section were approximated by linearizing

Table 10.2
Approximation Errors in Euler Equation

	DT Model		DS Model	
	$\sigma_c = 1$	$\sigma_c = 5$	$\sigma_c = 1$	$\sigma_c = 5$
Mean	1.0000	1.0001	1.0000	0.9998
SD	0.0030	0.0115	0.0027	0.0120
Minimum	0.9916	0.9550	0.9929	0.9610
Maximum	1.0086	1.0433	1.0067	1.0358

Note: The table lists for each of the four model variants summary statistics for the left side of the first-order condition (20) on a state-by-state basis. This ratio should be unity in the continuous economy.

the first-order conditions about the steady state and solving the associated system of linear difference equations (Kydland and Prescott 1982; King, Plosser, and Rebelo 1988a). This solution method was chosen for expositional purposes only, since it allows an easy interpretation of the expected adjustment of the economy to a shock by studying the impulse response functions. These impulse responses trace the effect on prices and quantities of a 1 percent increase in technology, assuming that the economy resides initially in the steady state. A detailed description of this method can be found in King, Plosser, and Rebelo (1987). Figure 10.1 presents the expected response to a temporary, but correlated shock to factor productivity in the DT model, starting from its steady-state level. In each panel, the lower dotted lines represents the steady-state growth of the economy due to exogenous technological progress, λ, and the upper dotted line corresponds to a growth path 1 percent above the steady state. An increase in productivity increases consumption demand at all future dates through a wealth effect. The desire for smooth consumption profiles leads agents to save (invest) in the early periods when there is high output and the return on capital is high, and dissave in later periods by consuming part of the capital stock. Although the wealth effect of the shock increases consumption demand more at near than at more distant future dates, consumption initially keeps rising before it returns to its steady-state level. This intertemporal substitution is motivated by high interest rates immediately following the shock, because of the autocorrelation of the shocks. Over time the accumulation of capital and the gradual decline in productivity lower the marginal product, and interest rates fall below their long-run level as consumption growth rates slow down toward the long-run trend path (see Figure 10.2). Figure 10.3 shows that increasing risk aversion, or lowering the elasticity of intertemporal substitution, leads to smoother consumption profiles. This is one of the key properties that distinguishes production models from the endowment models studied by Lucas (1978), Mehra and Prescott (1985), and Kandel and Stambaugh (1991): optimal consumption choices are not invariant

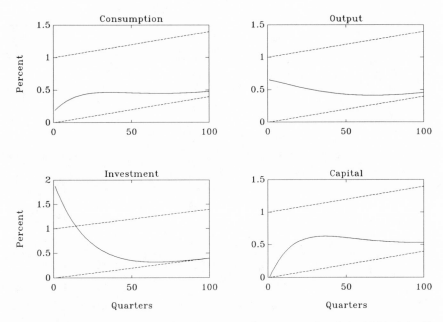

Figure 10.1 Quantity Responses to Temporary Technology Shock in DT Model with
$\sigma_c = 1$

Percentage deviations from steady-state growth path. Dotted line through origin shows steady-state
growth path in Figures 10.1 through 10.5.

to changes in risk aversion, which feeds back to the behavior of asset returns and
risk premiums. Increasing risk aversion tends to increase risk premiums, but this
effect is mitigated by a smoothing of optimal consumption plans.

A permanent improvement in technology (in the DS model) allows agents in
the long run to raise their consumption levels permanently. Figure 10.4 illustrates
that after the productivity shock, the stock of physical capital is below its long
run optimal level, stimulating investment demand. As capital is accumulated over
time and its marginal product falls, agents consume a larger fraction of the extra
output and reduce investment. Because consumption growth never falls below its
long-run rate, the interest rate never falls below its long-run level either (see Figure
10.5).

The important conclusion from studying these quantity dynamics is that shifts
in the investment opportunity set, temporary or permanent, give rise to temporary
movements in (consumption) growth rates and discount rates. Although the figures
show that the plans are smooth on an expected basis, they seldom are smooth ex
post because new information arrives, that is, shocks occur, forcing agents to
revise their plans. In the DT model, however, there exists no uncertainty about the
long-run trend path, whereas in the DS model, agents have to continuously adjust

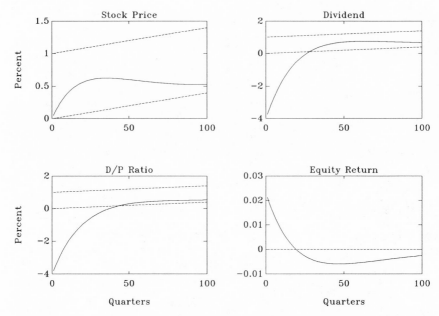

Figure 10.2 Price Responses to Temporary Technology Shock in DT Model with $\sigma_c = 1$
Percentage deviations from steady-state growth path; returns expressed in percentage deviations from long-run mean.

to a shifting long-run equilibrium path. This difference between the long-run properties of the models is potentially important for the analysis of long-horizon returns, which will be discussed shortly.

Figures 2 and 4 already give some important clues about the cyclical behavior of returns. Positive productivity shocks increase expected growth rates of consumption and hence increase the return on short-term discount bonds. Also, consumption growth rates are larger in the short run than in the long-run. Consequently short-term interest rates exceed the yield on long discount bonds. Although the yield on long-term bonds increases, the term structure slopes down following a positive productivity shock. The dividend-to-price ratio falls following a good shock in the DT model. Abstracting from the effects of operating leverage for the moment, the reason is that although output increases, the elastic investment (or "reinvested" dividends) response causes the dividend and the D/P ratio to decline. The behavior of dividends is sensitive to the persistence of the productivity shocks and the degree of risk aversion. In particular when the shocks become permanent, the investment response becomes smaller. The reason is that a temporary shock causes agents to increase their investment demand to save for future periods when productivity is expected to be lower. This intertemporal substitution effect becomes smaller as the persistence in the shocks increases. Figure 10.5 shows

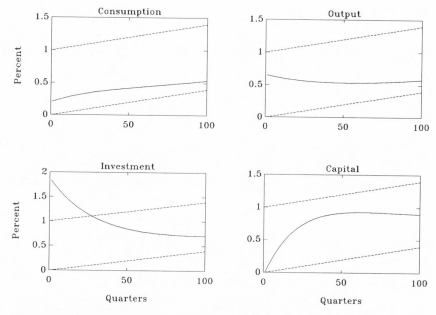

Figure 10.3 Quantity Responses to Temporary Technology Shock in DT Model with $\sigma_c = 5$

Percentage deviations from steady-state growth path.

that for $\sigma = 5$ as shocks become more permanent, 'reinvested dividends' are sufficiently small that the dividend to price ratio increases in response to a good shock.

Simulating Recessions and Expansions

To link the predictions of the model more directly to the cyclical behavior of returns, we simulated the numerical solution to the model by drawing a time series of shocks to the level of technology in the DT model, and to the growth rate in the DS model, using the transition probabilities given in equation (28). Starting from a randomly drawn level of the capital stock, we used the policy function for capital to create a sample path for the state vector. The optimal consumption and investment plans, as well as the equilibrium asset returns are computed as functions of the simulated state vector. In order to obtain predictions about the cyclical behavior of returns, it is necessary to take a stand on what constitutes a recession or an expansion. A recession is defined as an episode that starts at the beginning of a period during which output growth is negative for two or more consecutive quarters. A recession turns into an expansion when economic growth is positive for at least two quarters. This definition of recessions allows one to

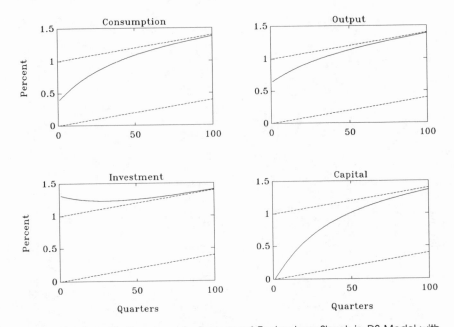

Figure 10.4 Quantity Responses to Permanent Technology Shock in DS Model with $\sigma_c = 1$

Percentage deviations from steady-state growth path. Upper dotted line represents new growth path.

identify cycles only ex post, similar to the practice used by the NBER. Because the economy is growing, expansions will on average last longer than recessions.

Average Returns

Table 10.3 presents some summary statistics of simulating 100 time series of 1,000 observations in the DT model. Part A illustrates the point made by Hansen and Singleton (1983) and Mehra and Prescott (1985) that consumption-based models have great difficulty in explaining the cross-sectional difference in mean returns. The model in this chapter is no exception and has similar difficulties in generating sizable risk premiums, despite the change in the definition of the equity claim and the presence of operating and financial leverage.[9] It is in some respects more difficult to explain risk premiums in a general equilibrium model than in an endowment economy. The reason is that the consumption choices are endogenously determined and not invariant to the level of risk aversion. Increasing risk aversion in a production economy leads to smaller changes in risk premiums because consumption itself becomes less variable, as can be seen by comparing Figures 10.1 and 10.3. Figure 10.3 suggests that increasing risk aversion even further, to around 30, as suggested by Kandel and Stambaugh (1991), would effectively remove any

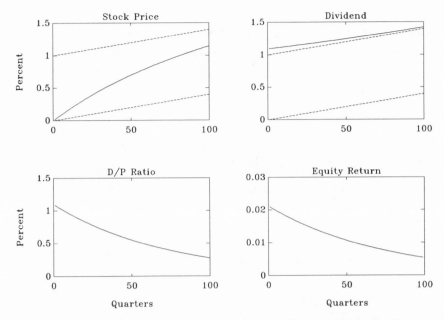

Figure 10.5 Price Responses to Permanent Technology Shock in DS Model with $\sigma_c = 5$

Percentage deviations from steady-state growth path; discount rates expressed in percentage deviations from long-run mean. Upper dotted line shows new growth path.

interesting consumption dynamics from the model. Although a sufficiently high level of risk aversion by itself can (perhaps) account for the mean return on equity, higher risk aversion will also raise the risk premium on long risk-free bonds, which has historically been small (or negative during the postwar period). It might be of some interest to see whether the proposed "solutions" to the equity premium puzzle (e.g., Rietz 1988; Constantinides 1990) can simultaneously rationalize a low excess return on long-term bonds and a high excess return on equity. Financial leverage effectively drives a wedge between the risk premium on equity and risk-free bonds. Unfortunately the current model does not assign an important role to leverage. This is best understood by returning to Figure 10.3 and examining the adjustment of the capital stock to a productivity shock. The adjustment of capital is extremely smooth, because technology allows agents to transform capital into consumption costlessly in each period. Consequently, the capital stock changes slowly between periods, which is reflected in the small variability of the return on unlevered equity shown in Table 10.3. Capital, or unlevered equity, is simply not a very risky claim in the model. Levering the firm to around 40 percent does not change this result. It takes unlikely high levels of leverage (> 0.9) for the bonds to even become risky and command a default premium.

Table 10.3
Return on Zero Coupon Bonds and Risky Equity: DT Economy

A. Average Returns

	$\sigma_c = 1$		$\sigma_c = 5$	
	mean	*SD*	*mean*	*SD*
Bonds, 1 qrt.	1.112	.254	1.093	0.9162
	(0.012)	(.013)	(0.065)	(0.053)
Bonds, 5 yr.	1.112	.379	1.093	1.042
	(0.020)	(.026)	(0.072)	(0.065)
Firm value	1.111	.145	1.099	0.206
	(0.010)	(.011)	(0.062)	(0.022)
Levered equity	1.112	.258	1.112	0.668
	(0.009)	(.018)	(0.062)	(0.063)

B. Cyclical Variation in Returns

	$\sigma_c = 1$				$\sigma_c = 5$			
	Recession		*Expansion*		*Recession*		*Expansion*	
	mean	*SD*	*mean*	*SD*	*mean*	*SD*	*mean*	*SD*
Bonds, 1 qrt.	1.050	.246	1.177	.243	0.998	0.940	1.197	0.871
	(0.020)	(.020)	(0.021)	(.022)	(0.064)	(0.077)	(0.075)	(0.097)
Bonds, 5 yr.	0.119	.379	1.104	.377	1.065	1.067	1.124	1.006
	(0.022)	(.037)	(0.021)	(0.40)	(0.072)	(0.088)	(0.080)	(0.117)
Firm value	1.023	.108	1.204	.115	0.990	0.165	1.218	.174
	(0.027)	(.009)	(0.024)	(.031)	(0.061)	(0.029)	(0.070)	(0.030)
Levered equity	1.006	.229	1.223	.237	0.995	0.703	1.240	0.598
	(0.022)	(.019)	(0.027)	(.026)	(0.062)	(0.078)	(0.071)	(0.081)
Leverage	0.406		0.396		0.399		0.399	
Term Spread	0.043		−0.046		0.055		−0.070	
	(0.099)		(0.010)		(0.019)		(0.025)	
D/P ratio (u)	0.008		0.006		0.008		0.006	
	(0.0002)		(0.0092)		(0.001)		(0.001)	
D/P ratio (l)	0.009		0.005		0.009		0.005	
	(0.0003)		(0.0004)		(0.001)		(0.001)	

Cyclical Variation in Returns

Short-term interest rates move procyclically in the model (see part B of Table 10.3). The return on bonds is higher during recessions. Recessions are typically periods with a sequence of bad shocks. Bad shocks cause downward revisions of the discount rate; good shocks tend to increase discount rates. A decline in

Table 10.3
Continued

C. Cyclical Variation in Conditional Returns

| | $\sigma_c = 1$ | | | | $\sigma_c = 5$ | | | |
| | Recession | | Expansion | | Recession | | Expansion | |
	mean	SD	mean	SD	mean	SD	mean	SD
Bonds, 1 qrt.	1.054	.248	1.172	.243	1.006	0.936	1.188	0.876
	(0.019)	(.019)	(0.020)	(.066)	(0.079)	(0.077)	(0.075)	(0.093)
Bonds, 5 yr.	1.053	.376	1.173	.370	1.068	1.049	1.187	1.018
	(0.027)	(.033)	(0.030)	(.040)	(0.073)	(0.080)	(0.083)	(0.113)
Firm value	1.055	.130	1.171	.133	1.020	0.185	1.185	0.188
	(0.016)	(.012)	(0.018)	(.015)	(0.062)	(0.027)	(0.067)	(0.029)
Levered equity	1.056	.253	1.170	.248	1.040	0.712	1.191	0.602
	(0.015)	(.023)	(0.018)	(.028)	(0.064)	(0.082)	(0.067)	(0.076)
Leverage	0.407		0.395		0.401		0.398	
Term Spread	0.046		−0.049		0.057		−0.072	
	(0.011)		(0.010)		(0.020)		(0.026)	
D/P ratio (u)	0.008		0.006		0.008		0.006	
	(0.0002)		(0.0002)		(0.0002)		(0.0002)	
D/P ratio (l)	0.009		0.005		0.009		0.005	
	(0.0003)		(0.0004)		(0.0003)		(0.0004)	

Notes: Summary statistics from 100 simulated times series of 1,000 observations. Numbers in parentheses are standard deviations across the 100 replications. All returns are express as percentage per quarter and measured at quarterly intervals. SD is the standard deviation of returns, computed as deviation from the (conditional) mean. D/P ratio (u) and D/P ratio (l) are the dividend-to-price ratios on, respectively, unlevered and levered equity. The term spread is the difference between the yields on the five-year and one-quarter bonds. Leverage is defined as the ration of the value of a one-quarter risky bond and firm value. Part B lists the average returns over recessions and expansions. Because recessions and expansions are only defined ex post facto, part C lists the average returns conditional on agents' *knowing* the economy is in a recession or expansion. This essentially lags the turning points of the business cycle in part C by two quarters relative to part B.

short rates during a recession tends to drive up the prices of longer bonds, which explains their higher rate of return in recessions. This does not mean however that *expected* rates of return are also high in recessions. In fact, in a model with a single source of uncertainty expected returns are highly correlated. A less than perfect correlation of expected returns arises because the conditional covariance of the asset returns and the marginal rates of substitution changes over time because of nonlinearities in the model. As pointed out before, risk premiums are generally small at low levels of risk aversion. The small variation in expected excess returns implies that realized returns largely reflect discount rate revisions.

Recessions and expansions are defined only ex post, that is, after output growth has been negative or positive for at least two quarters, Part C of Table 10.3 shows the values yielded by the model for conditional returns, that is, average returns conditional on agents knowing whether a recession or expansion is underway.

Table 10.3 shows that the model predicts little variation in the cyclical volatility of returns, especially for $\sigma = 1$. Movements in leverage, stemming from variations in the relative value of bonds and equity, are small because relative rates of return show little variation. Consequently leverage cannot explain the large changes in conditional volatility of equity returns reported in empirical work by Schwert (1989). Only for $\sigma = 5$ does volatility increase by about 15 percent during recessions in this model. It is not surprising that the price of risk, measured as the excess return on equity divided by the standard deviation of equity, is also virtually constant across states. The summary statistics shown in part B of Table 10.3 confirm the intuition of Figure 10.2 that the dividend-to-price ratio and the term spread move countercyclically in the DT model. Leverage slightly reinforces the cyclical movements in the dividend-to-price ratio. Table 10.4 shows that these conclusions carry over to the DS model, with a few exceptions. The dividend-to-price ratio becomes procyclical, as illustrated in Figure 10.5, and recessions show a sharper increase in the return on bonds.

Thus far the discussion has centered around the behavior of mean returns and return variances over the cycle. The remaining part of this section will focus on the properties of low frequency movements in returns, in particular, on the ability of the term spread, D/P ratio, and lagged returns to forecast future (excess) returns on stocks and bonds.

Forecasting Returns

Fama and French (1988a, 1988b), Poterba and Summers (1988), and Campbell and Shiller (1987) observed that equity returns can be forecast. Fama and French (1988a) show that the R^2 from regressing stock returns on their lagged values increases with the interval over which the returns are measured. The regression slopes are reliably negative, which is interpreted as evidence that stock price movements have temporary components. Time-varying expected returns can explain 25 to 40 percent of three- to five-year return variances. More recent studies have raised some caveats about these findings: Kim, Nelson, and Starz (1991) have reported that including the Great Depression in the smaple period affected the results, and Richardson (1989) has questioned the testing methodology.

To evaluate the autocorrelation in returns over different horizons, 10 time series of returns of length 2,000 were simulated.[10] To avoid bias in the regression slopes, overlapping observations were dropped, and consequently fewer observations were used to estimate the slope coefficients for long return intervals than for short return intervals. Figure 10.6 shows the slopes and R^2s obtained by regressing returns on their lagged values in the DT model. The left panels show the average regression

Table 10.4
Return on Zero Coupon Bonds and Risky Equity: DS Economy

A. Average Returns

	$\sigma_c = 1$		$\sigma_c = 5$	
	mean	*SD*	*mean*	*SD*
Bonds, 1 qrt.	1.101	.284	0.974	1.171
	(0.027)	(.032)	(0.077)	(0.40)
Bonds, 5 yr.	1.100	.500	0.979	1.706
	(0.014)	(.051)	(0.054)	(0.754)
Firm value	1.101	.118	0.988	0.158
	(0.028)	(.011)	(0.064)	(0.024)
Levered equity	1.101	.235	1.013	0.864
	(0.030)	(.016)	(0.083)	(0.777)

B. Cyclical Variation in Returns

	$\sigma_c = 1$				$\sigma_c = 5$			
	Recession		*Expansion*		*Recession*		*Expansion*	
	mean	*SD*	*mean*	*SD*	*mean*	*SD*	*mean*	*SD*
Bonds, 1 qrt.	1.075	.312	1.105	.276	0.888	1.355	0.989	1.096
	(0.039)	(.109)	(0.026)	(.017)	(0.273)	(1.123)	(0.064)	(0.162)
Bonds, 5 yr.	1.509	.475	1.037	.465	1.620	1.989	0.878	1.555
	(0.040)	(.171)	(0.021)	(.031)	(0.297)	(2.240)	(0.079)	(0.282)
Firm value	0.987	.093	1.118	.112	0.875	0.137	1.005	0.154
	(0.030)	(.013)	(0.027)	(.011)	(0.067)	(0.027)	(0.063)	(0.024)
Levered equity	0.930	.217	1.128	.224	0.907	1.809	1.0281	0.729
	(0.032)	(.058)	(0.028)	(.013)	(0.304)	(1.994)	(0.075)	(0.293)
Leverage	0.388		0.400		0.368		0.379	
Term Spread	0.016		−0.001		0.017		−0.009	
	(0.023)		(0.010)		(0.202)		(0.034)	
D/P ratio (u)	0.007		0.007		0.005		0.006	
	(0.0002)		(0.0001)		(0.0002)		(0.002)	
D/P ratio (l)	−0.003		0.009		−0.002		0.008	
	(0.001)		(0.0003)		(0.004)		(0.0004)	

Table 10.4
Continued

	C. Cyclical Variation in Conditional Returns							
	$\sigma_c = 1$				$\sigma_c = 5$			
	Recession		Expansion		Recession		Expansion	
	mean	SD	mean	SD	mean	SD	mean	SD
Bonds, 1 qrt.	1.031	.306	1.112	.274	0.816	1.402	1.001	0.066
	(0.043)	(.110)	(0.025)	(.015)	(0.292)	(1.119)	(0.061)	(0.043)
Bonds, 5 yr.	1.030	.526	1.111	.485	0.855	2.117	0.997	1.531
	(0.034)	(.175)	(0.014)	(.025)	(0.197)	(2.224)	(0.045)	(0.225)
Firm value	1.034	.107	1.111	.116	0.918	0.147	0.998	0.156
	(0.033)	(.014)	(0.027)	(.010)	(0.069)	(0.028)	(0.063)	(0.024)
Levered equity	1.037	.235	1.111	.232	1.020	1.122	1.010	0.690
	(0.035)	(.056)	(0.012)	(.012)	(0.318)	(2.028)	(0.074)	(0.050)
Leverage	0.387		0.400		0.378		0.368	
Term Spread	0.021		−0.001		0.082		−0.019	
	(0.025)		(0.010)		(0.225)		(0.032)	
D/P ratio (u)	0.008		0.007		0.006		0.006	
	(0.0002)		(0.0001)		(0.0002)		(0.002)	
D/P ratio (l)	0.008		0.007		0.007		0.006	
	(0.001)		(0.0002)		(0.003)		(0.0004)	

Notes: See Table 10.3.

coefficients, and a band of twice the average standard error across the 10 replications. The top panels correspond to $\sigma = 1$, and the lower panels correspond $\sigma = 5$. The figures show that simulated returns are reliably positively correlated up to thirty quarters. Although returns are mean reverting, and stock prices have temporary components, the returns are positively autocorrelated. Increasing the parameter of risk aversion only reinforces the positive correlation, because the increased desire for smooth consumption plans leads to slower and more persistent deviations of capital about its steady state. Figure 10.2 shows that in the DT model, only after capital has been accumulated do equity returns fall below their long-run mean. Mean reversion is therefore slow and does not show up as negative correlations in the regressions up to a thirty-quarter lag. Figure 10.7 shows that considering leverage does not alter this basic conclusion. A second aspect of the figures is that the autocorrelation is counterfactually large, reflecting the fact that movements in asset prices are largely driven by movements in expected returns. A drawback of studying equity returns in a model with deterministic trend is that the model necessarily understates the importance of the random walk component of stock prices. Because the economy is ultimately expected to return to its long-run

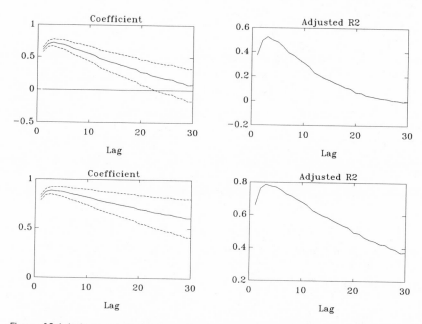

Figure 10.6 Autocorrelation in Long-Horizon Unlevered Equity Returns in DT Model
Top panels show $\sigma_c = 1$; bottom panels show $\sigma_c = 5$. Broken lines show a two standard error band.
Figures 10.6 through 10.15 based on regression results; see accompanying text for methodology.

trend path, there is no uncertainty about the long-run per se. In the DS model
in which technology is a random walk, uncertainty increases with the forecast
horizon. Although the long-run implications of a productivity shock are different
in the DT and DS models, the pattern of autocorrelations is very similar, as illustrated in Figure 10.8. The conclusion is therefore that the model does not support
a U-shaped correlation pattern.

Fama and French (1988b) have discussed the forecast power of dividends for
future. Their explanation centers around what they call the discount rate effect:
the offsetting adjustment of current prices triggered by shocks to discount rates and
expected returns. As just pointed out, this mean reversion is not immediate in the
model. First, productivity surprises cause both the stock price and the expected
return to increase. Consequently, unexpected returns and subsequent expected
returns are not negatively correlated. The neoclassical model, in which uncertainty
stems from supply shocks, does not capture the mechanism suggested by Fama and
French (1988b). Recent work by King (1991) indicates that interest rate dynamics
in a Keynesian model of business cycle fluctuations driven by monetary shocks
might not be fundamentally different from the interest rate dynamics presented
here. This suggests that explanations for mean reversion may have to go beyond
simple explanations based on demand or supply shocks.

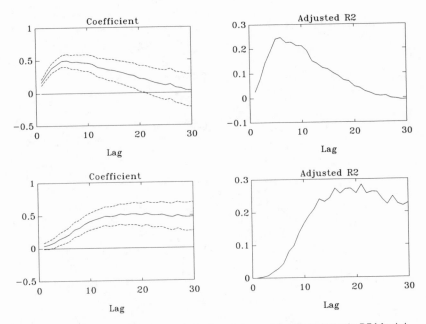

Figure 10.7 Autocorrelation in Long-Horizon Levered Equity Returns in DT Model

Top panels show $\sigma_c = 1$; bottom panels show $\sigma_c = 5$. Broken lines show a two standard error band.

Figures 10.9 and 10.10 show that the sign of the D/P ratio in predicting future returns depends on the level of risk aversion. As discussed previously and illustrated in figures 10.2 and 10.5, risk aversion and shock persistence affect the elasticity of reinvested dividends and therefore the cyclical behavior of the dividend-to-price ratio.

Forecasting Excess Returns

Fama and French (1989) provide evidence that excess returns on bonds and stocks can be forecasted by the D/P ratio, the term spread, and the default spread, the last being the difference between the yield on low-grade bonds versus the yield on high-grade bonds. Moreover, they argue that these forecasting variables have a business cycle interpretation. Fama and French suggest that (1) the term spread proxies for a risk factor that varies in a similar fashion for all bonds and stocks, and (2) the D/P-ratio tracks variation in expected returns that is larger for stocks than bonds. Empirically, the term spread is high when business cycle conditions are poor and low or negative at business cycle peaks. Similarly, the dividend-to-price ratio is high around troughs and low around peaks.

Figures 10.11 through 13 present the ability of these variables to forecast future excess returns in the DS model. Exploring this issue is difficult because average risk premiums are generally small in consumption-based models. To reduce the

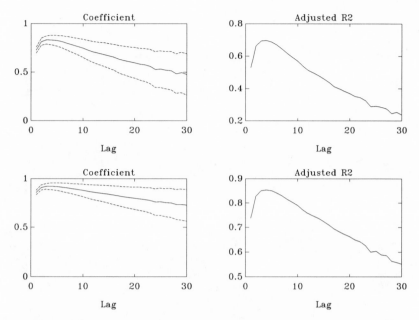

Figure 10.8 Autocorrelation in Long-Horizon Unlevered Equity Returns in DS Model

Top panels show $\sigma_c = 1$; bottom panels show $\sigma_c = 5$. Broken lines show a two standard error band.

potential bias caused by common approximation error in the excess return and the yield spread, excess returns starting at t were forecast by the yield spread at $t - 1$. The figures show that the forecast regressions perform poorly for both bonds and stocks, and do not support the empirical findings of Fama and French. Even over short horizons, the term spread does not predict future excess returns, which is at variance with the empirical evidence. Simulations with the DT model are not reported, but do not change this conclusion.

Financial Leading Indicators

Thus far the chapter has focused on the predictive power of the D/P-ratio and the term spread for future (excess) returns. In a recent paper, Stock and Watson (1988) compare a model of coincident economic indicators to the Index of Coincident Economic Indicators compiled by the U.S. Department of Commerce. This index includes measures of industrial production, personal income, manufacturing and trade sales, and employment. Stock and Watson find that financial prices and yields appear to have greater power to predict growth in the index than do measures of real output, real inputs or prices of foreign or domestic goods. Estrella and Hardouvelis (1991) document the ability of the slope of the term structure to forecast output several years into the future. Within my economy, a natural experiment to conduct is thus to regress output growth over various horizons on the yield on long bonds

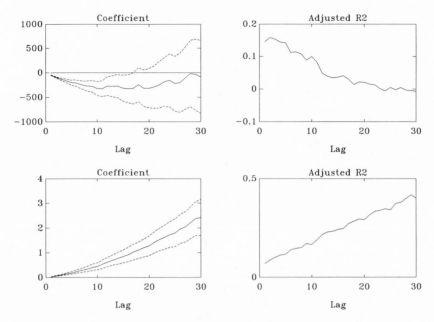

Figure 10.9 Forecasting Long-Horizon Unlevered Equity Returns with D/P Ratio in DT Model

Top panels show $\sigma_c = 1$; bottom panels show $\sigma_c = 5$. Broken lines show a two standard error band.

and the term spread. Figures 10.14 and 10.15 show that the long yield, but not the yield spread, forecasts future real activity.[11] Also, the yield explains a larger fraction of future output growth if the forecast horizon increases. This is not surprising because the yield itself measures expected consumption growth over the remaining life of the bond (five years).

5. Conclusions

This chapter presented a simple intertemporal model of production and consumption. Despite the model's relative success reported in previous literature in describing certain key features of business cycles, its asset pricing implications were often at variance with the stylized facts. Nevertheless the model provided important clues about elements that equilibrium models must incorporate for explaining the behavior of returns over the business cycle.

First, as was already known from earlier work by Mehra and Prescott (1985), the model was unable to replicate the cross-sectional differences in mean returns of bonds and stocks. In a way, it is more difficult to explain substantial risk premiums in a production economy, because consumption choices are endogenously determined and become smoother as risk aversion increases. Second, production

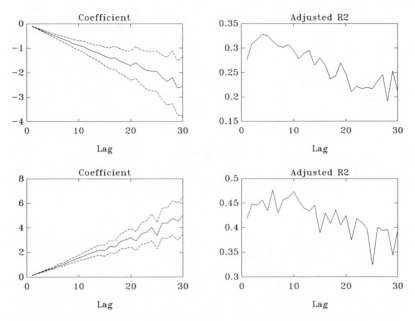

Figure 10.10 Forecasting Long-Horizon Unlevered Equity Returns with D/P Ratio in DS Model

Top panels show $\sigma_c = 1$; bottom panels show $\sigma_c = 5$. Broken lines show a two standard error band.

economies allow for a more natural definition of complex securities, such as equity claims. This chapter studied the effects of operating and financial leverage on risk premiums, but the capital stock (or its value) varies too little to match either the mean or the variance of the return on equity. This, of course, does not disrprove the importance of leverage for explaining risk premiums or cyclical variation in volatility. Movements in relative rates of return were simply too small for the influence of leverage to be significant. For instance, a number of recent studies have explored the avenue of changing preferences (e.g., Constantinides 1990) to explain relative rates of return by increasing the volatility of marginal rates of substitution. The effect on bond premiums, which have historically been quite small, have not yet been explored. Leverage might still be important because it effectively drives a wedge between the risk premium on bonds and stocks. Both findings on consumption smoothing and the low variability of equity returns motivate the study of technologies that allow less substitution in production, for instance by incorporating adjustment costs to drive a wedge between the replacement and the market value of equity capital.

Third, the problem of explaining the unconditional mean returns carries over to some extent into explaining the cyclical behavior of returns and volatility. Because expected returns move in a close lockstep, the role of leverage is small, and cannot

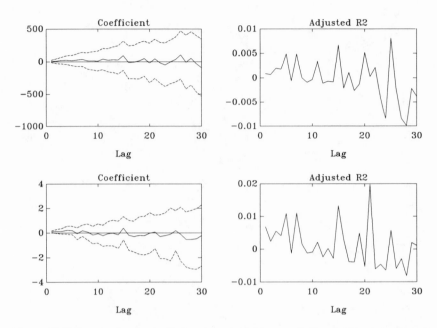

Figure 10.11 Forecasting Long-Horizon Excess Returns on Unlevered Equity with D/P Ratio in DS Model

Top panels show $\sigma_c = 1$; bottom panels show $\sigma_c = 5$. Broken lines show a two standard error band.

account for sharp volatility increases during recessions, as documented by Schwert (1989).

Fourth, the predictions of the model for low-frequency movements in returns were contrary to some empirical evidence that long-horizon returns are negatively autocorrelated. In both models with deterministic trends and those with stochastic trends, shocks induce temporary components in equity prices and mean reversion in returns, but the pattern of autocorrelations was uniformly positive for the variations of the model that were suggested by the data. However, recent work by King (1991) shows that Keynesian models of business cycles are likely to have return dynamics similar to those of the neoclassical model driven by technology shocks. This suggests that explanations for mean reversion in returns have to be found beyond simple models with demand and supply shocks.

Fifth, in the neoclassical model with a single source of uncertainty, expected returns closely follow variations in factor productivity, especially when (variation in) the risk premium is low. Also, the fraction of return variation explained by variation in expected returns is very high; "noise" is virtually absent from the model despite the presence of shocks and leverage effects in operations and financing. Aside from technologies that allow less intertemporal substitution, other model elements, which emphasize higher frequency movements in returns, will have to

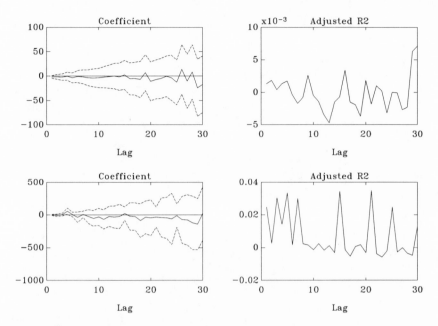

Figure 10.12 Forecasting Long-Horizon Excess Returns on Levered Equity in DS Model with Term Spread

Top panels show $\sigma_c = 1$; bottom panels show $\sigma_c = 5$. Broken lines show a two standard error band.

be incorporated to successfully describe the behavior of financial markets over the business cycle. Richer models with multiple sources of uncertainty or imperfect information might be required to explain the correlations between returns over short and long horizons.

On the basis of its relative success in describing the behavior of output, investment, and consumption over the business cycle, the neoclassical model was a natural first candidate for the study of the behavior of asset returns over the business cycle. Although the neoclassical model with technology shocks often provided an incomplete description of the behavior of returns at business cycle frequencies, its limitations point to important model elements that have to be included to increase our understanding of business cycles. This chapter highlights the role variations in productivity can play in this explanation.

Appendix

This appendix describes the method of constructing the state transition matrices for the shock process $\{z\}_{t=0}^{\infty}$. It is often of interest to compare the discrete approximation to the solution of a dynamic program to the solution obtained from linearizing

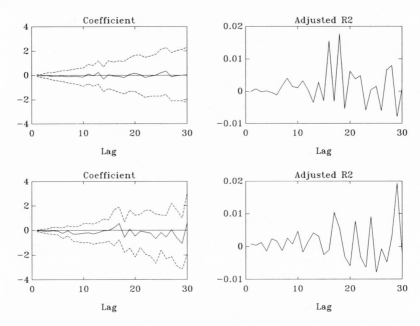

Figure 10.13 Forecasting Long-Horizon Excess Returns on Long-Term Bonds in DS Model with Term Spread

Top panels show $\sigma_c = 1$; bottom panels show $\sigma_c = 5$. Broken lines show a two standard error band.

the first-order conditions of the program. Examples of the latter approach can be found in Kydland and Prescott (1982) and King, Plosser, and Rebelo (1988a). Since the former method requires discretization of the state space, one would like to find a discrete approximation to a continuous distribution. This appendix discusses a family of Markov processes that can be used to approximate an AR(1) process. Under certain conditions, the limiting distribution of this Markov process is a symmetric binomial, which for fine discretizations can approximate a normal distribution arbitrarily closely.

The single parameter does not influence the stationary distribution, but serves to set the first-order serial correlation of the process. The two-state member of this family is

$$
\Pi_2 = \begin{bmatrix} p & (1-p) \\ (1-q) & q \end{bmatrix},
$$

with stationary distribution $\{(1-q)/[(1-p)+(1-q)], (1-p)/[(1-p)+(1-q)]\}$ and first-order serial correlation of $p + q - 1$. The three state member

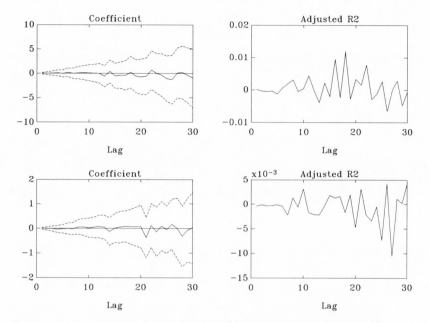

Figure 10.14 Forecasting Economic Growth with Term Spread in DS Model

Top panels show $\sigma_c = 1$; bottom panels show $\sigma_c = 5$. Broken lines show a two standard error band.

is

$$
\Pi_3 = \begin{bmatrix} p^2 & 2p(1-p) & (1-p)^2 \\ p(1-q) & pq + (1-p)(1-q) & q(1-p) \\ (1-q)^2 & 2q(1-q) & q^2 \end{bmatrix},
$$

which also has a first-order serial correlation of $p + q - 1$.

The Π_h case can be derived recursively from Π_{h-1} by applying the following two rules

Rule 1 Add the $(h \times h)$ matrices:

$$
p \begin{bmatrix} \Pi_{h-1} & \mathbf{0} \\ \mathbf{0}' & 0 \end{bmatrix} + (1-p) \begin{bmatrix} \mathbf{0} & \Pi_{h-1} \\ 0 & \mathbf{0}' \end{bmatrix}
$$

$$
+ (1-q) \begin{bmatrix} \mathbf{0}' & 0 \\ \Pi_{h-1} & \mathbf{0} \end{bmatrix} + q \begin{bmatrix} 0 & \mathbf{0}' \\ \mathbf{0} & \Pi_{h-1} \end{bmatrix}, \quad (29)
$$

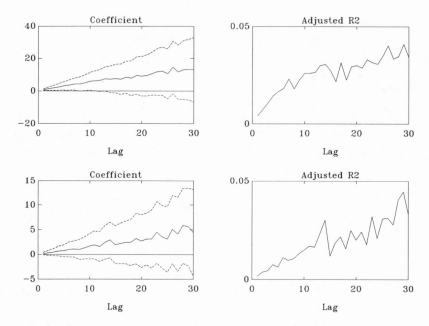

Figure 10.15 Forecasting Economic Growth with Bond Yields in DS Model

Top panels show $\sigma_c = 1$; bottom panels show $\sigma_c = 5$. Broken lines show a two standard error band.

where $\mathbf{0}'$ is a $(h - 1) \times 1$ row vector.

Rule 2   Divide all but the top and bottom rows by two to restore the requirement that the conditional probabilities sum to one.

Recursive application of these rules yields the transition matrix for any number of states, while maintaining the property that the first-order autocorrelation is $p + q - 1$. A special case is $p = q = \pi$, when the transition matrix is symmetric. It can be shown that in this special case the stationary distribution of the Markov process becomes independent of the single parameter π, which governs the first-order autocorrelation of the process: $2\pi - 1$. Assume that the shocks, z, can take on h values, $z_1, z_2, \ldots, z_h$, which are symmetrically and evenly spaced over the interval $\left[-\epsilon, \epsilon\right]$. The stationary probability of being in state z_j is given by

$$Pr(z = z_j) = \frac{\binom{h-1}{j-1}}{2^{h-1}},$$

where the variance of z is

$$\sigma_z^2 = \frac{\epsilon^2}{(h - 1)}.$$

The fourth central moment of z is:

$$\mu_4 = \frac{(3h - 5)\epsilon^4}{(h - 1)^3},$$

so that the kurtosis of the distribution is given by

$$\frac{\mu_4}{\sigma_z^4} = 3 - \frac{2}{(h - 1)}.$$

As $h \to \infty$, the kurtosis becomes 3. Therefore, for large h and choosing $\epsilon = \sqrt{(h - 1)}$, it is possible to obtain an arbitrarily close approximation to a standard normal distribution for the shocks, with autocorrelation $2\pi - 1$.

Notes

I thank Robert King, Charles Plosser, John Long, Jay Shanken, Marianne Baxter, John Campbell, Steven Cechetti, Tom Cooley, Mario Crucini, and Sergio Rebelo for helpful comments. Any errors are mine of course. Earlier versions of this chapter have circulated under the title *Asset Returns and Business Cycles: A General Equilibrium Approach*. This appendix draws heavily on joint work with Sergio Rebelo.

1. Examples of papers that do explore asset pricing include the studies of Chapman (1992), Cochrane (1991), Den Haan (1991), Donaldson, Johnson, and Mehra (1990), Marshall (1992), and Sharathchandra (1989).

2. Chapter 3, by Danthine and Donaldson, provides an overview of these methods. See Marshall (1992), Den Haan (1991), and Chapman (1992) for the term structure in production economies with money. Danthine and Donaldson (1986) discuss asset pricing in an exchange economy with money.

3. The arguments in this section closely follow Brock (1982).

4. The data used for the calibration were kindly provided by Larry Christiano and described in Christiano (1988).

5. Experimentation with specifications in which $p < q$ showed that conditional heteroskedasticity of the shocks will generally be translated into heteroskedastic asset returns. It is an empirical issue as to whether the shocks are indeed conditionally heteroskedastic. I applied Hamilton's (1989) regime-switching regression algorithm to the (detrended) Solow residuals computed from the data and found no evidence of conditional heteroskedasticity. Also, I thank Tim Bollerslev who spent some time estimating a GARCH model for the Solow residuals but found no evidence of time-varying volatility in the residuals. Choosing the distribution of shocks to be symmetric, helps to answer the question of whether the model contains propagation mechanisms to translate homoskedastic shock into heteroskedastic impulse responses.

6. During the postwar period, the average duration of a recession defined by the NBER was 4.6 quarters, and the average expansion was 14.3 quarters (Neftci 1984; Hamilton 1989). If the NBER dates recessions by a decline of output and output has an upward trend, recessions will be shorter than expansions even if the distribution of the shocks is symmetric. Therefore recessions in the model will, on average, also be shorter than expansions.

7. This assumption was made for computational simplicity: simultaneously searching for the optimal choices for h and k, increases the dimensionality of the problem considerably. Although labor supply is held fixed, the presence of labor still influences asset payoffs through operating leverage.

8. For a good survey of value function iteration and alternative numerical solution techniques, see Taylor and Uhlig (1990).

9. It should be pointed out, of course, that the claims studied in Mehra and Prescott (1985) and in this chapter do not exactly correspond to these empirical counterparts. For instance, a Treasury bill is not riskless in real terms because inflation is stochastic, and thus cannot directly be compared to a claim that pays off one unit of consumption with certainty. Incorporating money into general equilibrium models is a difficult problem, and no consensus has been reached about a satisfactory solution. An interesting problem is perhaps to turn the question around and ask what restrictions are required on the stochastic process for inflation to improve the model's match of the data. Also, valuing the risky bond in this model includes valuing a put option on the "index," which is different from the portfolio of puts required to value the aggregate value of all corporate bonds.

10. The number of replications was chosen to illustrate the basic workings of the model, rather than to try to replicate the sample moments reported by Fama and French (1988a, 1988b).

11. In empirical work the yield spread is more often used in forecasting regressions because it has the properties of an excess return and is therefore less sensitive to variations in expected inflation.

Chapter 11
International Business Cycles: Theory and Evidence

David K. Backus, Patrick J.
Kehoe, and Finn E. Kydland

1. Introduction

In modern developed economies, goods and assets are traded across national borders, with the result that events in one country generally have economic repercussions in others. International business cycle research focuses on the economic connections among countries and on the impact these connections have on the transmission of aggregate fluctuations. In academic studies this focus is expressed in terms of the volatility and comovements of international time series data. Examples include the volatility of fluctuations in the balance of trade, the correlation of the trade balance with output, the correlation of output and consumption across countries, and the volatility of prices of foreign and domestic goods.

We consider international business cycles from the perspective of dynamic general equilibrium theory, an approach adopted in a large and growing number of studies in international macroeconomics. In closed-economy studies, models of this kind have been able to account for a large fraction of the variability of aggregate output and for the relative variability of investment and consumption. See, for example, Prescott's (1986) review. In public finance, similar models have been used to assess the impact of fiscal policy on aggregate output, employment, and saving. Auerbach and Kotlikoff (1987) are a prominent example. In international macroeconomics, this approach has been used to account for some of the notable features of international data: the time series correlation of saving and investment rates (Baxter and Crucini 1993; Cardia 1991; and Finn 1990), the countercyclical movements of the trade balance (Backus, Kehoe, and Kydland 1994; Glick and Rogoff 1992; and Mendoza 1991), and the relation between the trade balance and the terms of trade (Backus, Kehoe, and Kydland 1994; Macklem 1993; and Smith 1993).

These efforts illustrate the insights dynamic theory has contributed to date, and is likely to contribute in the future. In our view, however, the most important aspects of this line of work for future research are those for which the theory remains significantly different from the data. These discrepancies between theory and data provide focus for future theoretical work in this area.

For this reason, we focus on two striking discrepancies between current theory and data. The first concerns the relations between business cycles across countries. In the data, correlations of output across countries are larger than analogous correlations for consumption and productivity. In theoretical economies, consumption and productivity correlations are larger than output correlations. The second discrepancy concerns the terms of trade, which we define as the relative price of imports to exports. Fluctuations in the terms of trade are much more variable in the data than in theoretical economies.

We examine cross-country comovements of aggregate quantities, including output and consumption, in the natural extension of Kydland and Prescott's (1982) closed-economy model to an international setting. In this extension, agents in the two countries produce and trade a single good. Fluctuations are driven by exogenous movements in productivity. Although the theory mimics some features of the data, the international comovements are much different from those in the data. Using parameters for the stochastic process for productivity shocks that we estimate from data for the United States and a European aggregate, we find that productivity is positively correlated across countries. In the model, however, shocks of this form give rise to output fluctuations that are less highly correlated than consumption and productivity fluctuations. The ranking of output, consumption, and productivity correlations is extremely robust: it survives large changes in a number of the model's parameters. Since these differences between theory and data are relatively insensitive to the choice of parameter values and even the model's structure, we term them collectively the consumption/output/productivity anomaly, or simply the quantity anomaly.

To examine fluctuations in relative prices, we extend the theoretical model to allow the outputs of the two countries to be imperfect substitutes. This extension allows the relative price of the two goods to differ from one. In the data, fluctuations in the terms of trade in the industrialized world have been very persistent and highly variable. These properties, and similar properties of the real exchange rate, are perhaps the most widely studied issues in international macroeconomics. We find that the model generates fluctuations in the terms of trade as persistent as they are in the data. The variability of the terms of trade, however, is generally much less in the model than in the data. We call this discrepancy the price-variability anomaly. If we lower the substitutability of foreign and domestic goods, we can increase the variability of the terms of trade, but this comes at the expense of reducing the variability of imported and exported goods far below what we see in the data.

The two anomalies concerning the behavior of international business cycles and relative prices pose a challenge for international business cycle research. With them in mind, we review a rapidly expanding body of work aimed at these and other issues and speculate on directions future work might take. Notable extensions of the theory include nontraded goods, incomplete markets, money, and imperfectly competitive firms. We argue that none of these extensions has yet to provide a persuasive resolution of the price and quantity anomalies.

2. Properties of International Business Cycles

We begin by reviewing some of the salient properties of international business cycles. These features of the data serve as a basis of comparison with theoretical economies. These properties, and others reported later, refer to moments of Hodrick-Prescott–filtered variables.[1] Our data are from the OECD's *Quarterly National Accounts* and *Main Economic Indicators* and the IMF's *International Financial Statistics*.

Table 11.1 shows a number of properties of business cycle experience since 1970 in ten developed countries and a European aggregate constructed by the OECD. We focus on volatility, measured by standard deviations; persistence, measured by autocorrelations; and comovement, measured by correlations, for a set of common macroeconomic time series. With respect to volatility, we find that while consumption has generally had about the same standard deviation, in percentage terms, as output, investment in fixed capital has been two to three times more volatile than output, and employment has been somewhat less volatile than output. There are, however, some differences across countries in the magnitudes. The standard deviation of output fluctuations ranges from a low of 0.90 percent in France to a high of 1.92 percent in the United States. We also find some differences in consumption volatility. The standard deviation of consumption, relative to that of output, is 0.75 in the United States, 1.09 in Japan, 1.14 in Austria, and 1.15 in the United Kingdom. The numbers are larger than those generally reported in studies of the United States, partly because consumption in this data set includes expenditures on consumer durables. If we exclude durables, which we can do for only five countries, the volatility ratios fall from 0.75 to 0.52 for the United States, from 0.85 to 0.59 for Canada, from 0.99 to 0.77 for France, from 0.78 to 0.61 for Italy, and from 1.15 to 0.96 for the United Kingdom. Some of these differences almost certainly reflect differences in the procedures used to construct aggregate data, but more work is needed before we can quantify the impact of disparities of measurement. In terms of persistence we see that in all countries the autocorrelation of output is high. It ranges from 0.57 for Austria to 0.90 for Switzerland.

There has been even greater variation in the volatility of employment (civilian employment from the OECD's *Main Economic Indicators*): the ratio of the standard deviation of employment to that of output ranges from 0.34 in Australia to 0.86 in Canada to 1.23 in Austria. At least some of this disparity appears to reflect international differences in labor market experience. Blackburn and Ravn (1992) and Burdett and Wright (1989) both note that fluctuations in total hours worked in the United States are largely the result of movements in employment, while in the United Kingdom changes in hours per worker are more important. We note

Table 11.1
Properties of Business Cycles in OECD Economies

Country	Standard Deviation (%)		Ratio of Standard Deviation to That of y					Autocorr.	Correlation with Output					
	y	nx	c	x	g	n	z	y	c	x	g	nx	n	z
Australia	1.45	1.23	0.66	2.78	1.28	0.34	1.00	.60	.46	.67	.15	−.01	.12	.98
Austria	1.28	1.15	1.14	2.92	0.36	1.23	0.84	.57	.65	.75	−.24	−.46	.58	.65
Canada	1.50	0.78	0.85	2.80	0.77	0.86	0.74	.79	.83	.52	−.23	−.26	.69	.84
France	0.90	0.82	0.99	2.96	0.71	0.55	0.76	.78	.61	.79	.25	−.30	.77	.96
Germany	1.51	0.79	0.90	2.93	0.81	0.61	0.83	.65	.66	.84	.26	−.11	.59	.93
italy	1.69	1.33	0.78	1.95	0.42	0.44	0.92	.85	.82	.86	.01	−.68	.42	.96
japan	1.35	0.93	1.09	2.41	0.79	0.36	0.88	.80	.80	.90	−.02	−.22	.60	.98
Switzerland	1.92	1.32	0.74	2.30	0.53	0.71	0.67	.90	.81	.82	.27	−.68	.84	.93
United Kingdom	1.61	1.19	1.15	2.29	0.69	0.68	0.88	.63	.74	.59	.05	−.19	.47	.90
United States	1.92	0.52	0.75	3.27	0.75	0.61	0.68	.86	.82	.94	.12	−.37	.88	.96
Europe	1.01	0.50	0.83	2.09	0.47	0.85	0.98	.75	.81	.89	.10	−.25	.32	.85

Notes: Statistics are based on Hodrick-Prescott–filtered data. Variables are y, real output; c, real consumption; x, real fixed investment; g real government purchases; nx, ratio of net exports to output, both at current prices; n, civilian employment; z, Solow residual, defined in text. Except for the ratio of net exports to output, statistics refer to logarithms of variables. Data are quarterly from the OECD's *Quarterly National Accounts*, except employment, which is from the OECD's *Main Economic Indicators*. The sample period is 1970:I to 1990:II.

that employment has been procyclical in all ten countries, but the magnitude of the correlation with output varies substantially across countries.

The last variable in Table 11.1 is the Solow residual, z, which we refer to as productivity. The Solow residual is defined implicitly in the Cobb-Douglas production function,

$$y = zk^\theta n^{1-\theta},$$

where y is real output, k is the stock of physical capital, and n is employment. This allows us to compute the Solow residual in logarithms by

$$\log z = \log y - [\theta \log k + (1 - \theta) \log n].$$

We set the parameter θ equal to 0.36, as explained in the next section. Since comparable capital stock data are not available on a quarterly basis, we omit the capital part of the expression. This is probably not a serious problem, since the capital stock contributes very little to the cyclical fluctuations of output (see, e.g., Kydland and Prescott 1982, tab. IV). Productivity, by this measure, is strongly procyclical. Its volatility is generally less than that of output.

Two exceptions to this tendency for aggregate variables to move procyclically are government purchases and net exports. Government purchases are procyclical in seven countries and countercyclical in three, but the correlations are small in all cases. The ratio of net exports to output, on the other hand, has been countercyclical in all ten countries, although both its standard deviation and its correlation with output vary substantially across countries.

In Table 11.2 we report statistics with more of an international flavor. In the first column we list the correlation of output fluctuations between each country and the United States. These vary in magnitude but are all positive. The largest is 0.76 for Canada. The correlations for Japan and the major European countries lie between 0.4 and 0.7. Table 11.2 also includes correlations of consumption, investment, government purchases, employment, and Solow residuals across countries. With respect to consumption, we find that the correlations are smaller than those of output for every country, but the difference is large only for Australia. The consumption correlation between the United States and the European aggregate, for example, is 0.51, while the output correlation is 0.66. The correlations of investment, employment, and productivity are also positive in most cases. We find that Solow residuals are generally less highly correlated across countries than output. In our data the differences are generally small. Finally, the cross-country correlations of government purchases vary in sign but are generally small.

We summarize briefly. Despite some heterogeneity in international business cycle experience across the major industrialized countries over the last twenty years, most of the regularities emphasized in Kydland and Prescott's (1982) closed-economy study stand up. More interesting from our point of view are statistics that capture comovements across countries. One is of particular interest to us: the correlations of output across countries are larger than those of consumption and

Table 11.2
International Comovements in OECD Economies

| Country | \multicolumn{6}{c}{Correlation of Each Country's Variable with Same U.S. Variable} |
	y	c	x	g	n	z
Australia	.51	−.19	.16	.23	−.18	.52
Austria	.38	.23	.46	.29	.47	.17
Canada	.76	.49	−.01	−.01	.53	.75
France	.41	.39	.22	−.20	.26	.39
Germany	.69	.49	.55	.28	.52	.65
Italy	.41	.02	.31	.09	−.01	.35
Japan	.60	.44	.56	.11	.32	.58
Switzerland	.42	.40	.38	.01	.36	.43
United Kingdom	.55	.42	.40	−.04	.69	.35
Europe	.66	.51	.53	.18	.33	.56

Notes: See Table 11.1.

productivity. The question for the next section is how these properties compare to those of a theoretical world economy.

3. A Theoretical Business Cycle Model

In our first theoretical economy, agents in two countries produce a single homogeneous good. The structure is a streamlined version of the model of Backus, Kehoe, and Kydland (1992) in which we have eliminated inventory accumulation and leisure durability, which in turn is a two-country extension of Kydland and Prescott's (1982) closed-economy real business cycle model.

In this economy each country is represented by a single agent. The preferences of the representative consumer in country i, for $i = 1, 2$, are characterized by an expected utility function of the form

$$u_i = E_0 \sum_{t=0}^{\infty} \beta^t U(c_{it}, 1 - n_{it}),$$

where c_{it} and n_{it} are consumption and employment in country i and $U(c, 1-n) = [c^\mu (1 - n)^{1-\mu}]^{1-\gamma}/(1 - \gamma)$.

Production of the good takes place in each country using inputs of capital, k, and domestic labor, n, and is influenced by the technology shocks, z. Output, or

GDP, in country i is

$$y_{it} = z_{it} F(k_{it}, n_{it}),$$

where $F(k, n) = k^\theta n^{1-\theta}$, the same relation we used to construct Solow residuals in the last section. Since the two countries produce the same good, the world resource constraint for the good is

$$\sum_i (c_{it} + x_{it} + g_{it}) = \sum_i z_{it} F(k_{it}, n_{it}),$$

where x_{it} is the amount of the good allocated to fixed capital formation and g_{it} is government purchases, both for country i. The trade balance, or net exports, in country i is then $nx_{it} = y_{it} - (c_{it} + x_{it} + g_{it})$, the difference between goods produced and goods used.

Capital formation incorporates the time-to-build structure emphasized by Kydland and Prescott (1982). Additions to the stock of fixed capital require inputs of the produced good for J periods, or

$$k_{it+1} = (1 - \delta)k_{it} + s_{it}^1,$$

and

$$s_{it+1}^j = s_{it}^1, \quad \text{for } j = 1, \ldots, J - 1,$$

where δ is the depreciation rate and s_{it}^j is the number of investment projects in country i at date t that are j periods from completion. We denote by ϕ_j, for $j = 1, \ldots, J$, the fraction of value added to an investment project in the jth period before completion. We set $\phi_j = 1/J$, so that an investment project adding one unit to the capital stock at date $t + 1$ requires expenditures of $1/J$ for the J periods prior to $t + 1$. Fixed investment at date t is

$$x_{it} = \sum_{j=1}^{J} \phi_j s_{it}^j,$$

the sum of investment expenditures on all existing projects.

The vectors $z_t = (z_{1t}, z_{2t})$ and $g_t = (g_{1t}, g_{2t})$ are stochastic shocks to productivity and government purchases, respectively, which we model as independent bivariate autoregressions. The technology shocks follow

$$z_{t+1} = Az_t + \epsilon_{t+1}^z,$$

where $\epsilon^z = (\epsilon_1^z, \epsilon_2^z)$ is distributed normally and independently over time with variance V_z. The correlation between the technology shocks, z_1 and z_2, is determined by the off-diagonal elements of A and V_z. Similarly, shocks to government purchases follow

$$g_{t+1} = Bg_t + \epsilon_{t+1}^g,$$

where $\epsilon^g = (\epsilon_1^g, \epsilon_2^g)$ is distributed normally with variance V_g. Technology shocks, z, and government spending shocks, g, are independent.

It is straightforward, but notationally burdensome, to define a competitive equilibrium for this economy with complete contingent claims markets. In it consumers use these contingent claims markets to diversify country-specific risk across states of nature. By so doing, consumers end up equating the marginal utility of consumption across countries. Such an equilibrium is, of course, Pareto optimal and we can characterize the equilibrium allocations by exploiting this feature. We compute, in particular, the equilibrium associated with the optimum problem: maximize $u_1 + u_2$ subject to the technology and the resource constraint. In this optimum problem the marginal utility of consumption is also equated across countries for each state of nature, and thus country-specific risk is optimally diversified. We approximate this problem with one that has a quadratic objective function and linear constraints. Details of this procedure are described in Backus, Kehoe, and Kydland (1992, sec. II).

Quantitative properties of this theoretical economy depend to a large extent on the values of the model's parameters. Our benchmark parameter values for this economy are listed in Table 11.3. With the exception of the parameters of the shocks to productivity and government spending, they are taken from Kydland and Prescott's (1982) closed-economy study. The parameters of the technology process are based on Solow residuals for the United States and an aggregate of European countries, as described in our earlier paper (Backus, Kehoe, and Kydland 1992, sec. III). They imply that the productivity shocks are persistent and positively correlated across countries. For the time being, we set $g_t = 0$, thereby eliminating government purchases from the model.

Table 11.3
Benchmark Parameter Values

Preferences	Discount factor, $\beta = 0.99$
	Consumption share, $\mu = 0.34$
	Curvature parameter, $\gamma = 2.0$
Technology	Capital share, $\theta = 0.36$
	Depreciation rate, $\delta = 0.025$
	Time-to-build, $J = 4$
Forcing Processes	Technology shocks, $A = \begin{bmatrix} a_{11} & a_{12} \\ a_{12} & a_{11} \end{bmatrix} = \begin{bmatrix} 0.906 & 0.088 \\ 0.088 & 0.906 \end{bmatrix}$
	var $\epsilon_1^z =$ var $\epsilon_2^z = 0.00852^2$,
	corr$(\epsilon_1^z, \epsilon_2^z) = 0.258$
	Government spending, $g_t = 0$

Table 11.4
Business Cycles in Theoretical Economies

A. Business Cycle Properties

Economy	Standard Deviation (%)		Ratio of Standard Deviation to That of y				Autocorr.	Correlation with Output				
	y	nx	c	x	n	z	y	c	x	nx	n	z
U.S. data	1.92	0.52	.75	3.27	.61	.68	.86	.82	.94	−.37	.88	.96
Benchmark	1.50	3.77	.42	10.99	.50	.67	.62	.77	.27	.01	.93	.89
Transport cost	1.35	0.37	.47	2.91	.47	.75	.61	.81	.92	.23	.92	.98
Autarky	1.26		.54	2.65	.91	.99	.62	.90	.96		.91	.99

B. International Comovements

	Correlation of Foreign and Domestic Variables				
Economy	y	c	x	n	z
U.S. data	.66	.51	.53	.33	.56
Benchmark	−.21	.88	−.94	−.94	.25
Transport cost	−.05	.89	−.48	−.48	.25
Autarky	.08	.56	−.31	−.31	.25

Notes: Statistics are based on Hodrick-Prescott–filtered data. Variables are defined in notes to Table 11.1. Entries are averages over twenty simulations of length 100. The data column refers to the United States in part A and to correlation between the United States and Europe in part B.

Properties of this theoretical world economy are reported in Table 11.4. The entries are means of various statistics across 20 stochastic simulations of the economy, each for 100 periods. As with the data, the statistics refer to Hodrick-Prescott–filtered variables.

We find, first, that the variability of output in this economy is somewhat less than we see in U.S. data, but larger than that of Europe in aggregate, as well as the component European countries. The differences between theory and data in this respect are not large compared to the differences among countries. The behavior of some of the output components, however, differs substantially from the data. The variability of consumption relative to output is smaller in the model economy than in U.S. data when durables are included (0.40 versus 0.75). Since the model disregards durability, a comparison with the volatility of U.S. nondurables consumption may be more appropriate. In this case most of the discrepancy disappears (the volatility of U.S. nondurables consumption is 0.52). Investment, on the other hand, is more than three times more variable relative to output than we see in U.S. data (10.99 versus 3.28). The standard deviation of net exports is about seven times larger than in U.S. data and much larger than for any country in Table 11.1. The net exports component is essentially uncorrelated with output (with a contemporaneous correlation of 0.01), and not countercyclical as it is in the countries in Table 11.1.

We can get some intuition for these properties of the model by examining the dynamic responses pictured in Figures 11.1 and 11.2. These figures illustrate the responses in the benchmark economy to a one-time increase of one standard deviation in the home country's technology innovation, ϵ_1, starting from the steady state. In these figures, productivity is measured as a percentage of its steady-state value; the remaining variables are measured as percentages of steady-state output. Figure 11.1 shows what happens in the home country. There, the technology innovation is followed by a rise in productivity, which subsequently slowly decays. The increase in productivity is associated with increases in domestic investment, consumption, and output. The movement in investment is by far the largest, and it leads to a deficit in net exports.

In Figure 11.2, we see that the innovation to domestic productivity leads eventually, through the technology spillover, to a rise in foreign productivity. Despite this, foreign output and investment both fall initially. Roughly speaking, resources are shifted to the more productive location, the home country. This happens both with capital, as investment rises in the home country and falls abroad, and with labor, which follows a similar pattern. This tendency to "make hay where the sun shines" means that with uncorrelated productivity shocks, consumption will be positively correlated across countries while investment, employment, and output will be negatively correlated. With productivity shocks that are positively correlated, as they are in our model, all of these correlations rise, but with the benchmark parameter values none change sign. This helps to explain why the correlations of foreign and domestic output, employment, and investment

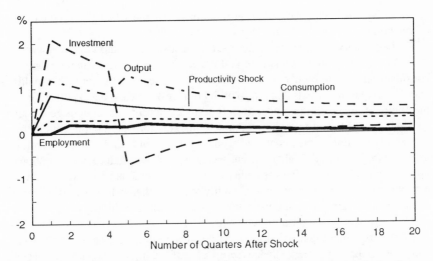

Figure 11.1 Effects of a Productivity Shock in the Benchmark Model on the Home Country

Figures 11.1 and 11.2 show percentage changes after a one-standard-deviation innovation in the home country's productivity shock. Change in productivity shock is measured as percentage of its steady-state value; change in other variables is measured as percentage of steady-state value of output.

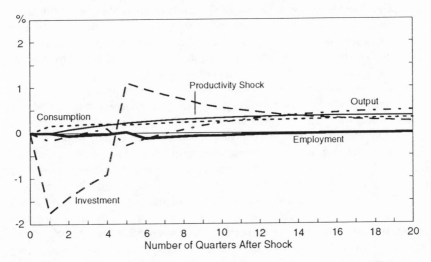

Figure 11.2 Effects of a Productivity Shock in the Benchmark Model on the Foreign Country

are negative, and why the output correlation is smaller than the productivity correlation.

The benchmark economy, then, differs from postwar international data in several respects. In the model, investment and net exports are more variable, whereas consumption is more highly correlated across countries, and output is less highly correlated. Our intuition is that the volatility of investment and net exports reflects the ability of agents in the model to shift perfectly substitutable goods costlessly between countries and to trade in complete markets for state-contingent claims. The ability to shift resources allows agents to shift capital and production effort to the country with the higher current technology shock; that movement shows up in the model as excessive variability of investment and negative correlation of output across countries. Consumers' ability to insure themselves against adverse movements in their own technology shocks suggests that the shifting of production will not be reflected in consumption plans.

We therefore investigate frictions in the physical trading process and the market structure. In the experiment labeled *transport cost*, we impose a quadratic cost on goods shipped between countries. The average cost, in equilibrium, is less than 1 percent, so that if one unit of the good is exported from country 1, more than 0.99 units arrive in country 2. As we see in Table 11.4, this cost reduces the variability of net exports substantially: the standard deviation of the ratio of net exports to output falls from 3.77 percent in the benchmark economy to 0.87 percent with transport costs. The transport cost also lowers the standard deviation of investment relative to output by a factor of almost four, from 10.99 to 2.91. Output's correlation across countries rises from -0.21 to -0.05, while consumption's correlation rises from slightly, from 0.88 to 0.89. In short, this type of friction greatly reduces the variability of net exports and investment but has little effect on the difference between the cross-country correlations of output and consumption.

In our next modification of the theory, we consider limitations on agents' ability to share risk across countries. With complete markets, we know that if preferences are additively separable between consumption and leisure, as they would be if we set $\gamma = 1$, then the ability of agents to trade in markets for contingent claims leads to a perfect correlation across countries. The nonseparability lowers this correlation, in our benchmark economy, to 0.88, which is far larger than we saw in Table 11.2. Here, we consider an extreme experiment, labeled *autarky*, in which we eliminate from the model all trade in goods and assets. The only connection between countries in this case is the correlation between technology shocks. We see in Table 11.4 that this reduces the consumption correlation to 0.56, which is only slightly larger than the correlation of 0.51 between the U.S. and Europe. Output, on the other hand, remains much less highly correlated than it is in the data. Even in this extreme experiment, the difference between theory and data is considerable. Our intuition for the large consumption correlation in the benchmark economy was that it reflected agents' ability to share risk internationally. Under autarky, risk sharing is prohibited, yet we still see a positive correlation. This correlation seems to reflect, instead, the operation of the permanent income hypothesis. The foreign agent knows that a rise in productivity in the home country will spill over to the foreign country and raise the foreign agent's own future productivity and income. In anticipation of this, the foreign agent chooses to increase consumption immediately and postpone some investment.

One way to increase the correlation between foreign and domestic output is to make the productivity shocks more highly correlated. In the benchmark economy, the correlation of productivity shocks is 0.23. If we vary the correlation of innovations we can make this correlation as large or as small as we like. In Figure 11.3 we graph the correlations of consumption, output, and productivity for different values of corr(ϵ_1^z, ϵ_2^z). We see that as we increase the correlation of the productivity innovations, we raise the correlation of productivity shocks, as well as the correlations of consumption and output. For different values of the correlation of the productivity innovation, the model can replicate either the consumption correlation in the data or the output correlation, but not the two together. In this sense, the discrepancy between theory and data is the relative size of the consumption and output correlations, rather than either one separately. We refer to these differences between cross-country correlations as the consumption/output/productivity anomaly, or the quantity anomaly.[2]

In short, the theoretical economy generates fluctuations that differ sharply in some respects from what we see in the data. The most interesting differences, we think, concern correlations across countries. In contrast to the data, the theory generally produces output fluctuations that are less highly correlated across countries than those of consumption and productivity. We return to this issue later

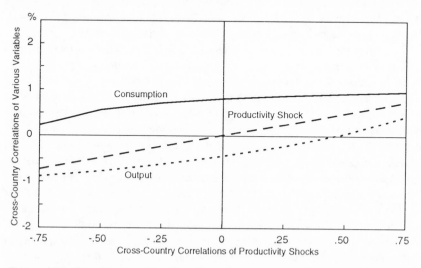

Figure 11.3 How Changes in Cross-Country Correlation of Productivity Shocks Change Cross-Country Correlations of Quantity Variables in the Benchmark Model

in the context of a theoretical economy in which foreign and domestic output are imperfect substitutes. For now we note that these properties are not unique to international economies: similar features should hold in multisector models of closed economies. The tendency for output fluctuations to be less highly correlated than productivity fluctuations, for example, should be more pronounced in a closed-economy where labor is mobile across sectors, yet we know that sectoral outputs are strongly correlated in the data. Similarly, consumption fluctuations should be strongly correlated across regions or individuals. Atkeson and Bayoumi (1991), Crucini (1992), and van Wincoop (1992b) are among those who compare related theories to data for regions within countries. Their work suggests that the one-sector methodology has also masked some interesting features of closed-economy business cycle behavior.

4. Properties of International Relative Prices

We turn now to the behavior of international relative prices, which has been one of the leading issues in international macroeconomics since the collapse of the Bretton Woods system of fixed exchange rates. The terms of trade, labeled p, is the ratio of the implicit price deflators for imports and exports—the relative price of imported goods. This definition is the inverse of the definition used by trade theorists, but corresponds to the convention applied in international macroeconomics to the real exchange rate. The deflators are from the OECD's *Quarterly National Accounts*. The exchange rate, denoted e, is the trade-weighted domestic currency price of one unit of foreign currency: the MERM effective exchange rate in the IMF's *International Financial Statistics*. As in Section 2, we measure the trade balance, labeled nx, as the ratio of net exports to output, with both measured in current prices as reported in the national income and product accounts. Real output, as before, is labeled y. Statistics for p, e, and y refer to logarithms.

We note in Table 11.5 a number of regularities in the behavior of the terms of trade. First, the terms of trade has been highly variable. The standard deviations vary somewhat, but are always greater than those of output (Table 11.1), sometimes by a factor of two or three. A second regularity is the persistence of relative price movements: the terms of trade is highly persistent, with an autocorrelation in the neighborhood of 0.8 for most countries. Finally, we find that the contemporaneous correlation between the terms of trade and net exports is negative in most countries. In France, Italy, Japan, Switzerland, and the United Kingdom the correlations are less than -0.4. The United States is the only country in our table for which these two variables have a sizable positive contemporaneous correlation.

In short, we find a number of regularities in the behavior of net exports and the terms of trade for eleven OECD countries. Prominent among them are the large standard deviations of international relative prices and the high degree of persistence of these variables.

Table 11.5
Properties of the Terms of Trade in OECD Economies

			Correlation of:	
	SD	$Autocorr.$		
Country	$p(\%)$	p	(p, nx)	(p, y)
Australia	5.78	.82	$-.10$	$-.27$
Austria	1.73	.46	$-.24$	.04
Canada	2.99	.85	.05	$-.05$
France	3.52	.75	$-.50$	$-.13$
Germany	2.66	.85	$-.08$	$-.11$
Italy	3.50	.78	$-.66$	.38
Japan	7.24	.86	$-.56$	$-.22$
Switzerland	2.85	.88	$-.61$	.41
United Kingdom	3.14	.80	$-.58$	.09
Europe	3.68	.83	.30	$-.20$

Notes: Statistics are based on Hodrick-Prescott–filtered data. Variables are p, terms of trade, relative price of imports to exports; y, real output; nx, ratio of net exports to output, both at current prices. Except for the ratio of net exports to output, statistics refer to logarithms of variables. Most variables are from the OECD's *Quarterly National Accounts*. The sample period is 1970:I to 1990:II.

5. Relative Prices in a Theoretical World Economy

A theory of relative price movements of foreign and domestic goods requires, obviously, that they be different commodities. Accordingly, we modify the economy of Section 3 so that the two countries produce different, imperfectly substitutable goods. As in Section 3, the preferences of the representative agent in each country i are characterized by an expected utility function of the form

$$u_i = E_0 \sum_{t=0}^{\infty} \beta^t U(c_{it}, 1 - n_{it}),$$

where c_{it} and n_{it} are consumption and hours worked in country i and

$$U(c, 1 - n) = [c^{\mu}(1 - n)^{1-\mu}]^{1-\gamma}/(1 - \gamma).$$

The technology changes as follows. Each country specializes in the production of a single good, labeled a for country 1 and b for country 2. Each good is produced using capital, k, and labor, n, with linear homogeneous production functions of the same form. This gives rise to the resource constraints,

$$a_{1t} + a_{2t} = y_{1t} = z_{1t} F(k_{1t}, n_{1t}),$$

and

$$b_{1t} + b_{2t} = y_{2t} = z_{2t} F(k_{2t}, n_{2t}),$$

in countries 1 and 2, respectively, where $F(k, n) = k^\theta n^{1-\theta}$. The quantity y_{it} denotes GDP in country i, measured in units of the local good, and a_{it} and b_{it} denote uses of the two goods in country i.

Consumption, investment, and government spending in each country are composites of the foreign and domestic goods, with

$$c_{1t} + x_{1t} + g_{1t} = G(a_{1t}, b_{1t}),$$

and

$$c_{2t} + x_{2t} + g_{2t} = G(b_{2t}, a_{2t}),$$

where $G(a, b) = [\omega a^{1-\alpha} + b^{1-\alpha}]^{1/(1-\alpha)}$. The parameters α and ω are both positive, and the elasticity of substitution between foreign and domestic goods is $\sigma = 1/\alpha$. This method of treating foreign and domestic goods, widely used in computable static general equilibrium trade models, is due to Armington (1969) and the resulting function, G, is called the Armington aggregator.

We simplify the capital formation process by setting the time-to-build parameter, J, equal to one. The capital stocks then evolve according to

$$k_{it+1} = (1 - \delta)k_{it} + x_{it},$$

where δ is the depreciation rate.

To develop some intuition for this economy think of good a as aluminum and good b as bricks. Thus, country 1 specializes in making aluminum using capital and domestic labor, while country 2 specializes in making bricks using capital and domestic labor. Country 1 keeps a_1 units of aluminum for domestic use and exports the rest, namely a_2. It then imports b_1 units of bricks from country 2 and combines the bricks and aluminum to make $G(a_1, b_1)$ units of country 1 goods. One can think of G as a function that simply transforms the aluminum and bricks into a country-1–specific good, which is then used for consumption, investment, and government spending in country 1. Likewise, country 2 imports a_2 units of aluminum from country 1 and combines them with b_2 units of bricks, which it produced to make $G(b_2, a_2)$ units of country-2–specific goods. These goods are used for consumption, investment, and government spending in country 2.

As before, we compute equilibrium quantities by finding an optimal allocation. If q_{1t} and q_{2t} are the prices of the domestic and foreign goods, respectively, then the terms of trade is $p_t = q_{2t}/q_{1t}$. In equilibrium, this relative price can be computed from the marginal rate of substitution in the Armington aggregator,

$$p_t = q_{2t}/q_{1t} = \{\partial G(a_{1t}, b_{1t})/\partial b_{1t}\}/\{\partial G(a_{1t}, b_{1t})/\partial a_{1t}\}$$
$$= \omega^{-1}(a_{1t}/b_{1t})^{1/\sigma}, \tag{1}$$

evaluated at equilibrium quantities. The trade balance of country 1, expressed in units of the domestic good, is

$$nx_{1t} = (a_{2t} - p_t b_{1t}).$$

Properties of this variable in Tables 11.6 through 11.8 refer to the ratio of net exports, nx_{1t}, to domestic output, y_{1t}.

With these elements and some parameter values, we can approach the behavior of the terms of trade. Relative to Table 11.3, our benchmark parameter set includes $J = 1$ and the parameters of the Armington aggregator: the elasticity of substitution, σ, which we set equal to 1.5, and the steady-state ratio of imports to GDP, which we set equal to 0.15 by choosing ω appropriately. In this benchmark version of the economy, foreign and domestic goods are better substitutes for each other than they would be with Cobb-Douglas preferences. Our choice of σ is consistent with a large number of studies, as documented by Whalley (1985, ch. 4). The import share is slightly larger than we see in the United States, Japan, or an aggregate of European countries (with intra-European trade netted out).

A number of properties of the theoretical economy with alternative parameter settings are reported in Table 11.6. Consider, first, the autocorrelation of the terms of trade. The autocorrelation for our benchmark parameter values is identical to that in U.S. data in Table 11.5: 0.83. This property is not especially surprising: the variables of the model, including the terms of trade, inherit the high degree of persistence observed in technology shocks in the data and incorporated into our technology shock process.

A second property of the model is the contemporaneous correlation between net exports and the terms of trade. Recall that in the data this correlation is generally

Table 11.6
Properties of the Terms of Trade in Theoretical Economics

			Correlation of:	
	SD	*Autocorr.*		
Country	$p(\%)$	p	(p, nx)	(p, y)
U.S. data	3.68	.83	.30	−.20
Benchmark	0.48	.83	−.41	.49
Two shocks (technology and				
government spending)	0.57	.67	−.05	.39
Large import share	0.66	.83	−.41	.55
Small elasticity	0.76	.77	−.80	.51

Notes: Statistics are based on Hodrick-Prescott–filtered data. Variables are defined in the notes to Table 11.5. Entries are averages over 20 simulations of length 100. The data column refers to the United States.

negative (see Table 11.5). In the theoretical economy, we find, for the benchmark parameter values, that the correlation is −0.41. This number is in the middle of the range observed across the countries in our sample.

Finally, consider the standard deviation of the terms of trade. With our benchmark parameter values the standard deviation is 0.48 percent, which is a factor of more than seven less than we see for the United States in Table 11.5. This large difference between the standard deviation in the model and the one in the data is our second anomaly: the terms of trade, or price-variability, anomaly.

Like the consumption/output/productivity anomaly, the price-variability anomaly is robust to reasonable changes in parameter values. We add government spending shocks in the experiment labeled *two shocks*. In this experiment, we calibrate the government spending process to U.S. data: the mean value of g in each country is 20 percent of steady-state output, $B = \text{diag}(0.95, 0.95)$, and the innovations are assigned standard deviations equal to 2 percent of mean government purchases, or 0.004. These shocks are independent across countries and of the productivity shocks, as they tend to be in international data (see Table 11.2). With these shocks added to the model, the standard deviation rises from 0.48 to 0.57, which remains far below what we see in the data. In another experiment, labeled *large share*, we raise the average share of imported goods to GDP from 0.15 to 0.25. In this case, the standard deviation of the terms of trade rises to 0.59. Nevertheless, the variability of the terms of trade in the model remains well below what we see in the data.

The variability of the terms of trade is also influenced by the elasticity of substitution between foreign and domestic goods, $\sigma = 1/\alpha$ in the Armington aggregator. In the *small elasticity* experiment we lower σ from 1.5 to 0.5; the standard deviation of the terms of trade rises from 0.48 percent in the benchmark economy to 0.76. In the theory, prices are related to quantities by the first-order condition,

$$\log p_t = -\log \omega - \sigma^{-1} \log(b_{1t}/a_{1t}), \tag{2}$$

where b_1 is imports and a_1 is output minus exports in country 1. Given a fixed amount of variability in the import ratio, b_1/a_1, we can increase the variability of p without bound by lowering the value of σ. In Figure 11.4 we see that as σ approaches zero the standard deviation of the terms of trade approaches values similar to those we see in the data. Closer inspection suggests, however, that raising the complementarity between foreign and domestic goods does not resolve the anomaly. The problem is that the variability of the import ratio in the data is not much different from that of the terms of trade. Thus choosing a small value of σ "resolves" the price variability anomaly only by making the variability of b_1/a_1 much smaller than it is in the data. Given the first-order condition, (2), it is impossible to separate the problem of insufficient variability of the price, p, from that of insufficient variability of the quantity ratio, b_1/a_1.

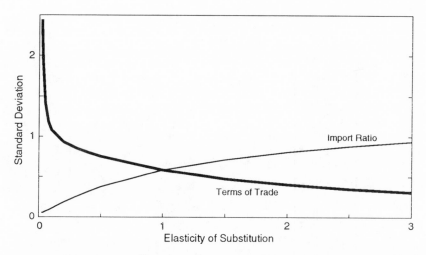

Figure 11.4 Effects of Varying the Elasticity of Substitution between Foreign and Domestic Goods on the Volatility of the Terms of Trade and the Import Ratio

Mussa (1986) adds another wrinkle to this puzzle. He argues persuasively that an important ingredient in the price variability puzzle is the sharp difference in price behavior between fixed and floating exchange rate regimes. As he shows, and we report in Table 11.7, the variability of the terms of trade has been much higher in the post–Bretton Woods period than before. By our estimates, the standard deviation of the terms of trade is higher by a factor of about three in the major countries for which we have long data series available. Mussa (1986) also notes that there has been greater price variability in other periods of floating exchange rates (for example, in Canada between 1952 and 1962), so the distinction between fixed and floating rate regimes is not simply one of time period. In our theory, and others in which there is a similar first-order condition relating prices and quantities, the standard deviation of the terms of trade is directly related to quantity variability: if the standard deviation of the import ratio doubles, then the standard deviation of the terms of trade also doubles. With this in mind, we note that while there has been greater quantity variability in most countries (Japan is an exception) in the post–Bretton Woods period, the increase has been much smaller than that for the terms of trade. The issue, then, is how to account for the sharp increase in price variability without generating a similar increase in the variability of quantities. At the very least, one must abandon the tight connection between prices and quantities implied by first-order conditions such as (1).

Finally, we return briefly to the consumption/output/productivity anomaly of Sections 2 and 3. We have noted that complementarity between foreign and domestic goods influences the variability of the terms of trade. It also influences the model's business cycle properties. As we see in Table 11.8 and Figure 11.5, the

Table 11.7
Properties of Four Economies by Subperiod

Country	Period	Standard Deviation (%)						Correlation with Same U.S. Variable	
		p	y	nx	im	ex	$im/(y-e)$	y	c
Canada	1955–90	2.44	1.48	0.79	5.25	5.52	3.85	.71	.52
	1955–71	1.19	1.38	0.78	4.83	2.89	4.13	.53	.59
	1972–90	3.05	1.54	0.79	5.44	4.64	4.75	.79	.48
Japan	1955–90	5.69	1.61	1.01	6.64	4.50	6.29	.20	.27
	1955–71	2.29	1.93	1.06	7.54	3.74	7.01	−.07	−.02
	1972–90	7.12	1.19	0.92	5.87	4.91	5.63	.57	.36
United Kingdom	1955–90	2.64	1.48	1.07	3.85	3.15	3.50	.46	.35
	1955–71	1.45	1.25	0.74	3.04	2.85	2.53	.15	.05
	1972–90	3.05	1.67	1.22	4.34	3.36	4.16	.57	.35
United States	1955–90	2.92	1.70	0.45	4.90	5.52	3.85		
	1955–71	1.26	1.23	0.32	3.38	5.23	3.16		
	1972–90	3.79	1.94	0.54	5.88	5.61	4.38		

Notes: Statistics are based on Hodrick-Prescott–filtered data. Variables include im, real imports; and ex, real exports. Other variables are defined in notes to Tables 11.1 and 11.5. Except for nx, statistics refer to logarithms of variables.

Table 11.8
Business Cycles and International Comovements in Theoretical Economies

A. Business Cycle Properties

Economy	Standard Deviation (%)		Ratio of Standard Deviation to That of y					Autocorr.	Correlation with Output					
	y	nx	c	x	g	n	z	y	c	x	g	nx	n	z
U.S. data	1.92	.52	.75	3.27	0.75	.61	.68	.86	.82	.94	.12	−.37	.88	.96
Benchmark	1.38	.30	.47	3.48	0.00	.42	.75	.63	.88	.93	.00	−.64	.94	.99
Two shocks	1.33	.33	.62	4.29	1.95	.42	.78	.65	.78	.89	.16	−.57	.79	.97
Large import share	1.36	.85	.47	4.70	0.00	.38	.76	.64	.86	.84	.00	−.59	.95	.99
Small elasticity	1.33	.37	.50	3.41	0.00	.37	.77	.63	.92	.93	.00	−.66	.94	.96

B. International Comovements

Economy	Correlation of Foreign and Domestic Variables					
	y	c	x	g	n	z
U.S. vs. Europe Data	.66	.51	.53	.18	.33	.56
Benchmark	.02	.77	−.58	.00	−.54	.24
Two shocks	.00	.83	−.64	−.02	−.62	.32
Large import share	.05	.83	−.76	.00	−.42	.24
Small elasticity	.10	.68	−.54	.00	−.36	.24

Notes: Statistics are based on Hodrick-Prescott–filtered data. Variables are defined in notes to Table 11.1. Entries are averages over 20 simulations of length 100. The data column refers to the United States in part A and to correlation between the United States and Europe in part B.

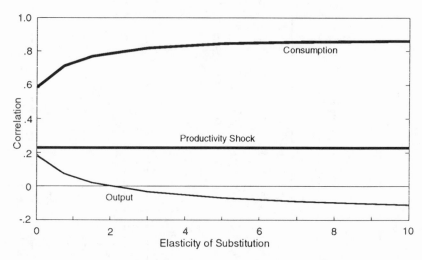

Figure 11.5 Effects of Varying the Elasticity of Substitution between Foreign and Domestic Goods on the Cross-Country Correlations of Selected Variables

correlation between consumption in the two countries of our theoretical economy falls as we reduce the elasticity of substitution between foreign and domestic goods. At the same time, the correlation between foreign and domestic output rises. Nevertheless, for values of σ above 0.025 (the smallest value we've been able to use) the consumption correlation exceeds the output correlation. The productivity correlation, of course, is not affected by our choice of σ: it equals 0.23 throughout. Thus for reasonable values of σ, there remains a substantial difference between the cross-country correlations of output, consumption, and productivity in the theory and those in the data. Imperfect substitutability between goods does not appear to resolve the consumption/output/productivity anomaly documented earlier.

In short, we find that we must add relative price variability to our list of anomalies. An interesting wrinkle to this finding is that the anomalous behavior of the relative price is closely connected, in our theory, to anomalous behavior of quantities.

6. Related Work and New Directions

We have documented two striking differences between theory and data, which we label the consumption/output/productivity and price variability anomalies. Our review of these issues has focused on our own work, but international macroeconomics has been one of the most active areas of business cycle research and includes studies that go far beyond the theoretical economies of Sections 3 and 5. Although these studies have addressed a wide range of issues, we find it useful to review them from the perspective of the two anomalies. We start by listing some of the prominent theoretical innovations, and then go on to consider their possible roles in accounting for the character of aggregate fluctuations and relative price movements.

Recent studies in international business cycle research have extended the theory in at least five directions. One of the more popular extensions has been to introduce nontraded goods. We are often reminded that haircuts and other services cannot be traded across cities, much less across countries, so this approach has some natural appeal. A second extension adds other sources of shocks including oil shocks and taste shocks. A third popular extension of the theory introduces restrictions on asset trade so that agents' ability to hedge risk is more limited than in our complete market economies. A fourth extension of the theory adds money to economies that are otherwise much like those we studied in Sections 3 and 5. A final extension introduces imperfect competition.

Adding nontraded goods does not seem to help explain either anomaly. Consider the consumption/output/productivity anomaly. Nontraded goods can, in principle, lower the cross-country consumption correlations, since the correlations between the nontraded components of consumption are not directly connected by trade in goods. They may, in addition, lower the correlation of the consumption of traded goods if the utility function is nonseparable between traded and nontraded goods consumption, as it is in Ravn (1992) and Stockman and Tesar (1991). The effect is similar to that of leisure in our models when utility is not additively separable between consumption and leisure. In both our work (Section 3) and in Ravn and Stockman and Tesar the effect of the nonseparability is quantitatively small. In Stockman and Tesar, the result of nontraded goods is that traded goods consumption, rather than total consumption, is more highly correlated across countries in the models than in the data. The anomaly, in other words, is simply pushed onto the traded component of consumption. Backus and Smith (1993) note, as well, that these models imply close connections between consumption differentials and relative prices that are not observed in aggregate data.

One of the by-products of this work has been a reconsideration of the impulses generating fluctuations. Costello and Praschnik (1992) introduce oil shocks, which increase the variability of the terms of trade in oil-importing countries and lowers the correlation of consumption across countries. They find, however, that the terms of trade for manufactured goods remains less variable in the model than we see in the data and that the cross-country correlation of manufactured goods consumption is much higher than in the data. Stockman and Tesar (1991) suggest shocks to preferences. They add a shock to the first-order condition that links consumption quantities and relative prices. This shock lowers the correlation of aggregate consumption across countries, and of consumption of traded goods alone. It has little effect, however, on the variability of the terms of trade. To date there has been no attempt to quantify such shocks, which makes it difficult to assess the effects of adding them to our models. One step in this direction might be to compute preference shocks as residuals from agents' first-order conditions, much as we compute productivity shocks as residuals from production functions.

Economies with incomplete markets would also seem to have the potential to account for low correlations of consumption across countries. With complete markets, as in the models of Sections 3 and 5, agents use asset markets to equate marginal rates of substitution across dates and states of nature. With separable preferences, this leads, as we have seen, to a perfect correlation of consumption across countries. When agents have limited ability to use international financial markets to share risk, marginal rates of substitution are not equated for all dates and states. One might guess, then, that the consumption correlation would be smaller than with complete markets. Thus Conze, Lasry, and Scheinkman (1991) show that in an economy in which agents can trade a single asset, the consumption correlation falls and the output correlation rises. Nevertheless, they still find that the consumption correlation exceeds the output correlation for most parameter values. Our autarky experiment in Section 3 makes the same point in an economy with even more limited trading opportunities. Kollmann (1990, tab. 1.1.3) studies an economy in which two agents trade a single, risk-free bond. In this economy he finds much smaller consumption correlations than with incomplete markets, but the correlation of investment across countries is sharply negative when productivity shocks are persistent, as they are in the data, and the consumption correlation remains higher than the output correlation. Baxter and Crucini (1992, tab. 4) also consider an economy in which agents trade a single risk-free bond and find that output is more highly correlated across countries than consumption, but the correlations of consumption, investment, and employment are negative. Thus these models have, to some extent, transferred the consumption/output/productivity anomaly onto other variables.

None of these models have accounted for the variability of international relative prices, like the terms of trade. The fourth extension, including money, was done with price variability explicitly in mind. Both Grilli and Roubini (1992) and Schlagenhauf and Wrase (1992) adapt Lucas's (1990c) liquidity model to the open economy. In these economies, asset markets and goods markets are separated for one period, and shocks to the stock of money have a one-period effect on interest rates, currency prices, and relative prices of goods. Thus the theory generates greater variability of relative prices than we would see in an analogous model without the segmented market structure. In its current form, however, this structure generates relative price movements with very little persistence, and thus fails to mimic this important feature of the data. The next step in this line of research is to specify a mechanism to generate the persistence we see in the data.

Another class of monetary models considers labor or goods contracts that fix wages or prices in advance. In closed-economy studies, such as Cho and Cooley (1992), this magnifies the effects of some shocks on employment and output. In open economies, one might guess that it could generate additional relative price variability, particularly if we added segmentation across national markets. This intuition has yet to be tested, but Cho and Roche (1993) and Ohanian and Stockman (1993) have made some progress in developing international business cycle models of this sort.

Imperfect competition is the final extension of the theory, and it might bear on the price variability anomaly. If imperfectly competitive firms sell their output in markets that are internationally segmented, then price discrimination might lead to greater changes in relative prices than we see with perfect competition. Studies of industries by Giovannini (1988) and Lapham (1991) show that this can lead to per-sistent movements in relative prices across countries, but the theory has yet to be extended to general equilibrium settings at the level of aggregation considered in Section 3 and 5. Perhaps Hornstein's (1993) or Rotemberg and Woodford's (Chapter 9, this volume) general equilibrium treatment of monopolistic competition in a closed economy could be adapted to the open economy.

All of these innovations help bring the quantitative implications of the theory closer to observed properties of international time series data. In our view, they have yet to resolve the two anomalies, but perhaps future efforts along similar lines will be more successful in this regard.

7. Final Thoughts

We have reviewed recent work on international business cycles, emphasizing two striking differences between theory and data. The first we call the consumption/output/productivity anomaly: in the data we generally find that the correlation across countries of output fluctuations is positive, and larger than the analogous consumption and productivity correlations. In theoretical economies we find, for a wide range of parameter values, that the consumption correlation exceeds the productivity and output correlations. The second anomaly concerns relative price movements: the standard deviation of the terms of trade is considerably larger in the data than in theoretical economies.

These anomalies have been met with a large and imaginative body of work in which the dynamic general equilibrium framework has been extended in ways that go well beyond the two-country versions of Kydland and Prescott (1982) that started this line of study. Our guess is that five years from now the models that have been developed will differ from this starting point in fundamental ways.

Notes

We thank Tom Cooley, John Donaldson, Tiff Macklem, Klaus Neusser, Patricia Reynolds, Julio Rotemberg, Gregor Smith, and Kei-Mu Yi for helpful comments on earlier drafts, and the National Science Foundation and the Center for Japan–US Business and Economic Studies NEC faculty fellowship program for financial support. We hope to make our data available shortly in machine-readable format.

1. See King and Rebelo (1993) and Prescott (1986) for descriptions of this filter and its relation to others.

2. Reynolds (1992) argues that our assessment of the theory is unduly pessimistic, in part because uncertainty about the parameter values makes the theory's predictions less precise. In her view, a model with multiple traded goods "is capable of replicating and explaining both the output and consumption correlations" (Reynolds 1992, abstract). Most of her point estimates, however, imply that the output correlations in her theory are smaller than the consumption correlations, and in one case the difference is significant in a statistical sense.

Chapter 12
Policy Analysis in Business Cycle Models

V. V. Chari, Lawrence J.
Christiano, and Patrick J. Kehoe

1. Introduction

In this chapter we study the quantitative properties of fiscal and monetary policies in business cycle models. We set out a theoretical framework and use it to
analyze two kinds of policies: exogenously given policies and optimal policies
with commitment. We illustrate how this framework can be applied in practice by
computing the quantitative properties of optimal policies.

Our framework builds on the so-called primal approach to optimal taxation
in the public finance literature (see, e.g., Atkinson and Stiglitz 1980; Lucas and
Stokey 1983; and Chari, Christiano, and Kehoe 1992). Using this approach we
characterize the set of allocations that can be implemented as a competitive equilibrium with distorting taxes by two simple conditions: the resource constraint and
an implementability constraint. The implementability constraint is an infinite-
horizon version of either the consumer or the government budget constraint in
which the consumer and firm first-order conditions are used to substitute out the
prices and policies. Thus, both constraints depend only on allocations. This
characterization implies that optimal allocations are solutions to a simple programming problem. We use these solutions to compute the optimal policies and
the equilibrium prices.

It is interesting to study the business cycle properties of economies with exogenously given policies. In the business cycle literature the quantitative properties
of economies with exogenous tax systems have been studied by Braun (1992),
Chang (1990), Greenwood and Huffman (1991), and McGrattan (1992). These
authors use the consumer and firm first-order conditions and the resource constraint
to solve for the allocations given the exogenous policies. This procedure either
assumes that lump sum taxes are available or leaves the initial debt obligations
of the government as a free variable determined in equilibrium. We show how
the first-order conditions and the resource constraint can be used together with
the implementability constraint to compute competitive equilibria within a class
of policies. Ruling out lump sum taxes and fixing the initial debt are especially
important when making welfare comparisons across alternative policies. We show

by way of an example that welfare rankings of alternative policies can be reversed when initial conditions are fixed.

Using the general approach, we analyze fiscal and monetary policy in two related models. We specify the parameters for preferences and technology to be similar to those used in the public finance and business cycle literature. The stochastic processes for technology shocks and government consumption are chosen to mimic those in the postwar U.S. economy. With these specifications, we show that the optimal policies for our model economies have four properties:

1) Tax rates on labor are roughly constant over the business cycle.

2) Capital income taxes are close to zero on average.

3) The Friedman rule is optimal; nominal interest rates are zero.

4) Monetary policy responds to shocks; money is countercyclical with respect to technology shocks; the growth rate of money responds negatively to technology shocks and positively to government consumption shocks.

In terms of the properties of fiscal policy, optimal tax policies should smooth distortions over time and states of nature. For reasonable parameter values, smoothing tax distortions turns out to imply that tax rates on labor (or consumption) should be essentially constant. Smoothing tax distortions also implies that capital tax rates should be close to zero on average, a result reminiscent of one in the deterministic literature (Judd 1985; Chamley 1986). Shocks to the government's budget constraint are absorbed by appropriately varying the ex post tax on capital income or the ex post return on government debt.

In terms of the properties of monetary policy, if the models had lump sum taxes, then following the Friedman rule would be optimal. Phelps (1973) argues that in models with distorting taxes, it is optimal to tax all goods, including the liquidity services derived from holding money. Hence, Phelps argues that in such models the Friedman rule is not optimal. In our monetary model, however, even though the government has distorting taxes, the Friedman rule turns out to be optimal. In our model, deviating from the Friedman rule amounts to taxing a subset of consumption goods, called *cash goods*, at a higher rate than that for other consumption goods. Optimality requires that all types of consumption goods be taxed at the same rate; thus, optimality requires following the Friedman rule.

The cyclical properties of optimal monetary policy amount to requiring that the government inflate relatively in bad times and deflate relatively in good times. In effect, then, such a policy allows the government to use nominal government debt as a shock absorber. In the model, the government would like to issue real state-contingent debt in order to insure itself from having to sharply raise or lower tax rates when the economy is hit with shocks. The government achieves this outcome by issuing nominal noncontingent debt and then inflating or deflating to provide the appropriate ex post real payments. In bad times, inflating is optimal, so the real debt payments are relatively small. In good times, deflating is optimal, so the real debt payments are relatively large.

We discuss some of the computational issues associated with the analysis of one of the models in the paper. We describe our basic procedure, which is based on the minimum weighted residual method described by Judd (1991). This procedure is more cumbersome to implement than procedures based on standard linearization techniques, such as the one described in Christiano (1991). For this reason, it is useful to compare results based on the two methods. It turns out that both methods deliver essentially the same results for allocations but are quite different for policies. The reason is that the policies depend upon ratios of allocations and small errors in computing allocations turn out to make large differences for computed policies.

The plan of this chapter is as follows. In Section 2, we describe a version of a standard business cycle model with shocks to government consumption and technology and define a competitive equilibrium and a Ramsey equilibrium. In Section 3, we characterize the set of allocations that can be implemented as a competitive equilibrium with distorting taxes. We also show how a competitive equilibrium can be computed when policies are restricted to lie in a given class. In Section 4, we characterize Ramsey equilibria and compute the associated policies and allocations in a standard quantitative business cycle model. In Section 5, we compute Ramsey equilibria for a version of Lucas and Stokey's (1983) monetary economy. In Section 6, we discuss computational issues, and in Section 7, we set forth our conclusions.

2. A Real Economy

Consider a production economy populated by a large number of identical infinitely lived consumers. In each period $t = 0, 1, \ldots$, the economy experiences one of finitely many events, s_t. We denote by $s^t = (s_0, \ldots, s_t)$ the history of events up through and including period t. The probability, as of time 0, of any particular history s^t is $\mu(s^t)$. The initial realization, s_0, is given. This suggests a natural commodity space in which goods are differentiated by histories.

In each period t there are two goods: labor and a consumption-capital good. A constant-returns-to-scale technology is available to transform labor, $\ell(s^t)$, and capital, $k(s^{t-1})$, into output via $F[k(s^{t-1}), \ell(s^t), s_t]$. Notice that the production function incorporates a stochastic shock. The output can be used for private consumption, $c(s^t)$, government consumption, $g(s^t)$, and new capital, $k(s^t)$. Throughout we will take government consumption to be exogenously specified. Feasibility requires that

$$c(s^t) + g(s^t) + k(s^t) = F[k(s^{t-1}), \ell(s^t), s_t] + (1 - \delta)k(s^{t-1}), \qquad (1)$$

where δ is the depreciation rate on capital. The preferences of each consumer are given by

$$\sum_{t,s^t} \beta^t \mu(s^t) U[c(s^t), \ell(s^t)], \tag{2}$$

where $0 < \beta < 1$ and U is increasing in consumption, decreasing in labor, strictly concave, and satisfies the Inada conditions.

Government consumption is financed by proportional taxes on the income from labor and capital and by debt. Let $\tau(s^t)$ and $\theta(s^t)$ denote the tax rates on the income from labor and capital. Government debt has a one-period maturity and a state-contingent return. Let $b(s^t)$ denote the number of units of debt issued at state s^t and $R_b(s^{t+1})b(s^t)$ denote the payoff at any state $s^{t+1} = (s^t, s_{t+1})$. The consumer's budget constraint is

$$c(s^t) + k(s^t) + b(s^t) \le [1 - \tau(s^t)]w(s^t)\ell(s^t) + R_b(s^t)b(s^{t-1}) + R_k(s^t)k(s^{t-1}), \tag{3}$$

where $R_k(s^t) = \{1 + [1 - \theta(s^t)][r(s^t) - \delta]\}$ is the gross return on capital after taxes and depreciation and $r(s^t)$ and $w(s^t)$ are the before-tax returns on capital and labor. Competitive pricing ensures that these returns equal their marginal products, namely,

$$r(s^t) = F_k[k(s^{t-1}), \ell(s^t), s_t], \tag{4}$$

and

$$w(s^t) = F_\ell[k(s^{t-1}), \ell(s^t), s_t]. \tag{5}$$

Consumers' purchases of capital are constrained to be nonnegative and the purchases of government debt are bounded above and below by some arbitrarily large constants. We let $x(s^t) = [c(s^t), \ell(s^t), k(s^t), b(s^t)]$ denote an allocation for consumers at s^t and let $x = [x(s^t)]$ denote an allocation for all s^t. We let $(w, r) = [w(s^t), r(s^t)]$ denote a price system.

The government sets tax rates on labor and capital income and returns for government debt to finance the exogenous sequence of government consumption. The government's budget constraint is

$$b(s^t) = R_b(s^t)b(s^{t-1}) + g(s^t) - \tau(s^t)w(s^t)\ell(s^t) - \theta(s^t)[r(s^t) - \delta]k(s^{t-1}). \tag{6}$$

We let $\pi(s^t) = [\tau(s^t), \theta(s^t), R_b(s^t)]$ denote the government policy at s^t and let $\pi = [\pi(s^t)]$ denote the policy for all s^t. The initial stock of debt, b_{-1}, and the initial stock of capital, k_{-1}, are given.

Notice that for notational simplicity we have not explicitly included markets in private claims. Since all consumers are identical such claims will not be traded in equilibrium, and hence their absence will not affect the equilibrium. Thus, we can always interpret the current model as having complete contingent private claims markets.

Given this description of an economy, we now define a competitive equilibrium. A competitive equilibrium is a policy π, an allocation x and a price system (w, r) such that given the policy and the price system, the resulting allocation maximizes the representative consumer's utility, (2), subject to the sequence of budget constraints, (3); the price system satisfies (4) and (5); and the government's budget constraint, (6) is satisfied. Notice that we do not need to impose the feasibility condition, (1), in our definition of equilibrium. Given our assumptions on the utility function, (3) is satisfied with equality in an equilibrium, and this feature together with (6) implies (1).

Consider now the policy problem faced by the government. We suppose there is an institution, or *commitment technology*, through which the government can bind itself to a particular sequence of policies once and for all at time zero. We model this by having the government choose a policy, π, at the beginning of time, and then having consumers choose their allocations. Formally, allocation rules are sequences of function $x(\pi) = [x(s^t|\pi)]$ that map policies, π, into allocations $x(\pi)$. Price rules are sequences of functions $w(\pi) = [w(s^t|\pi)]$ and $r(\pi) = [r(s^t|\pi)]$ that map policies, π, into price systems. Since the government needs to predict how consumer allocations and prices will respond to its policies, consumer allocations and prices must be described by rules that associate government policies with allocations. We will impose a restriction on the set of policies that the government can choose. Since the capital stock at date 0 is inelastically supplied, the government has an incentive to set the initial capital tax rate as high as possible. To make the problem interesting, we will require that the initial capital tax rate, $\theta(s_0)$, be fixed at some rate. For similar reasons we also require that the initial return on debt, $R_b(s_0)$, be fixed at some rate.

A Ramsey equilibrium is a policy, π, an allocation rule, $x(\cdot)$, and price rules, $w(\cdot)$ and $r(\cdot)$, such that

1) The policy maximizes

$$\sum_{t,s^t} \beta^t \mu(s^t) U[c(s^t|\pi), \ell(s^t|\pi)]$$

subject to (6) with allocations and prices given by $x(\pi)$, $w(\pi)$, and $r(\pi)$;

2) For every π', the allocation $x(\pi')$ maximizes (2) subject to (3) evaluated at the policy π' and the prices $w(\pi')$ and $r(\pi')$; and

3) For every π', the prices satisfy

$$w(s^t|\pi') = F_\ell[k(s^{t-1}|\pi'), \ell(s^t|\pi'), s_t] \tag{7}$$

and

$$r(s^t|\pi') = F_k[k(s^{t-1}|\pi'), \ell(s^t|\pi'), s_t]. \tag{8}$$

Notice that we require optimality by consumers and firms for *all* policies that the government might choose. This requirement is analogous to the requirement of subgame perfection in a game. To see why this requirement is important, suppose we had not imposed it. That is, suppose we required optimality by consumers and firms only at the equilibrium policies, allowing allocation and price rules to be arbitrary elsewhere. It is possible to show that the set of equilibria would be much larger. For example, allocation rules that prescribe zero labor supply for all policies other than some particular policy would satisfy all the equilibrium conditions. Since the government's budget constraint is then satisfied only at the particular policy, the government optimally chooses that policy. We think that such equilibria do not make any sense. That is, we think the requirement that consumers and firms behave optimally for all policies is the sensible way to solve the government's forecasting problem.

3. Characterization of Competitive Equilibrium

We now turn to characterizing the equilibrium policies and allocations. In terms of notation, it will be convenient here and throughout this chapter to let $U_c(s^t)$ and $U_\ell(s^t)$ denote the marginal utilities of consumption and leisure at state s^t and let $F_k(s^t)$ and $F_\ell(s^t)$ denote the marginal products of capital and labor at state s^t. We will show that a competitive equilibrium is characterized by two fairly simple conditions: the resource constraint,

$$c(s^t) + g(s^t) + k(s^t) = F[k(s^{t-1}), \ell(s^t), s^t] + (1 - \delta)k(s^{t-1}), \qquad (9)$$

and the implementability constraint,

$$\sum_{t,s^t} \beta^t \mu(s^t)[U_c(s^t)c(s^t) + U_\ell(s^t)\ell(s^t)] = U_c(s_0)[R_k(s_0)k_{-1} + R_b(s_0)b_{-1}], \quad (10)$$

where $R_k(s_0) = \{1 + [1 - \theta(s_0)]\}[F_k(s_0) - \delta)]$. The implementability constraint should be thought of as an infinite-horizon version of either the consumer or the government budget constraint where the consumer and firm first-order conditions have been used to substitute out the prices and policies.

Proposition 1 (competitive equilibrium allocations). The consumption, labor, capital allocations, and the date 0 policies (that is, $\theta[s_0]$ and $R_b[s_0]$) in a competitive equilibrium satisfy (9) and (10). Furthermore, given allocations and date zero allocations, which satisfy (9) and (10), we can construct tax policies, prices and debt policies that together with the given allocations and date 0 policies constitute a competitive equilibrium.

Proof. We first show that a competitive equilibrium must satisfy (9) and (10). To see this, note that we can add (3) and (6) to get (9), and thus feasibility is satisfied in equilibrium. Next, consider the allocation rule, $x(\pi)$. The necessary and sufficient conditions for c, ℓ, b, and k to solve the consumer's problem are given as follows. Let $p(s^t)$ denote the Lagrange multiplier on constraint (3), then by Weitzman's (1973) and Ekeland and Scheinkman's (1986) theorems, these conditions are constraint (3) together with the first-order conditions for consumption and labor,

$$\beta^t \mu(s^t) U_c(s^t) \le p(s^t) \quad \text{with equality if } c(s^t) > 0, \tag{11}$$

and

$$\beta^t \mu(s^t) U_\ell(s^t) \le -p(s^t)[1 - \tau(s^t)] w(s^t) \quad \text{with equality if } \ell(s^t) > 0, \tag{12}$$

the first-order conditions for capital and bonds,

$$\left[p(s^t) - \sum_{s_{t+1}} p(s^{t+1}) R_b(s^{t+1}) \right] b(s^t) = 0, \tag{13}$$

and

$$\left[p(s^t) - \sum_{s_{t+1}} p(s^{t+1}) R_k(s^{t+1}) \right] k(s^t) = 0, \tag{14}$$

and the two transversality conditions. These conditions specify that for any infinite history s^∞,

$$\lim p(s^t) b(s^t) = 0, \tag{15}$$

and

$$\lim p(s^t) k(s^t) = 0, \tag{16}$$

where the limits are taken over sequences of histories s^t contained in the infinite history s^∞.

We claim that any allocation that satisfies (3) and (11)–(16) must satisfy (10). To see this, multiply (3) by $p(s^t)$, sum over t and s^t, and use (13)–(16) to obtain

$$\sum_{t,s^t} p(s^t)\{c(s^t) - [1 - \tau(s^t)] w(s^t) \ell(s^t)\} = p(s_0)[R_k(s_0)k_{-1} + R_b(s_0)b_{-1}]. \tag{17}$$

Using (11) and (12) and noting that interiority follows from the Inada conditions, we can rewrite equation (17) as

$$\sum_{t,s^t} \beta^t \mu(s^t)[c(s^t) U_c(s^t) + \ell(s^t) U_\ell(s^t)] = U_c(s_0)[R_k(s_0)k_{-1} + R_b(s_0)b_{-1}]. \tag{18}$$

Thus, (9) and (10) are necessary conditions, which any competitive equilibrium must satisfy.

Next, suppose that we are given allocations and date 0 policies satisfying (9) and (10). We construct the competitive equilibrium as follows. First, note that for an allocation to be part of a competitive equilibrium it must satisfy (3) and

(11)–(16). Multiplying (3) by $p(s^t)$, summing over all dates and states following s^r, and using (11)–(16), we get

$$b(s^r) = \sum_{t=r+1} \sum_{s^t} \beta^{t-r} \mu(s^t|s^r)[U_c(s^t)c(s^t)+U_\ell(s^t)\ell(s^t)]/U_c(s^r) - k(s^r). \quad (19)$$

Thus any competitive equilibrium debt allocation must satisfy (19). Hence (19) defines the unique debt allocations given consumption, labor, and capital allocations. The wage rate and the rental rate on capital are determined by (4) and (5) from the capital and labor allocations. The labor tax rate is determined from (5), (11), and (12) and is given by

$$-\frac{U_\ell(s^t)}{U_c(s^t)} = [1 - \tau(s^t)]F_\ell(s^t). \quad (20)$$

We can use (3), (11), (13), and (14) to construct the capital tax rate and the return on debt. From these conditions it is clear that given the allocations the tax rate on capital and the return on debt satisfy

$$\mu(s^t)U_c(s^t) = \sum_{s^{t+1}|s^t} \beta\mu(s^{t+1})U_c(s^{t+1})R_k(s^{t+1}), \quad (21)$$

$$\mu(s^t)U_c(s^t) = \sum_{s^{t+1}|s^t} \beta\mu(s^{t+1})U_c(s^{t+1})R_b(s^{t+1}), \quad (22)$$

and

$$c(s^t) + k(s^t) + b(s^t) = [1 - \tau(s^t)]w(s^t)\ell(s^t) + R_b(s^t)b(s^{t-1})$$
$$+ R_k(s^t)k(s^{t-1}), \quad (23)$$

where $R_k(s^t) = \{1 + [1 - \theta(s^t)][r(s^t) - \delta]\}$. It turns out that these conditions do not uniquely determine the tax rate on capital and the return on debt. To see this, suppose that s_t can take on one of N values. Then counting linearly independent equations and unknowns in (21)–(23) gives $N + 1$ equations and $2N$ unknowns at each date and state. Thus the tax rate on capital and the return on debt are not uniquely determined if there is uncertainty.

One particular set of policies supporting a competitive equilibrium has the capital tax rate not contingent on the current state. That is, suppose for each s^t,

$$\theta(s^t, s_{t+1}) = \bar{\theta}(s^t) \text{ for all } s_{t+1}. \quad (24)$$

We can then use (21) to define $\bar{\theta}(s^t)$ and use the date $t + 1$ version of (23) to define $R_b(s^{t+1})$. It is straightforward to check that the constructed return on debt satisfies (22). Another set of policies supporting the same competitive equilibrium has the return on debt not contingent on the current state (for details, see Chari, Christiano, and Kehoe [1991a]).

From the proof of the proposition it is clear that certain policies are uniquely determined by allocations and date 0 policies that satisfy (9)–(10) while others are not. Specifically, the labor tax rate is determined while the state-by-state capital tax rate and return on debt are not. From (21), however, it is clear that the value of revenues from capital income taxation at date $t + 1$ in terms of the date t good are uniquely determined. To turn this variable into a tax rate, consider the ratio of the value of these revenues to the value of capital income, namely,

$$\theta^e(s^t) = \frac{\sum q(s^{t+1})\theta(s^{t+1})[F_k(s^{t+1}) - \delta]}{\sum q(s^{t+1})[F_k(s^{t+1}) - \delta]}, \tag{25}$$

where $q(s^{t+1}) = \beta\mu(s^{t+1}|s^t)U_c(s^{t+1})/U_c(s^t)$ is the price of a unit of consumption at state s^{t+1} in units of consumption at s^t. We refer to $\theta^e(s^t)$ as the ex ante tax rate on capital income.

Next, in defining the last variable that is uniquely determined by the theory it is useful to proceed as follows. Imagine that the government promises a state non-contingent rate of return on government debt, $\bar{r}(s^{t-1})$, and levies a state-contingent tax $v(s^t)$, on interest payments from government debt. That is, v and $\bar{r}$ satisfy

$$R_b(s^t) = \{1 + \bar{r}(s^{t-1})[1 - v(s^t)]\} \tag{26}$$

and $\sum q(s^t)v(s^t) = 0$, where $q(s^t)$ is the price of a unit of consumption at state s^t in units of consumption at state s^{t-1}. Thus, $\bar{r}(s^{t-1})$ is the equilibrium rate of return on a unit purchased in period $t - 1$ at s^{t-1} that yields a noncontingent return $\bar{r}(s^{t-1})$ in all states s^t. It is clear from (23) that the theory pins down $R_b(s^t)b(s^{t-1}) + R_k(s^t)k(s^{t-1})$. Given our definition of v it is clear that the theory pins down the sum of the tax revenues from capital income and the interest on debt, which is given by

$$\theta(s^t)[F_k(s^t) - \delta]k(s^{t-1}) + v(s^t)\bar{r}(s^{t-1})b(s^{t-1}). \tag{27}$$

We transform these revenues into a rate by dividing by the income from capital and debt to obtain

$$\eta(s^t) = \frac{\theta(s^t)[F_k(s^t) - \delta]k(s^{t-1}) + v(s^t)\bar{r}(s^{t-1})b(s^{t-1})}{[F_k(s^t) - \delta]k(s^{t-1}) + \bar{r}(s^{t-1})b(s^{t-1})}. \tag{28}$$

We refer to this as the tax rate on private assets. Next, we turn to discussing how Proposition 1 can be used in practice. Proposition 1 completely characterizes the competitive equilibrium allocations as long as there are sufficient degrees of freedom in setting policies. In some situations it may be reasonable to restrict the set of policies. For example, it may be reasonable to restrict tax rates to be less than 100 percent. Such restrictions can be easily imposed. We illustrate how to impose them in the following examples.

Example 1 (capital tax rates bounded by unity). Suppose that capital tax rates are at most 100 percent. Then in addition to satisfying (9) and (10), an allocation must satisfy an extra condition to be part of a competitive equilibrium. Rewrite (21) as

$$\mu(s^t)U_c(s^t) = \sum_{s^{t+1}|s^t} \beta\mu(s^{t+1})U_c(s^{t+1})$$

$$+ \sum_{s^{t+1}|s^t} \beta\mu(s^{t+1})U_c(s^{t+1})[1 - \theta(s^{t+1})][F_k(s^{t+1}) - \delta]. \quad (29)$$

Then if an allocation satisfies

$$F_k(s^{t+1}) \geq \delta, \quad (30)$$

and $\theta(s^{t+1}) \leq 1$, (29) implies

$$\mu(s^t)U_c(s^t) \geq \sum_{s^{t+1}|s^t} \beta\mu(s^{t+1})U_c(s^{t+1}). \quad (31)$$

If an allocation satisfies (9), (10), (30), and (31), then there exists a set of policies, prices, and debt allocations that together with the given allocation constitute a competitive equilibrium that satisfies the restrictions on capital tax rates.

Example 2 (noncontingent capital taxes and return on debt). Suppose that neither capital tax rates nor the return on debt can be made state contingent. Then the additional restriction that the allocation must satisfy so that we can construct a competitive equilibrium is given as follows. Substituting (19) and (20) into the consumer's budget constraint yields (after some simplification),

$$\frac{\sum_{t=r} \sum_{s^t} \beta^{t-r}\mu(s^t|s^r)[U_c(s^t)c(s^t) + U_\ell(s^t)\ell(s^t)]}{U_c(s^r)}$$

$$-\{1 + [1 - \theta(s^{r-1})][F_k(s^r) - \delta]\}k(s^{r-1}) = \bar{R}_b(s^{r-1})b(s^{r-1}), \quad (32)$$

where $\bar{\theta}(s^{r-1})$ satisfies

$$U_c(s^{r-1}) = \sum_{s^r} \beta\mu(s^r|s^{r-1})U_c(s^r)\{1 + [1 - \bar{\theta}(s^{r-1})][F_k(s^r) - \delta]\}. \quad (33)$$

The requirement that the debt not be state-contingent is then simply the requirement that the left side of (32) with $\bar{\theta}(s^{r-1})$ substituted from (33) be equal for all s^r. Then if an allocation satisfies this requirement together with (9) and (10), a competitive equilibrium can be constructed that satisfies the restriction that neither the capital tax rate nor the return on debt be state contingent. Clearly, computing equilibria with noncontingent capital taxes and return on debt is a computationally difficult exercise.

Example 3 (exogenous tax policies). Suppose next that we are given a policy for tax rates on capital and labor income, and we want to ask whether there exists a state contingent return on debt and allocations that together with the tax policies constitutes a competitive equilibrium. Then, the additional restrictions are simply the relevant first-order conditions:

$$-\frac{U_\ell(s^t)}{U_c(s^t)} = [1 - \tau(s^t)]F_\ell(s^t), \tag{34}$$

and

$$U_c(s^t) = \sum_{s^{t+1}} \beta\mu(s^{t+1}|s^t)U_c(s^{t+1})[1 + (1 - \theta(s^{t+1}))(F_k[s^{t+1}] - \delta)]. \tag{35}$$

Thus, if an allocation and the given tax policy together satisfy (9), (10), (34), and (35), then there exist state contingent returns on debt and debt allocations such that the returns and allocations together constitute a competitive equilibrium.

The general approach to characterizing competitive equilibria with distorting taxes described thus far is known as the primal approach to taxation in the public finance literature (see Atkinson and Stiglitz 1980). The basic idea is to characterize an equilibrium in terms of allocations as far as possible. This approach can be useful when we study optimal taxation. This approach is also useful in studying exogenous tax systems.

We find it useful to first describe the traditional approach to studying the business cycle implications of exogenous tax systems followed by Braun (1992), Chang (1990), Greenwood and Huffman (1991), and McGrattan (1992), among others. In this approach, stochastic processes for the labor tax rate and the capital tax rate are chosen to mimic those in the postwar U.S. data. The consumer's first-order conditions, (34) and (35) and the resource constraint, (9), are used to compute the stochastic processes for the allocations. This procedure is widely used in public finance. Of course, for a variety of reasons including problems in measuring and estimating tax processes, the allocations and policies computed this way will not typically satisfy the government budget constraint, or its analog, the implementability constraint. One interpretation of the procedure is that lump sum taxes are available and are appropriately used to ensure that the implementability constraint is satisfied.

Here we outline how this procedure can be modified to compute a competitive equilibrium when there are no lump sum taxes. Such a modification is especially important when making welfare comparisons across alternative policies. The basic idea is to consider a class of tax policies with enough degrees of freedom so that the implementability constraint can be satisfied. For simplicity, consider Example 3 and assume the state follows a Markov chain. Suppose that the capital and labor tax rates depend only on the inherited capital stock, k, and the current state, s. Suppose also the capital tax rates are a given function, $\theta(k, s)$, and the class of labor tax rates are given by $\tau(k, s; \alpha) = \alpha + \phi(k, s)$, where ϕ is a given function and α is a parameter that will be varied to satisfy the implementability constraint. Notice that by varying α, we are varying the mean of the labor tax while keeping its other moments unchanged. Given this class of policies and the Markov assumption on the state, it follows from the resource constraint, (9), and the first-order conditions (34) and (35) that the consumption, labor, and capital allocation rules can be described as stationary functions of the inherited capital stock and the current state. Denote these functions as $c(k, s; \alpha)$, $\ell(k, s; \alpha)$, and $k'(k, s; \alpha)$, respectively. Notice that in order to compute these functions, we do not need to know the debt allocation rule or the return on debt. Next we verify (10). One way of verifying this condition is to simulate a large number of sufficiently long strings of the state s^t. Obviously, this procedure is cumbersome. An alternative procedure is to use (19) to define a recursive law of motion for the debt allocation. Notice that given that consumption, labor, and capital are stationary functions of (k, s), (19) makes it clear that the debt allocations are also stationary functions. From (19), the debt allocations can be recursively written as

$$U_c(k, s)b(k, s) = \sum_{s'} \beta\mu(s'|s)[U_c(k', s')c(k', s')$$
$$+ U_\ell(k', s')\ell(k', s') + U_c(k', s')b(k', s')$$
$$+ U_c(k', s')k'] - U_c(k, s)k', \tag{36}$$

where $k' = k'(k, s)$ and $U_c(k, s)$, $U_\ell(k, s)$ are marginal utilities of consumption and labor and where we have suppressed the dependence on α. Notice that (36) defines a linear operator mapping bond allocation rules into themselves. Thus, from a computational perspective, once we have the consumption, labor, and capital allocations, it is relatively straightforward to compute the bond allocation rules. This procedure gives the end-of-period debt for all periods. Next, given k_{-1} and the date 0 policies, the allocation rules can be substituted into the consumer's budget constraint, (3), evaluated at date 0 to obtain the value of the initial debt, $\hat{b}_{-1}$. Of course, given an arbitrary α, the value of this debt, $\hat{b}_{-1}$, will not equal the given debt, b_{-1}. The parameter α is then adjusted until $\hat{b}_{-1} = b_{-1}$.

Next we illustrate this procedure in an example where we compute welfare under alternative cyclical policies. We begin with a naive procedure, which compares welfare across alternative policies without requiring that the initial debt be the same across these policy experiments. We show that imposing the government budget constraint can have sizable effects on the welfare comparisons.

Example 4 (cyclical policies and welfare). Consider an economy with preferences of the form

$$U(c, \ell) = (1 - \gamma) \log c + \gamma \log(1 - \ell),$$

where L is the endowment of labor. The production function is of the form

$$F(k, \ell, z, t) = k^\alpha (e^{\rho t + z}\ell)^{(1-\alpha)}.$$

The parameter ρ incorporates deterministic growth and the variable z is a technology shock that follows a symmetric two-state Markov chain with states z_1 and

Table 12.1
Parameter Values for the Exogenous Policy Analysis in
Example 4

Model	Parameters and Values		
Preferences	$\gamma = .75$		$\beta = .98$
Technology	$\alpha = .34$	$\delta = 0.08$	$\rho = .016$
Initial conditions	$b_{-1} = .2$	$k_{-1} = 1$	
Government consumption	$g = .07$		
Markov chains for			
technology shock	$z_l = -.04$	$z_h = 0.04$	$\pi = .91$
Baseline policy	$\tau = .24$	$\theta = 0.27$	

z_2 and transition probabilities $\text{Prob}(z_{t+1} = z_i | z_t = z_i) = \pi$, for $i = 1, 2$. Government consumption is given by $g_t = ge^{\rho t}$, where g is a constant. The parameters for preferences and technology are given in Table 12.1.

We begin by considering a baseline policy with a constant capital tax rate, $\theta(s^t) = 0.27$, and a constant labor tax rate, $\tau(s_t) = 0.24$. The implied value of initial debt is $R_b b_{-1} = 0.2$. We consider a countercyclical policy experiment. In this experiment, the tax rate is low when the current realization of the shock is low and high when the realization of the shock is high. This policy is intended to stimulate employment in the low state and reduce employment in the high state relative to our baseline policy and thus stabilize output. A naive approach to policy evaluation is to set the tax rate on labor in the higher state at its baseline level and reduce the tax rate on labor in the low state by a given amount. We conducted such an experiment and set the tax rate in the low state to 0.18, a decrease of 0.06 from its baseline level.

To evaluate welfare, we compute the constant percentage change in consumption relative to the baseline levels in all dates and states, keeping labor at its baseline levels, required to yield a utility level equal to that in the policy experiment. In Table 12.2 we report the results of this exercise. Note that welfare increases by 0.65 percent, the standard deviation of output falls to 31 percent of its baseline level, and the standard deviation of employment rises to 153 percent of its baseline level. Next we consider a similar policy exercise except that we require the implementability constraint to be satisfied. The class of policies considered in this experiment is described as follows. We set the tax rate in the high state at τ, a number to be determined. The tax rate in the low state is set at $\tau - 0.06$ and thus the difference in taxes between the high and low states is the same as in the naive experiment. Here, however, we adjust τ so that the initial debt is the same as in the baseline setting. The equilibrium value of τ is 27 percent. In terms of the volatility measures, we find that we get results very similar to the naive case. The standard deviation

Table 12.2
Countercyclical Policy Exercise in Example 4

	Naive	Budget Balance
Taxes		
τ_H	0.24	0.27
τ_L	0.18	0.21
Welfare relative to baseline policy	0.65	−0.1
Standard deviation of output relative to baseline policy	0.31	0.27
Standard deviation of employment relative to baseline policy	1.53	1.64

Notes: The welfare measure is the percent increase in baseline consumption level that gives the same utility as does the policy exercise.

of output falls to 27 percent of its baseline level, and the standard deviation of employment rises to 164 percent of its baseline level. More interestingly, we find that welfare decreases by 0.1 percent relative to its baseline level. Thus requiring budget balance reverses the welfare ranking of the policy experiment relative to the baseline policy. To see why this reversal occurs, notice that in the naive approach, the labor tax rates are lower in both states than in the policy requiring budget balance, and thus the present value of tax revenue is lower in the naive approach. It follows that if the naive policies are part of a competitive equilibrium, either the initial debt must be lower than under the baseline or lump sum taxes must be used to make up the lost revenues.

4. Ramsey Equilibrium

Given our characterization of a competitive equilibrium, the characterization of the Ramsey equilibrium is immediate.

Proposition 2. The allocations in a Ramsey equilibrium solve the following programming problem:

$$\max \sum_{s^t} \sum_t \beta^t \mu(s^t) U[c(s^t), \ell(s^t)] \tag{37}$$

s. t. (9) and (10).

It will be convenient to write the Ramsey allocation problem in Lagrangian form:

$$\max \sum_{t,s^t} \beta^t \mu(s^t) W[c(s^t), \ell(s^t), \lambda] \quad \text{s.t.} \quad (9). \tag{38}$$

The function W simply incorporates the implementability constraint into the maximand. For $t \geq 1$, we have

$$W[c(s^t), \ell(s^t), \lambda] = U[c(s^t), \ell(s^t)] + \lambda[U_c(s^t)c(s^t) + U_\ell(s^t)\ell(s^t)], \tag{39}$$

and for $t = 0$, W equals the right side of (39) evaluated at s_0, minus $\lambda U_c(s_0)[R_k(s_0)k_{-1} + R_b(s_0)b_{-1}]$. Here, λ is the Lagrange multiplier on the implementability constraint, (10). The first-order conditions for this problem imply that for $t \geq 0$,

$$-\frac{W_\ell(s^t)}{W_c(s^t)} = F_\ell(s^t), \tag{40}$$

and

$$W_c(s^t) = \sum_{s_{t+1}} \beta\mu(s^{t+1}|s^t)W_c(s^{t+1})[1 - \delta + F_k(s^{t+1})], \quad t = 0, 1, 2, \ldots. \tag{41}$$

A useful property of the Ramsey allocations is the following. If the stochastic process on s follows a Markov process, then from (40) and (41) it is clear that the allocations from date 1 onwards can be described by time-invariant allocation rules $c(k, s; \lambda)$, $\ell(k, s; \lambda)$, $k'(k, s; \lambda)$, and $b(k, s; \lambda)$. The date 0 first-order conditions include terms related to the initial stocks of capital and bonds and are therefore different from the other first-order conditions. The date 0 allocation rules are thus different from the stationary allocation rules that govern behavior from date 1 on.

We begin our analysis of optimal fiscal policy for this model by considering a nonstochastic version of the model in which the stochastic shock in the production function is constant. Government consumption is also constant, so $g(s^t) = g$. Suppose that under the Ramsey plan the allocations converge to a steady state. In such a steady state, W_c is constant. Thus, from (41),

$$1 = \beta(1 + F_k - \delta). \tag{42}$$

The consumer's intertemporal first-order condition is

$$U_{ct} = \beta U_{ct+1}[1 + (1 - \theta_{t+1})(F_{kt+1} - \delta)]. \tag{43}$$

In a steady state, U_c is a constant, so (43) reduces to

$$1 = \beta[1 + (1 - \theta)(F_k - \delta)]. \tag{44}$$

Comparing (42) and (44), we can see that in a steady state the optimal tax rate on capital income, θ, is zero. This result is due to Chamley (1986).

In Chari, Christiano, and Kehoe (1991a), we show that an analogous result holds in stochastic economies; namely, the value of tax revenue across states of nature is approximately zero in a stationary equilibrium. However, the state-by-state capital taxes are not uniquely determined (see the proof of Proposition 1) and can be quite different from zero. In Chari, Christiano, and Kehoe (1991a), we explore the quantitative properties of optimal policy in a parameterized version of the model. We consider preferences of the form

$$U(c, \ell) = [c^{1-\gamma}(L - \ell)^{\gamma}]^{\psi}/\psi, \tag{45}$$

where L is the endowment of labor. This class of preferences has been widely used in the literature (Kydland and Prescott 1982; Christiano and Eichenbaum 1992; and Backus, Kehoe, and Kydland 1992). The production technology is given by

$$F(k, \ell, z, t) = k^{\alpha}[e^{\rho t + z}\ell]^{(1-\alpha)}. \tag{46}$$

Notice that the production technology has two kinds of labor-augmenting technological change. The variable ρ captures deterministic growth in this change. The variable z is a technology shock that follows a symmetric two-state Markov chain with states z_{ℓ} and z_h and transition probabilities $\text{Prob}(z_{t+1} = z_i | z_t = z_i) = \pi$, $i = \ell, h$. Government consumption is given by $g_t = ge^{\rho t}$, where ρ is the deterministic growth rate and g follows a symmetric two-state Markov chain with states g_{ℓ} and g_h and transition probabilities $\text{Prob}(g_{t+1} = g_i | g_t = g_i) = \phi, i = \ell, h$. Notice that without technology or government consumption shocks, the economy has a balanced growth path along which private consumption, capital, and government consumption grow at rate ρ and labor is constant.

We consider two parameterizations of this model (see Table 12.3). Our *baseline* model has $\psi = 0$ and thus has logarithmic preferences. Our *high risk aversion*

Table 12.3
Parameter Values for the Real Models

Model	Parameters and Values			
Baseline Model				
Preferences	$\gamma = 0.80$	$\psi = 0$	$\beta = .97$	$L = 5,475$
Technology	$\alpha = 0.34$	$\delta = 0.08$	$\rho = .016$	
Initial conditions	$b_{-1} = .2$	$k_{-1} = 1$		
Markov chains for				
government consumption	$g_l = 350$	$g_h = 402$	$\phi = 0.95$	
technology shock	$z_l = -0.04$	$z_h = 0.04$	$\pi = 0.91$	
High risk aversion model				
Prefernces	$\psi = -8$			

Source: Chari, Christiano, and Kehoe 1990.

model has $\psi = -8$. The remaining parameters of preferences and the parameters for technology are the annualized versions of those used by Christiano and Eichenbaum (1992). We choose the three parameters of the Markov chain for government consumption to match three statistics of the postwar U.S. data: the average value of the ratio of government consumption to output, the variance of the detrended log of government consumption, and the serial autocorrelation of the detrended log of government consumption. We construct the Markov chain for the technology parameters by setting the mean of the technology shock equal to zero and use Prescott's (1986) statistics on the variance and serial correlation of the technology shock to determine the other two parameters.

For each setting of the parameter values, we simulate our economy starting from the steady state of the deterministic versions of our models. Table 12.4 shows some properties of the fiscal variables for both models. The baseline model values

Table 12.4
Properties of the Real Models and the U.S. Economy

	Model		U.S. Economy
Tax Rates	Baseline	High Risk Aversion	
Labor			
Mean	28.77	25.55	24.76
Standard deviation	0.10	0.09	2.39
Autocorrelation	0.83	0.90	0.77
Capital			
Mean	0.00	−0.11	28.28
Standard deviation	0.00	2.64	8.75
Autocorrelation		0.83	0.74
Private assets			
Mean	1.46	−1.27	0.00
Standard deviation	84.94	70.29	0.73
Autocorrelation	−0.01	0.00	−0.32

Note: All statistics are based on 400 simulated observations. The means and standard deviations are in percentage terms. For the U.S. economy, the labor tax rate is measured by the average marginal tax rate of Barro and Sahasakul (1983), the capital tax rate is measured by the effective corporate tax rate of Jorgenson and Sullivan (1981), and the tax rate on private assets is defined in (28). The capital tax rate is the ex ante tax rate on capital income; see equation (25). For the baseline model, the ex ante capital tax rate is zero; thus, its autocorrelation is not defined.

indicate that the tax on labor income fluctuates very little. For example, if the labor tax rate were approximately normally distributed, then 95 percent of the time the tax rate would fluctuate between 28.57 percent and 28.97 percent. The ex ante tax rate on capital income is zero. This is to be expected from the analytic results in Chari, Christiano, and Kehoe (1991a), since with $\psi = 0$, the utility function is separable between consumption and leisure and homothetic in consumption. For such preferences, that paper shows that the tax on capital is zero in all periods but the first.[1] In the baseline model, the tax on private assets has a large standard deviation. Intuitively, the tax on private assets acts as a shock absorber. The optimal tax rate on labor does not respond much to shocks to the economy. The government smooths labor tax rates by appropriately adjusting the tax on private assets in response to shocks. This variability of the tax on private assets does not distort capital accumulation, since what matters for the capital accumulation decision is the ex ante tax rate on capital income. This can be seen by manipulating the first-order condition for capital accumulation, (21).

In Table 12.4 we also report some properties of the fiscal policy variables for the high risk aversion model. Here, too, the tax rate on labor fluctuates very little. The tax rate on capital income has a mean of -0.11 percent, which is close to zero. We find this feature interesting because it suggests that our analytical result approximately holds for the class of utility functions commonly used in the literature. This feature also suggests that Chamley's (1986) result on the undesirability of the taxation of capital income in a deterministic steady state approximately holds in stochastic steady states of stochastic models. As in the baseline model, we find here that the standard deviation of the tax rate on private assets is large.

To gain an appreciation of the magnitudes of some of the numbers for our model economies, we compute analogous numbers for the U.S. economy. In Table 12.4, we report these as well. For the labor tax rate, we use Barro and Sahasakul's (1983) estimate of the average marginal labor tax rate. The standard deviation of this rate is 2.39 percent, which is approximately twenty-five times the standard deviation in our baseline model. For the tax rate on capital income, we use Jorgenson and Sullivan's (1981) estimate of the effective corporate tax rate. This number probably underestimates the ex ante rate, since it ignores the taxation of dividends and capital gains received by individuals. The mean effective rate in the data is 28.28 percent while our baseline model has an ex ante tax rate of zero. Finally, the standard deviation of the innovation in the tax on private assets in the baseline model is about six times that in the data.[2]

5. A Monetary Economy

In this section we study the properties of monetary policy, using a version of Lucas and Stokey's (1983) cash-credit goods model. This economy is a version of the real economy of Section 2 with money but without capital. Here we focus on optimal monetary policy. For a study of various exogenous policies in a related model, see Cooley and Hansen (1989, 1992). Here we study both the mean inflation rate and its cyclical properties. Friedman (1969) has argued that monetary policy should follow a rule: set nominal interest rates to zero. For a deterministic version of our economy, this would imply deflating at the rate of time preference. Phelps (1973) argues that Friedman's rule is unlikely to be optimal in an economy with no lump sum taxes. His argument is that optimal taxation generally requires using all available taxes, including the inflation tax. Thus, Phelps argues that the optimal inflation rate is higher than the Friedman rule implies.

In Section 4, we showed how real state contingent debt can serve a useful role as a shock absorber. Here we allow the government to issue only nominal state-noncontingent debt. We examine how the government should optimally use monetary policy to make this debt yield the appropriate real state contingent returns.

Consider, then, a simple production economy with three goods. The goods are labor, ℓ, and two consumption goods: a cash good, c_1, and a credit good, c_2. A stochastic constant-returns-to-scale technology transforms labor into output according to

$$c_1(s^t) + c_2(s^t) + g(s^t) = z(s^t)\ell(s^t), \tag{47}$$

where $z(s^t)$ is a technology shock and, again, $g(s^t)$ is government consumption. The preferences of each consumer are given by

$$\sum_t \sum_{s^t} \beta^t \mu(s^t) U[c_1(s^t), c_2(s^t), \ell(s^t)], \tag{48}$$

where U has the usual properties.

In period t, consumers trade money, assets, and goods in particular ways. At the start of period t, after observing the current state, s_t, consumers trade money and assets in a centralized securities market. The assets are one-period, state-noncontingent nominal claims. Let $M(s^t)$ and $B(s^t)$ denote the money and nominal bonds held at the end of the securities market trading. Let $R(s^t)$ denote the gross nominal return on these bonds payable in period $t + 1$ in all states s^{t+1}. After this trading, each consumer splits into a worker and a shopper. The shopper must use the money to purchase cash goods. To purchase credit goods, the shopper issues nominal claims, which are settled in the securities market in the next period. The worker is paid in cash at the end of each period.

This environment leads to this constraint for the securities market:

$$M(s^t) + B(s^t) = R(s^{t-1})B(s^{t-1}) + M(s^{t-1}) - p(s^{t-1})c_1(s^{t-1})$$
$$- p(s^{t-1})c_2(s^{t-1}) + p(s^{t-1})[1 - \tau(s^{t-1})]z(s^{t-1})\ell(s^{t-1}). \tag{49}$$

The left side of (49) is the nominal value of assets held at the end of securities market trading. The first term on the right side is the value of nominal debt bought in the preceding period. The next two terms are the shopper's unspent cash. The next is the payments for credit goods, and the last is the after-tax receipts from labor services. Besides this constraint, we will assume that the real holdings of debt, $B(s^t)/p(s^t)$, are bounded below by some arbitrarily large constant. Purchases of cash goods must satisfy a cash-in-advance constraint:

$$p(s^t)c_1(s^t) \leq M(s^t). \tag{50}$$

Money is introduced into and withdrawn from the economy through open market operations in the securities market. The constraint facing the government in this market is

$$M(s^t) - M(s^{t-1}) + B(s^t) = R(s^{t-1})B(s^{t-1}) + p(s^{t-1})g(s^{t-1})$$
$$- p(s^{t-1})\tau(s^{t-1})z(s^{t-1})\ell(s^{t-1}). \tag{51}$$

The terms on the left side of this equation are the assets sold by the government. The first term on the right is the payment on debt incurred in the preceding period, the second is the payment for government consumption, and the third is tax receipts. Notice that government consumption is bought on credit.

The consumer's problem is to maximize (48) subject to (49) and (50) and the bound on debt. Money earns a gross nominal return of one. If bonds earn a gross nominal return of less than one, then the consumer can make infinite profits by buying money and selling bonds. Thus, in any equilibrium, $R(s^t) \geq 1$. The consumer's first-order conditions imply that $U_1(s^t)/U_2(s^t) = R(s^t)$; thus, in any equilibrium, this constraint must hold:

$$U_1(s^t) \geq U_2(s^t). \tag{52}$$

This feature of the competitive equilibrium constrains the set of Ramsey allocations.

A Ramsey equilibrium for this economy is defined in the obvious way. As is well-known, if the initial stock of nominal assets held by consumers is positive, then welfare is maximized by increasing the initial price level to infinity. If the initial stock is negative, then welfare is maximized by setting the initial price level so low that the government raises all the revenue it needs without levying any distorting taxes. To make the problem interesting, we set the initial nominal assets of consumers to zero. Let $a(s_0)$ denote initial real claims that the government holds against private agents. The Ramsey allocation problem is

$$\max \sum_t \sum_{s^t} \beta^t \mu(s^t)U[c_1(s^t), c_2(s^t), \ell(s^t)]$$

s.t.   (47), (52), and

$$\sum_t \sum_{s^t} \beta^t \mu(s^t)[U_1(s^t)c_1(s^t) + U_2(s^t)c_2(s^t) + U_3(s^t)\ell(s^t)]$$

$$= U_2(s_0)a(s_0). \tag{53}$$

For convenience in studying the properties of the Ramsey allocation problem, let

$$W(c_1, c_2, \ell, \lambda) = U(c_1, c_2, \ell) + \lambda[U_1c_1 + U_2c_2 + U_3\ell], \tag{54}$$

where λ is the Lagrange multiplier on the implementability constraint, (53). The Ramsey allocation problem is, then, to maximize

$$\sum_t \sum_{s^t} \beta^t \mu(s^t) W[c_1(s^t), c_2(s^t), \ell(s^t), \lambda]$$

subject to (48) and (52). Consider utility functions of the form

$$U(c_1, c_2, \ell) = h(c_1, c_2)v(\ell), \tag{55}$$

where h is homogenous of degree k and the utility function has the standard properties.

Proposition 3 (the optimality of the Friedman rule). For utility functions of the form (55), the Ramsey equilibrium has $R(s^t) = 1$ for all s^t.

Proof. Consider for a moment the Ramsey problem with constraint (51) dropped. A first-order condition for this problem is

$$\frac{W_1(s^t)}{W_2(s^t)} = 1. \tag{56}$$

For utility functions of the form (55),

$$W = hv + \lambda[c_1h_1v + c_2h_2v + \ell hv'].$$

Since h is homogenous of degree k, $c_1h_1 + c_2h_2 = kh$. Thus, $W = h(c_1, c_2)Q(\ell, \lambda)$ for some function Q. Combining this feature with (56) gives

$$1 = \frac{W_1}{W_2} = \frac{U_1}{U_2}. \tag{57}$$

Since the solution to this less constrained problem satisfies (52), it is also a solution to the Ramsey problem. Then the consumer's first-order condition $U_1(s^t)/U_2(s^t) = R(s^t)$ implies that $R(s^t) = 1$.

In Chari, Christiano, and Kehoe (1991b), we show that the Friedman rule is optimal for more general utility functions of the form

$$U(c_1, c_2, \ell) = V[h(c_1, c_2), \ell],$$

where h is homothetic. We also show that the Friedman rule is optimal for economies with money in the utility function and for transaction cost economies that satisfy a similar homotheticity condition.

The intuition for this result is as follows. In this economy, the tax on labor income implicitly taxes consumption of both goods at the same rate. A standard result in public finance is that if the utility function is separable in leisure and the subutility function over consumption goods is homothetic, then the optimal policy is to tax all consumption goods at the same rate (Atkinson and Stiglitz 1972). If $R(s^t) > 1$, the cash good is effectively taxed at a higher rate than the credit good since cash goods must be paid for immediately but credit goods are paid for with a one-period lag. Thus, with such preferences, efficiency requires that $R(s^t) = 1$ and, therefore, that monetary policy follow the Friedman rule.

This intuition is not complete, however. As we mentioned earlier, the Friedman rule turns out to be optimal even in many models with money in the utility function or with money facilitating transactions. In such models, money and consumption goods are taxed at different rates. Specifically, money is not taxed at all, while consumption goods are. Thus, the Phelps (1973) argument turns out to be more tenuous than it first appears. (For analyses of optimality of the Friedman rule in various deterministic models of money with distorting taxes, see Kimbrough 1986, Faig 1988, and Woodford 1990.)

We turn now to some numerical exercises that examine the cyclical properties of monetary policy in our model. In these exercises, we consider preferences of the form

$$U(c, \ell) = [c^{1-\gamma}(L - \ell)^\gamma]^\psi / \psi,$$

where L is the endowment of labor and

$$c = [(1 - \sigma)c_1^\nu + \sigma c_2^\nu]^{1/\nu}.$$

The technology shock z and government consumption both follow the same symmetric, two-state Markov chains as in the model in Section 3.

For preferences, we set the discount factor $\beta = 0.97$, we set $\psi = 0$, which implies logarithmic preferences between the composite consumption good and leisure, and we set $\gamma = 0.8$. These values are the same as those in Christiano and Eichenbaum (1992). The parameters σ and ν are not available in the literature, so we estimate them, using the consumer's first-order conditions. These conditions imply that $U_{1t}/U_{2t} = R_t$. For our specificaton of preferences, this condition can be manipulated to yield

$$\frac{c_{2t}}{c_{1t}} = \left(\frac{\sigma}{1 - \sigma}\right)^{1/1-\nu} R_t^{1/1-\nu}. \tag{58}$$

With a binding cash-in-advance constraint, c_1 is real money balances and c_2 is aggregate consumption minus real money balances. We measure real money balances by the monetary base, we measure R_t by the return on three-month

Treasury bills, and we measure consumption by consumption expenditures. If we take logs in (58) and run a regression using quarterly data for the period 1959–1989, we get $\sigma = 0.57$ and $\nu = 0.83$.

Our regression turns out to be similar to those used in the money demand literature. To see this, note that (58) implies that

$$\frac{c_{1t}}{c_{1t} + c_{2t}} = \left[1 + \left(\frac{\sigma}{1-\sigma} \right)^{1/1-\nu} R_t^{1/1-\nu} \right]^{-1} . \tag{59}$$

Taking logs in (59) and then taking a Taylor's expansion yields a money demand equation with consumption in the place of output and with the restriction that the coefficient of consumption is 1. Our estimates imply that the interest elasticity of money demand is 4.94. This estimate is somewhat smaller than estimates obtained when money balances are measured by $M1$ instead of the base.

Finally, we set the initial real claims on the government so that, in the resulting stationary equilibrium, the ratio of debt to output is 0.44. This is approximately the ratio of U.S. federal government debt to GNP in 1989. For the second parameterization, we set $\psi = -8$, which implies a relatively high degree of risk aversion. For the third, we make both technology shocks and government consumption i.i.d.

In Table 12.5 we report the properties of the labor tax rate, the inflation rate, and the money growth rate for our monetary models. In all three, the labor tax rate has the same properties it did in the real economy with capital: it fluctuates very little, and it inherits the persistence properties of the underlying shocks.

Consider next the inflation rate and the money growth rate. Recall that for these monetary models the nominal interest rate is identically zero. If government consumption and the technology shock were constant, then the price level and the money stock would fall at the rate of time preference, which is 3 percent. In a stochastic economy, the inflation rate and the money growth rate vary with consumption. Therefore, the mean inflation rate depends not only on the rate of time preference, but also on the covariance of the inflation rate and the intertemporal marginal rate of substitution. This effect causes the inflation rate and the money growth rate to rise with an increase in the coefficient of risk aversion.

In the monetary models, the autocorrelation of the inflation rate is small or negative. Thus it is far from a random walk. The correlations of inflation with government consumption and with the technology shock have the expected signs. Notice that these correlations have opposite signs, and in the baseline and high risk aversion models, this leads to inflation having essentially no correlation with output. The most striking feature of the inflation rate is its volatility. In the baseline model, for example, if the inflation rate were normally distributed, it would be higher than 20 percent or lower then -20 percent approximately a third of the time. The inflation rate for the high risk aversion model is even more volatile. The money growth rate has essentially the same properties as the inflation rate.

Note that our results are quite different from those of Mankiw (1987). Using a partial equilibrium model, he argues that optimal policy implies that inflation

Table 12.5
Properties of the Monetary Models

	Model		
	Baseline	*High Risk Aversion*	*I.I.D.*
Labor tax			
Mean	20.05	20.18	20.05
Standard deviation	0.11	0.06	0.11
Autocorrelation	0.89	0.89	0.00
Correlation with			
Government consumption	0.93	−0.93	0.93
Technology shock	−0.36	0.35	−0.36
Output	0.03	−0.06	0.02
Inflation			
Mean	−0.44	4.78	−2.39
Standard deviation	19.93	60.37	9.83
Autocorrelation	0.02	0.06	−0.41
Correlation with			
Government consumption	0.37	0.26	0.43
Technology shock	−0.21	−0.21	−0.70
Output	−0.05	−0.08	−0.48
Money growth			
Mean	−0.70	4.03	−2.78
Standard deviation	18.00	54.43	3.74
Autocorrelation	0.04	0.07	0.00
Correlation with			
Government consumption	0.40	0.28	0.92
Technology shock	−0.17	−0.20	−0.36
Output	0.00	−0.07	0.02

should follow a random walk. It might be worth investigating whether there are any general equilibrium settings that rationalize Mankiw's argument.

6. Computational Issues

Our computational techniques use Propositions 1 and 2 to compute the equilibrium allocations, and then use the constructive procedure outlined in the proof of Proposition 1 to compute the equilibrum policies. We illustrate our procedure by describing how we compute the Ramsey equilibrium for the real economy with capital accumulation. We assume that the transition probabilities for the state follow a Markov chain and that the exogenous state variables, s, take on S values, $s = 1, \ldots, S$. Our computational procedure begins by fixing an initial value for the Lagrange multiplier, λ, on the implementability constraint, (10). Given this value of λ, it is clear from the resource constraint, (9), and from (40) and (41) that the consumption, labor, and capital allocations for $t \geq 1$ are stationary functions of the capital stock and the exogenous state. We denote these functions by $c(k, s; \lambda)$, $\ell(k, s; \lambda)$, and $k'(k, s; \lambda)$, respectively. There are a variety of standard methods for computing approximations to these functions (see Baxter 1988; Bizer and Judd 1989b; Coleman 1990; and Judd 1991). We investigate two methods: the minimum weighted residual method described in Judd (1991) and the log-linearization method described in Christiano (1991). Both approaches yield approximations to the stationary allocation rules. We then use these, together with the appropriate resource constraint and Euler equations, to compute the date 0 decisions. Finally, we adjust λ until the implementability constraint is satisfied. In what follows, we describe some details of these algorithms, and after that we compare results based on the minimum weighted residual method to those based on the log-linearization method.

We use (9) and (40) to solve for consumption and labor as functions of (k, k', s) and denote these functions as $\hat{c}(k, k', s)$ and $\hat{\ell}(k, k', s)$. (Here, and in what follows, we suppress dependence on λ.) We then substitute these functions into (41) to obtain

$$H(k, k', s) = \sum_{s'} \beta \mu(s'|s) G(k', k'', s'), \qquad (60)$$

where $H(k, k', s) = W_c[\hat{c}(k, k', s), \hat{\ell}(k, k', s), s], G(k, k', s) = H(k, k', s)(1 + F_k[k, \hat{\ell}(k, k', s), s) - \delta]$, and k'' denotes the capital stock at the end of the next period. Substituting the stationary capital accumulation decision rule, $k'(k, s)$, into (60) gives

$$H[k, k'(k, s), s] - \sum \beta \mu(s'|s) G(k'(k, s), k'(k'(k, s), s'), s') = 0 \qquad (61)$$

Then, for a given λ, our task is to find a function $k'(k, s)$ that solves (61). Given such a function, the consumption and labor decision rules are simply $c(k, s) = \hat{c}[k, k'(k, s), s]$ and $\ell(k, s) = \hat{\ell}[k, k'(k, s), s]$. Finding a function $k'(k, s)$ that solves (61) is complicated by the fact that k is a continuous variable. As a result, (61) is a continuum of equations in a continuum of unknowns, with equations and unknowns being indexed by all possible k, s pairs. Solving such a system is usually infeasible. The version of the minimum weighted residual approach that we adopt approximates $k'(k, s)$ by a finite parameter function based on polynomials, and requires evaluating (61) at only a finite number of points. The parameters of the function are adjusted until appropriately weighted averages of the left side of (61) are set equal to zero.

We consider decision rules of the form

$$k'(k, s) = \exp \left[\sum_{i=0}^{M-1} \alpha_i(s) T_i\{g[\log(k)]\} \right], \qquad (62)$$

where $\alpha_i(s), i = 0, \ldots, M - 1, s = 1, \ldots, S$ are the parameters of the decision rule and $T_i(\cdot)$ is a Chebyshev polynomial of order i that maps $(-1, 1)$ into $(-1, 1)$.[3] The function g maps the range of the log of the capital stock that we consider, $(\log k_1, \log k_N)$, into the interval $(-1, 1)$, and is defined by

$$g(\log k) = (2 \log k - \log k_N - \log k_1)/(\log k_N - \log k_1). \qquad (63)$$

Next, we construct a grid of capital stocks, $\{k_1, \ldots, k_N\}$, such that $k_1 < k_2 < \ldots < k_N$.[4] Substituting (62)–(63) into (61) and evaluating the resulting expression at the $N \times S$ values of (k, s) gives $N \times S$ equations in $M \times S$ unknowns, namely

$$R(k, s; \alpha) = 0, \quad k = k_1, \ldots, k_N, \quad s = 1, \ldots, S, \qquad (64)$$

where $\alpha = (\alpha_i(s))$. We adopt the Galerkin version of the minimum weighted residual method, under which $M < N$. Since there are more equations than unknowns, we consider $M \times S$ linearly independent combinations of the $N \times S$ equations. More specifically, let $R(s; \alpha)$ be a vector of length N, namely, $R(s; \alpha) = [R(k_1, s; \alpha), \ldots, R(k_N, s; \alpha)]'$. Let A be a matrix of dimension $M \times N$, where $A = (a_{ij})$, with $a_{ij} = T_{i-1}\{g[\log(k_j)]\}$. The parameters α are chosen to solve

$$AR(s, \alpha) = 0, \quad s = 1, \ldots, S. \qquad (65)$$

We also approximate the capital accumulation decision rule, using a standard log-linearization procedure, described in, for example, Christiano (1991). The procedure works with a modified version of (61) in which $H(\cdot)$ and $G(\cdot)$ are replaced by functions that are linear in the exogenous shocks and in the log of the capital stock. These functions are obtained by computing a suitable Taylor series expansion of $H(\cdot)$ and $G(\cdot)$ about the unconditional means of the exogenous shocks, and the log of the nonstochastic steady-state capital stock. It is then straightforward to solve the modified version of (61) exactly for a log-linear function, $k'(\cdot)$.[5] We used this procedure to obtain starting parameter values for the mimimum weighted residual algorithm and to set the bounds, k_1 and k_N, on the capital grid. These bounds are chosen to include the initial stock of capital and the ergodic set generated by the log-linear decision rule.

Either procedure described above gives us decision rules for a fixed value of λ. Next, we need to adjust λ until the implementability constraint, (10), is satisfied. Our algorithm exploits the stationarity and the recursive structure of the debt decision rule for $t \geq 1$. Recall from (36) that the debt decision rule satisfies

$$U_c(k, s)b(k, s) = \sum_{s'} \beta\mu(s'|s)[U_c(k', s')(c(k', s') + b(k', s') + k')$$

$$+ U_\ell(k', s')\ell(k', s')] - U_c(k, s)k', \tag{66}$$

where $k' = k'(k, s)$. This equation defines a linear map from debt allocation rules into themselves. In practice we approximated the debt rule by a piecewise linear function of the capital stock for each value of the state s. We then used (66) to define a linear map from the space of the parameters of piecewise linear debt rules into itself. The fixed point of that map is a system of linear equations in the parameters of the debt rule, which is straightforward to solve. (See Chari, Christiano, and Kehoe 1991a for details.)

Next we substitute the resulting bond decision rules together with the other allocations into the consumer budget constraint, (3), evaluated at date 0. Using the equality between the marginal rate of substitution between consumption and labor and the after-tax wage rate and setting $\theta(s_0)$ to its given value, we calculate a value for $R_b(s_0)b_{-1}$. We then iterate on λ until the desired initial value for $R_b(s_0)b_{-1}$ is attained.

We found that the minimum weighted residual and the log-linearization methods gave very similar results for the allocations. For the policies, however, the minimum weighted residual method improved substantially the accuracy of the solutions. The reason is that the policies depend on ratios of the derivatives of the utility function and small errors in computing the allocations can lead to large errors in computing the policies. One way to compare the relative accuracy of the two methods is to check how close the residual function, $R(k, s, \alpha)$, is to zero. Recall that ideally the intertemporal Euler equation would hold exactly for all

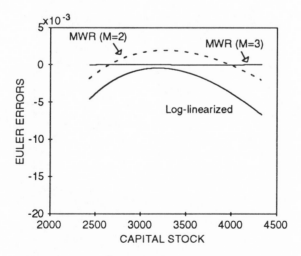

Figure 12.1A Residual Functions for First Exogenous State

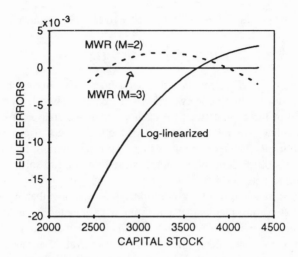

Figure 12.1B Residual Functions for Second Exogenous State

values of (k, s), and thus this function would be identically zero. In Figure 12.1 we plot this function against the capital stocks in the interval (k_1, k_N) for each of the four states in our baseline model. These are ordered as follows: $s = 1$ corresponds to (g_ℓ, z_ℓ); $s = 2$ corresponds to (g_ℓ, z_h); $s = 3$ corresponds (g_h, z_ℓ); and $s = 4$ corresponds to (g_h, z_h). We plot the residual functions implied by the minimum weighted residual (MWR) method for $M = 2$ and $M = 3$ and the residual functions implied by the log-linearization method. (For the MWR

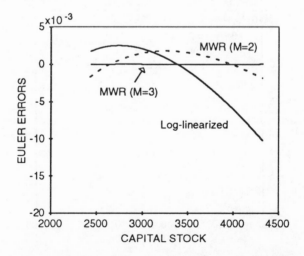

Figure 12.1C Residual Functions for Third Exogenous State

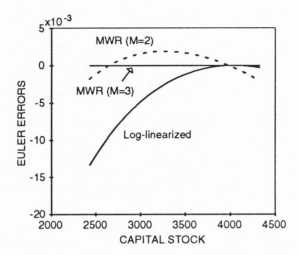

Figure 12.1D Residual Functions for Fourth Exogenous State

computations in Figure 12.1, $N = 20$.) Though the MWR ($M = 2$) and the log-linearization decision rules are both log linear, they still differ in two respects. First, the MRW rule allows both the constant and slope terms to differ for different values of s, while the log-linearized rule allows only the constant term to shift. Second, each method has a different criterion for choosing the coefficients of the decision rule, with the MRW method being focused exclusively on the behavior of the residual function. These two differences explain why the MRW ($M = 2$) residual function looks closer to zero in Figure 12.1 than does the residual function corresponding to the log-linearized decision rule. Note also that increasing M from 2 to 3 moves the residual function closer to zero by a couple of orders of magnitude, so that MWR ($M = 3$) appears in Figure 1 as a straight line at zero. The maximum of the absolute value of the residual function implied by the log-linearized decision rule is 0.02, while it is 0.002 and 0.00002 for the MWR ($M = 2$) and MWR ($M = 3$) methods. All other calculations for the growth model with capital reported in this paper set $M = 10$ and $N = 41$, and the value of the resulting residual function is at most 10^{-10} in absolute value.

Figures 12.2 through 12.4 illustrate that the differences in the accuracy of the two methods can have significant effects on the accuracy of the computed policies. In Figure 12.2 we plot the autocorrelations of the labor tax rate against the autocorrelations of the shocks for two values of the risk aversion parameter, ψ. Figure 12.2B shows that when $\psi = 0$, the two methods give quite different values for the autocorrelation of the labor tax rate when government consumption is close to i.i.d. In Figure 12.3, we plot the standard deviation of the labor tax rate against the

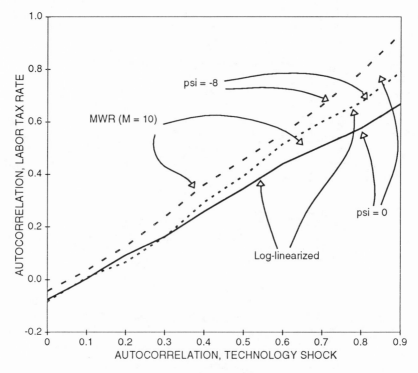

Figure 12.2A Persistence of Labor Tax Rate by Technology Shock

risk aversion parameter for the two methods. We find that the two methods can give quite different answers, especially when the risk aversion parameter is around −4. In Figure 12.4, we plot the mean and standard deviation of the ex ante capital tax rate and the private assets tax rate against the risk aversion parameter. Figure 12.4A shows that the log-linear method performs worse in terms of the mean of the ex ante capital tax rate for high values of risk aversion. Figure 12.4B illustrates that the log-linear approach performs worse in terms of the standard deviation of the ex ante capital tax rate for low values of risk aversion. The case $\psi = 0$ is of particular interest, since in this case we know theoretically that the mean and standard deviation of the ex ante tax rate on capital must be zero. Figure 12.4 indicates that when $\psi = 0$, then the minimum weighted residual gets these statistics right, while the log-linear method gets them wrong. Figure 12.5A illustrates that the log-linear approach works worse in terms of the mean of the private assets tax rate for high values of risk aversion; Figure 12.5B shows the standard deviation. Taken together, these figures suggest that the two methods give quite different answers for policies, and that the minimum weighted residual method is preferable for the issues we consider.

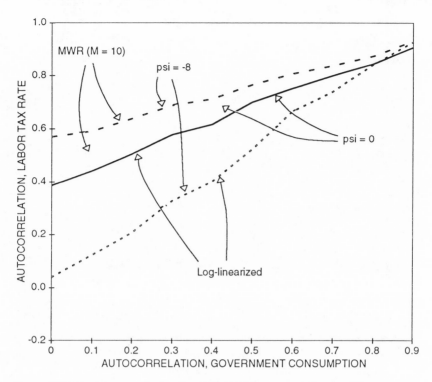

Figure 12.2B Persistence of Labor Tax Rate by Government Consumption

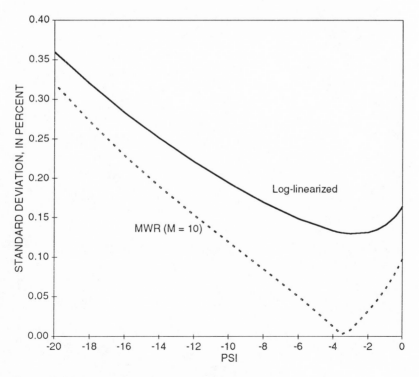

Figure 12.3 Standard Deviation of Labor Tax Rate

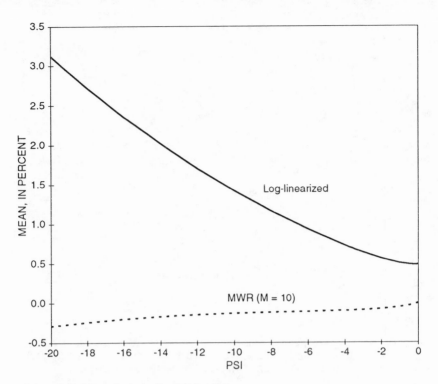

Figure 12.4A Mean Ex Ante Capital Tax Rate

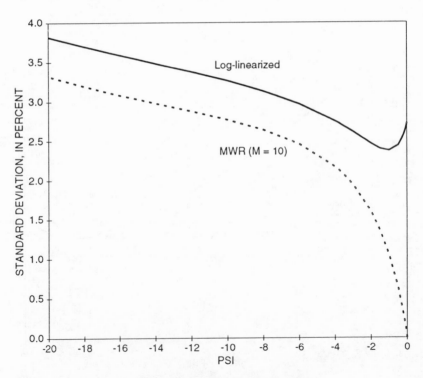

Figure 12.4B Standard Deviation of Ex Ante Capital Tax Rate

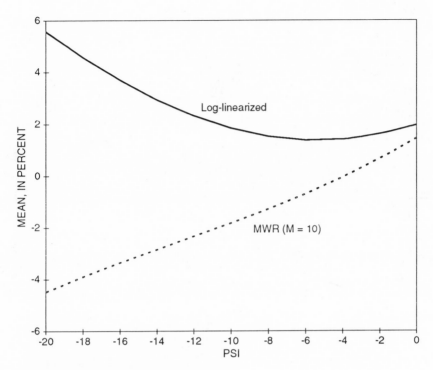

Figure 12.5A Mean Private Assets Tax Rate

7. Conclusions

In this paper, we have analyzed the quantitative properties of policies in business cycle models. We have abstracted from a host of issues. We have considered a representative-agent model. It would be interesting to explore the quantitative implications of policies in dynamic models with heterogeneous agents. For example, Auerbach and Kotlikoff (1987) have analyzed the quantitative implicatons of fiscal policies in overlapping-generations models (see also Escolano [1992] for an analysis of optimal policy in such models). In our model growth is exogenous. For some interesting work on optimal policies in endogenous growth models, see Lucas (1990b), and Jones, Manuelli, and Rossi (1991).

Our work and the related work mentioned above takes as given that the government has available only proportional taxes to finance its spending. A different approach, stemming from Mirrlees (1971), derives optimal policies given the restrictions imposed by incentive constraints due to private information. A fruitful area for research is to derive the quantitative implications for optimal fiscal policies in dynamic economies with private information.

Finally, we have assumed there is a technology for commitment by the government. It should be clear that the Ramsey policies in these economies are not time

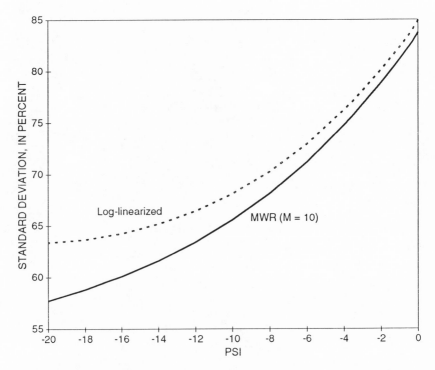

Figure 12.5B Standard Deviation of Private Assets Tax Rate

consistent. Perhaps the most promising area for research is to consider economies in which policy decisions are made sequentially and to analyze the quantitative properties of equilibrium policy and allocations. For recent theoretical discussions see Chari and Kehoe (1990, 1992) and Stokey (1991).

Notes

We are grateful to the National Science Foundation for financial support. The views expressed herein are those of the authors and not necessarily those of the Federal Reserve Bank of Minneapolis, the Federal Reserve Bank of Chicago, or the Federal Reserve System.

1. Separability between consumption and leisure and homotheticity in consumption are the well-known conditions under which the optimal policy is uniform consumption taxes in all periods except the first. See Atkinson and Stiglitz (1972) for an analysis in a partial equilibrium setting. In our model, uniform consumption taxes are equivalent to zero capital income taxes; thus, with $\psi = 0$, the result that capital income taxes are zero in a stochastic steady state is not surprising. More interesting is the result that, even for the high risk aversion model, which is not separable between consumption and leisure, the mean of the capital income tax is close to zero in a stochastic steady state.

2. We compute the tax on private assets by first constructing a value for total debt. Following Jorgenson and Sullivan (1981), we note that the present value of depreciation allowances is a claim on the government similar to conventional debt. We thus define total debt to be the sum of the market value of federal debt and the value of depreciation allowances. For further details, see Chari, Christiano, and Kehoe (1991b).

3. These polynomials are recursively defined by $T_0(x) = 1$, $T_1(x) = x$, and $T_{i+1}(x) = 2xT_i(x) - T_{i-1}(x)$ for $i \geq 2$. See Press, et al. (1989) for details.

4. This grid is computed as follows. Let z_i denote the ith zero of $T_N(z)$, $i = 1, \ldots, N$. Then, $\log k_i = g^{-1}(z_i)$, $i = 1, \ldots, N$.

5. There are actually two $k\prime(\cdot)$ that solve the log-linearized version of (61). We chose the solution which implies that for fixed s and any initial k_0, $\beta^{1/2}k_i \rightarrow 0$, where $k_i = k\prime(k_{i-1}, s)$, $i \geq 1$.

BIBLIOGRAPHY

Abreu, D. 1986. "Extremal Equilibria of Oligopolistic Supergames." *Journal of Economic Theory* 39:191–225.

Adelman, I., and F. L. Adelman. 1959. "The Dynamic Properties of the Klein-Goldberger Model." *Econometrica* 27:596–625.

Aiyagari, S. R. 1993. "Uninsured Idiosyncratic Risks and Aggregate Saving." Working Paper 502, Federal Reserve Bank of Minneapolis. Reproduced.

Aiyagari, S. R., and M. Gertler. 1991. "Asset Returns with Transactions Costs and Uninsured Individual Risks." *Journal of Monetary Economics* 27:311–32.

Akerlof, G. 1982. "Labor Contracts as a Partial Gift Exchange." *Quarterly Journal of Economics* 97:543–69.

Akerlof, G., and J. Yellen. 1985. "A Near-Rational Model of the Business Cycle with Wage and Price Inertia." *Quarterly Journal of Economics* 100:823–38.

Altig D., and C. T. Carlstrom. 1991. "Inflation, Personal Taxes, and Real Output: A Dynamic Analysis." *Journal of Money, Credit and Banking* 23:547–71.

Andolfatto, D. 1992. "Business Cycles and Labor Market Search." Working Paper no. 9225, Department of Economics, University of Waterloo. Reproduced.

Armington, P. 1969. "A Theory of Demand for Products Distinguished by Place of Production." *International Monetary Fund Staff Papers* 27:488–526.

Atkeson, A., and T. Bayoumi. 1991. "Do Private Capital Markets Insure against Risk in a Common Currency Area: Evidence from the U.S." Reproduced.

Atkinson, A. B., and J. E. Stiglitz. 1972. "The Structure of Indirect Taxation and Economic Efficiency." *Journal of Public Economics* 1:97–119.

———. 1980. *Lectures on Public Economics*. New York: McGraw-Hill.

Auerbach, A. J., and L. J. Kotlikoff. 1987. *Dynamic Fiscal Policy*. Cambridge: Cambridge University Press.

Auerbach, A. J., L. J. Kotlikoff, R. P. Hagemann, and G. Nicoletti. 1989. "The Economic Dynamics of an Aging Population: The Case of Four OECD Countries." *OECD Economic Studies* 12:97–130.

Avery, R. B., et al. 1986. "The Use of Cash and Transaction Accounts by American Families." *Federal Reserve Bulletin* 72:87–108.

———. 1987. "Changes in the Use of Transaction Accounts and Cash from 1984 to 1986." *Federal Reserve Bulleting* 74:179–108.

Backus, D. K., and P. J. Kehoe. 1992. "International Evidence on the Historical Properties of Business Cycles." *American Economic Review* 82 (September):864–88.

Backus, D., P. Kehoe, and F. Kydland. 1992. "International Real Business Cycles." *Journal of Political Economy* 101:745–775.

———. 1994. "Dynamics of the Trade Balance and the Terms of Trade: The J-Curve?" *American Economic Review* 84:84–103.

Backus, D., and G. Smith. 1993. "Consumption and Real Exchange Rates in Dynamic Exchange Economies with Nontraded Goods." *Journal of International Economics* 35:297–316.

Barro, R. J. 1974. "Are Government Bonds Net Wealth?" *Journal of Political Economy* 82:1095–1117.

――――. 1978. "Unanticipated Money Growth, Output and the Price Level in the United States." *Journal of Political Economy* 86:549–80.

――――. 1979. "On the Determination of the Public Debt." *Journal of Political Economy* 87:940–71.

――――. 1981. "Output Effects of Government Purchases." *Journal of Political Economy* 89:1086–1121.

Barro, R. J., and C. Sahasakul. 1983. "Measuring the Average Marginal Tax Rate from the Individual Income Tax." *Journal of Business* 56:419–52.

Basu, S. 1992. "Intermediate Goods, Menu Costs, and Business Cycles." Reproduced.

Baxter, M. 1988. "Approximating Suboptimal Dynamic Equilibria: A Euler Equation Approach." *Journal of Monetary Economics* 27:173–200.

Baxter, M., and M. Crucini. 1992. "Business Cycles and the Asset Structure of Foreign Trade." *Working Paper no. 316*, Rochester Center for Economic Research, University of Rochester.

――――. 1993. "Explaining Saving/Investment Correlations." *American Economic Review* 83:416–36.

Baxter, M., J. Crucini, and K. Rouwenhorst. 1990. "Solving the Stochastic Growth Model by a Discrete-State-Space, Euler-Equation Approach." *Journal of Business and Economic Statistics* 8:19–22.

Baxter, M., and R. King. 1991. "Productive Externalities and The Business Cycle." University of Rochester. Reproduced.

Becker, G. S. 1965. "A Theory of the Allocation of Time. *Economic Journal* 75:493–517.

――――. 1988. "Family Economics and Macro Behavior." *American Economic Review* 78:1–13.

Becker, R. A. 1985. "Capital Income Taxation and Perfect Foresight." *Journal of Public Economics* 26:147–67.

Beggs, A., and P. Klemperer. 1992. "Multi-Period Competition with Switching Cost." *Econometrica* 60:651–66.

Benabou, R. 1992. "Inflation and Markups: Theories and Evidence from Retail Trade Sector." *European Economic Review* 36:566–74.

Benassy, J. P. 1991. "Monopolistic Competition." In W. Hildenbrand and H. Sonnenschein, eds., *Handbook of Mathematical Economics*, vol. 4. Amsterdam: North Holland.

Bencivenga, V. R. 1991. "An Econometric Study of Hours and Output Variation with Preference Shocks." *International Economic Review* 33:449–71.

Benhabib, J., and R.E.A. Farmer. 1992. "Indeterminacy and Increasing Returns." Reproduced.

Benhabib, J., R. Rogerson, and R. Wright. 1991. "Homework in Macroeconomics: Household Production and Aggregate Fluctuations." *Journal of Political Economy* 99:1166–87.

Benveniste, L. M., and J. Scheinkman. 1979. "On the Differentiability of the Value Function in Dynamic Models of Economics." *Econometrica* 47:727–32.

Bertsekas, D. P. 1976. *Dynamic Programming and Stochastic Control*. New York: Academic Press.

Bils, M. December 1987. "The Cyclical Behavior of Marginal Cost and Price." *American Economic Review* 77:838–57.

——. **November** 1989. "Pricing in a Customer Market." *Quarterly Journal of Economics* 104:699–718.

——. 1991. "Indexation and Contract Length in Unionized U.S. Manufacturing." In R. W. Eberts and E. L. Groshen, eds., *Structural Changes in U.S. Labor Markets: Causes and Consequences.* London and Armonk: Sharpe.

Bils, M., and J. O. Cho. 1994. "Cyclical Factor Utilization." *Journal of Monetary Economics*, 33, 319–354.

Bizer, D., and K. L. Judd. 1989a. "Capital Accumulation, Risk, and Uncertain Taxation." Working Paper, John Hopkins University. Reproduced.

——. 1989b. "Taxation and Uncertainty." *American Economic Review* 79:331–36.

Blackburn, K., and M. Ravn. 1992. "Business Cycles in the UK: Facts and Fictions." *Economica* 59:383–401.

Blanchard, O. J., and C. M. Kahn. 1980. "The Solution of Linear Difference Models under Rational Expectations." *Econometrica* 48:1305–13.

Bodie, Z., A. Kane, and R. McDonald. 1983. "Why Are Real Interest Rates So High?" NBER Working Paper. Reproduced.

Boldrin, M., and L. Montrucchio. 1986. "On the Indeterminacy of Capital Accumulation Paths." *Journal of Economic Theory* 40:26–39.

Braun, R. A. 1990. "The Dynamic Interaction of Distortionary Taxes and Aggregate Variables in Postwar U.S. Data." University of Virginia. Reproduced.

——. 1992. "Fiscal Disturbances and Real Economic Activity in the Postwar United States." Federal Reserve Bank of Minneapolis. Reproduced.

Breeden, D.T. 1979. "An Intertemporal Asset Pricing Model with Stochastic Consumption and Investment Opportunities." *Journal of Financial Economics* 7:265–96.

——. 1986. "Consumption, Production, Inflation and Interest Rates: A Synthesis." *Journal of Financial Economics* 16:3–39.

Brock, W. 1979. "An Integration of Stochastic Growth Theory and the Theory of Finance. Part 1. The Growth Model." In J. Green and J. Scheinkman, eds., *General Equilibrium, Growth, and Trade.* New York: Academic Press.

——. 1982. "Asset Prices in a Production Economy." In J. J. McCall, ed., *The Economics of Uncertainty*, Chicago: University of Chicago Press.

Brock, W. A., and L. J. Mirman. 1972. "Optimal Economic Growth and Uncertainty: The Discounted Case." *Journal of Economic Theory* 4:497–513.

Burdett, K., and R. Wright. 1989. "Unemployment Insurance and Short-Time Compensation: The Effects on Layoffs, Hours per Worker, and Wages." *Journal of Political Economy* 97:1479–96.

Burns, A. F., and W. C. Mitchell. 1946. *Measuring Business Cycles.* New York: National Bureau of Economic Research.

Burnside, C., M. Eichenbaum, and S. Rebelo. 1993. "Labor Hoarding and the Business Cycle." *Journal of Political Economy* 101:245–73.

Caballe, J., and M. Santos. 1993. "On Endogenous Growth with Physical and Human Capital." Journal of Political Economy 101:1042–67.

Campbell, J. Y. 1986. "Bond and Stock Returns in a Simple Exchange Model." *Quarterly Journal of Economics* 101:785–803.

Campbell, J. Y., and R. J. Shiller. 1987. "The Dividend Price Ratio and Expectations of Future Dividends and Discount Factors." Princeton University. Reproduced.

Cardia, E. 1991. "The Dynamics of a Small Open Economy in Response to Monetary, Fiscal, and Productivity Shocks." *Journal of Monetary Economics* 28:411–34.

Castañeda, J., J. Díaz-Giménez, and J.-V. Ríos-Rull. 1994. "Unemployment Dynamics, Aggregate Fluctuations, and Income Distribution." University of Pennsylvania. Reproduced.

Chamberlin, E. 1933. *The Theory of Monopolistic Competition.* Cambridge, Mass.: Harvard University Press.

Chamley, C. 1986. "Optimal Taxation of Capital Income in General Equilibrium with Infinite Lives." *Econometrica* 54:607–22.

Chang, L. 1990. "Corporate Taxes, Disaggregated Capital Markets and Business Cycles." Graduate School of Management, Rutgers University. Reproduced.

Chapman, D. 1992. "Bond Yields, Returns, and Aggregate Activity." Ph.D. diss., University of Rochester.

Chappell, H. W. Jr., and R. P. Wilder 1986. "Multiproduct Monopoly, Regulation and Firm Costs: Comment." *Southern Economic Journal* 52:1168–74.

Chari, V. V., L. J. Christiano, and P. Kehoe. 1990. "Optimal Taxation of Capital and Labor Income in a Stochastic Growth Model." Federal Reserve Bank of Minneapolis. Reproduced.

———. 1991a. "Optimal Fiscal Policy in a Business Cycle model." Federal Reserve Bank of Minneapolis. Reproduced.

———. 1991b. "The Friedman Rule in Economies with Tax Distortions." Federal Reserve Bank of Minneapolis. Reproduced.

———. 1991c. "Optimal Fiscal and Monetary Policy, Some Recent Results." *Journal of Money, Credit and Banking* 23:519–40.

———. 1992. "Notes on the Primal Approach to Optimal Taxation." Federal Reserve Bank of Minneapolis. Reproduced.

Chari, V. V., and P. Kehoe. 1990. "Sustainable Plans." *Journal of Political Economy* 98:783–802.

———. 1992. "Sustainable Plans and Debt." Federal Reserve Bank of Minneapolis. Reproduced.

Chari, V. V., P. Kehoe, and E. C. Prescott. 1989. "Time Consistency and Policy." In R. Barro, ed. *Modern Business Cycle Theory.* Cambridge: Harvard University Press.

Cho, J. O. 1990. "Money, Nominal Contracts, and the Business Cycle: I. One-Period Contract Case." Queen's University. Reproduced.

Cho, J. O., and T. F. Cooley. 1992. "The Business Cycle with Nominal Contracts." University of Rochester. Reproduced.

———. 1994. "Employment and Hours over the Business Cycle." *Journal of Economic Dynamics and Control,* 18:411-32.

Cho, J. O., T. F. Cooley, and L. Phaneuf. 1994. "The Welfare Implications of Nominal Wage Contracting." University of Rochester. Reproduced.

Cho, J. O., and L. Phaneuf. 1993. "Optimal Wage Indexation and Aggregate Fluctuations." Queen's University. Reproduced.

Cho, J. O., and M. Roche. 1993. "An International Business Cycle Model with Money." Queen's University. Reproduced.

Cho, J. O., and R. Rogerson. 1988. "Family Labor Supply and Aggregate Fluctuations." *Journal of Monetary Economics* 21:233–46.

Christensen, L., and W. Greene. 1976. "Economics of Scale in U.S. Power Generation." *Journal of Political Economy* 84:655–76.

Christiano, L. J. 1988. "Why Does Inventory Investment Fluctuate So Much?" *Journal of Monetary Economics* 21:247–80.

———. 1990. "Solving a Particular Growth Model by Linear Quadratic Approximation and by Value-Function Iteration." *Journal of Business and Economic Statistics* 8:23–26.

———. 1991. "Modelling the Liquidity Effect of a Money Shock." Federal Reserve Bank of Minneapolis *Quarterly Review*, Winter, 3–34.

Christiano, L. J., and M. Eichenbaum. 1992. "Current Real Business Cycle Theory and Aggregate Labor Market Fluctuations." *American Economic Review* 82:430–50.

———. 1993. "Liquidity Effects, Monetary Policy and the Business Cycle." Northwestern University. Reproduced.

Christiano, L. J., and J.D.M. Fisher. 1994. "Algorithms for Solving Dynamic Models with Occasionally Binding Constraints." Department of Economics, Social Science Center, University of Western Ontario. Reproduced.

Citibank. 1992. "Citibase Macroeconomic Database." New York: Citibank.

Cochrane, J. H. 1991. "Production Based Asset Pricing and the Link Between Stock Returns and Economic Fluctuations." *Journal of Finance* 46:209–37.

Coleman, W. J. 1988. "An Algorithm to Solve Intertemporal General Equilibrium Models." Federal Reserve Board. Reproduced.

———. 1990. "Solving the Stochastic Growth Model by Policy-Function Iteration." *Journal of Business and Economic Statistics* 8:27–30.

———. 1991. "Equilibrium in a Production Economy with Income Taxe." *Econometrica* 59:1091–1104.

Constantinides, G. M. 1990. "Habit Formation: A Resolution of the Equity Premium Puzzle." *Journal of Political Economy* 98:519–43.

Constantinides, G. M., and D. Duffie. 1991. "Asset Pricing with Heterogeneous Consumers: Good News and Bad News." Reproduced.

Conze, A., J.-M. Lasry, and J. Scheinkman. 1991. "Borrowing Constraints and International Comovements." University of Chicago. Reproduced.

Cooley, T. F., and G. D. Hansen. 1989. "The Inflation Tax in a Real Business Cycle Model." *American Economic Review* 79:733–48.

———. 1991. "The Welfare Costs of Moderate Inflations." *Journal of Money, Credit and Banking* 23:483–503.

———. 1992. "Tax Distortions in a Neoclassical Monetary Economy." *Journal of Economic Theory* 58:290–316.

Cooley, T. F., and L. Ohanian. 1991. "The Cyclical Behavior of Prices." *Journal of Monetary Economics* 28:25–60.

Costello, D., and J. Praschnik. 1992. "The Role of Oil Price Shocks in a Two-Sector, Two-Country Model of the Business Cycle." University of Western Ontario. Reproduced.

Cox, J. C., J. E. Ingersoll, Jr., and S. A. Ross. 1985. "An Intertemporal General Equilibrium Model of Asset Prices." *Econometrica* 53:363–84.

Crucini, M. 1992. "International Risk Sharing: A Simple Comparative Test." Reproduced.

Danthine, J. P., and J. Donaldson. 1981. "Stochastic Properties of Fast vs. Slow Growing Economies." *Econometrica* 49:1007–33.

———. 1985. "A Note on the Effects of Capital Income Taxation on the Dynamics of a Recursive Economy." *Journal of Public Economics* 28:255–65.

————. 1986. "Inflation and Asset Prices in an Exchange Economy." *Econometrica* 49:1007–33.

————. 1990. "Efficiency Wages and the Business Cycle Puzzle." *European Economic Review* 34:1275–1301.

————. 1991a. "Methodological and Empirical Issues in Real Business Cycle Theory." *European Economic Review*, forthcoming.

————. 1991b. "Risk Sharing, the Minimum Wage, and the Business Cycle." In W. Barnett, B. Cornet, C. d'Aspremont, J.J. Gabsewicz, and A. Mas-Colell, eds., *Equilibrium Theory and Application*. New York: Cambridge University Press.

Danthine, J. P., J. Donaldson, and R. Mehra. 1989. "On Some Computational Aspects of Equilibrium Business Cycle Theory." *Journal of Economic Dynamics and Control* 13:449–70.

————. 1992. "The Equity Premium and the Allocation of Income Risks." *Journal of Economic Dynamics and Control* 16:509–32.

Danthine, J. P., and M. Surchat. 1991. "Consequence macroeconomiques du vieillissement demografique." Cahiers de recherches economiques, Universite de Lausanne, no. 9103. Reproduced.

Deaton, A. 1992. *Understanding Consumption*. Oxford: Oxford University Press.

Debreu, G. 1954. "Valuation Equilibrium and Pareto Optimum." *Proceedings of the National Academy of Science* 40:588–92.

Den Haan, W. 1991. "The Term Structure of Interest Rates in Real and Monetary Production Economies." Working Paper, University of California, San Diego. Reproduced.

————. 1993. "Solving Heterogeneous Agents Models: An Application to Asset Pricing with Incomplete Markets." Paper presented at conference, Models with Heterogeneous Agents, September 17 and 18, 1993, Federal Reserve Bank of Minneapolis.

Den Haan, W., and A. Marcet. 1990. "Solving the Stochastic Growth Model by Parameterizing Expectations." *Journal of Business and Economic Statistics* 8:31–34.

Devereux, M., A. Gregory, and G. Smith. 1992. "Realistic Cross-Country Consumption Correlations in a Two-Country, Equilibrium, Business-Cycle Model." *Journal of International Money and Finance* 11:3–16.

Díaz-Giménez, J. 1990. "Business Cycle Fluctuations and the Cost of Insurance in Computable General Equilibrium Heterogeneous Agent Economies." Working Paper, Universidad Carlos III de Madrid. Reproduced.

Díaz-Giménez, J., and E. C. Prescott. 1989. "Asset Returns in Computable General Equilibrium Heterogeneous Agent Economies." Working Paper, Federal Reserve Bank of Minneapolis. Reproduced.

Díaz-Giménez, J., E. C. Prescott, T. Fitzgerald, and F. Alvarez. 1992. "Banking in Computable General Equilibrium Economies." *Journal of Economic Dynamics and Control* 16:533–59.

Dixit, A., and J. Stiglitz. 1977. "Monopolistic Competition and Optimum Product Diversity." *American Economic Review* 67:297–308.

Dixon, H. 1987. "A Simple Model of Imperfect Competition with Walrasian Features." *Oxford Economic Papers*3 39:134–60.

Domar, E. D. 1946. "Capital Expansion, Rate of Growth and Employment." *Econometrica* 14:137–47.

Domowitz, I., R. G. Hubbard, and B. C. Petersen. 1988. "Market Structure and Cyclical Fluctuations in U.S. Manufacturing." *Review of Economic Statistics* 70:55–66.

Donaldson, J. B., T. Johnsen, and R. Mehra. 1990. "On the Term Structure of Interest Rates." *Journal of Economic Dynamics and Control* 14:571–96.

Donaldson, J. B., and R. Mehra. 1984. "Comparative Dynamics of an Intertemporal Asset Pricing Model." *Review of Economic Studies* 51:491–508.

Dotsey, M. 1990. "The Economic Effects of Production Taxes in a Stochastic Growth Model." *American Economic Review* 80:1168–82.

Dotsey, M., and C. Mao. 1992. "How Well Do Linear Approximation Methods Work? The Production Tax Case." *Journal of Monetary Economics* 29:25–58.

Dreze, J. 1981. "Inferring Risk Tolerance from Deductibles in Insurance Contracts." *The Geneva Papers on Risk and Insurance* 20:48–52.

———. 1989. *Labor Management, Contracts, and Capital Market: A General Equilibrium Approach*. Oxford: Basil Blackwell.

Eichenbaum, M. 1991. "Real Business Cycle Theory: Wisdom or Whimsy?" *Journal of Economic Dynamics and Control* 15:607–26.

Eichenbaum, M., and Lars Peter Hansen. 1990. "Estimating Models with Intertemporal Substitution Using Aggregate Time Series Data." *Journal of Business and Economic Statistics* 8:53–69.

Eisner, R. 1988. "Extended Accounts for National Income and Product." *Journal of Economic Literature* 26:1611–84.

Ekeland, I., and J. Scheinkman. 1986. "Transversality Conditions for Some Infinite Horizon Discrete Time Optimization Problems." *Mathematics of Operations Research* 11:216–29.

Englund, P. M. Persson, and L.E.O. Svensson. 1992. "Swedish Business Cycles: 1861–1988." *Journal of Monetary Economics* 30:343–71.

Epstein, L. G. 1983. "Stationary Cardinal Utility and Optimal Growth under Uncertainty." *Journal of Economic Theory* 31:132–52.

Escolano, J. 1992. "Optimal Taxation in Overlapping Generations Models." University of Minnesota. Reproduced.

Estrella, A., and G. A. Hardouvelis. 1991. "The Term Structure as a Predictor of Real Economic Activity." *Journal of Finance* 46:555–76.

Evans, C. 1990. "Productivity Shocks and Real Business Cycles." Reproduced.

Faig, M. 1988. "Characterization of the Optimal Tax on Money When It Functions as a Medium of Exchange." *Journal of Monetary Economics* 22:137–48.

Fama, E. F., and K. R. French. 1987. "Forecasting Returns on Corporate Bonds and Common Stocks." Working Paper no. 220, University of Chicago. Reproduced.

———. 1988a. "Permanent and Temporary Components of Stock Prices." *Journal of Political Economy* 96:246–73.

———. 1988b. "Dividend Yields and Expected Stock Returns." *Journal of Financial Economics* 22:3–25.

———. 1989. "Business Conditions and Expected Returns on Stocks and Bonds." *Journal of Financial Economics* 25:23–49.

Farmer, R.E.A., and J. T. Guo. 1993. "Real Business Cycles and the Animal Spirits Hypothesis." Reproduced.

Farrell, Joseph, and Carl Shapiro. 1988. "Dynamic Competition with Switching Costs." *RAND Journal of Economics* 19:123–37.

Feenstra, R. 1986. "Functional Equivalence between Liquidity Costs and the Utility of Money." *Journal of Monetary Economics* 17:271–91.

Feldstein, M. S., L. Dicks-Mireaux, and J. Poterba. 1983. "The Effective Tax Rate and the Pretax Rate of Return." *Journal of Public Economics* 21:129–58.

Finn, M. 1990. "On Savings and Investment Dynamics in a Small Open Economy." *Journal of International Economics* 29:1–21.

Fischer, S. 1977. "Long-Term Contracts, Rational Expectations, and the Optimal Money Supply Rule." *Journal of Political Economy* 85:191–206.

Fisher, J.D.M. 1992. "Relative Prices, Complementarities and Co-movement." Manuscript, Northwestern University. Reproduced.

Flood, R. P., R. J. Hodrick, and P. Kaplan. 1986. "An Evaluation of Recent Evidence on Stock Market Bubbles." NBER Working Paper. Reproduced.

Friedman, M. 1969. "The Optimum Quantity of Money." In id., *The Optimum Quantity of Money and Other Essays*, 1–50. Chicago: Aldine.

Friedman, M., and A. J. Schwartz. 1963. *A Monetary History of the United States, 1867–1960*, Princeton: Princeton University Press.

Frisch, R. 1933. "Propagation Problems and Impulse Problems in Dynamic Economics." *Economic Essays in Honor of Gustav Cassel*. London: George Allen and Urwin.

Fuerst, T. S. 1992. "Liquidity, Loanable Funds and Real Activity." *Journal of Monetary Economics* 29:3–24.

Fung, S. C. 1992. "Inflation, Taxation and Home Production in a Real Business Cycle Model." Manuscript, University of Western Ontario. Reproduced.

Gali, J. 1992. "Monopolistic Competition, Business Cycles, and the Composition of Aggregate Demand." Reproduced.

Ghez, G., and G. S. Becker. 1975. *The Allocation of Time and Goods over the Life Cycle*, New York: Columbia University Press.

Giovannini, A. 1988. "Exchange Rates and Traded Goods Prices." *Journal of International Economics* 24:45–68.

Giovannini, A., and P. Labadie. 1991. "Asset Prices and Interest Rates in Cash-in-Advance Models." *Journal of Political Economy* 99:1215–51.

Glick, R., and K. Rogoff. 1992. "Global Versus Country-Specific Productivity Shocks and the Current Account." Federal Reserve Bank of San Francisco. Reproduced.

Gomme, P., and J. Greenwood. 1993. "On the Cyclical Allocation of Risk." *Journal of Economic Dynamics and Control*, forthcoming.

Goodwin, R. M. 1955. "A Model of Cyclical Growth." In E. Lundberg, ed., *The Business Cycle in the Post-War World*. London: Macmillian.

Gottfries, N. 1986. "Price Dynamics of Exporting and Import-Competing Firms." *Scandinavian Journal of Economics* 88:417–36.

Gray, J. A. 1976. "Wage Indexation: A Macroeconomic Approach." *Journal of Monetary Economics* 2:221–35.

Greenwood, J., and Z. Hercowitz. 1991. "The Allocation of Capital and Time Over the Business Cycle." *Journal of Political Economy* 99:1188–1214.

Greenwood J., Z. Hercowitz, and G. W. Huffman. 1988. "Investment, Capacity Utilization and the Real Business Cycle." *American Economic Review* 78:402–17.

Greenwood, J., Z. Hercowitz, and P. Krusell. 1994. "Macroeconomic Implications of Investment-Specific Technological Changes." Working Paper no. 6-94, Sackler Institute of Economics Studies, Tel Aviv University.

Greenwood, J., and G. W. Huffman. 1991. "Tax Analysis in a Real Business Cycle Model: On Measuring Harberger Triangles and Okun Gaps." *Journal of Monetary Economics* 27:167–90.

———. 1993. "On the Existence of Non-Optimal Equilibria in Dynamic Stochastic Economies." Working Paper no. 370, Rochester Center for Economic Research, University of Rochester. *Journal of Economic Theory*, forthcoming.

Grilli, V., and N. Roubini. 1992. "Liquidity and Exchange Rates." *Journal of International Economics* 32:339–52.

Gronau, R. 1977. "Leisure, Work and Home Production—the Theory of the Allocation of Time Revisited." *Journal of Political Economy* 85:1099–1123.

———. 1986. "Home Production—a Survey." In Orley C. Ashenfelter, and R. Layard, eds., *Handbook of Labor Economics.* Amsterdam: North Holland.

Guesnerie, R., and M. Woodford. 1992. "Endogenous Fluctuations." In J. J. Laffont, ed., *Advances in Economic Theory: Proceedings of the 6th World Congress on the Economic Solution,* Vol. 2. Cambridge: Cambridge University Press.

Hairault, J.-O., and F. Portier. 1992. "Money, New-Keynesian Macroeconomics and the Business Cycles." *European Economic Review* forthcoming.

Hall, R. E. 1987. "Investment under Uncertainty: Theory and Test with Industry Data." NBER Working Paper 2264. Reproduced.

———. 1988a. "Intertemporal Substitution in Consumption." *Journal of Political Economy* 96:339–57.

———. 1988b. "The Relation between Price and Marginal Cost in U.S. Industry." *Journal of Political Economy* 96:921–48.

———. 1990. "Invariance Properties of Solow's Productivity Residual." In P. Diamond, ed., *Growth, Productivity, Unemployment.* Cambridge: MIT Press, 71–112.

Hamilton, J. D. 1989. "A New Approach to the Economic Analysis of Nonstationary time series and the Business Cycle." *Econometrica* 57:357–84.

———. 1991. "Overhead Costs and Economic Fluctuations." Discussion Paper 547, Columbia University. Reproduced.

Hammour, M. L. 1988. "Increasing Returns and Endogenous Business Cycles." Chapter 1 of Ph.D. Diss., MIT.

Hansen, G. D. 1984. "Fluctuations in Total Hours Worked: A Study Using Efficiency Units." Working Paper, University of Minnesota. Reproduced.

———. 1985. "Indivisible Labor and the Business Cycle." *Journal of Monetary Economics,* 16:309–27.

———. 1986a. "Three Essays on Labor Indivisibilities and the Business Cycles." Ph.D. Diss., University of Minnesota.

———. 1986b. "Growth and Fluctuations." Working Paper, University of California, Santa Barbara. Reproduced.

———. 1989. "Technical Progress and Aggregate Fluctuations." Working Paper 546, University of California, Los Angeles. Reproduced.

———. 1993. "The Cyclical and Secular Behavior of the Labor Input: Comparing Efficiency Units and Hours Worked." *Journal of Applied Econometrics* 8:71–80.

Hansen, G. D., and A. .Imrohoroğlu. 1992. "The Role of Unemployment Insurance in an Economy with Liquidity Constraints and Moral Hazard." *Journal of Political Economy* 100:118–42.

Hansen, G. D., and T. J. Sargent. 1988. "Straight Time and Overtime in Equilibrium." *Journal of Monetary Economics* 21:281–308.

Hansen, G. D., and R. Wright. 1992. "The Labor Market in Real Business Cycle Theory." *Federal Reserve Bank of Minneapolis Quarterly Review*, Spring, 2–12.

Hansen, L. P., and T. J. Sargent. 1980. "Formulating and Estimating Dynamic Linear Rational Expectations Models." *Journal of Economic Dynamics and Control* 2:7–46.

———. Forthcoming. *Recursive Linear Models of Dynamic Economies.* Princeton: Princeton University Press.

Hansen, L. P., and K. J. Singleton. 1983. "Stochastic Consumption, Risk Aversion, and the Temporal Behavior of Asset Returns." *Journal of Political Economy* 91:249–65.

Harris, M. 1987. *Dynamic Economic Analysis.* New York: Oxford University Press.

Hicks, J. R. 1949. "Mr. Harrod's Dynamic Theory." *Economica* 16:106–21.

Hill, M. S. 1984. "Patterns of Time Use." In F. Thomas Juster and Frank P. Stafford, eds., *Time, Goods and Well-Being.* Ann Arbor: University of Michigan Press.

Hodrick, R., and E. C. Prescott. 1980. "Post-War U.S. Business Cycles." Carnegie Mellon University Working Paper. Reproduced.

Hopenhayn, H., and R. Rogerson, 1993. "Job Turnover and Policy Evaluation: A General Equilibrium Analysis." *Journal of Political Economy* 101:915–38.

Hornstein, A. 1993. "Monopolistic Competition, Increasing Returns to Scale and the Importance of Productivity Changes." *Journal of Monetary Economics* 31:299–316.

Hornstein, A., and E. C. Prescott. 1993. "The Plant and the Firm in General Equilibrium Theory." In R. Becke, M. Boldrin, R. Jones, and W. Thompson, eds. *General Equilibrium and Growth: The Legacy of Lionel McKenzie.* New York: Academic Press.

Hotz, J., F. Kydland, and G. Sedlacek. 1988. "Intertemporal Preferences and Labour Supply." *Econometrica* 52:335–60.

Huggett, M. 1993. "The Risk-Free Rate in Heterogeneous-Agent Incomplete-Insurance Economies." *Journal of Economic Dynamics and Control* 17:953–70.

Huh, C. G. 1993. "Causality and Correlations of Output and Nominal Variables in a Real Business Cycle Model." *Journal of Monetary Economics* 32:147–68.

Hurd, M. D. 1989. "Mortality Risks and Bequests." *Econometrica* 57: 173–209.

Ibbotson Associates. 1993. *Stocks, Bonds, Bills and Inflation: 1992 Yearbook.* Chicago: Ibbotson Associates.

İmrohoroğlu, A. 1989. "The Costs of Business Cycles with Indivisibilities and Liquidity Constraints." *Journal of Political Economy* 97:1364–83.

———. 1992. "The Welfare Costs of Inflation under Imperfect Insurance." *Journal of Economic Dynamics and Control* 16:79–91.

İmrohoroğlu, A., and E. C. Prescott. 1991. "Seigniorage as a Tax: A Quantitative Evaluation." *Journal of Money, Credit and Banking* 23:462–75.

Joines, D. H. 1981. "Estimates of Effective Marginal Tax Rates on Factor Incomes." *Journal of Business* 54:191–226.

Jones, L., and R. Manuelli. 1990. "A Convex Model of Equilibrium Growth: Theory and Policy Implications." *Journal of Political Economy* 98:1008–38.

Jones, L., R. Manuelli, and P. Rossi. 1991. "Optimal Taxation in Convex Models of Equilibrium Models." Northwestern University. Reproduced.

Jorgensen, D. W., and M. A. Sullivan. 1981. "Inflation and Corporate Capital Recovery." In D. R. Hulten, ed., *Depreciation, Inflation, and the Taxation of Income from Capital.* Washington, D.C.: Urban Institute Press.

Judd, K. L. 1985. "Redistributive Taxation in a Simple Perfect Foresight Model." *Journal of Public Economics* 28:59–83.

———. 1989. "Optimal Taxation in Dynamic Stochastic Economies: Theory and Evidence." Working Paper, Hoover Institution. Reproduced.

———. 1991. "Minimum Weighted Residual Methods for Solving Dynamic Economic Models." Federal Reserve Bank of Minneapolis Discussion Paper no. 99. Reproduced.

Juster, F. T., and F. P. Stafford. 1991. "The Allocation of Time: Empirical Findings, Behavior Models, and Problems of Measurement." *Journal of Economic Literature* 29:471–522.

Kaldor, N. 1957. "A Model of Economic Growth." *Economic Journal* 67:591–624.

Kalecki, M. 1935. "A Macrodynamic Theory of Business Cycles." *Econometrica* 3:327–44.

———. 1939. *Essays in the Theory of Economic Fluctuation.* New York: Farrar and Rinehart.

Kandel, S., and R. F. Stambaugh. 1991. "Modeling Expected Stock Returns for Long and Short Horizons." *Journal of Monetary Economics* 27:39–71.

Kehoe, T., D. Levine, and P. Romer. 1989. "Characterizing Equilibria of Models with Externalities and Taxes as Solutions to Optimization Problems." Federal Reserve Bank of Minneapolis Research, Working Paper. Reproduced.

Ketterer, J., and A. Marcet. 1989. "Introduction of Derivative Securities: A General Equilibrium Approach." Reproduced.

Keynes, J. M. 1936. *The General Theory of Employment, Interest and Money,* London: Macmillan.

Kim, K., and A. R. Pagan. 1993. "The Econometric Analysis of Calibrated Macroeconomic Models." University of Rochester. Reproduced.

Kim, M. J., C. R. Nelson, and R. Starz 1991. "Mean Reversion in Stock Prices? A Reappraisal of the Empirical Evidence." *Review of Financial Studies* 58:515–28.

Kimbrough, K. P. 1986. "The Optimum Quantity of Money Rule in the Theory of Public Finance." *Journal of Monetary Economics* 18:277–84.

King, R. G. 1990. "Observable Implications of Dynamically Optimal Taxation." Manuscript, University of Rochester. Reproduced.

———. 1991. "Money and Business Cycles." Working Paper, University of Rochester. Reproduced.

King, R. G., and C. I. Plosser. 1984. "Money, Credit and Prices in a Real Business Cycle Economy." *American Economic Review* 74:363–80.

King, R. G., C. I. Plosser, and S. T. Rebelo. 1987. "Production, Growth and Business Cycles: Technical Appendix." Working Paper, University of Rochester. Reproduced.

———. 1988a. "Production, Growth and Business Cycles. I. The Basic Neoclassical Model." *Journal of Monetary Economics* 21:195–232.

———. 1988b. "Production, Growth and Business Cycles. II. New Directions." *Journal of Monetary Economics* 21:309–41.

King, R. G., and S. T. Rebelo. 1993. "Low Frequency Filtering and Real Business Cycles." *Journal of Economic Dynamics and Control* 77:207–31.

Klemperer, Paul D. 1987. "Markets with Consumer Switching Costs." *Quarterly Journal of Economics* 102:375–94.

Kollmann, R. 1990. "World Business Cycles and Incomplete International Asset Markets." University of Chicago. Reproduced.

——. 1993. "Fiscal Policy, Technology Shocks, and the U.S. Trade Balance Deficit." University of Montreal. Reproduced.

Krusell, P., and A. Smith. 1994. "Aggregation in a Macroeconomic Model with Heterogeneous Consumers." University of Pennsylvania. Mimeo.

Kuznets, S. 1926. *Cyclical Fluctuations: Retail and Wholesale Trade*. New York: Adelphi.

——. 1946a. *National Income: A Summary of Findings*, New York: National Bureau of Economic Research (NBER).

——. 1946b. *National Product Since 1869*. New York: NBER.

——. 1953. *Economic Change: Selected Essays in Business Cycles and National Income*. New York: Norton.

Kydland, F. E. 1984a. "Labor Force Heterogeneity and the Business Cycle." *Carnegie-Rochester Conference Series on Public Policy* 21:173–208.

——. 1984b. "A Clarification: Using the Growth Model to Account for Fluctuations." *Carnegie-Rochester Conference Series on Public Policy* 21:225–30.

——. 1989a. "The Role of Money in a Business Cycle Model." Institute for Empirical Macroeconomics Discussion Paper 23, Federal Reserve Bank of Minneapolis and University of Minnesota.

——. 1989b. "Monetary Policy in Models with Capital." In F. van der Ploeg and A. J. de Zeeuw, eds., *Dynamic Policy Games in Economies*. Amsterdam: North Holland.

Kydland, F. and E. C. Prescott 1977. "Rules Rather Than Discretion: The Inconsistency of Optimal Plans." *Journal of Political Economy* 85:473–91.

——. 1982. "Time to Build and Aggregate Fluctuations, *Econometrica* 50:1345–70.

——. 1988. "The Workweek of Capital and Its Cyclical Implications." *Journal of Monetary Economics* 21:343–60.

——. 1990. "Business Cycles: Real Facts and a Monetary Myth." *Federal Reserve Bank of Minneapolis Quarterly Review* 14:3–18.

——. 1991a. "The Econometrics of the General Equilibrium Approach to Business Cycles." *Scandinavian Journal of Economics* 93:161–78.

——. 1991b. "Hours and Employment Variation in Business Cycle Theory." *Economic Theory* 1:63–81.

——. 1993. "Cyclical Movements of the Labor Input and Its Implicit Real Wage." *Federal Reserve Bank of Cleveland Economic Review* 29:12–23.

Lapham, B. 1991. "A Dynamic General Equilibrium Analysis of Deviations from the Laws of One Price." Queen's University. Reproduced.

LeRoy, S. F., and R. D. Porter 1981. "The Present Value Relation: Tests based on implied Variance Bounds." *Econometrica* 49:555–74.

Lintner, J. 1965. "The Valuation of Risky Assets and the Selection of Risky Investments in Stock Portfolios and Capital Budgets." *Review of Economics and Statistics* 47:67–92.

Long, J. B. and C. I. Plosser. 1983. "Real Business Cycles." *Journal of Political Economy* 91:39–69.

Lucas, D. J. 1990. "Estimating the Equity Premium with Undiversifiable Income Risk and Short Sales Constraints." Northwestern University. Reproduced.

Lucas, R. E. Jr., 1972. "Expectations and the Neutrality of Money." *Journal of Economic Theory* 4:103–23.

——. 1973. "Some International Evidence on Output-Inflation Tradeoffs." *American Economic Review* 63:326–34.

——. 1975. "An Equilibrium Model of the Business Cycle." *Journal of Political Economy* 83:1113–44.

——. 1977. "Understanding Business Cycles." In Karl Brunner and Alan Meltzer, eds., *Stabilization of the Domestic and International Economy*. Amsterdam: North Holland.

——. 1978. "Asset Prices in an Exchange Economy." *Econometrica* 46:1429–45.

——. 1982. "Interest Rates and Currency Prices in a Two-Country World, *Journal of Monetary Economics* 10:335–60.

——. 1987. *Models of Business Cycles*. New York: Basil Blackwell.

——. 1988. "Money Demand, A Quantitative Review." In K. Brunner and B. McCallum, eds., *Money, Cycles and Exchange Rates; Essays in Honor of Alan Meltzer*. Carnegie-Rochester Conference Series on Public Policy, vol. 29. Amsterdam: North Holland.

——. 1990a. "The Effects of Monetary Shocks When Prices are Set in Advance." Reproduced.

——. 1990b. "Supply-Side Economics: An Analytical Review." *Oxford Economic Papers* 42:293–316.

——. 1990c. "Liquidity and Interest Rates." *Journal of Economic Theory* 50:237–64.

Lucas, R. E., and L. A. Rapping. 1969. "Real Wages, Employment and Inflation." *Journal of Political Economy* 77:721–54.

Lucas, R. E., Jr., and N. L. Stokey. 1983. "Optimal Fiscal and Monetary Policy in an Economy without Capital." *Journal of Monetary Economics* 12:55–93.

——. 1987. "Money and Interest in a Cash-in-Advance Economy." *Econometrica* 55:491–514.

Lundberg, S., and R. A. Pollak. 1991. "Separate Spheres Bargaining and the Marriage Market." Manuscript, University of Washington. Reproduced.

Macklem, R. T. 1989. "Durable and Non-Durable Consumption Goods." Bank of Canada, Ottawa. Reproduced.

——. 1993. "Terms-of-Trade Disturbances and Fiscal Policy in a Small Open Economy." *Economic Journal* 103:916–36.

Mankiw, N. G. 1985. "Small Menu Costs and Large Business Cycles: A Macroeconomic Model of Monopoly." *Quarterly Journal of Economics* 100:529–39.

——. 1986. "The Equity Premium and the Concentration of Aggregate Shocks." *Journal of Financial Economics* 17:211–19.

——. 1987. "The Optimal Collection of Seigniorage: Theory and Evidence." *Journal of Monetary Economics* 20:327–41.

——. 1988. "Imperfect Competition and the Keynesian Cross." *Economic Letters* 26:7–13.

Mankiw, N. G., and S. P. Zeldes. 1991. "The Consumption of Stockholders and Non-Stockholders." *Journal of Financial Economics* 29:97–112.

Marcet, A., 1989. "Solving Non-Linear Models by Parameterizing Expectations." Carnegie-Mellon University. Reproduced.

Marcet, A., and R. Marimon. 1992. "Communication, Commitment and Growth." *Journal of Economic Theory* 58:219–49.

Marcet, A., and K. J. Singleton. 1990. "Equilibrium Assets Prices and Savings of Heterogeneous Agents in the Presence of Portfolio Constraints." Reproduced.

Marshall, D. A. 1992. "Inflation and Asset Returns in a Monetary Economy with Transactions Costs." *Journal of Finance* 47:1315–42.

McGrattan, E. R. 1989. "The Macroeconomic Effects of Tax Policy in an Equilibrium Model." Duke University. Reproduced.

―――. 1991. "Notes on Computing Competitive Equilibria in Linear Models." Duke University. Reproduced.

―――. 1992. "The Macroeconomic Effects of Distortionary Taxation." Institute for Empirical Macroeconomics Discussion Paper 37. Reproduced.

McGrattan, E. R., R. Rogerson, and R. Wright. 1992. "Estimating the Stochastic Growth Model with Household Production." Manuscript, Federal Reserve Bank of Minneapolis. Reproduced.

Mehra, R., and E. C. Prescott. 1985. "The Equity Premium: A Puzzle." *Journal of Monetary Economics* 15:145–61.

―――. 1988. "The Equity Risk Premium: A Solution?" *Journal of Monetary Economics* 22:133–36.

Mendoza, E. 1991. "Real Business Cycles in a Small Open Economy." *American Economic Review* 81:797–818.

Merton, R., 1973. "An Intertemporal Capital Asset Pricing Model." *Econometrica* 41:867–887.

Meltzer, L. A. 1941. "The Nature and Stability of Inventory Cycles." *The Review of Economic Statistics* 23:113–29.

Mills, F. C. 1936. *Prices in Recession and Recovery: A Survey of Recent Changes.* New York: NBER.

Mincer, J. 1962. "On-the-Job Training: Costs, Returns, and Some Implications." *Journal of Political Economy* 70:50–79.

Mirrlees, J. A. 1971. "An Exploration of the Theory of Optimum Income Taxation." *Review of Economic Studies* 38:175–208.

Mitchell, W. C. 1913. *Business Cycles.* Berkeley: University of California Press.

―――. 1927. *Business Cycles: The Problem and Its Setting.* New York: NBER.

―――. 1941. *Business Cycles and Their Causes.* Berkeley: University of California Press.

―――. 1951. *What Happens during Business Cycles, A Progress Report,* New York: NBER.

Mood, A. M., F. A. Graybill, and D. C. Boes. 1973. *Introduction to the Theory of Statistics.* New York: McGraw-Hill.

Morrison, C. J. 1990. "Market Power, Economic Profitability and Productivity Growth Measurement: An Integrated Structural Approach." NBER Working Paper 3355. Reproduced.

Mortensen, D. 1990. "Search Equilibrium and Real Business Cycles." Northwestern University Working Paper. Reproduced.

Mortensen, D., and C. Pissarides. 1992. "The Cyclical Behavior of Job Creation and Job Destruction." Northwestern University. Reproduced.

Murphy, R. 1984. "Capital Mobility and the Relationship between Saving and Investment in OECD Countries." *Journal of International Money and Finance* 3:327–42.

Murphy, K., A. Schleifer, and R. Vishny. 1989. "Building Blocks of Market Clearing Business Cycle Models." *NBER Macroeconomics Annual,* 247–87.

Musgrave, J. C. 1992. "Fixed Reproducible Tangible Wealth in the United States: Revised Estimates." *Survey of Current Business* 72:106–07.

Mussa, M. 1986. "Nominal Exchange Rate Regimes and the Behavior of Real Exchange Rates." In K. Brunner and A. Metzler, eds., *Real Business Cycles, Real Exchange*

Rates, and Actual Policies. Carnegie-Rochester Conference Series. Amsterdam: North-Holland.

———. 1990. "Exchange Rates in Theory and in Reality." International Finance Section, Princeton University.

Neftci, S. N. 1984. "Are Economic Times Series Asymmetric over the Business Cycle?" *Journal of Political Economy* 92:307–28.

Negishi, T. 1960. "Welfare Economics and Existence of an Equilibrium for a Competitive Economy." *Metroeconomica* 12:92–97.

Nosal, E., R. Rogerson, and R. Wright. 1992. "The Role of Household Production in Models of Involuntary Unemployment and Underemployment." *Canadian Journal of Economics* 25:507–20.

Ohanian, L., and A. Stockman. 1993. "Effects on Interest Rates and Exchange Rates and the Independence of Monetary Policy under Pegged Exchange Rates." University of Pennsylvania. Reproduced.

Panzar, J. C. 1989. "Technological Determinants of Firm and Industry Structure." in R. Schmalensee and R. D. Willig, eds., *Handbook of Industrial Organization.* Amsterdam: North-Holland.

Parkin, M. 1986. "The Output Inflation Trade-off When Prices Are Costly to Change." *Journal of Political Economy* 94:200–24.

Phelps, E. S. 1970. Introductory chapter in E. S. Phelps, et al., *Microeconomic Foundations of Employment and Inflation Theory.* New York: Norton.

———. 1973. "Inflation in the Theory of Public Finance." *Swedish Journal of Economics* 75:67–82.

———. 1992. "Consumer Demand and Equilibrium Unemployment in a Working Model of the Customer-Market Incentive-Wage Economy." *Quarterly Journal of Economics* 107:1003–32.

Phelps, E. S., and S. G. Winter. 1970. "Optimal Price Policy under Atomistic Competition" In E. S. Phelps et al., *Microeconomic Foundations of Employment and Inflation Theory.* New York: Norton.

Plosser, C. I. 1989. "Understanding Real Business Cycles." *Journal of Economic Perspectives* 3:51–78.

Pollak, R. A., and M. L. Wachter. 1975. "The Relevance of the Household Production Function and Its Implications for the Allocation of Time." *Journal of Political Economy* 83:255–77.

Poterba, J. A., and L. H. Summers. 1988. "Mean Reversion in Stock Prices: Evidence and Implications." *Journal of Financial Economics* 22:27–59.

Prescott, E. 1986. "Theory Ahead of Business-Cycle Measurement." *Carnegie-Rochester Conference on Public Policy* 24:11–44. Reprinted in *Federal Reserve Bank of Minneapolis Quarterly Review* 10:9–22.

Prescott, E. and R.E. Lucas, Jr. 1972. "A Note on Price Systems in Infinite Dimensional Space." *International Economic Review* 13:416–22.

Prescott, E. C., and R. Mehra. 1980. "Recursive Competitive Equilibrium: the Case of Homogeneous Households." *Econometrica* 48:1356–79.

Press, W., B. Flannery, S. Teukolsky, and W. Vetterling. 1989. "Numerical Recipes in Pascal: The Art of Scientific Computing." Cambridge and New York: Cambridge University Press. 12:36.

Ramsey, F. P. 1927. "A Contribution to the Theory of Taxation." *Economic Journal* 37:47–61.

Ravn, M. 1992. "Business Cycles in the UK: A Small Open Economy in an Interdependent World." Aarhus Universitet. Reproduced.

Reder, M. W. 1962. "Wage Differentials: Theory and Measurement." In *Aspects of Labor Economics*. New York: NBER.

Reynolds, P. 1992. "International Comovements in Production and Consumption: Theory and Evidence." University of Southern California. Reproduced.

Richardson, M. 1989. "Temporary Components of Stock Prices: A Skeptic's View." Working Paper, University of Pennsylvania. Reproduced.

Rietz, T. A. 1988. "The Equity Risk Premium: A Solution." *Journal of Monetary Economics* 22:117–32.

Ríos-Rull, J.-V. 1992a. "Life Cycle Economies and Aggregate Fluctuations." Working Paper, Carnegie-Mellon University. Reproduced.

———. 1992b. "Population Changes and Capital Accumulation: The Aging of the Baby Boom." Carnegie-Mellon University. Reproduced.

———. 1993a. "On the Quantitative Importance of Market Completeness." University of Pennsylvania. Reproduced, forthcoming *Journal of Monetary Economics*.

———. 1993b. "Working in the Market, Working at Home and the Acquisition of Skills: A General Equilibrium Approach." *American Economic Review* 83:893–907.

Rogerson, R. 1984. "Topics in the Theory of Labor Markets." Ph.D. diss., University of Minnesota.

———. 1988. "Indivisible Labor, Lotteries and Equilibrium." *Journal of Monetary Economics* 21:3–16.

Romer, P. 1986. "Increasing Returns and Long-Run Growth." *Journal of Political Economy* 94 1002–37.

Rotemberg, J. J. 1986. "The New Keynesian Microfoundations." *NBER Macroeconomics Annual* 1:69–104.

Rotemberg, J. J., and G. Saloner. 1986. "A Supergame-Theoretic Model of Price Wars during Booms." *American Economic Review* 76:390–407.

Rotemberg, J. J., and M. Woodford. 1991. "Markups and the Business Cycle." *NBER Macroeconomics Annual* 6:63–128.

———. 1992. "Oligopolistic Pricing and the Effects of Aggregate Demand on Economic Activity." *Journal of Political Economy* 100:1153–1207.

———. 1993. "Imperfect Competition and the Effects of Energy Price Increases on Economic Activity." Reproduced.

Salop, S. C. 1979. "A Model of the Natural Rate of Unemployment." *American Economic Review* 69:117–25.

Sargent, T. J. 1979. *Macroeconomic Theory.* New York: Academic Press.

———. 1987. *Dynamic Macroeconomic Theory.* Cambridge, Mass.: Harvard University Press.

Schlagenhauf, D., and J. Wrase. 1992. "A Monetary, Open-Economy Model with Capital Mobility." Arizona State University. Reproduced.

Schumpeter, J. A. 1939. *Business Cycles: A Theoretical, Historical and Statistical Analysis.* 1st ed. New York: McGraw-Hill.

Schweitzer, P. 1984. "Aggregation Methods for Large Markov Chains." in: G. Iazeolla et al., *Mathematical Computer Performance and Reliability.* Amsterdam: North-Holland.

Schwert, G. W. 1989. "Why Does Stock Market Volatility Change over Time?" *Journal of Finance* 44:1115–53.

Shapiro, C., and J. Stiglitz. 1984. "Equilibrium Unemployment as a Worker Discipline Device." *American Economic Review* 74:433–44.

Sharathchandra, G. 1989. "Asset Pricing and Production: Theory and Empirical Tests." Working Paper, Southern Methodist University. Reproduced.

Sharpe, W. 1964. "Capital Asset Prices: A Theory of Market Equilibrium under Conditions of Risk." *Journal of Finance* 19:425–442.

Shiller, R. J. 1981. "Do Stock Prices Move Too Much to Be Justified by Subsequent Changes in Dividends?" *American Economic Review* 71:421–36.

Silvestre, J. 1993. "The Market-Power Foundations of Macroeconomic Policy." *Journal of Economic Literature* 31:105–141.

Sims, C. 1989. "Solving Nonlinear Stochastic Optimization and Equilibrium Problem Backwards." Discussion Paper 15, Institute for Empirical Macroeconomics, Federal Reserve Bank of Minneapolis. Reproduced.

———. 1991. "Empirical Analysis of Macroeconomic Time Series: VAR and Structural Models—Comment." *European Economic Review* 35:922–32.

Slutsky, E. 1937. "The Summation of Random Causes as the Source of Cyclic Processes." *Econometrica* 5:105–146.

Smith, B. 1989. "A Business Cycle Model with Private Information." *Journal of Labor Economics* 7:210–37.

Smith, W. 1993. "Savings, Investment, and the Volatility of the Terms of Trade: The Laursen-Metzler Effect under Uncertainty." Memphis State University. Reproduced.

Smithies, A. 1957. "Economic Fluctuations and Growth." *Econometrica* 25:1–52.

Solow, R. 1956. "A Contribution to the Theory of Economic Growth." *Quarterly Journal of Economics* 70:65–94.

———. 1957. "Technical Change and the Aggregate Production Function." *Review of Economics and Statistics* 39:312–20.

———. 1959. "Investment and Technical Progress." In Arrow et al, eds., *Mathematical Methods in the Social Science*. Stanford University Press.

———. 1970. *Growth Theory: An Exposition*. New York: Oxford University Press.

Startz, R. 1989. "Monopolistic Competition as a Foundation for Keynesian Macroeconomics Models." *Quarterly Journal of Economics* 104:737–52.

Stiglitz, J. 1976. "Prices and Queues as Screening Devices in Competitive Markets." IMSS Technical Report no. 212, Stanford University. Reproduced.

———. 1987. "Pareto Efficient and Optimal Taxation and the New Welfare Economics." In Alan J. Auerbach and M. Feldstein, eds., *Handbook of Public Economics*, vol. 2. Amsterdam: North-Holland.

Stock, J. H., and M. W. Watson. 1988. "A Probability Model of Coincident Economic Indicators." Manuscript, Harvard University. Reproduced.

Stockman, A. 1981. "Anticipated Inflation and the Capital Stock in a Cash-in-Advance Economy." *Journal of Monetary Economics* 8:387–93.

Stockman, A., and L. Tesar. 1991. "Tastes and Technology in a Two-country Model of the Business Cycle: Explaining International Comovements." University of Rochester. Reproduced.

Stokey, N. 1991. "Credible Public Policy." *Journal of Economic Dynamics and Control* 15:627–56.

Stokey, N., and R. E. Lucas with E. C. Prescott. 1989. *Recursive Methods in Economic Dynamics*. Cambridge, Mass.: Harvard University Press.

Stone, R. 1947. "Definition and Measurement of the National Income and Related Totals." Appendix to Measurement of National Income and Construction of Social Accounts. Geneva: United Nations.

———. 1956. *Quantity and Price Indexes in National Accounts*. Paris: Organization for European Economic Cooperation.

———. 1975. *Towards a System of Social Demographic Statistics*. New York: United Nations.

———. 1977. *National Income and Expenditure*, 10th ed., London: Bowes and Bowes.

Summers, L. 1981. "Taxation and Corporate Investment: A q Theory Approach." *Brookings Papers on Economic Activity* 1:67–127.

Svensson, L.E.O. 1985. "Money and Asset Prices in a Cash-in-Advance Economy." *Journal of Political Economy* 93:919–44.

Swan, T. 1963. "On Golden Ages and Production Functions." In Kenneth Berril, ed., *Economic Development with Special References to Southeast Asia*. London: Macmillan.

Tauchen, G. 1986. "Finite State Markov-Chain Approximations to Univariate and Vector Autoregressions." *Economics Letters* 20:177–81.

Taylor, J. 1979. "Staggered Price Setting in a Macro Model." *American Economic Review* 69:108–13.

———. 1980. "Aggregate Dynamics and Staggered Contracts." *Journal of Political Economy* 88:1–24.

Taylor, J. B., and H. Uhlig. 1990. "Solving Nonlinear Stochastic Growth Models: A Comparison of Alternative Solutions Methods." *Journal of Business and Economic Statistics* 8:1–19.

Tellis, G. J. 1988. "The Price Elasticity of Selective Demand: A Meta-Analysis of Econometric Models of Sales." *Journal of Marketing Research* 25:331–41.

Telmer, C. I. 1992. "Asset Pricing Puzzles and Incomplete Markets." Working Paper, Queens University. Reproduced.

Tinbergen, J. 1937. *An Econometric Approach to Business Cycle Problems*. Paris: Harmann and Cie.

Van Wincoop, E. 1992a. "International Risk Sharing." Manuscript, Boston University. Reproduced.

———. 1992b. "Regional Risksharing." Manuscript, Boston University. Reproduced.

Watson, M. 1993. "Measures of Fit for Calibrated Models." *Journal of Political Economy* 101:1011–41.

Weitzman, M. L. 1973. "Duality Theory for Infinite Horizon Convex Models." *Management Science* 19:783–89.

Welch, F. 1979. "Effects of Cohort Size on Earnings: The Baby Boom Babies' Financial Burst." *Journal of Political Economy* 87:65–97.

Whalley, J. 1985. "Trade Liberalization among Major Trading Areas." Cambridge, Mass.: MIT Press.

Woodford, M. 1986. "Stationary Sunspot Equilibria: The Case of Small Fluctuations around a Deterministic Steady State." University of Chicago. Reproduced.

———. 1988. "Expectations, Finance and Aggregate Instability." In M. Kohn and S.-C. Tsiang, eds., *Finance Constraints, Expectations and Macroeconomics*, Oxford: Oxford University Press.

———. 1990. "The Optimum Quantity of Money." In Benjamin M. Friedman and Frank H. Hahn, eds., *Handbook of Monetary Economics*, vol. 2. Amsterdam: North-Holland.

————. 1991. "Self-Fulfilling Expectations and Fluctuations in Aggregate Demand." In N. G. Mankiw and D. Romer, eds., *New Keynesian Economics*. Cambridge, Mass.: MIT Press.

Yun, T. 1993. "Nominal Price Rigidity, Endogenous Money and Business Cycles." University of Chicago. Reproduced.

Zin, S. 1992. "Incomplete Markets and the Representative Agent." Carnegie-Mellon University. Reproduced.

AUTHOR INDEX

SUBJECT INDEX